Mostly
Morgenthaus

Henry Morgenthau III

Mostly Morgenthaus

———— ✦ ————

A Family History

FOREWORD BY
ARTHUR M. SCHLESINGER, JR.

Ticknor & Fields · New York · 1991

For information about permission to reproduce selections
from this book, write to Permissions, Ticknor & Fields,
215 Park Avenue South, New York, New York 10003.

Library of Congress Cataloging-in-Publication Data
Morgenthau, Henry.
Mostly Morgenthaus : a family history / Henry Morgenthau III.
p.   cm.
Includes index.
ISBN 0-89919-976-3
1. Morgenthau family. 2. Morgenthau, Lazarus, 1815–1897.
3. Morgenthau, Henry, 1856–1946. 4. Morgenthau, Henry, 1891–1967.
5. Capitalists and financiers — United States — Biography. 6. Jews —
United States — Biography. 7. Jews in public life — United States.
8. United States — Politics and government — 20th century. 9. United
States — Foreign relations — 20th century.   I. Title.
CT274.M673M67   1991
973'.04924022 — dc20   90-32445
[B]   CIP

Printed in the United States of America

Book design by Robert Overholtzer

HAD 10 9 8 7 6 5 4 3 2 1

All photographs are from the author's collection unless otherwise noted.
Photographs credited to the FDR Library are reprinted courtesy of the
Franklin D. Roosevelt Library, Hyde Park, New York.

For Ruth,
Sarah, Ben, and Kramer,
with love

Contents

Foreword

I FIRST MET Henry Morgenthau, Jr., in the spring of 1947. These were still the days of the all-purpose weekly magazine. The two most popular were the *Saturday Evening Post,* which was generally hostile to Franklin Roosevelt and his works, and *Collier's,* which was usually in the New Deal camp. *Collier's* had recently contracted with the former secretary of the treasury for a series of articles based on the diaries he had so diligently kept during his years in the Roosevelt administration.

These diaries were only partly a diary in the usual sense of the word — that is, a personal record of the day's or week's experiences. The Morgenthau diaries had some of this, but the nine hundred volumes also included letters, memoranda, government documents, and transcripts of phone conversations — in effect, the contents of the secretary's daily in box and a treasure trove for historians.

Several writers had tried their hand at extracting a series of articles from this staggering mass of material. The various efforts had satisfied neither Mr. Morgenthau nor the peppery editor of *Collier's,* Walter Davenport, a pungent reporter of the old school. The series had been advertised; the deadline was approaching; and I was brought in at the last moment in the hope that something could be put together.

Henry Morgenthau, Jr., was then only fifty-six years old, but he seemed much older; it never occurred to me throughout our acquaintance to call him anything but "Mr. Morgenthau." He was a tall, heavyset, nearsighted, partly bald man of grave courtesy, slow in speech, often hesitant and wary in reaction, always apprehensive and not seldom gloomy but possessed of great stubbornness and drive. His son surmises that he had a learning disability in the era before dyslexia was readily diagnosed, and his occasional inarticulateness caused people to underrate his basic intelligence. In public he tended toward worry and suspicion, and his government career mingled insecurity and aggressiveness. But in private relations, once he had given his confidence, he was a person of much delicacy and warmth.

Ours was an intensive collaboration lasting three or four months. I would submit drafts of each proposed piece; he would go over them with anxious concern not just line by line but word by word. On occasion my formulations troubled him. It would sometimes take a while before one understood the nature of his objection, but almost always he had a point. I came away from this experience with great affection for Mr. Morgenthau and also with enhanced respect for President Roosevelt, who had so early discerned Morgenthau's solid abilities and had used them to such good effect.

The pieces were completed in time, and *Collier's* ran them in the autumn of 1947. They were a reasonable first take but were in time superseded by the three volumes of John Morton Blum's fine account of Mr. Morgenthau's public life, *From the Morgenthau Diaries.* Now Henry Morgenthau III has provided the personal context in this sensitive and absorbing story of the Morgenthau family in America.

Mostly Morgenthaus is, as Henry Morgenthau III observes, a tale of three patriarchs. It is a peculiarly American tale — American in the family's vitality and optimism, in their determination to embrace the new land and enter fully into its aspirations and opportunities, in the sense of social responsibility that moved them to help the less lucky and the less capable.

Lazarus Morgenthau, who brought his family from Germany to New York in the year after Appomattox, had his share of vicissitudes in life. But the first Henry Morgenthau, arriving in America at the age of ten, seized the world before him with joyous determination. He made his mark in business, then in reform and philanthropy, and, half a century after he set foot in the United States, was Woodrow Wilson's ambassador to Turkey.

"Uncle Henry," as Henry Morgenthau, Sr., became affectionately known throughout the Democratic party, was his son's opposite: he was short, articulate, cocky, outgoing, and merry. One always felt that the domination of a powerful, adored, and irrepressible father explained some of the son's evident insecurities. No doubt Henry Jr. struggled throughout his life under the weight of heavy parental expectation. But his father's — and later his gifted wife's — belief in him gave him the strength to overcome uncertainties and perplexities, and his career was in the end more distinguished than his father's.

I don't know that the tale of patriarchs continues unto the fourth generation; but the current Morgenthaus are carrying on the family tradition of public service and private concern and are making significant if perhaps nonpatriarchal contributions to American life. Robert Morgenthau is today the able, incorruptible, and unbeatable district attorney of New York and Henry Morgenthau III, after successes as a television producer, is the author of this perceptive book. *Mostly Morgenthaus* is a splendid demonstration of the possibilities of life in America.

Arthur M. Schlesinger, Jr.

Introduction

EARLY IN LIFE I sensed my parents' malaise in their Jewish-ness, which they mocked good-humoredly while remaining fiercely alert to attack from outsiders. In the adjustments I made over the years I moved through stages of self-hatred, anger, assertiveness, and, eventually, acceptance leading to a positive re-identification.

When I was a child in the 1920s growing up on the West Side of Manhattan, being Jewish was something that was never discussed in front of children. Unlike sex, which of course was also unmen-tionable, it held out no secret delights or dark pleasures. It was a kind of birth defect that could not be eradicated but with proper treatment could be overcome, if not in this generation then prob-ably in the next. The cure was achieved through the vigorous life-long exercise of one's Americanism.

To this day I can remember an incident that occurred in Central Park when I was about five.

An afternoon outing in the park was a daily ritual. A child's nurse would wheel her charge in a baby carriage out to meet her friends. They would sit on park benches, rock their carriages, and gossip. But when their children were old enough to play with others, the nurses instinctively began to cluster with nurses who worked for the relatives and friends of their employers. The popular meeting place was called the Rambles, slightly east of center.

At five I was in transition. My nurse, Nana, still met with her friends conveniently near Central Park West, close to a hilltop with a granite tower called the Belvedere. Below were the Shakespeare Gardens.

One of Nana's friends took care of a little girl about my age, and we became accustomed to playing and chatting comfortably. Once, though, she innocently asked me a question that was still bothering when I returned home. I told my mother about it.

"A girl asked me what religion I am."

Mother didn't answer. I didn't look at her, but I knew there was pain in her face.

"What's my religion, Mother?"

Then came a deliberate statement: "If anyone ever asks you that again, just tell them you're an American."

The issue was closed, never to be reopened. As though hermetically sealed, the picture remains clear in my memory to this day, long after many seemingly more important events have faded.

Throughout my childhood and adolescence I was horribly uncomfortable in my ambivalence. Yet on the one hand I was encouraged to sublimate the Jewish urge. To deny being a Jew would have been an unpardonable sin, tantamount to self-destruction. It would also have meant disregarding an elaborate infrastructure paralleling the mainstream, predominantly WASP institutions which acted as a reassuring safety net.

I don't remember ever being told in so many words that I was Jewish. It just seeped into my consciousness. Over a half century later my wife and I had occasion to visit my mother's surviving elder sister, Margaret, whom we called Aunt Peggy, then in her eighties. A large, tinseled Christmas tree dominated the living room of her expansive Fifth Avenue apartment. I told Aunt Peggy that we had stopped celebrating Christmas. In our home we observed Chanukah; we didn't want to confuse our children with mixed signals.

Aunt Peggy bristled, stating that she liked Christmas, it had *always* been her favorite holiday. But then, with no apparent sense of contradiction, she said, "I can remember when we had our first Christmas tree. Grandma Lehman was coming to call on us, and we were all scared that she would be furious. Aunt Clara had had one the year before. She always did things first. But no one had dared tell Grandma. When she came in, we all held our breath. At first she didn't say anything. Then she looked at the tree and turned to my mother and said, 'Isn't it lovely?' We were all terribly relieved. Of course we have had a Christmas tree ever since. Your mother always had a tree."

• • •

Writing this book about my family has been an odyssey of self-discovery. I began with strong preconceptions regarding the cast of characters based on direct association, stories handed down from older generations, and passing acquaintance with family memoirs and other written accounts. As I undertook to sift through the wealth of resources ready to be weighed, I found my point of view continually shifting. But, throughout, there was always one constant — that elusive, amorphous something called "being Jewish." Generating love, hate, pride, or fear, it remains inescapably present.

The experience of Jewish rebirth, although always intensely personal, is a phenomenon shared to some extent by all American Jews today in reaction to the Holocaust. After the stunning denouement of the final solution, Jews found common cause in support of the state of Israel. There was a revival of pride not only in the newborn nation, but also in the very condition of being Jewish. Depending on family background and position, and on the extent of self-knowledge, this state of grace had many ramifications. In my case, it inspired a kind of social-archaeological dig that I have chronicled here from my own perspective. It is a tale centered on three principal characters. The first was my great-grandfather Lazarus Morgenthau, born in 1815 into abject poverty in Bavaria. Fiercely ambitious, he never hesitated to cut corners. In midlife, after astonishing success, he found his finances grossly overextended and transplanted his large family to New York to make a fresh start.

His son, my grandfather, Henry, was the eighth among Lazarus's twelve surviving children. Born in Mannheim at the zenith of his father's career, he was rudely tossed out on his own in the New World when the Morgenthau fortunes plunged. It was his ambition to restore his family to what he believed was its rightful position in the world and then to launch it permanently into orbit on a much higher plane.

The final principal in this odyssey is my father, Henry Jr., my grandfather Morgenthau's only son. From what at first appeared to be unpromising clay, Grandpa was determined to mold a thoroughly American paragon who would make good on all of his own unfulfilled ambitions.

In grappling with the abundance of raw material available to me, I discovered the Morgenthau addiction to autobiography. It involved a strong sense of family and yearnings for distinction that existed both in the present and as admonitions to future generations. The three family patriarchs I am particularly concerned with, each in his own way, had a sense of destiny. Each seemed to believe that he would be able to improve not only his personal and family life but also the condition of his fellow man. What could not be achieved in his own lifetime might be accomplished by his children. Life was a relay race, with each succeeding generation getting off to a running start, snatching the baton for the next lap.

By the time I came into the world all significant vestiges of ethnicity in my family had been thoroughly camouflaged, and the Morgenthaus had assumed protective coloration to blend in with Protestant America. We had discarded all the ritual dietary laws and holidays and replaced them with Christian counterparts. As a matter of course we cheerfully ate bacon and ham, celebrated Christmas with a tree and carol singing, and Easter with bunnies and a hunt for colored eggs. My mother found her uncle Irving Lehman's mezuzah, displayed on the doorpost at his home, and his Passover seders rather painful to explain. But as chief judge of the New York State Court of Appeals, he could hardly be ignored.

These attitudes were more or less standard in our circle of second- and third-generation middle-class German Jews. My parents were on the leading edge of these mores of accommodation. We tended to avoid the network of institutions that gave Jews a comforting sense of community. Unlike their parents, my parents never went to the Harmonie Club in New York or to the Century Country Club. We had substituted for the usual "country place" in Westchester County a two-thousand-acre working farm "beyond the pale" in Dutchess County. We did not go to Temple Emanu-El even on Yom Kippur. We did not confide our health care exclusively to the network of physicians and surgeons associated with the Mount Sinai Hospital and the Jewish dentists and other specialists. We did use the Jewish law firm of Greenbaum, Wolf & Ernst, specifically Eddy Greenbaum, a boyhood friend of my father, who possessed an acerbic Groucho Marx–like humor coupled with wise compassion.

In the month of August when it was traditional to cool off at an Adirondack Mountain camp or in the sea breezes at the Jersey shore, we chose instead to penetrate some of the less fashionable New England resorts, gaining entry through my mother's Vassar College chums, a number of whom were daughters of Protestant clerics. Thus we spent several seasons at the Quaker-owned Weekapaug Inn, a few miles down the Rhode Island coast from tightly restricted, posh Watch Hill and light years away from Newport.

We were also engaged in significant pioneering in the public sector. "Don't stick your neck out," Jews admonished one another. Today one would call it keeping a low profile, avoiding publicity and controversy. But by the 1920s quite a few Jews were willing, even eager, to step into the limelight. Some, like my grandfather Morgenthau and Oscar Straus, had done so a generation earlier.

I was encouraged to take pride in these adventurous relatives: my mother's two uncles, Irving and Herbert Lehman, and among the Morgenthaus, my grandfather the ambassador and then my father, who became Franklin Roosevelt's secretary of the treasury. "All my ancestors are living," I would boast.

What might appear to be a tale of thoroughgoing assimilation really involved complex social adjustment. The Jews who arrived in New York in the mid-nineteenth century from southern German villages and cities made close connections. They did business, played, and built social institutions together. They followed a strict unwritten code dictating, among other things, that they should marry within the group. When it helped consolidate business, as in the case of Lehman Brothers, first cousins married; at Goldman Sachs, two Goldmans married two Sachses. These uptown Jews were also keenly aware that Christian social equals would not favor intermarriage.

My father and mother were born only a few doors apart on West Eighty-first Street between Central Park West and Columbus Avenue. I was raised in an apartment on that same block. In my parents' generation, the boys went to Sachs Collegiate Institute, which was "mostly all Jewish," as Edward M. M. Warburg put it. The school operated under the severe Germanic discipline of Dr. Julius Sachs, a brother of the banking Sachses and of Dr. Bernard Sachs, known for his description of the Tay-Sachs disease. Bernard's bright, attractive daughter Helen was a student there, too, before marrying Nathan Straus, Jr., the insecure yet ambitious son of the first Nathan Straus. That was the way things were intended to be.

Habit, rather than any driving cohesive force, sustained this pattern of relationships and marriages in my own generation. During my formative years my parents' closest friends continued to be couples with the same solid German Jewish heritage. In turn, their children were thrown together. My best friend was Jerome (Jerry) Straus. His grandfather Nathan Straus was my grandfather's close friend and later his bitter enemy. Nathan Straus's father-in-law, Dr. Gutherz, had been the Morgenthau family physician in Mannheim.

Jerry's father, Hugh Grant Straus, often told me that he had wanted to marry my mother. He was especially fond of saying this in front of his wife, Flora. Dr. Stieglitz, Flora's father, was the beloved physician of a lot of people we knew, though never for members of my immediate family. He had two famous brothers: Alfred, the photographer, and Julius Oscar, the chemist.

Jerry Straus and I planned to go to Princeton together after preparing at Deerfield Academy, largely because both his father and his uncle Nathan had been in Princeton's class of 1910. But in our senior year at Deerfield, Jerry attempted suicide by ingesting a potentially lethal quantity of a strong alkaline solution that was stored in the chemistry lab. He seriously injured himself and was unable to take college boards; he went on to Dartmouth, where the boards were not required. I was unaware of the things that were troubling Jerry and was deeply shocked and saddened when he succeeded in taking his life as a Dartmouth freshman.

My mother believed that all forms of disturbed behavior were hereditary. "Never marry one of the Lewisohn girls," she warned my brother and me. "There is insanity in the family." The four otherwise highly nubile sisters were the daughters of Sam and Margaret Lewisohn. The disappearance of Sam's brother remained a tightly guarded family secret. Margaret was a great beauty, but her mother, a Mrs. Seligman, had been committed by her family to a private cottage at Dr. Slocum's fashionable sanitarium in Beacon, New York, near Fishkill Farms, our family place in Dutchess County.

Before I entered Princeton I was rarely aware of the anti-Semitism that intensified during the period leading up to World War II. The German Jewish network, even as it was disintegrating, had provided me with a cushion that was about to be yanked away.

My cousin Barbara Tuchman (then Wertheim) recalled her experience with Swarthmore sororities, which was similar to what I went through with the Princeton clubs. She was as unprepared as I had been when she discovered she was to be excluded solely because she was Jewish. Having therefore decided to quit Swarthmore at the end of her freshman year and transfer to Radcliffe, she was sent to see the college president. "He was really astonished . . . you know, it never occurred to him that anybody in beautiful Swarthmore could suffer that kind of disability." She was much more forthright than I had been, and her action contributed to the decision to abolish sororities at Swarthmore a few years later.

It was no consolation to me that the year after I was rejected by the Princeton clubs my younger brother, Robert, was initiated at Amherst into Alpha Delta Phi, one of its two most prestigious fraternities. It had no formal rule barring Jews, but no one could recall that any had ever been admitted. This was a predicament that worried Frank Boyden, the headmaster at Deerfield and an Amherst alumnus. Bob had been president of his class and was an all-around outstanding Deerfield boy. Anything short of his full acceptance at college would be a slap at the school. Therefore, before he entered, Mr. Boyden managed (through intermediaries) to solicit the good offices of H. Stuart Hughes, an old Deerfield boy, grandson of the Chief Justice of the U.S. Supreme Court and president of the Amherst Alpha Delt chapter, in easing the way. Bob was accepted and went on to become chapter president himself.

Among all of us in the family it was my father who eventually reacted most forthrightly to the oppression of the Jews in our time. When President Roosevelt died, April 12, 1945, less than a month before V-E Day, I was in Patton's Third Army in Europe. In Washington, my father, after having served FDR from the beginning of his presidency, was to end his career in government with a brief, unhappy coda in the Truman administration. During the final years of the war, the plight of European Jewry had been brought home to him in a sudden painful revelation by information confided to him by three ardent Christian subordinates. He became uncompromisingly aggressive in his outrage. Like most of the Jews who wielded New Deal power and had had ready access to the president, my father had cautiously avoided Jewish issues. His fundamental change of heart, which emerged in 1943, must have sprung from something hidden deep within his conscience. From that point on, he maintained his lonely stance, enlisting few cohorts and many detractors.

At the end of the war in Europe, after the truth of the Holocaust was revealed, American Jews became united as never before. Out of public office, my father was a natural choice to lead the American effort on behalf of the remnants of world Jewry and the anticipated establishment of the state of Israel. A destiny that had been awaited for two millennia now seemed to be just around the corner. There was no messiah in sight, just a band of impatient Zionist leaders. Chaim Weizmann and Vera, his elegant, sophisticated wife, called on my parents at Fishkill Farms. Strolling outdoors after lunch, my father pointed to a great oak tree. He recalled the scenes that had taken place under its wide, sheltering branches. Every year during his presidency, Franklin Roosevelt and a large summer White House entourage had driven south in a motorcade from Hyde Park for a clambake, a traditional rural feast in which clams, corn, and lobsters were steamed over an open fire. On the last such occasion, during the war, FDR had been accompanied by his guest Winston Churchill, returning from the meeting at Quebec, where both had initialed the controversial "Morgenthau Plan" for a weakened, deindustrialized postwar Germany.

Returning from the war, I was a free spirit. As a consequence of the lessons learned in Germany, the Jewish cause and my father's top-level position in the reconstituted Jewish establishment held a strong attraction for me. So when he was general chairman of the United Jewish Appeal, I became head of the UJA, Junior Division, in New York. This work steadied me during a moment of transition. Still, I knew that something important was missing. All of that pro-Israel zeal, while providing positive results, was still rooted in the old negativism. Everyone seemed to be scolding everyone else and himself as well for not doing more, while Jews who had strayed too far down the byways of assimilation were welcomed back into the fold as returning prodigals. It was at that point that I began to explore a world of Jewish life and tradition which had been sealed shut.

Very few of my childhood associates married within the German Jewish network. Indeed, many married out of the faith. The children of these alliances, invariably cut off from Jewish tradition, were left in a religious vacuum. Furthermore, the German-American Jews avoided their Eastern European brethren. Yet most of the considerable Jewish infusion into American artistic and intellectual life, Yiddish culture, and the Labor Movement must be attributed to Eastern European Jewry. Though their background was strictly Orthodox, many of them had become militant atheists.

My marriage to Ruth Schachter in 1962 was a drastic departure from customary practice on both sides of the family. "Your father-in-law treats you like a Presbyterian," one of my old friends observed. Both of Ruth's parents, steeped in the Orthodox Jewish tradition, were born in a small town in Galicia, a Polish province of the Austro-Hungarian Empire. After the First World War they settled in Vienna, where they raised two daughters and prospered. For them, as for so many other Jews in Germany and Austria, Hitler's final solution was at first beyond belief. When they made their eleventh-hour exit, it was with the allowable five marks. Almost all their relatives who remained in Poland perished.

The Jewish rituals and laws that my wife's family followed were largely unknown to me. So too was the matter-of-fact, often joyous participation in the festive religious occasions that punctuated their everyday lives. When our three children arrived, it became even more important to make a commitment, as a family, to those Jewish traditions and values that we wished to preserve. For my part it was an arduous expedition on seemingly alien terrain. Clues that I unearthed as I tried to retrace my family tree were often hard to interpret, especially when they were in Hebrew. I was fortunate to get lots of help on the journey.

In the end it proved to be a liberating, though painful, rebirth. Along the way I developed a strong urge to uncover — or perhaps I should say discover — the road that my family had taken away from long-standing tradition. Why had the German Jews in the United States opted to homogenize and to camouflage themselves beyond recognition? There had been widespread acculturation within all immigrant groups. But the religious experience of Protestant and Catholic immigrants tended toward institutionalization rather than dissolution. This question, which had been in the back of my mind for a long time, inspired a search for answers which led me to the writing of this book.

Henry Morgenthau III
Saunderstown, Rhode Island
1991

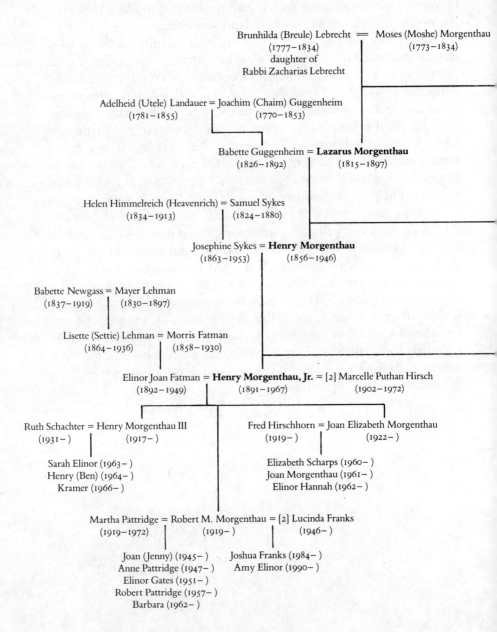

Brunhilda (Breule) Lebrecht == Moses (Moshe) Morgenthau
(1777–1834)   (1773–1834)
daughter of
Rabbi Zacharias Lebrecht

Adelheid (Utele) Landauer = Joachim (Chaim) Guggenheim
(1781–1855)   (1770–1853)

Babette Guggenheim = **Lazarus Morgenthau**
(1826–1892)   (1815–1897)

Helen Himmelreich (Heavenrich) = Samuel Sykes
(1834–1913)   (1824–1880)

Josephine Sykes = **Henry Morgenthau**
(1863–1953)   (1856–1946)

Babette Newgass = Mayer Lehman
(1837–1919)   (1830–1897)

Lisette (Settie) Lehman = Morris Fatman
(1864–1936)   (1858–1930)

Elinor Joan Fatman = **Henry Morgenthau, Jr.** = [2] Marcelle Puthan Hirsch
(1892–1949)   (1891–1967)   (1902–1972)

Ruth Schachter = Henry Morgenthau III   Fred Hirschhorn = Joan Elizabeth Morgenthau
(1931–)   (1917–)   (1919–)   (1922–)

Sarah Elinor (1963–)   Elizabeth Scharps (1960–)
Henry (Ben) (1964–)   Joan Morgenthau (1961–)
Kramer (1966–)   Elinor Hannah (1962–)

Martha Pattridge = Robert M. Morgenthau = [2] Lucinda Franks
(1919–1972)   (1919–)   (1946–)

Joan (Jenny) (1945–)   Joshua Franks (1984–)
Anne Pattridge (1947–)   Amy Elinor (1990–)
Elinor Gates (1951–)
Robert Pattridge (1957–)
Barbara (1962–)

Gerson (1809–1872) Regina (1823–1911)
Bernhard (1812–1882) Babette (1825–?)
Zacharias (1818–1898) Heinrich (1830–?)
Mengo (Max) (1820–1893)

Minna Morgenthau = Gustave Heidelberg Bertha Morgenthau (1844–1894) Recha (1855–1895)
(1850–1878) (1847–1916) Maximilian (1847–1936) Caesar (1857–1858)
  Pauline (1848–1915) Julius Caesar (1858–1929)
Louise M. Heidelberg (1877–1969) Siegfried (1851–1885) Mengo (1860–1927)
Max (Maxwell Hyde) (1878–1936) Gustave (1853–1925) Adele Louise (1861–1863)
  Ida (1854–1925) Richard Nathan Paul (1867–1891)

Mortimer J. Fox = Helen Sykes Morgenthau George W. Naumburg = Ruth Morgenthau ══ [2] John Knight
(1874–1948) (1884–1974) (1876, divorced 1936) (1894–1972) (1899, divorced 1951)

Henry M. (1907–1988) George W. Jr. (1918–)
Mortimer J. Jr. (1909–) Phillip H. (1920–)
Therese J. (Eastman) (1915–1990) Ellin (London) (1923–)

Maurice Wertheim = Alma Josephine Morgenthau = [2] Paul Lester Wiener
(1886–1950) (1887–1953) (1896, divorced 1948)

Josephine A. (Pomerance) (1910–1980)
Barbara (Tuchman) (1912–1989)
Anne R. (Werner) (1914–)

PART I

Lazarus: Up and Out

Trying to Survive in
Early Nineteenth-Century
Bavaria

RECENTLY I DISCOVERED a photograph of my great-grandfather Lazarus Morgenthau taken two years before he died at the age of eighty-two in 1897. He appears as something of a dandy, sitting erect in a straight-backed chair, immaculately groomed in a Prince Albert jacket, the loose trousers of the day flaring over glossy patent leather shoes buttoned to the ankle. With a hand of playing cards, displaying four kings fanned out toward the camera, he is smirking slightly behind his curled mustache as he gazes triumphantly at an obligingly defeated partner, an elegant young man. This hokey scene was no doubt staged for the occasion by the old man himself. Pasted on the back of the photograph is a calling card printed to resemble engraving in bold script: "Lazarus Morgenthau," and below, in smaller letters, "der achtzigjahrige Jungling, geboren den 17 August 1815, New York 15 August 1895" (the eighty-year-old youngster born 17 August 1815, New York 15 August 1895).

His granddaughter Louise Heidelberg (1877–1969, daughter of my grandfather's sister Minna) recalled Lazarus's "extreme personal fastidiousness. . . . He greatly disliked deshabille and once when he had invited some of his grandchildren to a tea party and a cold obliged him to remain in bed, he wore a dickey and his white tie over his night shirt rather than to postpone the party or to be seen undressed." This idiosyncrasy must have covered up many painful memories of a threadbare childhood.

In 1842, when he was twenty-seven, Lazarus Morgenthau wrote a short memoir that has become a kind of Rosetta Stone of clues and connections that unlock the early history of the Morgenthau families.★ This book was translated into English from the original Bavarian dialect by Louise Heidelberg. The German and English text, along with a "Foreword" and concluding "Sketch," written by Ms. Heidelberg, were printed privately by my father. Her "Sketch" covers the remainder of Lazarus's long, eventful life. It is primarily based on the recollections of his oldest son, Max, set down for this purpose at Ms. Heidelberg's request. At that time Lazarus was hard at work pulling himself up by his bootstraps. "If it is God's will that I should prosper in future years," he noted, "this little book may be read through often in order that neither pride nor arrogance may gain a foothold in my family — for the rich man can never have any concept of how the poor man lives unless he has been poor himself."

Prophetic or presumptuous, these words were fashioned when Lazarus's rise to a brief period of affluence still lay ahead of him. They were written just a year before he married Babette Guggenheim, the attractive seventeen-year-old offspring on her mother's side of the Landauers, the leading Jewish family in the southern Bavarian hamlet of Hürben. Perhaps the *Diary* was inspired by Lazarus's concern to establish his own identity before the wedding. We know that around the same time he obtained an officially stamped copy of his parents' death certificates.

No one in our immediate family ever spoke of Lazarus Morgenthau. There was a copy of his *Diary* in our library at home, but the pages remained uncut. It didn't occur to me that there was anything mysterious about this silence. Lazarus had died four years before my father was born so that he had no memory of his grandfather. My grandpa Morgenthau, usually bubbling with entertaining reminiscences, never mentioned his father. I later came to understand why, but in my youth I never inquired; I was too thoroughly

---

★ *The Diary of Lazarus Morgenthau* is the title printed on the cover of this little volume. But on the title page Lazarus himself described it more accurately and fully as *Lebens Geschichte von Lazarus Morgenthau aus Hürben bei Krumbach, von ihm selbst geschrieben Speyer, den 30ten November, 1842* (*The Life Story of Lazarus Morgenthau, of Hürben near Krumbach, written by himself, Speyer, the 30th November, 1842*).

mesmerized by Grandpa himself, progenitor of Morgenthau success.

My first glimpse of the territory where Lazarus had grown up
came at the end of World War II, when the U.S. forces became the
army of occupation. Our second cavalry group was stationed in the
forest hamlets, guarding the Czech border. In the army hierarchy,
the Twelfth Corps, to which we were attached, was in Regensburg,
the ancient Danube city that was once a Roman military outpost.
General Patton's Third Army headquarters was in Munich, the capital of Bavaria, whence I knew my great-grandfather had come. But
given the opportunity, I missed it; unfortunately in those days I had
no interest in tracing family roots. I also lacked the knowledge and
tools to launch such an exploration. I knew only that the Morgenthaus had emigrated from Mannheim. It would be thirty-five years
before I would have a second chance — in the summer of 1982.

In the *Diary,* which I studied before beginning my quest in
earnest that year, Lazarus had indicated distances in days and hours
of walking or cart riding. The communities he wrote about were
within a well-defined area of southern Germany, primarily in Bavaria. The cities and towns were in the river valleys: the Main, the
Rhine, the Neckar, the Danube, and their tributaries. Today the
autobahns cut straight through the craggy mountain forest, and cars
whiz along from point to point. In Lazarus's time roads followed
the meandering rivers, and one would find hamlets separated by a
kilometer or two and at every juncture of two streams.

Most of the great German cities like Mannheim had been leveled
to rubble by American bombers at the end of the war, while outly-
ing hamlets were left almost entirely intact. There, traditional half-
timber and stucco buildings with steeply pitched tile roofs huddled
in narrow streets and around small, cobbled squares. The only
ravages evident today were incurred by the rebuilding generated by
postwar German prosperity.

In 1982 I planned my trip through territory described in Lazarus's *Diary.* On this journey I was accompanied by Benno Szklanowski, a graduate student at the Hochschule für Jüdische Studien in
Heidelberg, who was completing his thesis on the Jewish cemetery
in Heidelberg. He was fluent in English, German, and Hebrew, and
was the owner of a station wagon, all of which were indispensable
assets for my Bavarian safari. Whenever we approached a targeted
town, Benno would home in on its Jewish cemetery. To my great

surprise many cemeteries, though neglected, had survived the Nazis. They were generally located in secluded spots on the outskirts of town, often serving a number of small neighboring communities.

The headstones, we discovered, were usually fashioned in a soft brown sandstone with a flaky surface that peels off. The more recent inscriptions were in German. Earlier inscriptions combined German and Hebrew. The earliest, however, dating from before 1850, had been worn away to the point of illegibility. Still, they often provided clues toward further elucidation through town records, which had also survived the upheaval intact. In line with characteristic German orderliness, the Jewish records were usually there along with all the others, and the younger generation of local officials tended to be solicitous in offering assistance. I once remarked on this to my good friend Rabbi Ben-Zion Gold, an Auschwitz survivor. "Yes," he responded, "they kept the records but not the people."

Lazarus Morgenthau's forebears had made a living through the performance of religious obligations — as rabbis, cantors, Hebrew teachers, or ritual slaughterers. Lazarus's father, Moses, intended his sons to continue this tradition. But with declining interest in Jewish ritual, they shifted to crafts and trade. Lazarus, who received only two years of schooling, appeared singularly ambitious and resourceful, seemingly guided by a mystical sense of destiny. "It must have been ordained by God," he declared, "that I was to write the story of my life."

Lazarus wrote that his father, Moses, was born in 1773 in the little Bavarian village of Gleusdorf, a few kilometers north of where the river Baunach flows into the Main, and still another few kilometers from the ancient city of Bamberg.

Moses was the first Morgenthau of record. Following laws established by Napoleon, Jews were required to take family names when they became citizens. Therefore it is likely that Moses took the name of Morgenthau sometime after 1813, when Bavarian Jews were granted citizenship, although some family names can be traced to an earlier date. (*Morgen Tau* is "morning dew" in German. My grandfather told a story, handed down to him — perhaps from his father — about a family member who was waiting in line at the town hall in the damp predawn to be assigned a family name. While pondering possible choices he noticed the dew on the ground and decided that the sound of *Morgen Tau* had an appealing ring.)

The Morgenthaus meanwhile were prosperous enough to have been granted limited rights of residence in Gleusdorf. This was a privilege, not an absolute right, proffered or withheld by local authority and subject to capricious revocation. To retain the right of residence one had to stay in the authorities' good graces, make special payments, and suffer many restrictions, including certain rules governing occupation and marriage. The number of Jewish families permitted to live in each community was very small. Thus, residence conferred high status: it meant that people could establish families and conduct their lives in an orderly fashion.★

Moses had four older brothers who jealously guarded their residence rights and in so doing unceremoniously shoved him out into the world. In later years, Lazarus responded to these uncles with bitter consternation. He wrote that his father "left home at sixteen years of age to become a teacher of Hebrew and a cantor." He later became a *shochet* (a ritual slaughterer), a position of high status.†

As an itinerant worker, Moses struggled for several years until he had saved a little nest egg of two hundred gulden (52.5 gulden were coined out of 500 grams of fine silver). He received a position in Hobach, in Untermain, which is part of the rabbinical district of Friedberg. The head rabbi was Zacharias Lebrecht, who claimed, as have countless others, that he was a descendant of Rashi, famous for his commentaries on the Holy Scriptures and the Talmud.

"My father," Lazarus continued, "had often to visit the head rabbi, and soon it came to pass that the daughter became his wife." The wedding took place in Hobach in 1808. Moses' marriage to Brunhilda (also called Breule) Lebrecht was a big step up in the world.★★

Moses and Brunhilda's third son, Lazarus, was born in Kleinwaldstadt on August 17, 1815. Two years earlier his father had

---

★There was a considerable Jewish underclass that did not have permission to live anywhere. Some became drifters and engaged in criminal activities. A few, mostly women, married Christians and converted. More frequently the community took responsibility for its homeless brethren, providing temporary board and lodgings. The women became house servants and the men, according to their skills, fulfilled various religious occupations, especially as teachers.
★★As rabbi for the district, Zacharias was the leader of the *Landgemeinde,* the organization that supervised the Jewish life of the scattered congregation and represented the community in its dealings with the civil authorities.
†The *shochet* was required to pass exacting exams on the ritual of slaughtering and the laws of *kashruth* as well as the underlying Talmudic tractate.

accepted an invitation to serve there as the town's *shochet*. The salary was somewhat larger than what he had been paid in Hobach but was barely enough to feed his rapidly expanding family.

During the course of my explorations in 1982 I stopped at Kleinwaldstadt, a small Bavarian market town on the east bank of the Main River where the valley widens into a flat plain and the Odenwald forms a dark, steeply rising backdrop. On a spur off the heavily trafficked highway and extending to the river's edge is one of those little communities that remains quietly untouched by the bustle of industrial progress in the region. On our arrival, we went to the rathaus and announced our mission to the bürgermeister. He responded with more than perfunctory courtesy, sending a secretary scurrying to bring in the oldest town ledgers. The search for a Morgenthau entry proved fruitless. However, many of the buildings either date back to the time of Lazarus's birth or have been rebuilt to look much as they must have at the time of Lazarus's infancy. The small Jewish community had for the most part emptied out of town, heading for the larger cities long before Hitler. But our host pointed out a narrow street labeled Synagogengasse, that extends from the marketplace in front of the rathaus to the riverbank where the shul (synagogue) was located. The old houses with attached barns and fenced courtyards form solid walls that lean into either side of the narrow street. Constructed of plastered stone and timber window and door frames elaborately carved to resemble drapery folds, they bulge as though ready to burst open and spill out people, barnyard fowl, and the family cow. Early in the nineteenth century, the Jews in Kleinwaldstadt were prospering modestly in the river trade in textiles and cattle and as butchers. Although it had enough families to support a shul and a boys' Hebrew school, the community did not have its own cemetery and was compelled to bury its dead at Rebernau, a downstream town.

In 1818 Lazarus's brother Zacharias was born. Lazarus wrote that "soon after the town of Hobach regretted having let my father go and agreed to write and offer him a better salary. My parents accepted this proposal" and returned to Hobach.

In another two years, after the birth of a fifth son, Mengo, the family was again on the move when Moses received a letter from the congregation in Hergershausen, in the duchy of Darmstadt, asking whether he would "consent to come there in the capacity of teacher, cantor, and *shochet*." The position was a very good one, but life remained very difficult for his growing family.

At an early age Lazarus became sensitive to his mother's hardships. His first recollection — he was four — was of his infant brother Zacharias spilling a pot of boiling coffee on himself "so that his abdomen was laid open and the intestines could be seen. One foot was very much injured and the right hand incapacitated to the present day because the nerves contracted immediately." The accident cost his parents several hundred gulden they could ill afford. During the convalescence Brunhilda got no rest. "She was always alone, she never had a maid except during her confinements and then four days was the longest period that they were with her. After that she no longer considered herself on the sick list."

In 1822 Lazarus himself "was attacked by an acute stomach trouble that lasted a whole year." The doctor diagnosed it as a dangerous colic for which he could do nothing. In his torment Lazarus remembered that he "threw over chairs and was doubled up with agony." Later he recalled that "often when I sat alone by her side she reminded me of this moment, no physician was able to help, only my mother with God's help. She prepared a household remedy and soon after that I recovered."

A year later, with the addition of the first daughter, Regina, the family moved to Obersimmern, where in 1825 an ordinance was issued, stating "that no alien would be tolerated in the Grand Duchy of Darmstadt." Moses, a Bavarian, was ordered to leave within forty-eight hours. "My mother being pregnant," Lazarus recounted, "went to see the Duke and received permission to remain there one year longer. That same year my sister Babette was born. We were now seven children and no favorable prospects in view."

In desperation, Moses determined to send his sons to Frankfurt, where they could earn money as cantors. "The idea was a good one and we acted upon it. The oldest brother [Gerson] was fifteen, Bernhard was twelve and I was ten years old."

The three young brothers "went gaily off to Frankfurt," where they sang in private homes. They were so small that they had to stand on chairs, but "they were much complimented and earned quite a lot of money." In order to save as much as possible, they begged lodgings from the local *shochet*. He gave them a bundle of straw to sleep on and his "smeary coat," which was not wide enough to cover all three of them so that one was always left out freezing. After three weeks on tour, their pockets full, they returned home.

The joyful reunion ended abruptly when the family received

notice from the town that "the year of grace" was up. "My parents were obliged to remove to the home of my Father, that is to Kleis- dorf [was in fact Gleusdorf] Konig Bad in Untermaingruss in Ba- varia." In his *Diary,* Lazarus recalled the grueling trek as the family of nine with all their possessions lumbered back to Gleusdorf for ten freezing days in an uncovered wagon hired for the occasion.

When they were an hour's distance from their home, Lazarus and his father went ahead on foot "to give notice of our arrival." His mother "went to my Father's four brothers who locked their doors against her and declared that Moses 'could go back where he came from.' The carter wanted to drive on, so our household possessions had to stand for several hours on the public highway until the innkeeper took pity on my Mother and gave her a room."

After Moses failed in his attempts to resolve the family housing problem, it was left to Brunhilda. Lazarus recorded, "On the fol- lowing day in the forenoon we met my Mother and one of my brothers on the way to the county courthouse." After Brunhilda had pleaded with the authorities, "the county judge at once ordered the Bürgermeister . . . and the same day we drove to our lodgings."

During the journey, Lazarus was deeply depressed by his moth- er's failing health: "a catarrh of one eye, a watery condition due to her many worries." He watched her try to hold the family together while his father seemed to be losing his grip and giving up. It was a nightmare that he could never expunge from his memory.

As their father's earnings repeatedly fell short of the family's barest needs, the boys' singing group went on the road more fre- quently. When they were at home for three or four weeks between trips, they foraged in the woods and went "to the farmers and begged for potatoes, peas, beans and lentils." Their parents, though too ashamed to admit it, were secretly doing the same thing. Ger- son, the eldest brother, often gave his mother money privately. Lazarus made the observation that "as is usual in marriages where there is little money, there had been some quarreling" between his parents.

But their meager existence was enlivened by the joyful rituals of their faith.

For breakfast each child received three or four potatoes and a small piece of bread. Very rarely coffee. At midday potatoes, soup and veg- etables. One pound of meat had to suffice for nine individuals, each child received a piece of meat the size of an egg yolk. And this occurred not daily but four times per week. But I can assure my dear ones that when we were gathered together on Friday evening our appetites barely half satisfied and our Father and Mother began to sing the Sabbath songs and we children joined in, that there could be nothing better or more beautiful. We thought neither of hunger or money, briefly, it never entered our heads.

Before the Industrial Revolution reached the German states, the majority of the population was struggling for survival in rural communities. Extreme malnutrition and outright starvation during times of famine were not unusual. Jews didn't own farmland. They were not much interested in agriculture, although when they could they would keep a cow and chickens for family use. The rural Christians were scarcely better off. Both Christian and Jewish families tended to be large — ten or fifteen children was normal. Jews were especially attentive to sanitation, meaning more surviving children, more mouths to feed.

As the catarrh in Brunhilda's eye began to abscess and her health declined, her impatience with Moses mounted. She couldn't let him forget how poorly he measured up to her father, the revered Rabbi Zacharias Lebrecht. It was a merciful God, she reminded Moses, who had spared the rabbi from living to see his daughter and grandchildren wandering across Bavaria begging.

From the very beginning of her marriage Brunhilda established herself as the stronger partner. Her willfulness, which matched the determined set of her dark, heavy features, gave her a haughty, disagreeable bearing. The children learned to depend on their mother. Lazarus worshipped her.

Moses, though handsome and charming, with considerable knowledge of Jewish ritual, lacked confidence. The more his wife goaded him, the more he retreated into his feelings of inadequacy, which became self-fulfilling prophecies. But what ultimately defeated him was his failure to recognize changed cultural and economic circumstances.

Moses had grown up at the very dawn of an era when the new opportunities for Jews in a predominantly Christian society were still uncertain and fraught with danger. While powerful rulers promoted Jews from the status of stranger to citizen, capricious local authorities reimposed all kinds of restrictions. Jews skilled in crafts and manufacture, which had recently been opened to them, and which would benefit the local economy, were favored. Failing to understand this, Moses continued to seek employment in the shrinking market for his skills in Jewish ritual. At the same time he groped to find ways for his sons to follow in his footsteps, arranging to have them trained as cantors.

Moses became a kind of negative role model. Ultimately, Lazarus decided not to pursue his career as a cantor, and as he matured he gradually departed from strict observance of Jewish law and rituals. Later, with great daring and flair, he headed into the mainstream of German society. During the metamorphosis his strong mystical attachment to his mother was mixed with a sense of guilt. At times he confused her powers with those of the Almighty. But he also believed, as she herself insisted, that with her death he would be released to go out in the world and prosper.

By the time Lazarus was fourteen, Brunhilda's health had deteriorated so much that her family could no longer rely on her to hold them together. Overwhelmed by self-pity, Moses gave up. "Time is passing," he told his children. "You are getting big, and to come right down to it, you really know nothing. What is to become of you? . . . I want to go on a long journey with you and it shall be the last. I will try to place you en route in spite of its being very hard on me for then I can no longer rely on you for help. But I trust in God and he will not forsake me."

Moses traveled with his three older sons to towns large and small. They even tried their luck in Munich but, Lazarus recounted, "were not permitted to sing because there was a rule against strange cantors singing there. Nevertheless we earned some money in private houses."

In the course of their wanderings they stopped in Hürben, where there was a thriving Jewish community. After an audition the boys were invited to sing in the Saturday services. "If anyone there had told me, 'You will some day be a citizen of this place,'" Lazarus noted, "I would really not have believed it, but everything is possible to God Almighty."

In the town of Grieshaben, between Hürben and the great city of Augsburg, they went to see Cantor Rafael Sänger, who was greatly impressed by Bernhard's voice and agreed to take him for training. A year later, when Sänger was appointed head cantor and religious instructor in Hürben, he took Bernhard with him to be an assistant cantor.

As their mother's health steadily worsened, Gerson, the oldest, was needed "as the maid of all work." He continued to live at home in Gleusdorf while apprenticing himself in the lowly trade of shoe-maker in Mursbach, a half-hour walk. "In the early morning," Lazarus recorded, "he made the beds and prepared the breakfast for the family. He had to be at his master's at eight o'clock, and in the evening he went home and cooked supper. Thus the sick mother was obliged to lie many a day, the whole day without anything to eat."

Lazarus was the last son to be farmed out. He noted, on reaching Bamberg, that his father learned "that teacher Stern from Bayreuth was there and was seeking a few good singers for the newly orga-nized choir. . . . My father sought him out and found him at Rabbi Rosenblatt's. An hour later I was called and the daughter of the Rabbi had to test my voice. . . . She played piano and I sang. She told Mr. Stern that she could use me as an alto."

The education that Lazarus obtained at Mr. Stern's was the only formal schooling he ever received. "I learned how to read correctly, how to write correctly and how to do sums correctly. And I was able to do the same in religion. I tried very hard and the little I have acquired I learned in two years."

When the singing course was over, a number of the students went off to the seminary in Bamberg. Lazarus then made an impor-tant decision, one that affected the rest of his life. "I realized," he wrote, "that no object would be gained even if I achieved the position of cantor in ten years. I went home and told my parents I wanted to learn a trade. That was satisfactory to them. So I selected tailoring and apprenticed myself to a master tailor." Thus, he en-tered the world of commerce.

"My parents laid their hands solemnly on my head and blessed me," he noted. His mother wept and reminded him of his duty to God. She was preparing to go to the Julien Hospital in Würzburg, so Lazarus set out to find work nearby. "About two hours from Gleusdorf I met a preacher of whom I asked aid and he gave me nine kreuzer. What a joy, now I had a whole gulden! I continued my journey to Würzburg begging what I needed each day, and even saved a few gulden for I slept on straw every night, lived on a whole loaf of bread and one kreuzer's worth of brandy. I didn't find work in Würzburg and therefore went to Lauterbach near Karlstadt and found work at a [Christian] master tailor named Spisz."

People began to warn Lazarus that his master was a vicious

drunkard who often "trounced his apprentices out of bed in the middle of the night." Experience soon bore out their direst predictions when, as Lazarus reported, "he came home three or four nights and broke down the doors and smashed everything." Lazarus huddled in bed "half dead with fright." Nevertheless he stuck to his job and started sending money home, although he managed to find lodgings with an "Israelite."

A few months later he received word that his mother, accompanied by the dutiful Gerson, had been admitted to the Julien Hospital. Lazarus became increasingly depressed with morbid forebodings. Eventually he set out to visit her in the hospital. By chance he discovered that she was lying in bed at a village inn that he was passing. As it happened, she had left the hospital to visit him. He recounted their meeting in his *Diary*.

> "I wanted to see you once more. . . . For surely this is the last time." I asked her how things had gone at the hospital.
>
> "Badly, my child, the doctors give me little encouragement. I am past help and I would gladly die if only my little ones were provided for."
>
> "God will help," I said. Where the world over was another such mother to be found who with one foot already in the grave yet for love of me, her son, wanted to see me once more.

By this time, Bernhard had moved to Hürben, accompanying his teacher, Rafael Sänger. Bernhard had gained employment as a turner's apprentice in addition to his responsibilities as Sänger's assistant. In August 1832 he wrote to Lazarus: "Dear Brother: I received your letter promptly and you ask me whether I do not advise your coming here; I can give you no advice other than this: if you can think of no other solution, then come here." Lazarus gave this reluctant welcome the most positive interpretation.

To reach Krumbach today, heading east on the autobahn from the city of Ulm toward Augsburg, one branches off on minor roads to the south. The Kammel River, which passes through Krumbach, of which Hürben is now a part, is a mere four or five meters wide. The Kammel's northern flow toward the Danube is barely rapid enough to propel the waterwheels of the mills once located along its course. Today Krumbach is a neat, modernized town, host to a number of light industrial plants. But considerable evidence of

Lazarus's Hürben remains. At the town hall I was shown photographs of the old marketplace and the synagogue. The latter, which had been rebuilt for the last time shortly before Lazarus's arrival, was a handsome white stucco building in the neoclassic style of that era. Although increasingly in disuse, it remained standing until it was torched and leveled by the Nazis on Kristallnacht in 1938. A granite monument testifying to its existence and destruction has been placed in a grassy plot on the street that has regained the name of Synagogengasse.

Just outside Krumbach on the road to Augsburg one can pick up an almost hidden path to the Jewish cemetery, which is protected by a high wall and a locked iron gate. We obtained the key at the town hall and let ourselves in. Situated on a grassy, wooded knoll, the cemetery is peacefully forlorn. Many of the inscriptions are faded, but there are still many legible Landauers, Guggenheims, and Guggenheimers.

In this same town, in the late fall of 1832, as Lazarus was arriving, it began "to snow hard" and "walking on slushy roads was bad." It was "on Thursday afternoon at two o'clock," he noted in his *Diary,* that he "asked for the master turner who lived opposite the Sternwirt [Star Inn]." Nothing would dampen his spirits — not the harsh weather nor the ambiguous welcome in his brother Bernhard's letter. Lazarus was full of optimism and the energizing stimulus of taking a calculated risk. What he had no way of knowing was that the growth and prosperity of this Jewish community was just then at its zenith and that he would encounter the onset of its decline.

There were no Jews living in Krumbach itself, although many walked across the bridge from Hürben to work there, as Bernhard Morgenthau did.★ Half the population in Hürben was Jewish. This arrangement of satellite, or sister, towns was to be found throughout the German and Central European states. But unlike the East European *shtetls,* these communities were not rural ghettos.

As Lazarus tried to settle in with his brother, he soon learned

---

★While the German Jews were totally excluded from many cities and towns, in those where they were granted residence rights they lived in close proximity to Christian neighbors. When they attained a critical mass, they organized their own religious and communal institutions. Jewish families isolated in tiny hamlets had to survive on their own under the guardianship of an itinerant district rabbi, like Brunhilda Morgenthau's late father, Zacharias Lebrecht. The sixty thousand Jews then inhabiting Bavaria were less than 1 percent of the total population.

that opportunities for outsiders were extremely hard to come by. "I tried to get work at several tailors in Hürben and Krumbach," he wrote, "but without success." The day came when he was prepared to leave in despair.

> It was exactly half past eleven when I came out of Isaac Levinger's house with my brother. My eyes turned to the sky and my heart beat very rapidly. I saw winter passing and I was to set forth once more. I thought of my mother's words: "Trust in God." As I reached the end of the street a voice called out: "Bernhard, come up a bit with your brother."
>
> It was baker Feisel. They were just eating their midday meal and invited me at once to partake, but I did not feel like eating, my low spirits did not permit. As luck would have it, tailor Funder happened to be there.
>
> "Mr. Funder," Feisel said, "you must oblige me and take this lad into your employ; you need not give him board, lodging or a ten thaler salary."
>
> "All right," said Funder, "but I don't have much to do."
>
> "At least, you have probably enough old trousers to patch."

Lazarus worked for half a year and later received a meager salary. He made a little extra brushing and mending clothes in the Abraham and Samuel Landauer households. He had a fortnightly schedule of free meals — an obligation assumed by the community — which he ate on appointed days at different households, mostly Landauers and Levingers.

For three years, his lodgings with Isaac Haimann were also free, save when he had to go to market with him to help him sell his goods. But he learned much in the process. "I worked day and night in order to send home one ducat every month to my sick mother, and to make myself some clothes."

Impatient with the regulations designed to slow the progress of apprentices and keep control in the hands of the masters, Lazarus was constantly on the lookout for shortcuts and ingenious innovations. One day at the end of the meal at the Landauers' home, opportunity knocked. Mrs. Landauer said to Lazarus, "Come, go for me to Krumbach to master tailor Nagele and tell him he should finish my jacket or else I will bring a charge against him."

Lazarus dutifully crossed the bridge to Krumbach and delivered the message.

"Everything would be all right if I could only get enough journeymen," Nagele complained.

"What would you give me per day if I came to work for you?" Lazarus inquired.

"Nine kreuzer."

It was a deal and a good one, more than doubling the twenty-four kreuzer per week that Funder paid him. Then, in the second week on the new job, Nagele gave Lazarus a wedding coat to quilt. Observing that "every bridegroom had to wear a quilted coat and this kind of work paid well," Lazarus cut a pattern for himself, "in order that if any work of this kind should ever come my way I would be able to handle it well."

Impatient to take advantage of his newfound skill, he implored his pregnant landlady, Yette Haimann, to let him quilt a jacket for the expected infant.

"If I thought you could really do it, yes."

"I'll pay for the material if I spoil it for you," Lazarus responded.

The order was his, and he pushed himself to complete it, working on his own "a few hours early in the morning and in the evenings." The jacket was finished none too soon. Yette was prematurely delivered of a daughter, and the jacket was laid on the cradle, where it was much admired by all her visitors.

Encouraged by his success, Lazarus resolved to make a man's jacket of white percale and raffle it off with ninety chances at eighteen kreutzer each. All the chances were sold in two days, earning him thirteen gulden. Lazarus made more jackets and tefillin★ as well. All sold for a profit.

Working alone in the black, silent hours, the youth was sometimes overwhelmed with a feeling of emptiness he could not explain. "Do you not lack some other kind of knowledge?" he asked himself. "You know very little of your religion." Save for the two years' studying in Bayreuth, he had received little formal religious training. In response to an inner urging, he now committed Saturday afternoons to reading the Pentateuch, which gave him "infinite satisfaction." Encouraged to go further, he engaged Abraham Steppacher from Kleinmundlichen, who was studying in Hürben with Rabbi Salomon Schwabacher. Lazarus then gave up his night work

---

★Phylacteries: two small leather boxes containing biblical inscriptions, worn by Jewish men on the left arm and head during prayer.

"for sheer love of studying," often working with Steppacher until three o'clock in the morning.

Lazarus engaged a second tutor to give him a rudimentary secular education. Twin certificates, both dated September 11, 1839, attest to his diligence. The primary document, signed R. B. Sänger, "school teacher in religion and cantor," states:

> During his seven-years stay here, from November 1832 until now, Lazarus Morgenthau of Gleusdorf Royal Regional Court of Baunach received intensive instruction in religion, especially in the Torah; since his interest in religion is especially great, as everyone in this town will testify, he made excellent progress, which is attested by the undersigned with the special mention in all truth that his moral and ethical conduct is most commendable.

The companion document certified that "journeyman tailor Lazarus Morgenthau . . . received from the undersigned the prescribed instruction in all elementary school subjects, and that he made very good progress."

Having accumulated a fortune of ninety-three gulden, he went to old Bathan and begged him to invest his money with a hog dealer: "Bathan liked me well for I had often been sent to his house by my master, Nagele. He went straight to the hog dealer, Lib, and on the same day, a Wednesday, Lib gave me a note that in the space of half a year I would receive exactly one hundred gulden for my ninety-three. How delighted I was to be worth one hundred gulden."

At the same time, Lazarus sent as much money home as he could spare to help cover his mother's expenses at the Julien Hospital. He knew that it was not enough, and often dire presentiments flooded his imagination. One evening as he left Bendick Gumb's house, where he had been taking supper,

> it was somewhat dark and it seemed to me as though I had seen something white walk in front of me; my depression increased. I again saw something white and this continued until I reached my lodgings. . . . On Saturday . . . a letter came for me and my brother Bernhard. It brought the sad tidings that my good mother had passed away on Wednesday.

In his grief, Lazarus remembered his mother saying, "Child, as soon as I die you may be sure that I will pray to the Almighty, and all will surely be well with you." He did feel liberated, although he could hardly bear to admit it to himself. Wracked by a chilling shudder, he experienced a flash of psychic awareness, which he accepted as a legacy of his mother's piety and a reward for his loving devotion. "On the very day when she departed from this world I already did one good stroke of business." It was on this day that the hog dealer, Lib, paid him the full one hundred gulden for the ninety-three.

A week after Lazarus's mother died, his father passed away without any warning. The orphaned brothers and sisters at home were quite helpless; the youngest, Heinrich, also called Heyum, was only four years old. Moses' four brothers, who had failed to aid him, seemed to construe his destitution as an insult to the family honor. What feelings of guilt they may have had upon his death were expressed in self-righteous outrage, as they distanced themselves from the calamity. Two weeks earlier, when Brunhilda lay dying, they had tried to absolve themselves by writing to inform her oldest son, Gerson, that it was time for him to come home. He left his job and returned home immediately, but by the time he got there his mother had been buried and his father too had died.

Lazarus told us that as Gerson, on his return, hurried down the street where the family lived, he sensed that people were staring at him. Entering the house, he found his father's corpse lying on the floor and his five young brothers and sisters sitting around it.

Gerson assumed responsibility and soon made it his business to have the children learn something. As Lazarus noted, "Every week he came to look after brother Mengo, who was learning to be a weaver in Memmelsdorf. Sister Regina was educated in Rechendorf." Meanwhile Moses' four brothers played out their roles in character. On the way home after the interment, they scolded their weeping young nephews and nieces, warning, "'If you do not do what we want we will have you placed at Plankenberg [orphanage].' Very consoling and kind words indeed!"

Lazarus observed the year of mourning in strict accordance with Jewish law but had little time for introspection. Indeed, his memoir was a notice of his resolve that never again would his family be so sorely tried; above all, that no wife of his should ever be exposed to the kind of bitter humiliation that his mother had endured.

· 2 ·

An Ambitious Tailor
Cuts a Few Corners

WITH HIS NEWFOUND FREEDOM, Lazarus focused all his energy and determination on promoting himself. He found a new master, the tailor Abraham Mühlschneidersohn. Learning quickly, he was able to cut and finish garments on his own at the end of six months. By then he was confident and ready to go into business for himself, but to do so he needed to find a master "who would let me use his name." He managed to make a deal with a tailor in Hürben named Kolb, who was totally blind. After a successful half year, however, complaints were lodged against the arrangement by Kolb's peers, and he did not want to continue.

Just at this time, a journeyman ladies' tailor, who sometimes made cravats for Christian gentlemen, came to work for Kolb. Lazarus "paid very close attention when [the journeyman] worked and began to experiment." It was a time when men's fashion prescribed austere black and gray in reaction against the bright plumage associated with prerevolutionary, fashionable French aristocrats. In the aftermath, one of the few permissible displays of color was in a man's cravat, "made very stiff so that one could not move the head [when the cravat was wound] around the neck." Lazarus made such a cravat for himself, and one Saturday, he

> went to the synagogue and stood in the middle of the temple where the Holy Scripture is read for I was there as a singer. The teacher, Hochstadter, stood at the same place.
> "Where did you get that cravat?" he asked me.
> "I made it myself."
> "So, well, you must make me one like that, too."

Lazarus set right to work that Sunday, reporting, "God now sent me the following thought: I went to tailor Funder, who was also a merchant and a dealer of second hand goods, bought a scrap of silk that was, however, old . . . for nine kreutzer. I made 3 cravats. The first went to Samuel Landauer for one gulden 12 kreutzer. The second went to Fogel for one gulden, the third to Bernhard Levinger."

Lazarus had long since made it his practice to call on God for assistance in overcoming all the vicissitudes of daily existence, but notwithstanding his acknowledged appeal for aid from the Almighty, he was, in practice, inclined to rely on his own nose for new opportunities and on his innate ability to exploit them. Thus, as he had used an infant's cradle to show off a quilted jacket, he advertised his cravats from the bimah★ in the synagogue.

His entrepreneurial talent enabled him to expand his markets. He bought wholesale "a considerable amount of goods for about fifty gulden." He started a small manufacturing operation, hiring "several girls who could sew," whom he supervised between trips. Up until this point, he had operated as a door-to-door peddler, occasionally selling from an inn. The next step up was to sell at county fairs or in large towns on market days. He hired a booth in each place as he made the circuit along the Danube valley from Ulm to Regensburg and north to Nördlingen, then south to Augsburg and the great Bavarian capital, Munich. "I took my whole case and also a good sized box full of cravats on my back, the load becoming so heavy that I felt where the straps had cut into both my shoulders for more than a fortnight."

Though he was weighed down physically, his spirits remained buoyant. He adjusted his general appearance to suit his cosmopolitan customers. He allowed himself to go bareheaded, his blond locks flowing down his neck in the romantic manner. His sharp blue eyes were deep-set and partially hidden under a low, receding brow. His mustache was full, but at twenty-one he could be excused for shaving off what would otherwise have been a scruffy beard. He was not handsome in the conventional sense but exuded an electric self-assurance that attracted attention on the road as it did in Hürben. Above average in height, he moved with an energetic swagger, his well-proportioned figure displayed to advantage in expertly

★A raised platform in the center of the synagogue, with a desk for the reading of the scroll of the Jewish law.

tailored trousers and jacket. He had made a calculated decision to abandon the Jewish uniform of black, loose-fitting garments. To wear one of his cravats would have made him intolerably hot while he hiked through the countryside, but he always put one on as he entered town, serving at once to add to his dignity and to model his merchandise.

As Lazarus moved about in the south Bavarian markets, he discovered that in restricting himself to doing business with Jews only he was needlessly opting out of the lion's share of the market. That spring he made arrangements to go to Landshut, where the Fair Committee did not know in advance whether he was a Jew. Lazarus recalled: "Therefore they held two booths in readiness, one in the Jewish section and one in the Christian. . . . I went to the police station to find out where my booth was situated. The Commissioner said: 'Oh, there are no more to be had, but I could give you a very good booth in Grubstrasse where the Christians stand.'" Lazarus reports that he did "very good business" and went from there to the Regensburg fair.

While Lazarus tested the waters in the mainstream of Christian commerce, he held fast in his scrupulous observance of Mosaic law. He perceived no conflict in his conduct. His actions seemed reasonable in a compartmentalized world. So when he went to Nördlingen, he found lodgings with his teacher's parents, noting that "they lived in Klein Nördlingen, a half hour's distance from Nördlingen where the Fair was held. I did this only in order to lodge with Jews." Every morning he put on *tefillin,* and when he was between trips he went to the synagogue to pray in the afternoon.

While he was at the Fürth fair, someone he did business with, seeing what a good salesman he was, suggested that he add dressing gowns to his line of merchandise. Lazarus acquiesced, and "this speculation turned out quite well." His business continued to expand. He "engaged several more girls to work and rented three rooms in another story at J. S. Landauer's."

When Lazarus Morgenthau arrived in Hürben in 1832, a miserable, half-frozen seventeen-year-old whose toes stuck out of worn boots, the Landauers had been among the first to take pity on him. A half-dozen years later, pity changed to admiration. Entirely on his own, drawing on his nimble wit and boundless energy, he had become a man of substance. In turn, Lazarus observed the progress of the

Landauers. He noted that there was a firm bond of trust within the family, and apprehensive mistrust, or at least an air of detachment, regarding everyone else. Even within the Jewish community, to which the Landauers gave generously — of themselves and their means, and were in turn much respected — it was always family first. The family unit must remain free to move on as the times dictated.

In communities like Hürben, there were always a few families that constituted a kind of establishment. They did business with one another, jointly assumed responsibility for religious and communal life, and cemented relations through multiple marriages. Very often two or more siblings married opposite numbers in other families. If a husband or wife died, the surviving spouse often married an in-law.

The Hürben experience was replicated in other southern German towns, where my ancestors and those of family friends in the United States resided before they eventually found their way to the New World. Most of these towns were situated on the banks of the Main, Danube, Rhine, and Neckar rivers or their tributaries. The communities great and small were connected by roads that followed the river valleys, providing the easiest passage for the traveler on foot or in a horse-drawn cart, for the men who were peddlers and purveyors of Jewish ritual, and for entire families forced to move in response to the uncertainties and restrictions of residency rights. As the Jewish communities were sometimes very small, marriages were often arranged between parties living at some distance. Beyond these formalities, no one had time or money for casual socializing. As a result, one finds little evidence of acquaintanceship among most of the families in this area who, after they were transplanted to the United States, established such a tight network of intricate, multiple connections.

The pecking order among families from Germany would be radically altered in the New World. Those who had faced the most adverse circumstances in Germany were the first to emigrate. Their early arrival gave them a head start, and they were often able to sustain their lead over those who could afford to be more leisurely in their departure. Thus German Jews in America, who had not known each other in the old country, shared a vast heritage of common experiences that were important in cementing their relationships in the United States. Fiercely preoccupied with adapting, they had little time for reminiscing. Still, there was a comfortable consensus regarding what they chose to remember and, more significantly, what they had decided to forget.

Four more years would elapse before Lazarus felt able to make his move, years that again took him far afield. His *Diary* provides the bare bones of the story. It was completed on November 30, 1842, in Speyer. In it he makes few references to his residence there, but it seems he was experimenting with the possibilities of city life. Speyer, then the capital of the Bavarian Palatinate, is situated at the confluence of the Rhine and the Speyerbach rivers in what was then a richly productive agricultural area. One of the important crops was tobacco. Lazarus probably noticed that Speyer was a burgeoning center of tobacco manufactures, including cigars, and that some of the recent entrants into the business were Jews.

The following spring, back in Hürben, Lazarus became engaged to marry Babette Guggenheim. Babette's mother, Adelheid (Utele), was, on her mother's side, a member of Hürben's first family, the Landauers, who had so readily befriended Lazarus ten years earlier. Babette's father, Joachim Guggenheim, had been born in Lengnau, Switzerland, in 1770 and later emigrated north to Bavaria.★

Among my grandfather Morgenthau's papers I found a penciled note in his hand stating that he was named for his grandfather Joachim, or Chaim, Guggenheim. It was the habit of Jews at that time to give children the Christian names that were suggested — sometimes quite vaguely — by their Hebrew names. Thus Chaim seemed to suggest Joachim and, in later generations, Heyum, then Heinrich, which was ultimately translated into English as Henry.

I have an ink sketch of Joachim Guggenheim, his craggy facial features crowned with an ornamented, high-crowned yarmulke. He and Babette's mother had married in 1820, when he was fifty and she thirty-nine. Both had survived previous spouses. From Adel-

---

★Lengnau, at the time of Joachim's birth, was one of the two remaining Jewish communities in German-speaking Switzerland. The Swiss had imposed severe limitations on Jewish settlement, causing many Jews to head for Germany and France, where restrictions had eased somewhat in the immediate post-Napoleonic era. But by the middle of the nineteenth century, with Europe once again in turmoil, Swiss Jews were joining the multinational wave of immigration to the United States. Thus in 1848 Meyer Guggenheim of Lengnau went to New York, where he and his nine sons established the eminent American Guggenheim family. Odds are that Joachim Guggenheim was a blood relative of Meyer, although there is no absolute proof.

heid's first marriage, to a Levinger, there was at least one son, Bernhard, to whom Lazarus refers as his brother-in-law in his *Diary*. Together Joachim and Adelheid produced three children. Babette, the youngest, was more like a granddaughter to her father, who indulged her with that special autumn fondness an older man reserves for a blossoming female. He was reluctant to give her away in marriage but was persuaded by his wife, who had been encouraged by her Landauer relatives. They had observed Lazarus's advance and recognized him as a man who would, with God's help, go far.

According to Louise Heidelberg's account, Lazarus "had known Babette as a child and had watched her grow into womanhood." He was especially taken by "her poise, tact and extraordinarily sweet nature." Meanwhile, he was employing all his energy and skill to present himself as a suitable bridegroom.

During the final weeks before the wedding, the flurry of preparations under Adelheid's competent supervision was building to a dizzying crescendo. Marriage was a family affair — too serious business to involve the whims of a seventeen-year-old bride. Immediately after the week of nuptial celebration, she would be departing with her husband on a long journey to take up residence in Speyer.

As Babette looked forward to this strange world, her curiosity outweighed her fears. She was confident that she would be a good wife. Older women in the family had often complimented her on her sewing and cooking abilities. Her father had encouraged her love of reading and music. There were not many in Hürben who were familiar with Heine and Lessing, as she was. People spoke of her cultured taste with awe, although some thought it scandalous. Babette had heard that in the city all the women who could afford a servant spent time reading during the day. Some, like her, played the piano.

While Babette's primary concerns were connected with her projected move away from Hürben and the endless wedding details, she was by no means indifferent to the man she was marrying. She had been pleasantly aware of Lazarus Morgenthau for as long as she could remember, whereas some girls she knew had been married off to total strangers. When their families had been unable to find a suitable man in Hürben, they had used the services of a marriage broker to find a bridegroom in one of the bigger towns — Ulm,

Augsburg, as far away as Regensburg. It was the broker's responsibility to match the families as fairly as possible. The size of the bride's dowry was of primary consideration, as well as the social and financial status of her family. Of great value was the right of residence in a community, the number of new households the family was allowed to establish, and ownership of a house.

Lazarus and Babette were married on November 2, 1843, and set up housekeeping in Speyer. The town was buzzing with the news that Ludwig I, the Bavarian king, had announced his intention to build a new city endowed with his name. Ludwigshafen was located on the Rhine, directly opposite Mannheim, the great port city of the independent grand duchy of Baden.

Lazarus was intrigued. Furthermore, incentives were being offered to businessmen (including a limited number of Jews) to settle there. It was just the kind of gamble he was looking for. So a few months after her arrival in Speyer, the pregnant Babette was on the move again. In December 1844 their firstborn, Bertha, was delivered in Ludwigshafen.

In the following year, Lazarus found developments disappointingly slow. He fixed his gaze across the Rhine on the bustling city of Mannheim. On the riverfront he could see ships unloading and loading. Small barkentine-rigged sailboats plying their traffic floated down from the southern headwaters and relied on the erratic breezes to fight their way back upstream against the strong, steady current. On the docks their cargoes were reloaded onto sturdier ships and barges together with the manufactured goods of the city and the agricultural produce of the hinterland to proceed downstream toward the North Sea.

· 3 ·

Mannheim:
Success and Failure
in the Cigar Business

TOWARD THE END of 1847 the ferment of revolution was in the air. In Baden the liberal reforms under Archduke Leopold had encouraged the Radicals to press for ever bolder demands. In the winter of 1848, with news of the revolution in Paris, serious disorder spread like wildfire in Baden. By the following year, there was near-total anarchy. Following an insurrection by the army, the archduke fled, escaping from the civilian mobs that had taken control of the cities.

Lazarus left few details of his activities during these years. However, it is clear that he moved his family to Mannheim, into the eye of the storm. His third child, Pauline, was born there on December 8, 1848, and in the city register of 1849, Lazarus Morgenthau, "merchant," is listed as residing at M1-10, where he remained for eight years.

Many other Jewish families out in the countryside were doing the same thing. The harvest of 1847 had been disastrous, and during the resulting famine, Jews in the rural towns were, as usual, scapegoats. According to the *Allgemeine Zeitung,* Mannheim's Jewish journal, "Swarms of fugitives from the country entered the cities, particularly Mannheim where they had friends." Their plight was noted in proclamations signed by prominent members of the Jewish community, deploring "acts of blind destruction and endangering of lives and property against our Jewish citizens. The light of freedom is endangered by humiliating excesses."

The local Jewish community went on the line to welcome their brethren, which had not always been the case in situations of this kind. They had recently formed the elite Association for Patriotic Union, which also published proclamations.

When Lazarus took up residence in Mannheim he also completed the shift in his business activities from cravat manufacturing to cigars. In October 1849 he received a passport issued by the Bavarian authorities permitting him to carry on his new trade. Granted permission by the Baden Ministry of the Interior in 1854 to manufacture as well as to sell cigars, he took his "oath of allegiance and fealty" in Mannheim in 1857.

Lazarus's entry into the cigar business was consistent with earlier leaps into fresh fields of endeavor that appeared promising. Another contemporary document vouches that he was licensed to operate as an insurance agent. Every one of these shifts in his business activities required courage, imagination, and enterprise. His success was especially remarkable since it was achieved without capital or family support. At times, he was able to dip into his wife's dowry. But as his enterprises expanded, they provided opportunities — and obligations — for other family members.

In 1849 Lazarus's younger brother Mengo, more often referred to by his given name, Max, responding to the enticement of gold discoveries in California, decided with the approval of his elder brothers to head for San Francisco. After a short stopover in New York, he continued west, arriving at his destination the following year in time to share in the great bonanza.

To the Morgenthaus back in Mannheim, Max became the fabled "'gold uncle'; exotic gifts arrived — a cane for the Archduke of Baden, its head a piece of gold-bearing quartz." At his brother's behest, Lazarus, still a tobacco and cigar merchant, decided to become a manufacturer as well. Until then his only industrial experience had been the operation of cravat sewing rooms. This was in fact a useful apprenticeship; the manufacture of cigars at that time was a relatively unsophisticated industry. No machinery or power supply was needed. It was a matter of painstaking labor carried out under close supervision. Most of the workers were women, who sat at tables cutting and rolling tobacco, with scissors and knife as their only tools. In its monotony, it was not much different from the sewing rooms. Sometimes readers were employed to edify the workers and keep them awake with selections from journals and books.

When brother Max (also called Mengo) wrote from San Francisco suggesting that Lazarus manufacture cigars for the American market, sending him samples and offering to finance the undertaking, Lazarus jumped at the opportunity and began to experiment, copying both Cuban and American brands. There was a plentiful supply of good tobacco grown in the Palatinate, but the quality of cigars made for home consumption was very poor. In Europe cigars were just becoming popular but were still considered ungentlemanly. Pipes were much more socially acceptable, as snuff had been in the century before. Lazarus's oldest son (also Max) described the situation:

> The problem with which my Father was confronted was not only to imitate the fine workmanship but also to secure and produce boxes equally fine and made of cedar wood, labels in colors of high standard, etc. After a great many experiments he succeeded in solving the various problems and was able to make cigars which could be retailed to the miners and others at from fifty cents to one dollar a piece. As the duty was not high the profit was very large. Mengo not only paid for the cigars but he forwarded additional funds to enable my Father to increase his factories and the two brothers formed a partnership under the title "Gebrüder Morgenthau" [Morgenthau Brothers].

A small quantity of large cigars imitating the very best Cubans was sold for the top price of a dollar to the miners, some of whom were earning $2.50 a day. The factory workers who produced this luxury item were paid ten times the regular wage, and the foremen who inspected them before they were packed "rejected about two thirds on account of trifling defects." As the business expanded, sales were no longer confined to California; large quantities were sold in New York.

During the 1850s the Morgenthau Brothers business grew rapidly; three branch factories were located in the towns of Bensheim, Heppenheim, and Lorsch, connected by railroad to Mannheim. It had become a family enterprise that included not only Max in San Francisco but Lazarus's older brother, Bernhard, who remained for some years in Ludwigshafen, and his youngest brother, Heyum; a nephew, Carl Schnaitoucher, ran the Bensheim plant.

In Mannheim, as Lazarus and Babette continued to produce a

new Morgenthau almost yearly, they began to look for a headquarters suitable to their rising station in life. The city itself was expanding. It was a fluid society; Jews were not restricted as to where they could live. The best real estate in town was available to anyone who could meet the price.

Mannheim, located at the confluence of the Rhine and Neckar rivers, had long been a prize of great strategic and commercial importance and a temptation to invaders from west and east. As a result, it had been repeatedly destroyed and rebuilt. At the beginning of the nineteenth century, the grand duke of Baden had leveled the ancient protecting wall and built a broad Ringstrasse, as Franz Josef had done in Vienna.

According to the Mannheim Stadtarchiv records, the Morgenthau house was A2,4. Outside the Ringstrasse to the south was a massive palace compound. Just inside was the baroque Jesuit church. Facing it across an open square was the great National Theater, beloved throughout the German states for its early espousal of Friedrich von Schiller, the poet-playwright, popular in his time for his articulation of the spirit of German freedom and nationalism.

On one corner opposite the theater was a grand residence with twenty-three windows on the street, owned by Baron Heinrich von Überbruck-Rodenstein and his wife, Anna, née Countess Forini. On November 6, 1856, title to this property passed to "Lazarus Morgenthau, cigar manufacturer, and his wife Babette, née Guggenheim." The purchase price was 24,000 gulden with a 4,000-gulden down payment and a mortgage at 4 percent for the balance, to be paid semiannually.

This house, the Morgenthaus' last residence in Germany, remained standing until it fell victim to the bombs dropped from the bays of American planes at the end of World War II. A woodcut print showing the side entrance to the National Theater includes a glimpse of the mansion, depicting it as a squat, two-story baroque structure, surmounted by a dormered third-floor garret. A pilaster on the corner supports a niche on the second floor, framing the sculptured figure of a saint. This building, laid out around a large interior courtyard, became the headquarters for both family and business. The ground floor was used for offices, sales rooms, and storage. The entire *bel étage* above was occupied by the Morgenthau household. The top floor became a cigar factory.

In 1857, the year after Lazarus took over these extravagant

quarters, business slumped, but "he was not seriously embarrassed and continued to prosper," his son Max recalled. Indeed, that year marked a visit from the reigning Grand Duke Friedrich of Baden and the grand duchess, Louise, the only daughter of Wilhelm I of Brandenburg-Prussia, who was to become kaiser.

The Morgenthau Brothers factory had been designated by the mayor and common council of Mannheim for a state visit, having gained a reputation as "the best equipped and systematically organized plant" in the city. After the inspection of the factory, Lazarus invited the grand duke and duchess to meet his large family. "Everything was prearranged and when he entered the salon with the royal highnesses," Max related,

> sister Bertha was seated at the piano and played the [national] hymn and the rest of us were arranged on one side, according to age, with brother Henry [Heinrich] as the last, carried by his governess. Mrs. David Oppenheim, the wife of the well known banker, assisted our mother in receiving the royal guests, and the committee from the city. The Grand Duke spoke to several of us and I remember his remark to my mother, namely that it reminded him of a row of organ pipes, when he saw the line of the children.★

According to Louise Heidelberg, Lazarus regarded this visit "as one of the greatest events of his life." These very considerable Mannheim data have validated the stories that were handed down to me. They allayed many of my unfounded suspicions, attributable to Lazarus's flamboyant style, that his accounts had been overstated. They helped me to understand how fast and far he had advanced.

At the time of the royal visit, or perhaps because of it, Lazarus was granted the full rights of a free citizen of Mannheim by a resolution dated July 3, 1857,† and confirmed with documentation of an "oath of allegiance and fealty" sworn on September 9.

• • •

★An article in the *Mannheimer Anzeiger* of May 25, 1860, also describes the royal visit: "Their Excellencies spent half an hour in Morgenthau's cigar factory and inspected all rooms with the greatest interest. . . . The illustrious visitors were surprised with an attractive scene from the factory owner's family life: His ten children were placed side by side in accordance with their age and made their lovely curtseys before the illustrious pair of potentates."

†It declares: "The Israelite manufacturer Lazarus Morgenthau of Friesenheim is granted Grand Ducal citizenship of Baden, based on documents furnished by him, for the purpose of taking up residency in Mannheim for himself and his family." (In the Stadtarchiv, Mannheim.)

The Jews of Mannheim had begun to participate broadly in civic and political affairs. Sober Jewish burghers accepted their new status with caution. They reacted with a display of chauvinism and civic virtue that outdid that of the Christians; above all, they were striving to be 100 percent German. At the same time the majority of them were committed to a radically reformed Judaism designed to dispel impressions of separateness. Lazarus was no exception.

When Lazarus arrived in Mannheim in 1848 the Reform Hauptsynagoge had already attracted most of the new mercantile class. Its congregation had outstripped the older Claus-Synagoge, the staunch redoubt of the Orthodox. The Hauptsynagoge was presided over by a charismatic, controversial young rabbi, Moses Prager, who sometimes pushed things further than his most devoted supporters desired. Nevertheless, suffering from growing pains, the congregation began to plan in earnest for a new synagogue that would be a handsome embodiment of their reforms.

The money was raised, and construction was carried out between 1851 and 1855. An opulent neo-Moorish style in vogue at the time had been selected as suitably unevocative of traditional synagogue architecture. But as the structure rose, so did second thoughts. Some congregants thought the facade suggested a cross; others complained that it was "too Catholic" or simply "too beautiful." Moreover, the women were to be seated in the same chamber with the men, and the *almemar* (a raised platform, or *bimah,* where the Torah and haftorah scrolls were read) was moved from the center to the east end of the building in front of the Holy Ark. This arrangement reflected the Christian tradition of locating the altar at the east end of the church. There was also to be a choir of both men and women. Finally, as the structure neared completion, a storm broke over the installation of a pipe organ, the first in a synagogue in Baden.

The dedication of the new Hauptsynagoge took place in 1855 with great pomp and ceremony. The previous day, the council made donations to the Mannheim poor — Jews and Christians alike — of two hundred florins each. The service started at six o'clock on the Sabbath evening. All the city dignitaries had accepted invitations. The Catholic and Protestant clergy and the high-ranking civil and military officers marched in the procession to the Holy Ark, led by the women of the mixed choir dressed in white robes with garlands of roses in their hair. Behind them followed the venerable rabbis of the Baden Council, bearing Torah scrolls under elaborately ornamented covers. The organ blasted forth, accompanying the choir in the performance of a cantata commissioned for the occasion. The words had been written by Rabbi Leopold Stern of Frankfurt, the music by the fifteen-year-old prodigy Hermann Levi.

The sermon, delivered by Rabbi Prager on the text "How Beautiful Are Thy Tents, Jacob," focused the spirit of this occasion on what was indeed at the very heart of the Reform theology: "The word of God is eternal, unchanging," Rabbi Prager proclaimed. But "the words with which we speak to God are an expression of our needs at a particular time and are perennially subject to change."

Lazarus Morgenthau was a member of the Hauptsynagoge at the time of the formal dedication. Louise Heidelberg describes his move from strict traditionalism to "extreme freedom of religious thought" as having taken place that same year, after he witnessed a performance of Lessing's *Nathan the Wise*. The synagogue ledger reveals that in 1856 he paid 660 gulden — 600 in dues and 60 in head tax.

Once again Lazarus's conversion, described as taking place after a revelation experienced in the theater, suggested a tendency toward self-dramatization. I was fascinated, therefore, to find a playbill in the Mannheim Theater Museum of a performance of the Lessing play at the very time he had claimed to have seen it.

At about that same time, in a burst of ecumenical enthusiasm, he "had a portal erected in the Catholic church and donated the first bell, which he called Babette, to the Protestant church in Ludwigshaven. To the Society of Freedom of Religion he gave benches and chairs, while the synagogue of Mannheim received a valuable ceremonial robe."

Lazarus's magnanimity was not limited to matters of faith. Like other successful Mannheim businessmen, he was an avid supporter of the performing arts, especially the music and drama staged in the palatial National Theater.

In the year 1859 the centennial of Schiller's birth was celebrated all over Germany, but the citizens of Mannheim didn't get around to it until three years later. Mannheimers had been identified with the great poet-playwright ever since the city had debuted his first play, *The Robbers*. In 1862, on Schiller's birthday, November 10, a celebration was planned to include a revival of *The Robbers* and the unveiling of a larger-than-life statue of him, commissioned from the Munich sculptor Friedrich von Miller. Lazarus Morgenthau plunged into the spirit of the occasion.

As the program called for a daylight procession, which would pass by the Morgenthau residence, and general illumination at night, Lazarus made extensive plans. He arranged to have five hundred of his women employees, dressed in white, march, and to have his house elaborately decorated. Unfortunately, during a test of the lighting, a fire destroyed a great part of the decorations. But Lazarus could not be persuaded to give up any of his plans and wired to his nephew Carl Schnaitoucher, the manager of his Heppenheim factory, for people to assist in the restoration. Carl arranged for a special train, which arrived with a big force the next morning. The helpers worked all night and had everything in perfect order by November 10.

From the moment Lazarus arrived in Mannheim, his business and social advances had been truly phenomenal, and he had become manic in his enthusiasm for expansion. According to his son, Max, "The zenith of his success in business was reached in the year 1859; he was in the full vigor of life — 44 years old." But by the end of 1862 he had begun to suffer serious financial reverses. The Morgenthau Brothers cigars were almost exclusively geared for export to the United States. The German and European market was slim, especially for the high-quality, expensive cigars that were a Morgenthau specialty.

During the U.S. presidential campaign of 1860, Abraham Lincoln had been a persistent advocate of high protective tariffs. "Vote yourself a tariff" and "Vote yourself a farm" were the slogans leading to the first Republican presidential victory. Even before Lincoln's inauguration in 1861, the Republican Congress passed the first of its protective measures. In the cigar industry, the tobacco growers in the Connecticut River valley particularly (rather than those in the South) wanted to cut off the competition from manufacturers of cheap German cigars that were entering the U.S. market through the ports of New York and Baltimore.

Max, who was thirteen years old at the time, remembered his father's alarm:

> In November of that year [1860] he was greatly interested in the result of the election. Prior to that time he sent his nephew to New York to

open an office for Morgenthau Bros. This nephew had instructions to give him prompt information (there was no cable at the time but [one could] wire to Halifax and again from Queenstown to Germany). I remember that I took a walk in the Schloss park and that during this walk we were stopped by a messenger from the bureau who brought the telegram announcing Lincoln's election. He turned to me and explained . . . that this was very serious to his large business. This information was followed by wires from San Francisco from his brother urging him not to discharge any help and work at full force so that he may have a large stock of goods on hand [in the United States] when the new tariff would go into force, which would probably not be before May, 1861.

With the outbreak of the Civil War in the United States, the demand for revenue as well as for protectionism caused import duties to climb even more rapidly than Lazarus had anticipated. In 1862 he realized that a new tariff on cigars would mean the end of his export business. He delivered as much as he could before the law went into effect. An account of what happened has been handed down by Lazarus's son Henry, my grandfather: "Unfortunately, the slow freighter that carried the last and biggest shipment arrived one day too late — the day's delay meant the difference between profit and disaster to my father. The cigars, which, when duty free, would have yielded a good return, were a dead loss."

In the face of extreme adversity — not unknown to him — Lazarus reverted to his talents for invention and innovation. His large tract of woodland in the Black Forest became the source of raw material for a nicotine-free cigar (far ahead of its time), bathing extract, and candy made from pine needles. "He took out patents at home and abroad and after submitting these articles to the Grand Duke of Baden and Hesse, secured the title of 'Purveyor to the Court.'" Increasingly desperate, he became ever more adventurous. He went to Paris to have an audience with Napoleon III, "and though," as his son Max reports, "he did not speak a word of French, he was invited to dine in the Tuileries."

A form letter printed in English and dated January 20, 1863, announced the opening of a branch office in London for the purpose of selling and distributing his pine needle candy manufacture throughout the United Kingdom and its colonies. The letter was signed by both Lazarus and Max, who was to be in charge of the Mannheim home office while Lazarus himself was to be in London.

Lazarus's failure to make a comeback probably had more to do with his business style than with the abrupt closing of the U.S. market for imported cigars. This era of German prosperity generally worked to the advantage of Mannheim businessmen — Jews and Gentiles alike. Lazarus was boldly creative. He could sense an opportunity and move quickly. He was also a good salesman and an incorrigible promoter. But operating a factory and managing finances he found less exciting, even boring. He enjoyed being family patriarch and liked to parcel out key management positions to brothers, nephews, and eventually his sons — family was considered to be more trustworthy and controllable than outsiders. Further, by keeping the profits within the family, its social status could advance. That is, of course, if things went well.

One of Lazarus's biggest problems while his business was expanding had been that even in his large extended family no one quite had his flair and energy; nor was anyone as skillful an overseer. Brother Mengo had chalked up a respectable record for himself in San Francisco; but when he died in 1893, he left little. Moreover, to judge from his obituary, the partnership probably ended during the Civil War, and there is no record of any commercial relationship between the West and East Coast branches of the family in later years.

Today all records of these relatives whom Lazarus drew into his orbit have vanished. Nephew Carl Schnaitoucher, manager of the Heppenheim plant, and indeed the three branch operations in Bensheim, Lorsch, and Heppenheim were never mentioned again.

As the pressure of business reverses mounted, Lazarus continued to maintain his posture of self-confidence. He managed to keep up prompt payment of the biannual installments owed to Überbruck-Rodenstein for the house. But at home he regularly subjected his family to irrational outbursts. He complained that Babette's extravagances were ruining him, and that she was to blame for allowing the children to take everything for granted, which was in fact exactly what he himself had encouraged them to do.

Finally, when all seemed about to collapse, Lazarus decided to do what he had always done at critical times in his life: move. He would emigrate to the United States, where he could start life afresh. If he must assume a more modest posture, it would be in new surroundings where there would be no loss of face. With his usual bravado, Lazarus managed to convert this final disaster into the start of an adventure. The family's mood lifted immediately, and the community attitude changed from suspicion to admiration.

In January 1866, less than five years after the birth of his four-teenth — and twelfth surviving — child, Lazarus dispatched three of the older children as an advance party. His oldest son, Max, eighteen, daughter Mina, fifteen, and son Siegfried, fourteen, were to establish a family beachhead in Brooklyn. The festive atmosphere of the departure is preserved in one of the very rare scraps of writing in Lazarus's hand. A cheerful piece of doggerel, it is addressed to "My dear son" (probably Max) and dated Mannheim, November 29, 1865. A free, unrhymed translation is as follows:

> You are parting from us today for a little while [*Zeit* in German]
> May you be the first to bring us hope and joy [*Freude* in
>   German, but *Freit* in Yiddish]
>
> Through diligence and righteousness you will succeed
>   [*bellingen*]
> To bring your parents, brothers, and sisters a happy future
>   [*bringen*]
>
> Go with God's blessing and arrive in good health
> This, wishes your loving father.

Nine-year-old Heinrich was not innocent of the deeper implica-tions behind this front of gay optimism. Later on, he noted, "My father [was] during my early childhood in very good circumstances, but the cause of our leaving Germany was the loss of a great deal of money."

The Morgenthaus
Transplanted in New York

W HEN LAZARUS MORGENTHAU ARRIVED in New York in 1866 he discovered that its Jewish community was firmly controlled by a network of families, most of whom had emigrated from Germany a generation earlier, notably the Seligmans, Loebs, and Lehmans. They were soon to be joined by Schiffs, Strauses, and others. Some, like the Sulzbergers and Seligmans, intermarried with New York's small aristocratic band of Sephardic Jews: Cardozas, Hays, Nathans, and Seixases. Others drifted into the Christian mainstream.

Lazarus was more concerned with the impression that he and his family would make in the New World than he was with their immediate comfort. Eight months after his arrival, he moved from his Brooklyn quarters to a larger dwelling in Manhattan at 1121 Second Avenue, on the corner of Fifty-ninth Street, "a three story, high stoop, brownstone house, rows of which were then being erected." It was on the fringe of the city's fashionable East Side, and it was a luxury he could ill afford.

Just before his departure from Germany, Lazarus had invested in a shipment of German wines. "At our arrival," his son Heinrich (whose name was anglicized as Henry) noted later, "my father had a wine business on Cedar Street, but this was not enough to cover the expenses of so large a family." To help make ends meet, "the back parlour had to be rented as a doctor's office and shortly after my mother decided that it was her duty to take in boarders."

Like Lazarus himself years earlier, Henry was deeply distressed by his mother's parlous situation, and the other children, unhappy with their father's self-indulgent pride, rebuked him for their mother's humiliation. As a result, Lazarus tried a variety of wildly implausible business schemes in the desperate hope of staging a spectacular comeback. Why he never returned to cigar manufacturing is not clear. On both sides of the Atlantic, as the market burgeoned, tobacco was again a thriving business.

All in all, the $30,000 nest egg that he had brought from Mannheim should have been more than sufficient for Lazarus to re-establish himself. But his tremendous ego got in the way. He was not satisfied just to make it — he had to make it big. So he plunged into increasingly risky gambles.

He invented, among other oddities, a tongue scraper, a toilet article that did not appeal to the public. Next he spent a great deal of time on a gum label machine, which his son-in-law William Ehrich helped him to finance but which also proved to have equally little commercial value. Always stimulated by publicity and seeing his name in print, Lazarus ordered a variety of business cards: one read "L. Morgenthau, Director of Bathing Establishment," and another, "L. Morgenthau, Special Physician to Cure Rheumatism."

Nevertheless, Lazarus did engage in one successful business venture. Ironically, it derived from his worst American disaster, a fire that destroyed his wine business. "In the course of settling the fire loss," Henry recalled, Max dealt with an agent, Mr. H. C. Gordon, who "also had an agency from the National Life Insurance Company." At his father's urging, Max entered the business and became a general agent. But that was not all. "His father took an active interest in the organization too; in fact he succeeded in issuing more policies than either Mr. Gordon or Max."

Lazarus had gained some experience in the insurance business in Germany. In New York, Lazarus separated from his son and Gordon and became an outstandingly successful agent for the New York Life Insurance Company. "He knew the power of fear," Henry recalled, "and he used it with great effect. For example he would show his clients notices of sudden death clipped from the newspapers and point out the terrible danger of leaving a family unprovided. He would importune, cajole and threaten his clients but few were offended by his methods and many came to admire his wit and to be carried away by his eloquence."

Since Lazarus spoke little English, he made his sales pitch in German. This was not a crippling handicap, however, at a time when many of the city's immigrants continued to speak their mother tongues. Germans, both Jewish and Christian, who had arrived in increasingly large numbers from the 1840s on, read the local German-language press and conducted their business, social, and religious affairs bilingually.

Attempting to recapture the grand lifestyle he had enjoyed in Mannheim, especially since his daughters, according to the custom, were to be wed at home, Lazarus decided to make yet another move, to a large brownstone just off the much more fashionable Lexington Avenue at 161 East Sixty-first. To maintain the house, the older children were all obliged to find employment, and Mrs. Morgenthau continued to take in boarders.

Lazarus meanwhile had joined Congregation Adas Jeshurun.* Lazarus felt very much at home there. The services were conducted in German and tended toward the radical Reform he had espoused in Mannheim. The rabbi, Dr. David Einhorn (1809–79), a flamboyant orator, was well known in Europe and the United States for his controversial extremism. Rabbi Einhorn became closely associated with the Morgenthau family. He officiated at three weddings in 1871 and 1872: Pauline to Edward Simon, Ida to William Ehrich, and Max to Fannie Ehrich, sister of William (Bertha had been married to Gustave Zittel in 1866). Dr. Einhorn was a frequent guest in the Morgenthau home and was available to make public pronouncements favoring Lazarus's charitable ventures.

Of the latter, there were many. At the end of November 1870 a great fair was held in the Armory on Fourteenth Street for the benefit of the Mount Sinai Hospital and the Hebrew Orphanage. Mount Sinai had already become a major draw for German Jewish benefactors. Headed by the Seligmans, other leading families vied with one another in their largesse. Social status was measured by support for sectarian institutions, a tradition that continues to this day.

Lazarus was quick to latch on to this system; he had already seen it work in Mannheim. Though virtually broke, he invented an

---

*Congregation Adas Jeshurun was formed in 1866. Its rabbi, David Einhorn, remained when it amalgamated with another congregation to become Temple Beth El in 1874. Its German congregants were a social cut below those of Temple Emanu-El. (Jacob Schiff, the arbiter of New York Jewish life, joined both congregations as a gesture of noblesse oblige.) Later the two congregations merged, retaining the Emanu-El name only.

ingenious scheme for elevating himself as a prominent benefactor. He would use "The Golden Book of Life" to capitalize on the honorable ostentation of Jews eager to display their generosity. His idea harnessed human vanity to the biblical metaphor of the Book of Life, in which names are entered on Rosh Hashanah and sealed on Yom Kippur.★ For the beneficiary of the moment he prepared an elaborate volume, similar to a large ledger, bound in red morocco and handsomely inscribed, called *The Golden Book of Life.* This book he dedicated and presented to the beneficiary; then he would start out to solicit contributions by subscription. As his enterprise gained momentum, the *Jewish Times* observed that every Sunday "the High Priest of the 'Golden Book,' L. Morgenthau, robed in the habiliments of his office, the white neck-tie, is faithfully in attendance to receive the pilgrims and their offerings."

If no one else enjoyed the fruits of the golden books quite as much as the high priest himself, the idea was nonetheless a lasting contribution to the art of fund-raising. Lazarus had the books copyrighted in Washington as *The Book of Life, The Golden Book of Life,* and *The Silver Book of Life,* and for the next ten years he continued to sell the idea to Jewish charitable institutions in New York, Baltimore, Philadelphia, and Chicago. All told, the scheme raised $250,000, although no single event quite equaled the inaugural effort at the 1870 Charity Fair, which raised $18,000. (Two-thirds went to Mount Sinai Hospital and one-third to the orphanage.)

After Lazarus's efforts had furnished $7,000 of the orphanage's annual expenditure of $93,613 in the spring of 1871, "the Board of Directors resolved to tender Mr. Morgenthau a suitable expression of their appreciation of his devotion to the cause of charity, and on Wednesday evening they assembled at the residence of the gentleman and presented him with a silver sugar case and a set of resolutions." Lazarus, replying in German, according to the *Jewish Times,* "could hardly find suitable expression for my feelings. The Memorial which you have presented to me immortalizes you in the hearts of my family, it will be cherished by them as the dearest legacy. Your present will remind me to be liberal in handing cigars to all who shall be willing to have their lives insured for the benefit of the

---

★ *The American Israelite* noted that when Lazarus "retired from active business life," he began to work on his charitable schemes (*The American Israelite,* New York, September 1, 1897, editorial, "Death of L. Morgenthau").

Asylum." Dr. Einhorn eulogized the merits and services of the host, his successful raids on the pockets of the people.

The toasting and feasting continued late into the night of Wednesday, March 22, 1871. Nothing in the *Jewish Times* indicated that Lazarus's financial straits were so dire that three days beforehand he had forced Henry to quit City College and go to work, although Henry wrote later that year, "Father had the intention of letting me go all through." In view of Lazarus's own bitter experience, the abrupt termination of Henry's innocence was an especially cruel act. For some time, Henry, along with his siblings, had remained loyal to his father, but the old man's excessive demands and violent temper were becoming intolerable. Still, throughout these and later tribulations, Henry was loath to criticize Lazarus. Part of his anguish no doubt derived from a realization that they were, in some ways, very much alike. In the years ahead Henry would try to guard against those drives that had led to Lazarus's undoing.

To Lazarus Morgenthau, recalling as he often did, the state visit to his home in Mannheim of the archduke of Baden, it seemed quite natural to expect no less from his new ruler, the American president. On learning that Ulysses S. Grant was coming to New York on September 23, 1872, he wrote explaining the purpose of *The Golden Book of Life,* "requesting of him an interview in case he would approve of it and would be desirous of adding his name to the list, in order to give it strength and popularity."

Having lived in America for only six years, Henry was understandably awed by President Grant. "This day ought to be remembered by me as a very remarkable one," he noted in his journal. "At 11:00 A.M. Max, Papa and I rode down in a carriage to the Fifth Avenue Hotel to see U. S. Grant. . . . Max sent up his card and we were admitted immediately, Mr. G. asking us to be seated." Because Lazarus was unsure of his English, Max did most of the talking "about the institutions and the object of the books etc." Henry's English was more polished than anyone else's in the family, so he was taken along. The conversation ended "by [Grant] subscribing to both books." Max thanked him, and "Father said, 'I hope you will be President again and live a hundred years more' or something to that effect." Later that month Henry described Grant as "a mere tool in the hands of the party."

Lazarus also founded the "Temple of Humanity," an institution devoted to assisting "orphan girls who were about to be married or showed an inclination to be married." Marriage, according to Jewish tradition, was the greatest mitzvah (good deed). To support his project, Lazarus established the "Non-Sectarian Dowry Fund," and got out another *Golden Book of Life* "for the purpose of raising enough funds to make the institution perpetual." The project, however, went somewhat awry, because "about seventy-five young men and women who participated in an entertainment given for the benefit of the fund in Terrace Garden, and who afterward sued Mr. Morgenthau for services rendered, but unsuccessfully, as he proved that they had offered their services gratuitously."

In May 1876 Lazarus and Babette and five of their six unmarried children left the Sixty-first Street mansion and moved to 723 Lexington Avenue, where they kept a "*regular* Boarding House." Lazarus expected to make about two or three thousand dollars a year, but Henry noted the family "barely paid expenses and we are all uncomfortable. Papa sees the last traces of his big name gained by his working for Asylums, Hospitals, etc. daily grow less and less." At the same time he had lost his standing as an insurance broker, "so that he earned but very little, he is therefore very despondent."

Everything and everyone seemed to have turned against Lazarus. Keeping a boardinghouse was considered jarringly déclassé. Henry, who for the most part refrained from saying anything negative about his family, in a rare moment of unvarnished candor found occasion to take them to task one by one. In July 1876, when Americans were celebrating the one-hundredth anniversary of their independence, the twenty-year-old Henry wrote an eight-page memorandum entitled "A Centennial Reminiscence." "The object of this is to refresh my memory in the future," he starts out, "when I desire to think of these times as they *really were* and not as they might *appear* to *have been*. The most extensive and exact memory will not be able to recall matters as they really were at any particular period, the changes being so gradual as to be imperceptible." In this memo he remarked on the news of scandals involving Lazarus's son Siegfried and son-in-law Gus Heidelberg, which, he believed, would "likely cut one of the last threads upon which [his reputation] hangs."

"He tells me," Henry wrote, "that Siegfried he disowns, G.H. he despises, Gust. M[orgenthau] he considers a stupid fool, JCM [Julius C. Morgenthau] he hardly notices, the only one he has faith in is Mengo. Recha he wishes married and Richard he deems spoiled and considers his habit of stealing and lying incurable."

Though providing us with Lazarus's list of indictments, Henry never mentioned what he thought was his father's assessment of him. At the same time he pulled no punches in placing full responsibility for the family debacle: "a fearful and very much to be avoided result of Father's mode of bringing up his children. Has a man who cannot give a great deal of his time to their education, a right to raise a family of 12?" Recalling the comforts of his own early childhood, he found it "awful to realize that a man who has lived the way Father lived in Mannheim should end his life with such prospects for his family."

Henry then went on to issue his own bill of indictments, even more devastating than his father's. Brother Gustave was a "light headed fickle minded" wastrel whose ambition to marry a rich girl Henry believed "may be his best chance for salvation." Gustave had been neglecting a good business opportunity with Mandel Brothers in Holyoke, Massachusetts, while he "plays billiards, whores and makes love to the store girls one of whom he is even at present corresponding with in most loving terms." With an ingrained tendency to live beyond his means, Gustave frequently turned to Henry for financial aid. In a diary entry for June 6, 1872, Henry noted that he "had made an agreement with Gus to lend him $25 and he said he would give me $1.50 in interest. I thought it over very long. And at first I considered it usury to take so much interest, but after I had reckoned it, I found that I would lose about 40 cents by taking the money out of the Six Penny Savings Bank and that money would bring me about 20 cents interest . . . also it was Gustave who proposed it, and not I."

Recha's difficulty in finding a husband was a concern that Henry shared with their father. Henry wished that she would "fall in love with someone, marry, and be happy as she deserves." He had explored the possibilities of promoting a match with the nephew of his Simon in-laws (the family of sister Pauline's husband), but Carl Simon proved to be something of a degenerate and scarcely an adequate provider.

The next target of Henry's withering contempt was his brother Julius, two years his junior. "Julius is a queer person, displeasing, not at all amiable and makes more enemies than anyone else — though by some he is thought very highly of, perhaps overestimated." At that time, Julius was an undergraduate at City College, and Henry predicted "will graduate with honor, turn teacher, and perhaps his ambition to be a United States Senator will be realized. I doubt it as he lacks the power of organizing a party. He may attain a high position if he [illegible] some person with more practical sense than he has to push and eulogize him."

Among all these angry attacks leveled against members of his family, this one is especially surprising. For Julius was the only one of Henry's brothers who managed to pursue his education to the point of realizing his full intellectual capacities. In later years Henry showed his admiration for Julius in praises tinged with condescension. But at this point, when he was still sensitive about his own lack of education, he may have been jealous of Julius, who proceeded to sail through City College with flying colors.

Other members of the family could be disposed of more readily. Henry thought his sister Bertha's husband, Gustave Zittel, a "schlemiel." "Bertha has to live off Prof. Uboski's board and from money sent to her by the folks who I believe are each contributing $1 a week."

Max, who had married into the wealthy Ehrich family and now had two children, was at New York University "studying law and what else he is doing I don't know. I don't think he has $500 of his own and yet he lives at the rate of $2,500.00."

Henry departs briefly from his litany of sour comments to write a few pleasant words about his sister Pauline and her husband, Edward Simon, who are "the happiest of the whole family — satisfied with each other." Yet they were "swindled" into a house that was too large for them. Edward "failed a year ago and is now worth nothing at all though he carries on the coal business on credit — where there is so much love success will be the reward."

Siegfried, the most disreputable member of the clan, "embezzled money in San Francisco. We have but to wait developments for he is sure to give some more trouble."

Henry then seems to have lost steam, or perhaps in his depression decided that he'd better desist. Thus William Ehrich, Ida's husband, who was the most affluent member of the family and was already sponsoring Henry's activities, and Mengo, his brother, both rated "OK."*

---

*That summer Mengo, finding life with father intolerable, had flown from the family nest intending to become a farmer. Copies of Henry's letters to him indicate that things were far less than "OK" in Henry's censorious view. Henry continued to exercise control over

As things went from bad to worse, the Morgenthau children were plagued by Lazarus's increasingly disturbed behavior. It all seemed to stem from his inability to regain his former dominance over his family. In desperation he shifted from the unreliable to the felonious. Henry noted in his diary that he "met with LM from 3 to 5 P.M., told him that he ran the risk of being arrested for lottery business," and warned that he intended to absent himself from any proceedings. But Henry's greatest fear was that Lazarus would physically hurt Babette.

Eventually, the family had Lazarus removed to a "lunatic asylum" while they arranged for a marital separation. Opinions differed as to just how dangerous he was. Henry was the most apprehensive. "As I claimed all along," he wrote his brother Max, "as soon as Mama is out of the way and he is deprived of the opportunity of using threats to her in order to frighten us, he would be comparatively quiet."

Babette was persuaded to move to Chicago — a seemingly safe distance — to live with Max and Fannie, who had moved there earlier. She also had the company there of her sons Gus and Mengo, who were working in Max's store. After being released from custody Lazarus went to live in Paterson, New Jersey, with Bertha, who became his strong partisan. "Not a single line of Bertha's letter is true," Henry wrote his brother Max. "It was dictated by father and enlarged upon by her. She does her utmost to incite father against all . . . LM is not at all angry at you . . . but in his insanity he does not know what he says, and Bertha opens all his letters and tells him the contents, colored of course as she deems best."

This outbreak of civil war within the family couldn't have come at a worse time for Henry, whose wedding day, May 10, 1883, was only weeks away. But, as usual, he jumped in to manage the situation. This understandably served to bring all of Lazarus's fury down on his head, as the old man was convinced that Henry had dared to usurp his patriarchy. But when Henry realized that Lazarus was trying to disrupt his impending marriage, he was furious: "Father

---

Mengo, treating him as a missile to be guided by letters brimming with advice, moralizing, goading, censuring, and manipulating to keep him within a controllable orbit. When in later years Henry encouraged his own son to find himself on the land as a farmer — considerably off the beaten track pursued by most of his peers — my grandfather may have had his brother Mengo's experience in mind. Both were young men and blood relatives for whom he had a special fondness.

had a long talk with Mrs. and Willie Sykes [the in-laws-to-be] and told them that either they must not invite any of the family that called to congratulate me or he would have nothing to do with me and them. They have decided not to comply with his request. If he is sane and makes that demand, he is too contemptible to be spat upon, if he is insane — the greater fools would we be, were we to allow our conduct to be regulated by a lunatic."

Lazarus was being treated by a Dr. Nichols, a "specialist," and by Bertha's family physician, Dr. Thompson. As Lazarus began to show signs of improvement, Henry became all the more alarmed because Babette, who continued to show pity and even longing for her husband, was inclined to return to him as she had done following earlier separations. "It was the greatest mistake for Mama ever to attempt to live with him again, he hates her most bitterly and is fit to do her all sorts of harm when he comes into contact with her. Mama must stay away for the present and no letters ought to reach her. She must admit now that had she followed my advice the last time and kept aloof from him things never would have come to the pass they did."

As the nuptials approached, Henry asked Julius Ehrich, his brother-in-law's brother, to retain the services of the Pinkerton National Detective Agency to follow Lazarus on the day of the wedding and to apprehend him if he showed up and became violent. Two operatives, provided with an identifying photograph, tailed him from the time he "left his residence at 11 A.M. on the morning of May 10th as he proceeded on foot to the residence of his physician." Lazarus never did appear at either the ceremony or the reception. Still, the Pinkertons were not dismissed until early the following morning.

Henry had dealt with his father's aberrant behavior in a practical manner. As far as he was concerned, it was then time to move on. "I will have nothing more at all to do with the matter," he wrote Julius, regarding the exclusion of his father from the festivities. "I will hence forth never allude to it again and will try to have the whole matter fade from my memory as quickly as possible." He was not inclined to dwell on anything except the prospects of married life.

Lazarus and Babette continued to live apart. Sometime after their son Henry's wedding, however, she returned to New York City from Chicago. At age sixty-six she died while on vacation in the Catskill Mountains, on August 14, 1892.

During these years and thereafter, Lazarus, in robust health, lived out his life with as much bravado as he could muster. When the son of Archduke Friedrich of Baden died, Lazarus sent condolences: "From your never forgetting friend, L. Morgenthau, formerly of Mannheim now of 318 East 18th Street." The archduke cabled back promptly, "Deeply moved by your faithful sympathy." Lazarus saw to it that the news of his exchange of greetings with his noble friend got out to the press, prompting a long interview by the German-language newspaper *M. N. Figaro*. A reporter with the initials H.A.L. wrote a comprehensive profile, including an account of the Morgenthau family's visit from the archduke and his wife to their home in Mannheim, and mentioning Lazarus's intimate "contact with other high personalities."

On the occasion of his eightieth birthday, Lazarus produced a calling card announcing himself (in German) as "the eighty year old youngster." Two years later, Lazarus Morgenthau died late Monday night, August 31, 1897, at the Mount Sinai Hospital "of a complication of diseases." At that time the hospital was located between Sixty-sixth and Sixty-seventh streets on Lexington Avenue. During those final years, Lazarus, living alone, had moved frequently. Three or four weeks before he was hospitalized for the final two days of his life, he had settled in nearby at 1013 Lexington Avenue.

According to a long obituary in the *American Israelite* (September 1), "Charity and philanthropy of every conceivable nature were the great objects of Mr. Morgenthau's life." He was credited with being "in comfortable circumstances though not very wealthy." (This was of course a gross overstatement.) The obituary did mention, though, that his "individual gifts soon made large inroads upon his comparatively small capital."

As a young boy, Lazarus had been shoved out into the world literally to sing for his supper. From then on, left to his own devices, he developed a driving ambition for upward mobility. Through his sharp wits and a quality I remember my grandfather (his son Henry) called "gumption," he achieved remarkable success. In his haste, however, he developed a tendency to overextend himself, causing the collapse of a newly gained fortune. Furthermore, in his impatience to get ahead in the world he failed to sort out his values. Although committed to establishing his family in a state of prosperous well-being, he often ended up sacrificing them in favor of his personal vanity. He sometimes commingled business and charitable funds to the point of illegality. In the end he lost the respect of his children, lingering on, in their view, as a specter of unspeakable embarrassment. He deserved better. He had, after all, given his family a sense, however ephemeral, of what a comfortable, assimilated way of life could be. He left them securely transplanted from the Old World to the New. He had made a name for himself and, though not always a good one, it hardly went unnoticed.

PART II

Henry's
Self-Improvement

· 5 ·

Ambition and Idealism

A
T A VERY early age, Henry gained his mother's special attention. Babette's ninth child, he was delicate at birth, but evinced a vigorous will to survive. When he arrived in 1856, the family's tide of good fortune had been rushing in. In Mannheim their most ambitious dreams were becoming reality. Lazarus asked nothing of his wife but that she preside over their amply appointed home. His blossoming family was convincing proof of his success. He regretted only that his mother could not bear witness to it.

Baby Heinrich had his father's reddish blond hair and blue eyes. From the beginning he seemed to have an instinct for attracting people and making them smile. As soon as he was old enough to toddle, his mother enjoyed showing him off to friends.

In 1860 the young archduke of Baden, Friedrich I, issued an Easter proclamation making regulations for Jews more liberal than in any other German state. In gratitude, the Jews of Mannheim established a charitable foundation, the "Friedrich Stiftung," for the purpose of subsidizing the salaries of teachers of religious education, regardless of creed. The city scored another first with the establishment of nonsectarian community schools. This meant the closing of Jewish elementary schools. Because of Saturday classes, Jewish children were hard-pressed to celebrate the Sabbath, even though the school council technically gave the children free time to attend religious services. However, even Orthodox parents did not insist on this exemption, as they were afraid their children would miss too much school. To solve the problem, a special children's service on Saturday afternoons was initiated.

Heinrich Morgenthau obtained his elementary education at the Grand-Ducal Lyceum of Mannheim, a community school on this order. His report card for the year 1865–66, when he was ten, shows that the head teacher recognized him as a serious-minded, energetic student, if not an accomplished scholar. He ranked twentieth among his forty-five classmates. He was rated "good" in math, diligence, and deportment; "good to fairly good" in Latin; "fairly good" in religion, German, geography, gymnastics, and writing; and "mediocre" in drawing. Among the subjects offered that he did not take that year was spoken Hebrew.

Heinrich was short in stature, which made him as determined to push his wiry, compact body to its limit as he was to train his mind. In later years he recalled: "We were given regular exercises and great was my pride when I passed the 'swimming test' one summer's day by holding my own for the prescribed half hour against the Rhine current and so winning the right to wear the magic letters R.S. — 'Rhine-Swimmer' — on my bathing suit."

But the months following the outbreak of civil war in the United States made Heinrich's last term at the lyceum a nightmare never to be forgotten. Born into affluence, he took it for granted. Indeed, his father had done everything within his considerable power to convince his children that the style of living to which their parents had recently become accustomed was to be their natural, permanent way of life. During Heinrich's early years, both his physical surroundings and his family's euphoria established the father's dream as the impressionable child's reality.

Heinrich was at first undismayed by his family's financial setback. In a serial letter addressed to his brothers in the United States, he wrote:

Mannheim, Aug. 2, 1866

Dear Gustav!

I was very happy when I saw that what had been promised you has come true. As I have read in Julius's letter that you have got a job, you can get me a house with several butlers, several maids, several bathrooms, you can lend it to me and I will send you the money later on. I better close this letter or it will cost too much money.

Your incorrigible brother
Heinrich

Dear Max!

I was delighted when I opened your letter and found the dollar in it and I want to thank you very cordially. . . . I will be able — with the help of Miss [illegible] — to write you a letter in English because that will make you all very happy.

Referring to this cheerful family correspondence many years later, Heinrich, then Henry, recalled: "These letters gave us fresh thrills of emotions and new materials for our active fancies. Then my father abandoned his now unprofitable business, sold his factories and home, packed our household goods and furniture, and possessed of about thirty thousand dollars in cash — all that remained of his fortune [a very substantial amount at that time] — led his wife and remaining eight children upon the expedition."

They set sail from Bremen on the North German Lloyd steamer *Hermann,* first-class, arriving in New York eleven days later. "On the stormiest day of our passage," Heinrich was proud of being "the only child well enough to eat his meals, and the Captain honored me with a seat beside him at his table." In later years he would not have thought of sitting anywhere else.

When the family was reunited in Brooklyn, the youngest children, though attending school, were also compelled to earn some money. Mrs. Morgenthau, instead of presiding over household servants as she had in Mannheim, joined her daughters in performing housekeeping chores not only for the family but for their paying guests as well.

Like his father's before him, Henry's bond with his adored mother was colored with mystical overtones. His feeling of helplessness in the face of the humiliation she was to endure would be ingrained in his memory, a sharp reminder as he plotted his own course.

"I could not speak of my mother as she was during these trials without the deepest emotion," he wrote years later, at the peak of his success. "There is nobody to whom I owe so much; there was no debt which so profoundly affected my entire career." Before he was twelve years old, he felt "manfully responsible, . . . lest my mother, who was my idol, and who was so superior in accomplishments and knowledge to the people that boarded with us, might in the course of her duties, be compelled to render quasi-menial services." He was mindful of "the efforts his sisters made to ease their mother's situation." Indeed, when he himself became the family patriarch he did not permit their filial devotion to go unrewarded. But at the time Henry was again reminded of his father's anguish when as a youth his impoverished family fell apart and his mother's distress proved beyond his powers of aid and comfort.

On the other hand, Henry's pleasant memories of his Mannheim childhood provided a sense of security that would stay with him all his life. Nothing that happened afterward dislodged his deep-seated feelings of what life could and should be. With self-confidence fueled by great energy, he remained optimistic in the face of all challenges and frustrations: the ebb of the family fortunes in the New World inspired his irrepressible ambition: "to restore my mother to the comforts to which she had been accustomed, to save myself from an old age of financial stress such as my father's, to give my own children the chances in life that were all but denied to me, and to try to attain standards of thought and conduct consonant with the fine concepts that characterized my mother's mind and lips."

What happened a few years later in young Henry's life, when Lazarus's fortunes failed completely, was a shock but not a defeat. In fact, he seemed to enjoy addressing adversity with a self-discipline that was positively masochistic and with an optimism that at times seemed as unrealistic as his father's pretentious egotism. On reflection, he admitted, "I was full of energy, and had tremendous hopes as to my future success, which gave me a certain assurance that was often misconstrued into conceit, but which was really a conviction of the necessity to collect religiously a mental, moral, physical, and financial reserve guaranteeing the realization of my best desires."

His "best desires" were double-edged swords fashioned both for personal advancement and for a guarantee that never again would the family — particularly its women — be subject to the indignity of poverty. In his earnest prose, he sounded terribly pompous, but in person, my grandfather displayed a sense of humor and zest that got lost in his writing. As an older man, "he was fun to be with," recalled his granddaughter Barbara Tuchman — although there were those who sometimes found him rather hard to take.

At a very early age, Henry had been taught the importance of education. Eventually he would come to look on it not as a route to intellectual development but as an instrument for practical "self-improvement." In Mannheim he had hoped to become a good citizen of Baden, a good German. In New York he schooled himself to become a worthy citizen of the United States, a hundred percent American.

In the New York public school where he rose to the top of his class, his teachers, like their German predecessors, commended Henry for his "industriousness." He had a quick mind that made him especially adept in numbers, but less so in language skills and conceptualization.

He began at the Degraw Street Public School in September. Eight months later, when the family moved to Manhattan, he transferred to "Grammar School No. 18, on Fifty-first Street near Lexington Avenue. . . . I had my little difficulties," he recalled. Aside from the language barrier was the "double handicap of being both a Jew and a German." And, although the school put the greatest stress on arithmetic, his forte, he was frequently bullied by some of the older, Irish boys, until he demonstrated that he had the guts to defend himself with "sheer unscientific force."

At the age of eleven, Henry made up his mind to go to City College and looked for a better school in which to prepare himself. The two top-rated schools were full. The next in line, No. 14, on Twenty-seventh Street near Third Avenue, admitted him in the fall of 1868. Here "it required no effort on my part to keep the lead in mathematics," while he devoted his spare time "to improving my pronunciation and mastering the spelling of English." He managed to earn "100 percent perfect marks" and was well up among the three hundred selected for admission to City College in September 1870. He was fourteen.

City College, located at that time on Lexington Avenue at Twenty-third Street, combined high school and college curricula. It was therefore not unusual for students to enter at this young age. Some came right out of grammar school; starting as "sub Freshmen," they could cram an entire high school education into one year. Nevertheless, many dropped out before taking their bachelor's degree, for financial as well as academic reasons. Free tuition was not enough at a time when many youngsters were called upon to help support their families.

When young Henry entered the class of 1875, it was with far more than the minimum requirements. He had "joined the Mercantile Library in the previous February." His reading of a wide selection from American and English literature and philosophy, as noted in his journal for 1871, included Cooper, Dickens, Mill, and Hume. He was also attending Cooper Institute classes in education and debating, and he later "secured instruction in grammar and composition at the Evening High School on Thirteenth Street."

So that he could afford to go to City College in the fall, Henry had taken a part-time summer job as "errand boy and general utility lad in the law offices of Ferdinand Kurzman at $4.00 a week." Thus when he started classes he was able to plunge into his studies with energy and enthusiasm. "Though 'stumped' in anatomy and chemistry through my unfamiliarity with the long words employed, I stood well on the general roll and was No. 11" in a class of 286.

Henry had begun to emerge as the family prodigy, and he kept detailed, uninhibited records of his progress. While still an obedient son and devoted brother, he was discovering that if he wanted to control his own destiny, he had to distance himself from his undisciplined, emotionally driven father and siblings.

Though he tried to leave nothing to chance, the important moves in his life were largely determined by external circumstances. Henry used situations, both good and bad, to his advantage by always keeping his objective in view. When the tide pushed him back, he gained strength by swimming against it. When the tide was behind him, he rode on the crest of the wave.

His determination was buttressed by strong faith; the year after his confirmation in Rabbi Einhorn's liberal synagogue, he felt that his religious education had been much too perfunctory and began searching for a more profound application of his beliefs. The notion of public service emerged. His reward would be acceptance and esteem by fellow citizens in his adopted land. Accumulation of wealth, not to be an end in itself, would put wind in his sails to speed him on his course.

Money could be a strong temptation, but as an active teenager, he found his appetite for sweets and sex more threatening. Both demanded vigilant suppression. Even in the most private circumstances, the word *sex* was, of course, never uttered or written.

Henry left little direct evidence of his sensuality and of how he responded to it. On one rare occasion he described a daydream while riding the train from Albany to New York City. Gazing out the window at Peekskill, where he had once spent a summer vacation, he contemplated "how so rich a scenery, witnessed by male and female together in company [illegible] of about the same age, will surely create feelings of love etc. I imagined myself wandering by the Hudson on the mountains making love to [illegible]." However, Henry's many written comments upbraiding his relatives and friends for their loose morals give a strong hint of his concern about his own self-control.

• • •

The avant-garde Judaism of Dr. Einhorn had hit young Henry during his impressionable years. At Temple Beth El, services were held on Sunday. Men with bare heads worshipped alongside women, while listening to the music of the mixed choir and organ. With his considerable scholarly background, Dr. Einhorn made a convincing case for Talmudic law as merely symbolic and for his allegorical interpretation of biblical text. Altogether he stressed the consonance of his preaching with that of his Protestant peers, urging his congregation to go forth and make this discovery for themselves. He intended to put them at ease with their Judaism in the American Protestant climate.

During the spring and summer of 1870, while he was busy preparing for City College, Henry noted that he "had taken very seriously" his "confirmation in the Thirty-Ninth Street Temple Beth El." After his confirmation, Henry reports that he "formed the habit of visiting churches of many denominations and making abstracts of the sermons I heard delivered by Henry Ward Beecher, Henry W. Bellows, Rabbi Einhorn, Richard Storrs, T. DeWitt Talmage, and R. Alger, and many others of the famous pulpit-orators who enriched the intellectual life of New York." He was also influenced by a hunchbacked Quaker doctor, Samuel S. Whitall, who rented quarters at the Morgenthaus'.

> He was the physician at the coloured hospital who gave half his time to charitable work among the poor. I frequently opened the door for his patients and ran his errands, and we became friends. I remember his long religious talks, and how deeply I was impressed by Penn's *No Cross, No Crown,* a copy of which he gave me. Largely because of it I composed twenty-four rules of action, tabulating virtues that I wished to acquire and vices that I must avoid.

Henry kept a detailed chart of some twenty-four "maxims," a list of commandments that was a mixed bag of warnings and goals. Infractions were indicated each day with an "X," possible violations with a question mark. Each day was graded numerically, ranging from 95 to 40, and sometimes with a general comment appended: "This day was not so well spent," or "Spent a pretty nice day." The maxims covered a wide range of sins and virtues. "Swearing" was the sin most frequently noted, along with "slang phrases." The more positive comments included "sweet or [illegible] good," "think," "study and read in the bible," "gratefulness," "truthfulness" and "cleanliness." All told he gave himself small margin for self-indulgence.

While he noted that at times he was considered "egoistic," he realized that he could not afford the luxury of gentlemanly false modesty. He did record some bouts of depression verging on paranoia, which he analyzed with precocious maturity and immediately dispelled. His sensitivity seemed to be intensified by the turbulent family environment and what today would be called "culture shock." He responded by conquering the obstacles through the strenuous exercise of willpower.

Henry was deeply shaken when only a few months after he entered City College his father made him quit and go to work to support himself and to contribute to the family's welfare. Meanwhile he had fixed his sights on becoming a lawyer and gave himself a timetable, which he managed to adhere to with amazing precision. Yet there were moments when the challenges overwhelmed him. One Sunday morning he recorded in his journal, "Sitting at my desk in my room on the top floor back room in the house, 161 East 61st Street, looking through a diary for 1871 and college chemistry notes, I was thinking how awful it was that I had left college over one year ago and was still so very foolish and stupid, instead of being studious and settled." But in the next sentence he picks himself up: "I consider some change for the better, positively and understandably necessary in order that I should succeed in this world."

After leaving college, Henry worked at a variety of odd jobs. He didn't much like any of them, particularly because they interfered with his goal of becoming a lawyer. His father had urged him to take up engineering, and he went to work for Mr. G. Weissenborn, a civil engineer. But Henry quickly determined that he "lacked the requisite mathematical foundation." The stay was very brief, indeed — March 29 to April 1 — "when I left as I did not like it." Later that month he went to work for his brother Max and Max's partner, Gordon Schwartz, who were operating the uptown office of the Phoenix Insurance Company. He was paid six dollars a week as errand boy and assistant bookkeeper. He stayed with them "til September 16th when the firm was dissolved." A few days later, "I improved myself by securing a $10 position with Bloomingdale & Company who were then in the wholesale 'corset and fancy goods' business on Grand Street near Broadway. I kept the books and also helped to pack hoop-skirts, bustles and corsets, until the firm's financial difficulties gave me an excuse for turning my ambition again to the law."

In January 1872, Henry again went to work for the lawyer Ferdinand Kurzman, an acquaintance of his father's. The summer before he entered City College, he served papers and was sometimes sent to the district court "to answer the calendar and occasionally fight for an adjournment." When Kurzman observed that his eager young assistant wrote with a strong, clear hand, he gave him the added assignment of copying documents. "Stenographers and type-writers being practically unknown, the lawyer would dictate and his clerk transcribe in longhand, make the required number of copies with pen and ink and then compare the results and correct any errors." With this experience, Henry developed the beautiful handwriting that he retained even in old age. It also inspired his habit of making drafts or copies of all his correspondence, including the most personal.

At the same time, Henry often made himself useful straightening out other people's accounts. Lazarus was much in need of his son's services. Henry and his brothers were also kept busy making the rounds collecting money for *The Golden Book of Life,* which had become the principal family enterprise. To Henry's distress, the line that Lazarus drew between charitable affairs and his personal business was somewhat fuzzy. There is no doubt that he raised large sums for several worthy causes, and while he always made a "generous" contribution himself, "he seems to have deducted something for his expenses, and sometimes commingled his business and 'benevolent' activities." Henry notes that his father also incurred problems "when his individual gifts . . . made large inroads upon his comparatively small capital. He declared that the profits from the manufacture [of his pine products] would be devoted to charity entirely, with the exception of the actual expense of his sustenance."

The period of Henry's employment with Kurzman also marked the birth of his intense interest in public affairs. At this time, Grant was campaigning for re-election. His bitter opponent was Horace Greeley, the brilliant editor of the *New York Tribune,* then the most widely read and influential publication in the nation. Young Henry, fascinated by the spectacle of the American political free-for-all, was sympathetic to the assaults from idealists like Greeley and Carl Schurz on the corruption and the punitive anti-Southern policies of the Grant administration. He also appears to have been sensitive to the manipulative power of the press. "I shall relate to you my experience in this campaign," he wrote his friend Sam Schlessinger, the week after he had met Grant.

> At first I was very much for Greeley and denounced Grant very bitterly, but the expression used in the papers and organs of both parties in regard to each other showed me conclusively that there was nothing to be learned from politics as the editorials in the papers were all political, and always of a slandering character. . . . [T]herefore I take no interest at all in this campaign and do never express an opinion as I think I do not know enough acts of either to judge which is better, but I think there are a good many persons who know as little about either as I do, but yet they denounce either Grant or Greeley according to the papers they read and to the speeches that are the loudest.

In the privacy of his journal, Henry was even more critical: "[Grant] is a mere tool, in the hands of the party. . . . But enough of Grant, as in a single interview I cannot be expected to know all the traits of the man's character, that is expecting too much. The impression his appearance made on me may have prejudiced me against him." Later he recalled talking about Grant to his brother-in-law Gustave Zittel, saying, "If any of our family would ever come into power he would appoint just as many relatives."

Politics as a power game had begun to surface in Henry's writings. More and more he began to consider the possibilities of public service as a complement to business or even as an alternative. As a new American, he was deeply grateful to find American democracy, however flawed and corrupt, to be a reality. The United States was a place where immigrants, despite handicaps, were not treated as outsiders, as Jews had been treated in Europe. Yet there must have been something humiliating, even terrifying, about the family's departure from Europe.

But he wasted no time brooding; on the contrary, he determined to ensure his security as an American by overpaying his debt of gratitude. He also sensed that this course of action could have enormous benefits. While others were blindly slugging it out in the marketplace, he would reinforce his endeavors with the leverage of political force. He would also bask in the warmth reserved for those who serve the public interest at some personal expense. The way his father had turned charitable acts to personal glory had been

marked by his son. Henry was not deterred by the absence of Jews
in the public sector. In America, one could expect almost any kind
of change within a single generation, or so he believed.

In the storm of emotional chaos within the Morgenthau family,
Henry had begun to look outside for a confidant and mentor. At
first he had turned to the Quaker doctor who boarded in his home.
When Dr. Samuel S. Whitall presented him with William Penn's *No
Cross, No Crown,* Henry was inspired by the Quaker call to conscience and social action. In its advocacy of the individual's responsibility to the community, it was close to the radical Reform preach-
ings of Rabbi David Einhorn.

Henry made a note of a two-hour session in which Whitall spoke
of the spirit within, saying that it was each person's duty to retain
his individual spirituality. Thereupon Henry resolved to read pas-
sages in the Penn text every night. "This will help me more than
writing down everything I do as though it was positive that I must
succeed. I intend to commence actual work at once (as acts are better than words) tomorrow, by really doing what my conscience
prompts me, not what my pride dictates."

At this stage in Henry's life, however, this resolve led to more
punishing self-denial of what he loved most: food. There was no
letup in the written confessions in his journals and correspondence.

"I eat for my supper merely two eggs, three pieces of black
bread, and a cup of coffee, and resolve to sacrifice after having read
of Abraham, Moses, Job, and Jesus, denying themselves, sacrificing
what was most dear to them to obey the will of God. I feel very . . .
contented with my behavior . . . go to bed now at 8 so as to
be up early tomorrow and commence my work in content, and I
pray." Henry, though much attracted to Christian beliefs, especially
when separated from ritual trappings, gave no indication that he
ever considered cutting his bond with Judaism. His furthest departure was his affiliation with the secularized Judaism of Felix Adler,
founder of the Society for Ethical Culture. The "ethical" implied a
moral righteousness that atoned for the sins visited upon Henry by
his father. It also stood for personal purity (sexual abstinence) and
proved a bulwark against youthful temptation. "Culture" implied
the kind of "self-improvement" that paved the route to complete
Americanization.

Later in life Henry became fascinated with Christian Science.
The idea of substituting will power for faith seemed to validate his

confidence in the ability of human beings to overcome their frailties. But when some of his relatives actually embraced the creed, he facetiously called them "Jewish Scientists."

Meanwhile, in the law office of Ferdinand Kurzman, Henry found his duties "very various" but "interesting." There were a large number of criminal and small claims cases. "We have all kinds of clients." Some were "pretty liberal"; others "mean and miserly, some men and some women and even some mere boys who commence business and get into trouble with their creditors." They handled suits for "payment of $50 promissory notes . . . divorce and seduction and bankruptcy." He found it a good education in human nature, but on the whole it was "an assembly of the worst class of people, and I thought rather than being a criminal lawyer . . . I would like to be a real estate lawyer."

In due course, the real estate cases came his way after Kurzman, in an extraordinary show of confidence, sent his young chief clerk to Albany to appear in court to obtain an injunction in a case of real estate fraud. The proceedings and Morgenthau's success in court were reported at length in the New York English- and German-language press — probably the first time that Henry Morgenthau's name appeared in print.

Kurzman had a busy practice handling the buying and selling of middle-class residences during the real estate boom that soared through the year 1872. He took in a distinguished Kentucky gentleman as his partner. George H. Yeaman had been a member of Congress and U.S. minister to Denmark, and subsequently was a lecturer at Columbia Law School. Henry felt lucky in being chosen to take his dictation, which helped him learn how to do title searches. Then, without informing Kurzman, Henry reorganized his boss's account books. "[I] shall never forget his surprise and appreciation," Henry noted, "when at the end of the year, I showed what he had earned and the sources and also the accounts still due him."

At the end of the summer in 1873, most people, having ignored the early warning tremors, went into shock when the American economy shattered in a ruinous financial collapse. "No man that lived through the Panic of '73 can ever forget it," Henry recalled years later. The expansion of the railroads had fueled optimism "that bordered on hysteria." Encouraged by the glowing success stories of manipulative entrepreneurs, "clergymen, school teachers and small professional men" had plunged into the stock and bond markets. Real estate too was booming, stimulated by "the recently created middle class."

People who had made investments funded with loans and mortgages were wiped out. The banks that had financed them operated without any government protection. As the bad news spread, the rush to withdraw personal savings brought on an avalanche of failures. At the end of the week in mid-September when Henry was standing in line to make his usual deposit at the German Uptown Savings Bank, his sharp gaze through the teller's cage detected "the president of the bank in earnest conversation with three other men." He couldn't hear what they were saying but noticed that "the president seemed worried, and those with him also showed uneasiness." When Henry reached the teller's window, "on a sudden impulse I thrust my dollar bill that I intended to deposit back into my pocket, presented my pass book and told the clerk that I wanted to withdraw the entire $80 that was to my credit." The bank closed three days later. Depositors ultimately settled for fifty cents on the dollar.

Kurzman was badly bruised by his investment in Northern Pacific Railroad bonds, but his law practice continued to prosper. Where the office "had once been almost rushed to death with drawing mortgages," they found themselves instead "hard pressed to keep pace with foreclosure proceedings." Henry felt that he was profiting from the experience and the 10 percent of the gross fees he received as commission. He made up his mind never, never to be tempted into speculation. On later reflection, he believed that if he "had not lived through the Panic of '73," he would have become "either many times richer . . . or what is more likely penniless."

This decision, however, did not stop Henry from paying another kind of price.

· 6 ·

An Eye-opening
Return to Germany

WORKING LONG HOURS under bad lighting conditions in
Kurzman's offices, Henry had become alarmed by painful eyestrain. He found that his condition was further
irritated by tobacco smoke. Finally, in desperation, he accepted his
doctor's orders for a long sea voyage. In June 1874, after the financial panic had subsided, he embarked for Hamburg from the Jersey
Flats. His ultimate destination was Kiel, the resort seaport on the
Baltic. To finance this holiday he relied on his own meager resources. They could hardly have amounted to more than double the
eighty dollars he had withdrawn from his savings account. He had
been attracted therefore by an advertisement seeking a few passengers on the sail-and-steam-powered freighter *Dora:* thirty days for
thirty-five dollars.

On disembarking in Hamburg, Henry was greeted by the Simon
family, who had been designated as his German hosts. Edward
Simon was married to Henry's older sister Pauline. He had emigrated to New York from Rendsburg, where the substantial Simon
family had their base.

The first week, before proceeding to Kiel, Henry made daily
visits to Dr. Salomon in Hamburg for his eyes, which pained him
enormously while reading and writing. He recorded payment to the
doctor and for medicine and an "eye brush." In one instance he
accidentally used lead instead of zinc ointment, with excruciating
results. Thus restrained from his usual heavy reading schedule,
Henry opened his senses to all that was emanating from his new
environment.

In Kiel, Henry was impressed by the Prussian bustle, so different from the easygoing ways of the Mannheim he remembered. The Franco-Prussian War had ended in 1871, leaving Germany newly unified under a Prussian kaiser as the dominant power in Europe. "Everywhere there were the beginnings of commercial and military activity; everywhere there was preached the doctrine of world power."

That August the entire city and harbor were decked out with flags to greet Field Marshal Helmuth von Moltke, whose skill in mobilizing and commanding the German forces had been deservedly credited with achieving the victory over Napoleon III's poorly organized command.

Henry marched with some soldiers on their way to the maneuvers being staged for the hero's welcome, and "got an idea of how they carry on skirmishes." The celebration came to a climax in the evening with a torchlight parade that proceeded to the Germania Hotel, where Henry "plainly saw Moltke three times and heard him speak" of all classes joining together in support of German unity.

During his holiday Henry remained under the guardianship of the Simons. Life in this backwater trading post was provincially conservative. As opposed to the liberalized Reform Judaism subscribed to by the majority of big-city Jews, Henry was subjected here, for the first time in his life, to the ways of Orthodoxy.

He recalled a Saturday morning with the Simons when he went to synagogue, "where I listened to the prayers. Firstly, I was surprised at the shabby appearance of the men, then at the loudness of their prayers, kissing their talles and [illegible] and touching the torath and then kissing their hand; selling at auction the mitzvas and offering the first calling up [illegible]. Don't understand, took a bath and visited the Museum." On Sunday afternoon, after taking a nap, he and Carl Simon "conversed about religion and the soul, future life, etc. Then went to the Confectionary, took some ice cream and cake."

A few years Henry's senior and completely different from him in personality and physique, Carl Simon was slight, affecting an elegantly languid manner. "C.S. weighed 104 and I 133 German lbs.,"★ Henry recorded in his diary. During the weeks they were together, Henry discovered Carl to be a moody libertine with liter-

★One German pound equals 500 grams. One U.S. pound equals 373.2 grams.

ary pretensions, a taste for gambling, and a disrespect for women. On the evening of August 18, Henry noted,

> CS and I drank coffee, took a nap, then went walking out of the northern part of Kiel along the Knooperweg. Saw the drum corps practice. . . . In the evening went to No. 60 Dammenstrasse, a house of ill repute which was very finely fitted up. We took some Brause lemonade and I felt very bashful and awkward. Then we went to concert saloon where we heard them sing. The girls were dressed up grand. Then we took some beer and gave two shillings to the singers. Then went home, had a conversation with CS whereabout we totally disagree.

Henry had chosen not to visit any of his blood relatives in southern Germany. Most of the German Jewish families that had prospered in the United States had maintained personal and business ties with their relatives in the old country, through frequent visits and a steady flow of correspondence, ending only with the outbreak of World War I. Then again, during the Hitler period, many American Jews made a special effort to rescue family members who had tarried in Germany. There are good but hardly sufficient reasons why Henry rejected this custom in the summer of 1874 and thereafter. The sojourn in Kiel had made demands on his tight budget, and the doctor's prescription for a seaside vacation was meant for rest. The fact that all four of his grandparents were deceased could have been another factor. What is mystifying is that all ties between the American branch of the Morgenthau family and the German appear to have been severed: no visits, no correspondence. Over the years, Henry nurtured a fierce hostility toward Germans, which his descendants have sustained. During the previous summer he witnessed scenes of intense Prussian military preparation that left him forever wary of Teutonic aggression.

Studying Law at Columbia

W HEN HENRY came back to New York in the fall of 1874, he did not return to Kurzman's dingy office, where he had suffered eyestrain. Instead he entered the "new well lighted quarters" of Chauncey Shaffer, an attorney with a national reputation for his colorful ways.

In serving his apprenticeship, which was then an acceptable way of preparing for the bar, Henry soon came to the conclusion "that obtaining a knowledge of the law in this scrappy, unsystematic fashion was unsatisfactory." In the summer of 1875 he left Shaffer's employ to enter Columbia College Law School that fall.

As he needed to support himself while earning his degree, he sought a job teaching night school. After several rejections, he discovered that such assignments were handed out as political plums. A well-connected friend then wrote a letter on Henry's behalf to a Charles H. Wilson, Esq.:

> Although we have been associated politically for some years, I do not think I have ever asked a political favor of you. There must always be a first time and this is my first time. The bearer Mr. Henry Morgenthau, desires an appointment as a teacher in night school. He is a graduate of Public School No. 14 and has been a year at the New York College. I think he is qualified, mentally, morally and physically for the position . . . if you can aid him by your influence on the Board of Trustees to secure the appointment you will confer a very great favor on yours very truly . . .

The fifteen-dollar-a-week job he obtained teaching night school on Forty-second Street near Third Avenue was no sinecure. The students, aged eighteen to forty-five, were "hard working carpenters, brakemen, butchers, a plumber's assistant, a coachman and a blacksmith intent on learning." There were also some disruptive ruffians throwing tobacco quids and playing cards whenever the teacher turned his back on the class to write on the blackboard. Henry, a husky 180-pound nineteen-year-old, made an example of one of these bullies when he "forcibly ejected him from the classroom." Maintaining discipline and class attendance were requisites for Henry's keeping the job that was his sole means of support.

At law school Henry "joined the Columbia Club and was one of the team to debate with the Barnard Club, all of whose members were college graduates."★

During the second year of the two-year program he chose not to continue teaching night school but instead found a job with "that fine Southern gentleman, General Roger A. Pryor, who had been Congressman and Minister to Spain, and finally became a Judge of the Supreme Court of the State of New York." When Theodore Tilton came to consult Pryor concerning the morals charges he was preparing to bring against the Reverend Henry Ward Beecher, Morgenthau served as secretary and took dictation.†

In 1876 the hotly contested Hayes-Tilden presidential race resulted in what many considered an unfair decision in favor of the Republican candidate, Rutherford Hayes. Henry, while still just under voting age, had made some speeches for the Democratic candidate, Samuel J. Tilden, the wealthy, reform-minded governor of New York. Henry noted that "the country [is being] damned and called rotten and its future existence as a republic is in doubt. But all this will blow over." As a defensive booster of his adopted country, he deplored those who would "make you think it is the worst place in the world." This argument he attributed to those who were living beyond their means "and condemn it as a place where no poor man can rise and prophesy the inevitable result a regular aristocracy — now this is all moonshine."

Henry believed that for those who worked hard and lived pru-

★Named in honor of Frederick Augustus Porter Barnard (1809–99), then president of Columbia. The women's college that was later named in his honor was not yet in existence.
†Beecher, the spellbinding preacher, whose favorite theme was love, had been accused by his old friend Tilton of having made improper advances toward Mrs. Tilton. Although the charges were eventually dropped, they stirred up a furor that became one of the sensations of the era.

dently the rewards in America were unlimited. The disaster in store for spendthrifts is a recurring theme in his writings, which is no wonder, considering his bitter personal experience. "The Family was never so low and its prospects so poor. I ask why? Simply because they have lived beyond their means for the last few years while money was plentiful and times good." His only words of praise were reserved, as usual, for his mother.

Henry had assumed that he was solely responsible for the restoration of the family, "even if I have to sacrifice a great deal of my time to introduce different principles, ideas, and modes of living. Morally the family is also very low, none of the older ones believe that Religion is the true guide to a moral life. Honesty is a thing that is preached but not practiced except for policy's sake."

Although he sounded uninhibitedly judgmental, Henry was in fact driven but modest, never laying claim to any special talent. What some mistook for conceit was a necessary display of self-assurance that gained him the confidence and support of others. Above all he was a man of strong faith in the ultimate goodness of man and the power of individual will to overcome personal faults. His theology had been transformed from traditional Judaism to the ethical democracy to which all Americans supposedly aspired. He sought favor in the eyes of God and his fellow Americans through service to democracy — his true religion, or a substitute for religion.

Henry's idealism was tempered by faith in the power of wealth. Money, in his view, was not the soul of democracy, but it was certainly its lifeblood. Accordingly he set out to amass a decent-size fortune so that he could afford the public virtue to which he aspired. Without cynicism he was convinced that everything and everyone had a price. While impatient to regain his lost status, he prudently avoided the reckless gambling that had ruined his father; he was well aware that the appetite for gain could become an addiction. Like other passions, this one would require stern self-discipline to stay in check.

· 8 ·

On the Bumpy Road
to Love

I N JUNE 1877 after graduating from Columbia Henry was admitted to the New York bar. At the age of twenty-one he had
achieved a degree of professional acceptance just short of full
collegiality by the ruling clique of Protestant lawyers. His rapid
advance had been phenomenal, although not unique. Oscar Straus,
born in Rhenish Bavaria six years before Henry, had graduated four
years ahead of him at Columbia Law School. Though both were
bound to the intimate society of German Jews, their personal relationship remained guardedly cool and occasionally hostile. Perhaps
each was concerned that the world outside the perimeter of their
inner circle couldn't accommodate them both. As keenly competi-
tive first-generation Americans, they eyed each other warily. Although some of their descendants developed close friendships, the
adversarial attitude between the two families never entirely disappeared.

One telling difference between the two young men, as they
started off in life, was that while Henry was left to his own resources, Oscar had effective backing from his family. The Strauses
were close, to the point of suffocation, but there was a chemistry
within the family that worked to the benefit of each individual.
Oscar's two older brothers, Isidor and Nathan, recognized his intellectual proclivities and proceeded to make sure that he got the best
education obtainable. In contrast to Henry, whose pattern of formal
education was erratic, Oscar with solid family support had been
able to graduate from Columbia Grammar School and Columbia

College as well as the law school. Though their advances were closely parallel, their paths seldom crossed.

After earning his degree, Henry went back to work for his old boss, Ferdinand Kurzman. Kurzman then had two principal associates, George H. Yeaman and Alfred McIntire, "a New Englander of the very best type, considerably older than Mr. Kurzman, and regarded as one of the best conveyancers of the city of New York." Henry credits McIntire with having "graciously initiated me into the intricacies of his work" and having obtained for him clerkships with two other Gentile lawyers, Shaffer and Pryor. It was not then especially unusual for Christian lawyers to have Jewish partners. Only after the mass immigration of Eastern European Jews accelerated in the 1880s did the tide of anti-Semitism cause professional and commercial reorganization along religious and ethnic lines. Barred from association with Christians, German Jews in turn excluded their Eastern brethren. These ethnic and religious considerations were not yet compelling when Henry decided that he was ready to set out on his own. One Sunday afternoon he and McIntire rowed out on the Harlem River to discuss a partnership. As Henry recalled, "He was about six foot two in height and weighed fully 250 pounds, and I was to do the rowing. Our skiff had not proceeded fifty yards before I discovered that I could not pull such a load and get anywhere. I took this as an omen, and then and there resolved that when I did select a law partner, he should be of my own age and weight so that he could do some of the pulling."

A year and a half later Henry formed a partnership with two men cut to his specifications. His friendship with Abraham Goldsmith had begun when they were classmates at City College, and it continued at Columbia Law School, where another classmate, Samson Lachman, had graduated with top honors. What Henry failed to mention — probably because it seemed irrelevant — was that all three men were Jewish.

On January 1, 1879, Lachman, Morgenthau, and Goldsmith opened offices at 243 Broadway. The rent was $400 and the net income $1,500 for the first year. It would have been a meager existence had it continued. Fortunately Henry had other resources to fall back on. While clerking for Kurzman and Yeaman, he had obtained a favorable settlement for a client and with his employers' consent had accepted one share of stock in the Celluloid Piano Key Company. This company had secured the exclusive right to make celluloid piano and organ keys, and when the price of ivory sky-rocketed, so did the value of its stock. But as the business grew so did mistrust among its officers. The only thing they seemed to agree on was their confidence in their twenty-one-year-old counsel. Henry became secretary and eventually president of the company.

This was the first of many profitable ventures that began to turn Henry's attention from his law practice to business, primarily real estate. Before long he was handling mortgages and foreclosures. Many of them were in Harlem, an area popular with respectable middle-class householders, some of them Jews, who had been through the expansion and collapse of the 1870s. Thus by 1880 nearly all of Harlem was for sale. Henry began to buy "plots of three to five adjoining houses at a time, and quickly re-sell them for a small profit." With his only capital frozen in celluloid, he turned to his brother-in-law, William Ehrich, who, as a silent partner, advanced the required funds and received half the profits.

Ehrich himself had been very successful in running his family dry goods store but had had to retire when he developed symptoms of tuberculosis. He decided to invest his profits in New York City real estate under Henry's guidance while he and his wife, Ida, retreated to Davos, Switzerland, where the climate was reputedly beneficial.

On October 21, 1882, Henry wrote a long letter to Ida in Davos, supposedly confiding in her alone that he was wrestling with the idea of marrying a young woman, whose name he coyly withheld. What Henry really wanted was not the advice but the consent and applause of his nearest and dearest. He enjoyed portraying himself as a young man head over heels in love. But there had been nothing impetuous in the cool, rational way he had arrived at his decision. In good lawyerly fashion he had developed his arguments in writing and solicited the opinions of valued confidants. At the same time he was quite certain that he would gain his objective. As it turned out, however, the route to marriage proved unexpectedly rocky.

At twenty-six Henry had prudently postponed considering marriage until he had a firm grip on the ladder to success as a New York lawyer and businessman. With the family finances in disarray and his father's reputation clouded with scandal, he knew his eligibility would have to be assessed on his own achievements and promise. In this respect he was following both his grandfather and his father, who, twenty-eight when he married Babette Guggenheim, had waited until he was in a position to marry up the social scale.

Filed away among Henry's papers is a handwritten roster of more than 450 young women. He nowhere indicates how he compiled it. Perhaps it was a list of guests at the Harmonie Club balls (a club where the Sykeses were members and the Morgenthaus were not) or the Freundschaft (a less exclusive assembly), which Henry attended. Next to some of the names was a check mark; a few had double checks. Only one, Josephine Sykes, was awarded a triple check. It would seem to have been a case of "liking at first sight which easily turned into love," as Henry's brother Julius assessed the romance after it had blossomed.

Without mentioning Josephine by name, Henry gave Ida a sketch by comparing her to a mutual friend: "two inches smaller, somewhat thinner, a little livelier, with almost the same character accomplishments, adding to the latter a fair voice and a knowledge of some of the favorite German songs and you will have a fair idea. Her family is also similarly situated though somewhat larger."

"I neither expect to better my social standing nor my purse," he told his sister Ida. "I do not despise such as sell themselves into slavery for life, but I sincerely sympathize with them, for in their short sightedness and disregard of the future, they know not what they do." Henry's vehement denial that he included the social and financial standing of Josephine's family among her virtues has a slightly false ring. If he had been candid, he might have admitted that status was an item to be marked under assets on the balance sheet.

In selecting his mate, Henry, like his forefathers and descendants, looked for a woman with great inner strength and a modicum of sweetness. He sought a true companion equipped with the wit and cultural refinement needed to share and attain his limitless ambitions. The family would act as the mirror in which he would seek the reflection of his improved self. His wife's role in administering the household would be no demeaning task. Physical beauty was not a priority. Its cultivation was deemed frivolous; preoccupation with it, in either sex, a cause for suspicion. A married woman should have the dignity and the well-upholstered, richly ornamented look of fashionably overstuffed furniture.

At the end of a stormy courtship, Henry and Josie became engaged in December 1882. At that time Henry's younger brother,

Julius, was studying for a doctorate in archaeology at the university in Leipzig. Henry confided in him, in a somewhat surprising reversal of the contempt he had expressed six years earlier. Julius for his part could not contain his gushing affection and admiration for the brother who had "been more than a brother, a friend, almost-father." Julius wanted to be a member of the wedding. "Probably this will sound peculiar to you both," he wrote Henry and Josie, "but I have always considered you . . . a part of myself." He reminded Henry of their pledge "to give each other pictures of our minds." As brothers "in mind and body," he suggests, "if it is not impertinent," that Josie write to him "so that we two can learn to know each other better." Thereupon he confesses, "I always look upon my future as bound up in Henry's. I cannot imagine myself as separated from you, and you, Henry will understand me when I say that I want to know your wife." Josie's letter of December 1882 written without a salutation and attached to a letter from Henry was probably her answer to Julius's request.

"Ever since the second of October our courtship had been coming to a crisis very rapidly," Josie wrote. "On the third of December it concluded with a proposal. Oh, and such a proposal, it was too funny for anything." She proceeded to mock the scene that took place in her mother's back parlor:

> Henry sitting on the sofa leaning forward talking very earnestly and sincerely. I, a few paces distant, sitting in a big arm chair, my head turned away, not daring to look at him, under soft winter's twilight. To all of this (in what poetical phrase) do you suppose he asked? "Do you *like* me?" Wasn't that in harmony with the situation? But never mind, *love* was the big mountain we had to climb together. Now after our experience I fully believe in the old adage about true love never coming smoothly, for our road was a very crooked one.

The strain caused Henry and Josie each to lose about twenty pounds. All of this had been going on right under Mrs. Sykes's nose, while she was "utterly unconscious of what was passing between us."

Henry had asked Josie to keep their engagement secret, but a few days later he himself spilled the beans to her brother Willie, subsequently telling Josie he "thought it dishonorable that you should have a secret from your folks." A furious Mrs. Sykes forbade any further communication between the two and refused to receive Henry. The young couple, however, continued to write ardent letters to each other which were delivered clandestinely by friends.

"Be sure to let me know in some way whether you have received this note," Henry wrote, relishing the *Romeo and Juliet* turn of events. "I feel I must either see or write you every day, as your image is constantly before me and your spirit enters all my doings and thoughts."

His letters were full of strong arguments that he was confident would be read by his chief adversary.

> I insist on being treated fairly and honorably. I am willing to submit to the criticism and judgment of your entire family, and if they think they can detect the slightest flaws they ought to be pleased at the opportunity I am willing to give them.
>
> If they fear that our judgment is not mature enough (which I do not for one moment admit) I am satisfied to submit myself to the judgment of maturer persons (can I propose anything fairer), but how can they judge me unless they see me — I am as chivalric as any knight of old who willingly fights lions and tigers to win his lady-love.

To allay any suspicion of base motives Henry declared, "I ask *nothing,* absolutely nothing but *you* and the task and pleasure of making you happy."

Josie's mother, Helen Himmelreich Sykes, had become a wealthy widow at forty-six with a family of nine children. Her husband, Charles Sykes, had gained a windfall fortune in Detroit at the beginning of the Civil War manufacturing clothing for the Michigan state militia.

Dorothy Bloomfield, a distant cousin of mine, has a snapshot of our great-grandmother Sykes. It was taken by her mother when Dorothy was six. In her words, Great-Grandmother Sykes was a delight: "a tiny bit of a thing with enormous hips and narrow shoulders, barely taller than I was. She wore black always, and voluminous skirts with petticoats galore and deep pockets in the petticoats. She always had treasures hidden in those pockets."

In contrast with his wife, about whom there is much well-documented information, Samuel Sykes remains an elusive, shadowy figure. The only extant likeness of him, to my knowledge, is a family photograph that reveals him as a short, dark, compact man in the somber black clothes considered suitable for this sort of formal portrait. According to Louise Heidelberg's family tree, he was born in Manchester, England, May 28, 1824, and died October

9, 1880, presumably in New York City. On visits to Manchester in 1986 and 1989 I discovered that these assumptions were only partially correct. Three important clues have recently come to light which seem to solve this mystery: first, Samuel Sykes's death notices; second, a vine-choked gravestone in an abandoned cemetery; and finally, a bizarre account in the *Manchester Guardian* of a court settlement of a suit lodged by one brother against another.

In 1849, a Morris Friedlander (whose Jewish name was Moshe ben Shemarihu), the father of Samuel Sykes, arrived in Manchester from Prussia, whereupon he changed his surname to Sykes. (The practice of assuming an English surname and first name was common.) Sykes was accompanied by his wife Caroline (Simra, daughter of Zvi), one year his senior, and their two younger children: Susan, eleven, and Henry, seven. The Sykes family settled on Johnson Street, Red Bank. This "voluntary ghetto" held a concentration of the poorest newly arrived Jews. Sykes is credited as Manchester's first Jewish India-rubber waterproofer. This kind of work involved a simple process, developed in Manchester by Charles Mackintosh, of smearing cloth with vulcanized India rubber. It was one of the tinkers' trades that could be pursued without capital, expensive equipment, or special skills.

From this lowly beginning Sykes advanced rapidly. In the 1851 census he is listed as a tailor and had moved his residence to Berkeley Street among the petite bourgeoisie in the Strangeways district, where the family remained thereafter. In the 1861 *Directory of Professions* Sykes is listed as a clothier and in the 1871 census as a wholesale clothier.

On March 1, 1862, the *Manchester Guardian* published an article headed SINGULAR ACTION BETWEEN BROTHERS. It is a lengthy account of a jury trial that had taken place the day before in the case of *Friedlander v. Sykes*. It noted that "the plaintiff and the defendant are brothers and Jews." This rather demeaning account of two brothers squabbling over money reflects the kind of Dickensian anti-Semitism then pervasive in Britain. Nevertheless, it gives some important facts about the Sykes family not otherwise available, first and foremost corroborating the change of name from Friedlander to Sykes.

Scholar Bill Williams has noted that there was a great deal of confusion in the Manchester records as to whether particular Jews had emigrated from German-speaking Prussia itself, or from Polish territory then incorporated into Prussia where Jews spoke Yiddish. These arcane distinctions were of little importance in mid-nineteenth-century Manchester. However, the fact that the Sykeses were (or claimed to be) of German rather than of Slavic cultural origins was important later on to Samuel Sykes in seeking a wife in Bavaria and in establishing his family in Detroit.

As Morris Sykes rose in the business community, he became an influential member of the Great Synagogue on Cheetham Hill Road, serving on the governing board of this center of Orthodox worship. By that time Manchester also boasted an impressive Reform synagogue, frequented by the Anglo-Jews and some of the prosperous German Jews, and a Spanish-Portuguese synagogue for the Sephardic Jews. By the late 1860s Sykes had identified with the old guard of the Great Synagogue who felt the need to distance themselves from the ever expanding influx of impoverished newcomers. In the summer of 1872 he and a group of colleagues composing the new elite were deposed in a synagogue election by a solid majority of the new masses. Thereupon Sykes and his cohorts became the founding members of the secessionist South Manchester Synagogue.

Morris's son, Samuel Sykes, was twenty-five when his parents and two much-younger siblings arrived in Manchester in 1848. He himself probably went directly to the United States, the ultimate destination of most of the Continental emigrants. However, he was visiting his family in Manchester at the time of his death at the home of his sister, Mrs. Selig Jacobson, October 9, 1880.★

In 1853, Samuel Sykes went to Bavaria to consecrate what was probably a prearranged marriage with Helen Himmelreich. The Himmelreich home was in the village of Frensdorf, near Bamberg. Also near Bamberg was the hamlet of Gleusdorf, where Moses Morgenthau had been born in 1773. Abraham Himmelreich, Helen's father, born in 1779, appears to have planted his family on more solid ground than had the Morgenthaus. Whereas both men

---

★The *Jewish Chronicle,* Friday, October 22, 1880, reads, "Mr. Morris Sykes, Mr. Henry Sykes and Mrs. Selig Jacobson return thanks for cards, letters and visits of condolence received during the week of mourning for their late beloved son and brother, Mr. Samuel Sykes of New York City — 2 Petworth Street, Cheetham, Manchester." On October 11, the *Manchester Examiner and Times* "Deaths" column listed "Sykes, on the 9th instant at the residence of his sister, S. Jacobson, 2 Petworth Street, Cheetham, Samuel Sykes Esq. of New York, aged 55."

attempted to improve their lot through marriage, at that time only Abraham succeeded.*

Immediately after Samuel Sykes and Helen Himmelreich were married on March 3, 1853, they emigrated to the United States and went to Detroit, where Sykes established his men's clothing business. They maintained their living quarters over the store along with Sam Himmelreich (Heavenrich), Helen's younger brother, in a cramped, uneasy ménage. Helen capitalized on her brother's affection by forging an alliance with him against her husband, who could be quick-tempered at times. Nevertheless Heavenrich credits Sykes with recovering quickly and becoming contrite. The marriage had soon become fruitful, but the first two children were stillborn. During these trials, young Sam was a "help-mate to dear sister Helen, doing mostly all the marketing for her as it was customary for men to do that kind of work then. The love and affection which existed between us, lasted for all times — we never spoke a harsh word to each other, always living peacefully and happily together." These sentiments were recorded three-quarters of a century after the fact in the rosy twilight of Samuel Heavenrich's ninetieth year. At the same time they show the extent to which the willful Helen — given to bouts of depression and foul-tempered outbursts — managed to bamboozle her brother.

At the end of two years Sykes's store was prosperous enough for him to move to Macomb Street and then to fashionable Antoine Street. There he built a fine double brick house, living in one half and renting the other. William Wright, who had just arrived from

---

*According to a memorandum written by his son, Samuel Heavenrich (the name the family adopted in the United States), his maternal grandfather, whose name was Brüll, had a prosperous lumber business in Regensburg. When his daughter's marriage was arranged, there was an agreement "written out between himself and my father, to give the latter 1500 florins on the day when the wedding took place, on condition, that my father should be possessed of a good substantial stone house in the town of Frensdorf, free of any incumbrance, in which to take his bride, and that they were to be married inside of three years. . . . In the fall of 1832 the wedding took place, and immediately thereafter the young couple settled in their new home in Frensdorf, and were blessed with thirteen children, of which four died in infancy, and nine grew up into man and womanhood" (Samuel Heavenrich, 1839–1930, memorandum to his family, dictated in 1929; in the author's archives).

Samuel tells us that his mother had five sisters and one brother. All made good marriages in various parts of Germany, produced large families of their own, and lived to be over eighty. Aunt Fannie went to Vienna to marry a von Meyer, a Catholic. In accepting his religion, she became the first convert to Christianity recorded in the annals of the extended family. Apparently the match was acceptable on both sides. Samuel notes that when he took members of his American family on a grand tour in 1873 to visit his mother and other German relatives, they included a stop in Vienna, where Aunt Fannie von Meyer "paid us a great deal of attention."

England, where he had gained a reputation as an artist, received his first commission in the United States decorating the walls and ceilings of Sykes's splendid residence. During the same period the Sykes store was relocated twice.

In 1860, recognizing the entrepreneurial talent of his young brother-in-law, Sykes saw fit to give him an interest in the business. Then something very surprising happened. At thirty-eight, Samuel Sykes retired from business permanently. We can only speculate that this moody man, whose health was never robust, wished to leave Detroit, with its hostile climate and frontier tastes. His brother-in-law noted, "Sykes thought he would retire from business and go to Europe with his family. In 1862 I became sole proprietor."

On March 29, 1863, while the Sykeses were visiting Stuttgart, Helen gave birth to a baby girl. Josephine was the sixth of the Sykeses' nine surviving children. The family returned to the United States later that year, to live comfortably in New York City.

"The Sykeses were great snobs," according to Dorothy Bloomfield. When nineteen-year-old Josephine Sykes confided her intention to marry Henry Morgenthau, her mother grandly dismissed everything her impulsive daughter had to say in his favor. Josie shared her mother's tendency toward temperamental explosions and widening hips. Indeed mother and daughter were very much alike, which only seemed to exacerbate their mistrust of each other. Helen herself had made what was considered a risky alliance when she wed Samuel.

Helen was furious that the courtship had proceeded without her knowledge or approval. She was also uneasy about the rumors concerning Lazarus Morgenthau and the family's instability. Although she had heard about young Henry's bright promise, she found him awfully pushy. Josie was only nineteen, after all, and could afford to wait.

Notwithstanding all of this, Mrs. Sykes was soon persuaded to give in. According to Josie, "Henry asserted himself and after numerous consultations everything came to this happy ending." Henry's conquest of Mrs. Sykes was complete. Moreover, in winning her favor, he found that he had also gained the support of the entire Sykes clan. Josie's brother Willie became his particular champion. But this prenuptial euphoria was short-lived. Henry's family situation weighed heavily on everyone.

Henry had decided that because of his father's aberrant behavior, neither of his parents should attend the wedding. He traveled to

Chicago to visit his mother, after writing to give her his painful decision. "With Papa things are not good, as I expected," he wrote.

> His hatred of the family is now worse than ever, and his behavior is so erratic that it is positively crucial that you prolong your stay in Chicago until he improves. It would be unwise to try it, as I am convinced that it will be very bad with him as soon as he will get upset.
>
> Yesterday I visited Dr. Gottheil and discussed the situation with him. He recommends that we should have a very small wedding and that neither you nor Papa should be present and that it would neither appear suitable or right if you came without your husband. And Papa also threatens all kinds of things, which he would carry out if you were to come. How the prospect of a wedding without your presence pains my heart, you can hardly imagine. But we (you and I) have had to bear so much so that we shall be able to bear this too. Above all there has to be peace. . . . It is terrible that everything is being spoiled only by *him*.

With the strain of family affairs and the burdens of business and law practice, Henry felt cheated out of the pleasures of courtship. "The 5 months of my engagement I passed in a sort of dreamy state," he wrote to Julius in Leipzig,

> half fearing all the time to be rudely awakened by some volcanic eruption from sources, but too well known to you. This fear and the strain of my nerves received from other causes, such as late hours and the inconvenient distance I lived from Josie totally unfitted me to enjoy as I had anticipated the pleasant period of engaged life, and though the same was not devoid of many very pleasant instances and the trials we had enabled us to more searchingly study each other and taught us more fully to appreciate each other, yet I can't refrain, now when it is ended, to say that it was not fully satisfactory.

During these fretful times Henry complained of frayed nerves, sore throats, and other discomforts. But he somehow managed to harness adversity as a force to propel him forward on his predetermined course. He even went ahead with a private seminar he had arranged with an eminent Shakespearean scholar and writer on English usage, Richard Grant White, whose son, Stanford White, was on his way to becoming the favorite architect of New York millionaires. When the class started, Henry arranged to include Josephine Sykes.

The disorderly state of affairs in the Morgenthau family made Josie's mother all the more determined that her daughter's nuptials be carried off with the elegance appropriate to her station. Everything was planned in accordance with high American fashion, and all reminders of German culture and Jewish dietary laws banished. Helen, whose personal communications were confined to German, ordered the wedding invitations engraved in English and the banquet menus in French, inscribed on double-paged booklets bound in ruby satin, corded, fringed, and tasseled. (I found some of them among my grandfather's papers at the Library of Congress.) The first course, for example, was "clams" — a purely American dish, which of course violated the kosher prohibition against shellfish. This was followed by two soups (perhaps a choice), hors d'oeuvres, including "Timbales à la Rothschild," a fish course, and a "Relevé" of filet de boeuf aux champignons, after which things became truly serious with a double "Entrée" of chicken and veal. The "Sorbet" course at the bottom of the first page was intended to cleanse the palate and offer a pause before the wedding guests were urged on with roasts, vegetables, and a final deluge of sweets and ices. No doubt all of this nourishment was washed down with a quantity of wine and champagne.

But on the evening of May 10, 1883, the solemn propriety of the occasion commanded by Helen Sykes brought no comfort to the bridegroom, who was, with good cause, intensely nervous. Two days before the wedding he had written to Josie, "I received a note from [sister] Pauline in which she informed me that her *Papa* has concluded *not* to come to the wedding." Henry felt Bertha and Papa were not to be trusted. "The afternoon of my wedding day was the closing scene of the old life," he wrote to his brother Julius afterward. "At lunch, Max, Julie, Ehrich, Chas. Weil and I were in conference yet about L.M. as he had threatened to raise a [illegible] but everything passed off nicely and charmingly. I have requested Mengo to write you the details."

Henry took time out to write Julius a few hours after he and Josie began their honeymoon in the Grand Hotel on Broadway and Thirty-first Street: "My own sweet little wife is taking a short nap for the wedding was such a success and we, contrary to usual customs, remained so long (12:15) that she feels considerably fatigued." A few days later Henry reported to Julius in detail "how happy and *blissful* I feel . . . I can't realize the fact that I could ever have been happy with anyone else — how I would like to write you some of the little reasons why I am daily and hourly becoming more and more infatuated with her, but I can't, the pen is not capable of picturing them, they are too delicate and tender." But in the days and weeks to come Henry found little that was too delicate to reveal.

"My Honey-moon from the hour of our wedding has opened a new Chapter . . . That Josie and I are happy, very happy — happy beyond our fondest expectations was paradoxically speaking to be expected." Henry had promised to give Julius a "mental photo" of his connubial bliss. While finding this "impossible," he certainly needed to share his most intimate feelings. "Let me state right here," he boasted,

> that all the self-denial I have practiced for so many years has been more than amply repaid during the past 12 days. How I could ever have enjoyed the charming innocence of Josie, had I been in the habit of having intimate intercourse with other women. The thrill of pleasure, the ecstatic delight at beholding the beautiful, chiseled like form of Josie I can't describe — I never expected to find such a Venus in my wife. But it is as much of a treat to me to look at her as the finest statue — could this have been so had I been impure.

"But enough of this," he wrote as though trying to control himself. Yet the need to tell all seemed overpowering.

> We spend our time in the most varied manner imaginable. We talk earnestly, play childishly, kiss fondly and often, read Gibbon *Decline and Fall of the Roman Empire* (abridged Edition by Smith) and Rau's *Life of Mozart,* alternately play pool, walk along the beach, or into the Fortress [Fort Monroe was 100 yards from their hotel] and smilingly observe the soldier life they lead here. Many hours we spend in speaking of our future plans and of our absent friends and altogether it often astonishes us how quickly the time passes.

Henry had originally intended to make his wedding trip a "surprise visit" to Julius in Europe but had changed plans because of the illness of his law partner Abraham Goldsmith. After the first night at the Grand Hotel they enjoyed the remainder of the honeymoon at the Hygeia Hotel at old Point Comfort, Virginia. But Henry had no regrets. "We are both anxious not to live beyond our means and our European trip might have been a little extravagant" — and Henry's experience had convinced him that "one of the chief causes of domestic unhappiness is the living beyond your means." Then he added that "in order to be happy" husband and wife "must always be striving together to improve ourselves." With Josie to encourage him, he believed "there is scarcely anything beyond the reaches of my capacities. No doubt will ever enter again into my mind as to the ideal life we so often hoped to lead, for Josie is as anxious for it as I am."

At the time Josie married Henry her claim to superior social status was an asset that should have given her confidence, but somehow it did not. In contrast to Henry, with his contagious ebullience, Josie was haunted by self-doubts. While Henry continued to show his affection and his respect for her judgment, she began to question his sincerity. She tested him with complaints and demands, and by deliberately neglecting her personal appearance, putting on weight, and being less fastidious in her toilette.

Although nothing is known of Josie's formal schooling, there are many indications that she had cultivated a mind that nicely complemented her husband's. She could sing and accompany herself on the piano in the repertoire of German lieder. She also proved to be adept at languages. Her English had none of the guttural Germanic echoes of her husband's, even though she had been born in Stuttgart, spent her early years traveling abroad, and was brought up in a German-speaking household. She knew enough Hebrew to teach Sunday school classes and became fluent in French. The latter was a great asset when her husband joined the diplomatic ranks, in which French was the common language.

A year after they were married, their first child was born; she was named for Josie's mother, Helen Sykes. At regular intervals three more were born in the course of a decade. All were extraordinarily healthy, as was their mother. In an era when hiring wet nurses was a common practice, Josie chose to suckle her own babies. It was demanding, and at times she let her husband know it. "I remind myself of a cow who is milked every two hours," she complained to Henry a couple of months after giving birth to "your son and heir." But in the same letter she wrote that "baby is doing beautifully and looks like a lovely bud today, so rosy and healthy."

During the summer Josie and the children would leave the city for cooler surroundings, by the sea or in the mountains, while Henry continued with his affairs in town. This was common among the affluent middle class. Men frequently joined their families on weekends, sometimes taking long trips by train or steamship, with a final leg by horse and carriage. They would usually take a vacation during the entire month of August, when New York became a steamy tropical town.

All the summer resorts were restricted along ethnic, religious, and economic lines. Almost no one cared to challenge the established borders or felt especially deprived by them. There was enough room for everyone to find comfortable accommodations somewhere.

The railroads, the New York Central and the West Shore Line, opened up the North Country above Saratoga. As a very young man Henry had begun to seek the refreshment of invigorating country air at a boardinghouse with the Harpel family in Hopewell Junction in Dutchess County, New York. More than thirty years later, his son Henry Jr. assembled a large tract of farmlands — eventually two thousand acres — in East Fishkill, which had Hopewell Junction as its post office address. I have often wondered if this purchase, which so affected our family's destiny, might have been influenced by my grandfather's pleasant memories of vacations spent in this area.

When he became a prosperous family man, Henry shifted his vacationing from the boardinghouses north of the city to the Jersey Shore. During the week, while he stayed in town, he and Josie usually exchanged a letter a day, sometimes more. Henry was a prodigious correspondent. He also meticulously preserved his letters, frequently requesting their return, and he continued to make preliminary drafts. Always attentive to handwriting, style, and moral tone, he was concerned that he present himself favorably, as though posing for a photograph. Nevertheless, during the early years of their marriage his letters to Josie were candid expressions of his ambitions and self-doubts, supportive in response to her complaints and negative moods, and full of love for his children. Letters that were meant to ease the tension of their separation revealed — within the proprieties of Victorian expression — a healthy sensuality.

"My dear little fatty!" Henry wrote from the Sykes townhouse, where he and his brother-in-law Charles were keeping bachelor quarters.

> Last evening I slept in your virtuous couch, and I thought how little did you think two years ago when we got acquainted that I would once sleep there. I don't want to say anything against it, but it is just a little too hilly to be comfortable. Charley was my bed fellow and it was

amusing to hear him snore — so between the hilliness and the snores, I confess I slept not too well — although I would not tell Charley so — I got up very early and was in the Register's office about 7:40 A.M. and have been working steadily ever since.

Henry's energy penetrated every aspect of family life, while Josie sometimes retreated into childlike dependence. "With much love and kisses," she signed off, "and please bring me some molasses candy." On another occasion when his absence made her depressed and restless he responded with manly assurance: "I'll calm your stormy spirits when I come up on Friday and hereafter we shall not spend another such summer [apart]," a promise Henry was unable to keep. Josie accordingly began to express feelings of boredom and uselessness, with a touch of sarcasm. From Essex & Sussex on the Beach at Spring Lake, New Jersey, she wrote, "Yesterday was a big day, we were awfully busy. In the morning we had a bath, [sisters] Emma, Sophie and I, and in the afternoon we took a long drive to Asbury Park."

Though she was her husband's sharpest critic and was sometimes apprehensive about his business ventures, Josie also considered herself a full partner in his ambitions. Both of them believed that Henry's success would redound to the family's credit.

The Law, Real Estate, and Politics: Comfortable Bedfellows

A FTER HIS MARRIAGE, Henry saw the real estate business that he shared with William Ehrich continue to prosper. In the summer of 1889, however, Ehrich died at Saranac Lake, the Adirondack Mountain tuberculosis retreat, at the age of forty-five. From then on Henry had to build his own financial base. There was no more family support system than there ever had been. Quite the contrary, his own parents and siblings had become increasingly dependent on him. So too had some of Josie's family, a rude reversal of his expectations.

On May 26, 1891, two weeks after his son was born, Henry consummated his first big real estate deal. He had organized a syndicate to purchase a tract of sixteen city blocks in the neighborhood of 181st Street in Manhattan's Washington Heights. With $50,000 down, he secured an option to purchase the property for $1 million. The co-owner was Levi P. Morton, at that time vice president of the United States under President Benjamin Harrison.

There were "a number of fortuitous circumstances," Morgenthau recalled, "which helped make for success." On the day he arranged to auction off all the lots, "James Gordon Bennett, owner of the *New York Herald,* having large possessions in the neighborhood, directed that our sale receive generous attention in the *Herald.*" To help matters further, "the genial Vice President of the United States added: 'If there is anything I can do please call upon me.'" As things turned out, all the lots were sold at a profit without vice presidential assistance. The highest prices were paid by the ex-registrar of deeds, John Reilly. "He afterwards confided to me," Morgenthau recalled, "that he had succeeded where we failed in finding out that the subway was to go through St. Nicholas Avenue and there was to be a station at One Hundred and Eighty-first Street." Morgenthau was beginning to notice that business and politics need not make strange bedfellows. Although many successful businessmen held politicians in contempt, it was clear that friendly relations could be advantageous for both.

Soon after their victory in Washington Heights Morgenthau and some of his partners sank their profit of a half-million dollars into the apparently promising coal-mining town of Bridgeport, Alabama. While Henry was as ever optimistic, Josie wrote that she was "very, very anxious . . . please do not under any circumstances go in heavier than you already have." She enclosed an article from the *New York Times* about a friend's business failure, which "shows you that you ought to keep your money invested in *Real* [triple underline] Estate and not in mythical, bombastical schemes."

Henry appeared to take heed: "I have firmly adhered to my resolution not to increase my holding, and shall not do so under any circumstances." By August he was forced to concede that he had "made quite a blunder ever to take hold of Bridgeport, which is so very far from New York. But there is no use crying over spilled milk. All is not lost. I am young yet and shall make the future pay me for the expenses I obtained at Bridgeport."

On the whole, Henry's real estate activities and law practice seemed to be mutually supportive, as indicated in a letter of recommendation from an endorser (with an illegible signature) to the president of the New York Life Insurance Company, C. A. McCall, who was looking for "the infusion of new and younger blood in the Board" of trustees. This sponsor wrote McCall that he didn't "know any one among his people who would invite . . . confidence to any enterprise . . . more than [Morgenthau]; [he] has been fortunate in all his real estate enterprises while continuing a popular law practice, and he is probably one among the best judges of Real Estate in the City. He . . . has a large clientage among the best Hebrew firms . . . and I have learned to esteem him very much as a very broad gauge and upright man."

Much of Morgenthau's law practice involved untangling the

business and real estate deals of prosperous Jewish clients. In the dissolution of the Brooklyn dry goods business of Wechsler and Abraham, which later became Abraham & Straus, "we represented Wechsler, and William J. Gaynor, afterward Mayor of the City of New York, represented Abraham." Some years later "one of the greatest surprises in our practice was when Judge Horace Russell retained me as a business lawyer" to advise him on the near-bankrupt affairs of his brother-in-law, Judge Henry Hilton, who had gained control of Hilton Hughes & Company. This retail enterprise had succeeded to the business of A. T. Stewart & Company, the largest store in New York. Judge Hilton, who also operated the Grand Union resort hotel in Saratoga Springs, New York, had offended American Jews by refusing to accommodate Joseph Seligman at his inn. This episode became a cause célèbre. As a result, "most of the [Jewish] trade" went "to the rising firms of B. Altman & Co. and Stern Bros. and so strengthened them that they became great competitors of Hilton Hughes & Co. and precipitated its downfall." John Wanamaker bought Hilton Hughes & Company, but shrewdly advertised the Wanamaker store as the successor to A. T. Stewart & Company.

While Russell had availed himself of Jewish counsel, Hilton had retained Elihu Root as his personal attorney. During the final negotiations, Root and Russell sat up all night with Morgenthau to complete Hilton's terms of surrender. Morgenthau "felt a strange sensation to be present at the midnight demise of the great business of A. T. Stewart & Co. I could not help but think of the causes." He remembered Root's telling him "that night that it was unwise for any lawyer to devote himself entirely to politics, that he should, when called upon, render a public service, complete it, and then return to his profession, but then be ready for any further calls that might be made upon him." Morgenthau concluded that Root had "pursued that course most successfully."*

Morgenthau began to think of using his success in real estate as leverage on a grand scale. "Why not induce some leading financiers to join me," he asked himself, "in the formation of a real estate trust company which would do for real estate what banking institutions

---

*At that time Root had served as U.S. attorney, New York Southern District. Later he became, successively, secretary of war, secretary of state, a founder of the World Court at The Hague, and Nobel Peace Prize laureate.

have done for the railroads and industries?" It was the right move at the right time — in the middle of the decade 1896–1906 that would see the greatest expansion of the U.S. economy to date.

Morgenthau soon discovered that others were thinking along the same lines. Nevertheless his reputation made him attractive to some of the city's leading financiers who were ready to invest their money and their names in an enterprise with Morgenthau at the helm. As president of the Central Realty Bond & Trust Company, he was euphoric at finding himself "suddenly catapulted from my comparatively unknown law office," from which he had resigned, "into the very midst of high finance. . . . My associates were all leaders in their various pursuits, and gloried in the power and wealth that they had accumulated while struggling to reach these eminent positions. . . . They bought me on my past performances . . . I simply had to make good or be displaced."

Perhaps his biggest coup was in persuading James Stillman, president of the National City Bank, to become a director and member of Central Realty's executive committee. In addition to Stillman's personal accomplishments, his two daughters were married to two sons of William Rockefeller (John D. Rockefeller's brother), "and through this alliance [Stillman] gained all direct and indirect advantages of a favored position with the Standard Oil Company." Morgenthau also persuaded Hugh J. Grant, former mayor of New York, "to become Vice President of the Company . . . Grant's greatest faculty was in being able to 'sniff' success."

All of these big men who invested in the company prided themselves that in "joining the other eminent leaders in this enterprise [they] increased its chances of success." Three months after stock was issued to the public, the price had doubled. The secret lay in using real estate to lure diverse interests usually at one another's throats. At a time when the financial supremacy of the banks was being challenged by both the more recently arrived trust companies and the ever-expanding insurance giants, all three were eager to get their share of real estate profits.

By 1905, six years after his company had been launched, Morgenthau began to be apprehensive that the boom would end as it ran out of money for expansion. He had represented the East Coast extension of the Fuller Construction Company in the subway boom, which involved developing Bronx lots adjacent to the transit lines, and in the purchase of the Plaza Hotel. Nevertheless Morgenthau decided it was time to realize his gains: "We merged [Central Realty Bond & Trust Company] into the Lawyers' Title Insurance Company." He then personally purchased all the real estate holdings from his old company and formed the Henry Morgenthau Company with his twenty-eight-year-old nephew Robert E. Simon as partner, and "thus returned to the real estate business only on a much larger scale than I have ever operated before."

Henry had always proclaimed his intention of using his wealth toward altruistic ends. This was no idle boast. At a time when the ability to make money was admired by those who could and those who would, it was not easy to stop when one was succeeding. In Henry's case there is evidence that he prepared to disengage himself from business at the very moment his prospects were the rosiest. Anticipating the financial panic of 1907, he began to sever business ties and resolved to "devote the rest of my life to making good on the better resolutions of my boyhood." He was fifty at the time. Accordingly, he put half of his fortune in trust for his wife, and for protection of his children, who would receive the income after her death. The principal was then to be distributed to his grandchildren.

From the beginning of Morgenthau's rapid advance in the private sector, his strategies had involved making useful connections with public officials. Smelling the rank air of political corruption, he began to dream of becoming a crusading reformer. At the same time he was aware of the commercial advantages of political connections.

His first opportunity appeared in 1906, when Rabbi Stephen Wise returned to New York from the West Coast and founded the Free Synagogue. Henry Morgenthau became its president and principal fund raiser. Together they shared an enthusiasm for political reform and social action, especially that designed for relief of impoverished Eastern European Jews. The Free Synagogue, "pewless and dueless," with services held in Carnegie Hall, was a highly visible alternative to Temple Emanu-El, the cathedral synagogue of the German Jewish establishment. In a storm of noisy melodrama, Wise had rejected an invitation to become Emanu-El's preacher.

Stephen Wise was a lion of a man. His black mane, with the suggestion of a part in the middle flowing back from his high forehead, remained full and dark beyond its season. Arrogant, vain, manipulative, magnificently articulate, Wise over the years proved himself the most ardent, uncompromising, and effective American spokesman for Zionism.

In his mid-twenties Wise had been the rabbi of Temple Beth Israel in Portland, Oregon. Solomon Hirsch, a Republican business-man and politician, was president of the congregation. During the Harrison administration, Hirsch had served as minister to Turkey, the first American Jew to hold ministerial rank. It was from Hirsch that Wise, already a committed Zionist, began to understand the importance of having a Jew head the Turkish mission (the Ottoman Empire included a large Jewish population, as well as Palestine). By coincidence Hirsch had been well known to Morgenthau as the uncle of his law partner, Samson Lachman.

In 1911 Rabbi Wise and Henry Morgenthau invited the elo-quent, reform-minded governor of New Jersey, Woodrow Wilson, to a dinner in celebration of the synagogue's fourth anniversary. Henry seated himself between the two guests of honor, Governor Wilson and William Borah, the populist senator from Idaho. Then and there he decided to hitch his chariot to Wilson's rising star, offering Wilson his "unreserved moral and financial support."

Morgenthau's decision to leave the fast-flowing business main-stream and dive into the political whirlpool was a dramatic turning point in his career. But like everything else he did he had prepared for it with thorough calculations. As early as 1872, when he was sixteen, he wrote of visiting New York's City Hall and being im-pressed by the somber portraits in the Governors' Room. These men, he mused, had not only received "great honor and influence and self-satisfaction while alive, but . . . even after death they [were] honored, respected and revered by the Republic which they pro-duced."

By 1911 the time was right for a Jew to seek office. The ruling Protestant elite, while continuing to sound the high moral tone of its Puritan ancestors, had in fact become an aristocracy of wealth. The opportunities for amassing fortunes in banking, railroads, and mining were far more tempting than political plums. The lavishness of Fifth Avenue mansions and Newport "cottages" vastly outshone the lure of the White House in Washington, then a very provincial town. Moneyed barons were aware of the importance of maintain-ing control over the electoral process, but they chose to do so through a well-financed system of indirect rule.

Theodore Roosevelt's political ambition had distressed his patrician family. A generation later Sara Delano Roosevelt took a similar view of her son Franklin's aspirations. Both Roosevelt presidents were considered "traitors to their class" by their peers. There were other rare exceptions, but those families that had risen to the top of the financial heap — Morgans, Vanderbilts, Astors, Rockefellers, and the like — would not even in their nightmares have dreamed of a politician in the family.

The German Jewish elite, which in most respects tried to mirror their WASP peers, likewise avoided direct participation in public life.★ But there were important differences. The tenets of the reform movement, subscribed to by the vast majority of German Jews, dictated an activist idealism. Moreover, among those who had emigrated in the middle of the nineteenth century, some had been involved in the 1848 uprisings in Europe. Those who came a little later, including the Morgenthaus, had witnessed the liberalization of politics, as in the grand duchy of Baden, where Jews were permitted to hold elective office.

In the United States sporadic outrage against corruption had inspired waves of reform, during which professional politicians temporarily laid low and outsiders, including Jews, found an opportunity to gain political access. But while a few German Jews were beginning to get their feet wet in politics, the richest and most powerful families, like their Protestant counterparts, usually chose to remain on the sidelines. The exception that proved the rule was Henry's coeval Oscar Straus.

The Straus brothers, Isidor, Nathan, and Oscar, had advanced the family fortune. The two older brothers progressed from dry goods and crockery to ownership of the great Macy's department store in Manhattan and Abraham & Straus in Brooklyn. It was the youngest brother, Oscar, however, who was encouraged to devote almost undivided attention to pursuing a career in public life. There was a striking parallel in the careers of Henry Morgenthau and Oscar Straus, but after graduating from Columbia and becoming lawyers Morgenthau was diverted into real estate, while Straus moved directly into politics. He started as a reform Democrat, and having supported Grover Cleveland for president, he was awarded the post of minister to Turkey, the second in a long series of Jewish

---

★Joseph Seligman turned down an offer from President Ulysses S. Grant to be secretary of the treasury, which would have made him the first Jew to serve in the cabinet.

envoys to Constantinople. Greatly concerned about sound money, he opposed the Democrats' free silver policy and switched his allegiance to the Republicans. He became Theodore Roosevelt's secretary of commerce and labor, the first Jew to serve in a presidential cabinet. It was a dramatic gesture by Roosevelt in reaction to the Eastern European pogroms. In appointing Straus, he wrote: "I have a very high estimate of your judgment, and your ability, and I want you for personal reasons. There is still a further reason: I want to show Russia and some other countries what we think of the Jews in this country."

Morgenthau's involvement in public service began in 1911, when he became a member of the Committee of Safety; this citizens' group was formed in a moment of citywide trauma following the Triangle Shirtwaist fire. Flames had broken out on the eighth floor of the Asch Building, a modern, fireproof loft, not a notorious sweatshop. Five minutes before closing time, Saturday afternoon, March 25, the workers on the ninth floor were trapped between the fire on the floor below and the locked exit to the roof. The factory owners had secured the exits as a means of controlling their workers and barring entry to union organizers, after an unsuccessful strike by shirtwaist workers the preceding year. Most of the employees had been laid off and replaced with young Jewish and Italian women right off the boat. On that afternoon some 146 of them (the accounts vary) met a grisly death: they were burned, suffocated, or dashed to the street 110 feet below, attempting a leap to safety. Lurid photographs of the mangled remains laid out on the sidewalk covered the front pages of the newspapers. The next day more than 100,000 people passed through the morgue. A packed rally in the Metropolitan Opera House was addressed by financier Jacob Schiff, the Episcopal bishop, the Right Reverend David H. Greer, and Rabbi Stephen S. Wise. But it was a diminutive redhead, speaking in a heavily accented hoarse whisper, whose words have been remembered: "The life of men and women is so cheap and property is so sacred and there are so many of us for one job, it matters little if one hundred and forty of us are burned to death." Rose Schneiderman, born in a Polish ghetto, was a rising star in the Women's Trade Union League and would become a mentor and lifelong friend of a young volunteer social worker, Eleanor Roosevelt.

The Committee of Safety was given the mission of seeing that such tragedies would never happen again. Its members were powerful men and — most unusual in those days — a significant number of women. At the outset, sitting in the front row, so to speak, were high-minded members of the Protestant establishment, like George W. Perkins and John A. Kingsbury. Henry Stimson, who had served as U.S. attorney for the Southern District of New York and had been the unsuccessful Republican candidate for governor in 1910, was the committee president. Also included were J. P. Morgan's maverick sister, Anne, who had provided bail for the striking shirtwaist workers, the ubiquitous Lillian Wald, and a no-nonsense young woman from the Consumers League, Frances Perkins.

A couple of months after the committee got itself organized, on June 15, 1911, a front-page headline in the *New York Tribune* announced: NEW HEAD FOR SAFETY. HENRY MORGENTHAU SUCCEEDS HENRY L. STIMSON. The latter had resigned to take up duties as President Taft's secretary of war. Morgenthau, a member of the committee from its inception, was listed as "President of the Henry Morgenthau Realty Company, President of the Free Synagogue, Director of the Mt. Sinai Hospital . . . and director of many companies."

No one wanted to mention that almost all of the principals in the Triangle tragedy were Jews. Many of the workers and their union leaders were "Lower East Side" Jews, while "uptown" Jews owned the building and the shirtwaist company. When charges were brought against company officials, their attorney, Max Steuer, won acquittals for all of them. Becoming notorious for a long string of well-heeled clients, including the gangster Arnold Rothstein (later murdered) and the officers of the failed "pants pressers" Bank of the United States, Steuer was nicknamed *Geltschwessel* (money sweater).

At the same time, a movement was stirring within the Jewish community to right the injustices for which it felt partly responsible, with men like Morgenthau stepping to the fore. A month after taking over the reins of the committee, Morgenthau succeeded in having the state legislature appoint an official commission under the leadership of two of its most promising young lions, Robert Wagner, as chairman, and Alfred E. Smith, as vice chairman. Frances Perkins became their executive secretary.

Service on the Committee of Safety was a bonding experience for people like Morgenthau, who later became prominent in a generation of liberal Democrats whose ideals culminated in the New

Deal. By the time he arrived on the national political scene, Morgenthau could boast experience on two major investigatory bodies and proof of both his desire and ability to combat social injustice. For in addition to serving on the Committee of Safety, he became a member of the Committee on Congestion of Population in New York City, which was instrumental in bringing about legislation designed to correct some of the evils of the barbarous "old law" tenements. Clearly, Henry Morgenthau was well prepared for the future.

· 10 ·

*The Discomforting
Jewish Slot*

ORGENTHAU'S DECISION to cast his lot with Woodrow
Wilson was both a courageous gamble and a credit to his
ability to size up the talents of a dark-horse candidate. Yet
behind his public posture he was deeply ambivalent. On the one
hand, he held that he had earned recognition as a full-fledged American. On the other, he believed that he represented a rightful Jewish
communal demand for recognition in a pluralistic, democratic society. Furthermore, he expected the Jews to support him as their
candidate for honors. Like other German Jews who had succeeded
in the United States, he relied on the support of his Jewish peers.
There was indeed an active underground network crisscrossing political and regional lines which made concerted demands in behalf of
Jewish special interests.

The concept of a Jewish post, or representation as a "Jewish
slot," which Jews so abhorred, in fact resulted from Jewish demands. Oscar Straus was succeeded as secretary of commerce and
labor by Charles Nagel, appointed by President Taft. Nagel, a
prominent Republican lawyer who had been acting mayor of St.
Louis, was subsequently under consideration for appointment to
the U.S. Supreme Court. This news prompted one of his friends,
Ben Hillman, to write to Morgenthau that "the Secretary of Commerce and Labor is about to be appointed, according to the newspapers, to the Supreme Court bench and President Taft wants to
appoint one of our people as his successor." Hillman asked Morgenthau to assist him in promoting "my friend, the Honorable Nathan
Frank" as Nagel's successor. "I know that Mr. Frank is a very strong

personal friend of President Taft," Hillman wrote. "And from what I have been told if a few prominent people, like yourself, Mr. Schiff, Mr. Oscar Straus, and Capt. Greenhut, would advocate our friend Frank's appointment, it would be made." As things turned out, Nagel stayed in his cabinet job until the end of the Taft administration.

Morgenthau, at fifty-five, was, by his own account, "financially independent, and rich in experience, and recently released from the toils of materialism." With self-righteous enthusiasm, he held it to be his "duty to pay back in the form of public service, the overdraft which I had been permitted to make upon the opportunities of this country. Repayment in money alone would not suffice: I must pay in the form of personal service." But in doing so he would be forced to stomach the bitter irony that a wealthy man's offer to serve the public would be accepted as a privilege for which he was expected to pay according to his means.

Early in 1912, before the Democratic Convention, with the odds heavily stacked against Wilson, Morgenthau made good on his pledge to contribute five thousand dollars a month for four months. That support placed him securely in the ranks of major contributors. It was the kind of grand gesture that attracted attention. But Morgenthau was not only self-interested. He was a truly generous man. As early as 1903, Felix Adler, founder of the Society for Ethical Culture, acknowledged his gift of five thousand dollars to the building fund, expressing the hope that the cause of the society, "which appealed to you so strongly in the idealistic period of youth, may never entirely lose your sympathy and your support." A year later Morgenthau had contributed five thousand dollars to Rabbi Stephen S. Wise's Free Synagogue. He then made this sum an annual subvention. Indeed he appears to have contributed five thousand dollars to all those causes that were important to him.

At this time Morgenthau was very much influenced by his good friend Wise, a man of noble and determined convictions. Justine Wise Polier, the rabbi's late daughter, once recalled a moment when "Mrs. Morgenthau was very cross complaining that Wise had 'gotten Henry to waste five thousand dollars on Woodrow Wilson.'"

In the late spring of 1912, before the Baltimore Democratic Convention, Henry Morgenthau and his friend Abram I. Elkus, along with William Gibbs McAdoo and a tiny band of stalwarts, were among the few who continued to show up at the New York headquarters and shell out from their own pockets. Morgenthau, Elkus, and Samuel Untermyer were outbid only by a few of Wilson's wealthy Princeton cronies. His classmate Cleveland H. Dodge topped them all with donations totaling more than $50,000. But, all told, these men scraped together almost half of the $200,000 the spendthrift chairman, William F. McCombs, had disbursed before Baltimore.

After Wilson was nominated on the twenty-sixth ballot, everything changed. The lonely few who had stood by him found themselves jostled and crowded out by the "pros," who came swarming in. Morgenthau, battle weary and sensitive, felt let down when he was asked to be chairman of the Campaign Finance Committee. He told "the Governor" that he "was disinclined to be merely a money collector." He wanted to be treasurer or at least a member of the Campaign Committee itself. Wilson was able to woo him back by putting him on the committee and persuading him that his assignment was far more important than that of treasurer.

Headquarters was fraught with turmoil and internecine struggles. In the course of "the ill-humored rivalries of McCombs and McAdoo and their adherents," Morgenthau's loyalties placed him in the McCombs camp, where he enjoyed a warm working relationship with a boss somewhat his junior. (McCombs was at this time chairman of both the Democratic National Committee and the Campaign Committee.) McCombs began calling him "Uncle Henry," and for the rest of his life Morgenthau derived the greatest sense of camaraderie with political peers from this informal title. But when in midcampaign McCombs collapsed and McAdoo took over, Morgenthau began to feel pushed aside.

"Mr. Wells [treasurer of the Democratic National Committee] and I do not like the way we were asked to withdraw from the meeting at noon," he wrote McAdoo on August 15, 1912. "I understood distinctly from Governor Wilson that I was, ex-officio, a member of the Committee." He insisted that, having undertaken the task of financing the campaign, they were "entitled to be present at all consultations." In what might well have seemed rather threatening language to McAdoo, he demanded "an immediate conference between Mr. Wells, you and I to see if the matter can be adjusted without referring it to the Governor."

Because of this and other similar incidents and whatever else may have transpired, Morgenthau would later come to believe that he had made his most important political enemy. In fact, he was prob-

ably overreacting. McAdoo habitually tried to control his hench-
man with a tight rein, but he was not vindictive. Indeed, there is
every reason to believe that he appreciated Morgenthau's unswerving loyalty to Wilson and his unique contribution in organizing
campaign finances. In the end Morgenthau had personally donated
over $30,000 and along with McAdoo had solicited the financial
community when hopes for broad-based popular support foun-
dered. However, his signal contribution to the annals of politics was
that for the first time the campaign was put on an accountable,
businesslike footing. When it was all over and more than $1 million
had been spent, there was $25,000 left in the kitty.

The day after Wilson was elected president, Morgenthau was
among a select group of his supporters who sat down for an early
lunch in Princeton, at the Wilson home on Cleveland Lane. Morgenthau expected to be rewarded along with other veterans of the
campaign, like McAdoo, who became secretary of the treasury, and
Josephus Daniels, the North Carolina journalist, who became secretary of the navy. He wanted a policymaking job concerned with
finance or commerce, preferably a cabinet rank. Not only had he
paid his dues, as he saw it, but he had the personal qualifications.
He had completed his basic training in the law, succeeded in business, and served the public interest in New York. There was also
that matter of Jewish representation. While he resented being cate-
gorized as a Jew, he also demanded what he considered appropriate
recognition of "our People." In this respect, he saw himself as the
Democratic equivalent of Oscar Straus. On that premise he believed
he should be made secretary of commerce or perhaps the Treasury.

After the election he listened anxiously to the gossip being
bruited about among his peers and in the press about impending
presidential appointments. It was well known that Louis D. Brandeis was favored for *the* Jewish cabinet post: attorney general or
secretary of commerce. But when Wilson learned that there was
bitter opposition to Brandeis from business interests, who had gotten through to the Massachusetts congressional delegation (Brandeis's home state), he decided not to risk Senate confirmation.

The discomfort Morgenthau was feeling spread among his friends.
"Have you heard anything?" Stephen Wise, on vacation in Munich,
inquired. "One appointment after another and nothing for us. As
far as I have seen, no Jew has been appointed to a single place of
importance. It seems an almost deliberate slight. Have you led him
to feel that you would accept nothing?"

During the winter of 1913, before the March 4 inauguration, Morgenthau allowed the pressure among his supporters to mount. Judge Ben B. Lindsey, a Denver "Bull Mooser," wrote Wilson, "Since you are the second choice of so many of us, may I presume one step further and tell you how delighted I am to see in the newspapers that Henry Morgenthau's name is being considered for secretary of the treasury."

Right after the inauguration, when the juiciest plums had been handed out, Charles Strauss (a Christian) wrote "a personal line in re Henry Morgenthau" to Senator James A. O'Gorman of New York, who had been a key supporter of Wilson at the Baltimore convention. Strauss held that "Morgenthau's attitude has been manly and commendable throughout, and he deprecates any such sentiment, but he cannot control the newspapers, who advertise him as being full of pique and resentment, criticize the President for his ingratitude to a man who has rendered him such great personal service, and even introduce the suggestion of race prejudice, to which every well wisher of the Administration knows it is foreign."

A month later Senator O'Gorman telephoned Morgenthau, who recorded that "he had been requested by the President to offer me the ambassadorship to Turkey. I apparently astonished him when I told him . . . that I would not accept."

Morgenthau's aspirations, though supported by his friends, were in fact quite out of line with Wilson's firm intentions. An entry in the diary of Colonel Edward M. House, Wilson's éminence grise, makes note of the evening of May 2, spent with the president: "We talked of a multitude of matters at dinner . . . I told him that something should be done for Morgenthau or Elkus or perhaps both. He said he would offer Morgenthau the Turkish mission. I had heard that Morgenthau did not want it and would not be complimented by the offer. He replied that nevertheless he would offer it."

Having decided to turn down the president's offer, Morgenthau called on Wilson to discuss it. "The two posts that demand the greatest intellectual equipment in our representatives are Turkey and China," the president told him. "If that is the situation I should much prefer China, although it is only a ministership," Morgenthau replied. He argued that

the Jews of this country have become very sensitive (and I think properly so) over the impression which has been created by successive

Jewish appointments to Turkey, that that is the only diplomatic post to which a Jew can aspire. All the Jews that I have consulted about your offer have advised and urged me to decline it. Oscar Straus has been criticized by some of his co-religionists for accepting a second and even a third appointment to Constantinople. I don't mind criticism, but I share the feeling of other Jews that it is unwise to confirm that this is the only field for them in diplomatic service.

The president's reply "was aggressive in manner and almost angry in tone" and quite insensitive to Morgenthau's position. He stated that

in the first place, Constantinople is the point at which the interest of American Jews in the welfare of the Jews of Palestine is focused, and it is almost indispensable that I have a Jew at that post. On the other hand, our interests in China are expressed largely in the form of missionary activities, and it seems quite necessary that our minister there should be a Christian, and preferably a man of the evangelical type.

At the conclusion of the meeting, Morgenthau recalled that as he left, the president seemed "sadly disappointed that he had not been able to dominate my decision." Thus on June 12, 1913, a few days after they had confronted each other, Morgenthau wrote Wilson:

In compliance with your request, I saw Mr. Schiff and explained to him what induced you to offer me the Turkish mission and that you were not aware that our People were so strongly opposed to having any position made a distinctly Jewish one or having the impression continued that Turkey was the only country where Jews would be received as our country's representative.

Mr. Schiff was pleased to hear your views and I found that he shared my desire that no Jew be appointed as Turkish Ambassador.

He informed me that Secretary McAdoo had asked him over the telephone last Sunday to suggest a Jew for New York sub-treasuryship and that he had written McAdoo that he knew of none.

Senator O'Gorman asked me the same question last Friday and I declined to suggest anyone.

I wonder if they understand that this is diametrically opposed to your expressed policy of selecting men solely on their merits and not on account of their religion. Why should the Jews be treated differently than anyone else?

Would prominent Methodists or Baptists be told here is a position, find one of your faith to fill it?

I write you frankly because I know you regret mistakes of this kind as much as any of us.

This letter is included in Wilson's presidential papers. There is no indication that it was ever answered. The same day that Morgenthau wrote to the president, Josephus Daniels sent Morgenthau a warm note marked "personal" on his official stationery, urging him to accept "the post tendered" and suggesting that it "would offer you [a] rare opportunity for the exercise of your great talents and to perform a very great service to your country."

"Your letter . . . has come too late," Morgenthau replied two days afterward. "I have already definitely and irrevocably declined . . . and given the President my reasons for so doing." Typed on the back of the draft, perhaps to be incorporated into the letter, was this statement: "I consulted with fifteen of the most prominent Jews in the City and only one thought that I should accept." And there the matter rested, for the time being.

Meanwhile, in May 1913, having made his decision to refuse the president's offer, Morgenthau, accompanied by Josie and their youngest daughter, Ruth, headed for the French spa of Aix-les-Bains. After the excitement of the campaign, the election victory, and the heady expectation of sharing the spoils, Morgenthau felt tremendously let down. In midlife he had refocused his vision for the future on a new public career only to be faced with unwanted leisure. He soon realized that this was more of a readjustment than he was willing to make. Accordingly, he decided to reset his course and aim anew for a high-level policymaking position in Washington.

Having filled the cabinet seats, the president had turned his attention to drastic banking and currency reforms, proposing a plan for reorganization under a powerful new agency. But what would eventuate as the Federal Reserve system was then only an embryonic scheme that seemed likely to end up stillborn. Nevertheless, Morgenthau's uncanny nose for the big opportunity led him to seek out a position in the agency well before it had in fact been defined. He sent a telegraph to his friend Samuel Untermyer.

An attorney with a keen and flexible intellect, Untermyer had become spectacularly wealthy while fighting for liberal causes. Aside from his penchant for luxuries, he resembled a more famous counterpart, Louis Brandeis. Both men were frequently sought out by reform-minded politicians. At a later date they would be linked together as ardent Zionists.

During the long, hot summer of 1913, in pre-air-conditioned Washington, Wilson kept a reluctant Congress in session, demanding enactment of his bills. Untermyer, wearied with the thankless role of intermediary, had left for his customary European vacation. So it was that Morgenthau's telegraphed plea for help reached him as he was settling into his suite at Claridge's Hotel in London. Untermyer immediately responded to his friend in a letter assuring him, "You may rely on me to do everything possible to help. . . . I know of no post in our country that will be of greater importance and dignity unless it be that of the President himself. I want to see you exhaust every energy to secure it for I consider you peculiarly adapted for the satisfactory discharge of its vast responsibilities and that you would reflect credit on our race in that position."

Untermyer went on to offer some sound tactical advice. First and foremost, Morgenthau must re-establish rapport with McAdoo. Following the incident at campaign headquarters Morgenthau had not hesitated to express his bitterness. Acceding to Untermyer's counsel, he wrote McAdoo that "there has been some ill feeling between us," but asserted that he was "not looking for a vendetta." He plainly stated that he was "a candidate for the position of Governor of the Federal Reserve Board of Control" but that he would "abandon all further efforts if it is not entirely agreeable to you." Morgenthau concluded, "I am through with any rancor — I have pulled it out by the roots and I feel better for having done so."

On July 10, the same day he wrote to McAdoo, Morgenthau got off a long, thoughtful letter to Colonel House. He cautioned that the National Democratic Committee was not gearing up for the 1914 congressional election. He suggested that taking action on this front would reassure members of the present Congress and motivate them to support the president's programs.

Morgenthau's anxiety proved well founded. The Democrats, while maintaining their majority in the Congress, slipped precariously in the election that fall. Morgenthau believed that the Wilson-sponsored legislation to lower tariffs was "temporarily going to upset business." The confidence of the "well-to-do" would have to be restored. "The laborers, farmers and railroad and mine employees always have confidence as long as they have work."

Morgenthau's letter was calculated to appeal to Colonel House's affection for the rich and powerful, in contrast with McAdoo's doctrinaire liberalism. "It is all important that the head of the Board of Federal Control [sic; the governor of the Federal Reserve Board] must be the one who can secure the confidence and respect of the businessmen and bank presidents of the country. One who can talk their language. You can't expect me to elaborate much on this — as you know that I am a possible candidate for the position." Having revealed his hand, the suppliant signed off with a particularly high-minded flourish: "I am finished with moneymaking, and deeply feel the responsibility of the *debt* I owe to my country for the success, happiness and comforts it has showered on me. I am as determined and anxious to liquidate that debt as I ever was in accepting the gifts received. I believe in the Law of Compensation."

Colonel House's reply was polite but noncommittal. "Your sentiments of patriotism do you much credit," he wrote from Beverly, Massachusetts. "I expect McAdoo here in about two weeks and when he comes I will discuss with him the matter about which you write."

At Aix-les-Bains, Morgenthau, unaccustomed to the leisure and isolation of the luxurious spa life, had been beset with uneasiness. His gloomy, pessimistic wife and truculent youngest daughter, Ruth, were little comfort. When the American ambassador to France arrived at Aix on holiday, Morgenthau was bursting to talk politics with him. Myron T. Herrick, a wealthy industrialist and former Republican governor of Ohio, was a holdover from the Taft administration. Herrick told Morgenthau that he had found the diplomatic service highly congenial at his time of life (he was two years Morgenthau's senior) and that he believed Morgenthau had made "a grievous mistake" in turning down Wilson's ambassadorial offer. He insisted, as Morgenthau recorded, "that not only I, but my children and my children's children would benefit by my having held such a position."

This was all the urging Morgenthau needed. Suddenly everything was back in focus. For counsel he turned once again to his friend Stephen Wise, who at that moment was in Paris. Wise had just returned from his first visit to the Holy Land, an intensely moving experience for him. When Morgenthau informed him that he wanted to reconsider his rejection of the Wilson offer, if it was not too late, Wise was overjoyed. He suggested an immediate rendezvous at Lyons. During his sojourn in the Near East, Wise had been sorely disturbed by the misery of Palestinian Jews: "I knew, of course, that Palestine was a Turkish dependency not an Arab kingdom or province. But I had not understood how completely Palestine was under the suzerainty of the Turkish Empire." Wise had experienced personal indignities at the hands of the authorities, though armed with a letter of introduction "of warm friendliness from President Wilson" which "did not help me much."

Wise harbored no doubts that the U.S. diplomatic mission should be maintained as a Jewish outpost. Wilson thought of it as an opportunity — Wise as a necessity — for a Jewish ambassador to serve the interests of his people. The Wise persuasion took effect speedily. Following their rendezvous in Lyons, Morgenthau wrote to Wise, who was by then in England, that he would be willing to reconsider the president's original offer when he returned to the United States in September, if it was still open. That was not soon enough for Wise, who seized upon the letter as a signal to take matters into his own hands. On August 7 he wrote Morgenthau,

> I was tempted to telegraph to you that you might, if necessary, revise a cable message which I have already sent the President, but in view of your letter, I felt that I could exercise my discretion, such as it is, and so I cabled to the President as follows:
> "Have earnestly urged Morgenthau to accept your offer of the Turkish Embassy in view of importance of post for many reasons at this time. I would suggest immediate renewal of invitation to serve which I believe he would now accept. Could forward message to him."

At this point Morgenthau decided it was time for him to recapture the initiative himself, and he sent a cable to the "Honorable Woodrow Wilson." The penned draft in his papers reveals the process of firming his resolve. "Will accept," he wrote, followed by "if you still desire it" crossed out. The final version reads: "Have reconsidered. Will accept. Will be at the Reginapalast, Munich Monday, warm regards, Henry Morgenthau." When he arrived at the Reginapalast there was a cable waiting for him: SINCERELY GLAD YOU ARE WILLING TO ACCEPT. WILL BEGIN ARRANGEMENTS AT ONCE. WOODROW WILSON. Life was beginning anew for Henry Morgenthau.

Swept along by pressure from Wise, Henry had neglected communication with his most ardent supporter for a different post. When he belatedly informed Samuel Untermyer on August 12, his friend had already "seen the announcement." His response was critical but remarkably good-tempered in view of the way in which he had learned the news: "Now that you have taken the step it is hardly worthwhile to discuss it except to say that I am one of your few friends with the brutal frankness to say that I do not agree with its wisdom."

At about the same time, Morgenthau received a long-delayed answer to his letter to McAdoo. McAdoo claimed to have responded earlier with a wire that Morgenthau never received. Indeed there is doubt that it was ever sent. Nevertheless, McAdoo's letter, while cautious, seemed friendly: "I should be very glad to consider you in connection with the Federal Reserve Board . . . I am not able to commit myself now, because all the factors in the situation must be weighed carefully."

With Morgenthau committed to the Turkish post, McAdoo had gotten himself off the hook with good grace. Thus he could accept Morgenthau's apology and declare magnanimously "that it was most unfortunate that mischief makers had been able to gain any part of [your] confidence," adding, "I have never entertained anything but the kindest feelings for you, and was surprised when I learned that you had been expressing very different sentiments about me. However, I am very glad to receive your cordial expressions of friendship, and to assure you of the restoration of similar feelings on my part." He expressed his pleasure that Morgenthau was "going to accept the very great honor [the president] has tendered, namely, the Ambassadorship for Turkey. I congratulate you, and think you are very wise to take this great post."

Whether or not Morgenthau knew all the facts, future events would prove that he had indeed made a wise choice.

· 11 ·

The American Ambassador

A T THE END of the summer of 1913 Morgenthau returned
home to prepare himself for his diplomatic post with unreserved enthusiasm. His appointment was confirmed by the
Senate on September 4. Immediately thereafter he went to Washington for a month of concentrated instruction at the State Department, "crowned in October . . . by an official call on the Secretary
of State." This turned out to be a great anticlimax, as William
Jennings Bryan "knew no more about our relations with Turkey
than I did." The only thing Bryan had to say in a brief cheerful
meeting was that when he had made a pilgrimage to the Holy Land
he had "had great difficulty in finding Mount Beatitude. I wish you
would try to persuade the Turkish government to grant a concession to some Americans to build a macadam road up to it, so that
other pilgrims may not have the inconvenience which I did in
attempting to find it." As Rabbi Wise recalled the incident, Bryan
said, "Uncle Henry, you know a great deal about real estate. I wish
you would do this for me. Get an option on the purchase of the
mountain from which Jesus delivered the Sermon on the Mount."

When the ambassador called to say farewell to the president,
Wilson advised him to "remember that anything you can do to
improve the lot of your co-religionists is an act that will reflect
credit upon America, and you may count on the full power of this
Administration to back you up." Unlike Morgenthau's earlier visit,
when he had been deeply offended by a similar remark, this one
found him fully reconciled to being, among other things, the Jewish
ambassador to the Near East and, ironically, especially in the eyes
of his "co-religionists."

But Morgenthau was determined to make much more of his role. Just before he left he learned that several leaders of the Foreign Mission Boards — of the Presbyterian, Congregational, United Presbyterian, Methodist, and Episcopal churches — were sailing for Europe at the same time he was but on a different ship. He immediately rebooked his passage on the *George Washington*.

Morgenthau had learned something of the American missionary interests in the Ottoman Empire through a Princeton classmate of Wilson's, Cleveland Dodge, whose family were the principal supporters of Beirut's Syrian Protestant College (today the American University). The family deployed not only large portions of their copper fortune, but also the clan's most able members.*

Josephine Morgenthau, who remained unreconciled to diplomatic life, stayed behind ostensibly to launch her youngest daughter, Ruth, into society. In her stead the new ambassador invited his oldest daughter, Helen Fox, who worshipped him and was thrilled by the prospect of playing opposite him. Following in her wake were her husband, Mortie, and two young sons, Henry, age six, and Mortimer Jr. (Tim), age four. The November 1 entry in Morgenthau's diary reveals the full extent of his exhilaration: "10:30 A.M. Embarked on the George Washington. Mama and children saw us off. Mortie, Helen, Henry and Tim with me. Poor Henry Jr. and Mama and Alma felt very badly. I am delighted to go — feel greatly buoyed up by the love bestowed on me."

By the next day he had established contact with the clergy: Drs. Brown, Barton, and Watson, and Bishop Lloyd. James L. Barton had been a missionary in Turkey and president of the Protestant College in Harpoot. Charles Roger Watson "had been a missionary in the Turkish Protectorate of Egypt and his parents had been missionaries for half a century at Cairo." Together, for the benefit of their shipmates' souls, "they held splendid services. Helen played the piano for them." The shipboard conversations with these men were "a revelation." Morgenthau had "hitherto had a hazy notion

*Generations of Dodges have served as presidents and in other capacities at family-sponsored Middle East institutions, sometimes at considerable personal risk. In August 1916, Cleveland Dodge's daughter, Elizabeth, went to Robert College in Constantinople with her husband, George Huntington. They remained there until the end of the war. Cleveland Dodge's son, Bayard, became president of American University. His grandson, David S. Dodge, was kidnapped in Beirut, Lebanon, while he was serving as president of the university. He was subsequently released in Iran.

that missionaries were sort of overzealous advance agents of sectarian religion, and that their principal activity was the proselytizing of believers in other faiths."

This week of relaxed intimate association turned out to be a profitable investment in understanding and mutual trust which was destined to pay handsome dividends during Morgenthau's tenure in the Near East. Ambassador Morgenthau came to appreciate that, while these clerics were indeed "profoundly concerned in converting as many people as they could to what they sincerely believed to be the true faith," they also shared his commitment to education and social service. They were "advance agents of civilization," supporting hospitals, schools and colleges, and sanitation, and "bringing a higher conception of Christianity to the millions of submerged Christians in the Turkish Empire." This notion of religion as a social service obligation closely paralleled his own practice of Judaism. Suddenly many earlier experiences fell into place: boyhood conversations with the hunchbacked Quaker physician Dr. Samuel S. Whitall, the boarder in his home who gave half his time to caring for patients in "the colored hospital"; the tenets of the founder of the Ethical Culture Society, Felix Adler, who was bent on a universal application of Jewish values; and Lillian Wald's pioneering endeavors on New York's Lower East Side.

Disembarking in Plymouth on the morning of November 8, the ambassador and the Foxes took the boat train to London, arriving "about 4 P.M. Went to Claridge's. Evening supper at Ritz and saw Vaudeville."

The next day, he noted in his diary, he called at the American embassy and had a "nice talk" with his good friend the U.S. ambassador, Walter Hines Page. It was the first time he had set foot inside an embassy anywhere in the world. In the next couple of weeks he visited all the American and Turkish missions en route to Constantinople, making good use of the chance to observe diplomatic life.

During four heavily scheduled days, Morgenthau encountered a great variety of people. Accompanied by Ambassador Page, he called at the Turkish embassy and met Ibraham Hakki Pasha, previously grand vizier, who had been sent by his government to negotiate matters concerning the Persian Gulf and the scaling down of the former territorial rights of foreign governments known as the "Capitulations." He called at the Speyer Brothers banking house and talked with the Oppenheims, and a Mr. and Mrs. Moro, and a Mr. Cohen, who were concerned about the white slave trade.

From the moment he had nailed down the Morgenthau appointment, Stephen Wise had been scheming to mold the future ambassador as an instrument of Jewish interests in the Near East. On August 7 he had written Morgenthau that there were "certain persons" in London and Paris who were "particularly well-informed on Near Eastern questions." Ironically, not one of the men in Wise's European network, though sharing his tenets of liberal progressive Judaism, was a true Zionist. But in their opposition to political Zionism they were nonetheless sympathetic to the plight of oppressed and persecuted Jews and were no less active in seeking their liberation. Most of them supported the Jewish Colonization Association (ICA), an organization often pictured as a rival, or even an enemy, of Zionism. It in fact predated Herzl's movement.

Founded in 1891 by Baron Maurice de Hirsch, whose wealth grew to an incredible $100 million, the ICA received his munificent support. Good businessman that he was, de Hirsch incorporated the ICA in London as a charitable joint stock company, with Sir Ernest Cassel, the Goldsmids, Baron Edmond de Rothschild, and others among Europe's wealthiest Jews becoming shareholders. At its peak, the ICA was capitalized at around $40 million, at a time when Zionist funds were a pittance by comparison.

Those who favored the ICA were skeptical of Zionism because of its limitations rather than its objectives. The ICA favored settlement in North and South America where, it was believed, Jews could become farmers. Though not fundamentally opposed to settlement in Palestine, de Hirsch had been negatively impressed with the miserable conditions of the "oriental" Jews during the years he was developing his concessions for the railroad linking Europe to Constantinople. The notion of resettling Eastern Europe's Jews so that they would share the misfortune of their Palestinian brethren seemed to him like an act of utmost folly. In keeping with the times, the ICA proponents were colonialists rather than nationalists. Furthermore, in line with the rational universalist tenets of their progressive brand of Judaism, the ICA proponents failed to appreciate the mystical magnetism of the idea of returning to Jerusalem. The assimilated Reform Jews of Europe and the United States held to a tradition of rejecting the "next year in Jerusalem" concept as a kind of death wish. For them this implied a return to the ghetto, a renunciation of newly won rights and acceptance in the adopted homelands of their choice.

Claude Joseph Goldsmid Montefiore, the patrician gentleman who called on Morgenthau at the behest of Stephen Wise, was the epitome of all this enlightenment. As an heir to the Montefiore and Goldsmid fortunes — his antecedents included Sir Moses Montefiore★ — he was financially free to pursue his interests in liberal Judaism. He had been educated at Balliol College, Oxford, and by Solomon Schechter,† and his considerable scholarly work was directed toward a search for universal linkage between Judaism and Christianity.

As president of the Anglo-Jewish Association, which sponsored schools in "underdeveloped" communities in the Near East, including Jerusalem, Claude Montefiore was interested in meeting the new American ambassador, to whom he was quick to communicate his view of Jewish nationalism as a dangerous threat to universalism. Jews like Montefiore, who was almost exactly the ambassador's age, were new in his experience: men with the easy self-confidence derived from several generations of wealth and education, free to pursue altruistic interests, sometimes rather cavalier about money. In the United States most Jewish wealth belonged to those who had struggled for it, or was not more than one generation away from them.

On the same day Montefiore came to call, Morgenthau noted in his diary, "I[srael] Zangwill took supper with us and remained until 11:30 discussing territorialism and I.C.A." In contrast with the urbane, upper-class Montefiore, Zangwill was a flaming volcano, his small hat perched on a thick mop of curls, over strong, mobile features. Zangwill had been born to poor Russian immigrant parents and raised in London's heavily Jewish East End. But the British Establishment had a way of awarding instant honorary life membership to those with brilliant intellect and eloquence. It was one of the greatest sources of strength of their durable upper class.

Zangwill had made the social leap comfortably. As a popular novelist, he was a kind of Jewish Thackeray. He was also a spell-

---

★Sir Moses Montefiore (1784–1885) was the first English Jew to be knighted; he represented persecuted Jews worldwide.
†Solomon Schechter, whom he had brought to England as his private tutor, later became the president of the Jewish Theological Seminary in New York and the founder of Conservative Judaism.

binding orator. He had contributed to the *Jewish Quarterly,* financed and coedited by Claude Montefiore. As a friend and early Herzl enthusiast, he was an on-again, off-again Zionist. In the interim he had launched the Jewish Territorial Organization. The movement paradoxically envisioned self-governing communities that were to be at once superghettos and the instrument for the absorption of Judaism into a new universal religion of the future. On the middle ground between the ICA and Zionism, territorialism never seriously competed with either of them. Zangwill's only success had been the Galveston, Texas, project, with funds provided by the ubiquitous Jacob Schiff. It was not a community but a collecting point for the dispersal of immigrant Jews throughout the Southwest. By sending them to the port of Galveston, Schiff and others like him on the East Coast hoped to divert some of the massive influx of Eastern European Jews who were flooding into New York to the detriment, it was felt, of the established German Jews. Morgenthau was very much taken with Zangwill's ideas.

On arriving in Paris after the heady round of talks in London, Morgenthau went straight to the Ritz Hotel in the Place Vendôme and relaxed with old friends from New York: the Naumburgs (parents of his future son-in-law, George), the Herbert Lehmans, and their great-niece Margaret Fatman (his future daughter-in-law, Elinor's older sister), who was studying voice in Paris.

Claude Montefiore showed up to continue arranging meetings for Morgenthau's edification. In Paris, Morgenthau was introduced to Baron Rothschild by the Belgian financier and future president of the ICA, Franz Phillipson.

Edmond de Rothschild openly lived a double life. As a discriminating patron of the arts, with impeccable if extravagant taste, he was a dominant figure in the Parisian haute monde. He was also the leader of Jewish communal life in France, the beloved *Ha-Nadiv Ha-Yadu'a* (the well-known benefactor) in Palestine. However, Rothschild, like the other patrician English and French Jews Morgenthau met, had distanced himself from political Zionism and had some years earlier placed all of his settlements in Palestine under ICA supervision.

Morgenthau had never met a Jew anything like Rothschild. He looked rather like Jacob Schiff, but in his casualness about money matters, combined with his sartorial chic and elegant surroundings, made a sharp contrast with Schiff's humorless, Germanic self-importance. Rothschild, according to Morgenthau, was "not pessimistic — splendid man — fine palace, gave me his opera box for next Monday. He expects visiting Palestine in February."

The meetings with Jewish leaders were perhaps the most substantively informative part of the Paris visit in a schedule crowded with a great variety of activities. There was a courtesy call on the Turkish ambassador in the company of U.S. Ambassador Herrick; a call at the offices of Underwood Typewriter Company, of which Morgenthau was a director; an American Chamber of Commerce lunch held in his honor at the Ritz. There were also shopping expeditions with son-in-law Mortie Fox, tourist attractions, including a visit to Versailles, and a great deal of high living. But these endless frivolities soon bored Morgenthau. "Very frenchy . . . and I am getting a little tired of Vanity Fair and will not like it long — real virile men and women for me, they are sincere, others only scratch surface and pat their stomachs."

The Paris visit ended, and Morgenthau moved on. After a four-day stopover in Vienna, the ambassador and his entourage checked into the Budapest Ritz. Here Morgenthau received the first of many reports from the resident U.S. consul general reviling the U.S. consul in Jerusalem, Samuel Edelman. He also got his first whiff of the nationalist passions smoldering in the Balkans. "Saw quite some remnants of war — burned down villages and neglected fields," he observed on the final leg of his journey to Constantinople. But this was hardly sufficient evidence to alert him to the possibility that regional warfare could ignite Europe. Indeed, President Wilson and Secretary of State Bryan knew little and cared less about happenings in the Balkans and the Near East. Thus, while Morgenthau came well informed on Jewish interests, he knew little of what would be the core concern of his mission.

During the winter of 1913–14, when Morgenthau assumed his Turkish post, the United States was not yet party to the European jockeying for position in the dying Ottoman Empire, known as the "sick man of Europe," nor was it aware of the situation within the empire itself.

A few years earlier, in 1908, the Committee of Union and Progress (known as the Young Turks) had taken over the government with the promise of instituting reform, modernization, and equal rights for all citizens. A year later Abdul Hamid II was deposed, sent into exile, and replaced by his ineffectual brother as a figure-head. The Young Turks had received the enthusiastic backing of the Christians, especially the Armenians, as well as the Jews.

Morgenthau described his arrival at the Ottoman capital in his diary:

> Was met at station by entire staff. Hofman Phillip [chargé d'affaires] introduced me to all. . . . After a somewhat bewildering round of handshakings, Phillip, the Foxes and I stepped into a carriage and were driven to the Pera Palace Hotel, where Phillip gave us a Thanksgiving dinner.

The ambassador was eager to go to work. He opened a bank account and "deposited my first salary received since 1905." With "5 servants helping," he repacked to move from the hotel to the embassy, where he "took possession" of his new domain.

As a seasoned observer of human nature, Morgenthau realized that to accomplish anything he would have to move quickly and decisively. The "instinctive ambition of the attachés led them to try to keep the Ambassador from taking an active hand in the work of the Chancery." He sensed that foreign service personnel had put him down as a typical wealthy political contributor claiming as his reward the status of diplomatic high living at his own expense. "With great solemnity" they explained that an "embassy was not like other business offices." They mumbled about the delicacies of diplomatic protocol, which demanded years of training and experience. They had grievously misjudged their man.

"I made short work of this monstrous nonsense," Morgenthau recalled. "Business is business and details are the substance of larger concerns." He read through the records of the embassy like a good lawyer preparing a brief. "Common sense, judgment and energy are the desiderata of all business relationships, and I found no barrier in these affairs because of their so-called diplomatic nature." As things turned out, his seemingly high-handed self-confidence was justified. During the ensuing months, with communications uncertain, the ambassador would at critical moments be called on to act as a freewheeling agent. The State Department was especially slow to react to tremors on unfamiliar territory, and the foreign service officers were scarcely more in touch with their surroundings. Moreover, while the chief-of-mission slot was reserved for a Jew, its occupant was likely to find himself in a den of anti-Semites.

One way Morgenthau managed to avoid staff entrapment was by selecting as his personal dragoman (interpreter) an Armenian, Arshag K. Schmavonian, long-time legal adviser to the embassy. Wise in the ways of the diplomatic jungle, Schmavonian had become a permanent staff fixture, tolerated by his American colleagues with grudging respect. As a Christian minority in a Muslim nation, the Armenians had played a role similar to that of the Jews in Western society. Thus, the Turkish Schmavonian had, in placing himself in the American camp, burned all his bridges. Becoming a kind of private secretary in the British sense, he attached himself to Ambassador Morgenthau with fierce loyalty. Morgenthau had immediately spotted Schmavonian as an appropriately discriminating counselor and trusted interpreter. In addition, Schmavonian possessed knowledge of "every American interest in Turkey . . . He knew, also, all the Turkish officials . . . the names, characteristics of the leaders of the recent revolution; and, was versed in the niceties of diplomatic custom."

Having arrived in Constantinople without his wife, Morgenthau at first led a rather reclusive life, which was nevertheless carefully monitored by government agents. Quick to take note of Schmavonian's privileged relationship, they began trying to pump him.

"Who is your ambassador's mistress?" they demanded to know.

"The ambassador doesn't have a mistress," Schmavonian answered firmly.

"Impossible. We must have this information for the police records," they persisted.

When the agents pressed their interrogation, they were given the same reply. After some fruitless weeks had passed, one of the agents conceded to Schmavonian, "That ambassador of yours is really very clever. You know we still haven't been able to discover who his mistress is?"

It was Schmavonian himself who dutifully reported this incident to his boss. The ambassador often repeated it and with great relish.

At this time, Morgenthau found it appropriate to sit back and observe while the "Powers" occupied center stage, maneuvering for position as they lined up for the great war that by then seemed inevitable. In Constantinople the captains of the opposing factions were the German and British ambassadors, both perfectly cast for their roles. Baron von Wangenheim, though not a Prussian by birth, was, as Morgenthau observed, "Prussia and modern Germany embodied. . . . His bearing was that of an excitable Hindenburg." A tall, commanding figure, he was "overflowing with physical vitality, opinionated, . . . aggressive in conversation, somewhat flirtatious, proud [and] overbearing." By way of contrast, Sir Louis Mallet, the British ambassador, "exhibited the quiet force and cultivation which one naturally expects from a member of the English upper classes." He presided with easy grace over his cavernous embassy. His government "had spared no pains to make its public appearance there correspond with the splendor and importance of the British Empire."

These European diplomats had been accustomed to viewing the American ambassador as someone given to vulgar displays of newly acquired wealth. Morgenthau set out to shatter this image by doing "as nearly as I could directly the opposite of what was expected of me." Instead of riding about in an automobile — a conspicuous rarity — he used a carriage drawn by a pair of Arabian ponies. He managed the embassy frugally, outfitting it with furniture lent to him by a Mr. Levy, a local furniture dealer.

Morgenthau was not one to be restrained by convention or preconceived ideas. Neither his lack of traditional training and experience nor the strain on his finances, and certainly not his being a Jew among Christian peers in a Muslim country, would limit his exercise of full ambassadorial authority. This was not the first time in his life that he had advanced rapidly on an unfamiliar course. He was aware that his unconventional approach and exuberant self-confidence could be played to advantage, and he believed that by working hard enough he could overcome any handicap.

He started by trying to learn French, the language of diplomacy and the second language in this part of the Near East, taking daily lessons whenever he could. But try as he might, he never attained a serviceable French. On social occasions he depended on his daughter Helen and, later, on his wife and younger daughters.

To educate himself in the diplomatic niceties, the new ambassador found a willing tutor in an Old World aristocrat, Marquis Pallavicini, the Austrian ambassador, dean of the diplomatic corps in Constantinople. The Marquis reveled in diplomatic intricacies. Morgenthau found this Austrian with his "little upturned gray moustaches" and a "rather stiff, even slightly strutting walk" like the

"Marquis that was once a stock figure on the stage." Morgenthau proved himself a superior pupil.

Accompanied by Helen, whom her father found an apt and eager counterpart, Morgenthau attended his first formal diplomatic dinner at the British embassy. "You can't imagine my feelings," he wrote to his family in New York, "as I was ushered into the room in which there were thirty other guests including the Grand Vizier (chief minister), Talaat Bey, and three other Cabinet Ministers, the Wangenheims, D'Ankerswaerd [the Swedish minister and his American wife] and other Sirs and Ladies." Having arrived late, he felt as though they were all staring at him "when 'The American Ambassador' was announced. I felt, 'is it I or not?'"

Helen was thrilled. "Never in my life have I experienced anything so wonderful. . . . two marvellously uniformed *cavasses*★ stood at the door inside, where powdered footmen in knee breeches, about twenty of them, were also stationed." A young black page dressed like an Egyptian slave stood just outside the drawing room where they were received by the British ambassador, Sir Louis Mallet. The huge embassy was lighted entirely by candles: "In the dining room huge candelabra stand on mirrors surrounded by quantities of roses — all from Nice. . . . The polished silver platter seemed to be alive with shimmering reflections dancing in front of us as the meal was served in the usual rapid fire English style."

Helen was seated "next to the place of honor," with an elaborately uniformed Turkish cabinet minister on one side and Baron von Wangenheim on the other. Seated on the other side of the Turk was an English beauty wearing "the most gorgeous emeralds," Mrs. Harold Nicolson, née Victoria (Vita) Sackville-West. Although "heaps of people had been asked to stay for dancing," Helen was exhausted and left with Mortie at midnight.

Her father, however, was still going strong. "Wangenheim asked me to play bridge with him, a Turk, and a Greek banker — which I did until 1:30 when the dancing was over and they all went in for supper." Only then did he go home, leaving behind "a few revelers to dance until 2:30 or so." It had been an exhilarating induction into ambassadorial service. "I thoroughly enjoyed it," he wrote Josie. "I am *very glad* I came."

The dazzling, decadent capital of the Ottoman Empire that

★*Cavass*, or *kavass*, a Turkish police officer.

my grandfather confronted was literally a divided city. Built, like Rome, on a collection of seven hills, it was joined by two great bridges standing at the southern extremity of the Bosphorus, where Europe and Asia meet lip to lip. The American embassy, along with all the other foreign missions, was located in the Pera section, on the European side. From there, one overlooked the Golden Horn and the ancient city of Stambul, layer on decaying layer, a monument to its history of unceasing violence. Viewed from the Pera heights, the Stambul panorama was marked by the silhouettes of minarets, cupolas, and domes. From the distance one gazed on a fairyland, which quickly vanished when one descended into the narrow alleys, leading endlessly through piles of debris. Here the busy street life was at once aggressively predatory and mysteriously withdrawn, acrid, and perfumed. From sidewalk shops, haggling merchants assaulted the passers-by along with beggars displaying crippled limbs and festering sores. Veiled women slipped by silently and disappeared into dwellings hidden behind high walls and latticed balconies. Everywhere was the babel of Eastern languages and Turkish inscriptions lettered in graceful Arabic script.

By contrast, in Pera, the embassies, grand hotels, expensive restaurants, and bordellos were populated with sophisticated foreigners who controlled the commercial life, speaking French and other foreign languages.

Outside the charmed circle of the embassy, Morgenthau discovered an upside-down society, in which extraordinary rights and privileges were extended to foreign expatriates and residents of European lineage, making them far better off than the natives, and especially the non-Muslims.

As "people of the Book," Christians and Jews were permitted to govern themselves within their own communities throughout the Ottoman Empire. But in relation to Muslims, they found their rights rigorously curtailed. Their testimony was inadmissible in a Muslim court, leaving them open to victimization by their neighbors. On the other hand, residents of European ancestry had held special privileges called "the Capitulations" for hundreds of years; in the nineteenth century these were extended to Americans as well. These lucky residents had virtual diplomatic immunity from one generation to the next, even though they continued to live in Ottoman territories. They paid no taxes, either to their native countries or to the Ottoman government, and thus amassed enormous fortunes while the native Jews and Christians, burdened by Turkish taxes, paid excessively, and often large additional sums in cash or produce were extorted by corrupt local officials.

Since the days of Queen Elizabeth I, England and other European nations had engaged in trade with the Sublime Porte. Americans had entered the scene in significant numbers only after the first quarter of the nineteenth century, and then not as traders but as Protestant missionaries, having perceived an unparalleled opportunity to convert masses of Mohammedans to Christianity. These newcomers, virtually all sponsored by the American Board of Commissioners for Foreign Missions, had gone with high hopes only to discover why the field was wide open: under the law of the Koran, the penalty for conversion was death to the converted and converter alike. The missionaries were not deterred, however; they took the long view that "if it were possible to [imbue the native Christians] with a lively missionary spirit [for the Eastern churches did not proselytize] they will be the best and most effectual [future] missionaries, because native to the soil."

Oblivious to how Westernized Christians might be viewed by Ottoman rulers, the missionaries proceeded to build schools, dispensaries, and hospitals, even colleges, in every region where there were substantial numbers of Christians. It was apparent that their chief clients would be the Armenians. Greeks and a few other regional Christians also frequented the mission schools, though the Greek Orthodox Church discouraged such attendance. Still, Armenian girls as well as boys flocked to the mission schools in increasing numbers, although no more than about 10 percent formally converted to the evangelical brand of Christianity.*

Henry Morgenthau understood exactly how important these American institutions were to his government. They constituted the United States' major vested interest in the region. Deeply committed to them were some of President Wilson's wealthy Princeton cronies and biggest political contributors. Copper-rich Cleveland

---

*The missionary influence raised the standards of the traditional Armenian Apostolic Church schools. Church officials had at first resented missionary intrusion but came to an accommodation after considering the benefits, not the least of which they perceived as American interest in their plight and therefore American protection. By 1913, throughout Turkey alone, where most mission schools were located, there were 450 Protestant schools and numbers of dispensaries and, throughout the remaining empire, 8 colleges, including those in Turkey. See Robert L. Daniel, *American Philanthropy in the Near East* (Athens, Ohio: Ohio University Press, 1970), p. 94.

Dodge and Charles R. Crane of the Chicago-based Crane Plumbing Company were both active supporters of Robert College in Constantinople, the first and most prestigious of the colleges.*

"There were constantly two problems interesting me," the ambassador noted. "The first was the American missionary activities, whose ramifications reached into all parts of Turkey . . . My second problem was the Jewish question." The former he expounded on at great length. The latter he promised "to discuss in a separate chapter" in his autobiography *All in a Lifetime* but never did.† The problem that preoccupied him was the Armenian question.

At the time of Morgenthau's arrival in Constantinople, the Jews were less feared than the Christian minorities, whose condition had become increasingly precarious as successive nineteenth century revolutions tore first the Greeks, then the Bulgarians, Slavs, and Serbs from the empire, with the result that all the Ottoman territories in Europe were lost. This made the Ottoman rulers particularly wary of separatist movements in the remaining territories, a fear that bordered on paranoia under the rule of Abdul Hamid II in the late nineteenth century. (The sultan was known as "The Great Assassin" and "The Bloody Sultan" for his treatment of the Armenians.)

The Armenians, the most cruelly persecuted of the Ottoman minorities, were native to the Turkish northeast. At its height, in the century before the birth of Christ, the Armenian kingdom extended over what are now parts of Iran, the Caucasus region of the Soviet Union, and northeastern Turkey.

The Armenian people trace their presence in eastern Anatolia

---

*Robert College was incorporated in the 1860s by a nonsectarian board led by a deeply religious wealthy importer, Christopher Rhinelander Robert. Dodge's son, Bayard, was the son-in-law of the head of the Syrian Protestant College in Beirut.

†This much-heralded chapter never materialized. At the very outset of his previously published *Ambassador Morgenthau's Story,* he apologized that he had had to omit the story of the Jews in Turkey, and dismissed his failure to account for "the splendid activities of the American Missionary and Educational Institutions in Turkey" with the excuse that each subject "would require a book by itself." In fact, the latter topic is covered extensively in both text and photographs. And while there are numerous mentions of the condition of the Ottoman Jews, the only account of his expedition to Palestine — the first important event during his tenure — concerns his leading a delegation of Protestant notables to the caves of Machpelah. This omission appears consistent with my grandfather's reluctance to emphasize his Jewish identity in the American arena. Fortunately, he recalled the fascinating and far-reaching details of this trip in his diaries, letters, and supporting documents, which he carefully preserved for posterity.

(now part of Turkey) and the Russian Caucasus back to the sixth century B.C.E. In the early fourth century C.E., they became the first nation to adopt Christianity, later developing their own alphabet, and they took on a distinct national identity. Over the years, because of their faith and their occupation of a strategically important crossroads, they were continually vulnerable to persecution by waves of invaders.

Before the outbreak of World War I there were really two Armenias. Western Armenia, with a population of about 2 million under Ottoman rule, had its cultural and commercial center in Constantinople. Eastern Armenia, with a population of about 1,700,000 under Russian rule, had two enormously wealthy centers, Tiflis and Baku. The latter city supplied Russia with 90 percent of its oil.

The Turks in the dying Ottoman Empire especially feared the Russians, traditionally their enemies in any case. The czars had long coveted Constantinople as the Ottoman crown jewel and, even more important, as the only warm-water port near Russian borders.

To both Morgenthau and the German ambassador, Wangenheim, the Armenian presence in both of these opposing empires appeared to have many parallels with the Jewish presence among the opposing nations of Eastern Europe. As alien minorities, essentially powerless in themselves, both the Jews and the Armenians were always being accused of traitorous collaboration by the governments that ruled them.

By 1913 the Ottoman Armenians were scattered throughout the empire. Although the greatest concentration remained in the northeastern provinces, even here they were a diminishing majority. They were dispersing westward because of harassment by the rebellious Kurds, whom the imperial rulers encouraged to move into the Armenian provinces. As Muslims, the Kurds were given a free hand to invade Armenian homes, steal Armenian women and girls, and take whatever Armenian produce and chattel they pleased.

Meanwhile, Russia had become host to nearly half of the surviving Armenians. By the end of the nineteenth century, Russia was expressing a strong desire to act as "protector" of the Armenians across its frontier. These sentiments displeased not only the sultan but England and France as well. The European powers interpreted Russia's interest as a pretext to gain a foothold in Turkey, a move they had no intention of permitting. They expressed their solicitude for the Armenians, but took no active measures to protect them, nor would they allow Russia to take such steps. The resulting "Armenian Question" exacerbated the sultan's fury, leading him to order the greatest blood-bath to date. During 1895–96 some 300,000 Armenians were massacred, mostly in the northeastern territories nearest to Russia.

Armenians on both sides of the border fostered a dream of a united greater Armenia free of both Russians and Turks. But for the time being, the Armenian nationalists in Russia were content to call for the relief of their Turkish brethren from the sultan's tyranny. Turkish Armenians specifically wanted relief from extortion, from incursions by the Kurds and from periodic massacres. They asked for reforms in the Ottoman Constitution that would afford them something closer to the rights afforded Muslim citizens.

When the Young Turks seized power in 1908, they promised, and for a short time delivered, all of the above, and the Armenians, more than any single element of the Turkish population, were overjoyed. They gained two representatives to the Parliament and distinguished themselves in the Balkan Wars at the outset of the regime. But in 1909, 21,000 Armenians were massacred at Adana in an inexplicable reaction by extremists. By the time of Morgenthau's arrival a gang of militants was firmly in control of the Young Turk leadership; the "Committee of Union and Progress" had become a conspiratorial organization led by a trio of ruthlessly ambitious radicals.

Morgenthau was never deluded as to the underlying ambitions and venality of the CUP leaders. At the same time, however, he was determined to be as effective as possible in carrying out his ambassadorial duties, which required close personal relationships with the men at the top. Enver, Talaat, and Djemal had consolidated their joint dictatorial control over the opposition of more moderate cohorts. Of these three, Enver and Talaat were the two dominating figures. Together they had forged a team and continued to be mutually supportive.

When Morgenthau approached these men he used unconventional ways calculated to emphasize the contrast between himself, the American "shirt-sleeve" diplomat, and the snobbish aristocrats representing the Great Powers. His style was very much in tune with that of the self-made men who had seized the reins of Ottoman power.

While his hosts seemed amused by his display of American

idealism, Morgenthau remained hopeful that these Turkish revolutionaries would return to their earlier avowed pluralistic objectives. Before the demands of war stifled all such possibilities, this was not an absurdly naive dream. Morgenthau began to tempt the despairing Turks with talk of an economic recovery, modeled on the post–Civil War reconstruction of the American South which he had known in his youth, albeit from a Northern perspective. Publicly, he declared his "extreme desire to help them" and noted "the great sympathy that the American people felt for all struggling nations."

The ambassador also held out the possibility of infusions of American private capital. He went to Syria and Palestine (then still part of the Ottoman Empire) partly at the behest of the Turks as a way to gather firsthand information on investment opportunities. But privately he was much more pessimistic. "It is really pathetic," he wrote his family in New York, "to meet these men who are entrusted with the government and rehabilitation of its tremendous territory, with its great undeveloped wealth, evidently anxious to perform the task, but almost hopelessly handicapped by existing conditions created by their predecessors."

The pair of strong men in control, Talaat and Enver, were very different from each other in style and appearance, though much the same in their ruthless determination to succeed. Morgenthau learned how to play up to their weaknesses or take a firm stance as might be demanded.

Talaat, a great bear of a man, would pound his massive fists on the table while shouting out his disapproval. During one emergency the pajama-clad Talaat received the American ambassador in his bedchamber. His home was in the working-class neighborhood where he had lived before his rise to power. Next to his bed was a telegraph key with which he had earned his living not so many years earlier. He still preferred to tap out confidential communications on this device himself. He was by no means, however, an unsophisticated man.

Morgenthau's first private meeting with Talaat was in the home of his old friend the chief rabbi, Nahoum. After establishing himself on firm ground, Morgenthau shrewdly waited for Talaat to present him to his partner, Enver. The opportunity came at an Italian embassy ball. "Talaat Bey introduced me to Enver Pasha, and I had a nice talk in German with him," Morgenthau noted in a letter to the family in mid-January 1914.

Enver in fact enjoyed showing off his excellent German. He had served as an attaché at the Turkish embassy in Berlin, where he had acquired the elegant manners of diplomacy, polished to the point of foppishness, a taste for extravagant living, and an unswerving commitment to the German cause.

A few evenings later, at a Cercle d'Orient dinner hosted by Bustani, the Turkish minister of commerce, Morgenthau was "much surprised that we [himself, daughter Helen, son Henry, and a visiting U.S. commission] were the only Europeans, and that the other guests were Enver Pasha, Djemal Pasha, Talaat Bey, Halik Bey [president of the Parliament] . . . so that we were really being entertained by the leaders of the Party of Union and Progress and the ruling majority of the Cabinet." Morgenthau was delighted to be seated next to Enver and talked with him for nearly two hours. Perhaps naively, he found Enver "a very strong, determined young man" who said that "patriotism impels him to make every effort to save his country from disintegration; that if they failed and died in the attempt they will at least have the satisfaction of having done their duty."

But the facts of Turkish life, as Morgenthau soon discovered, irrevocably contradicted the numerous accounts popular abroad of the young revolutionaries who had triumphed over the bloody sultan. Always the optimist, Morgenthau at first pleaded, "Let us not criticize too harshly the Young Turks, for there is no question that at the beginning they were sincere in their ideal for a new Turkish State which it was evidently beyond their ability to translate into a reality." He pointed out some similarities between the undemocratic CUP rule and the bossism that "has at times flourished in American cities, mainly because the citizens have devoted their time to their private affairs and thus neglected the public good." But he hastened to add that he did "our corrupt American gangs a great injustice" by comparing them with the CUP, which "had added to their system a detail that has not figured extensively in American politics — that of assassination and judicial murder." The Young Turks had destroyed Abdul Hamid's regime only to adopt the sultan's favorite methods, so instead of having one Abdul Hamid, Turkey now had several.

Soon after he started on the job, Morgenthau began to hear the disturbing cries of minority voices, to which he seemed to be attuned with special sensitivity. While he had resented the role of

Jewish ambassador that was foisted on him by both Wilson and Stephen Wise, it was nevertheless precisely because he was a Jew and an immigrant that he empathized with other persecuted minorities. He furthermore found this an entirely appropriate way of expressing his Americanism. Later, reflecting on his Armenian partisanship, he would say, "I am not here as a Jew but as an American Ambassador. My country contains something more than 97,000,000 Christians and something less than 3,000,000 Jews. So at least in my ambassadorial capacity, I am 97 percent Christian."

Late in December 1913, a month after arriving in Constantinople, Morgenthau was visited by the Armenian patriarch, who told him about the murderous attacks on distant Armenian settlements in the interior by nomadic bands of Kurds who roamed between the cities and towns. It was customary for the representatives of the various *millets* (ethnic groups) to call on the foreign ambassadors. So the patriarch was constantly petitioning the Sublime Porte on behalf of his people for relief from these atrocities. Morgenthau wrote his wife, Josie, that the Kurds would "pounce down upon [the Armenians] from their mountain fortresses whenever they needed anything" and seize attractive young women to keep as concubines. He was shocked to learn that such brutish behavior was accepted, by victims, overlords, and foreigners alike, following a pattern ingrained in Turkish history.

Morgenthau found the cruelly treated Armenians very much like the Jews, "particularly [in their] stubborn adherence to their religion and very strong race pride." In very short order he began to forge a bond of compassion with the Armenian people that was to become his outstanding commitment during his ambassadorial tenure and, indeed, for the rest of his life.

· 12 ·

The Jewish Ambassador

FROM THE MOMENT he agreed to the Turkish embassy post, Morgenthau was besieged by Jewish leaders to represent their special interests. He was personally sympathetic to their concerns and stood ready to make bold moves on their behalf as long as they did not put him at odds with the broader American — essentially Christian — interests of his official mission. Hence, when he arrived in Constantinople, a "confidential" letter from Louis Marshall awaited him. Marshall was a prime spokesman and arbiter for the American Jewish establishment, a position he shared congenially with Jacob Schiff. Schiff earned respect for judicious and generous ecumenical donations from his great wealth, Marshall for his intellect and his natural gift of leadership.

Marshall and Morgenthau, exactly the same age, and of similar background, had met in the fall of 1876 when they were both studying law at Columbia. Marshall was born and raised in Syracuse, New York, of German immigrant Jewish parents. Like Morgenthau, he had little formal education, but this in no way impeded his enthusiasm for learning. He became Samuel Untermyer's law partner at Guggenheimer, Untermyer & Marshall while acquainting himself with the broader concerns of politics.

As an active Republican, Marshall influenced President Theodore Roosevelt to take a firm stand against the anti-Jewish practices of the Russian czarist regime. As president of the American Jewish Committee, he was, although never a political Zionist, nevertheless ardently committed in his support of an expanding Jewish community in Palestine. Now he hastened to alert the new ambassador to the "red passport," which the Turks had introduced to halt the expansion of Jewish settlement in Palestine.

Marshall was kept directly informed on these matters by highly irregular communications from the American consul in Jerusalem, Samuel Edelman. "You will of course treat what I say as personal and confidential," Marshall cautioned Morgenthau, "for I assume that you will be officially notified of these facts and at the same time you will protect Mr. Edelman from animadversion."

Edelman had given Marshall the alarming news that the Turks, while appearing to relax restrictions, had done just the opposite. They had abolished the practice of "requiring Jews on arrival to deliver up their passports to the Ottoman authorities" but had substituted "in return a red receipt permitting them to remain [only] three months in Palestine." Constantinople had ordered that foreign Jews post a bond to guarantee adherence to this procedure.

Edelman claimed that he had succeeded in having these orders rescinded. "'Of course, I reported these facts to my superiors,'" Marshall quoted Edelman, "'and am now on the anxious bench for fear I have exceeded my authority. I am awfully glad that a Jew is coming as Ambassador to Turkey; the moral effect is already felt all through the country [Palestine].'" Marshall added, "I think this will afford you a splendid opportunity for immediate service, not only to the United States, but also to our Jewish brethren."

At first, unconcerned by any appearance of impropriety, Morgenthau agreed. During his second week on the job, he wrote Marshall that he had asked Edelman to send him "a list of recent arrivals and how they have been treated." And he concluded, "It is encouraging to hear that the moral effect of my appointment is already felt in Palestine."

In the winter of 1914, Morgenthau made plans to visit "the Holy Land and the Mediterranean Coast of Asia." "Everyone urged me to go," he told his family. The missionaries and the Jews believed that his presence in their midst "would impress the local authorities" and augur favorable treatment by the Turkish authorities in Constantinople. For their part, these officials expected that on gaining firsthand acquaintance with the possibilities for industrial and agricultural development, the ambassador might be "useful to them in influencing Foreign Capital to invest in their prospects."

On March 22, 1914, Morgenthau and his party, which included Schmavonian and a retinue of Protestant missionaries, boarded the *Peter the Great,* a luxurious Russian steamship that sailed weekly between Odessa and Alexandria. He had ordered Captain McCauley, skipper of the U.S. gunboat *Scorpion,* which was assigned to the embassy, to precede him and be available as he journeyed along the Mediterranean coast, although the *Scorpion* served more for official entertaining than for security.

For his Protestant well-wishers especially, the high point of the ambassador's trip was his visit to the Machpelah caves, site of the burial ground that Abraham purchased for Sarah, and where he, Isaac, Rebecca, Jacob, and Leah were subsequently interred. The Muslims, who included these patriarchs and their wives among their most revered saints, jealously guarded this holy site, and for seven hundred years prohibited Jews and Christians from visiting the tombs. The only exception to the exclusion of non-Muslims was the privilege extended to royalty, heads of state and their ambassadors, and their entourages.

As soon as news of the Morgenthau pilgrimage became known, the ambassador found himself surrounded by a band of devout persons eager to share in this unique opportunity. Dr. W. W. Peet, the Mission Boards of America's financial representative in Constantinople, was the first to sign up, and he let the word get around in the higher Protestant echelons. The deputation, snowballing from an initial six to twenty-six, included the missionary and Arabic scholar from Beirut, Dr. Franklin Hoskins, and the president of the Protestant Syrian College, Dr. Howard Bliss, along with his daughter and son-in-law, the Bayard Dodges. Others who joined the party en route were Chancellor McCormick of the University of Pittsburgh and an earnest, "rather clerical looking Dr. Sayre," who identified himself as the brother-in-law of President Wilson's daughter, Jessie.

Schmavonian, the ambassador's "French-Turkish tongue," had pleaded and plotted to be included in the official party during the journey. He had been in the employ of the Americans for seventeen years and said he "expected to die in the service." As a Turkish Armenian, with no other place to go, he was anxious to maintain his role of indispensability. Morgenthau teasingly said he feared that if his aide were away from Constantinople, it "would interfere with the activities of the Embassy." Whereupon Schmavonian quickly responded, "You know that nothing important will be done in your absence without your consent, so why not have me with you at your elbow?" It was an irresistible rejoinder. Morgenthau later recalled that he "proved of invaluable assistance."

Morgenthau's daughter, Ruth, had her own view of the relationship. She wrote home to her brother, Henry Jr., "Schmavonian is continually worrying whether or not people are making [enough] fuss over the old man. It's always 'Mr. Ambassador,' and I don't believe he knows Pa's other name. Anyway, he is a nice old duffer, and means and does well."

Four days later the Morgenthau party disembarked in Alexandria, which, while remaining nominally a Turkish suzerainty, was then under firm British control. One of the Egyptian khedive's cousins was serving (also nominally) as the Young Turks' grand vizier, but Lord Kitchener, the British hero of Khartoum, held a firm grip on the reins of power. Morgenthau was eager to meet the great man. But he was also sensitive to the way Kitchener's authority was enforced outside official Ottoman channels. Forewarned, he proceeded to move through this diplomatic minefield with impeccable finesse.

The khedive had dispatched his private railroad car to transport the ambassadorial party to Cairo. Later that afternoon, Morgenthau drove out to see the Great Sphinx and the neighboring pyramids, and was reminded of his biblical heritage: "of what abject slavery must have existed at that time when one man could have compelled thousands and thousands of people to give up their entire lives to drag stones to that place in order to erect a monument to hide his mortal remains . . . It seems to me but a monument to brute force."

These reminders of long-term oppression, daily underscored Morgenthau's awareness that the Jews remaining in the lands of their ancestors were still battling for survival. The ambassador was often confronted with deputations of Jews. Even as the *Peter the Great* stopped over in Smyrna there were four delegates of the B'nai B'rith Lodge waiting on the dock. In Cairo he "received a deputation from the Maimonides Cairo lodges" who urged "my accepting a reception, which I did . . . They were all in full dress and considered it very important to their existence. I answered their addresses in German and we then discussed Zionism until after 11 o'clock. The members were mostly of the prosperous middle class, but not nearly as intellectual as those in Constantinople. They all are ardent nationalists."

Morgenthau managed to compartmentalize his obligations, attending to the missionaries with only an occasional bow to his persistent coreligionists. "The Jews absolutely leave Pa no peace," daughter Ruth complained to her brother, Henry. "Every station we arrive at, a mob of them turn out, sing, make speeches and a lot of noise."

In Cairo before making his official call on the khedive, Morgenthau allowed himself a brief meeting with Kitchener and had "a very nice frank talk with him. He thinks the orientals are unable yet to accept western methods. He is very strongly anti-Turkish and considers the English as the best and perhaps the only well-equipped nation for the administration of other countries."

By the spring of 1914 British power and confidence had reached a high-water mark. According to his biographer Philip Magnus, Lord Kitchener was the "embodiment of the patriotic ardor of the British nation." Morgenthau was impressed by his encounter with the living legend — who towered over him — "a forceful, courageous, intellectual giant. Though dominant in his manner, he is courteous. His attitude is that of an absentee landlord or investor." An administrator of both competence and confidence, he "talked of the Colonies in the same manner and from much the same viewpoint as I had been accustomed to hear among businessmen in New York who were developing some big business combination or trust."

Kitchener's reception of the ambassador seemed to be equally enthusiastic. He had himself wished to be appointed His Majesty's ambassador to Constantinople but had been compelled to settle for the rather anomalous position of consul general in Cairo and British agent. As such, his power in Egypt and the Sudan was supreme, but according to diplomatic protocol, he ranked below almost everyone with whom he was likely to associate. On state occasions he circumvented the problem by having himself declared host, and thereby assuming the place of honor.

Two days after their first meeting, Kitchener entertained the Morgenthaus at a luncheon in the luxurious residency, served by a large staff of servants turned out in scarlet and gold livery. The bachelor earl presided at one table while his sister, acting as hostess, sat at the head of a second table with the ambassador on her right.

At the time of Morgenthau's visit it was an open secret that Kitchener was bent on deposing "the wicked little Khedive," whom he had quite needlessly humiliated. As the vassal of the Ottoman sultan, himself a withered figurehead, Abbas Hilmi II exercised hardly more than ceremonial power. Yet with wounded Arab pride stirring, he remained a symbol of Egypt's glorious past and a lightning rod for anti-Christian feeling.

The khedive's face, heavily jowled and dissipated in appearance, made him look much older than his thirty-nine years, and reflected the self-indulgence and corruption that had colored the two decades of his regime. Nevertheless, he possessed "many attractive and amiable qualities" — along with a sharp intelligence, Morgenthau noted.

On returning to his Cairo hotel, Morgenthau found the royal carriage waiting to take him to the khedive's palace. En route, policemen had been posted at every cross street "so as to secure us the right of way and proper recognition." His Highness met the ambassador at the palace door and ushered him inside to a sofa, where they talked while sipping coffee. "It was a very curious experience to sit with one of the [world's] potentates on absolutely equal footing and talking good English."

This friendly visit prompted a subsequent call from the khedive's brother, Prince Mohamet Ali, who bore the name and the fierce pride of his famous forebear, the tyrannical pasha who had ruled Egypt throughout the first half of the nineteenth century.

> He talked about Egyptianism exactly as the Jews do about Zionism. I have seldom seen a clearer case of parallel thought. . . . His pride and patriotism feel hurt that the English are their protectors. He admits they have benefited [from] them, but claims that European customs and schools have depraved their children, that women are no longer to be trusted. He thinks they were much happier "before they read European novels" and became slaves to the "modes" and their dressmakers [who] act as procurors.

The following day, Morgenthau was escorted by a representative of the khedive to a Koranic school, where seven to ten thousand "pupils were seated on the floor studying, all of them apparently very poor, but very sincere and earnest. Conditions were extremely squalid. Pupils live on next to nothing, but seem perfectly contented. They come from India, Somaliland and all parts of Turkey and the provinces. There must have been ten different shadings of skin from absolute white to coal black."

On April 1 the Morgenthau party set sail from Port Said, Egypt, for Jaffa, the port of entry to the Holy Land. On shipboard Morgenthau met James (later Lord) Bryce, the eminent scholar and diplomat, and his wife. Morgenthau found Bryce "a very remarkable old man" and a relentless brain-picker with an unquenchable thirst for facts. Bryce had been elevated to the peerage a year earlier for his achievements in improving U.S.-Canadian relations while serving as British ambassador to Washington. As a young M.P. in the Gladstone era, Bryce had founded the Anglo-Armenian Society, and he remained the most constant and ardent advocate of the Armenians' cause.

· 13 ·

The Holy Land

A T SEVEN the next morning on April 2 the Morgenthau party made an uncomfortable landing at Jaffa "in a very rough sea . . . our vessel rocking most awkwardly, so that we practically had to be thrown into the little boat which took us to the port." Morgenthau's visit had been eagerly anticipated by the Jewish community in Palestine and, for his part, the ambassador, who seemed to have thrived on the turbulent sea voyage, was ready to plunge immediately into the full round of activities that had been planned for him. Despite some misgivings about Zionism, he was overwhelmingly attracted to the Holy Land. "Everyone who can afford it is a fool if he does not travel out here and learn of the birth of our people," he wrote home.

The ambassadorial party "drove to Tellavi [sic], a new suburb of Jewish residents of Jaffa, a splendid example of what can be done in five years." Arthur Ruppin, who ran the Zionist office in Jaffa, explained how he and a group of middle-class Jews had planned Tel Aviv as a garden suburb modeled along European lines. It had already grown rapidly to a population of two thousand, with families living in pleasant one-story houses on individual plots. Morgenthau found it "a clean nice little town and has an air of prosperity and comfort that would do credit anywhere in America, so that the first impression of Jewish activities in Palestine was a most favorable one."

From Tel Aviv, Morgenthau and his party pressed on to visit the agricultural village of Petah Tikvah. Here a group of religious Russian Jews had established a community of privately owned farms on the coastal plain. Overcoming the hostile natural environment, Arabs, Turks, and the rigid administrators of Baron de Rothschild's charity, they were proud and prosperous as they welcomed the ambassador. "Ten of them mounted on splendid horses met us at the boundary to escort us into their town." Among them were the first *Shomerim* (watchmen) — vigilante bands of Jews and some Bedouins, organized to ward off Arab marauders.

The settlers lived in neat, white stucco houses with red tile roofs grouped in rows behind alleys of trees that provided shade along the hot dusty streets. "They have raised oranges, almonds, wines, etc., many of them are very prosperous. We asked one who seemed to be particularly happy, whether he did not feel like a millionaire, and he said, 'Indeed, I do. I came here twenty years ago without a cent and I am now worth 40,000 francs and am altogether independent.'" Added to the community of 3,000 Jews were about 2,000 Arabs and 200 Yemenite Jews serving as laborers. "The latter are very peculiar: small, shriveled-up people of a most benevolent and amiable appearance, meek and submissive and very industrious."

As they rode back to Jaffa in their carriages, Dr. Ruppin filled Morgenthau's ears with the Zionist party line, telling him that they "desire to cater only to farmers who do their own work, that is, who till their land themselves and, if possible, to exclude all speculating and promoting tendencies. One of the main reasons why they wish to teach Hebrew is that they don't want the boys to emigrate and leave the colonies." Morgenthau had never before seen a community of Jews living healthy outdoor lives, combating the elements, and being prepared to defend themselves. Though he had encouraged one of his brothers and his son to take up farming, this pioneering spirit was entirely new to him. "The condition of the people is far superior to [that of] any city Jews that I have seen."

Next on the ambassador's itinerary was a four-hour train ride from Jaffa to Jerusalem, where the ambassador finished off the evening by organizing a kind of supper seminar. He came away with the impression "that there are no leaders in Jerusalem except those that are heads of institutions, that there is an absolute need of federating the charities and finding work for the Jews. Unfortunately, Jerusalem seems to be fast drifting into an international non-denominational poor house, of course the Jews predominating."

At the time Morgenthau arrived in Palestine, a seemingly eso-teric dispute over whether German or Hebrew should be used as the language of instruction at the new engineering school in Haifa had ignited an all-out war among the hostile factions within world Jewry. As the new building on Mount Carmel for the Technikum (now Technion) was about to open its doors, the Zionist minority on the governing board in Berlin demanding that instruction be conducted in Hebrew had been overruled by the German majority. The German argument against using modern Hebrew was that it lacked both technical vocabulary and texts, and that it would ex-clude all non-Jews from participation in an institution conceived as the first technical training center in the entire Near East region.*

The Zionists and their local allies were adamantly opposed. Most of the wealthy Jews who funded projects in Palestine were not Zionists. They had prospered and gained acceptance in their adopted homelands, where they had become stalwart patriots. They were united in their commitment to rescuing fellow Jews from the devastation of Eastern European pogroms and relocating them wherever they could become self-sufficient, but they were not com-mitted to founding an independent Jewish nation in Palestine. At that time most of the Jewish leadership wanted to help their op-pressed brethren to emigrate anywhere in the world where they would have a chance to thrive. Some cynics would claim this meant anywhere except to the homeland of the sponsor — an unfair gen-eralization, though it bore a kernel of truth. In the United States, German Jews had become alarmed when the gates were opened to the impoverished Eastern European Jews. Meanwhile, back in Je-rusalem in 1914, the conflicting interests of the principal European overlords, in Germany, Great Britain, and France, were increasingly linked with their own national concerns. Only the United States was still able to remain above the fray.

When conflict first erupted in the overseas-sponsored schools in Palestine, the strikers repaired to the building in Jerusalem that

---

*The Technikum was sponsored by the Berlin-based Hilfsverein der Deutschen Juden (Relief Organization of German Jews). The new institute had been launched with two large gifts: one hundred thousand rubles from the estate of a Moscow millionaire, and one hundred thousand dollars from Jacob Schiff. At that time the Hilfsverein was operating a number of elementary schools in Palestine. When the teachers and some of the students received word of the decision at Haifa they responded with strikes and in some instances violence. As a result the opening of the Technikum had to be postponed. Then, with the onset of the war, classes on a university level were delayed until 1924.

housed the Nathan Straus workshops. Straus was almost unique among his wealthy German Jewish peers in the United States in his firm commitment to Zionism, but the U.S. consul, Edelman, felt that the Straus building should not be sheltering perpetrators of a public disturbance.

Edelman was convinced that he had gotten things under control. In fact, he had resolved nothing and irritated everyone. Louis Lipsky, chairman of the Federation of American Zionists, wrote to Ambassador Morgenthau, "As an American organization interested in Palestine, we resent the intrusion of the American Consul in affairs which are beyond his jurisdiction."

Living at the end of the twentieth century when a sudden shift in the balance of power has cataclysmic implications, we are never surprised when some kind of an explosion in Israel sets the world on edge. Looking back at Palestine just before the First World War, it is astounding to observe a seemingly arcane dispute within the *yishuv* (the Jewish community in Eretz Israel prior to statehood) produce an international ripple effect. Certainly global links to Palestine were less strategically important than they are today, but even then sparks in this hot dusty land ignited passions halfway around the world, and the Jewish community in the Holy Land, small and miserable in 1914 compared with its counterpart today, has always depended on outside help.

"Isn't it a thousand pities that this nasty mess has come about in Palestine," Stephen Wise wrote Morgenthau. "I cannot help feeling that even though some of our Zionist friends may be a little hotheaded and overzealous they are right in resenting the Teutonic rather than the Jewish attitude of [the Haifa technical school's German-Jewish sponsors]. After the usual blundering manner of the Jews they have set out to be more German than the Germans and probably made promises and overtures to Imperial quarters in Berlin which could be carried out only at the expense and self-respect of the Jewish people."

Wise had anticipated that this "bitter and divisive spirit" would alienate rich Jews in Europe and the United States like Montefiore and Jacob Schiff. Indeed, shortly thereafter Wise wrote to say that Schiff had warned him that if Paul Nathan, the head of Hilfsverein in Berlin, were to quit "then Palestine will be a closed country to me."

Wise pushed Morgenthau to try to straighten things out, paradoxically warning "that it might be unwise" for him "to have any part in partisan strife." Morgenthau himself was ambivalent. "There are evidently two sides of this controversy," he wrote Wise. "I shall withhold my decision until I have been on the ground and discussed the matter with the various parties." He fully intended to see if he could "be instrumental in restoring harmony."

On his first full day in Jerusalem, Morgenthau's heavy schedule started at 8:30 in the morning. "I visited the school of the Alliance Israelite. We saw the workshops and the school rooms."★ One of the boys attending class that morning, thirteen-year-old Menache Eliachar, retains a vivid memory of that visit.

Eliachar boasted the most distinguished Sephardic lineage in the Holy Land, with a not uncommon pairing of scholarship and wealth. When I interviewed him in 1980, he was living in a spacious townhouse on a shady street in Jerusalem's most elegant old residential neighborhood. I was ushered into a drawing room with a high ceiling and marble floor, an oasis of cool dignity on a hot July morning in the bustling metropolis. He appeared frail, courtly, and wound up to talk. His British-inflected English was impeccable. As one often discovers with old people whose awareness of the present seems shadowy, his recall of his youth was vivid and lively. "The name of Morgenthau was very, very much known," he told me, "and considering the importance of the U.S. to the Turkish government before the U.S. joined the general war, he was given a very royal reception by the Turkish authorities. I remember it was announced by the town crier that everyone should go and receive the guest of honor. And many people, both Arabs and Jews, were in the streets to await the arrival of Mr. Morgenthau."

Eliachar also recalled being singled out in class to recite a poem for Ambassador Morgenthau. "I was considered to be one of the exceptional boys because I finished three classes in one year, studying at home to progress as much as I could. . . . When [the ambassador] heard about my success from the director of the school, he was so pleased that he asked me (through Mr. Farhi) to give him the poem in my handwriting as a souvenir."

Morgenthau was in a hurry to gather as many firsthand impres-

---

★The French-based Alliance Israélite Universelle, founded in 1860, was the first international organization of Jews in modern times. It had come into being in reaction to the notorious "Damascus affair." The Hilfsverein der Deutschen Juden was launched in 1901 as a German alternative to the Alliance.

sions as he could. At ten o'clock, after visiting the Alliance School, he received Homan, the governor of Jerusalem, "an energetic, bright young man, extremely fair minded and anxious to do what he can for Jerusalem." He also received a Yemenite delegation, toured the Armenian church and convent with the bishop of Jerusalem, and returned the governor's call at the municipal building, all before lunch.

At 2:00 P.M. he resumed with a visit to the grand rabbi, Moshe Franco. "His title is the biggest thing about him," Morgenthau observed. "He has a little bit of a building in a very much out of the way street and is not at all impressive." In contrast, the scene with "Ashkenashim Rabbi and community was a picture to see, twenty men dressed in old fashioned style with all colors of the rainbow, with long curly hair, intelligent fine heads gathered around a table to welcome me."

Next he managed to squeeze in a call on the Hadassah nurses before attending "a splendidly arranged reception" in his honor at the American consulate from 3:30 to 6:00 P.M. He had his picture taken with the "Consular Representatives of all the countries" while the American colony band played.

The embrace of the Jewish community in Jerusalem was a strange and discomforting experience for Ambassador Morgenthau. No sense of ambassadorial aloofness or lawyerly cool could dampen his emotions as a Jew. He could see only too clearly that this little band of impoverished Jews, if cut off from their frail, extended lines of support, would suffer the victimization reserved for the weak. And the threat of world war increased that danger. Already there were indications that the Turks and Arabs were biding their time until the European umbilical cord was severed. The Americans, still children in the game of international rescue, found the shoes they were required to step into a bit oversized.

On Morgenthau's first Friday in the Holy Land, out of respect for the predominantly observant Jewish community, he attended divine services, escorted by Ephraim Cohen, the Hilfsverein director, and Mrs. Cohen, as well as Dr. Peet, Dr. Hoskins, and Schmavonian. Afterward at supper they regrouped for a two-hour session on missionary affairs. They were joined by Dr. Thompson, who was in charge of the American Mission School in Jerusalem, and a Miss Gummue, "about whom serious complaints had been raised at the Sublime Porte" concerning the overzealous goings-on at her school for Arabs in Beersheba. Under Muslim law both converters and converted qualified for capital punishment.

"I finally convinced Miss Gummue that I was principally interested [in] her personal safety; that it was wiser for her to accept my advice and for a while, at least, dispense with her native evangelist's services, which she agreed to do." During the course of the evening, the ambassador believed he had "learned more about the internal workings of the branch missionary activities than I ever knew before."

On the Sabbath itself, Morgenthau dropped in and out of four synagogues and visited the Wailing Wall. Here he noted, "it would be a great thing and should be undertaken to remove the small houses opposite the wall and put a park there so that visitors would have room to move about and a chance to rest themselves between prayers."

It didn't take Morgenthau long to assess the abject misery suffered by much of Jerusalem: Jews, Christians, and, most desperate of all, the Arabs. "They informed me that 30% of the Jews in Jerusalem had trachoma, while 90% of the Arabian population are also suffering from it."

While Ambassador Morgenthau concentrated on assessing the intricate tangle of Jerusalem's Jewish affairs, the delegation of distinguished Protestants who had assembled to accompany him on his trip to visit the cave of Machpelah in Hebron had the opportunity of observing Holy Week within the walls of that holy city.

After the conclusion of the Christian holidays the Morgenthau party set out for Hebron. "At the end of the journey [we] had an experience which confirmed my apprehensions regarding the susceptibilities of the Arab Mohammedans." Since the road was blocked by carriages and wagons, "we all thought it was a Jewish funeral. Our outriders, which were four in number, and my carriage drove into the field, when we suddenly discovered that instead of a funeral it was the Jewish delegation that was waiting to escort us into the city."

The *kaimakam* (deputy governor), chief rabbi, and lay leaders of the Jewish community went out to the Hebron city limits to greet Morgenthau and his entourage, preceded by "a large contingent of armed soldiers on horseback" with "many soldiers and police under the command of the police commissioner deployed to keep order."

After a brief rest, they were winding through the narrow street approaching the cave, when a small Arab child ran out of a house and directly under the carriage wheels.

"Fortunately the child was extricated without having received any injury. If we had killed the child there undoubtedly would have been a riot." Grateful for his deliverance, Morgenthau continued, "But I shall not soon forget the black looks of instinctive hatred upon the faces of the Arabs in that throng, who looked upon us as infidel intruders. The same looks and deep murmurs of disapproval accompanied us as we entered the sacred portals of their mosque which covers the Caves of Machpelah."

Here was the ancient gravesite reputedly purchased by the shepherd-patriarch Abraham from the Hittite Ephron for four hundred silver shekels, as the place of burial for his wife, Sarah. The details of the negotiations are described in Genesis 23. Morgenthau the real estate lawyer noted this was the first legal contract of record. It was also "the first assignment of property to the Hebrew people in the Holy Land."

With the advent of Christianity and then of Islam, these patriarchs and their wives were revered by all three faiths, and Machpelah became a shrine that each claimed exclusively. The tombs held to have been erected over the gravesites were enclosed with a wall constructed of enormous granite blocks dating back at least to the reign of Herod. In the era of Byzantine Christendom the tombs were housed in a church. Under Muslim rule this structure was converted to a mosque. The Islamic rulers had been primarily interested in excluding Christians; for some 650 years prior to Morgenthau's visit the tombs had been accessible only to Muslims, with a few notable exceptions.*

Looking back at Morgenthau's visit to Hebron in 1914, it is apparent that the balance of ethnic and religious forces was destined to shift drastically but unpredictably. The Ottomans, in an effort to

---

*An important breakthrough had come in 1862 when, after much diplomatic negotiation, access to the tombs was granted to the British Prince of Wales (later Edward VII) during his visit to Egypt and the Holy Land. His admission to the Caves of Machpelah set a precedent for future visits by royalty and heads of state, or their ambassadors, with their entourages. In 1862, His Royal Highness was accompanied by an Anglican divine, the Reverend Arthur P. Stanley (later Dean of Westminster), who had engineered the visit. Stanley wrote a fascinating account of what he witnessed in his *History of the Jewish Church*, which had come to Morgenthau's attention when it was reprinted in 1913 by Charles Scribner in New York. In writing home, Morgenthau referred his family to the Stanley work, which I found many years later in his personal library.

stabilize their shaky empire, were preparing to make one last desperate attempt to rid themselves of all disloyal elements by staging their habitual massacres and deportations. This policy also placed Arab nationalism under Turkish suspicion, although in practice it was mitigated by the Arabs' overwhelming numbers and shared Muslim religion.

From the time the Muslims gained control of the Holy Land until the nationalist ambitions of the Zionists were fully revealed, the Muslims tolerated the Jews as an insignificant minority. For their part, the pre-Zionist Jews had been less interested in real estate than in protecting their Covenant from co-signers. Ephron, the Hittite, had at first offered Abraham the Machpelah caves as a gift. But Abraham insisted on the purchase in order to maintain the permanent separation of his family from the Canaanites. Later on, first Christianity and then Islam took form under the guidance of men who were ultimately rejected by the Jewish establishment. When the Muslims conquered the Holy Land, they claimed Jerusalem and Hebron as two of their four most holy places. As fierce guardians, they were expressing both their hostility toward infidels and fear of the patriarchs, who were believed to dwell eternally in their tombs in a state of "suspended animation."

When Morgenthau entered the restricted environs of Machpelah, guards held back an angry crowd who had delayed their noon prayers in favor of the honored infidels. "The same looks and deep murmurs of disapproval accompanied us as we entered the sacred portals of the mosque," Morgenthau noted. After inspecting the tombs of Abraham, Isaac, and Jacob, they were told that the tombs of Sarah, Leah, and Rebecca would be accessible only to the women in the party. "They explained that the Mohammedan rule, that men might not look upon the faces of women, applied to the dead as well as the living."

A few minutes later, Dr. Franklin Hoskins, the American Arabic scholar and missionary, suggested that Morgenthau invite the entire group to join in silent prayer.

"I did so, and there we stood, Moslems, Christians and Jews — all of us conscious of the fact that we were in the presence of the tombs of our joint forefathers — that no matter in what detail we differed, we traced our religion back to the same source, and the ten minutes to which this prayer extended were undoubtedly the most sacred that I have ever spent in my life."

Morgenthau's ecumenical euphoria continued through the evening, when he returned to Jerusalem to give a dinner for fifty-two at the Jewish Hotel Kamnitz. They all remained until after eleven o'clock at what turned out to be "an epoch-making affair," because of the "tremendous importance that people in Jerusalem are giving to the fight that is being waged between the factions as to which language should be the dominant one. I had become thoroughly familiar with the real feeling prevalent among the masses, and there is no doubt that it is overwhelmingly in favor of Hebrew." Consistently throughout his journey Morgenthau had been surprised to discover "the greatest enthusiasm for Hebrew and for nationalism. It does not seem to be a question of religion as much as it is a question of race."

Before leaving Jerusalem, Morgenthau had a farewell visit with the governor: "We had a very long talk about the Jews." The governor complained of "the absence of any leaders amongst them." He spoke of the need for "a leader whom they all recognize and with whom the authorities could deal." These were certainly Morgenthau's sentiments as well. He had found the misery of the people in Jerusalem deeply disturbing and in terrible contrast with the vigor of the Jews in the new agricultural settlements.

In Nablus, Morgenthau found that the governor had been prompted by a telegram from Talaat in Constantinople to extend every courtesy. The ambassador was weary of "Turkish dinners" and "formal receptions." But what really troubled him was the feeling that he was out of touch with the Muslim sensibilities in the community.

Honoring the ambassador's desire to rectify the situation, the governor of Nablus showed up at the hotel one evening to escort Morgenthau and his party on a tour of the Arab community. They set out on foot, preceded by the chief of police and three constables, "each carrying a table lamp instead of the ordinary lantern." As Morgenthau recorded in his diary, "We walked through the dark streets . . . here and there a shoemaker at work and a fruit store open . . . turning corners and twisting, breathing in a fine aroma, until we landed suddenly in a square with a fountain playing."

The party were all ushered into two well-illuminated rooms with cushion-covered divans and fine carpets on the walls. Some twenty-four Arab men sat cross-legged on the divans. They were discussing the effect the new railroad would have on their principal business, soap exports, when there would be larger shipments than could be transported by camel. The Arabs spoke with great pride of their lineage. "They looked, indeed, with their intelligent faces and dignified bearing, like men bred of good stock." One man claimed to have evidence that his family had resided in Nablus for five hundred years; another "traced his lineage back to the prophet Mohammed. . . . Nothing could have been more gracious or hospitable than their manner toward us." More to the point, Morgenthau believed he had been granted a brief, if carefully orchestrated, glimpse of how Arab men conduct themselves on their own turf.

On April 21 Morgenthau wrote Wise that these experiences had been "the most delightful . . . I have ever had in my life." In this moment he felt closest to his old friend and mentor, gripped in a bond of intimacy too tight to last, for Wise was attuned to the weaknesses in his friends and associates, manipulating them unconscionably on behalf of his passion, Zionism. Morgenthau was fundamentally opposed to an independent Jewish state, but at that point he was sympathetic and open to Zionist seduction. Always eager to make things happen, he proved all the more valuable to the Zionists because of his acknowledged skepticism.

"I am impressed that there must be a strong desire amongst the masses for nationalism, as otherwise they could not keep their agitation alive," he had written Wise from Constantinople. "It seems to me that recent victories of the Greeks and the practical independence of the Arabs in the Yemen district have much encouraged the Jews. They seem to feel that the only solution of their present trouble is in national independence." At the same time he was trying to ascertain "whether this desire for nationalism emanates from the masses or whether it is fanned by agitators."

Looking beyond his observations of the moment, Morgenthau remained fearful about the outcome of all he had witnessed. "Has it ever occurred to you," he asked Wise,

> that if the Jews again become a nation either in Palestine or elsewhere, while they are developing and before they reach (even if they ever could) such importance that they would have their own army and navy, they would in case of prosperity become a prey to the cupidity of some great power who is so equipped that it should easily destroy

them? Would it therefore not be a great deal better if they continued to spread amongst other nations and take advantage of the great results that they attained in the last fifty years in England, America, France, Italy and elsewhere?*

Morgenthau, the assimilationist, persisted in his belief that Jews would be better advised to "retain their religion and show their character and idealistic aims that Judaism stands for and would undoubtedly make an impression on all nations that absorbed some of them. If Christianity had been satisfied with a local national existence in the country of its birth, what would have become of it and where would it be now?" Finally, he advised Wise, "I want you to know that I am studying this problem, perhaps with greater advantages, though not with near the preparation that some of you folks have had, and that I shall unhesitatingly express my conclusions when they take definite shape."

As a fitting climax for Morgenthau's Palestine excursion, Wise had arranged a visit with the fabled pioneer agronomist Aaron Aaronsohn. Wise had met Aaronsohn in the United States when he came to Washington as a guest of the Department of Agriculture, following his discovery of wild emmer wheat growing in the Galilee. At that time, Aaronsohn was introduced to some of the United States' most powerful Jews, and he gained their support for his agricultural experiment station at Athlit, outside Haifa. Morgenthau was impressed by its all-star board of directors, which included Julius Rosenwald as president, and Paul Warburg, Henrietta Szold, Louis Marshall, and Judge Julian Mack.

The Aaronsohns were a tightly knit family of gifted, fiercely independent individuals. As a six-year-old, Aaronsohn had arrived with his parents and siblings from Romania, to settle in the fledgling farm community at Zikhron Jacob. Prior to meeting Morgenthau, Aaron had been a farm manager in Anatolia, Turkey, where he acquired an intense antipathy for the Turks.

Morgenthau and Aaronsohn hit it off immediately. Describing their first evening together, Morgenthau wrote to his family (and Stephen Wise), "Such a jontefdick [holidaylike] dinner I have not had in a long time. . . . I have never in my life seen Jewish men and

---

*Interestingly, Germany, where Jews had advanced so dramatically, was not included in his list of countries of opportunity.

girls look as fine, robust, honest, self-reliant and independent as these people did. They showed the result of honest toil and open air; and the way they danced, the decency thereof, puts to shame the gilded youth of America. There was not a sign of sensuality or impropriety. It was really a great delight, and I cannot speak too enthusiastically about it."

Then in the same paragraph, as though to put the brakes on his own euphoria, Morgenthau wrote of "a very long conference with some of the leaders of the colony" when they told him "they thought they might have to eventually drive out the Arabs," who at that time constituted a six- or seven-to-one majority of the population and owned about two and a half percent of the land. "This is one of the most troublesome questions in connection with the development of Palestine."

Ending their Palestine visit at Tiberias, the ambassador's party crossed the Sea of Galilee in a small boat and was escorted from there to the Syrian capital in Damascus. Palestine was then an undefined area within the Ottoman Syrian province, so there were no clear borders. Yet for all its geographic vagueness, Palestine signified something very specific, especially to the Jews and the British, which set off strong negative vibrations among Turks, Arabs, and Britain's European rivals. When Morgenthau called on the governor in Damascus, "he told us he had little hope for adjustment between Turks, Arabs, Kurds and Jews." The governor suggested "they should destroy all mosques, churches and synagogues and begin over."

At this time the Americans remained aloof from all the international power plays. The substantial presence of U.S.-sponsored Protestant institutions radiated an aura of high-minded idealism. In 1914 there was no significant conflict of interest between Jews and Protestants. In Beirut Morgenthau gave himself over to the Syrian Protestant College crowd, but without neglecting urgent summonses from the Jewish, Armenian, and Greek Orthodox communities. On the *Scorpion,* moored in the Beirut harbor, the ambassador and his wife entertained lavishly and ecumenically at an afternoon shipboard reception for "all the College faculty, the Hospital [associated with the college] people, the Jewish community, B'nai B'rith head, with 150 or so." The college catered to the proportionately large Christian population in Lebanon, many of whom had found refuge there from oppression in other parts of the Ottoman Empire. Others, including Jews but few Muslims, were attracted by the educational advantages.

At the end of April, when Morgenthau returned to the embassy in Constantinople on board the *Scorpion,* the Hebrew language daily, *Ha-Heruth,* printed an article stating that "all were suddenly notified that the American Ambassador had been urgently called back to Constantinople. It was said that Ambassador Morgenthau had been called to Washington where he would be appointed to a very high government post, perhaps Secretary of the Treasury . . . According to the press, the American government is planning to appoint a Jew, Mr. Ira Morris, as its representative in the Ottoman capital in place of Mr. Morgenthau."

It is difficult to understand how or why this story was written. One can only speculate, but the most likely source would have been Morgenthau himself or one of his traveling companions. The only light shed on this mystery is a letter to Morgenthau from Senator Hamilton Lewis dated April 27, 1914, and marked "Very Personal" (it was discovered among the Morgenthau papers at the Library of Congress).

"It is again bruited about from very reliable authority," the senator's letter began, that Morgenthau would be appointed to the board of the Federal Reserve New York District bank. "But as the responsible rumor goes, you are to be put in line for the successorship to Secretary [of the Treasury William Gibbs] McAdoo." The rationale was that McAdoo, who was engaged to marry President Wilson's daughter, Eleanor, would find it prudent to resign.

"Of course it will be necessary that you be present in the country and in touch with the finances as they are projected by the government in order that you not be passed over for *some one near at hand pressing themselves.*"

"The point of my writing to you this note," Lewis concluded, "is to ask you to co-operate with me in the designation of our friend *Ira Morris* as your successor . . . One prominent Jewish citizen in one of the big places — of financial responsibility in Government, and another — succeeding to a position in the diplomatic — would be a dignified and appropriate recognition of a great class of people — who will no doubt appreciate a Democratic administration in its effort to properly reward the Jewish people."*

---

*Whatever reasons Senator Lewis had for his speculations they were wildly off the mark. McAdoo stayed in the treasury until after the armistice in 1918. During the war years he

Senator Lewis's letter, dated April 27, must have been received long after the April 29 article in *Ha-Heruth*. Though it corroborates the prevalent rumors, it could not have been the source of the story. Accident or a "trial balloon," it would seem to have been awkwardly launched from a point of origin that would have been highly suspect if the letter had attracted attention. Yet, however fanciful, this kind of speculation points to Morgenthau's unfulfilled ambitions. Attesting to this are many newspaper clippings and letters that he preserved. They also underscore his ambivalence about demanding recognition as an American and expecting to collect tribute as a Jew.

Stephen Wise was convinced that Morgenthau's trip to the Holy Land was a win for the Zionist cause, or what he prudently referred to as "the new Palestine." He was "truly happy" to note that Morgenthau had been "converted to the view that the Jews be given a chance to develop their desire, as you put it, for a quasi-national existence." As though to lock in the profits of his qualified victory, he acknowledged that Morgenthau was "catholic and sympathetic enough to understand the depth of Jewish feeling in the matter, and that surely something will be gained by helping our fellow Jews to make this great experiment in the art of racial self-reliance." Wise relentlessly pressed his advantage. He had taken the initiative in organizing a commission with a vague mandate "to survey all the needs of the Jews of Palestine." He had also designated Morgenthau as a sponsor and personally obligated him for a portion of its financial support. Another sponsor, Jacob Schiff, had become alienated by the bitter "language dispute" that had brought the plans for the Haifa Technikum to a grinding halt.

Wise clearly realized that "the matter is really a very serious one." When they met in February 1914, Schiff had told him that if a minority of Jewish nationalists gained the upper hand in "the language dispute," Schiff would withdraw his support. Wise understood the broader implications: "Apart from my own little commission which might fall by the way . . . it would seem to me a very great injury to Jewish interests there if Schiff stepped out." Wise feared a domino effect, with rich Jews in the United States and

---

consolidated his power, taking on a number of additional key positions, including the chairmanship of the Federal Reserve Board, and was widely considered Wilson's political heir to the presidency.

Europe falling in line. Nevertheless, when Schiff did indeed act on his warning, Wise chose to take it as a personal insult.

The eminent rabbi proceeded to weep acid tears on Morgenthau's shoulder, expressing his customary sense of other people's obligations to his cause. In a May 18 letter he deplored Schiff's "failure to keep his promise which I asked not for myself . . . but for an undertaking which is as much his concern as it is yours or mine." In this way Wise managed to escalate their disagreement into a personal vendetta. "He will no longer exist for me," he wrote Morgenthau. "I have gotten along without him and I shall continue to do so. If the continuance of my work depended on his support I would rather that it end this hour. I thought that Schiff was big enough to see that having accepted nothing for myself I was merely inviting him to share an important burden."

Both parties called on Morgenthau to negotiate a cease-fire. But Wise, irrepressible in his righteous indignation, wrote Morgenthau, "Personally I would not speak to Mr. Schiff. For I would not ask anything of him. . . . But I thought that knowing the circumstances, you might write and ask him."

Despite his distress over the battle between these two willful titans, Morgenthau was unable to mediate their quarrel. "It is too bad you and he are not working in harmony for the furtherance of Jewish interest," he wrote Wise, "but I am afraid you are both of such positive natures that it is difficult for you to adjust to each other."

Eventually Morgenthau cut his links with the Wise Commission after he received a sharp letter of inquiry from the State Department. From the outset he had been "by no means enthusiastic" that the commission would discover anything beyond what had already been concluded — namely, "that there should be control over the money sent to Palestine and that something should be done to prevent Jerusalem from becoming an international poorhouse." Concerned that Wise might refuse to accept his no for an answer, Morgenthau warned,

> I am sure you are the last one who wants to do anything to jeopardize my standing with the [State] Department or my influence here, so I beg of you not to make any effort to obtain consent of Secretary Bryan [to re-establish Morgenthau's sponsorship of the commission] because he will think I asked you to do so. . . .

I am going very far in using my official position to benefit the condition of the Jews in Turkey, particularly in Palestine and Syria, and it would be a great pity if I was to take one step too far and by so doing undo the good that has been done.

But during the first days of August the Wise Commission issue — along with everything else in the Near East — was swept aside by the outbreak of war in Europe.

Witness to the Armenian Massacre

ORGENTHAU'S TWO-YEAR-OLD GRANDDAUGHTER Barbara Wertheim (later Tuchman), her parents, and two sisters were on board the *Sicilia,* a small Italian passenger steamer, in the Aegean Sea on their way to the American embassy in Constantinople for the family's summer vacation. The historic events that took place at sea and after they reached port "became a big family legend," Tuchman recalled. "I've told it many times, but I didn't remember it personally." Almost fifty years later, in *The Guns of August,* she described the scene without reference to its autobiographical connection, stating that "the daughter, son-in-law and three grandchildren [herself included] of the American Ambassador, Mr. Henry Morgenthau . . . brought an exciting tale of the boom of guns, puffs of white smoke, and the twisting and maneuvering of faraway ships." Indeed, the Wertheims had witnessed the exchange of fire between the British light cruiser *Gloucester* and the two elusive German warships the *Goeben* and the *Breslau.*

When Tuchman decided to "do a book about 1914 as a critical moment in modern history, really the start of the twentieth century," she had at first thought of simply writing about the escapades of the *Goeben,* but then decided that she needed a "broader canvas; certainly the family stories about the episode made the whole thing a lot more alive for me."

Although Tuchman had no recollection of the historic skirmish at sea, she retained "a memory of the visit to Constantinople, that seems almost impossible because I was only two. And yet I have a memory and I tested it a few years ago [1976] when I went to Turkey." She recalled a "white marble" building and "tall dark trees." In Istanbul, what had been the embassy in 1914 had later become the consulate. With great difficulty she managed to be driven there. "I just had a chance to look in and sure enough it was white marble and there were tall, dark graveyard trees." It was an impression that "must have been somehow stuck in my mind."

Stephen Wise wrote Morgenthau on August 13, "I hope with all my heart that the Wertheims big and little have reached you in safety and that you will all be comfortably housed throughout the crisis." He concluded, "The President is doing magnificently."

War had been fatalistically anticipated, like some dreaded natural disaster. Although almost no one believed it could be prevented, some were already calculating its effects and planning for the aftermath. As the contending parties raced toward collision, all claimed to have God on their side.

From his vantage point in Constantinople Ambassador Morgenthau saw the war fulfilling his darkest presentiments about German militarism. Throughout his life, he had staunchly maintained that the antidemocratic, bellicose German spirit seriously threatened world peace. Though some German Jewish families maintained links of blood and commerce with the *alte heimat,* the Morgenthaus had permanently severed all such ties as soon as they arrived in America.

Public opinion in the United States was mixed. As a Jew with substantial German connections, Jacob Schiff was adamantly neutral. His continuing bond with the Germans and a long-standing hatred of their enemy, czarist Russia, for its brutal treatment of Jews, seemed in harmony with his Americanism. Wise was also propeace at first and opposed Wilson's accelerated commitment to military preparedness.

Morgenthau began to observe the German warlord mentality, epitomized by Ambassador Wangenheim. Morgenthau's apprehension grew as he witnessed Wangenheim's blatant disregard for international agreements and manipulation of corrupt Turkish officials. But, as usual, prophetic vision was heeded too late.

Morgenthau could see Enver steering Turkey into the German camp, while Talaat remained skeptical about it. Djemal, the least consequential member of the triumvirate, preferred friendship with the

Allied powers. Single-minded and ruthlessly determined, Enver maneuvered his compatriots into making irreversible decisions binding Turkey to Germany, overlooking the risks of being swallowed up in the process.

Ambassador Morgenthau could see that the Germans intended to make Turkey not so much an ally as a vassal state under the skilled direction of Baron von Wangenheim, a complicated and explosive man, who dominated "not so much by brute strength as by a mixture of force and amiability."

Wangenheim held to the Prussian policy of keeping "our governing classes pure, unmixed of blood," but nevertheless went out of his way to cultivate the American Jewish ambassador and his family, whom under any other circumstances he would have found socially unacceptable. Morgenthau never allowed himself to be taken in by "the Kaiser's personal representative, fundamentally ruthless, shameless and cruel," but was admittedly "affected by the force of his personality."

Joining Wangenheim to help rebuild Turkey for German purposes, the extraordinarily talented General Liman von Sanders had come to Constantinople in December 1913 specifically to reorganize the Turkish army. His arrival attracted little notice. The Sublime Porte was accustomed to receiving German army and British naval missions. Like Baron von Wangenheim, General von Sanders found it prudent to ingratiate himself with Morgenthau. "I think Liman is one of the nicest men that I have ever met, and I expect to make quite a friend of him," Morgenthau wrote his family in New York. "He told me that the Emperor talked with him for two hours the day he asked him to accept this post, and for three quarters of an hour when he said goodbye to him. . . . He is a widower and has two daughters. I expect Ruth will have them as her friends." Things did not work out that way.

The ragtag army that the Turks handed over to General von Sanders was completely demoralized. The officers, with salaries three and a half years in arrears, could not afford uniforms. When Morgenthau invited some of them to an embassy reception, they begged to be allowed to wear evening dress; when the grand vizier vetoed this suggestion, they were obliged to absent themselves. The enlisted men could not even be drilled because they had no shoes.

Army conditions exemplified the general state of destitution in the empire. Whereas Enver was enthusiastic about the prospects for

Prussification, Talaat believed, as he told Morgenthau, "that he was using Germany, though Germany thought it was using him." However, with the infusion of German funds and expertise, the military transformation was phenomenal. One Sunday afternoon in January 1914, Morgenthau and his son were given a two-and-a-half-hour tour in the new French Panhard automobile owned by the heir-apparent to the sultan. "As you ride through the country," the ambassador noted, "you really think that you are passing through an encampment. We met at least six different regiments of soldiers drilling, exercising and maneuvering."

With all resources concentrated on mobilization, conditions for the general population grew ever more desperate. Out of 4 million adult males, more than 1.5 million were eventually conscripted. Soldiers were paid about 25 cents a month, and their families received an allowance of $1.20 a month. Evasion of military service was a crime punishable by death. One could obtain exemption by payment of about $190, a sum almost no one could afford.

Similarly, the requisitioning of supplies "amounted to wholesale looting of the civilian population." Most merchants were not Muslims, and Morgenthau thought the Turks seemed to find "a religious joy in pillaging the infidel establishments." Even more devastating was the requisitioning of livestock regardless of civilian needs. Thousands of people were left enfeebled and starving. Morgenthau later estimated that the empire had "lost a quarter of its Turkish population since the war started."

Enver, as minister of war, seemed without compassion for his people and was impressed only by "his success in raising a large army with practically no money." But his true strength lay in German hands. A rapid succession of dramatic events locked Turkey's destiny with Germany's, and it became clear that Turkey had forfeited its right to any independent choice of options.

Perhaps the outcome was inevitable. At the outbreak of war, on August 2, Turkey and Germany had signed a secret agreement to ward off aggression from Russia, for centuries the primary threat to Turkish security. Since England and France were allied with Russia, the Turks were obliged, however reluctant some might have been, to join the German-Austrian camp.

A week after the Wertheims observed the *Goeben* and the *Breslau,* the ships arrived at the straits of the Dardanelles. Having escaped the vastly superior British naval forces, the Germans had no choice but to enter neutral Turkish waters. To the British, such a violation of international law was unthinkable. But when the Germans demanded to have their warships take shelter in Turkish waters, Enver, with no time to consult his peers, single-handedly acceded. In what turned out to be an instant of momentous historic importance, Enver had resorted to a thinly disguised ploy permitting the Germans to "sell" their men-of-war to the Turks. On the rechristened *Jawus* and *Midilli,* the German officers donned fezzes and steamed through the straits to safe harbor. The kaiser now virtually held the Turkish government hostage.

Boisterous German arrogance knew no bounds. Ambassador Morgenthau made note of a day when "the *Goeben* sailed up the Bosphorous, halted in front of the Russian Embassy . . . The officers and men lined up on the deck . . . all solemnly removed their Turkish fezzes and put on German caps." Thereupon, the sailors, accompanied by a military band, serenaded the Russians with "'Deutschland Über Alles,' 'Watch on the Rhine' and other German songs" before once again donning their fezzes and steaming back to their station.

In the first weeks of the war, the Turks, maintaining their officially neutral position, deluded no one but themselves. Wangenheim boasted to Morgenthau that the Dardanelles could be closed to shipping within half an hour. On September 27, on the flimsiest of pretexts, the German general in charge at the mouth of the straits did just that. "Down went the mines and the nets. The lights in the lighthouses were extinguished." When Sir Louis Mallet and Morgenthau rushed to lodge their protests with the grand vizier, they were shocked to learn that his government had received no advance warning. In one stroke the Germans had severed Russia's only warm-water lifeline and isolated the country from its allies.

It took only one more stroke to maneuver the Turks into war. A few days after the straits were closed, three Turkish gunboats entered the harbor of Odessa, with German officers in command. It was the religious holiday of Baivam, and there were few Turks on duty. Without provocation, the Germans attacked Russian and French warships and shelled the town. Still it was only in late October that the Russians, faced with no alternative, declared war on Turkey.

The U.S. ambassador suddenly found himself confronted with challenges of far greater magnitude than he had anticipated. As the

Allied envoys left, they put their embassies and their nationals in his custody. At intervals he became responsible for safeguarding a total of eight national groups. The situation became particularly difficult when the Turks, furious with the British and French as their military forces tried to storm their way back through the Dardanelles, announced that they were sending the two or three thousand Allied citizens in Constantinople to Gallipoli "as targets for the English and French ships." At the time it seemed like "an ingenious German scheme to discourage the English blockading fleet, not unlike the stationing of Belgian men and women in front of the advancing German armies in Belgium." As the last mediator on the scene, Morgenthau, who had remained on good personal terms with Enver, went to bargain with him. Enver "finally consented to send only fifty and the youngest men be selected." Soon afterward Morgenthau's successful haggling for these hostages "brought the party back without loss."

The ambassador's greatest challenge came not in protecting enemy aliens, however, but in trying to stop minority persecution within the empire. As in earlier times of stress, the Turkish government resorted to scapegoating those who were neither Turkish nor Muslim. The only possibility for benign intervention seemed to be the neutral Americans.

Ambassador Morgenthau kept the State Department informed with cables describing Near East developments and his analysis of them. He received little feedback and less guidance except occasional cautionary admonitions, which he chose to interpret as a license to exercise his best judgment, consistent with American ideals. But while the voices in official Washington remained muted, the voices of private constituencies — especially Christian missionaries and Jewish organizations — came through loud and clear. They were all Morgenthau needed to be prompted to vigorous action.

Early in 1915 Turkish officials began to interfere with communications from the interior. Morgenthau meanwhile was receiving alarming news about Palestine from Grand Rabbi Nahoum in Constantinople and the organized Jewish community in New York. Furthermore, the Turks, while planning their "final solution" for the Armenians, seemed to have a similar fate in mind for the Jews and other minorities under their control.

When the war began, nearly everyone imagined it would end

quickly, probably with a settlement negotiated by the United States. This expectation hardly mitigated fears among Ottoman Christians and Jews that once they were cut off from the benevolent concern of the Europeans the Turks would destroy them. For the Jewish community in Palestine, heavily dependent on outside aid, the prospect of economic strangulation was especially frightening. No one was more disturbed than Ambassador Morgenthau, who had gained a thorough understanding of the precarious situation during his visit to the Holy Land.

On August 28, acting quickly and decisively, Morgenthau cabled Jacob Schiff in New York for help through official State Department channels:

> PALESTINE JEWS FACING TERRIBLE CRISIS. BELLIGERENT COUNTRIES STOPPING THEIR ASSISTANCE. SERIOUS DESTRUCTION THREATENS THRIVING COLONIES. FIFTY THOUSAND DOLLARS NEEDED BY RESPONSIBLE COMMITTEE.

Schiff passed the word to Louis Marshall, president of the American Jewish Committee, "suggesting" a meeting of the committee "at once."

The committee convened on August 30. Early on September 2, Schiff, on his own initiative, cabled Morgenthau "accepting your suggestion, and authorizing you to go ahead in carrying it out." Later that same day he notified Morgenthau: "We had a meeting of the executive committee of the American Jewish Committee, which approved of what I had done, contributing from their own funds $25,000, while I undertook to add $12,500 and it is expected that the American Federation of Zionists will furnish the remaining $12,500, but be that as it may, the entire $50,000 will be at your disposal as soon as we hear from you to whom to remit."

Ambassador Morgenthau arranged with the Standard Oil Company to have the initial gold payment from the United States released through Standard's representative in Constantinople. From there, it was transported aboard a battle cruiser, the USS *North Carolina,* with his son-in-law Maurice Wertheim serving as his personal emissary.

Delivering the American gold and seeing to its equitable distribution among the Palestinian Jews' was a difficult, highly visible assignment, which inspired mixed reviews from the local Jewish press. The Palestine Jews were acrimonious and fragmented, split between the Zionist agricultural colonies and the religious groups concentrated in Jerusalem. A supposedly representative committee led by Dr. Ruppin, head of the Zionist office in Jaffa, was authorized by donors in New York to set up a loan institute. At Morgenthau's suggestion, Aaron Aaronsohn, managing director of the Jewish Agricultural Experiment Station at Haifa, was added to this body. All of these men were ardent — though not necessarily political — Zionists, but religious Jews, the conspicuous minority in representation, were vocal in their claims.

The American battle cruiser *North Carolina* entered Jaffa harbor on Thursday, September 24, 1914, like a miraculous apparition. Dr. Ruppin, in the company of the new American consul, the Reverend Otis A. Glazebrook, welcomed Mr. Wertheim. "There was a large crowd on the land-station to witness the scene," Ruppin reported to Morgenthau. "The fact that the son-in-law of the American Ambassador on board an American cruiser has brought subsidies from the United States for the Jews of this country has deeply impressed the Palestinian population and will no doubt have a wholesome effect on people's attitude . . . and the people have become aware of the fact that, although the Jewish community here is not yet strong as far as the number of its members are concerned, it receives strong support from our co-religionists abroad."

The gold itself, which Wertheim carried in a suitcase, caused great excitement. According to Ruppin, it was immediately deposited in the Anglo Palestine Company Building. Barbara Tuchman recalled her father telling the story of locking himself in a room with the gold and refusing to come out until the loudly disputing parties reached an agreement.

The same day, Dr. Ruppin wrote Morgenthau that he had given Wertheim "the same tour which I have made with you of the Jewish colonies in the Jaffa–Tel Aviv area." Two days later, Saturday, Wertheim received the heads of several institutions in Jerusalem "and requested them to inform other Jerusalemites that the money was not intended for individuals who lived on charity, but to aid in its hour of need the *yishuv* which supported itself by productive work." Concerned with matters of life and death, these meetings appear to have been exempt from Sabbath restrictions. "On Sunday morning Mr. Wertheim visited the Haham Bashi [the title accorded by Ottoman rulers to the chief rabbis, and in Palestine to the chief Sephardic rabbi] and at two that afternoon the Haham Bashi accompanied by several members of the committee, returned the call." The following day the distribution committee went to Haifa to meet with Aaronsohn and make the final arrangements for apportioning the funds. Everything had been "done with lightning speed, in the American way."

Before the end of 1914 the Wertheim clan were all back home in New York. Wise wrote Morgenthau that he thought Wertheim's "visit to Palestine and what he did there will make a permanent difference throughout his life. We had the delight of seeing Alma as well as Maurice and those three lovely little girls."

Morgenthau had served as the catalyst in a feat of international social networking that momentarily saved the frail Jewish community from extinction. It was a historic benchmark but not a turning point in a battle during which mortal threats continued to mount.

By the beginning of November the Germans had finally manipulated the Turks into the war on their side, an alliance that never gained much popular Turkish support. Among the ruling triumvirate only the kaiser-worshipping minister of war, Enver Pasha, nicknamed "Napoleonik," was an unabashed enthusiast. Yet all three were flattered to be courted by the great powers.

Morgenthau recalled that in November 1914 "a great demonstration" was held at the Haidar Pasha Railroad Station. "All the members of the Cabinet and other influential people" had assembled to bid godspeed to Djemal, who, as minister of the marines, had been given the unlikely task of commanding the Fourth Turkish Army, with headquarters in Syria.

Morgenthau, who had established a personal bantering relationship with Talaat and Enver, could find no socially redeeming graces in Djemal: "His private life was profligate . . . his enormous vanity . . . his laugh, which disclosed all his white teeth, was unpleasant and animal like . . . he was undersized, almost stumpy and stoop shouldered." Though whenever "he shook your hand, gripping you with a vise-like grasp and looking at you with those roving, penetrating eyes, the man's personal force became impressive."

Morgenthau had received a letter from Dr. Ruppin in Jaffa dated October 19, which, while not mentioning Djemal by name, contained "alarming news from an absolutely reliable source" that the new kaimakam (deputy of the grand vizier) "who will leave Constantinople to come here, has been instructed by Talaat Bey to proceed against the Jews with great vigor, and hinder their work in the country as far as possible."

Djemal shouted bombastically to the crowd from his train as it jerked out of the station, "I shall not return to Constantinople until I have conquered Egypt." This melodramatic demonstration served to make it clear to Morgenthau that Djemal was only a somewhat embarrassing extremist in his advocacy of the Pan Turkish policy that was rapidly gaining the ascendency. "He despised the subject peoples of the Ottoman country — Arabs, Greeks, Armenians, Circassians, Jews; it was his determination to Turkify the whole empire."

On February 23, 1915, Morgenthau wrote Louis Marshall in New York, "The government here desires the Russian Jews to become Ottomans, and in order to bring this about they do not hesitate to use the worst kind of threats, smilingly telling me that they have no intentions whatever to carry them out."

The cat-and-mouse game the Turks were playing with the Palestinian Jews was nothing new. But with the abrogation of the Capitulations protecting foreign nationals and the removal of European protection under war conditions, the situation had become much more ominous. On the one hand, the Turks were threatening to deport their minorities; on the other, they were inclined to hold them hostage and set them up to attack each other. As a result, the Turks, no friends of the Arabs, encouraged Arab nationalism in a manner calculated to arouse Arab hostility toward the Jews, as they had encouraged the Kurds to slaughter the Armenians.

In January 1915 an official proclamation signed by Beha lel Din, Djemal's secretary, and directed against the Zionists, appeared in Jerusalem's Hebrew and Arabic papers. It proved highly effective in unleashing the Arabs, notably in the vicinity of Jaffa and Haifa. They began assaulting colonists on the pretext of their "insulting the name of the sultan" and being "traitors against the government." According to one report, "At one village about twelve or fifteen Arabs came in and began to create a disturbance. When asked why they had come they answered 'We want to prepare you for tomorrow, we are going to kill all of you!' In another colony the Turkish military officer directed a colonist to deliver to him a certain young girl."

As the Jews in the agricultural colonies in Galilee and the Jaffa region were rendered increasingly defenseless, many felt compelled to become Ottoman citizens. But in Jerusalem they were trapped in a Catch-22 situation. On January 6 Ruppin wrote Morgenthau that there were an estimated eighteen thousand Russian Jews in Jerusalem who were "wholly destitute and therefore unable to pay the tax of frs. 37.50." Later the amount was reduced to 25 francs, "but even this sum was above their means." Finally, it was rumored that all those who could prove they were without means would be exempt. Nevertheless, as Ruppin explained, several thousand Jews would be forced to leave Palestine, some because they had property in Russia, which would be confiscated if they became Ottomans, and others because "the interruption of all postal communications deprived them of remittances from Russia."

During the first critical months of 1915 the U.S. State Department and especially the Navy speedily responded to the plight of Palestinian Jewry. Secretary of the Navy Josephus Daniels, who had an abiding fondness for Morgenthau, acted with State Department approval to put naval craft in the area at the ambassador's disposal. One was the USS *North Carolina,* which had carried Maurice Wertheim and his satchel full of gold to Jaffa. The following January the USS *Tennessee* was ordered to Alexandria to confer with the U.S. consul and Jewish leaders. The *Tennessee*'s extraordinarily able captain, Commander Renton C. Decker, performed his task with enthusiasm beyond the call of duty. Strictly interpreted, his mission was to protect Americans and their personal interests, but he extended it to general mercy. Negotiations had been completed for the evacuation of Palestine Jews to refugee camps in Alexandria. Some one hundred imprisoned leaders were released, followed by an outpouring of thousands of destitute Jews. Ruppin had written Morgenthau that for those who "cannot afford to pay for their passage even in the third class, the sending of the USS *Tennessee* here with orders to receive all refugees and transport them to Egypt is of very great help, for which the Jews cannot be thankful enough." Morgenthau wrote home crowing, "It is a great thing to have a country back of you that puts a couple of warships at your command."

When the USS *North Carolina* steamed into Jaffa harbor in August 1914, its imposing presence was as significant as the satchel full of gold carried by the ambassadorial messenger. Later there would be much larger sums of money, and U.S. ships would bring in essential supplies and carry harassed refugees out to safety. The American mission was supported, not without complications, by the Allied powers, with much of the funding channeled through German banks, even when the war was on, aided by Schiff-Warburg connections.

The Jews remaining behind in the Palestinian farm colonies were determined to maintain a bridge to the future of Eretz Israel and were fully conscious of the risks involved. They knew their tiny foothold could be erased forever, and frankly told the captain of the American rescue ship, Commander Decker. Although he had no personal or cultural links to the tragedy, he reported to his superiors back in Washington with an amazing sense of urgency: "The existence of Zionism is at stake and all [the colonists'] efforts are concentrated on preventing its extinction. . . . if this great movement were killed now it [is] doubtful [whether] it could be revived."

At this point, Djemal, preparing the Turkish defense against the Egyptian campaign, stripped the Palestinian countryside and its inhabitants of all resources. Almost no one believed that his campaign would succeed, but many feared that if his troops were routed, they would take revenge on anyone in the path of retreat.

By the end of 1914 the Jews had been systematically disarmed. At first they were conscripted into the Turkish Army, but in short order the Turks relegated them to labor battalions, as they had with the Armenians, Greeks, and other minorities, rendering them impotent. The ruling Turkish triumvirate had further cleansed the government of all who quibbled with their uncompromising, hard-line policy, encouraged by their German overlords.

At his post in Constantinople, Morgenthau immediately responded to the Jewish community's desperate needs and worried that increasingly aggressive Zionist activities, both in the Near East and the United States, would trigger vicious reprisals, beyond his power to mitigate.

Morgenthau had good cause for alarm. Intending to flatter his old friend, Wise wrote, "We had a splendid meeting in Boston of the Zionist organization . . . Mr. Brandeis again and again made reference to the great help which you have rendered in safeguarding, as American Ambassador, all interests in Palestine." Morgenthau, not easily taken in, replied, "It is rather dangerous for [the Zionists] to say much at present about their ambitions as to Palestine." He informed Wise that the Halil Bey, the minister for foreign affairs, had reminded him,

"Just see how the Armenians are treated for their nationalistic tendencies!" As the Central Powers have at present the upper hand in this great conflict, the Turks . . . will not allow themselves to be trifled with and are apt to indulge in some more excesses if any provocation is given them. They are now hard at work trying to Turkify their country in every way, and I beg of you for the sake of all the Jews that are living here, that you try to exert your influence to have no bomb thrown from America. It is utterly impossible to convince the Turkish authorities that Zionism is anything else but a political move to create a Jewish state on Turkish territory.

I have no objections to your showing this letter to some of the others who are interested in Zionism, particularly Mr. Brandeis.

Morgenthau's fears of similar fates for the Armenians and the Ottoman Jews were never realized. In fact, it was the weight of a foreign presence — including his own — that proved the Jews' saving grace.

In 1915 Talaat and Enver raised state-sponsored massacre to the level of genocide.* As would happen a generation later in Germany, the prevailing philosophy relied on extreme chauvinism with a heavy overlay of mythic heroics. The intention in Turkey was to restore national pride through Ottoman absolutism, or "Turkification." Those who resisted or were deemed unworthy were condemned as enemies of the state.

While all Ottoman minorities were on that list, which included Jews, Kurds, and Arabs, the Armenians came first. Plans to exterminate the Armenians were already under way when World War I began. They were handy scapegoats and were doubtless longing for the freedom that voices from Russia and abroad were calling for. Moreover, Turkish philosophy, as expounded by Ziya Gokalp, set forth the idea of a pan-Islamic federation reaching into Russia and encompassing all the Turkish provinces along that country's southern flank, a thrust that would more than replace the lost European empire. Non-Turkic and non-Muslim, the Armenians stood directly in the way of this dream. They had to be eliminated: first in Turkey (under cover of the war), then across the Russian border.

In Turkish Armenia, most of the villages and small towns were inhabited by peasants and artisans, while in Constantinople and

---

*Although the term *genocide* had not yet been invented, Rafael Lemkin, a survivor of the Holocaust who coined the word after losing forty-nine members of his family to the Nazi terror, noted that the fate of the Turkish Armenians in World War I came under his definition of the word.

other urban centers many Armenians were well-educated and prosperous — bankers, civil servants, merchants, intellectuals, artists, and skilled craftsmen. The sophisticated Armenians who could afford it sent their children to Europe — especially Paris — to be educated.

Following the secret alliance with Germany, the Turks proposed at the congress of the Dashnak party for Armenian independence in Erzurum to grant the Armenians autonomy in exchange for their organizing a rebellion against the Russians in the Transcaucasus. But the Dashnaks, mistrusting the CUP, rejected the offer, though they did join with the Armenian churches in declaring loyalty to the Turkish state. The men enlisted or paid the exemption tax more willingly than the Turks themselves and submitted to requisitioning of their goods and livestock. As Ambassador Morgenthau noted in his diary, Talaat told him the CUP preferred the Armenians' financial resources to their military service.

Once the war had begun, the Turkish leaders became doubly apprehensive when the czar approved the formation of an Armenian volunteer corps to fight against Turkey and proceeded to tour the front himself. Overruling the top Dashnak leadership's cautioning, two high-profile Armenians, Karekin Pastermadjian (also known as Armen Garo), a member of the Ottoman Parliament, assisted in leading one corps, and the so-called Armenian Robin Hood, Shabin Karahissar, an Ottoman citizen, led another.

As early as February 1914 Talaat had begun to formulate secret plans for the total liquidation of the Armenians. In August the *valis* (provincial governors) received sealed orders outlining a scheme for extermination to be carried out by "special organizations" composed largely of hardened criminals released from prison. A Turkish general described them as "butchers of men saved from the gallows or impalement." They had been selected to "protect" the Armenian refugees as they fled.

In December 1914, in the dead of the freezing Caucasian winter, Enver committed his Third Army to an offensive from Erzurum to Sarikamish. Defeated more by weather conditions, with accompanying disease and starvation, than by the Russians, Enver nevertheless blamed Armenian treachery. Of the 90,000 soldiers sent into battle, about 15,000 returned. So it was that immediately after April 20, when the Armenians in the city of Van tried to defend themselves, the Turks began wholesale massacres on the pretext of deporting the Armenians from border areas where they were reported to be collaborating with the enemy. Many of the communities affected were in fact nowhere near the borders.

On the night of April 23, the Turkish government arrested some two hundred leading Armenians in Constantinople. They included a member of Parliament, later sent on a mission outside the city and assassinated, as well as business, educational and community leaders, and artists.

On April 24, Talaat Pasha, as minister of the interior, dined with Ambassador Morgenthau at the embassy. Talaat readily admitted that, knowing from his own experience how easy it was to stage a revolution, he planned to put the Armenian leadership "among Turks in the interior where they could do no harm." A few days later at the German embassy, Talaat acknowledged that his worry over an Armenian insurrection had been fabricated. But more arrests soon followed, including more than 650 of the Armenian elite in the capital. Still, because of their high visibility, most of the Armenians in Constantinople were left alone. Some of them, with means and connections abroad, escaped.

Since Armenian slaughter was nothing new, the world was in one sense conditioned to Turkish brutality. At the same time the murder of a nation — an enormity so far beyond human comprehension that it tended to be received with skepticism — was only gradually gaining credibility, so as the nations of the world stood by, the Turks proceeded with their plan.

Communications between the Turkish interior and the capital city, always difficult, had been virtually halted. Though the United States maintained diplomatic relations, the normal courtesy of allowing consuls to report to their embassies was ignored. Still, some news managed to leak out to Washington through missionaries and consuls in the field.

In Constantinople, Ambassador Morgenthau discovered that his best source of information was the German embassy staff, their Turkish allies having permitted them untrammeled communications. Thus on March 28 he learned from Wangenheim that the Turks were disarming Armenian soldiers under their command, and he soon discovered the full treachery involved. As soon as these soldiers were disarmed, they were segregated into work battalions, under surveillance of "Special Organization" gendarmes. They were then marched off and simply disappeared. Some were worked to death. Others were shot or clubbed to death after being forced to dig their own graves.

Deprived of their able-bodied men, the women, children, and old men were given short notice to dispose of their possessions and prepare for deportation. The dispersion was supposed to be a temporary security measure, but as soon as they were out of town, Muslim refugees from Europe were moved into the empty houses.

Morgenthau was horrified by the consistency in the tales he received of bands of defenseless, terrified people stripped of all their possessions, sometimes literally naked, marched south through rugged mountain and desert terrain. In the process many expired from starvation, thirst, disease, and attacks. Babies were born in dire circumstances, while women and girls were raped by Turks and Kurds and the gendarmes ostensibly provided to protect them.

When Ambassador Morgenthau knew the full extent of these Turkish atrocities, he took on the lonely role of self-proclaimed champion of the Armenian people. For want of alternatives, he turned in desperation to the Turks' German overlords. Despite German militarism's intransigent ruthlessness, he hoped that they could be persuaded to intercede on behalf of the Armenians as a Christian minority victimized by Islamic rulers. Since he had established a good working relationship with Wangenheim, Morgenthau felt emboldened to seek his cooperation in a scheme for massive Armenian emigration that had been approved by the Turks — for the time being.

Wangenheim refused. He had, however, one wry suggestion. If the Americans would take some Armenians to the United States, the Germans would send some to Poland. In exchange they would send some Polish Jews to Turkey, if they would agree not to participate in Zionist schemes. His motive was that he believed having Jews at the Polish-German frontier was undesirable. This cynicism was contrary to the views of many Germans, who, along with other Europeans, had a history of concern for Armenian Christians.

On July 31, 1915, Dr. Johannes Lepsius, president of the German Orient Mission, called on Ambassador Morgenthau at the U.S. embassy for what proved a fruitful exchange of information. With permission from Washington, Morgenthau opened his files to Lepsius, who proceeded to disclose the facts to the German people and the International Red Cross. A notable consequence was Franz Werfel's novel *The Forty Days of Musa Dagh,* based in large measure on documents Lepsius collected.

In March and early April defenseless Armenians in small, isolated northeastern communities fled to some of the larger centers. Van, capital of the Vilayet (province) on the Russian and Persian frontiers, became the major refugee asylum. In Van the Armenians constituted the majority. Considerably more prosperous than their Turkish and Kurdish neighbors, they lived in their own quarter. Until the war, relationships among these disparate groups had been reasonably harmonious, under the rule of a moderate *vali* (governor). He was replaced by Enver's brother-in-law, Djevdet Bey, who had been raised in Van, where he was known to be an unstable, treacherous character. Right after his appointment he served in the Turkish Army in the Russian offensive and shared in that humiliating defeat. He favored "nailing horseshoes to the feet of his Armenian victims," for which he became known as the "Horseshoer of Bashkale." This was an embellishment of a more common form of torture, the bastinado, which consisted of beating the soles of the feet with a thin rod until they gradually swelled and burst.

With the arrival of spring in 1915, the Russian troops who had advanced across the Turkish border retreated. Then, during a three-day period starting April 15, in about eighty villages north of Lake Van, some 24,000 Armenian men, women, and children were brutally violated and murdered. Some young women were handed over to Turkish custody. A few of the men escaped to Van.

On April 20, in Van, a couple of Armenian men who tried to save a few women from Turkish soldiers were shot dead — whereupon Djevdet Bey, with a well-equipped army of 5,000, opened fire on the Armenian quarters. Hastily organized, the Armenian resistance numbered only about 1,500, armed with three hundred rifles and a meager supply of ammunition. In time they would attempt to replenish this with homemade bullets made from melted candlesticks and the like. Some of the resisting Armenians eventually took refuge in the American missionary compound, which Turkish artillery subsequently bombarded, setting much of the town on fire.

Rumors filtered in to Van that the Russians were again advancing. For a month the little band of Armenians and missionaries, including young children, miraculously held their ground. On May 19 the Russians arrived and the Turks fled, leaving behind the rotting bodies of some 55,000 Armenian victims.

Joachim (Chaim) Guggenheim was born in Lengnau, Switzerland, in 1770. He immigrated to Hürben in southern Bavaria, where he married, prospered, and later died in 1853. His daughter, Babette, married Lazarus Morgenthau in Hürben in 1843.

Below left: In 1842 Lazarus followed his older brother Bernard to Hürben, where there was a thriving Jewish community. The brothers served as assistant cantors in the Hürben synagogue, which the Nazis destroyed on Kristallnacht, November 1938. *Below:* The marketplace in the 1920s. It had changed little from the time when Lazarus earned a meager living here as a young tailor.

In 1849 Lazarus Morgenthau moved from Bavaria across the Rhine River to Mannheim in the independent duchy of Baden, where he prospered briefly as a cigar manufacturer. This artfully enhanced photograph, taken in 1855, shows Lazarus and Babette with their burgeoning family the year before the birth of their ninth child, Heinrich (Henry Sr.).

Lazarus Morgenthau was a member of the reform Hauptsynagoge in Mannheim when the congregation moved into this handsome new home in 1855.

The building was gutted by fire on Kristallnacht, November 9 and 10, 1938.

After suffering business reverses in Mannheim, Lazarus Morgenthau moved to New York City with his family in 1866. *The Golden Book of Life* was a fund-raising scheme that he invented and administered with great success.

Lazarus playfully posed (with an unidentified man) for this photograph, referring to himself as "the eighty-year-old youth." He died at eighty-two in 1897 at the Mount Sinai Hospital in New York.

In 1870 the fourteen-year-old Henry Morgenthau (Sr.) worked in a law office for four dollars per week, serving papers and working as a copyist.

Henry Sr. (right) graduated from Columbia Law School with Samson Lachman (center) and Abraham Goldsmith (left). They formed the Lachman, Morgenthau, and Goldsmith partnership. In this 1886 photograph they are playfully masquerading as a mandolin trio.

Josephine Sykes (far right), her siblings, and parents, circa 1873. Her father, Samuel, was born in Prussia and later immigrated, via Manchester, England, to Detroit in 1853. Her mother, Helen Himmelreich (Heavenrich), was born in Frensdorf, Bavaria (near Bamberg), where she wed Josephine's father in 1853.

Courtesy of Joan Auerbach Dumont, granddaughter of Bella Sykes Buchman.

Josephine (center), before her wedding in 1883, with her widowed mother (third from left) and sisters.

Josephine and Henry Morgenthau, shortly after they were married in New York in 1883.

Henry Morgenthau, Sr., proud and loving father, with his only son, Henry Jr., born in New York, May 11, 1891.

In his dorm room at Phillips Exeter Academy, Henry Jr. was a handsome but extremely unhappy member of the class of 1908. Directly over his head is a photograph of "Pa." Below, to the right, is his favorite sister, Alma.

While Henry was struggling at Exeter, his future wife, Elinor Fatman, was getting top grades at Miss Jacobi's school for girls in New York. Later at Vassar, class of 1913, she became an accomplished amateur actress.

A few months after Henry Morgenthau, Sr., arrived in Turkey as the U.S. ambassador, he toured the Near Eastern Ottoman territories, including the Holy Land. In the garden of the U.S. consulate in Jerusalem, April 3, 1914, left to right, in Western garb: Consul Samuel Edelman; Ambassador Morgenthau; Richard Whiting, head of the American colony (missionaries); Josephine Morgenthau; A. K. Schmavonian, principal embassy attaché; and Miss Ruth Morgenthau.

A telegram from Ambassador Morgenthau, September 3, 1915, dispatched in the midst of the Turkish massacre of the Armenians, led to the formation of what later became the Near East Relief Committee, now the Near East Foundation.

Courtesy of the Near East Foundation.

After Morgenthau returned to New York he joined the relief organization's executive committee. In this 1919 photograph he is seated (left) next to Cleveland Dodge, Woodrow Wilson's wealthy Princeton classmate, who organized the committee at his own expense.

Courtesy of the Near East Foundation

Henry Morgenthau, Jr. (far left), in a Turkish army uniform. From the embassy in Constantinople the ambassador dispatched his son to inspect the German-Turkish positions on Gallipoli at the end of December 1915, just before the final British withdrawal.

Henry Jr.'s sisters (left to right), Alma, Helen, and Ruth, were bitterly jealous of the unabashed favoritism shown to him by their father. At the same time, they all adored "Pa."

The U.S. ambassador and his son are greeted by family in New York Harbor, February 22, 1916. Left to right: son-in-law Morty Fox, Ruth (back turned), Josephine, son-in-law Maurice Wertheim, and Alma.

Elinor Joan Fatman married Henry Morgenthau, Jr., on April 17, 1916, in her parents' brownstone house, 23 West Eighty-first Street in New York. The bridegroom's niece Josephine Wertheim was the flower girl, and his nephew Mortimer J. Fox, Jr., was the page.

Elinor's father, Morris Fatman, at the wheel, with two uneasy passengers, his wife, Settie, and older daughter, Margaret, in Mamaroneck, New York, circa 1910.

Mayer and Babette (Newgass) Lehman (seated in the center) were the maternal grandparents of Elinor Fatman Morgenthau. On the far right is their youngest son, Herbert. On his right (from back to front) are Elinor's parents, Morris and Settie (Lehman) Fatman and their older daughter, Margaret. On the far left (back to front) are Phillip, Hattie (Lehman) Goodhart, and daughter Helen (Altschul).

Elinor and her oldest son, Henry III, born January 11, 1917, were delighted with each other from the very beginning.

The future D.A., Robert M. Morgenthau, looks down disapprovingly as brother Henry clutches baby sister Joan, circa 1924.

Black Beauty, the Shetland pony that nearly did me in, with (left to right) Nana, our beloved nurse, at the reins, my brother, Bob, and me.

Above left: Top to bottom: Henry III, Jerry Straus, and Bob Morgenthau build a playhouse on the farm, circa 1927. *Above:* Henry Morgenthau, Jr., bought his Dutchess County farm in East Fishkill in 1913. This farmhouse was the Morgenthau family home until 1929.

Above: "The Homestead" was the Morgenthau family's Dutchess County home from 1929 on. Remodeling of this spacious abode was completed a few months before the October stock market crash. *Right:* All the Morgenthaus on horseback, 1934. Left to right: Robert, Henry Jr., Joan, Elinor, and Henry III.

Henry Morgenthau, Jr.,
always denoted his profession
as farmer.

Twice a year Fishkill Farms paid him dividends of sheer ecstasy: first when the delicately scented apple blossoms opened, around the time of his birthday, May 11.

And then in the fall, when the boughs were bent to the point of breaking, laden with red and golden fruit.

In June 1931 at Manchester, then a fashionable seaside resort north of Boston, some old Wilson Democrats were busy lining up party stalwarts behind a new Roosevelt-led team. Left to right: Senator David I. Walsh, Colonel Edward House, Governor Franklin D. Roosevelt, Boston Mayor James Michael Curley, Senator M. Coolidge, and Henry Morgenthau, Sr.

As Henry Sr. sought to secure a position for Henry Jr. in FDR's orbit, the old man looked for opportunities to enjoy life. But in this photograph, taken in 1929 in the Glendale motion picture colony of greater Los Angeles, he and his friend Adolph Ochs, publisher of the *New York Times,* both appear rather ill at ease posing with silent film star Madge Bellamy.

Rabbi Stephen S. Wise had been Henry Morgenthau, Sr.'s, close friend and mentor until they fought bitterly over Zionism. They had a momentary reconciliation at the White House in 1938.

The Old Guard on the first morning at Binghamton! 1928
Franklin D Roosevelt

Above: Henry Morgenthau, Jr., was active in all of FDR's political campaigns, from the 1920 vice presidential race on. During the 1928 gubernatorial campaign he served as Roosevelt's advance man.

Left: Henry III and Henry Jr. take a back seat, observing the preeminent politician at work.

Below: By the time Roosevelt reached the White House, Morgenthau was a fixture at his side. For Henry's wife, FDR had inscribed this picture "from one of two of a kind."

for Elinor from one of two of a kind
Franklin D Roosevelt

In June and July the situation seemed to improve, despite a typhus epidemic. But toward the end of July word came that the Russian troops were again falling back in the face of a Turkish counterattack. The Russian commander ordered all the Armenians and the missionaries to evacuate with his army. The missionaries, their caravan marked with the Red Cross insignia, were attacked by Kurds in a narrow mountain pass. This time Cossacks and Armenian volunteers came to the rescue. Finally, on August 10, the refugees arrived in Tiflis, over the Russian border, looking so filthy and ill that they were initially refused hotel lodging.

The first details came to Morgenthau by way of the German embassy. Immediately after the Armenian stand-off began on April 20, Morgenthau found the Turkish government referring to an Armenian revolutionary uprising, which from then on they would persist in using as the pretext for their relentless extermination efforts.

Although Morgenthau's previous intervention on behalf of Turkey's French and English nationals had succeeded, his Armenian appeals were flatly rejected. Relief funds for survivors, mostly from the United States, were sent to American nationals for field distribution. But Enver informed Morgenthau, "We don't want the Americans to feed the Armenians . . . it is their belief that they have friends in other countries which leads them to oppose the Government and so brings down upon them all their miseries. They must never know that they have any friends in the United States." Talaat, always more frank than Enver, told Morgenthau, "We have got to finish with them . . . No Armenian can be our friend after what we have done to them."

Talaat boasted, "I have accomplished more toward solving the Armenian problem in three months than Abdul Hamid accomplished in thirty years." Later Talaat demanded that Morgenthau provide a list of Armenians with American life insurance policies. Since they lacked heirs, Talaat reasoned, the Turkish government was their rightful beneficiary. Morgenthau, of course, refused.

On August 11, Ambassador Morgenthau cabled the State Department, "It is difficult for me to restrain myself from doing something to stop this attempt to exterminate a race, but I realize that I am here as an Ambassador and must abide by the principles of non-interference with the internal affairs of another country." He nevertheless proceeded to make suggestions for U.S. intervention.

First, a direct government-to-government appeal from the United States to Turkey that "on behalf of humanity" the present campaign should cease. Second, "if our present relations permit, that an official appeal be made to the Emperor of Germany to insist on Turkey, his ally, stopping this annihilation of a Christian race." Third, that "an official demand be made without delay" for opening channels of outside aid to "Armenians already affected by Government deportation."

Morgenthau received no response for almost two months. In the meantime Robert Lansing, who had succeeded William Jennings Bryan as secretary of state, was advised by the Division of Near Eastern Affairs that "however much we may deplore the suffering of the Armenians we cannot take any active steps to come to their assistance at the present time."

The State Department, however, had no objection to the ambassador himself going public with accounts of atrocities. When they found no way to deal directly with his appeals, they frequently turned his lurid cables over to private American religious and charitable agencies, to be published in support of their relief efforts.

On September 6, John Reed, an itinerant American journalist (later the most active American supporter of the Bolshevik revolution), interviewed Morgenthau in Constantinople. Reed queried him about rumors that he had offered to donate personally $1 million to fund an Armenian exodus. Morgenthau stated that in fact he had offered to raise money if the Turks would let the Armenians go. "I told him the U.S. might prove the Moses of the Armenians," Morgenthau wrote in his diary. Subsequently, when the Turks withdrew their offer to let the Armenians leave, the matter became moot. But as a result of widespread press attention, public support began for the Armenians' plight.

On September 16, the American philanthropist Cleveland Dodge convened a small meeting in his New York office of the Armenian Atrocities Committee, which had been organized primarily in response to Ambassador Morgenthau's pleas. What they imagined would be a short-term emergency operation would grow into the biggest effort for refugee relief to date. Harkening to the cry "Remember the starving Armenians," they would expand internationally to become the great Near East Relief Agency. Those who met with Dodge in the early stages were primarily Protestant clergy (plus Rabbi Stephen Wise, at Morgenthau's suggestion) and philanthropists. Unlike the parallel Jewish relief efforts, organized entirely by Jews, there appeared to be no Armenian-Americans with the wealth and prestige to participate effectively in fund-raising, and no Armenians were serving on the Armenian Atrocities Committee.

The Turks and Germans by then had collaborated in their grim answer to the Armenian question. Only a remnant survived. Over a million had perished.

In the autumn of 1915, a Dr. Nossig, newly arrived from Germany, came to call on the American ambassador. He claimed that the reason for his journey was to work against the Zionist. But it was soon evident to Morgenthau that he was a "German political agent." However, Dr. Nossig showed little knowledge of Morgenthau's nature when he tried to confide in him on a Jew-to-Jew basis. Nossig wanted to persuade Morgenthau that his activities on behalf of the Armenians were irritating the Turkish government to the point of their asking for his recall. "All of us Jews are proud of what you have done and we would hate to see it end disastrously."

Morgenthau dismissed this threat and sent Nossig scurrying back to Wangenheim with the stern pronouncement that he "could think of no greater honor than to be recalled because I, a Jew, have been exerting all my powers to save the lives of hundreds of thousands of Christians."

Nevertheless, as the year 1915 waned so did Morgenthau's inner sense of his effectiveness in Constantinople. "My failure to stop the destruction of the Armenians," he recalled, "had made Turkey for me a place of horror — I had reached the end of my resources."

In September the ambassador arranged for his wife, who was as shattered by the turn of events as he was, to return to the United States. Living alone in the embassy, cut off from all members of his family, Morgenthau became increasingly depressed. But in December he was cheered considerably by a visit from his son, for whom he had arranged an official (unpaid) State Department temporary appointment. On December 29 he sent Henry Jr. on a five-day tour of inspection of the German-Turkish positions on Gallipoli, an experience the young man would always remember. Only a few days later the hard-fought struggle for control of the Dardanelles was all over.

On January 17 there was a great victory celebration in Constantinople. The ambassador had come to realize that any hopes he harbored of being effective as the representative of a neutral United

States and the Allied powers were by then in vain. "You seem to represent all our enemies" Talaat told him cheerfully.

At the end of January 1916 Ambassador Morgenthau obtained home leave. Accompanied by his son and his devoted dragoman, Schmavonian, he boarded the newly completed Balkan Zug (train) to begin the first leg of his return trip to New York, with a stopover in Berlin, where the United States still maintained diplomatic relations with the kaiser.

· 15 ·

The Homecoming

AT ABOUT 7:30 A.M., February 22, 1916, the Danish liner SS *Frederick VIII* steamed into New York harbor. Standing on the bridge, anticipating the welcome in his honor, was the homebound American ambassador to Turkey, Henry Morgenthau. In his diary, Morgenthau noted, "Arrived at the quarantine at 5 A.M. We got up very early, had our breakfast and were on the lookout for the boat which was to call for me."

The ambassador dressed for the occasion in formal morning attire, wrapping himself in a mink-lined overcoat as protection against the raw wind.

The slender young man at his side, half a foot taller, was the ambassador's adored only son, Henry Jr., who had remained with his father in Constantinople during the siege of the Dardanelles, after his mother and sisters had been sent home. Both father and son wore the same rimless pince-nez, made fashionable by President Wilson, with strong lenses for their deep-set, nearsighted eyes. The glasses pinched the flesh of their prominent noses, making them ever so slightly less hawklike.

In the long years ahead, Ambassador Morgenthau would recall this hour of return to New York harbor among his finest. But at the time he was still brimming with ambitions that would prove elusive. Just before his return to the United States, the newspapers were speculating that he would be appointed secretary of war, replacing Lindley Garrison. The source of these rumors was not disclosed. But they prompted Morgenthau to announce on his arrival that things had quieted down in Turkey and he felt it was a good time to come to this country to consult with the authorities in

Washington and with Americans who have interests and philanthropies in Turkey. He had asked for two months' home leave. His hidden agenda, however, was quite different. In fact, he planned to tender his resignation and offer his services as fund raiser for the 1916 presidential campaign.

Morgenthau's hope of receiving a cabinet post or some other high-level administrative position in the political mainstream, which had been frustrated during Wilson's first term, now appeared more likely than ever. He believed he could capitalize on the high visibility he had attained as the courageous, would-be savior of the Armenians and as the protector, under the American flag, of the expatriates of all the Allied nations. This had, after all, gained him currency in the Protestant Establishment. Nevertheless, he continually found himself placed in context as a Jew, which was not meant as a put-down but rather as added praise.★

References to his special aptitude as a Jew always made my grandfather uncomfortable. He much preferred the kind of nonsectarian tribute he received from Nathan Straus. YOU HAVE THROWN LUSTER ON PURE AMERICANISM, proclaimed his old friend, IN STANDING UP FOR JUSTICE AND RIGHT, AS AGAINST OPPRESSION AND MIGHT. But when the Yiddish press declared "Mr. Morgenthau is our national hero. It would be most advisable and fitting to give [him] a Jewish welcome," he found it expedient to put aside his aversion to what seemed to him narrow parochialism. Indeed, he could hardly have prevented it.

On the morning of February 22, as the *Frederick VIII* slowed to a standstill, the ambassador observed the little Coast Guard cutter *Manhattan* maneuvering through the heavy veil of mist and spray, almost directly below the side of the great liner. Morgenthau caught sight of his good friend Cleveland H. Dodge, who was aboard the *Manhattan*. Morgenthau waved his arms in a broad, vigorous semaphore, which Dodge saw and returned.

Cleveland Dodge was a true Christian gentleman, the scion of a staunchly Presbyterian family. It was virtually inevitable that he

★For example, the *Christian Science Monitor* noted, "The genius of the Jew combined with his acceptability to the Turk, must have proved unquestionable assets to Mr. Morgenthau in his efforts to assist the Armenians during the last terrible persecution in the Near East. And when the history of the past few months can be told with safety to all concerned, it is perfectly certain that there are few men who will stand higher in the estimation of the American people than the American Ambassador to the Sublime Porte" (*Christian Science Monitor*, March 3, 1916).

would go to Princeton.* Though he continued in the family copper business, he committed his heart and considerable energies primarily to Near Eastern Protestant missionary educational institutions, for which his family provided stewardship as well as underwriting, and which included Robert College in Constantinople and the Protestant Syrian College in Beirut. Dodge's son, Bayard, was then working at the latter, having married the daughter of its president. At the time of Ambassador Morgenthau's return, Cleveland Dodge was anxious about his son's safety.

One of the journalists who had gone out on the cutter to cover the story described the ambassador's arrival: "Lowering himself on the ladder from the ocean liner to the cutter, Mr. Morgenthau belied his sixty years by the youthful agility with which he handled himself. He seemed in the prime of health and spirits as he pushed aside the crowd to embrace his wife and two daughters, Mrs. Wertheim and Miss Ruth Morgenthau."

Henry Jr. tagged along behind his father. Josephine Sykes Morgenthau reached out her arms first to her husband and then to her son, smothering them with passionate hugs and wet kisses. With her emotional guard down, she was quick to feel hurt when the response seemed unequal to her insatiable hunger for love, and she pushed back as impulsively as she had grabbed. Her lips were tightly compressed in a severe line, and her unstylish hat was planted squarely on her head; her figure had become shapeless. The whole effect seemed to defy the elegant formality of the occasion. This was abundantly obvious to her husband, who appreciated his wife's good taste in all other matters of beauty. Daughters Alma and Ruth were slim and modishly turned out in fur hats, their hands buried in matching muffs. Their sister Helen, oldest of the four siblings, had decided to wait on the dock.

A brief family reunion at Pier A ended abruptly when a drably dressed young man presented himself to the ambassador as a State Department courier and delivered a sealed envelope. Morgenthau, with the reaction of the lawyer he was, recoiled as though he were

---

*During his undergraduate years, in the famous class of 1879, Cleveland Dodge forged a close friendship with classmate "Tommy" (T. Woodrow) Wilson, who, according to another "'79er," sought out "certain wealthy and rather sporting men who were very influential in guiding the policy of the class and certain more general college matters" (*The Prince Remembers — One Hundred Years of the Daily Princetonian,* Judy Piper Schmitt, ed., "T. Woodrow Wilson, Managing Editor," by Nicholas A. Ulanov, p. 25). Wilson and Dodge both remained on campus to receive M.A. degrees in 1882.

being served with a subpoena; but in a second, his composure restored, he opened a letter from the secretary of state, Robert Lansing. It was intended to restrain Morgenthau's well-known undiplomatic conduct: "While I realize that a large number of our fellow citizens will wish to offer you testimonials as a recognition of the splendid work which you are doing, it would seem to me that, in view of the international situation, a public meeting, however carefully arranged, might have unhappy results."

This letter had been triggered by an inquiry from a group called the Central Committee for the Relief of Jews Suffering Through the War which wished to offer public recognition of services Morgenthau had rendered in Palestine and Turkey. The secretary concluded, "Please pardon me for this suggestion, and also in giving you a word of warning in regard to newspaper reporters, who may misrepresent you and whom it is well to avoid as far as possible."

Morgenthau slipped the Lansing letter into his jacket pocket and went right ahead to expound volubly to the press while posing for pictures with his family and members of the welcoming committee.

The full membership of the mayor's welcoming committee, as it was published in all the newspapers the next day, was a glittering roster of more than sixty men and one woman who would not often find themselves in one another's company. Not all of them managed to be present. Jacob Schiff, who made it a practice to meet other Jews on his own turf, wrote that he would be happy to receive Morgenthau at home the following week so that they could have a good tête-à-tête. The Jewish Establishment was nevertheless well represented by three old Morgenthau colleagues, Rabbi Wise, Louis Marshall, and Lillian Wald, and by leaders of the financial community, including James Speyer, Isaac Seligman, and Adolph Lewisohn.

At a time when the city abounded with newspapers, the press barons were enlisted on the welcoming committee in strength. Adolph Ochs, publisher of the *New York Times,* was a close family friend, and Morgenthau had served as his real estate broker in acquiring the Forty-second Street property on what became known as Times Square. The *New York World* was represented on the committee by its second-generation scion, Ralph Pulitzer, as was the *Tribune* by its publisher, Ogden Reid.

Also on the committee were leaders of the city's institutions of higher learning, including the despot of Morningside Heights, Columbia University president Nicholas Murray Butler; Seth Low, who had left the Columbia presidency to become mayor of New York; and John Huston Finley, who had been president of the College of the City of New York, and was at this time state commissioner of education (he would later become associate editor of the *New York Times*).

Dodge had rounded off the committee with a sprinkling of politicians, some of Morgenthau's business and law associates, and a goodly representation of his own peers in the Protestant Establishment. Some of them, like Frank Vanderlip, president of the National City Bank, were staunch Republicans. Others, like Charles R. Crane, had joined Dodge in contributing early and heavily to the Wilson treasury, under Morgenthau's stewardship.

Dodge's remarks in introducing Morgenthau to the assemblage were emotional and personal: "I could trace the history of this man and tell how he made his own way from poor boy, . . . untried, to a most difficult post, where he has proved himself the peer of the greatest diplomats of Europe."

The press noted the following day, "Mr. Dodge's son [Bayard Dodge] is associated with the college at Beirut and is said to be dependent for his safety on the diplomacy of the Ambassador to Turkey, which accounted for the emotion shown by Mr. Dodge who began to sob."

Morgenthau rose to the occasion in his response: "When I went to Constantinople I had only one interest to look after. However, it soon became necessary for me to make an umbrella of the American flag. I was the man with the umbrella. . . . The first people to come under the umbrella were of course the Americans in Turkey, and because I was a Jew, came the Jews of all nationalities. Then the English, French, Belgian, Serbian, and Swiss citizens crowded under. The Armenians tried to come under the umbrella, but since they are Turkish subjects I could not give them official protection."

Morgenthau took pains to make the journalists in attendance aware of the "confidential" letter he had received from Secretary Lansing. Just short of reading it out loud, he referred to it in a way that heightened the drama of his return, as the front-page stories the next day made clear.

"As [Morgenthau] stated . . . in his speech to the reception committee, this letter warned him to be guarded in what he said. At the first opportunity, Mr. Morgenthau got on the long-distance telephone and had a brief talk with Washington." The *New York World* reported that, denying "with sharp emphasis that any basis existed for a report that he might succeed to the War portfolio, the Ambassador said 'I have been at my post for two years and four months. . . . All that I can say is that I had an unusual opportunity to serve my country and I have gloried in the doing.'"

There seemed to be no stopping the ambassador, so intoxicating was the spirit of the occasion: "If this reception is a sign of the way public service is appreciated in this country, it ought to be an encouragement to other men."

Then, someone interrupted, shouting, "How are the Jews being treated by the Turks?" Morgenthau snapped back, "They are being treated very well, there is no trouble about that."

It was time to go home for lunch. The ambassador pushed his way through to the back of the crowd to Josie and his daughters, escorted them to a waiting limousine, and ordered the chauffeur to drive to 30 West Seventy-second Street. His goodbye wave was cheerfully regal.

At home Henry and Josie's big extended family assembled in the ample oak-paneled dining room for lunch and a private celebration of the public events that had reflected honor on them all.

Only Henry Jr. was conspicuously absent. He had slipped away unnoticed sometime during the course of the morning. In the middle of lunch the father was summoned from the table to talk with his son on the telephone. What Henry Jr. had to say signaled a turning point in his life that would be as memorable in the annals of the family as this landmark day of distinction in the career of the ambassador.

The Secret Mission

BETWEEN THE TIME of his triumphant return from Constantinople in February 1916 and President Wilson's re-election in November, Morgenthau was back at his old post raising campaign funds. He was again magnificently successful. Once victory came at the polls in November and the United States entered the war in April 1917, all kinds of special tasks beckoned to eager patriotic leaders. But to his dismay and disappointment Morgenthau was again completely passed over.

On May 16, 1917, in an office overlooking the west side of the White House, Secretary of State Robert Lansing received the sixty-one-year-old ex-ambassador to Turkey. Morgenthau, who knew from past experience that the cautious Lansing regarded him warily, opened the conversation by apologizing that he had come to make a proposition the secretary would probably consider fantastic and visionary. He had come to suggest "a separate peace with Turkey." "That is not fantastic," Lansing answered immediately, "though the way to go about it may be."

Morgenthau believed the Turks might be open to a secret approach from the Americans. He held that the Turks were tired of their German allies and of the war. Only the likelihood of German retaliation and the certainty of financial dependency kept the Ottoman Empire fighting. Men like Talaat, grand vizier and leader of the most nationalistic faction in the ruling triumvirate, and Enver, the pro-German minister of war, might be wooed by bribes or pacific overtures. If so, Morgenthau thought they could be persuaded to allow Allied submarines to slip past the mines and submarine nets in the Bosphorus and destroy the German warships

Goeben and *Breslau,* whose guns dominated Constantinople; and, as Morgenthau pointed out, the Turks could conceive of no greater disaster than its bombardment. With the Germans de-fanged, he argued, a hastily negotiated separate peace might be possible "on very favorable terms for the Allies."

Lansing found this plan "to say the least startling." Morgenthau's motives undoubtedly included a wish to do something spectacularly important. Earlier that day Lansing had had a long conversation with Henry Alsberg, the young, Harvard-educated private secretary of Abram I. Elkus, who had succeeded Morgenthau in Turkey until diplomatic ties were severed in April, when the United States declared war on Germany. Alsberg had heavily stressed the war-weariness in Constantinople. Food shortages as well as dislike of the Germans and apprehensions about Turkey's future militated against continuing Turkish participation in the war. Significantly, Alsberg had said that only the threatening presence of the German warships *Goeben* and *Breslau* kept the Turks fighting. The heart of any settlement would be the preservation of Constantinople; the Turks would probably "give up Palestine, Syria, and Armenia in order to hold Constantinople, even though it were under a practical protectorate like Egypt."

Whether Morgenthau had earlier conferred with Alsberg before meeting Lansing is unknown, but Morgenthau had spoken with Louis D. Brandeis, Supreme Court Justice, leading American Zionist, and highly influential Wilson adviser. The matters discussed between them most likely were related to Morgenthau's Turkish proposals.

Morgenthau had some reason to believe he was on good terms with Brandeis, although he was not a Zionist himself. In the first place, he had been Wilson's emissary to Capitol Hill in the uphill campaign to get Brandeis confirmed on the Court. He had also shown a great willingness to participate in Zionist fund-raising efforts after returning from Turkey. Nevertheless, there was a certain coolness between the two men. Morgenthau had wanted Brandeis to run for the Senate from Massachusetts against Henry Cabot Lodge shortly after Brandeis's confirmation to the Court. He believed Brandeis could easily beat Lodge, giving the Democrats a valuable seat. It seems inconceivable that Brandeis would have considered making the shift, but Morgenthau later attributed Brandeis's refusal to a lack of courage. Quite simply, Brandeis was little interested in conventional party politics, preferring to remain aloof from certain aspects of political struggles. Though Brandeis and Morgenthau had in common their backgrounds as prosperous, self-made lawyers who had shifted their talents to public service, the gap between them widened as their opposing positions on Zionism deepened.

The night after Lansing met with Morgenthau and Alsberg, the secretary decided their suggestions were worth passing on to the president. Cautioning that there was less than "one chance in fifty of success," he concluded that "we ought not to ignore any chance, however slight, of gaining so tremendous an advantage as would result from alienating Turkey from the Teutonic Alliance."

On May 21, after having received the Lansing memo, the president dropped in at Lansing's home, where they discussed the Morgenthau proposal and hastily concluded that it "possessed sufficient merit to warrant attempting it." If it succeeded, it would be a significant factor toward ending the war. If it failed, the situation would be no worse than before. The two men agreed that Lansing should discuss the matter with the British foreign secretary, Arthur Balfour, who was at that moment making the rounds in Washington to drum up American support for the British war effort.

Balfour was a high-minded but pragmatic intellectual Scottish aristocrat. Nearing his seventieth year, he had served Conservative and wartime coalition cabinets in a variety of posts, including prime minister. His firm commitment to Zionism harmonized with his aspirations for defending and strengthening the British Empire.

At their meeting Lansing got the impression that Balfour favored the proposed Morgenthau mission. This was never the case, although perhaps Balfour, when meeting with Wilson earlier, had been led to believe that this was a pet White House project and so decided to play along. With Britain and France near exhaustion by 1917, Balfour was very eager to bring the Americans into close support. Significantly, Balfour had also met for the first time with Brandeis early in May. The two men had greatly impressed each other, and in this way an apparent meeting of the minds emerged.

Given the go-ahead, Morgenthau began to prepare himself for an initial meeting in Switzerland with Turkish representatives sanctioned by their government. He proceeded methodically to update his information in briefing sessions with Alsberg, who had left the Sublime Porte on April 7, the day after the United States severed diplomatic ties with Turkey. Ambassador Elkus, having contracted typhus, had left earlier and was recuperating in Paris. During the weeks before his departure, Morgenthau was continuously in contact with Leland Harrison, third assistant secretary at the State Department, who was assigned to facilitate the implementation of his plans.

An important bargaining chip Morgenthau intended to use in his negotiations was the release of two important Turks, Ayoub Sabri and Zinnoun, who had been held as prisoners of war by the British at Malta since the outbreak of hostilities. While Morgenthau had been serving as ambassador in 1914, Talaat had hounded him to use his influence to gain the release of these two men, especially his old and close friend Ayoub Sabri.

Lansing authorized Morgenthau's plan to go to Switzerland, "where he could get in touch with two former members of the Turkish Cabinet, and through them arrange a secret meeting between him and either Enver or Talaat." It was implicit that whatever proposals were made would be sweetened with substantial bribes for any of the top Turkish leaders involved.

Meanwhile Balfour had proceeded from Washington to Canada, on the morning of May 28. He had the chargé of the British embassy in Washington inform Lansing that since Switzerland was overrun with spies, it would be better to try to get in touch with Turkish officials in Egypt. Morgenthau "readily agreed to the change," and the word was given out that he was going to Egypt "to attempt to alleviate the conditions of the Jews in Palestine."

We don't know how Morgenthau really felt about this suggestion. He had started out with a patriotic scheme to save the lives of American boys by shortening the war. Now, once again, he found himself being sent as a Jew on what would be portrayed as a Jewish rescue mission, even though in fact this was only a cover. In any case, he told Lansing that to make the mission palatable to American Jews it must include a committed Zionist. (Morgenthau's having played a key role in saving the Jews of Palestine would not be enough to satisfy the Zionists.) Accordingly, Felix Frankfurter was designated a member of the mission.

Frankfurter, a thirty-five-year-old Harvard Law School professor, was currently serving as an assistant to Secretary of War Newton Baker; he often represented Justice Brandeis on Zionist business and operated behind the scenes for him. (Wilson had told Lansing to see Brandeis about the Morgenthau mission, and it seems quite plausible that it was Brandeis, rather than Morgenthau, who initiated the idea of sending Frankfurter.) Frankfurter accepted the assignment with great reluctance, but he believed that he was acting under presidential orders, that he had been sent along to "control" Morgenthau, to prevent him from "being any more foolish than could possibly be avoided."

From the time he joined the mission, Frankfurter served as a Zionist mole bent on informing, leaking, and eventually blowing the mission out of the water.

In June, while the mission was preparing for a speedy departure, Frankfurter began his negative reports to Brandeis. Information calculated to fuel the suspicions of American Zionists was also transmitted to British Zionists, who had found common cause with the British government. This in large measure resulted from the skilled maneuverings of Chaim Weizmann. Born in an isolated shtetl twenty-five miles from the predominantly Jewish city of Pinsk in Russian Poland, he had managed to obtain a first-rate education, mostly in Germany, as a chemist, later moving to Manchester, England. His inventions, which led to the efficient production of smokeless gunpowder, earned him recognition from David Lloyd George, then minister of munitions.

Weizmann had been a Zionist zealot since boyhood. While honing the practical application of his scientific abilities, he had vigorously struggled for the cause. In wartime Britain he was able to link his newfound favor in the highest government circles with his ambitions for Zionism and his personal ambition to become the leader of the movement.

By 1917, Lloyd George, as prime minister, and his foreign minister, Arthur Balfour, were both convinced that a strong Jewish presence in Palestine would buttress their hold on the Suez Canal — that all-important passage to India. For the same reason they also favored a strong Arab presence. Yet they naively failed to appreciate the potential for conflict in this dual sponsorship, unlike Morgenthau, who, during his visit to Palestine in 1914, had been fully sensitized to the brooding hostility of the Arabs against the Jewish presence.

During the early spring of 1917, Weizmann found that he had moved the British government tantalizingly close to declaring themselves in favor of a Jewish homeland in Palestine. This achievement had been reached over the firm opposition of most of the English Jewish establishment, with Lord Rothschild (Lionel Walter) as a notable exception.

By the beginning of June, Weizmann had heard something about the proposed Morgenthau mission. Looking for further information from American Zionists, he found them suspicious of Morgenthau, a declared non-Zionist. Weizmann thereupon began to slander Morgenthau at the Foreign Office. "I am expecting to see Mr. Morgenthau employed in some intrigue for a separate peace with Turkey and believe he is coming to Europe for this purpose. If so the whole thing is a German move," he declared.

Weizmann then spread the news of the Morgenthau mission to other interested parties, including the British ambassador in Washington, Sir Cecil Spring-Rice.

On June 9, Ambassador Spring-Rice fired off a long cable from Washington warning that Morgenthau, a person of some influence at the White House, was "closely connected with Germans in the United States [and with] many influential people in Turkey especially the Jews . . . and probably like most Jews wishes to save the Turkish Empire." Pursuing this rather contorted and wrong-headed reasoning, Spring-Rice went on to say that "Morgenthau's sympathies are probably more German than British but he is opposed to German militarism." In London a Foreign Office official noted, "Mr. Morgenthau is out to play a part quite Jew, and . . . his views cannot be other than tainted as he may be expected to subordinate everything to his wish to play a big part."

It is ironic to find the anti-German, non-Zionist Morgenthau, heroic defender of the Armenians, protector of British and all Allied expatriates, set upon by an alliance of anti-Semitic but temporarily pro-Zionist British foreign service officers and the international Zionist movement, along with Armenian and Arab nationalists. Why had almost everyone who had initially supported the Morgenthau mission now turned against it? The answer seems to be in the matter of timing. The possibility of detaching the Turks from the war, at first viewed as a worthy adventure with nothing to lose, now showed itself a destabilizing threat to a network of special interests.

The spring of 1917 was a desperate low point for the Allies. On the Western Front was a debilitating stalemate, which had stirred mutiny among the French troops (though this was largely concealed from Britain). Unlike the British, the French government remained supportive of the move for a separate Turkish peace. They believed British troops fighting in the Near East could be relieved for much-needed redeployment on the Western Front. The French also had rival interests in the area and wanted to be in a position to stake out their own claims at the end of the war;* and they were less strategically poised than the British.

Nevertheless, Britain's edge appeared far from decisive. In the Near East the war had gone particularly badly for the British, who had hardly any Allied assistance. British forces had been soundly defeated at Gallipoli at the beginning of 1916 and had more recently been driven back from Baghdad. In June 1917, as the Morgenthau mission prepared to leave for Egypt, a British advance that had stalled at Gaza blocked Morgenthau's rendezvous with the Turks.

Weizmann, meanwhile, was concerned that the Germans were trying to woo the Zionists into their fold. He felt that anything threatening the delicate balance in the Near East had to be ruthlessly stamped out, and the mission for a separate peace with the Turks seemed just such a threat to both the Zionists and Prime Minister Lloyd George. But, while one group in the Foreign Office supported the government position, the goal of a separate peace remained very much alive with other statesmen, who favored anything that would undermine German strength. As a result the new government-Zionist alliance strove to equate anti-Zionism with a pro-German and in some instances pro-Turkish position. This ploy was designed to counter all those leaning toward a separate peace, including the French and the Americans.

Without much appreciation for the intricacies of this political game and without useful guidance from the State Department, which showed little concern, Morgenthau continued preparing to lead his mission to Egypt. He had no idea that his efforts were being undermined by Frankfurter, and even permitted him to recruit two ardent Zionists to the mission: Max Lowenthal, a young friend of Frankfurter's, who came along as the mission's secretary, and Lithuanian-born Eliaha Lewin-Epstein, a well-known figure in U.S. and international Zionist circles.

On June 19, two days before the mission set sail from New

---

*The secret Sykes-Picot agreement of 1915, undisclosed to the Zionists, had provided for a Palestine divided into British and French zones.

York, the *New York Times* carried a story, cleared by the State Department, reporting that Ambassador Morgenthau and Professor
Felix Frankfurter "will proceed to Egypt and from there conduct an
investigation to ascertain the means of relieving the situation among
the Jews of Palestine." A follow-up story affirmed that "Jacob
Schiff, Felix M. Warburg, Louis Marshall and thirty other members
of the Joint Distribution Committee had added 'unlimited funds' to
the $800,000 already sent for the relief of Jews in Palestine." An
attempt would be made to send millions should the avenue be
opened, and Morgenthau and his associates would have utter discretion as to the disbursement of the funds.

By this time an agreement had been reached for the Morgenthau
mission to stop in Gibraltar en route to Egypt to consult with
British and French government representatives. Balfour had originally intended to send Sir Louis Mallet, the former ambassador to
Turkey, who favored the idea of separate peace. But after leaks to
the press about the mission, Balfour decided to send a less conspicuous figure, and Weizmann emerged as the ideal candidate. His
presence would be consistent with the subterfuge that the mission
was concerned exclusively with Palestine relief. Furthermore, he
would give the impression that the primary objection to the mission
emanated from Zionists rather than the Foreign Office.

Two other facts affected the mission's outcome. One was a letter
to Morgenthau from Colonel Edward House, President Wilson's
closest adviser and sometime alter ego, dated June 13; it seems to
have arrived too late for Morgenthau to act on. House warned that
Morgenthau's plan to stop at Gibraltar to confer with Weizmann
and the French representative, Colonel Weyl, also a Zionist, was a
great mistake. He fully understood that as Zionists both of these
men would oppose Morgenthau's plan for a separate peace with
Turkey. As an alternative he suggested Morgenthau meet them on
his return journey. This was indeed a wise suggestion from the most
astute and best informed of Wilson's advisers. Colonel House was
well acquainted with what Morgenthau was up to, and Morgenthau
had generally sought House's counsel and aid. But this time he had
played the game according to the rules, reporting only to the secretary of state and to the president.

The other fact — a curious footnote — was a call Morgenthau
received the day before he sailed from a special agent for the Department of State, William Yale. In addition to reporting to the depart-

ment, Yale was an oil prospector and an agent for the Standard Oil Company. At the Peace Conference in 1919 he would serve as an expert consultant to the pro-Arab, anti-Zionist King Crane Commission. Being attached to that commission sometimes objectively criticizing the Jews has earned him the reputation of being anti-Zionist; but, in fact, he filed a minority report with the commission declaring that "Jewish energy, Jewish genius, and Jewish finance will bring many advantages to Palestine." He also predicted that "a Jewish state will inevitably fall under the control of American Jews who will work out, along Jewish lines, American ideals and American civilization."

In 1917 Morgenthau's and Yale's views on the Middle East situation apparently converged, for Morgenthau explained the nature of his mission to Yale and invited him to come along. Yale's up-to-date information from Turkey, combined with his vast knowledge and his keen objectivity as a Gentile among so many Jews, would have made his presence extremely valuable. But there was no time for him to accept this last-minute invitation.

On June 21 the Morgenthau party departed on the SS *Buenos Aires,* flying the neutral Spanish flag. Morgenthau was accompanied by his wife, the other members of the mission, eighteen trunks, and $400,000 in gold, entrusted to him by the Joint Distribution Committee. Plying a sea infested with German U-boats, the ship kept all its lights burning at night to declare its neutrality. But in the face of real danger during the uneasy journey, Morgenthau, buoyed by a sense of the importance of his mission, harbored no fear of losing lives or treasure.

On June 25, four days after receiving a cable from Walter Hines Page, the U.S. ambassador in London, which noted British concerns, Lansing ordered Page to inform Balfour that Morgenthau would reach Cadiz about July 1. Undoubtedly prompted by a telegram Frankfurter had sent to Leland Harrison, Lansing urged Page to "leave nothing undone" in arranging for Chaim Weizmann to meet Morgenthau at Gibraltar. At the same moment, Lansing ordered the American consul in Cadiz to inform Morgenthau that "British and French representatives will meet him in Gibraltar." It seems likely that the president and the secretary of state were now looking for a way to rein in their ill-timed expedition.

The American mission did arrive in Cadiz on July 1 and drove down to Gibraltar, where Morgenthau established his headquarters.

Frankfurter soon moved across the bay to a Spanish hotel. Weizmann arrived on July 3, having come down by train, picking up a "tail" of German spies in the process. In addition, Weizmann had met Professor A. S. E. Yahuda on a street corner, "the one man I wanted to avoid in Madrid." The British ambassador had already informed Yahuda of British opposition to Morgenthau's mission. Yahuda, who was on poor terms with Weizmann, took the opportunity to question him about the opposition. According to Yahuda, Weizmann attacked Morgenthau as an "assimilationist" who would ruin Zionist plans for Palestine. Years later, Morgenthau told Yahuda of his bitterness and denied that he had opposed the settlement of Jews, particularly Eastern European Jews, in Palestine.

On July 4 and 5, Morgenthau and Frankfurter met the British and French representatives — Weizmann for the British and Colonel Weyl for the French. Weyl was a staff member of the Ministry of Munitions; his prewar role as the head of the Turkish state tobacco monopoly and his fluent Turkish gave him an excellent understanding of Turkish affairs. The British government arranged to have one of the buildings constructed within the "Rock" itself for use as a conference room. Gibraltar in July was blistering hot, and the windows were left open. Because Weyl spoke no English and Morgenthau had no French, the conversations took place in German, which added to the difficulties of communication. Arshag K. Schmavonian, the Armenian who had been Morgenthau's most trusted adviser in Constantinople, was also present. He had arrived from Switzerland, bringing the latest available information on the Turkish situation; he also had had numerous conferences with the reputedly propeace ministers Djevdet Bey and Taalat Pasha. Weizmann conceived an immediate and intense dislike for Schmavonian, probably because of his closeness to Morgenthau.

The American representatives opened the talks by laying out the background and intentions of the mission.* Morgenthau offered an exposition of the desperate military and economic situation of Turkey, largely based on the reports of Schmavonian. Having perceived some slight possibility of detaching the Turks from their alliance with the Germans and having won the approval of the other Allies,

---

*Lewin-Epstein, who was suffering from ill health, was left behind in Cadiz during the time of the Gibraltar meetings. He had been brought along purely as Zionist window-dressing and was never enlightened as to the true nature of the mission.

he explained, President Wilson had dispatched the Morgenthau mission, under the guise of an inquiry into the situation of the Palestinian Jews. "From this it will be evident that we are instructed to make soundings; we have no definite plan to propose for penetrating into the Turkish situation, much less any program of terms for dealing with the Turks."

Discussion then turned to the course of action the Americans proposed. Frankfurter recalled that Morgenthau placed great faith in his ability to persuade the Turkish leaders by force of personality. At the same time, Weizmann found that Morgenthau "became very vague and no amount of discussion and question could elucidate any definite plan or programme." Weizmann and Weyl posed two specific questions. First, did Morgenthau

> think that the time has come for the American government, or for the Allies through the American government, to open up negotiations of such a nature [that is, peace negotiations] with the Turkish authorities? In other words, whether he thinks that Turkey realizes sufficiently that she is beaten or is likely to lose the war, and is therefore in a frame of mind to lend itself to negotiations of that nature? [Second,] assuming that the time is ripe for such overtures, has [Morgenthau] a clear idea about the conditions under which the Turks would be prepared to detach themselves from their present masters?

Pressed hard on these points, Morgenthau may have chosen to remain vague. The purpose of his mission was after all simply to establish contact with the Turks and test the waters for possible future negotiations. But Weizmann was critical of the fact that Morgenthau had "received no instructions from the President or Lansing about [the terms for a separate peace] and has not considered the matter at all." He recognized that there was no reason to believe the Turks would accept a separate peace if they were compelled to yield Armenia, Syria, Mesopotamia, and Palestine.

At the end of two days, Weyl joined Weizmann in opposing the continuation of the mission. They both argued that the situation had changed recently and that the time was "not ripe" for initiating conversations with the Turks. The British advance through Gaza in Palestine had been stalled. Revolution had disrupted politics and military operations in Russia, easing pressure on Turkey's eastern front and restoring confidence in an eventual victory by Germany and its allies. And Britain's failure to make headway against the

Turks in Mesopotamia had resurrected belief that the outer parts of the empire might be defended. All these facts combined to increase Turkey's hopes and resolve.

On July 6, after the two-day session, Weizmann reflected that "in view of the fact that Mr. Morgenthau had no plans and no clear notions of what he is going to do, it seemed to us that the only thing possible is to try to prove to Mr. Morgenthau that it is useless to begin dangerous and important work of this kind without a full consultation of the English and French governments, and without communicating with his Government and obtaining from them a clear expression of their views."

As a result of the relentless opposition he encountered from Weizmann, Morgenthau decided to abandon the trip to Egypt. He also gave up the idea of trying to make contact with Turkey through the numerous Turkish officials who visited Switzerland during the war. Instead, he decided to go to France, confer with General Pershing, and await further instructions.

Morgenthau and Frankfurter jointly cabled from Madrid on July 8 the collective views of the four representatives. This was immediately followed by a cable from Frankfurter to Frank Polk, acting secretary of state, and Brandeis. Frankfurter urged that Morgenthau be called home. The timing of the cable seriously damaged Morgenthau's standing in Washington. Secretary of State Lansing had lately departed for a monthlong vacation, leaving the State Department in the charge of an incompletely briefed assistant secretary. Polk apparently found himself at a loss to understand just what Morgenthau's instructions had been.

A month after the start of the mission, on July 13, after receiving several reports from "Special Agents" Morgenthau and Frankfurter (including the cable of July 8 from Frankfurter urging Morgenthau's recall), Wilson felt compelled to repudiate Morgenthau. The president privately asked Sir William Wiseman★ to explain to Balfour that Morgenthau had badly exceeded his instructions. Wilson claimed that Morgenthau had been sent to do "relief work." He was only to contact Turkish leaders discreetly and to "sound them on the subject of peace" if the opportunity appeared. Wilson wanted

---

★Sir William Wiseman, the chief British military intelligence officer stationed in Washington, regularly communicated with Colonel House, circumventing official diplomatic channels.

Balfour to know that "Morgenthau was not authorized to express his views to anyone, or to approach any Turkish leader officially." Wilson had told Morgenthau of his ideas on Turkey, but privately. Wilson "had no idea that they would be repeated, and certainly did not authorize Morgenthau to communicate them to anyone."

The next day, Frank Polk cabled Morgenthau, informing him that the State Department had been "surprised and disturbed" by his belief in a larger mission than that of dealing with the Jews in Palestine. Morgenthau was instructed to proceed to Cairo in company with Frankfurter, to get on with the relief mission, and to pursue no independent initiative. Thereafter Polk, Lansing, and Wilson were puzzled about what face to put on the adventure. Polk regarded it as a fiasco but was uncertain about whether something might be salvaged by allowing it to proceed to Cairo. Colonel House advised that Morgenthau be recalled directly from France.

On July 17, Morgenthau cabled Lansing from Paris that he had not exceeded instructions "in the remotest degree" and had done nothing to give Wilson or Lansing reason to feel disturbed. He suggested that Frankfurter return to brief the president, while he would await further instructions.

Morgenthau became the target for criticism from both sides of the Atlantic. Yet at the same time the British were putting out peace feelers to the Turks. Despite his intense personal dislike for Schmavonian, Weizmann appears to have found the information on the condition of the Turkish war effort credible enough to pass along to the Foreign Office. The original terms discussed in Lansing's office suggested that the Turks would sacrifice their peripheral territories if they could get out of the war while keeping Constantinople. However, the British and the Zionists were united in seeing the mission as a danger that had to be stopped. In all likelihood, the Morgenthau mission threatened to open up a discussion among all of the Allies — French, Italian, and Russian — about the future of the Turkish Empire at a critical moment in the war. The British defeats in the Middle East were less important than the general crisis of the war that occurred with the outbreak of revolution in Russia and the near stranglehold of the German submarines on Britain's supply lines. Hard-pressed on every front, the British probably wished to avoid any possible disputes within the coalition.

The Americans' motives are only slightly less clear. The Wilson papers show that, from the first, the discussion of Palestine relief work was a cover and the real purpose was in fact to sound out the Turks about an accommodation. In the numerous discussions before Morgenthau's departure, neither Wilson nor Lansing seems to have given the ambassador any detailed instructions, nor did either open his mind on the subject of a future peace to him. Nor, for that matter, did either of them pose exact and demanding questions about procedures and intentions. Wilson seems to have approved the mission in a cavalier fashion. He then followed up his approval with an amazingly careless lack of concern about details. The possibility of negotiation with the Turks, moreover, seems strangely at odds with the commitments Wilson had so recently given to Brandeis to accept and support the creation of a Jewish homeland under a British protectorate hewn from the Ottoman Empire.

It is normal and acceptable procedure for the president of the United States to step aside from any operation that fails, and to find a scapegoat down the line, especially in matters of international relations. An attempt to induce Turkey to pull out of the war was from the beginning marked as a long shot by all concerned, including Morgenthau himself. If it had succeeded the president would certainly have claimed the victory.

But what probably caused the administration in Washington to label the Morgenthau mission "a fiasco," rather than simply ignore it, was that Morgenthau had claimed to be speaking for the president, exposing Wilson and his closest advisers to criticism. Morgenthau was also blamed for the leaks on both sides of the Atlantic which quickly found their way into the press. He did have a reputation for seeking public acclaim but in this instance had been extraordinarily discreet — most of the so-called loose talk appears to have been planted by American and British Zionists. As the Zionists and the British Foreign Office became increasingly apprehensive that Morgenthau could upset their plans for Palestine, they looked for ways to discredit him and scuttle his mission, including leaks to the press that were calculated to destroy the necessary element of secrecy.

Morgenthau himself remained uncharacteristically tightlipped about the entire affair. His only public mention of it seems to be a terse reference in his autobiography: "In July, 1917, the President asked me to go abroad upon a secret diplomatic errand, which I am not even yet at liberty to disclose further than to say that I learned that what the President hoped for could not be accomplished."

Morgenthau was embittered by the way Brandeis, whom he greatly admired, had treated him, and even more by the betrayal of Frankfurter, whom he had trusted completely. The effect on Morgenthau was apparent in his increasingly angry opposition to Zionism.

Toward the end of 1917 history moved on in ways that seemed to affirm the intentions of those who had opposed the Morgenthau mission. Before the Morgenthau plans were developed, Wilson had been conditioned by Brandeis to support Zionist objectives in Palestine. By mid-October the president informed Colonel House that he approved of the draft statement submitted by the British. A public statement by the United States remained simply a matter of timing. Then on November 2, in a sixty-seven-word letter from Foreign Secretary Balfour to Lord Rothschild (Lionel Walter), the Balfour Declaration endorsed "the establishment in Palestine of a national home for the Jewish people."

On December 10 General Edmund Allenby, having routed the Turkish forces, led the triumphant entry of British soldiers into the holy city of Jerusalem. This dramatic, highly symbolic shift of Allied fortunes in the Near East seemed to confirm, at least at that moment, the British insistence on a military rather than a diplomatic solution in the region. The next day Morgenthau wrote a long letter to the editor of the *New York Times,* noting that "the 10th of December, 1917, will be remembered as a day of profound historical interest, and, I hope also of large meaning for the future." He observed that "after twelve centuries of almost uninterrupted Mohammedan rule" Christians would rejoice that the Holy Land "so well known to them through both the Old and New Testaments has been restored to the civilized world." Having spoken on behalf of Christians, he proceeded to speak for "all Jews, both the Zionists and those of us who do not take part in the advocacy of the entire programme of the Zionists." His central tenet, which he believed he shared with "a majority of those of my faith in America, is that we are 100 percent Americans, and wish to remain so, irrespective of the fact that some of our blood is Jewish and some of [it] is German, Russian or Polish. To us and our children America, too, is veritably a Holy Land."

Morgenthau foresaw a Palestine given a "very large measure of self-government" under "an international and inter-religious commission." But since "the whole world is now moving away from . . .

extreme nationalism," it would be an error to "set up a limited national state."

On Sunday, March 3, Rabbi Stephen Wise headed a "delegation of representative Jewish leaders" which went to the White House to confer with Woodrow Wilson. After meeting for an hour the president announced that he had approved Zionist plans "for the creation of a National Jewish Commonwealth." Rabbi Wise had invited Morgenthau to take over the pulpit of the Free Synagogue — of which he was the founding president — on that very Sunday in Carnegie Hall, informing Morgenthau only that he was going to Washington on business. Morgenthau was understandably hurt and angered by what he considered to be a deceitful betrayal. He phoned Dr. Wise immediately and resigned from his affiliation with the congregation that he had done so much to build.

· 17 ·

The Polish Mission

A FTER THE NOVEMBER 1918 armistice, Jews in the United States decided to join an international delegation to speak for Jewish religious and civil rights, particularly in Romania, Poland, and Russia. Morgenthau was elected as a representative to a Philadelphia congress, which would in turn select the American delegates to go to Paris. But as soon as he arrived in Philadelphia, he determined that the Zionist minority had taken control of congressional votes. He left immediately, joining a rump delegation of "seventy-five prominent Jews" from thirty-seven states who declared their "objections to the organization of a Jewish state in Palestine" and the "segregation of the Jews as a nationalistic unit in any country." They concluded with a vehement repudiation of the "double allegiance" they believed lay in "the establishment of a sovereign state for the Jews of Palestine."

As an Allied victory became inevitable, Morgenthau had looked forward to playing an active role on the peace conference. Although he resented the thought of again traveling the Jewish route, he was prepared to accept this as inevitable. Felix Frankfurter recalled that, as he was crossing the Atlantic with Morgenthau in the summer of 1917, Morgenthau was already speculating as to whom the president would send to the peace table. He supposed the delegation would "have to have a Jew." Frankfurter, who admittedly delighted in being "outrageously mean," steadfastly refused to suggest that the man should be Morgenthau.

In May 1919 there were published reports of atrocities (euphemistically referred to as "excesses") against Polish Jews, which stirred angry protest among Jews in the United States and Britain.

A rally that packed New York City's Madison Square Garden, with an overflow of thousands in the surrounding streets, was addressed by Charles Evans Hughes (Wilson's Republican opponent in the 1916 election). Resolutions were passed calling on President Wilson to act.

A few weeks earlier Wilson had appointed Hugh Gibson as the U.S. minister to the newly reconstituted Polish nation. Gibson, with all the earmarks (including politely muted anti-Semitism) of a promising young foreign service professional, was hastily called in to report on the alarming "excesses." His job, as he saw it, was to make a case for Poland as just another example of the new postwar democracies, playing down the "yarns" of anti-Jewish incidents as "foreign manufacture for anti-Polish purposes." But he soon discovered that he had stepped into a hornet's nest of Jewish outrage.

Realizing he was in deep trouble, Gibson retreated to Paris to report to Colonel House, who was there with the president (not to Secretary Lansing, his official boss). Arriving for his audience, he found the colonel with Felix Frankfurter and Justice Brandeis. Frankfurter had come to Versailles as an American member of the international Jewish (pro-Zionist) delegation, and Brandeis, the associate justice of the Supreme Court, just happened to be passing through on the way to his first visit to Palestine. No sooner had Gibson arrived in the colonel's suite than his host departed, leaving him at the mercy of two irate American Jewish lawyers. Frankfurter did most of the talking, making clear to Gibson that he "had no right," because of his limited knowledge, "to make reports to the [State] Department on Jewish matters." Gibson believed that Frankfurter had made "a scarcely veiled threat that the Jews would try to prevent my confirmation by the Senate."

At this point an idea surfaced — possibly initiated, and certainly supported, by Gibson — of sending an American mission to Poland to investigate the excesses against the Jews. Heading the Polish delegation to the Paris Peace Conference was the new Polish premier, the great pianist and patriot Ignace Paderewski, who seized on the idea of a mission, to be appointed jointly by President Wilson and himself, as an instrument for gaining American — especially Jewish — amity.

Morgenthau was attending the Peace Conference in what he referred to as a "semiofficial capacity." In May he arranged to visit the occupied Rhineland. Stopping in Koblenz, he addressed an assembly of American soldiers in the Liberty Hut, causing quite a stir back home. He warned the doughboys that at present "we are enjoying only a suspension of hostilities . . . within fifteen years America will be called on really to save the world." It was not far off the mark, and certainly not what anyone wanted to hear. He warned, furthermore, that the United States should foster a cooperative unity between capital and labor so that "we can save civilization from annihilation."

With Morgenthau there on the fringes of the Peace Conference, it occurred to the Wilson insiders and the State Department that he was the man to repair the damage wrought by Hugh Gibson. According to Brandeis and Frankfurter, Gibson "had done more mischief to the Jewish role than anyone who had lived in the last century."

Wilson was determined that the Polish mission be headed by a Jew. Morgenthau was certainly not the choice of Brandeis and Frankfurter or any of the Zionists. By then an unmitigated anti-Zionist and something of a loose cannon, he was also mistrusted by the Jewish Establishment, which was seeking a quiet accommodation leading toward Jewish unity. Louis Marshall and Cyrus Adler suggested that no Jew serve on the commission. On July 3, the ubiquitous Jacob Schiff fired off a purportedly chastening cable to Morgenthau, "While I thoroughly appreciate your independence of judgement may I not withstanding in exceedingly friendly spirit caution you against being misled by Poles for the eyes of Jewry are upon you." To which Morgenthau responded, "I realize that the truth will probably displease both sides — but console myself with the knowledge that just decisions seldom please either of the contending parties."

On June 26 Morgenthau had gone to see President Wilson to try to beg off from his assignment. But when the president stated that he would definitely appoint a Jew, Morgenthau believed he had received a command that "as a good citizen" he could not disobey. He proceeded to fill the commission with very able men who, however, lacked any special knowledge of or special sensitivity for the mission at hand. They included General Edgar Jadwin, one of the United States' finest engineers, and Homer Johnson, a lawyer and politician. Serving as counsel was Arthur Lehman Goodhart, a brilliant young lawyer (and incidentally my mother's first cousin).

He kept a detailed diary of the commission's work which he later published.

No one on the commission staff knew Polish or Yiddish, the two principal languages in which the hearings would be conducted, nor were they familiar with the intricacies of Polish and Jewish culture and the long-standing history of interethnic animosity. Morgenthau, however, did have the experience of effective dealings with Orthodox, Zionist, and nationalistic Jews in the Ottoman Empire, particularly in Palestine.

Just before the members of the commission left Paris for Warsaw, Paderewski gave them a dinner at the Ritz. In the middle of this ceremonial meal, the host and two of his guests, Secretary of State Robert Lansing and Roman Dmowski,★ rushed off to the railway station where President Wilson was departing on the first leg of his journey back to Washington. Then all three men returned to the Ritz, plus Hugh Gibson, the controversial American diplomat, and settled down for a serious discussion with Morgenthau.

When the commission arrived in Warsaw, Morgenthau learned that Frankfurter planned to conduct his own investigation. Morgenthau cabled to Paris asking that Frankfurter be headed off, but Joseph C. Grew, secretary of the American Peace Delegation, answered that it was too late and that it wouldn't do any harm to gather additional testimony. In the end, though, nothing significant was heard from Frankfurter.

The Morgenthau Commission of 1919 carried clear, written instructions from Secretary Lansing officially approved by President Wilson, Premier Paderewski, and Mr. Gibson stating that it was to look into all matters affecting Jewish/Polish relations, including "massacres, and other excesses alleged to have taken place, the economic boycott, and other methods of discrimination." Beyond the investigation itself, the mission was to discover underlying causes "with a view to finding a possible remedy." The assumption was that anything done for the benefit of either group, the Jews or the Poles, would automatically benefit the other.

Wilson, prompted by Colonel House, was responding to Jewish demonstrations in the United States protesting Polish pogroms

---

★Dmowski, a powerful political leader, extreme Polish nationalist, and acknowledged anti-Semitic activist, had been the Polish cosigner of the Versailles Treaty with Paderewski.

and anti-Jewish boycotts. But American government officials held that a strong, unified, democratic Poland was essential to separating Germany and Russia. No one understood the importance of this better than Morgenthau.

Paderewski valued this mission as an instrument to build confidence and generate economic and political support. Unlike the other leaders of the new Polish state, Paderewski was a man of the world. He understood that American Jews were more powerful and vocal than the Polish-Americans who outnumbered them. He foresaw that Poles would need U.S. support to retain the generous allotment of territory granted them at Versailles. It was this knowledge that gave the Morgenthau Commission some leverage in a climate hostile to outside (especially Jewish) interference in Polish affairs.

The Jewish population in Poland was about 11 percent. Morgenthau had never before been confronted with such a large concentration of Jews, nor such deep-seated traditions and divisiveness along political, cultural, and class lines. The vast majority were Orthodox, and the men, especially, were conspicuous in long black kaftans and a variety of headgear, from yarmulkes to broad-brimmed, fur-trimmed hats, uncut beards, and side curls. Many were poor beyond anything Morgenthau had seen on New York's Lower East Side. With their own language (Yiddish), strict observance of religious ritual and dietary laws, they lived separately and were despised by many of their Christian neighbors.

The more modernized Jews were nationalists, who wanted a separate and protected existence within Poland, and Zionists, who wanted a Jewish homeland in Palestine. Then there were the assimilationists, who hoped their Jewishness would dissolve as they floated into the social mainstream. But to the Poles none of these distinctions mattered. In their newly reunited country, which had previously been parceled out to Austria, Prussia, and Russia, an intense spirit of Polish nationalism and anti-Semitism was firmly rooted in both church and state. The Polish-Jewish alienation resembled the hatred that Morgenthau had witnessed between Muslim Turks and Christian Armenians. The arch anti-Semite Dmowski, though he had spoken softly to Morgenthau in Paris, pursued a hard line. He invited all the ethnic minorities within the new expanded Polish borders to assimilate. But the Jews, for whom he could see no hope of assimilation, were to be persecuted and driven out or destroyed.

When the Morgenthau Commission arrived it was welcomed by all the Jews and berated by the Poles. The bitterest attack appeared in *Mysl Niepodlegla,* the leading weekly, in an editorial complaining that Wilson ought to know that his delegation "takes the part of the Shulhan-Aruch★ people against the people of Kosciuszko and Mickiewici. The nation of the Shulhan Aruch live upon usury, fraud, receiving of stolen goods, white slavery, counterfeiting and wilful bankruptcy." Meanwhile "the daily *Robotnicza*" demanded, "The Polish public must take up anti-Semitic action which means an economic fight . . . a boycott in friendship and in our everyday life . . . we do not wish to be acquainted with the Jews; . . . we buy nothing from them nor sell anything to them. If a man desires to remain healthy he should isolate himself from disease. For on this very day our health and the health of the whole nation is at stake." Morgenthau and General Jadwin had issued a statement of good will: none of the Polish papers printed it, but all four of Warsaw's Jewish newspapers published it and asked for further interviews.

Morgenthau and Jadwin decided to invite the press to meet the mission. About twelve reporters showed up. "At first they were stiff and suspicious," Goodhart noted in his diary, "but after a while Mr. Morgenthau succeeded in establishing friendly relations." He confessed to the journalists that the mission's motives were not entirely unselfish, as it was in the interest of the Allied countries that there should be a strong Poland that could keep Russia and Germany apart. And a strong Poland must be free of internal strife. The next day the papers were warily more favorable. One said that "if Mr. Morgenthau was a friend he was a very charming one, but that if he was an enemy he was extremely dangerous."

Although the Polish press seldom printed any U.S. news, while the mission was in Poland they carried front-page accounts of race riots in Washington and Chicago. Arthur Goodhart noted that someone had "suggested that a Polish Mission be sent to America to investigate the Negro problems." In 1915 Ambassador Morgenthau's reports on the Armenian massacres and his suggestion that only the Germans could curb the Turks had drawn a similar response. The German ambassador to Washington, Count Johann von

---

★*Shulhan-Aruch* (Hebrew, meaning prepared table) is the standard code of Jewish law and practice.

Bernstorff, began making comparisons between Armenian atrocities and the lynching of Negroes in the South. The *Frankfurter Zeitung* pointed out that "the Armenian affair is no more Germany's business than the lynching of the Negroes is Germany's business."

In striking contrast, the Polish Jews welcomed Morgenthau "as a second Moses Montefiore." The first Friday evening after arriving in Warsaw, Ambassador Morgenthau, General Jadwin, Captain Goodhart, and other commission members decided to attend services at the principal synagogue, where they found five or six thousand people gathered in front of the building. There was great cheering, principally for Morgenthau, but also for General Jadwin (whose name they had difficulty pronouncing), President Wilson, and America. The crowd closed in so that they had difficulty in getting through the doorway until Jewish Boy Scouts armed with sticks cleared the way. Inside, the synagogue was packed to overflowing, with the men on the main floor and women in the gallery, according to Orthodox custom. The orderly service and the chanting by the cantor and the boys' choir impressed the visitors with the grave symbolic importance of the occasion. After the service, when Morgenthau and his party tried to leave, the crowd in front of the synagogue, now about ten thousand, was unyielding. The militia had to fire shots over their heads to clear a path. "Everyone took the shooting calmly, as if it were quite an ordinary affair," Goodhart commented.

During their two months' stay, the commission submitted to a relentless barrage of testimony from the Jewish community and counterclaims from Polish officials. The commission members also felt a great deal of pressure to complete and report on their assignment quickly, so they divided into teams. During the first two weeks the teams remained in Warsaw, listening to the appeals that came in from all over the country. Much of the rest of the time they spent at trouble spots throughout Poland, followed by a final week of recapitulation in Warsaw.

In conducting his hearing, Morgenthau noted that among the Jews, the best organized and most vocal were the Zionists. They "were our first callers, they were also our most constant," he recalled. "The Zionism of most of them was simply advocacy of Jewish nationalism." In making demands for emigration to Palestine, they hoped to refocus attention on the wrongs done them at home. Despairing of gaining equality with the ethnic Poles, they sought protection through a form of separate rights under the provisions of the Versailles Treaty.

The largest group of Polish Jews, the Orthodox, held to no political agenda at all. According to their belief, the return to Zion awaited the call of the Messiah. Most of them wished to remain where they were, unmolested, but Morgenthau and Goodhart believed that along with the Zionists many Orthodox Jews, if given the choice, would go to New York. This was indeed the case for the most desperately poor; the more affluent preferred Vienna and other Western European cities where they felt more at home.

The third and smallest group of Jews was the "assimilators," who had chosen to identify with and merge into the mainstream of Polish culture and politics. This group included many affluent business and professional people, who regarded "Judaism as a matter of faith" only. Morgenthau believed that these assimilated Jews "mingled on an equal footing of social equality with the Christians." This was the way of life he had chosen for himself in the United States, and, downplaying both the intensity of anti-Semitism and the depth of Yiddish culture, he conceived of it as the way out for all Polish Jews. But he was, as always perhaps, more a wishful thinker than a naif. He reported with amusement on a great banquet given for him by an aristocrat who had joined the Polish government. His host "ransacked the entire neighborhood" to invite some prominent Jews. At the table Morgenthau held the place of honor. His hostess's eighteen-year-old niece, who was seated next to Captain Goodhart, whispered, "It seems strange to me to see a Jew treated with such consideration in our home. You know I just detest the Jews, don't you?" When Goodhart identified himself as a Jew, "the little Countess was all confusion."

General Jadwin and Captain Goodhart arrived at Pinsk just as Polish troops temporarily took the city from the Russian Bolsheviks on August 8. Ninety percent of the shops in Pinsk were owned by Jews. It was a classic example of a situation in which looting and violence were countenanced on the false premise of Jews' aiding and abetting Bolsheviks. There had been warnings of impending events, and it was hoped that the presence of an American general could help prevent them. The Americans, who saw widespread looting, did personally round up some of the culprit soldiers and run them in. Realizing, however, that this was neither a practical nor safe solution, they reported a number of incidents to the Polish commander. He begged off on the grounds that neither he nor his officers could control the "disobedience" of their noncoms — soldiers and civilians. During the next few days, soldiers killed thirty-one Jews and plundered 377 Jewish shops; many homes were broken into and the residents beaten and robbed. Without General Jadwin on the spot, there might have been even more such excesses. The government reported that four Polish soldiers lost their lives and that subsequently some of the rioters were executed.

Reporting on a separate incident, Morgenthau wrote, "I wish I could adequately describe the scene that I witnessed in Pinsk." It haunted him as an "expression of the misery and injustice which is prevalent over such a large part of the world today." A few months earlier, seventy-five Jewish community leaders (including six women) had assembled to arrange for distribution of matzo meal that the American Joint Distribution Committee had sent them for Passover. As the meeting was breaking up, the Polish town commander, a Major Luczynski, and fifteen of his men broke into the hall where the Jewish leaders were gathered and arrested everyone on the unsubstantiated charge that the Jews of Pinsk had aided the Bolsheviks. Less than an hour later, without any investigation of the charges or identification of the people arrested, thirty-five of them were lined up in the town square against the cathedral wall and shot. The next morning when three were discovered still alive they were shot again. All the bodies were thrown into a common grave without any religious ceremony. Until the arrival of the commission no Jews had been permitted to visit the unconsecrated mass grave. The evening Morgenthau attended services in the great Pinsk Synagogue it was mobbed. The approximately eighteen thousand Jews of Pinsk represented about 75 percent of the total population. As the grief-stricken congregation "cried and screamed," Morgenthau wrote, "This was the first time I ever completely realized what the collective grief of a persecuted people was like."

Forty-eight hours before the commission was scheduled to leave Poland, Count Zoltowski, vice minister for foreign affairs, notified Morgenthau that he would be receiving a large number of affidavits from witnesses in Vilna who claimed to have seen Jews firing on Polish soldiers. Morgenthau was furious. The commission had spent over a week in Vilna and the government had produced not a single witness concerning these alleged shootings. Morgenthau and General Jadwin went to call on Pilsudski, who was temporarily residing there. This stern, hulking soldier had spent years in Russian and German prisons as a result of his uncompromising patriotism. He deemed the Morgenthau mission, created at the Versailles Peace Conference, which Pilsudski had not attended, an insult to Polish honor. After listening to a ten-minute tirade, Morgenthau began his rebuttal with good humor, arguing that in "his official capacity, [he] was no Jew, was not even an American, but was a representative of all civilized nations and their religions." Pilsudski switched to laughter, and before the audience ended he had promised to release the Jewish prisoners taken into custody since April 1919.

But in Warsaw, on the eve of departure, the tables seemed to have turned. The Vilna affidavits were not withdrawn. Morgenthau threatened to return to Vilna and reopen the hearings, a move no one wanted. The next morning Count Zoltowski informed him that the Polish government would not press the matter of the affidavits. That night the count headed a delegation of Polish officials who came to the railroad station to speed the commission on its way home. A delegation of leading Zionists was also on hand for the occasion. As the train pulled out, these two tight little clusters of men were left standing on the platform still distinctly apart from each other.

Morgenthau had anticipated before going to Poland that his findings would please no one. His forebodings were amply borne out, especially since his official report and his subsequent comments were unmistakably colored by his anti-Zionist sentiments. "One of the deep and obscure causes of the Jewish trouble in Poland," the report concluded, was the "Nationalist-Zionist leadership that exploited the Old Testament prophecies to capture converts to the Nationalist scheme." Morgenthau compared the militant Zionists to labor unions' "walking delegates," who "agitate in order to maintain their leadership." The majority of Polish Jews were Orthodox. Morgenthau criticized them for their alien ways, their separatism, and their Yiddish (akin to the language of Poland's German-speaking enemies) as cause for Polish resentment. Furthermore, he pointed out that Article 93 of the Versailles Treaty (advanced by the international Jewish delegation in Paris, which Morgenthau had shunned) had exacerbated Polish resentment against the Jews in general; it guaranteed protection of minority rights in Poland and elsewhere.

Perhaps as a sop to the Polish government, which had reluctantly cosponsored his mission, Morgenthau advanced an "official" excuse for the "excesses," which he described in harrowing detail. It was claimed that the responsibility lay with "undisciplined . . . Polish recruits" and their "inexperienced" and "timid officers," who sought to profit "at the expense of that portion of the population which they regarded as alien and hostile to Polish nationality and aspirations." In sum, the Polish acts against the Jews were "political rather than anti-Semitic."

Morgenthau had inadvertently used the language of confirmed anti-Semites, like Roman Dmowski. To have it appear in this report inflamed American Jews from Eastern Europe, who knew, often from personal experience, exactly what these code words meant. It was they who were the most numerous, the most concerned, and the most vocal among the American Jews. As for the assimilated German Jews — the powerful, prosperous elite — they would have preferred to have no report at all, to bury the findings in silence. But while Morgenthau was suffering attacks for having gone too far in trying to justify Polish acts and attitudes, his two fellow commissioners, Jadwin and Johnson, held that he had not gone far enough. They refused to sign the Morgenthau report and eventually filed a separate one of their own.

Morgenthau continued to attract criticism from all directions with a number of widely publicized speeches. "American public opinion has been a great restraining force on anti-Semitic feeling in Poland," he told the Reform Rodeph Shalom congregation. But he went on to conclude that, though "an outrage to civilization," the number of deaths reported had been overstated and that the Polish government was "eager to make amends if that were possible."

In an address to the Vassar College alumnae appealing for U.S. aid to Poland as a "strong barrier" against a "German–Russian alliance," he referred to General Pilsudski as a "high class pirate." A "Dear Henry" letter from Undersecretary of State Frank Polk indicated that the Poles had protested bitterly, demanding that Morgenthau be removed from office. Morgenthau wrote back to Polk that he was "sorry" but added privately and prophetically that in Pilsudski's character "there is that defiance of law and restraint which may someday make him a very troublesome factor in mid-European politics."

· · ·

The Polish mission was Morgenthau's last important assignment for the U.S. government.* In March 1920 Wilson appointed him ambassador to Mexico, but he failed to receive Senate confirmation.† However, he received a flood of congratulatory letters. Robert Lansing, himself out of office, wrote that "in that land of turmoil and revolution" he did not envy Morgenthau his new post but admired his "patriotic spirit." Of special interest was a letter of "a thousand congratulations" from Morgenthau's estranged friend Stephen Wise for having "broken through the old 'encirclement'" (of jobs available to Jews).

In 1923 Morgenthau accepted an appointment from the League of Nations to be chairman of the Greek Refugee Settlement Commission, which was charged with the task of resettling Greeks who had been expelled from Smyrna by the Turks. Morgenthau proceeded to coordinate the job of housing and rehabilitating what amounted to about a 25 percent increase in the population of Greece. The task required a practiced outside hand. Altogether, the time Morgenthau spent in Greece on behalf of the League of Nations proved to be one of his happier and most effective ventures.

Morgenthau experienced one final truculent round with the Zionists. On April 2, 1921, Chaim Weizmann arrived in the United States to wrest the leadership of the American Zionists from Brandeis and his powerful elitist cohorts, and to place it in the hands of the Eastern European Jewish leaders. In June Weizmann marched on to the convention of the Zionist Organization of America in Cleveland, where, by a vote of more than two to one, the old guard was roundly defeated. Over forty Brandeis men quit, including Felix Frankfurter and Stephen Wise. Weizmann crowed over his fallen enemies: "I do not agree with the philosophy of your Zion-

---

*In 1933 the seventy-seven-year-old Morgenthau was appointed by President Roosevelt to serve as a member of a large U.S. delegation to an economic conference in London. His was a largely ceremonial assignment. Nevertheless, thrilled with the opportunity to get back in harness, Morgenthau canceled family plans to celebrate his and his wife's golden wedding anniversary and took off.

†For a number of reasons the Senate never voted on the Morgenthau appointment. First, the Republican-controlled Senate was disinclined to have diplomatic relations on the ambassadorial level with the "revolutionary" Mexican government. Second, there was reluctance to confirm lame duck appointments at the tail end of the Wilson administration. Finally, there were the maneuverings of the Republican senator from New Mexico, Albert B. Fall, on the Foreign Relations Committee (later convicted for his participation in the Teapot Dome scandal).

ism, your conception of Jewishness. We are different, absolutely different. There is no bridge between Washington and Pinsk."

Morgenthau might have delighted in the repudiation of this distinguished band of his fellow "uptown" Jews who had treated him so shabbily. But he too was rather disturbed by the unbridgeable gap between Washington and Pinsk. He mounted a vitriolic counterattack.* "Zionism is the most stupendous fallacy in Jewish history," he began, "wrong in principle and impossible of realization." In a mounting crescendo of fury he attacked it as an "eastern European proposal" that could "cost the Jews of America most [of what] they have gained."

The Balfour Declaration, Morgenthau warned, "is a shrewd and adroit delusion . . . The British Government favors the establishment of a homeland for the Jewish people in *Palestine*. But this does not say that the Jews shall have the right to dispossess, or to trespass upon the property of those far more numerous Arab tenants." Morgenthau foresaw with deadly accuracy that the "British Government has no intention of evicting Arab owners of the soil in favor of the Jews. Nor . . . have the Arab owners any intention of selling their holdings to the Jews, for they are fully aware of the Zionist programme, are very resentful of it, and intend to use every means at their command to frustrate it."

Morgenthau proceeded to draw on his firsthand experience and observation. He could never forget his 1914 visit to the Cave of Machpelah where the tombs of the patriarchs "are revered alike by Jews, Christians and Mohammedans," where he had been confronted with "the mutterings of discontent" and the "threatening looks . . . of devout Mohammedans." In Jerusalem he had observed that "exactly the same political issue of religious fanaticism applies to the question of Christian sensibilities." A Jewish state would, Morgenthau believed, only "concentrate, multiply and give new venom to the hatred which [the Jew] already endures in Poland and Russia, the very lands in which most Jews now dwell, and where their oppressions are the worst."

In the end he reverted to the old battle cry of assimilationism: "We enjoy in America exactly the spiritual liberty, the financial success, and the social position which we have earned." In his

---

*Morgenthau wrote "Zionism a Surrender, not a Solution" in June 1921, and it was published in the July *World's Work*.

euphoria Morgenthau had exaggerated the facts of American life in the 1920s; indeed, these conditions would not be realized until the last decades of this century and then not altogether as he would have had it. "The Jews of France have found France to be their Zion. The Jews of England have found England to be their Zion. We Jews of America have found America to be our Zion. Therefore, I refuse to allow myself to be called a Zionist. I am an American."*

When the defeated old guard marched out of the Cleveland convention, Samuel Untermyer, newly converted to Zionism and formerly one of Morgenthau's closest friends and mentors, believed he could reconcile the two warring factions. When that failed, he was designated to rebut Morgenthau. But Untermyer's "A Reply to Henry Morgenthau" (published in *Forum*, September 1921) was not simply a rebuttal. It was loaded with snide personal invective, designed to cast doubt on Morgenthau's motives and credibility. Untermyer concluded that "Mr. Morgenthau's article seems to have been written in a mood of personal egotism and a sort of moral vacuum." In passing, he sneered at Morgenthau's usefulness as a diplomat and as president of the Free Synagogue. He also attacked Morgenthau's contention that the ultimate Zionist objective was a Jewish state in Palestine. "If Mr. Morgenthau is acquainted with Zionist plans for a sovereign Jewish state, he has possession of secrets that are not shared by the Zionist leaders themselves."

After this bitter contretemps, Morgenthau quite understandably withdrew permanently from all involvement with organized Jewry. His position was very different from that of the Brandeis contingent which walked out of the Cleveland convention. All of them, including Brandeis himself, while remaining aloof from direct involvement in the Zionist political organization, re-established themselves in a variety of agencies designed to support Jewish activities in Palestine. Then, with just a touch of irony, only a few years later Morgenthau and his old enemies were back on common turf as Democrats: enthusiastic supporters of Al Smith and Franklin Roosevelt. But as these two presidential hopefuls became rivals, their Jewish supporters again became divided.

Back in the days of the Wilson presidency, my grandfather had identified the young, aristocratic charmer who was assistant secre-

---

*Morgenthau republished this article, "Zionism a Surrender, not a Solution," in 1923 as the final chapter of his autobiography, *All in a Lifetime*. I take it as an indication of the depth of his feelings about Zionism and indirectly of his sense of personal betrayal.

tary of the navy as a man of great political promise. Morgenthau had loyally supported the Cox-Roosevelt ticket in 1920 and, Al Smith in 1924. But when Smith was determined to have a second shot as the Democratic candidate in 1932, Morgenthau was firmly in the Roosevelt camp. No less energetic than before, he had, however, shifted his ambition from himself to his son, Henry Jr. The senior Morgenthau, doing what he knew best and what was expected of him, plunged into the always unenviable task of fund-raising.

PART III

Henry Jr., the 100 Percent American

· 18 ·

Great Expectations

JOSIE MORGENTHAU gave birth to four healthy infants, each separated by three years and some months. Henry Jr., her third child, born May 11, 1891, was the only boy. Accordingly, the mantle would pass to him.

From the outset there was between the self-possessed, quick-witted immigrant father and the gentle, somewhat diffident, totally American son a bond of trust and affection. Even in his adolescence young Henry confided in his father, who in turn left no stone unturned in seeking advantages for his son. But, although Henry Jr. played along with his father's sermonizing and relentless expressions of ambition for him, the boy was by nature fun-loving, given to practical jokes and displays of bravado, and brimming with personal charm. He enjoyed the limelight without any need for a star performance, a feat for which his oldest sister never forgave him.

Helen, starting life as an only child, was her father's favorite until her brother appeared seven years later. Throughout that time her father had craved a son, and after he succeeded in producing such an attractive one the family balance shifted. Once Henry became the center, the family matured as an unstable nucleus, subject to violent explosions of jealous rage. The situation was exacerbated by the father's tactless expression of his priorities. "I'll handle the boy," he told his wife. "You can take care of the girls."

The first Henry's concern for his son's education — he organized a kindergarten class in their West Seventy-fourth Street house when Henry Jr. was four — flew in the face of an intractable problem: although obviously bright, the boy suffered from what today would be called a learning disability. After kindergarten Henry Jr. was enrolled in the Sachs Collegiate Institute, where he suffered and did poorly. Despite hard work, the boy developed an aversion to conventional schooling. To sister Helen, "Henry Jr. was a disappointing kid brother who didn't amount to much." In 1904 Henry Sr. sent the boy to boarding school at Phillips Exeter Academy in New Hampshire. There young Henry was absolutely miserable. His father had intended for him to stay for the full four years and graduate with the class of 1908, but before the first year ended his son was begging to be allowed to quit. During his second year he campaigned even more relentlessly for freedom.

His father chose to blame outside forces. One of his favorite excuses was that young Henry had been weakened by growing too fast — six inches within a year — when he was merely experiencing a typical adolescent growth spurt. But there are many indications that Henry Jr. was functionally handicapped. He had difficulty with language skills and handling arbitrary symbols. His apparent dullness was as frustrating for him as for his teachers, parents, and peers — because he was actually intelligent. He seized the essence of every subject, though he had trouble with details. His mind would jump ahead, forming grand plans of unusual imagination and originality.

Yet the father never gave up on his son, and as a result the boy never gave up on himself. His father's criticism was always balanced with love and indulgence. Henry Jr. grew to count on his father's support. Even as a young man he sought his father's approval in the most personal matters. He once wondered if for a certain young woman's birthday he "ought to send her a small box of candy or something else" and sought his father's advice. "I don't seriously object to your sending Louise Leve a box of candy," Henry Sr. responded. "I suppose you want Huylers, the most expensive brand."

At Exeter, Henry Jr. was homesick, but was diverted by occasional weekend visits in Boston to his mother's oldest sister, Carrie, and the Filene, Eiseman, and Dreyfus cousins — families of Carrie's three daughters by Charles Weil, whom Carrie married in 1874.

But such diversions did not fire his academic performance, and at the end of the school year, in 1906, Henry Sr., Henry Jr., and Exeter agreed that young Henry would not return in the fall. Instead, he was readmitted to the Sachs Collegiate Institute, this time under the tutelage of Otto Koenig, a Prussian martinet notorious for cramming required academic skills into a select group of German Jewish skulls.★

On returning from Exeter, young Henry moved into the new home his parents had built at 30 West Seventy-second Street. With its limestone facade and elevator, it was a notch above the Seventy-fourth Street brownstone — an impressive residence and an appropriate cap to Henry Sr.'s real estate successes. My grandparents were still living there when I was a child. I can remember that it seemed grand indeed by comparison with my maternal grandparents' more modest brownstone and our own cramped apartment a few doors away.

Henry Jr. occupied a large room on the third floor, where he could retreat from "the many family activities that were constantly going on in our house."

After two years under Dr. Koenig, Henry was ready to graduate but was still not qualified to enroll as a student of architecture at Cornell, the route that he and his father had chosen. To ease the transition, he attended Cascadilla, a cram school in Ithaca, outside the walls of the college. Edward Bernays, the public relations genius, was Henry Jr.'s age and was among his classmates at Cascadilla (and then at Cornell). The diminutive Bernays remembers looking up admiringly to Henry: "He was tall, handsome, very personable; no table pounder or 'go-to-hell' kind of person, affable and gentle."

Eventually Henry Jr. was accepted by Cornell, where a private tutor engaged by the Morgenthaus remained on duty. When Henry's grades were poor and he failed to get into a fraternity, his father blamed the tutor. He had not "delivered his money's worth," he wrote to his son.

Henry soon realized that he was once again fighting a losing battle. His father had dreams of a partnership in building construction. His experience in real estate, law, and business would be appropriately complemented by an architect son, and, further, his own father had tried to steer him toward a civil engineering career. He had even worked briefly in an engineer's office, only to give it up, convinced that he "lacked the requisite mathematical foundation."

★Years later Edward M. M. Warburg, the youngest child of the "royal union" of Felix ("Fizzy") Warburg of Hamburg and Jacob Schiff's only daughter, Frieda, recalled that Dr. Koenig kept order by closing his eyes and screaming until his face turned red.

By the spring of 1911, Henry Jr., discouraged by his books and drawing board, left Cornell. Having determined that a hands-on approach to the building business would be more to his liking, he became a timekeeper on a construction job and he much preferred open-air employment to the confinement of the classroom. However, his desultory commitment to this new course of action was no match for Henry Sr.'s conviction that his son had taken a giant step in the wrong direction. Henry Sr. suggested that if he wanted to see how the other half lived, he should volunteer his services at the Henry Street Settlement House on Manhattan's Lower East Side. Henry Street operated under the compassionate stewardship of Lillian Wald, a trained nurse of German Jewish antecedents from Rochester, New York.

Henry Street had started as a visiting nurse service, under the quiet patronage of Jacob Schiff. It expanded into a social service and cultural haven for the flood of desperately poor Eastern European Jewish immigrants. Operated almost entirely by volunteers — sons and daughters of wealthy, established families — it became recognized as a kind of social service finishing school for those who aspired to careers in public life, like Herbert Lehman. Elinor Fatman, later Henry's wife, worked in the settlement's Neighborhood Playhouse.*

For Lillian Wald's wealthy patrons, Henry Street was more than noblesse oblige. From 1881 on, the pogroms in Russia and Poland had triggered an exodus of impoverished, uneducated Jews, most of whom arrived at Ellis Island in New York harbor. Some were extremely Orthodox in their religious observance, others were militant atheists and socialists. The East European Jews far outnumbered their German brethren, most of whom had arrived in the United States a generation earlier. Soon this new majority became the Jewish stereotype in the eyes of the community at large, as all Jews found themselves the victims of a new, virulent strain of anti-Semitism.

---

*The Henry Street Settlement was a magnificent instrument for Americanizing recent immigrants, a paradigm that was emulated at the Grand Street Boys Club, the Educational Alliance, and elsewhere. Later, when Henry Morgenthau, Sr., was active in Bronx real estate, Lillian Wald convinced him that the Bronx needed a "Henry Street." He responded by helping to organize Bronx House on Washington Avenue, a few blocks east of the Grand Concourse (the Fifth Avenue of the Bronx). As Henry Street was enhanced by the reputation of its adjunct Neighborhood Playhouse, Bronx House received acclaim for its music school, nurtured by Henry Sr.'s wife, Josephine, herself an accomplished amateur musician.

Leaders of the "uptown" Jews, who were disturbed by what was happening on the Lower East Side, reacted with benign hostility. Realizing that there was nothing they could do to stem the tide of immigration, they took steps to speed the Americanization and general well-being of all newcomers as rapidly as possible. At the same time, of course, they tried to maintain their own exclusive and superior status.

Henry was not content to remain in New York. After his Henry Street stint in the summer of 1911, he got a job in Hartford as a laborer with the Underwood Typewriter Company, where his father had made a hefty investment and was a director. A few days after he started he became seriously ill with typhus. When he recovered, "Pa insisted that I should go out to a Texas ranch for several weeks of recuperation." There, Henry experienced more than physical mending. Suddenly he knew what he wanted to do with his life. He would be a farmer. With this purpose clearly in mind, he returned to Cornell to enroll in the School of Agriculture for what would be his final round of formal education.

In the fall of 1913, a few months after finishing up at Cornell (without a degree), Henry Morgenthau, Jr., then twenty-two, acquired some one thousand acres of farmland in the township of East Fishkill, about fifteen miles south of Poughkeepsie, New York. The nearest post office was Hopewell Junction. His father calculated the risk and gave it his blessing. He was affording his son the chance to escape on a short leash.

The farm seemed everything that Henry Jr. had been reaching for all his life. Working outdoors, free from the glib, aggressive, verbal city life, he was reborn. He thought he had discovered a world where his father, his relatives, and his German Jewish peers would not trespass.

But he was mistaken. His father continued to intervene, to offer unsolicited advice, and to finance him, while pulling the farmboy back into his own glamorous orbit. But this time Henry Jr. had set sail on his own course, and his father was quick to recognize the difference between his son's commitment to this new venture and previous false starts. He tried to exercise self-control in his irrepressible urge to act for his son. Always one to start with the head man, he sent his son to seek advice from David F. Houston, President Wilson's secretary of agriculture. Houston arranged for a junior staff member, Carl Schurz Schoffield, to take a leave of absence so that Henry could retain him as an adviser. So the two men, accompanied by Schoffield's male secretary, J. A. Taylor, took off on a transcontinental grand tour.

Perhaps it was more than a coincidence that after exploring opportunities nationwide, Henry Jr. discovered his Canaan at the East Fishkill valley, fifty miles north of New York City. As a young man, before he got married in 1883, Henry Sr. had occasionally sought rest and fresh country air in Hopewell Junction, boarding with the Harpel family. Sometime after that he had contemplated going into farming there himself. Now, although the senior Morgenthau had no intention of becoming actively engaged with the soil himself, owning country acres had a strong appeal for him. Besides, had not his own father once owned a sizable tract in the Black Forest? The Fishkill farms, paid for by the senior Morgenthau, was at first a joint father and son enterprise.

Young Henry's taste for the outdoor life undoubtedly was influenced by summer vacations at the family's Eagle Nest camp in the Adirondacks as well as his experience of convalescence in Texas. In 1904 a group of German Jewish families that knew each other in New York City bought property in the Blue Mountain Lake region of the Adirondack Mountains and formed the Eagle Nest Club. At a time when Jews were not welcome in the "better" resort hotels, this clubbing together of companionable families proved to be a pleasant solution. The general practice, with many variations, was for each family to build a log cottage as living quarters and to eat together with the others in a shared casino. One of these clubs, Knollwood, on Upper Saranac, still functions today, with descendants of the founding Blumenthal family among those in residence.

Henry Jr.'s closest friend was a contemporary at Eagle Nest, Harold Hochschild. Their fathers were founders, and Harold's mother was a Knollwood Blumenthal. Harold had also been a classmate of Henry Jr.'s in kindergarten and at the Sachs school.

Many years later the Hochschilds bought out everyone else and took over the entire property for themselves. Harold had quietly become an enormously wealthy tycoon as the CEO of American Metals Climax.*

---

*A classmate of one of Harold Hochschild's nephews at Oberlin College, E. L. Doctorow, vacationed at Eagle Nest. His *Loon Lake* is a marvelously aberrant fictional version of the Eagle Nest way of life during Harold's reign.

As teenagers early in the twentieth century, Harold Hochschild, Henry Jr., and three other boys formed a club of their own. All achieved outstanding distinction thanks, in no small measure, to family connections. Arthur Sulzberger married Adolph Ochs's daughter and sole heir, Iphigene, and succeeded him as publisher of the *New York Times*. Alfred Jeretzski followed his father into a law partnership at Sullivan & Cromwell. The other lawyer in the group, "General" Edward S. Greenbaum, whose father had been a New York Supreme Court judge, established the firm of Greenbaum, Wolff and Ernst.

Two younger brothers, Walter Hochschild and David Sulzberger, were awarded junior membership in what came to be called the Poker and Pretzel Club. All seven managed to get together once a year for the rest of their lives, to play poker for low stakes. Because they were "the babies," the two junior members always received invitations with little pink bows, David Sulzberger's widow, Louise (née Blumenthal), recalled. "The only trouble was that the babies were better gamblers than the seniors; they had done more of it."

All the families at Eagle Nest had motorboats made by the Lozier Company in Plattsburg, New York, which could speed across the lake at about seven or eight miles an hour. When Henry Sr. bought one that could do twelve miles an hour, and named it the *Henry Jr.*, the young owner became the envy of all, not only for his sleek mahogany craft but also for his frequent passenger, a gorgeous redhead, Bernice Marx. She had a habit of sitting on the railing of her porch overlooking the lake and swinging her long, bare legs in a way that attracted adolescent boys from miles around. At the age of eighty-six, Harold Hochschild remembered Bernice as "the most beautiful girl I've ever seen. But I was never on the same basis with [her] that your father [Henry Jr.] was," he confided ruefully.

Henry and Ellie

IN 1909, the year after Henry Jr. went to Cornell, Bernice Marx matriculated at Vassar College in the class of 1913. But it was a Vassar classmate of hers, Elinor Fatman (called Ellie by her family and friends), who, somewhere in the course of events, became the focus of Henry's ardent attentions. There is no record of just how Henry and Ellie met — although opportunities had abounded. Both were born on West Eighty-first Street between Central Park West and Columbus Avenue. Both had worked at the Henry Street Settlement House. They had traveled in the same social crowd. Elinor Fatman was no match for Bernice according to conventional standards of beauty. But she had an arresting presence attesting to her keen intellect and later enhanced by her experience on the stage at Vassar. In the all-female casts she had often played the male lead. She had a short, rounded figure, clear white skin, and deep-set, dark brown eyes emphasizing her large nose, which she described as "Roman." In her well-modulated, musical voice she could converse equally well in German and English, and quite comfortably in French. She later studied Spanish and Russian.

Ellie was a good athlete and kept herself in shape, although with due consideration for feminine niceties, as a girl she rode horseback sidesaddle rather than astride. When she played tennis, she employed an underhand serve calculated to avoid the unladylike stretching of the bosom required in the execution of a man's overhand serve. This stroke had a nasty cut and flat bounce which, when properly placed, limited her opponent's return to an impotent high lob.

Ellie went to Miss Jacobi's private school for girls in New York.

She excelled in the humanities — math and science were not required — and graduated near the top of her class.

I don't know what put the idea in my mother's head of going to Vassar. Though not unheard of, it was still very much the exception for women of her generation to leave home for college. Among the prosperous New York families it was held that if one's daughter insisted, she could commute to Barnard. Nevertheless, Ellie managed to gain parental consent.

There had been a similar situation in the Morgenthau family when my father's oldest sister, Helen, an intelligent, fiercely independent person, announced her intention to go to Vassar. She received some encouragement from her father, who made all the important decisions in the family. Her mother was dead set against it. She felt that a girl who went to college would turn out to be "a blue stocking, . . . that she would just do teaching . . . and probably never get married." Helen graduated from Vassar in the class of 1905, got married, and produced three children.

I suspect that in Elinor Fatman's case, as with Helen Morgenthau, it was her father who overruled her mother's misgivings and permitted her to go. Morris Fatman, who would dearly have loved to have had a son, lavished some of the special attention generally reserved for boys on the favorite of his two daughters. He had missed gaining a college education himself and was eager to provide this opportunity for his intelligent and ambitious offspring.

At Vassar Ellie had made close, lifelong friends, like Gabrielle Elliot Forbush, a collateral descendant of President Rutherford B. Hayes.

"Nobody knew Ellie well freshman year," Gabrielle recalled. "It must have been quite an ordeal for her because she was so completely unprepared for it.

"Dear old Mrs. Fatman had never had anyone in her family go to college. She thought of it like a swell finishing school. So she had outfitted Ellie with all these lovely clothes. . . . [Ellie] hung all those dresses in the closets without really looking at them.

"One evening early in freshman year she went down to dinner as usual wearing an old brown sweater, brown skirt, and white blouse. . . . That evening everybody at her table was all dressed up. Ellie was quite hurt. She thought someone was having a party off campus and had left her out. Finally she turned to one of the girls and said, 'Do you mind my asking where you got that dress? I think

I have one like it.' Whereupon the entire table burst out laughing. It seems they had all gone into her closets and 'borrowed' her gorgeous dresses, sweaters, and shoes. Elinor hadn't really recognized them at all. So that kind of broke the ice with the girls. Ellie always loved to tell that story on herself. She had a keen sense of humor.

"During Ellie's sophomore year we decided to stage *Beau Brummel*. We had trials for the roles. Ellie got the part of the Prince of Wales. It was a good part, and she came out of obscurity with it.

"I remember my senior year three of us had a suite together with a study and three bedrooms. Ellie had a freshman who was very devoted to her. We had 'crushes' in those days. Ellie came into the study and dropped into the easy chair gasping, 'I've seen fresh freshmen in my day but this is the freshest freshman ever.'"

Elinor's best friends at Vassar came from Protestant families of modest means. They had been sent to college because it seemed prudent that they be prepared to "do something" in life.

Elinor had never felt wealthy at home. The Fatmans were comparatively poor relations of the Lehmans, on her mother's side, the Einsteins on her father's side, and such family friends as the Blumenthals, Margaret Seligman, and Carola Warburg.

But, "to us at Vassar," Gabrielle recalled, "she was rolling in money. But you really didn't know unless you were an intimate.

"I remember once I was staying up at Vassar over vacation because I had been in too many plays and was behind in my work. She invited me to come down just for the day to see *Parsifal* at the Met. She had borrowed her aunt's little carriage and horse and coachman. During the intermission we drove over to Maillard's and had chicken sandwiches and hot chocolate and then tooled back to the Opera House. . . . Well, those are the things that kind of opened your eyes. That was a lovely time."

According to Gabrielle, the matter of Ellie's being Jewish did not matter to her friends. "It was ignored completely. I know my mother and hers got together on that once. Mother thought that I had lost my faith at Vassar, and Mrs. Fatman was complaining that Ellie never would go to temple. They were two mothers mourning over their young. I don't think Mrs. Fatman went herself. Of course she was deaf. That would let her out of many things. There weren't many Jewish girls at Vassar then. The Marx girl, Bernice, was very beautiful. She was always the marshal in Ellie's class, 1913. Ellie had no use for her. I don't know why."

Ellie's four years at Vassar constituted the one period in her life when she was permitted to operate independently in a world of her own. Though a closed, protected society, a women's college allowed women to play all the important roles, including those usually reserved for men. She was an above-average student. However, it was the stage that became the consuming passion of her college career. During her junior year, she was elected president of the Philathesis, the dramatic society. At college she experienced the possibilities and limitations of social relationships: competition, negotiation, and the exercise of power. She formed a network of friends — mostly fellow students, but a few teachers as well — that lasted the rest of her life. Vassar was a success story that began to fade as she returned to the outside world. Never again would she assert herself with the same confidence and demonstrable potential. It was not yet a time when a woman could play the same role as a man, and any woman wanting to try would have been required to sacrifice any notion of becoming a wife and mother. And such a sacrifice was certainly not what her family or Ellie herself had in mind. All the same, when she returned home to West Eighty-first Ellie continued to nurture some dreams of a theatrical career. She performed with an amateur company in New York City and taught at the Neighborhood Playhouse, then an adjunct of the Henry Street Settlement on the Lower East Side.★

Ellie graduated from Vassar in 1913, and Henry purchased his farm that same year; their romance began to blossom sometime after that. In 1915, when he went to Constantinople to serve as the ambassador's aide, Henry Jr. revealed his intentions. His father had serious misgivings — not about Elinor Fatman, whom he knew and liked — but on general principles.

"Disregard women or give yourself up as vanquished," the senior Morgenthau had admonished himself in his diary in 1877. Then twenty-one, he managed to postpone this dreadful fate for another six years. "I have often thought lately what a mistake it would have been for you to have married too young," he had written his son in 1914.

★The Henry Street Neighborhood Playhouse was directed and financed by two Lewisohn sisters, Irene and Alice. Later on, relocated in midtown, it thrived as a professional theater school. Under the motherly management of Rita Wallach Morgenthau, divorced wife of my father's cousin Max, it trained Gregory Peck and a generation of aspiring actors, many of whom must have been inspired by the Yiddish theater, thriving on Second Avenue.

You are just now soaring onward and upward and no matter who you would have married, you would have developed your physical desires more than your intellectual and altruistic tendencies, and almost any smart girl would have cajoled and controlled you and dwarfed and stunted your growth. This is an inexplicable condition that arises with 9 out of 10 men, and I want you to be the tenth who escapes. The path of enjoyment is so much pleasanter than that of duty, so that most men are only too willingly guided to adopt it and once following it, seldom leave it.

For the first time in his life Henry Jr. proceeded to override his father's advice. Indeed it appears that part of Ellie's appeal was that he was beginning to rely on her strength of character as an alternative source of reassurance against his self-doubts. In 1915 Henry Jr. was writing to Ellie from Turkey somewhat boastful, hardly passionate letters, indicating that he was sharing confidences, about his father, with someone other than the old man himself. "This is strictly sub, sub [sub rosa]. Pa is in a very difficult frame of mind. And I am glad to say that I can and am being helpful to him in one of the most crucial moments of his life. We are trying to think out the best possible way to get him home [from Constantinople] this spring. Pa dictated a letter to Colonel House for me which I then wrote and signed on that subject."

A week later he again shared his father's dreams with Ellie, revealing that his father expected to "have some wonderful opportunities in the next few years, and we will all live to see the day when he will have accomplished even greater and bigger things than he has here [in Turkey]. Just as after the Civil War the generals and soldiers held all the political positions for twenty years, now the successful War ambassadors will be the ones sought after in fields of political endeavor."

So it happened that after returning to New York on February 22, 1916, while the dockside welcoming ceremonies for the returning ambassador were in progress, Henry Jr. slipped away unnoticed. He proceeded immediately to the Fatman brownstone at 23 West Eighty-first Street to call on Ellie. She was pleased but not surprised to see him. Henry, however, was speechless. She suggested a walk around the Central Park Reservoir. After they had silently circled the entire half-mile perimeter of this artificial pond, "I broke the ice by proposing marriage. Henry was greatly relieved."

He immediately telephoned his father, who was summoned

from the family celebration in the dining room. "Pa, I want you to be the first to know. Ellie and I are engaged!"

The older Morgenthau was only a little surprised at his impulsive son's precipitate timing. He accepted the news with characteristic optimism, banishing his considerable misgivings, for at twenty-four, his son still appeared to him erratic and unpredictable.

The Morgenthaus and the Fatmans, faced with the inevitability of their children's marriage, found each other mutually acceptable. Elinor's parents were both second-generation Americans. Morris Fatman had been born in Cincinnati, his wife, Settie, in Montgomery, Alabama. More important, Settie was a Lehman. After the Civil War, her father, Mayer Lehman, had moved his family to New York, where he and his brother converted their cotton brokerage business into the great banking house of Lehman Brothers. Morris and his bachelor brother Solly (Solomon Aaron) manufactured "shoddy" (a feltlike woolen cloth) in the Raritan Woolen Mills in Somerset, New Jersey, on the Raritan River.

Nevertheless, "Ellie's not strong enough to have a baby," Settie protested. "It's really dangerous, awfully dangerous." Perhaps her misgivings had something to do with her older daughter, Margaret, who was still single. Or perhaps she was simply experiencing the anxiety and regrets of a woman thrust toward grandmotherhood.

Settie Fatman viewed a good marriage as the primary goal for both sexes. But once coupled, the two partners were expected to run on entirely separate tracks. A man headed for advancement in his career; a woman's place was in the home — when she went out in the world, it was to play a clearly defined supporting role. One measure of a husband's worth was the extent to which he relieved his wife of all household labor. The ultimate achievement was an idle woman who would venture forth at her husband's beck and call, laden with expensive jewelry and heavy furs, advertising his success. At home she supervised a staff of full-time help and occasional specialists.

The Morgenthau women chafed at this stereotype with varying degrees of manifest indignation. Not so Elinor's mother. Without a qualm she wedged herself into the mold humorlessly. She was, after all, a *geborene* Lehman; what more could one aspire to? Settie had the Lehman look that endowed men and women alike with the appearance of an angry squirrel: paunchy gray cheeks, deep-set eyes, and dark, bushy brows that joined in a permanent scowl.

What Settie Fatman lacked in natural beauty she made up by her sense of style. She wore well-cut black high-neck dresses with a choker of grosgrain silk ribbon ornamented with pearls and diamonds. Her serious demeanor was perfectly suited to one of her favorite activities: the recounting of what she called her "rows" — disputes, generally with tradespeople, though sometimes with family and friends. These battles, as in Shakespearean tragedy, took place offstage. Settie would warm to the retelling while presiding over the tea table, her passionate anger exploding at some innocent guest who had the nerve to show that she was something less than a totally sympathetic ally.

Moments later, the temper storm spent, Settie would make a peace offering. "Have a chocolate leaf," she would suggest, passing a plate of almond wafers coated with bittersweet chocolate shaped and veined to resemble oversized oak leaves. They were one of the expensive delicacies, along with the chocolate éclairs and cream puffs, which were delivered as a standing order from Dean's Pastry Shop.

Bonded in a true love match, Henry and Elinor were convinced that their approaching marriage had been made in heaven. For their parents and the German Jewish community it had been made appropriately on Central Park West.

The nuptials took place on April 17, 1916, less than two months after they became formally engaged. For the occasion the partition between the two back-to-back dining rooms was removed in the adjoining houses that Mayer Lehman had built for two of his daughters, Settie Fatman and Hattie Goodhart.* With the two houses as one on that day only, Settie prepared to accommodate more guests than she had bargained for.

Gabrielle Forbush had a vivid memory of this "most impressive" wedding. "It was a great crush. . . . Poor Mrs. Fatman was utterly snowed under with both families."

Ellie invited a number of her Vassar friends. Ethel Freeman, her classmate, was the maid of honor. Henry's niece, Josephine Wertheim, was the flower girl. His nephew, Tim Fox, was the page.

The bride was serenely beautiful. Having lost a lot of weight

---

*Hattie (Mrs. Phillip) Goodhart is the "Aunt Hattie" whom Stephen Birmingham credits with the title of his book *Our Crowd*. It was her notion of a euphemistic way of referring to that select group of her German Jewish relatives and friends: "people you visited."

just before the wedding, she was ethereal in a tight-bodiced white satin dress and a veil made of yards of gauze. She carried an enormous bouquet of lilies of the valley and trailing ribbon.

The nervous bridegroom was nonetheless aware that he looked very handsome in the cutaway tailored for the occasion — that is until his mother looked him up and down. Her eyes settling critically on his middle section, she commented dryly, "Henry, you've got my hips." Years later he had not forgotten his mother's blessing on that day. Meanwhile, the older Morgenthau, who had dispensed with all of his misgivings, took center stage as his son's best man. Rabbi Stephen Wise performed the wedding ceremony, "a stage character," Gabrielle recalled, "that beautiful voice and presence." Margaret, Ellie's older sister, who was singing small roles at the Metropolitan Opera, sang Wagner's "Wedding March."*

After the wedding Henry Jr. received a cordial invitation from Walter Hines Page, U.S. ambassador in London. "When it becomes safer, come over here and spend your honeymoon. You'll find the latch at No. 6 Grosvenor Square hanging on the outside. All good luck. My regards to your father."

By the time the letter arrived Henry and Elinor had already returned from a wedding trip motoring through the Shenandoah Valley and the Blue Ridge Mountains in the sporty red Stutz Bear Cat that Henry had selected as a wedding present from his father after watching it win a road race. (Ellie owned a Model T Ford coupé, purchased with one thousand dollars from her father.)

A married woman, deeply in love, Elinor was enthusiastically ready to venture forth hand in hand with her husband into a brave new world beyond Manhattan. She shared his partiality to the outdoors and to his father's high ideals. He was determined to make his farm a financial success.

On January 11, 1917, just short of nine months after the wedding, Elinor delivered a healthy 6-pound, 8-ounce baby boy. Her mother's doubts and worries about her daughter's reproductive capacity shifted abruptly to embarrassment. "Ellie had a fall just a week before the baby was born," Settie Fatman said, feeling it her

*According to Gabrielle Forbush, "Margaret sang 'Ave Maria,' which was a strange selection . . . but it was kind of an old war horse for her." Perhaps she sang this number as well as the "Wedding March."

duty to explain the "premature birth." I was the last member of our family to be born at home rather than in a hospital. A few years later I would have my tonsils and adenoids removed at home, then a much-favored procedure. But my brother Robert was delivered in 1919 and my sister Joan in 1922 in hospitals, by then the preferred practice.

Home was an apartment on Broadway in the Seventies. In those days unless one owned a brownstone — co-ops were rare and considered risky — it was the custom to move from one rented apartment to another as the size of the family and its financial circumstances dictated.

For our tribe all this movement was inside a loosely defined West Side ghetto. The choicest apartments were on Central Park West from Central Park South to Eighty-sixth Street. Houses and smaller apartment buildings were on the side streets. West of Columbus Avenue, with its noisy, dirty, rattletrap El, the quality of life descended, picking up again, as the Broadway musical lyrics told us, "Way Out West on West End A-ven-ue," and on Riverside Drive.

However, as the 1920s peaked, "our crowd" was increasingly moving to the East Side. Although many of the properties had restrictive covenants, it wasn't difficult to find something if they had the money and many of them did. Some arriving a little overextended got caught in the 1929 crash, and exited via the window like the father of a friend of mine, from a Park Avenue co-op.

The senior Morgenthau was unabashedly overjoyed when his grandson was anointed — without benefit of a *bris* (ritual circumcision) — Henry III. He himself had cheerfully violated the dictum of Ashkenazi Jews against giving a child the name of a living relative. Now he could hardly wait to have the three Henrys photographed together. "Mr. Morgenthau playfully refers to this picture as the Morgenthau dynasty," the caption reads under this photograph, which is reproduced in his autobiography.★

★Years later when I was a mature bachelor living with my grandfather, who was then approaching his terminal ninetieth year, he offered me a handsome financial incentive to produce a legitimate Henry the Fourth. Some considerable time after he died I did so. Although my son's legal name is Henry, my wife and I began referring to him as Ben Henry (Hebrew for "son of Henry"). We thought this would please both my father and my father-in-law, a devout Orthodox Jew. But like most compromises it only aroused suspicion and resentment on both sides.

My grandfather used the authentic German pronunciation *Morgen-tow*. Later it was corrupted to *thow* and finally to *thaw*. One thing he would not tolerate was the appendage "senior." He was simply Henry Morgenthau, his son Henry Jr., and his grandson Henry III. My mother referred to me as "little Henry," "Hen," or "Heine." Later, when she noted that I was knock-kneed she would chant, "Heine Heine, mit der krumme Beine."

In a decorus volume, "Annals of Babyhood," bound in turquoise blue leather and silk embossed with gold, my mother recorded details of my birth and hesitant beginnings, with the unique devotion of a mother for her firstborn. Never again, neither at the advent of her second son nor her daughter, did she trouble to preserve all the evidence so unsparingly. Amidst all these data, locks of hair, photographs, letters, and telegrams of congratulation is noted "Father's occupation: farmer."

Ellie's dual role as mother and farmer's wife terminated any of her premarital ambitions for a career in the theater. On Rita Morgenthau's insistence, Elinor did teach sporadically at the uptown Neighborhood Playhouse School, but by then her energies were harnessed to activities supportive of my father's career. She would soon discover that her theatrical skills could be transplanted from the stage to the political arena, and she later became a popular speaker for the state Democratic Committee, Women's Division.

Most of the time she was serene in her bucolic Dutchess County environs. No regrets — at least not until much later — even though she was abandoned to her own devices just a few months after I was born. After all there was a war on.

When the United States joined the Allies in April 1917, patriotic fervor was rampant. UNCLE SAM WANTS YOU posters were everywhere. Many men jumped into uniform. The young Morgenthau tried to enlist but was turned down because of poor eyesight.

My parents then redoubled their efforts in cultivation, preservation, and marketing of farm produce in Dutchess County.

My mother, who had never stepped inside the kitchen either in her mother's home or in her own, applied herself diligently to learning the technique of canning as though it were another foreign language, and she was soon teaching it. At around the same time my father became chairman of the Dutchess County Committee on Conservation and Food. But his father kept prodding him to find a broader field for his endeavors, and opportunity soon presented itself.

At the time the United States entered the war, the nation was shipping large quantities of food to France, under difficult and dangerous circumstances. With all the horses and able-bodied men ages eighteen to fifty at the front, one-fourth of the tillable uninvaded French soil lay fallow. Young Morgenthau envisaged batteries of tractors in France manned by those unfit for service aided by expert American mechanics as a way of restoring France's ability to feed its populace. The idea seemed so simple and obvious that Morgenthau thought it must have occurred to others or that he had overlooked some major problems. So of course he tested it out on his father.

The old man was duly impressed, seeing the scheme as a great opportunity for his son. He went straight to President Wilson. The president referred him to Secretary of Agriculture Houston, who was not impressed. But the senior Morgenthau persisted, going on to see the newly appointed food administrator, Herbert Hoover. This time he hit pay dirt. Hoover was enthusiastic and promised to have the proposal implemented.

In mid-December 1917, in response to a summons from a Hoover assistant, Lewis Strauss, young Morgenthau arrived in Washington to effect his plan under the aegis of the Food Administration. It was a bold and complex undertaking for an inexperienced twenty-six-year-old.

The French high commissioner in Washington (and later premier of France), André Tardieu, expressed the French government's willingness to purchase tractors with funds loaned by the U.S. government. Then the Red Cross stepped in. They coordinated a meeting of the French high commissioner, the acting secretary of agriculture, and representatives of the Food Administration, along with Red Cross officials and young Morgenthau. In the meantime Morgenthau went to Detroit to call on Henry Ford, the leading tractor manufacturer, and secured his promise of cooperation.

Early in February the first three hundred American tractors were shipped to France on board the U.S. Navy transport *Lake Tahoe*. At the end of the month, Tardieu wrote to Food Administrator Hoover to inform him that in response to his "suggestion of sending a large number of agricultural tractors to France . . . [of the] 1500 tractors purchased by the French Government, some are now in France and more will be shipped before the end of this month." The high commissioner went on to say: "I feel that this gratifying result is largely due to Mr. Henry Morgenthau, Jr., who has kept in touch with the transaction through all the stages of allotting contracts, manufacture and shipping by rail and water.

"With a view to carrying this enterprise to a successful issue, may I suggest that it would be advisable to have Mr. Morgenthau go to France."

Two weeks later Morgenthau set sail on board the French liner *Espagne* with a shipload of civilians bent on doing their part for the war effort. There were a number of notables among them, and the handsome young American attracted considerable attention, for which he felt bound to account to his wife:

> I am the only married man on board I have seen so far who wears a wedding ring and I am proud of it. Agnes Nicholson said she and some of the other girls talked me over and decided I was very nice. Especially in that I was so different from most husbands because I guess I am always talking about you and Henry III.
>
> Did I tell you that Agnes N. told me in confidence that she is engaged to be married to a man who is in the wholesale farm seed business. Miss Lauder is also engaged. So my two little playmates on the ship are quite harmless.

Nevertheless, he felt constrained to keep Elinor advised that he was behaving himself. "Girls no longer mean anything to me," he wrote several days later, "as I have only one girl as she is by my side all the time darling. You know sweetheart I am ever so glad that you came on board to say goodbye. Because I always look over to the place on the couch where we sat and said goodbye and I feel closer to you then."

Morgenthau arrived in Paris the morning of April 14, booked himself a room at the Hotel Crillon, checked in at the American embassy, and in the evening went to the opera. He was surprised to find in the extreme gravity of the war situation the Parisians carrying on as usual, even though the Germans were near enough so that French Army replacements were being sent to the front by taxi and one could occasionally hear the burst of a long-range German shell.

After reporting everything to Elinor, Henry was dismayed by her somewhat chiding response. "For some reason, the fact that I went to the Opera the first night struck my wife as extremely funny, though it seemed to me a natural thing to do," he noted in his journal. Henry had also written Elinor that "fighting was only the least part" of winning the war. She wrote back, "I must say I don't entirely agree with you and think every man ought to just enlist in the active fight, then if he is refused let him do what he is best fitted for, just as you have done. Ideas are all very nice, but fighting men must win the war."

Elinor had encouraged her husband's adventure abroad, yet she couldn't help reminding him that while he was enjoying Paris her life on the farm was pretty austere — albeit with a nurse, a cook, and a maid. She was spending a good deal of time managing the farm, especially minding the accounts. She was also taking a daily course in automobile mechanics in preparation for ambulance driving and repair. Among other things, she had mastered the task of changing a tire — no mean trick in those days when it meant removing the shoe from the rim and replacing or patching the inner tube before remounting and inflating the entire assembly. In later years she would sometimes remind her husband that never in his life had he changed a tire.

The second day Morgenthau was in Paris he met with a Captain Goudard, the chief of Culture de Terre, to discuss the tractor project. He was generally hostile, although Morgenthau accepted the merit of many of his objections: there were serious problems with spare parts and qualified mechanics, even with the three-wheel tractors themselves, which were difficult to turn on wet ground. Morgenthau was at first nonplussed, but he soon came to appreciate that "our tractor plan must have appeared to Goudard as a criticism of his agency."

The following week Morgenthau met with the minister of agriculture, Victor Boret, who surprised him with his excellent English, his patient explanation of some of the real problems, and his determination to convince Herbert Hoover that the French government would do everything in its power to increase crop production. While in France Henry Jr. also visited a factory that turned out forty thousand shells per day. He noted in his journal, "Women do not receive equal pay for equal work. Wages fixed by Minister of Munitions. Pace terrific. Women look none too well. 75% of workers are women."

In May, Morgenthau returned to the States. With the delivery of the tractors he had essentially completed his responsibility for the mission. He wisely chose not to become further involved with the French bureaucracy in implementing the project. Back home on the farm, not wanting to be considered a "slacker," he immediately appealed to his father to help him get into uniform, requesting a waiver of his physical deferment. Pa first went to the secretary of war, Newton Baker. But before Baker had acted, the secretary of the navy, Josephus Daniels, who had warmly befriended Ambassador Morgenthau, proposed to get his son a commission for service in the Naval Quartermaster Corps. In short order Louis Howe, assistant to Assistant Secretary of the Navy Franklin D. Roosevelt, informed the young man that the Bureau of Navigation had waived his deferment.

The bureau authorized the commandant of the Third Naval District to enroll Henry as a lieutenant, junior grade. On September 3, he was sworn in and assigned to New York headquarters for duty under the general inspector, Naval Transportation Service. Thus, for the final two months of the war, looking rather handsome in his blue serge uniform, he busied himself inspecting cargo on the city docks, returning each evening to his wife and son at their apartment on Broadway.

· 20 ·

Morgenthaus, Fatmans, and Lehmans

SINCE EVERYONE on both sides of my family had come to the United States from Germany, during my childhood the immigrant forebears were still around, if not physically, at least in memory. My relatives through my parents' generation spoke German until the United States went to war, although German Jews continued to emphasize their Germanness at least as much as their Jewishness. Much later in life I understood that this was designed as a barrier they used to separate themselves from the impoverished "hordes" of East European Jews who had flooded these shores from the end of the last century until after World War I. At the same time, like other German Americans, German Jews found no inconsistency in affirming their unshakable loyalty to the United States and ultimately to the Allied cause. The kaiser's government had expected the descendants of immigrants from the Fatherland to stir up American sympathy for the Central Powers. These hopes were dashed.

When I was three and my brother Robert was six months old, we moved to an apartment at 35 West Eighty-first Street, only two or three doors away from the Fatman and Goodhart brownstones. As a baby Bob was mischievously angelic, a blue-eyed blond with delicate features not yet dominated by the prominent family nose. Our mother didn't have the heart to have Bob's crown of golden curls cropped, as was held befitting to a boy, until he was five. At that stage of life I had sported a page-boy bob well suited to my dark, perfectly straight locks that were preserved for about the same length of time.

During those early years, we spent the winter months in New York City and the summer on the farm. Later on, when we children were at school, we resided in the city during the academic year, although we generally went to the farm on weekends and holidays. Our building on West Eighty-first Street, the Orvista Apartments, was for the most part a way station for Jewish families with ideas of better places to be. The entire twelfth, top floor was the love nest of a notorious playboy. The flamboyant decor included a huge bed decorated with carved dragons. My cousins, the Frank Altschuls, eventually took over this choice apartment.★

West Eighty-first Street in the 1920s was in a well-established, unpretentious neighborhood, cozy and convenient. Settie Fatman's teas were served in the second-floor parlor, which extended across the entire front of her brownstone at number 23. A bay window facing south overlooked the small park behind the Museum of Natural History. It was crammed full of comfy, overstuffed furniture upholstered in soft velour, in rich browns and grays. Faded where the sun filtered in through the lace curtains, the bulky chairs and couches were old friends. A big carved oak desk supported an array of silver and leather-framed family photographs, an ivory desk set, carved and monogrammed, which included a magnifying glass, letter opener, and other unused objects, all surrounded by stacks of old letters and postcards inscribed with brief factual accountings of summer vacations in Europe and the Adirondacks.

On the dark green damask-covered walls above the oak-paneled wainscoting were oil paintings of the Barbizon School, French landscapes, embedded in heavy gilt frames and embalmed under a glaze of yellowed varnish.

In one corner there was an oil portrait of a proud patriarch with a full gray beard and piercing black eyes that seemed to follow you and demand attention.

"Who is that old man?" I got up enough nerve to ask my grandmother on one occasion. Grandma was hard of hearing, reputedly a hereditary Lehman trait. She wore a hearing aid that was wired into a black box designed like a handbag, and it squealed back at my

★Helen Altschul was the daughter of my aunt Hattie Goodhart, who lived down the street at number 21. Frank Altschul's sister Edith was married to Aunt Hattie's and Grandma Fatman's youngest brother, Herbert Lehman. Frank was at Lazard Frères on Wall Street. With a good nose for investments and a considerable financial leg up from both sides of the family, he was on his way to amassing a huge fortune. When the Altschuls moved to the East Side, we took over the twelfth-floor apartment.

question when I got too close. "Who is that old man?" I shouted insistently. Grandma glared at me, answering in an annoyed tone that precluded further inquiry, "He's an Old Testament prophet." Hanging on the back of the door next to him was a silk Muslim prayer rug.

Along one wall there were several mahogany bookcases with glass doors protecting sets of English, American, and German authors. In handsome leather bindings were the complete works of Shakespeare, Walter Scott, Mark Twain, Edgar Allan Poe, and, in German, Schiller, Lessing, Heine, and Henrik Ibsen (translated from the Norwegian). In a separate two-tier case in soft black leather gold-embossed binding was the great eleventh edition of the *Encyclopaedia Britannica* (published 1910–11).

Every inch of space displayed a valued object. A vacuum was no more abhorrent to nature than was empty space to the post-Victorian generation. Of course they never worried about collecting dust because there were always servants armed with feather dusters and rags to spread it around. The brass was polished regularly, as was the silver. A mysterious man appeared once a week to wind and regulate all the clocks, a responsibility beyond the powers of ordinary mortals.

Most households had more full-time servants than family members. In a cramped apartment like ours, sustaining this balance could demand considerable sacrifice in comfort and privacy for both master and servant. Nevertheless servants were considered a necessity — the status of a family freed from all manual labor had to be upheld at all costs. Wages paid to the help were meager, although their physical needs were supplied: lodgings, food, uniforms, hand-me-down clothes for "days off," medical services. Mother refused to have anything to do with my father's physician, Dr. Kessel, because he thought it was beneath him to care for servants, leaving this chore to his assistant, Dr. Hyman. Later, when Dr. Kessel died, Harold Hyman became the family physician for all of us.

Servants had no rights, only privileges and a homemade safety net of sorts. Most were single women. A few had been deserted by men. None were expected to have any close relationships with the opposite sex.

Buried under Settie Fatman's angry tantrums there was a sensuous aspect of her nature, well hidden from her grandchildren. Louise Sulzberger, whose father, Hugo Blumenthal, and Uncle Gus were Morris Fatman's closest friends, had a "peculiar story" she related with some trepidation. "I had to ask my children if it was all right to tell you. Two said yes and one said no." She continued.

"In those days, one of the great liberal ideas was that couples did *not* sleep in double beds. No one could get over that the Fatmans slept in a double bed. It was *the* talk of the town. They were the only married couple in that generation that still had a double bed. It was just something that one didn't do, you know. The twin bed had come in and that was liberation — that was as liberated as anyone could possibly be.

"I don't remember my parents ever *not* having twin beds. It was the time when everything had to be French. They had a huge blue satin canopy that extended over the two beds that were right next to each other and covered with one big blue bedspread.

"It was the fact that the Fatmans slept in a double bed that no one could understand. That was a very important thing."

It was only after her husband died that we began to notice that Grandma Fatman was quite a flirt. Her daughters, especially Margaret, the elder, became very worried when their mother encouraged the attentions of a Mr. Sollinger, a courtly widower. I suspect that she may have been concerned more with the orderly flow of her inheritance than her mother's happiness.

Grandma's generosity was something we took for granted. At the end of summer, when she returned from Europe, she lavished extravagant presents on us. One of her specialties was large Egyptian cotton pocket handkerchiefs embroidered with elaborate monograms. As they seemed too good to use, I stored them away. Some remain to this day in mint condition.

Settie Fatman's generosity frequently extended beyond the family circle. She was known to arrive at the home of a sick friend with her favorite remedies: a roast squab and a container of chicken soup.

My cousin Frances Lehman Loeb recalls that one day at noon during the Depression, her aunt Settie left her apartment at the Savoy Plaza for a walk. Outside, she noticed a woman selling apples from a small stand. Settie bought a nice McIntosh for five cents and began to ask the woman about herself. Settie was very hard of hearing, but she had her ways of communicating, doing most of the talking herself. She asked the woman when she was going to lunch. The woman indicated that she had neither time nor money for lunch. Whereupon Settie gave her a dollar and told her to go off and buy herself some lunch while she minded the apple stand. During the hour or so that Settie Fatman was dutifully manning her post, she was observed by several friends in the neighborhood, who were shocked by what they were seeing. Later that day word went out on the telephone that "poor Settie had gone balmy. She seems to think she has lost all her money and is out on the street corner selling apples."

When we were living at 35 West Eighty-first, Yehudi Menuhin, the violin prodigy, and his remarkable family were quartered in a seedy apartment hotel on the corner of Eighty-first Street and Columbus Avenue, which is still there, still seedy. I don't know how we knew about Menuhin's presence, but we did. He was almost exactly my age, and he practiced violin four hours a day, I was told. Soon he would have a Carnegie Hall debut and join the ranks of celebrated Russian Jewish prodigies, following in the footsteps of Jascha Heifetz and Mischa Elman.

We had no musician in the family, but I had a vague, disquieting feeling that our nuclear family was different from the families of our relatives and friends. Sometimes I thought it was money. We had less than most of them. They had straight-eight Cadillacs and twin-six Packards. We had a six-cylinder Buick and later on a LaSalle, which General Motors had produced for those who couldn't quite afford Cadillacs. The Nathan Strauses had the ultimate, sixteen-cylinder Cadillac inherited from their grandfather, Nathan Straus (Sr.). Shortly before he died, he had ordered it with a special body designed so that he could walk in without bending over. When his descendants took it over they had it cut down to normal size, giving it a strange, sliced-off look.

I didn't realize it at the time but my parents were then preparing for a bold adventure that would permanently remove us from the safe havens of the German Jewish establishment. We had not yet slipped our moorings, but we had loosened the bonds. We were leading a double life. In the city my mother maintained warm relations with a network of her relatives and family friends, and we were close to my Morgenthau grandparents. We were poor but not discredited relations.

In Dutchess County we were on undiscovered territory. Most of our crowd flocked to Westchester County for weekends and summers. There they occupied country estates of varying degrees of grandeur, downplayed with bucolic names like "Little Farm," "Four Wind Acres," and "Hill & Dale." When not entertaining one another, they would get together at the Century Country Club, where they could be outdoors golfing, playing tennis, or swimming, or indoors during this Prohibition era developing a taste for dry martinis, Manhattans, and Bacardi cocktails.

When these same solid citizens wanted to go farther afield, they gathered in small clusters in Adirondack "camps." Some still went to Elberon and other ports of call along the Jersey shore. But whenever they migrated to the suburbs, to the mountains, or to the seashore, it was always in a flock. There was always a critical mass.

In the 1920s, my father was engaged in money-losing occupations — farming and publishing a farm magazine, the *American Agriculturalist*. Living in space far from grand, the family and hired hands were on intimate terms. Everyone had to know his place. There was a basic cadre of five live-in maids, plus a full-time chauffeur and a caretaker. Later, during the Depression, when my father became a government official, there was also a gardener, a groom, and in the summer a college-student tutor for my brother and me.

The center of gravity in our nuclear family was not my father but my father's father. Grandpa Morgenthau, ever an outrageously lovable egotist, believed he could shape the world to his liking and take the credit. He was so successful in blotting out the spectre of his own father, Lazarus, whose world had finally collapsed around him, that not until after his passing did I divine what a haunting, driving force it had been throughout his lifetime.

On Sunday afternoons I enjoyed cruising around Manhattan with Grandpa in his big, royal blue Lincoln limousine. This was adventurous luxury. Most wealthy Jews avoided Lincolns because the manufacturer, Henry Ford, had published anti-Semitic vitriol in his *Dearborn Independent*. They opted instead for Cadillacs or, like my grandfather Fatman, a Pierce Arrow.

From the rear seat Grandpa Morgenthau directed his chauffeur like a commanding general to streets where he would recall past real estate conquests with contagious relish. It was Grandpa's successful real estate deals in Manhattan and the Bronx that had put enough wind in his sails for him to embark on uncharted seas leading to a public career in the Woodrow Wilson administration.

"What are your ambitions?" Grandpa would ask me. The question hung like a threatening stormcloud throughout my childhood. Being pushed to make a choice when opportunities seemed to be without limit was terrifying. "You can do, you can be anything you want to," my mother tried to reassure me. She didn't. Yet for all the trauma of feeling inadequate to his hopes and expectations for me during my early years, my grandfather was the powerfully attractive, loving father figure in my life.

My true father had a rich baritone voice. As a young man he took singing lessons, and people said he had real talent. It was probably inherited from his mother, a disciplined pianist and singer. But a musical career was the last thing in the world my grandfather had in mind for his only son. Music was all right, though, for the girls. Alma, one of my father's three sisters, trained her voice to the edge of professionalism; later she became a discriminating and demanding patron of avant garde composers like Arnold Schönberg and Aaron Copland.

"I'm forever blowing bubbles," my father warbled from behind the shower curtain, his voice right on pitch, resonating in the white tiled bathroom where to me, at three and a half, everything loomed large. I could just barely see over the top of the wash basin. Standing naked in the bathtub, wrapped securely in the white canvas shower curtain suspended from a shaky chrome ring, my father was briefly a happy and free man. As he lingered singing in the shower, the steam billowing and filling the tight confines of the bathroom, I had a fleeting sense of intimacy with my father as I perched on the closed toilet cover. The joyous singing was accompanied by the rush of water, which made uneven, ripping sounds against the canvas, like heavy rain, bouncing off my father's body as he moved in a slow, sensuous dance soaping himself.

> I'm forever blowing bubbles
> Pretty bubbles in the air
> They fly so high
> They reach the sky
> Then like my dreams
> They fade and die.

My father's voice trailed off. A hand appeared and snapped back the curtain. He stepped out of the tub carefully and awkwardly. Now much too close, I felt uncomfortable, fearful of the unpredictable, sudden mood swings that veered from warm affection to flashes of cold fury. He could be set off by a seemingly odd assortment of circumstances. It might even be the most innocent challenge to his intellectual capacity. On other occasions he would blow up when someone close to him was physically endangered or hurt.

Except when my father was in the shower, he seemed to have a great many things on his mind that bothered him. He suffered frequent migraine attacks. "Your father has one of his sick head-aches," Mother would inform us once or twice a week. "Try to be very quiet." Daddy meanwhile would be stretched out on a couch in his darkened dressing room, quietly or not so quietly suffering. There seemed to be no relief, though all kinds of remedies were tried.

I identified with my father's headaches; however, my pains and distress were in my stomach rather than in the skull. "I have a headache in my tummy," I would wail.

Fear of ill health and early death preoccupied middle-class families between the two world wars. In my grandparents' generation, couples commonly had a dozen or more children, expecting some to die in infancy, others while maturing or in early adulthood, from ill-ness or accident. Among the survivors would be some physically or emotionally handicapped or unable to reproduce. But sheer strength of numbers increased the possibility that enough would live to continue the family line. Those who survived, after a regulated mourning period, closed ranks and marched forward.

My grandparents all came from what in my generation were considered very big families. I can't remember anyone talking about those who had died young. There were, however, ready explana-tions for the inadequacies of the living. Grandma Fatman's two youngest brothers, Irving and Herbert Lehman, were sterile, sup-posedly because they were the youngest members of a large family. I accepted the theory that the male reproductive capacity had some-how run dry at the end of the line like an overtaxed well. Then there was Grandpa Fatman's bachelor brother, Uncle Solly. After asking why he had never married, I was told that it was because he had caught a bad cold after getting very wet on a hunting trip, an explanation I found no need to question further.★

In my parents' generation the number of offspring in a middle-

---

★Solomon Aaron Fatman, my uncle Solly, wanted to settle $100,000 (an enormous fortune at that time) on my brother if my parents would name him Solomon Aaron. My mother said she had rejected what seemed like an offer one couldn't refuse because "it would be terrible to go through life with that kind of a name." Instead my parents hit on what I can now appreciate as an ingenious solution to their problem. They named my brother Robert Morris, which within the family meant that he was named for Mother's father, Morris Fatman, but in the outside world he was associated with Robert Morris, a signer of the Declaration of Independence and a principal financier of the American Revolution.

class Protestant or Jewish family (Catholic families were often larger) seldom exceeded three or four. Two children, as in the case of my mother's family, or an "only child" were not unusual. With parents playing against very thin odds, children received a heavy overload of anxiety and expectation of achievement. Parents were at once afraid for and of their children. One moment they would be overprotective, the next permissive. Children reacted to the confusing signals with behavior that was willful and lacking in self-discipline and confidence.

· 21 ·

Henry and Franklin,
and Elinor and Eleanor

D URING THE YEARS between the end of the First World War and the election of Franklin Roosevelt as president of the United States in 1932, Henry Morgenthau, Jr., emerged, to the great surprise of his family and close friends, ready to become a major player on the New Deal team. My father seemed to be driven to push himself beyond the limit of his resources. There were times when he would be consumed by migraine headaches, which induced spasms of excruciating pain and nausea. None of the medications or purgatives he ingested daily in increasing doses brought him relief. But eventually he learned how to accept these insults to his system and resume his battles. Indeed these recurring physical attacks may have taught him to deal effectively with the challenges he faced daily in the public arena.

Into the 1920s the senior Henry Morgenthau continued to proclaim that he had found his Zion in America. Often frustrated in his own efforts, he shifted the weight of his ambitions to the shoulders of his son and heir. Among those few who very early on had no doubt (against heavy odds) of another Roosevelt presidency, my grandfather was determined that in a Roosevelt administration his son would have the cabinet post of which he himself felt deprived by Wilson. Pragmatic optimist that he was, he soon saw his daughter-in-law, with her talents and qualifications, as an ally in his campaign to advance his son. Elinor shared her father-in-law's vision of unlimited opportunity and became his congenial co-conspirator.

My mother had a way of engaging men in conversation which made her seem interesting but not threatening. She was a subtle flatterer. It was a talent she honed to a fine art, using it to build confidence in her diffident young husband and to massage the ego of her self-satisfied father-in-law. She could adjust her verbal response to a wide range of dinner partners, including Franklin Roosevelt and Albert Einstein. Once she found herself seated next to the great scientist at a White House dinner. As President Roosevelt told one of his long amusing stories, Elinor tried to interpret what he was saying. At the end, when everyone was finished laughing, Einstein turned to Elinor and remarked ruefully, "I understand each individual word that he says. But when he is finished I don't know. Does he mean yes or does he mean no?"

In the 1920s, my mother's friendship with Eleanor Roosevelt developed into a firm alliance that proved to be enormously helpful to my father. Whenever he felt uncertain about his relationship with FDR — which was often — he could count on back-door access to his boss through the Elinor-Eleanor team.

My recollections of my parents' public life are mixed with those of the cloudy mysteries of day-to-day existence. I took it for granted that they were very much in love with each other, although they permitted almost no outward display of affection. Yet, sometime early on I had observed that my parents slept in adjoining twin beds with small tables on either side. Other people's parents, I noticed, slept in twin beds separated by a bedside table.

In 1915, two years after buying his Fishkill farm and four months before he was married, Henry Jr. wrote Elinor from the U.S. embassy in Constantinople that he and his father had reached a satisfactory agreement permitting the junior partner to test the practicality of their joint enterprise as a profitable business proposition. My father had selected two principal endeavors: dairy farming and apple growing. During the first years he concentrated on his dairy, beginning by building up a herd of registered Holstein cattle. Acquiring a bull with a distinguished pedigree, affectionately nicknamed "Old Dutch," he proceeded to breed his heifers and soon had reached the desired level of fifty head. For a short time he sold his milk, very profitably, a few miles down the Hudson River to the West Point Military Academy.

The start-up time for an apple orchard was in those days considerably longer than for a dairy. The business of maintaining an orchard was always fraught with problems, from late spring frosts that nipped the delicate buds to hailstorms that could ruin mature fruit in seconds. My father frequently called on the expertise of distinguished professors of pomology at Cornell who would arrive to consult and introduce new varieties and methods with which they were experimenting.

In the years to come Henry Jr.'s passionate attachment to the orchard deepened. He loved nothing better than to ride horseback through the rows of apple trees at all seasons. Twice a year the problems dissolved in a moment of sheer ecstasy. For a few spring days — usually bracketing his birthday on May 11 — the trees would burst forth in a pink-white haze of delicately scented blossoms. Then, at the end of the season, the boughs would be bent down, heavy with red, golden yellow, and green apples ready to be plucked for market. These few days made all the drudgery, disappointment, and expense worth enduring.

As if making a statement that his farm was a serious business and no rich man's hobby, Henry Jr. effected a scruffy, no-frills appearance. Shabby barns and sheds were painted and repaired only when absolutely necessary. Unstinting in his expenditures for the latest equipment — tractors, spray rigs, mechanical apple sorters, and so forth — he spent no money on extras or fancy amenities. It was a perfect stage set on which to play out the myth that Fishkill Farms was a money-making business. In fact the farm sustained huge losses most of the time, but its fabled success was accepted by almost everyone. I think my father came to believe in it himself, although he was always very thin-skinned when anyone dared to question him closely on this score. Of course my grandfather knew the truth. But he began to see other ways for his son, the farmer, to make a name for himself.

One of my father's new friends in Dutchess County was the sometime gentleman farmer and rising young Democratic politician Franklin Delano Roosevelt. At the time, Roosevelt was serving as assistant secretary of the navy in Washington. Prior to that he had been elected to the state senate as a Democrat in a staunchly Republican stronghold. Throughout 1914 he kept in close touch with events at home because he was thinking of running for the U.S. Senate. He also had the responsibility and pleasure of overseeing "Springwood," the family estate at Hyde Park north of Poughkeepsie.

It isn't known exactly how or when Franklin Roosevelt and

Henry Morgenthau, Jr., met. The first piece of evidence that they had established a trusting (but still rather formal) relationship is a "confidential" letter dated December 11, 1914, typed on the letter-head of the assistant secretary of the navy, addressed to "My Dear Mr. Morgenthau." Roosevelt was inquiring about "John Dugan, the Blacksmith," the candidate of the county Democratic powers for postmaster in Fishkill. He understood that there was some opposition: "I should much like to have your personal and confiden-tial judgment on the matter . . . of course, if possible I should like to have everybody united in the Township of East Fishkill." After writing about the problems in great detail, Roosevelt concluded, "We are all proud of your father's work."

This letter is a revealing early sample of the Roosevelt political style: careful attention to detail, and a kind of case study approach to the judgment and skill of someone he was considering for mem-bership on his team. From the beginning of their acquaintance these two men, so different in background and personality, seemed to hit it off. But just as important, if not more so, they shared similar ideals and ambitions. Roosevelt in a fond, unpatronizing way al-ways treated Henry Jr. like a younger brother. They were never rivals. But as Roosevelt continued to be tied down by his navy job during the war, he began to rely on his friend to take care of some of the political matters in the county. Increasingly he came to appreciate Morgenthau's dogged determination to carry out any chore he was assigned and his habit of obtaining the best expert advice before making a move. "He is an awfully nice fellow," FDR wrote to Louis Howe, "and one who will be a tremendous asset to us in the county . . . certainly we ought to do everything possible to keep him interested." Roosevelt believed the myth that Henry had made his farm pay and frequently referred to this achievement in the years to come. But he also knew that Henry had outside financial resources that gave him the independence to operate free from the concerns of earning a living. Above all Roosevelt valued the trustworthiness that came with absolute loyalty.

My father saw that his farm could be profitable in ways that would not show up on the balance sheet. Roosevelt wanted to win the support of the upstate farmers by balancing their interests against those of the powerful New York City bosses, and my father gradually began to discern a role for himself in mustering farming interests and expertise for Roosevelt. All of this politicking de-lighted my grandfather.

Henry discovered too that with Elinor's help he could move ahead on the political path with a quicker and surer step than he had been able to under his father's pushing and manipulation. Elinor, he found out, had her own weaknesses and insecurity. While she was prepared to do almost anything for her husband, she had little confidence in acting for herself. Granted, the opportunities open to women in this era were narrowly limited. Yet even within these limits she tended to become worried and depressed in the face of real or imagined confrontations. Long before the pill balanced the cycle of women's lives, Elinor Morgenthau suffered physically and emotionally from extremely heavy menstruation. In writing to my father about what she called "the curse," she protested that she was "put out of business two weeks out of every month."

The balance of Elinor's weaknesses and talents against Henry's made them an effective team. As Elinor leaned on her husband for strength and courage, she made a man out of him. In any kind of public situation Henry Jr. was painfully shy. All of the practical joking, the fun-loving, high spirits he displayed among his intimates were submerged. He faced the world with a scowling inarticulateness that made him appear brusque and arrogant to outsiders. The idea of addressing a small collection of fellow farmers at a local Grange meeting or a clambake was enough to bring on one of his sick headaches. So Elinor, who had tamed her stage fright while acting in plays at Vassar, found a new role for herself, speaking lines she attributed to her husband. She took lessons in public speaking and soon began to impress her audiences with her intelligence and charm. When Henry took her to call on Franklin Roosevelt's grande dame mother, Sara Roosevelt found herself pleasantly surprised by the young couple. "Young Morgenthau and his wife called this pm," she wrote her daughter-in-law, Eleanor, "and while they were here Mrs. F.W.V. [Mrs. Fredrick W. Vanderbilt] came bringing 5 people and we had a pleasant tea. Young Morgenthau was easy and yet modest and serious and intelligent. The wife is very Jewish but appeared very well."

While serving out his term in Washington, Franklin Roosevelt was careful to maintain his political ties to New York, staying in close touch with a small cadre of loyal supporters that included the Morgenthaus. FDR's model and inspiration as he contemplated his political destiny was his distant cousin, Eleanor's Uncle Teddy. Following in TR's footsteps, FDR won the vice presidential nomination in 1920. Henry Jr., as chairman of the Notification Ceremonies Committee at Hyde Park, carried off his first important political assignment with aplomb, marshaling an estimated eight thousand enthusiasts. Sara complained about the crowd that trampled her front lawn, though after the ceremony she received about five hundred of them into her house, including such party notables as Al Smith, William Gibbs McAdoo, and FDR's old boss, Secretary Josephus Daniels.

The following August, when the Roosevelt family was summering at Campobello, FDR was stricken with polio. Almost everyone assumed his public career was finished. Only a small, hardy band of loyalists was ready to carry on for him. First among them was Louis Howe, who had the unlikely idea of pushing shy, homely Eleanor Roosevelt onto center stage, as a stand-in for her crippled husband. At first her painfully earnest speeches were disconcerting, as her voice rose out of control in high, nervous giggles. But she was determined to improve, and slowly, with Howe's patient coaching, she did.

In the fall of 1922, two years after women's suffrage had taken effect, there were a lot of New York State Democratic women who were eager to make their vote count for Al Smith in the upcoming gubernatorial race. In the segregated fledgling women's division of the party, Eleanor, with the boundless energy and generous spirit that were to become her trademarks, soon found herself a magnet for like-minded peers. Elinor Morgenthau was an early entry into this charmed circle. Eleanor Roosevelt, who greatly regretted having been deprived of a college education, respected Elinor as a Vassar graduate and admired her hard-won poise on the speakers' platform.

When Eleanor married Franklin she had privately shared her mother-in-law's class-bred anti-Semitism, while Franklin seemed to have outgrown such feelings, as did Eleanor with a vengeance. Elinor Morgenthau was an obvious exception to Eleanor's earlier stereotype of Jewish devotion to "money, jewels and sables." Both women shared a disdain for fashion. My mother seldom wore any jewelry other than her diamond engagement ring, gold wedding band, and occasionally an amber or crystal necklace or a small brooch. And the house at Fishkill Farms was in every way unostentatious.

Unlike my parents, a lot of the Roosevelt camp followers were loners without family ties. Many of Eleanor's crew were single women — unmarried, widowed, or divorced. Franklin's political destiny was a joint enterprise for him and "the Missus." The Roosevelts maintained separate, and increasingly rivalrous, courts, but my parents managed to bridge the gap. In this and in other respects they were unique, as they were in never placing their devotion to the Roosevelts ahead of their own family commitment. The Roosevelts, their own family in some disarray, seemed to respect and admire the Morgenthau family solidarity.

My parents' financial independence cleared the way for both of them to work unstintingly for the Roosevelts. They also made financial contributions, reinforced by Grandpa Morgenthau's generosity; but money never played the role that it had in the senior Morgenthau's political career. Our resources were modest compared with the political competition from Herbert and Irving Lehman, Jesse Straus, and such kingmakers as John J. Raskob and Bernard Baruch. Furthermore, my father lacked business connections and the magic of his father's touch had worn thin, so that my parents were not in a position to raise a lot of money. Nor could they provide the kind of lavish entertainment, like the cruises on Vincent Astor's floating palace the *Nourmahal,* which Franklin adored and Eleanor despised. Perhaps the secret of my parents' success was simply that they were always there, though there were constantly tests to be met and turf to be guarded.

In 1922 Al Smith, a New York City Tammany Hall candidate for governor, courted upstate support and the Roosevelts who could deliver it to him. Both Morgenthaus gleefully fell into line behind them. At a luncheon in Dutchess County with Eleanor Roosevelt presiding, Elinor proposed an anti-Hearst resolution, which was given unanimous support. From the state convention in Syracuse, Louis Howe telegraphed the boss at Hyde Park:

AL NOMINATED WITH GREAT ENTHUSIASM. MORGENTHAU AND YOUR MISSUS LED THE DUTCHESS COUNTY DELEGATION WITH THE BANNER THREE TIMES AROUND THE HALL.

After Smith was elected governor he appointed Roosevelt chairman of the Taconic State Parkway Commission, mandated to build a highway set in continuous parkland from Westchester County to Albany. FDR, with an open touring car rigged up so that he could operate it entirely with his hands, set out to negotiate some of the proceedings himself. Sometimes my father would accompany him.

While they were working their way through southern Dutchess, FDR and Eleanor would often come to our farm for dinner. My mother always made sure it was a good one. On those occasions when Eleanor Roosevelt wrested control of the household from Sara, the table tended to be unappetizingly frugal. (Perhaps subconsciously this was one of the ways she punished her husband for his extramarital indulgences.) In any event there was never a better example of finding a way to a man's heart through his stomach than that of the food and drink served up in our crowded little dining room.

In a letter to Elinor dated July 16, 1925, FDR wrote: "We are looking forward to the pool and supper with you on Saturday . . . I will telephone you from Hyde Park on Friday (to confirm how many of us are coming) so you can kill the fatted calf for us! — p.s. Missy [his secretary, Marguerite LeHand] reminds me that I shall have to bring Roy [his valet] with me to get in and out of the pool and dress me — that means that you will have to provide 15 or 16 newly caught fish for him."

The entrance to our Fishkill home was by way of four rickety wooden steps. Roosevelt, without his leg braces, waited to be carried from his car into the house by his valet and my father. In the middle of the difficult maneuver up the steps, Roosevelt, knowing that my father was uncontrollably ticklish, would begin to poke him. My father, scared beyond his wits that he would drop his precious burden, would cry for mercy while Roosevelt roared with laughter. I think the tickling was done partly to tease my father and partly to turn the embarrassment of displaying himself as a cripple into a joke on someone else.

By the time all the grown-ups had finished their cocktails and sat down to dinner, I had been sent to bed. I can remember creeping down to the landing to listen to the cheerful chorus of conversation. I couldn't catch the words, but every once in a while Roosevelt's sonorous baritone would take over in the telling of one of his favorite stories. It would invariably end with "Don't you love it?" and a burst of his contagious laughter, cuing everyone else to join in.

If Henry Jr. were to become Roosevelt's farm expert, his own farm, alone, would not suffice; he must broaden his base. In an undated letter (1921 or 1922) he wrote to his father, "There is nothing I would rather do than own an agricultural paper." So in

1922 he purchased the *American Agriculturist,* a New York State farm weekly. Losing money, it was competing against the entrenched *Rural New Yorker.* This enterprise must have required a substantial additional capital injection from the senior Morgenthau, who kept a keen eye on the balance sheet.

My father found his editor, Ed Eastman, to be competent and congenial. He himself knew nothing about either the editorial or the business side of newspaper publishing. In need of help from someone he could trust, he brought in Elinor's Vassar College friend Gabrielle Elliot (later Forbush). "Gay" wrote with breezy fluency. She had inherited editorial skills from her two journalist parents. When my father invited her to come on board, she insisted that she was a city girl who knew nothing about farming, so he made her the women's editor. She made one other contribution, which she later grew to regret. When Henry Jr. began looking for a personal secretary, Gabrielle suggested Henrietta Stein, a twenty-one-year-old with "lovely ash-blonde hair which she rolled up over the ears in what they used to call cootie garages." She had been brought up very strictly by her Orthodox Jewish mother.

Henrietta Stein always remembered her first meeting with my father. "He looked at me and he said, 'Yes, I'll hire you, how much were you earning?' I said I was earning thirty-five dollars a week, and he said, 'Well, I'll start you with thirty dollars.' . . . I think if your father had asked me to jump off the roof I would have done it . . . because he was a gentleman and he was a wonderful human being. But he was a very very inhibited person, and having gotten to know your grandfather I understood a great many things." She believed that my father's suspicious and mistrusting nature derived from his father. But "when he trusted you, it was forever." After she had been on the job about a week, her boss asked her to bring in a particular file folder. As she opened it a five-dollar bill fell out. "I gave him the money and thought nothing of it." Two weeks later he asked her to bring in a certain book. As she took it out of the bookcase a ten-dollar bill fell out. She again turned it over to her boss. That was the end of that kind of nonsense. "Later he gave me power of attorney and everything," she told me.

Gabrielle believed that my father "always had that suspicious vein" but Henrietta brought it out in him. She wanted to protect him, and she was fiercely loyal. But she viewed everyone and everything in a narrowly personal way.

Once Henrietta started working for my father at the *American Agriculturist,* "from then on they were together." Sometime after that Henrietta married Herman Klotz. "She never treated him as anything but an appendage," Gabrielle told me. She had really wanted to marry his brother, Jules, who ended up marrying her best friend.

Henrietta Klotz had one daughter who was born without any irises in her eyes, resulting in seriously impaired vision. The over-dependent relationship that developed between the two of them became the tragedy of their lives. Henrietta named her Elinor, after my mother.

From mid-1922 until mid-1924, while my father was working very hard to make a success of his farm and the *American Agriculturist,* my mother was tied to family and household duties. Her last child, my sister, Joan, was born October 9, 1922.

The next summer I suffered an accident on the farm which derailed the whole family for a while. At six I had learned to ride a Shetland pony controlled by a leading strap held either by another rider or someone on foot. One evening the pony, impatient to get back to the stable, broke away and bolted for home. I started to fall off, but my left foot caught in the stirrup, and at the gallop I was dragged with my head bouncing on the ground. When the pony came to a standstill in the barn I was unconscious. Upon his arrival the local GP, Dr. Coburn, pronounced me dead. But my parents, unwilling to accept the doctor's verdict, scooped me up and with my father at the wheel and me stretched across my mother's lap, headed for the Vassar Hospital in Poughkeepsie. I later regained consciousness, with a fractured skull.

Over the course of the rest of the summer of 1923 I completely recovered the use of a partially paralyzed left leg. However, my parents decided that my health called for our family's spending the winter of 1923–24 in the warmer environs of Augusta, Georgia. So Mother and her three children and her staff moved into a comfortable, rented, yellow brick house. My father stayed in New York to attend to his paper and his farm.

That winter a reputedly unprecedented blizzard in Augusta caused my mother to doubt the wisdom of dislocating the family for the benefit of my health. Separated from friends, relatives, and the opportunities to work, she began to brood over the decisions she had made, first to quit the theater, and then to cut herself off from the beginnings of a career in Democratic politics in New York State. Several times a week she wrote to her husband that she had "become awfully morose and depressed . . . without you nothing is really worthwhile." Some days later she complained, "You write me the world's skimpiest letters." But she was "always happy to hear your voice on the phone, even though speaking at such a distance and for such a short time is very unsatisfactory." "Don't let's ever be separated so long again — ever — ever — ever!" she wrote.

When my parents were together, which was most of the time, their life was carefully regulated. Away in distant Augusta, Elinor clearly missed her husband. "I found a certain little blue package of yours left in a drawer in the bureau Hilda Altschul [a visiting relative] is going to use. I blushed! I didn't quite know what to do with [it]. So I wrapped it up and put it in with your collars. You certainly are a casual person about your belongings." (The blue package contained condoms, which in those days could only be mentioned furtively to a druggist and purchased under the counter. Later when I was an adolescent I discovered these blue packages stowed "casually" in my father's top bureau drawer.)

Elinor encouraged her husband to occupy evenings in New York dining out with some of their mutual women friends. She didn't expect him to flirt and there is no indication that he did. However, when he told her that he had taken the glamorous Margaret Lewisohn to the theater she wrote back, "You certainly always knew how to pick them, except when it came to me."*

During the winter in Augusta Elinor made few new acquaintances, but a number of female friends and relatives paid extended visits as house guests. Between these occasions she chose to spend much of the time in the company of her children. When the local Jewish women persisted in trying to draw her into their circle she retreated defiantly.

I don't remember much about what happened during that atypically cold winter in Augusta. But a letter Elinor wrote to my father postmarked December 14, 1923, when she was busy preparing for Christmas, suggests that some of her mixed feelings about her family and her Jewishness had seeped into my imagination. "This morning Henry wanted to tell me a story. . . . It was about Kings,

---

*Margaret Seligman, who had married the wealthy eccentric Sam Lewisohn, was known to her friends as a stunning beauty and a great flirt.

Queens, and Princes who lived in a castle that was bigger than the Bon Air [the largest hotel in Augusta]. Their name was Lehman." My mother thought I must have been subjected to some of Grandma Fatman's "propaganda about how wonderful the Lehmans are." In my story I had endowed them with a Rolls-Royce, and so my mother "suggested that they were so disgustingly rich they must be very unhappy [with] nothing to wish for." So I decided to have them sell the Rolls-Royce and buy a Buick, like ours. "Then they went for a long trip and went up the mountain where Jesus lived."

In one of her letters to my father, my mother said she thought they would indeed have to go to temple when he came for a visit in Georgia, but I don't think they did. In fact I can't recall my parents ever going to temple during all the years that I was growing up. In another letter Mother wrote that I had been asking questions about God that left her in a difficult predicament: "I do wish I weren't such an agnostic myself, but it's so hard to teach one's children when one doesn't believe in much one's self."

After her unwanted sabbatical from New York State politics, Elinor Morgenthau and her husband were back on the campaign trail in the fall of 1924 for Governor Smith's re-election. Their previously rather formal relationship with the Roosevelts grew warm and intimate. As a member of Eleanor Roosevelt's team, running the Women's Division of the Democratic State Committee, Elinor Morgenthau chaired the Committee on Clubs and was vice president of the *Women's Democratic News,* with Eleanor Roosevelt as editor and treasurer.

An article in the August 1925 issue under Elinor's by-line exhorted women to "organize — city, town, village, county; solidify — then attack the issues — not each other." Before publication she had received a complimentary note from Eleanor: "I can't thank you enough for having everything in such good shape for me, and the best things in the 'news' next month will be yours." But no accolades from her mentor were enough to assuage Elinor's anxieties. "I didn't say half I wanted to when we were talking the other day," Eleanor tried to reassure her. "I've grown to love you and to feel that you and Henry were not only 'our' but 'my' real true friends and tho I can't take away the feeling you have it makes me unhappy to feel that it is worrying you and I want to put my arms about you and keep away all the disagreeable things which have made you feel this way."

Elinor should have been delighted. "Much, much love dear to you, and Franklin wants to send you and Henry all kinds of messages. He wants you to wine and dine as soon as he arrives!" During those years my parents dined frequently and were guests on the Roosevelt houseboat, *Larooco,* anchored off the Florida Keys, as well as at Hyde Park. Yet neither of them ever felt secure. In their work relationships each of the two Roosevelts had individual ways of keeping supporters off balance.

FDR consciously stirred rivalries among those he put in positions of power, ultimately leaving himself in control. His magnetic personal charm made this tactic a success. It was a technique he had learned handling the conflicts between his mother and his wife.

On one occasion in the 1920s while touring upstate New York with two other aides, my father wrote to my mother that at the end of the day they had two double hotel rooms reserved for the four of them. "We flipped coins to see who would sleep with the boss. I won and before we went to bed we had a grand rough house."

The uneasiness in Eleanor's entourage was quite different. She neither calculated nor encouraged rivalries among her friends and was always distressed by infighting, yet, with her unconscious needs for affection, she unwittingly excited a swirl of emotions that constantly spilled over from personal into work relationships.

In 1924, when my mother committed herself to the New York State Democratic organization, there were two women who seemed to control Eleanor's team and influence her personal life. Eleanor had built a stone cottage on the Roosevelt property a mile or so distant from "the Big House." Franklin had encouraged the project as a practical way to free Eleanor from Sara's domination while keeping his wife at Hyde Park. Knowing that she wouldn't want to live alone, he was delighted to have her take in two women partners who were her good friends and Democratic party co-workers. Marion Dickerman conformed to the popular stereotype of the genteel, dour schoolteacher for young ladies that she was. Nancy Cook wore her wiry curls in a short bob, spoke in a gruff, deep voice, and had a penchant for woodworking. Joseph Lash (Eleanor's biographer and intimate) saw the relationship between Nancy and Marion as what Henry James termed a "Boston marriage." Mother found these two women, especially the more aggressive Nancy, a disagreeable stumbling block, jealously possessive and exploitive of Eleanor. But my mother soon learned that Eleanor, who seldom showed her anger, could become incensed when her friends criti-cized each other.

While Elinor remained politically active, my father struggled to keep his head above water with the *American Agriculturist,* which continued to run in the red. On January 20, 1924, his own father, who was in Athens heading a League of Nations Commission, wrote bluntly, "It is not much of a business that produces $185,000 and costs over $200,000 to do so . . . Don't forget you are now in the midst of good times and yours, like all other enterprises, will have to weather some severe business storms when the reaction comes. So make hay while the sun shines — size up the prospects and act accordingly." But my grandfather continued to put up with the drain on family funds as long as his son grew in stature as FDR's agricultural adviser.

In the summer of 1928 both Roosevelts threw the combined weight of their forces behind the nomination of Al Smith for presi-dent. On April 26 Eleanor had written to Franklin, "Elinor and Henry Morgenthau are like children in their joy that she should be made a delegate at large." The next day she continued, "I never realized anyone could care so much."

Henry and Elinor were the only husband-and-wife delegates at the Houston convention. Henry wrote to his father, "There was no doubt from the beginning that Smith was to be the candidate . . . Elinor presented planks for the Women's Democratic Union before the Resolutions Committee and Senator Wagner . . . the member from New York was extremely kind to her. Elinor made quite a hit with everybody and they were particularly impressed with her ability and knowledge of political affairs.

On returning from Houston, my father, in tune with the con-ventional wisdom, predicted incorrectly to his father that "Franklin will definitely not run for Governor." He went on to say that there was some talk that he himself would be picked to run as lieutenant governor on a ticket headed by Senator Wagner. In the same letter he noted that "with Herbert [Lehman] and Franklin as members of the Executive Committee and Eleanor Roosevelt, Chairman of the Women's Advisory Committee, Elinor and I are able to keep in close touch with what is going on in national campaign headquar-ters."

When Roosevelt ended up running as the Democratic candidate for governor, Lehman, who was Elinor's uncle, ran for lieutenant governor. From then on FDR always referred to Lehman as "my good right arm." As a girl Elinor had been especially devoted to her mother's youngest sibling, a cheerful, outgoing man fourteen years Elinor's senior, who was more like an older brother to her than an uncle. After he married Edith Altschul they both encouraged the budding Henry-Ellie romance.* However, when the Lehmans and Morgenthaus began competing for favor in the Roosevelt camp, the familial camaraderie cooled. My mother's lifelong resentment of the Lehman wealth resurfaced, and I think both my parents harbored the uneasy feeling that they might be outbid in their political ambitions, especially because of the unspoken fear that there was some kind of Jewish quota at the top. On the other hand, my parents remained on very cordial terms with Herbert's older brother, Irving Lehman, judge (later chief judge) of the New York State Court of Appeals.†

During the 1928 campaign Henry Morgenthau, Jr., was the Democratic gubernatorial candidate's advance man. He traveled across the state sizing up the political situation in the places where FDR planned to appear. When Roosevelt arrived, Morgenthau would often be there to brief him. Sometimes Elinor accompanied her husband, having become increasingly unhappy with Nancy Cook's domination of the Women's Division. Then, on October 17, about two weeks before election day, Henry overstepped the bounds, perhaps with Elinor's coaching. From the Hotel Arlington in Binghamton he telegraphed a long "day letter" to Eleanor Roosevelt in New York.

> Very much disturbed on learning today that Women's Division has been making independent arrangements for Roosevelt Lehman tour. At Franklin's request Elinor and I have seen men and many women in each county . . . Very much surprised to learn today that Women's Division has sent out a lot of telegrams to women chairmen and committeemen making arrangements for trip. If Elinor and I are to be held responsible for the success of this trip I must ask . . . that I be consulted before any future plans are made . . . When I spoke to Nancy [Cook] she told me that the above mentioned telegrams were sent out at your explicit instructions.
>
> Henry Morgenthau, Jr.

*Edith Altschul's brother, Frank, married Helen Goodhart, who was Elinor Morgenthau's cousin and Herbert Lehman's niece.
†Irving Lehman's wife, Sissie Straus, was the oldest child of the wealthy Zionist Nathan Straus, the close friend and client and later an archenemy of Henry Morgenthau, Sr.

At 6:00 that evening Eleanor, stepping over Morgenthau's head, telegraphed her response directly to her husband.

HENRY TOLD NAN THAT HE WISHES CAROLINE [O'DAY] MYSELF AND NAN TO KEEP OUR HANDS OFF AND NOT MAKE ARRANGEMENTS FOR WOMEN SPEAKERS ON YOUR TRIP STOP NAN IS SENDING HIM THE SCHEDULE FOR WOMEN SPEAKERS WHICH I TOLD YOU LAST NIGHT WE HAD ARRANGED . . . AT YOUR REQUEST WILL CANCEL EVERY WOMAN SPEAKER THAT WE HAVE ARRANGED FOR AND CAROLINE AND I WILL RESIGN IMMEDIATELY.

ELEANOR

At 7:00 P.M. a second telegram arrived at the hotel addressed to Morgenthau and signed Mrs. Daniel (Caroline) O'Day. It specified all the women speakers who had been booked. At this point Franklin jumped in to calm the tempest. On the back of the typewritten draft of Henry's day letter to Eleanor he penciled his own response aimed at getting his wife to back off from her furious ultimatum. Typical of his writing style, it picked up the reassuring cadence so characteristic of his speech.

Perfectly simple situation. Entirely approve list [of] lady speakers given me before I left. Carry this through but let Henry know in advance of any change of plans. All well.

Meetings great success.

Much love
FDR

Roosevelt knew that his wife, who championed the underdog, Al Smith, had little enthusiasm for his own candidacy. But he was determined, as always, not to let her get away from him. His note charmed her back on board. A contrite Elinor Morgenthau was devastated by the realization of what she and Henry had done. It must have seemed to her that in a single stroke of foolish arrogance they had destroyed the relationship that meant everything to them. She immediately wrote Eleanor a letter that seems to have been both a despairing plea for forgiveness and a counterattack aimed primarily at Nan. Though Elinor's letter has disappeared we can surmise its contents from Eleanor's compassionate but scolding answer.

To say that your letter amazed me would be mild, somehow I always forget how tragic things seem to you . . . You don't realize how objective all the happenings of the past few weeks have been, work is always interesting in itself and while I'm doing a job that swallows up everything . . . Gov. Smith's election means something but whether Franklin spends 2 years in Albany or not matters as you know comparatively little. It will have pleasant and unpleasant sides for him and the good for the State is problematical.

Now as to what you have done [she went on to address Elinor's misery in having committed a grievous faux pas], you haven't done anything as far as I know. Henry sent me a message and a telegram which annoyed me extremely but that is over long ago as far as any feeling I had goes — I quite realize now that he was trying to do his job . . . My real annoyance was with Franklin . . . however I straightened that out with him . . . As far as I'm concerned the whole thing is over and forgotten. I realize that you both did a wonderful piece of work and you know that both Franklin and his mother realize it also and we are deeply grateful . . . Frankly I wasn't keen to talk over any of those things until we all had time to cool down and forget — I am devoted to you and Henry and I don't wish to talk of it anymore — As for your saying you have had a "rotten deal" I don't know what things happen[ed] and if you want to resign, that is your choice but no one has forced you to do it. I have worked more years than you have with Caroline, Nan and Marion and enjoyed it . . . I resign now only because I know that if I take any part in politics everyone will attribute anything I say or do to Franklin and that wouldn't be fair to him. Now, you say Nan's "continuous and insidious propaganda" and I have no idea what you mean. Nan and I are both too busy and have too much that must be done to dwell over any petty difficulties long . . . if you don't like her there is no reason why you should not say so but I don't intend to referee in the matter . . . I am devoted to her and it will be wiser for you not to talk to me about it as you cannot expect me to agree with you or to be influenced by your feelings.

This letter in its candor and unvarnished display of irritation was quite uncharacteristic of Eleanor Roosevelt. But she did have her limits. She let Elinor know in no uncertain terms that she had gone too far.

I have always felt that you were hurt often by imaginary things and have wanted to protect you. But if one is to have a healthy, normal relationship I realize it must be on some kind of equal basis, you simply cannot be so easily hurt, life is too short to cope with it! Cheer up and forget about it all . . . I'll be home for lunch tomorrow and Thursday at 1:30 but must work from three on.

Thus matters rested. Eleanor was never one to nurse a grievance. After some pruning back, her friendship with Elinor and Henry resumed and flourished.

I believe my mother had come to understand that the best way to maintain her friendship with Eleanor Roosevelt was on a one-to-one basis, rather than in an office or group association. Eleanor frequently invited my mother along on her strenuous jaunts. Mother would return thrilled and exhausted. In these kinds of contacts my mother realized she could be most effective in guiding and protecting her husband's relationship with FDR, which became her primary occupation after 1928. These were also years when she was kept busy on the home front.

After recuperation in Augusta, Georgia, I started second grade at the Lincoln School, near Morningside Park. It had been conceived as a John Deweyesque experiment and an adjunct to the nearby Teachers College at Columbia University. Lincoln was intended as a kind of laboratory for New York City schools. But though it was located on the edge of Harlem, it did not include a single black pupil or teacher, and a kind of white racism seems to have been accepted without a twinge of conscience. In the school cafeteria all the busboys were Japanese students living in the nearby International House. Lincoln and the International House had both been funded by the Rockefellers. Nelson and David Rockefeller both graduated from the school a few years ahead of me. About half of the students at Lincoln were from affluent Jewish families and were transported from downtown in chauffeur-driven limousines.

My brother, Bob, and sister, Joan, also attended Lincoln. Growing up in a nuclear family that severely limited contacts in the outside world, Bob and I were close friends. Yet early on I was compelled to recognize that he was clearly the one marked for leadership. Bob's fifth grade teacher reported: "He seems to want to cooperate in all things, but likes to lead so well that he makes a poor follower. Robert's work habits are good. He is honest and trustworthy." But by the end of the second term this same teacher reported: "Robert still is a good leader, and seems now very willing to follow where another is leading. He has done a good year's work."

I don't think Bob's achievement ever came easily. He was diligent in everything he pursued. Our mother wisely encouraged the two of us to operate on separate tracks. I was encouraged to follow my artistic bent. Bob was tone deaf and couldn't carry a tune, but he was good in most sports. In his teens he practiced his tennis serve by the hour. The only sport I was good at was swimming. Bob had developed ear infections that kept him out of indoor pools. In those days there were no antibiotics, so infections were very dangerous.

During the winter of 1925, when our parents were traveling in Spain, Bob developed a lingering ear infection that began to loom as life-threatening. My grandfather Morgenthau visited daily to consult with the doctors. I remember one evening when our beloved Nana, under the strain of serving in loco parentis, burst into tears. Terrified, I began to cry with her. That illness was the first of several close brushes with death for Bob.

Our sister Joan often seemed to be left out of family activities, partly because she was the youngest and partly because in many ways we were favored as boys. But Joan never gave up. Our father named his horse "Me Too" in Joan's honor. When my large, flat feet continued to grow after I had stopped gaining height, he gave me the endearing nickname of "Big Foot." Only my brother retained his regular moniker, Bob.

Joan was naturally drawn to her father. Our mother tried to treat all three of us in an even-handed way. She continued to take violin lessons in order to play with Joan. "I think it is remarkable how well Joan plays," she wrote my father. "I think my practicing with her is going to be a real bond between us."

In 1926, after my mother inherited some money from her father, who had succumbed to heart failure, my parents were prepared to establish themselves in a more elegant Dutchess County homestead. A gingerbread Victorian mansion located in the middle of the farm acres came on the market. The property was shaded by mature maple trees and a huge, ancient oak on the south lawn. The north side commanded a view of an artificial pond that had supplied neighborhood icehouses before the advent of the refrigerator. Other buildings on the property included a boathouse, a sawmill, and a large barn with box and straight stalls for horses. For the next couple of years, supervising the remodeling and furnishing of the house and the landscaping of the grounds occupied a great deal of my mother's time.

Rather wisely as it turned out, my parents proceeded to get the whole job done without delay. In an era when Victorian design was generally abhorred, a fashionable architect, Aymar Embury, completely redesigned the exterior and interior as a dignified Georgian manor house. My mother, whose taste ran to rustic colonial cottages, held the line against what she considered the pretensions of marble fireplaces and mahogany furniture, opting instead for brick and pine. At the time, I was doing a lot of reading and observing concerned with residential design, and became very much involved with my mother in building our family home. It was not a usual pursuit for a ten-year-old boy, who was supposed to be outdoors playing ball, but I loved it.

The move into our new aggrandized country seat was completed during the summer of 1929 just before the October crash on Wall Street which heralded the Great Depression. Luckily we had made all the outlays in advance and had no mortgages or loans. I can't recall any retrenchment in our family's way of life during the Depression years, although as the watchdog of family expenditures my mother continued as always to be extremely careful. The farm and the *American Agriculturist,* which had been debtor operations all along, didn't seem to be losing any more money than usual. Morris Fatman, my mother's father, had fortuitously sold his woolen manufacturing business a few years before he died and prudently invested his profits and his wife's Lehman inheritance in securities that produced relatively stable yields. Similarly, the senior Henry Morgenthau had on the whole retired from active business.

The overwhelming defeat of Al Smith in the presidential election of 1928 was a crushing blow to Eleanor Roosevelt. Franklin's squeaking in as governor held no consolation for her. Indeed she seemed to take it as adding insult to injury. Henry and Elinor, however, were overjoyed with this new beginning. Franklin appointed Henry to fill the seat (but not the chairmanship) he had vacated on the Taconic State Parkway Commission. He also made Henry chairman of the new Agricultural Advisory Commission. There was no salary and no office space. Henry set up headquarters at a clerk's desk just outside the governor's office, and he and Elinor maintained a suite at the DeWitt Clinton Hotel, Albany's finest. The Agricultural Commission sponsored studies of farm problems and initiated a broad program of legislation, much of which was enacted within the two-year gubernatorial term. Up until then, the Democrats, beholden to the New York City bosses, had ignored the farmers. Roosevelt made them his friends.

But the onset of the Great Depression turned everything upside down. In the 1930 election the Roosevelt-Lehman ticket was re-elected by a huge majority, and FDR became the presidential front-runner. Al Smith's resounding defeat in 1928 could be credited to prosperity and anti-Catholic bigotry. As 1932 approached, the first factor no longer applied, but the second still did. Foreseeing that almost any Democrat could win in 1932, Smith dearly wanted a second chance, but savvy Irish Catholic politicians like Jim Farley and Ed Flynn, along with other powerful Democrats, were turning to Roosevelt.

In March 1931 FDR agreed to have Louis Howe set up a small office in New York City to raise funds and organize. He got started with contributions of five thousand dollars each from three stalwart optimists: the senior Henry Morgenthau, Frank C. Walker, a Roosevelt friend, and William H. Woodin, a wealthy industrialist destined to become the New Deal's first secretary of the treasury.

In his second term as governor, Roosevelt promoted Morgenthau to his first important administrative assignment: conservation commissioner in charge of wildlife and the preservation of vast forest lands, a job Morgenthau had coveted and was by experience and talent well qualified to execute.

After his decisive victory in 1930, Roosevelt began to use Albany as a place to test ideas and men for his intended move to Washington. Morgenthau was intensely aware of the opportunity handed to him, as was his wife. "I feel tremendous joy and pride in your giving Henry the important post of 'Conservation Commission,'" she wrote the governor. "While you are moving on in your own work . . . it gives Henry a chance to grow, so that your friendship can continue to be cemented by a community of interest as well as by the deep affection with which he holds you." Roosevelt gracefully accepted these rather heavy-handed compliments with his own calm humor. Henry had taken to reaching the outposts of his vast wildlife domain in a single-engine, open cockpit Conservation Department plane. When Henry complained about getting airsick during low, bumpy flights, Roosevelt warned everyone not to stick their heads out the windows when they heard Henry's plane flying over Albany.

Meanwhile Henry was proving himself to be an able administrator. He sought out the best advice and put it to good use. He learned how to delegate authority. He was generous in crediting his subordinates, with their share in his accomplishments. Indeed his wife frequently urged him to be less modest. He also showed a penchant (which would resurface in Washington) for rigorously prosecuting wrongdoers. At times he carried it to the absurd as when he insisted on finding the Long Island Sound fishermen trafficking in under-sized lobsters. Though he had a great deal of patronage at his disposal he was generally uncompromising in hiring only the best-qualified candidates, regardless of party affiliation, to the point where he became known "as probably the world's worst politician."

The vast reforestation program Morgenthau successfully pur-sued in the Adirondacks was particularly close to his boss's heart. But Roosevelt, who was as concerned with the conservation of humans as of natural resources, was especially pleased when Morgenthau joined forces with Harry Hopkins, chairman of the State Temporary Emergency Relief Administration. Together in the spring of 1932 they arranged to have ten thousand young, unem-ployed men work in the forests. This and some of the other work they initiated served as pilot projects for the future CCC (Civilian Conservation Corps) and the NYA (National Youth Administra-tion).

During the critical election year of 1932 both Morgenthaus sus-tained an intimate closeness with both Roosevelts. "Elinor, I want to know what makes Henry argue so. Don't he get a chance at home to make his opinions known?" FDR scrawled on the program for the luncheon celebration of his fiftieth birthday at Hyde Park on January 30. The following week he dictated a letter that he undoubt-edly composed himself: "In the excitement of the party on Saturday I don't know whether or not I really thanked you and Henry for the very useful birthday gift. . . . I hope you will both come down and use the cups while I am in Warm Springs."

On May 11, while spending his own forty-first birthday at Warm Springs, my father received a letter from his wife:

> I hope it will be a happy day in that you . . . get a lot of interesting information, and I also hope with all my being that if you have any all consuming wish that you get your heart's desire. That is if Franklin should be President, I hope you go along with him in whatever capac-ity you most want. As far as Franklin is concerned however I think his chances are very slim, but you have done so wonderfully in your own name that I think you should go very far, if only you will sometimes take a little credit to yourself and not always hand all your ideas and work to some one else.

From Warm Springs Roosevelt dispatched Morgenthau on a swing through the Middle West and Southern farm belt to gather opinions on the causes of and cures for the agricultural depression and on the Roosevelt candidacy. "My trip is going fine," he reported to the boss. "I am meeting a lot of very interesting farm leaders. Most are Republicans but are ready to vote for you, if given the opportunity. Our New York story on agriculture has reached them and they all admit New York has done more for the farms than any other state."

In the meantime my mother had jumped back into the fray to work for the Women's Division at Democratic Headquarters in New York. In October she wrote to me at Deerfield Academy, where I had started classes that fall: "This week has been an unusually busy one for me. The radio work piled up heavily as I have had to get women speakers not only for New York, but for almost every state in the union." By this time she had become much more optimistic about the elections. "Things on the whole look most promising," she wrote. "I think that Uncle Herbert [Lehman] will carry the State by close to half a million and the Governor [Roosevelt] will surely be elected and carry New York also."

· 22 ·

Passing the Baton

WHEN GOVERNOR FRANKLIN D. ROOSEVELT was elected president of the United States in 1932, my father was still serving as his conservation commissioner in Albany. Although both my parents had been key workers in the campaign, it was my grandfather who was still the recognized public figure. My first cousin Barbara Tuchman told me she remembers coming down from Radcliffe to be with him election night:

> I will never forget the night Roosevelt was elected because Grandpa took me to headquarters with him at the Biltmore Hotel. It was terribly crowded and very exciting . . . A policeman at the hotel saw Grandpa and began pushing the crowd away saying "Come on, Uncle Henry, I'll get you in." Everybody knew him . . . We went right into the room where the governor was sitting at the head of a long, long table. It seemed to me about thirty feet long with people on both sides. Mrs. Roosevelt was standing in the corner with [Jim] Farley.
>
> Grandpa took me right up to the governor and said I had worked on the campaign the previous summer . . . Roosevelt looked up at me as if I was the one person in the world he wanted to see. "How nice it was of you to come down from college to see me elected." He had this way of making you feel important.

Barbara remembered "waiting around for Hoover to concede, which he didn't for the longest time . . . My beau had a bottle with him, [the kind] people used to carry in the rumble seat. We went and sat with Grandpa at a table at Childs and ordered tea cups and poured the liquor into the white china tea cups. I can remember we all had a drink to the president's health."

The Roosevelt inauguration on March 4, 1933, marked a rite of passage in the Morgenthau family. Henry Sr. at seventy-six, having given his son a good running start in the intergenerational relay race for political power, professed to be ready to pass the baton. Yet he continued to act as though his young teammate were still not entirely capable of operating on his own. The ambassador had set out to have his son given a cabinet post.

Henry Jr. had been groomed to become secretary of agriculture, but there were a number of strikes against him. On the national scene the image of Wall Street obscured the fact that upstate New York was in fact one of the country's major farm regions. Furthermore, with a New York governor moving into the White House, the notion of a Jewish secretary of agriculture from New York State was anathema in the Midwest and the Southern farm belt.

Earlier that year, while my father was visiting me at Deerfield Academy, Grandpa was in New York pressing negotiations on behalf of his son. Henry Jr. had himself sought the support of Eleanor Roosevelt. "Please at least talk to him," she had written to her husband.

At a prearranged time my father called his father from a pay phone in Deerfield to get the news. The door of the booth squeaked closed, and I watched his lips moving silently through the streaked glass panels. It was not long before the door squeaked open again and my father stepped out pale and crestfallen. True to character, his father had tried to present the bad news in a positive light. Roosevelt was not going to put him in his cabinet, but he had something much better in store. He wanted Henry Jr. to organize a new Farm Credit Administration and take over as governor of the old Hoover Farm Board as well. My father, who always discussed serious matters in a slow monotone, was especially glum.

For all his show of optimism, the senior Morgenthau found the bad news — too reminiscent of his own disappointment — hard to take. According to his private timetable, the moment had come for a Jew in the cabinet. Oscar Straus, Theodore Roosevelt's secretary of labor and commerce, had been the first and only one to rise to that level.*

---

*Ironically, FDR was considering Jesse Straus, the president of Macy's department store and the nephew of Oscar Straus, as a possible secretary of commerce. This bitter turn of events was more than Henry Sr. could swallow. He was so delighted when he learned that FDR was persuaded to appoint someone else to that post that he could not resist the temptation to break the bad news to Straus himself. Straus was furious, not so much at

Meanwhile Grandpa had invited all his grandchildren to join him on a safari to Washington to attend the inaugural celebration. It was his last hurrah before his son gained pre-eminence in the family.

Washington was flooded with well-wishers, but Grandpa had managed to get choice locations everywhere. We had rooms at the Mayflower Hotel, where Roosevelt himself had a suite. And we all had front-row seats for the various ceremonies. As we shoved and elbowed our way through the masses of people, many old-timers cheerfully greeted Grandpa as "Uncle Henry." He loved it.

On that gray, chill Saturday morning when Franklin Delano Roosevelt was sworn in as president by Chief Justice Charles Evans Hughes against the backdrop of the Capitol, my parents were seated in the stands with the official party — the Roosevelt family and personal friends. With Grandpa and his flock, I was packed in at the front of the crowd directly facing the players on stage. At sixteen, I had only a vague sense that I was on the periphery of history in the making, although, invisibly wired to my parents, I could feel the electric surge of the moment. My parents, with Grandpa's backing, had bet everything on Roosevelt and they had won, but they had no personal base of power, no constituency. If they strayed behind — perhaps only for a moment — the sidelines were crowded with those ready to step in and replace them. Along with the excitement I could feel their insecurity.

When Roosevelt moved into the White House he took many of the old Albany crowd along with him, though not all who would have liked to join him. As each of the chosen settled into his new post (Frances Perkins, secretary of labor, was the only woman), there was more to worry about than just protecting one's turf. In her first interview in the White House, Mrs. Roosevelt told her journalist friend Lorena Hickok, "No one close to people in public today can fail to realize that we are all facing extremely critical times."

The pervasive mood of the country was isolationist, with strong sentiments favoring disarmament and pacifism. International relations had not produced any major campaign issues, but Roosevelt,

---

the decision but at the way he was informed. The Roosevelt inner circle was very much annoyed with Morgenthau Sr.'s gauche move. It took some adroit maneuvering to smooth Straus's ruffled feathers. He finally agreed to accept the French embassy as a consolation prize.

who was very much interested in preserving peace, was nevertheless uneasy about Japanese aggression and the danger posed by German rearmament (Hitler had become chancellor that January).

I remember my grandfather coming to visit me in the spring of 1933 at Deerfield, shortly after the FDR inauguration. Such occasions were always welcome breaks in long, woebegone stretches of captivity in an institution for adolescent boys in an idyllic but remote part of western Massachusetts. On this visit he gave me a recently published book that predicted the collapse of the postwar German Republic. To this day I have in my possession a long-since faded copy of Edgar Ansel Mowrer's *Germany Puts the Clock Back,* which bears a firm, gracefully penned inscription on the flyleaf, "To my grandson Henry Morgenthau 3rd with love from his Grandpa." Quoting Adolf Hitler's prophecy "All that I say and do is history," Mowrer warned that Hitler "could conceivably become dictator of Germany, another Mussolini, the peer of Stalin, Pilsudski and Kemal Pasha."

At that time, when the majority of Americans were manic in the midst of the New Deal honeymoon, news from abroad filtered through to the American consciousness with difficulty. It was certainly not a concern preoccupying most affluent teenage boys. But for reasons that I find difficult to explain, Mowrer's book made a deep and lasting impression on me. I believe it was in part my love and admiration for my grandfather. I was eager to echo his thoughts.

At Deerfield, I was a loner, unnoticed and much given to reveries. When my parents gave up our family apartment in Manhattan in anticipation of joining the new Roosevelt administration in the nation's capital, I was compelled to leave the "progressive" Lincoln day school, which I adored, for the tradition-bound boarding school, which I found confining.

It was during the depths of the Depression, and almost any boy whose family could pay the tuition was acceptable. During the reign of its charismatic despot of a headmaster Frank Boyden, Deerfield had grown to assume a position of solid respectability in the ranks of private secondary schools. It did not, however, have the assurance of an upper-class WASP clientele guaranteed to some of the older schools like Groton. The latter admitted few if any Jewish students into their notoriously anti-Semitic environment — St.

Paul's took one a year — but Deerfield was welcoming a substantial block of my German Jewish peers. Whatever anti-Semitic passions might have been harbored in schoolboy breasts were somehow miraculously suppressed even during those rare unsupervised moments in the dorms when boys could harass each other with impunity.

My loneliness at Deerfield had less to do with my Jewishness than with a painfully self-conscious struggle with adolescence. It was as though my concept of Jewish alienation had permeated my sensibilities as an antidote to an uncontrollable personal malaise. Reading Mowrer's book was an exciting revelation that unlocked a new identity. When Mowrer said that "the aim of [the Hitlerites'] barbarous campaign was the extermination, permanent subjection or voluntary departure of the Jews from Germany," I was chilled to the marrow of my bones.

My brother's experience at Deerfield was quite different from mine. The year before he started he was afflicted with a second very serious ear infection, this one leading to mastoiditis. On recovery he was left almost completely deaf in the afflicted ear. Following surgery he had to drop out of Lincoln School, and he spent the hiatus profitably on the farm. A companionable tutor, John Fox, enabled him to keep up with his school work; he also became accomplished at chopping wood and at other healthy outdoor activities. When Bob entered Deerfield in the fall of 1933 he was in great shape intellectually and physically. In the four years spent there he rose to the top of his class and before graduation was elected its president.

When my brother and I were securely parked at Deerfield, my parents became totally immersed in Washington officialdom.*

Soon after his inauguration, FDR began to feel his way toward establishing diplomatic relations with the Soviet Union, as a potential check against Japanese and German expansionism. At first he encountered strong opposition from the State Department. Holding to his simplistic solution for all international problems through reciprocal trade agreements, Secretary of State Cordell Hull, along with the firmly anti-Bolshevik foreign service regulars, was ex-

*My sister, Joan, living at home, attended the Cathedral School. Later, she was a boarder at Miss Madeira's School in Virginia.

tremely unsympathetic. Roosevelt therefore turned to his old colleague Henry Morgenthau, Jr., now installed as governor of the new Farm Credit Administration. On the pretext of initiating negotiations for the purchase of U.S. agricultural commodities with the Soviet state trading corporation, Morgenthau was ordered to begin preliminary wide-ranging diplomatic discussions. This early instance of operating outside established channels was to become a hallmark of the twelve-plus years of the Roosevelt presidency.

Soon my father found himself sitting down in Washington with a senior Soviet diplomat, Maxim Litvinov. The moon-faced, roly-poly Jew (officially an atheist) had been a prerevolutionary Bolshevik-in-exile along with Lenin. In England, Litvinov had married Ivy Low, a member of a respectable family of British intellectuals who had fled from Hungary after the failed 1848 revolution.

Morgenthau hit it off well with Litvinov, finding him "a warm, friendly man, sparkling in conversation, abundant in hospitality." But he was appropriately cautious, understanding that no Russian was ever granted personal discretion in negotiations. "If the deal worked out well," he told Roosevelt, "he [Morgenthau] would be a hero, but if it flopped, he would have to leave Washington. 'Well, of course, you know that I stand back of you in these negotiations,' Roosevelt replied, 'and if you have to leave Washington I will leave with you.'"

Much to Morgenthau's relief, the negotiations were eventually placed in the hands of William C. Bullitt, the State Department's Soviet expert. Bullitt thereafter worked directly for the president and behind Hull's back. Well versed in his mission and a master of intrigue, Bullitt would appear to have been the right man for the job. He had married and then divorced the widow of the American Communist John Reed, the only American buried in the Kremlin wall. Passionate and mercurial in his attachments, he was then very much a Soviet partisan. He was an interesting balance for Litvinov, whom the hard-line Soviets always suspected of harboring pro-Western sympathies. When the barriers between the two nations eventually came down, each man became his country's ambassador to the other.

After his initial disappointment in failing to win a cabinet post, Morgenthau soon came to realize that he had been handed an assignment in the Farm Credit Administration at least as challenging as heading the Department of Agriculture. The farmers of the United States were going broke. The FCA was designed to bail them out and get them back on their feet. This was Henry Jr.'s first venture into public finance, and it was conspicuously successful. Even some of his closest and most loyal associates were surprised.

Roosevelt's first secretary of the treasury, William Woodin, meanwhile, had fallen mortally ill with cancer, and in 1934 the undersecretary, Dean Acheson, was put in charge. Acheson proved to be obdurate in his opposition to Roosevelt's hope to stem plummeting commodity prices by purchasing gold.

Acheson and Roosevelt were of the same breed of patrician gentlemen, both firmly committed to liberal political beliefs. Both had attended Groton. But whereas Roosevelt had learned to charm, compromise, and manipulate to achieve what he considered honorable ends, Acheson was aloof, arrogant, and unyielding in adhering to principle. His attitude toward public service was one of noblesse oblige, in the best sense.

In any case, when FDR became aware that here was a Groton boy who could not be had, he began to look elsewhere for an ally. He knew from their days together in Albany that my father combined the virtue of absolute loyalty with an uncanny ability to get things done, sometimes in extremely unorthodox ways, using aides who were themselves idiosyncratic in their approach to problems.

Dean Acheson held that the president's announced intent to purchase gold was illegal, unethical, and economically unsound. So, for that matter, did almost everyone else. Morgenthau, from the rather oblique perspective of the Farm Credit Administration, came to the rescue. His brilliant, eccentric chief counsel, Herman Oliphant (who had been recommended by my father's old friend and personal attorney Edward S. Greenbaum), found some arcane legal precedent that was enough to enable Roosevelt to start operating even without sanction from the Department of Justice.

The president hated to fire anyone. Thus from June until November, Acheson, while remaining consistent in his opposition to the president, and having submitted an undated letter of resignation, stayed on the job. But when, after a White House breakfast conference on November 13, 1934, Roosevelt told Morgenthau that he was to replace Acheson, his faithful lieutenant was completely "dumbfounded" and "broke out in a cold sweat." Looking back on this fateful day many years later after he had retired from public life, my father was able to philosophize that "the President wanted a

Secretary [of the Treasury] who would be loyal and would try to get things done."

At forty-three, after serving briefly as under- and acting secretary, my father attained the second-highest-ranking seat in the cabinet and became the first Jew to serve in the cabinet since Oscar Straus. He was overwhelmed. But my grandfather felt no such diffidence. There was no question in his mind that his son's achievement was not because he was Jewish but in spite of it.

In 1933 my mother went to Washington with my father to advance his career and, vulnerable person that she knew him to be, protect him. For her, Washington, like going away to college, was yet another radical departure from the way of life her mother had intended for her. As at Vassar her approach was again one of earnest, purposeful reserve.

That first year of the New Deal my parents resided in a three-room suite in the Shoreham Hotel overlooking Rock Creek Park, while my brother and I were conveniently tucked away at Deerfield Academy. But my sister Joan was still a day student at Lincoln, so we kept the family apartment at 35 West Eighty-first Street. When my father advanced from Farm Credit to the Treasury, Mother felt firmly enough rooted in Washington to rent a furnished house on fashionable Kalorama Road. My father persisted in his fear that he would lose his grip at the top of the ladder in Washington, and so we moved every couple of years, renting one furnished house after another, never daring to buy one.

There was a rigidly prescribed role for cabinet wives, often performed *en bloc*. All ten of them would line up and be seated according to the rank of their husbands, starting with Mrs. Hull, wife of the secretary of state, then my mother, and so on down the line. Frances Perkins, as the first woman to serve in the cabinet, was an anomaly. No one would have suggested that her husband take his place with the cabinet wives. "Madame Perkins," wanting to do the right thing, gave in to the suggestions of the protocol officers and attempted to perform all the social obligations of both cabinet officer and cabinet wife. The situation reached the height of absurdity during the 1934 Gridiron dinner, a stag affair at which the Washington press corps — exclusive of its own female members — roasted the politicos, from the president on down, in their presence. Mrs. Roosevelt retaliated by holding the first annual White House gala for the "Gridiron widows." The ladies were invited to come in costume. Mrs. Roosevelt received them dressed as a Romanian peasant. Mother was attired as a court lady of the eighteenth century. Secretary Perkins, excluded from the stag Gridiron dinner, came to this widows' gala wearing academic cap and gown, as a brain truster.*

Eleanor Roosevelt, never troubled by foolish consistency, established a role for the first lady, unmatched before or since, which was at once regal and populist. Early in life, as the niece of the other Roosevelt president and the wife of Woodrow Wilson's assistant secretary of the navy, she had become well versed in official Washington etiquette and performed all her official duties with meticulous correctness. But she was happiest when she could be out in the field serving as Franklin's eyes and ears, observing the New Deal in action, or visiting places where she thought government service was needed. Striding ahead in flat-heeled shoes and practical, unfashionable clothes, she felt that she was at once performing a useful role and carrying out her long-standing rebellion against her patrician relatives' insensitivity to social injustice.

My mother loved every moment she spent with Eleanor Roosevelt. For the most part this meant engaging in political and social service activities. But there were private occasions as well. The two women frequently went horseback riding in Rock Creek Park. And whenever Mrs. Roosevelt went to a Broadway show she counted on Mother, with her theater background, to select the play and get the tickets.† When the two of them were in New York together, Eleanor sometimes took her friend Elinor to dine at the Colony Club. When she learned that Mother would be interested in joining, she put her up for membership. But in those days the Colony Club wasn't interested in having Jewish members. Mother was blackballed. Both women were shocked, and Eleanor Roosevelt resigned.

My father's Treasury appointment was accepted as though it were a family achievement, and none of us hesitated to bask in the warm glow of prestige by association.

I had the first taste of extended "perks" traveling abroad dur-

---

*After dinner Mrs. Roosevelt was featured as "Apple Mary" in a skit written for the occasion by my mother and her Vassar College friend Gabrielle Elliot Forbush. At the time Gabrielle was employed at the Treasury to answer the secretary's voluminous mail.
†Getting tickets for Mrs. Roosevelt was not difficult, as I discovered for myself during the post–White House years when I was her TV producer. If one made it known that the tickets were for Eleanor Roosevelt, the only problem was getting anyone to accept payment for them.

ing the summer of 1934 with my best friend Jerry Straus and his mother, Flora. My passport was "Special," just short of "Diplomatic." The attention it attracted from obsequious petty public servants gave me an exhilarating sense of being quite above the ordinary tourist. As the three of us moved around Europe, we were received like an official mission by U.S. ambassadors and consuls. We touched base in many of the major cities, having deliberately excluded the Fascist capitals, Rome, Berlin, and Madrid. We arrived in the Soviet Union by train from Helsinki at the Finland station in Leningrad, less than a year after the two countries had resumed diplomatic relations. The U.S.S.R. was not equipped to receive many tourists, but we were well accommodated, as a gesture of appreciation for my father's role in the negotiations with Litvinov. In Moscow we were entertained by William Bullitt, the enigmatic American ambassador. From there we traveled by railroad to Warsaw, stopping at the splendid Hotel Europjedski. Poland seemed a luxurious garden of plenty in contrast to the U.S.S.R.

From Warsaw we took the overnight train to Vienna. The first evening we dined at a night club that had a dramatic, panoramic view of the city. The dance band leader, wishing to please American customers, crooned a hit tune of the season, "Haf You Efer Zeen a Dream, Danzing?"

The next day we visited the "Karl Marx Hof," a large housing complex where socialist workers had been under siege earlier that year and where we inspected the outer walls, which were pitted from the machine-gun fire of the attacking police. A week after we departed, the Austrian chancellor, Engelbert Dollfuss, a right-wing Catholic, was assassinated during a failed Nazi putsch.

· 23 ·

Princeton,
a Painful Awakening

B Y THE TIME I returned from Europe for my senior year at Deerfield in the fall of 1934, I assumed that after graduation I would go on to college at Princeton. With my parents transplanted from New York to the nation's capital, Princeton was geographically more convenient than the New England colleges favored by most of the Deerfield boys. But initially the deciding factor was that my friend Jerry Straus intended to go to Princeton.

By the 1930s Princeton had fully recovered from the righteousness of its zealous idealist president, Woodrow Wilson. Not long after assuming office in 1902, he had declared in the stern rhetoric soon to be familiar across the land, "I have told the authorities I will not be president of a country club. Princeton must either be an educational institution or I will not remain."

Eight years later, a consortium of uneasy trustees and the megalomaniac Dean West of the Graduate College eased him out and into the New Jersey governorship, which led two years later to his presidency of the United States.

The sons of Old Nassau whom I joined in the fall of 1935 were confronted with a man in the White House who seemed to them far more dangerous than Wilson with his overly generous offer to make the world safe for Democracy, American style. At a moment of economic and social chaos, Princetonians perceived FDR as a threat to the sacred free enterprise system. They resented his tendency to play up to the masses, and denounced him as a traitor to his class.

Princeton was too distant from any urban center to accommodate the students who commuted from the impoverished inner city, as they did at Harvard and Columbia. At Princeton, where there was a propensity to identify with one's captain-of-industry father or the father-in-law one hoped to become accustomed to, there was little danger of being infected with the left-wing virus that was sweeping the country.

Princeton undergraduates in those days were men of heritage and men of ambition. The former, though not a majority, had the upper hand. They set the style poignantly glamorized by F. Scott Fitzgerald in *This Side of Paradise*. I soon learned that the campus abounded with scions of the great American baronies. My contemporaries included the heirs of the presidents of Du Pont, Pennsylvania Railroad, Hershey Chocolate, Borden Milk, Benton & Bowles and the D'Arcy advertising agencies, and the Engelhard mineral interests. We were in between waves of Firestones and Rockefellers.

The roster also rang with history. One learned not to blink when faced with a genuine Washington Irving or a Benjamin Franklin sporting a button-down shirt collar, tweed jacket, and dirty white shoes. Since Princeton was the farthest north a Southern gentleman could safely venture for a good education, it was not surprising that our ranks included descendants of Martha Washington, Henry Clay, and Robert E. Lee.

Our mixed bag of "sons of" boasted one each of architect Raymond Hood, Wendell Willkie, and union leader John L. Lewis, and a nephew of John Foster Dulles, '08, and Allen W. Dulles, '14. One of our classmates who left freshman year because of illness was the second son of the Wall Street tycoon and first chairman of the SEC, Joseph P. Kennedy. When he recuperated, Jack Kennedy decided to enter Harvard.

There were a few young men who, though duly accredited students, were accepted as and behaved like guests of the university. Prince Fumitaka Konoye, son of the Japanese premier, roomed on the floor above me my freshman year in Pyne Hall. Fumi threw himself into college life with an abandon that frequently left his American roommate, who tried to keep up with him — particularly in alcohol intake — in the shower shaking with D.T.'s. Fumi played a pretty good game of golf. He perfected his swing on the college links laid out between the Princeton Inn (now Forbes Hall) and the grad school. One summer he invited the entire Princeton team to Japan as his guests. During the war he was pressed into active service in the army and was killed in Manchuria.

By contrast, the majority of my contemporary fellow Prince-tonians came from unspectacular middle-class families. Sending their sons to Princeton was an investment — sometimes made at considerable sacrifice — in their sons' future security. They were ambitious to join the men of heritage or supplant them. Although this was a period of increasing intolerance, it was also one of rapid social mobility. In the depth of the Depression, while some fortunes were being lost, others were being made. It was also a time when there was new respect and opportunity for intellectual accomplish-ment in government. Roosevelt didn't invent the term *brain trust,* but he brought it into the vernacular while placing professors on the Supreme Court and in the ambassadorial ranks. Most of them came from Harvard and the University of Chicago.

At Princeton the men who set the social tone were a core of white Protestants, many from the South. There were a respectable number of Catholics, particularly those of Scottish and Germanic descent, and a very few others. Indeed Princeton felt secure in choosing its undergraduates from this preferred group without any qualms about who was excluded. No women were allowed, of course, not even as visitors. An undergraduate known to have gotten married would be automatically expelled. No blacks either, although Paul Robeson had been born and raised in Princeton, son of the pastor of the Witherspoon Street Presbyterian Church dur-ing Wilson's presidency at Nassau Hall. Between the Civil War and World War II blacks were not even considered for admission to Princeton. Robeson went to Rutgers, where he became an All-American football player with a Phi Beta Kappa key.

In 1935 Princeton didn't have a sign out NO JEWS NEED APPLY, but very few did — so few that Princeton was never faced with a "Jewish problem" like Harvard.

All of us in that tiny minority of Jewish students in the class of '39 came from families that had opted for assimilation to varying degrees. Indeed, going to Princeton was often a significant factor in the process. It was first of all a place to get a good education — always a high Jewish priority — and it also provided access to the mainstream.

For some of us, assimilation had progressed to the point where we had lost all positive sense of Jewish identity. We were the most vulnerable. When others discovered our Jewish identity for us, we had nothing to fall back on. But there were those who had preserved a solid knowledge of where they came from and a more realistic sense of where they were heading. They came to Princeton from just the opposite extreme, totally inoculated against the scourge that awaited us.

Bud Redpath's "Class History" in the 1939 *Nassau Herald* noted that "with the turn of the year there was only one thought in the Sophomore mind — clubs. All too soon were we initiated into the most distinctive of Princeton institutions." Bud was one of about 75–80 percent of our class who "signed our names in mysterious books, shook the hands of impressive presidents and donned new ties of varying types."

The process in which upper-class clubmen select and negotiate with sophomore prospects for coveted membership in the Prospect Street eating clubs is called "bicker." It involved none of the violence and horseplay associated with fraternity hazing. It was a mannered ritual with a strict dress code. For those who indulged, it was a polite, sadomasochistic experience from which they never totally recovered. Pain can be blocked out, but some subliminal memory of it remains. If I had sorted out my values, I would probably have wanted to weigh in with the 20 percent who chose or were chosen to survive outside the clubs. With a rearview mirror and the perspective of over a half century I can see this clearly.

Joining a Princeton club seemed like just another step into the new, barrier-free social whirl I had discovered in Washington. It would be there for the asking. Without further thought and with no cultivation and cementing of appropriate friendships, no leveraging of family and alumni connections, I lined up for the slaughter with arrogant optimism. For those critical bicker weeks I prepared each night to sit in my room.

Each club sent around teams of "callers." I waited for the sound of footfalls trudging up the stairs. Some nights there were none. Sometimes they approached and passed on. Then they would stop; there was a knock on another door, an exchange of muffled voices, a door clicking shut, and silence. As the nights and weeks succeeded one another, I knew that things were not going well for me.

Then there was a final Walpurgisnacht of wild celebration and despair, followed by the merciless dawn of reality. It was all over. When the pain subsided, a new numbness set in. From then on, I was a social paraplegic. The "good" clubs and the middle tier had passed me by, and those at the bottom of the pecking order —

Court, Gateway, and Dial Lodge — had been equally silent. I supposed they didn't think I was interested in them. Later on, after the bids had gone out, we made some awkward, uncomfortable maneuvers toward each other. But it was more than I could take. It had been an emasculating experience that left me feeling that I was something less than a Princeton man. On the one hand, I was filled with self-hate in the realization that I would do anything to get into a club, and on the other hand, frustrated by the knowledge that no act of self-mutilation would enable me to succeed.

At the time of this traumatic incident only three classmates had identified themselves on the record as Jewish. But there were a total of sixteen who caused my ethnic divining rod to bend decisively in their direction. Of these, five did not join any club, three signed up with Court, three with Gateway, and five joined one of five other clubs.

There was no Jewish life as such at Princeton in those days, and most of us wouldn't have wanted it any other way. Right after the club debacle, I have a faint memory of looking in on the Jewish service conducted by a classmate who was a rabbi's son. A handful of students was gathered in a dim, shadowy corner in the vast Gothic Milbank Chapel. I felt even more alienated there and never returned.★ The rabbi's son roomed with someone he remembers "as a very plain Jewish boy from Uniontown, Pennsylvania, utterly unspectacular. One day when he was walking down Prospect Street, he threw a snowball at the cannon in front of Cannon Club. It landed squarely in the mouth of the namesake cannon. On the front lawn the whole street full of kids cheered. That was the high point of his career."

Some of us who were not in clubs, either by choice or popular demand, formed a small group that contracted for regular meals at the Peacock Inn in town. It was technically possible, but hardly desirable, to continue eating in Commons with the succeeding crops of freshmen. The rabbi's son remembered "our class Quaker, [who] used to bow his head and say grace before eating at Commons — when he looked up, all the food was gone. That always impressed me immensely with the disadvantages of praying while other people are grabbing."

★I heard later that some of the boys who attended the Friday evening Jewish services were Christians who could thereby avoid compulsory Sunday chapel. This enabled them to enjoy a full weekend off campus.

Six years before my experience at Princeton, my cousin Barbara Tuchman had discovered as a freshman at Swarthmore that the sororities that dominated campus social life didn't pledge Jews. She told me that this was the first evidence she had encountered, involving her personally, that there was a difference between Jews and others. It seemed to her not so much traumatic but idiotic. As she put it, "Here was something that was affecting me over which I had absolutely no control. It had nothing to do with my personality or capacities. It was just automatic, without rationale. That angered me. So I decided to leave at the end of the year. . . . I went to Radcliffe, because from what I could find out, it seemed to have no organized social life, no sororities, no groupie stuff."

It was a new and enjoyable beginning for Barbara. Being Jewish at Radcliffe wasn't important, except, as she noted, she didn't go out on dates along with her group of women friends who lived on the fourth floor of Briggs Hall. "It seemed a little strange, but I didn't push it," she recalled.

The handicap of being shut off from the Prospect Street club way of life shunted me into a stream of other activities in the Princeton community. I don't think it ever occurred to me to leave. I'm glad I didn't. The faculty was lively, humane, and challenging. Some of them, especially Dean Christian Gauss, were actively supportive.

During my junior year at Princeton I set up a special backdoor relationship with some of the best clubs on Prospect Street. This came about when I joined a classmate, Archie Leonard, who organized a program to collect leftover food from the club kitchens and distribute it to hungry Princeton families. As manager of the Student Refreshment Agency, which helped him work his way through college, Archie had the rare privilege of being permitted to operate a truck. Thus a number of Archie's recruits collected vats of cooked cereal and other perishables, and transported them to "needy" families identified for us by the local relief agency.

These handouts dispensed from Archie's truck were accepted by the recipients with as much dignified gratitude as seemed appropriate under the circumstances. A good many of the hungry poor were members of the Princeton black community, descendants of the "body servants" who had accompanied Southern gentlemen to Princeton in an earlier era.

One of the most conscientious members of our squad of volunteers was a handsome, long-legged Dutchess County squire who summered in Newport, Rhode Island, Claiborne Pell, '40. His grandmother had been a friend of Sara Delano Roosevelt. His father, Herbert C. Pell, as congressman and New York State Democratic Committee chairman, had become friendly with my parents as fellow Roosevelt supporters. Claiborne and I encountered each other not only on the food distribution route but also while running for the cross-country team.

When Fascism was ravaging Europe, Princeton became a magnet for some of its most distinguished displaced intellectuals. Thomas Mann, voluntary exile from Hitler's Germany, transplanted his family and his haute bourgeois lifestyle to a spacious lower Nassau Street mansion protected by a forbidding, high brick wall. He delivered a series of Jovian lectures in magnificently ponderous English. Erwin Panofsky, the art historian, and Albert Einstein both came to Princeton to join the Institute for Advanced Study. At that time, the Institute had no quarters of its own, so its members were truly guests of the university.

Despite his shy, unassuming manner, one could never say that Einstein had a low profile on campus. In the era of crew cuts and knitted ties, his trademarks were his crowning shock of wildly tangled silver hair and a fountain pen clipped to his shirt at the throat. One could pick him out wandering about the campus or at a concert in McCarter Theater. If he particularly enjoyed what he heard, he would without any suggestion of pretentiousness, walk directly from his orchestra seat up the steps on the side of the proscenium to express his appreciation to the artist.

My grandfather Morgenthau, who generally found a way of hobnobbing with renowned personages wherever they were, was acquainted with Einstein. So, on one of his visits to me at Princeton, we went to call on Einstein at his modest, wood frame house on Mercer Street.

Einstein turned to me with sincere interest and asked what I was studying. I said history of art. He began to question me further. Behind the soft, kindly eyes there was something that automatically focused on the truth, cutting through the small talk. Unintentionally he was giving me an overpowering challenge from which I retreated. Moments later when we departed, I felt diminished. I had lost the moment to respond in the presence of greatness.

Joe Schein, '37, got Einstein to come to Murray-Dodge Hall and talk to all the Jewish students. About twenty-five showed up. A math major who had come said that at the time he resented what he considered the extremely parochial tone of Einstein's talk. Einstein had said he didn't know how to explain himself, it was nothing he understood, but that he was always powerfully stirred by his feelings of Jewish identity.

The class of 1939 was the last to graduate before the outbreak of World War II. While some of my classmates seemed gifted with prescience, this had little influence on our collective views. In response to the question "Would you fight for your country at home?" in a class poll, 431 voted yes, 20 no. But when asked "Would you fight for your country abroad?" 141 voted yes, 247 no.

A total of 293 thought Hitler was the outstanding personality of the preceding year; 57, Chamberlain; 21, Roosevelt.

The ROTC was popular, particularly among those who wanted to face the inevitable military service as officers and gentlemen. But the antiwar society also had strong support. It in turn gave birth to a Veterans of Future Wars movement, and an auxiliary started at Vassar which particularly enraged parents: The Future Gold Star Mothers.

Walter Lord, who became the best-known historian in our class, noted twenty-five years later that after graduation "Europe seemed full of cycling '39ers, many of them bound for places that would later have a strange ring for vacationing — Budapest, Warsaw, Bucharest. Toward the end of summer there was even an informal class reunion in Hitler's rathskeller in Munich."

Most of us had little appreciation of the profound changes in store for us. We certainly failed to realize that after the war we would never go back to Old Nassau as we knew it. But our class orator, Phil Davison, stood above us with an eerie clarity of foresight:

> We shall see what happens when Hitler and Mussolini die or are killed. We shall probably see the break up of the British Empire; perhaps we shall see the unification of China and the rise of one of the world's most powerful states.
>
> We shall all be able to watch the process of the centralization of power and the reaction to this process; we shall probably see a religious revival, or some similar reaction against the increasing mechanization of life. Progress in science is . . . taken for granted.

While my brother and I were at Amherst and Princeton, respectively, our Christmas vacation calendar was crowded with invitations to one or more Washington parties almost every night. On

New Year's Eve 1938 "everybody who is anybody," in Washington, according to the young gossip columnist Igor Cassini, attended the dance given by Mrs. Demarest Lloyd for her daughter, Angelica. Some four hundred guests at the Lloyds' lingered on until 7:00 the next morning. Bob and I had been invited to a dinner before the ball for one hundred guests at the Sulgrave Club, given by "post-deb" Eleanor Flood for her debutante cousin from Virginia, Maggie Byrd. Igor Cassini and his brother Oleg, czarist Russia emigrés descended from diplomat parents who were stranded in the United States after the revolution, were prominent on the Washington social scene themselves. Igor's "Petit Point" column, which was generally simply a flood of frivolous one-liners, described young Eleanor Roosevelt, the niece and namesake of the first lady, as "dancing dignifiedly with quick-witted Henry Morgenthau [III]."

As the Lloyd New Year's Eve ball was picking up momentum around 11:00 P.M., my brother and I, escorting Eleanor Flood and young Eleanor Roosevelt, slipped away to the White House to join our parents before midnight to see the old year out. The four of us arrived at the north portico in one of the two Cadillac limousines assigned to the secretary of the treasury. We were not asked to produce any kind of identification but were questioned by a Secret Service guard much more closely than I had recalled on other similar occasions. The Secret Service, charged with protecting the president's life, was under the wing of the secretary of the treasury. It was an awesome responsibility, and my father was always grimly aware of it. Moments after my brother and I and our dates entered the White House, we were ushered into the family quarters upstairs. My father, who came out to greet us, was in a high state of agitation. He had left instructions with the Secret Service detail on duty that when we arrived we should be ushered right in.

Earlier that night a sixteen-year-old Washington high school student, Joe Measell, his date, Beatrice White, and his fourteen-year-old brother had been at a party where they accepted a dare to go to the White House and get autographs from the president and the first lady. They managed to drive right up to the main entrance at 1600 Pennsylvania Avenue in the family car where Measell "told the policeman there we wanted to see the President." The Secret Service officers mistook him for one of the expected Morgenthau sons, and he and his date were ushered upstairs where everyone had just finished watching a movie.

According to Measell, FDR did not appear at all taken aback by his presence "until some men whom I suppose were Secret Service men rushed into the room and hurried me out." Meanwhile Beatrice had been taken in to see Mrs. Roosevelt and obtained her signature.

In her "My Day" column a few days later Mrs. Roosevelt commented at length on the interrupted celebration at the White House. Just before midnight, "my niece Eleanor Roosevelt came from the dance she had been attending accompanied by Robert and Henry Morgenthau and Miss Eleanor Flood." It was "the President's custom as the midnight hour strikes, to drink the first toast of the year . . . 'to the United States.' After that come personal toasts, but I rather think few people who have the privilege of drinking the first toast in this historic house can do so without a thrill."

Eleanor Roosevelt expressed her annoyance at "the rather unfortunate incident which a thoughtless boy and girl brought about by their intrusion on New Year's Eve. Their rude and unmannerly behavior" could have resulted in truly unfortunate consequences. She had been saddened "to have young people grow up at present so thoughtless and unmindful of others."

· 24 ·

World War II
Shall Not Take Place

I N MIDSUMMER 1938 the Morgenthau family embarked on the August vacation that had been an unbroken tradition as far back as I can remember. Our safari, though paid for privately, was eased with all the perks of an official deputation. On board the Dutch liner *Stattendam,* we were bunked in three spacious first-class cabins — one for my parents, one for my brother and me, and one for my sister and my mother's Scottish maid, Janet Crawford, who was combining her usual duties with a visit to her relatives near Glasgow.

In the *Stattendam* dining salon our family was assigned to a table served by an especially efficient steward whom my father was convinced was a German spy. We all reacted to Daddy's suspiciousness with great amusement. In an odd turn of events at the end of the war I discovered that my father's hunch was uncannily close to the mark.★

After disembarking from the *Stattendam* at Boulogne, en route to the Côte d'Azur, we stopped off at the American embassy in Paris as guests of the ambassador, William Bullitt. I had met him

★Shortly after V-E Day in 1945, my mechanized cavalry unit was stationed on the Czech border of Bavaria and was loosely guarding the surrendered German Eleventh Panzer Division, giving them freedom to roam around the village we were occupying. I was approached there by a German corporal, who addressed me in excellent English. "I am Karl, your dining room steward on the *Stattendam,*" he informed me. Karl claimed that he was a Dutch national but that all his identity records had been destroyed during the bombing of Rotterdam and, left without identification, he had been drafted into the German army. Perhaps my father's suspicions in 1938 had been well founded.

previously when he was the first American envoy to the postrevolutionary Soviet Union. In Paris, which was much more to his taste for high living luxury than Moscow, he could indulge his penchant for grand intrigue, spinning tales of official corruption highly seasoned with private scandal.

At his country retreat in Chantilly, Bullitt had created a veritable stage set for weekend entertaining. Situated in a corner of a vast park attached to that of the principal chateau, his Renaissance lodge overlooked a small reflecting pond. We were invited to this elegant abode for Sunday lunch to fulfill my father's wish to meet with Léon Blum, leader of the socialist, anti-Fascist Front Populaire. Blum had become France's first Jewish and first socialist premier two years earlier. Then out of office (and later back in for a month), he remained a formidable left-wing presence until he was sent to a concentration camp by the Germans during their occupation of France.

The following week the French government took the opportunity to show my father its appreciation for his efforts on behalf of the nation's faltering economy and indeed in rescuing France from the brink of bankruptcy. Among other things, there was a well-attended press conference in the American embassy garden.

Later, the minister of national economy, Patenôtre, was selected to give my father a lavish official dinner. We were all invited. He lived very grandly in a *hôtel particulier,* supported by the fortune he had inherited from his American mother. The multicourse banquet was served by a platoon of waiters who kept grabbing dishes from under my nose, allowing me scarcely a moment to savor their delicately complicated flavors. Just as we were about to depart, Mme. Patenôtre asked my brother and me to stay on and go out on the town with her and her sister. I pressed for parental approval, which was granted reluctantly, especially by my mother, who was very apprehensive at the thought of her sons being led astray by two older, married French women.

In the early morning hours, at the end of a thrilling but quite innocent evening, the women dropped us off at the U.S. embassy, where we found our parents sitting up waiting for us in a state of great anxiety. It seems that Bill Bullitt had regaled them with a lurid tale of M. Patenôtre's sodomizing a kitchen boy in his household. Somehow it caused a fatal injury to the lad and resulted in a large settlement on the boy's family. What relevance this event had to our night of divertissement with the two women was never made clear. But it undoubtedly triggered my mother's concern about our susceptibility to the corrupting influence of decadent international life. Bullitt was devilishly amused. He seemed to take special delight in stressful situations, sometimes rooted in homosexual intrigue.

In the spring of that year Hitler had marched back into his native Austria and gained 7 million subjects without firing a shot, while the British and French, then vastly superior in military strength, stood by in silence. That fall, Neville Chamberlain boasted of achieving "peace in our time" as Germany gained a critical slice of Czechoslovakia and another 3.5 million citizens. In between these events the French and British ruling elites were telling themselves that this was their last summer, and they set out to enjoy it with cynical fatalism. With governments torn and demoralized, those in positions to do so were preparing to make private deals to protect their own interests. As things turned out, they had yet one more summer before war broke out in September 1939.

In mid-July 1938, during the post–Bastille Day *fermeture annuelle* in Paris, the French prepared themselves for the inevitability of war with a kind of eleventh-hour bacchanal. Everyone who was anyone headed for the sunny Côte d'Azur. Beatrice Lillie, idol of New York's Broadway and London's West End musical theater audiences, said it all in the lyrics of one of her show tunes, "A Marvelous Party": "Quite for no reason, I'm here for the season and frightfully gay. . . . [We were] in the fresh air and we went as we were [rhyming with hair] and we stayed as we were, which was hell."

Headquarters for all these goings-on was Cap d'Antibes, a rocky promontory between Cannes and Nice, jutting out on the sea side of the highway and railroad that hug the pebbly Mediterranean beaches. Here at Eden Roc, the select were well protected from all intrusions in a shady garden of delights. During the daylight hours it was frequented by those of us who were stopping at the Hôtel du Cap, about one hundred meters up the hill, and by families living in nearby villas. There was a central pavillion — white stucco walls and decks with metal railings — suggestive of the great steam yachts resting in the harbor. It was surrounded by a collection of cabanas, affording more privacy. From the stone cliffs, incised with convenient steps, one could walk down directly into the calm, clear, tideless sea. There was also a swimming pool for those who preferred fresh water.

Cap d'Antibes was a most unlikely spot for the family Morgen-thau to congregate, especially for my mother, who was attracted to weatherbeaten, shingled New England Protestant understatement. But there we were. It had all happened in response to my father's inquiries directed to the Treasury's man at the U.S. embassy in London, a bon vivant by the name of William Walton Butterworth. "Buttsy" got a vicarious kick out of making arrangements of this sort for those who could afford to live beyond *his* means.

For the privileged younger generation, Cap d'Antibes provided a field day of adventure. Bea Lillie's son, Robert Peel, had arrived with his sporty little British roadster. A rangy, good-looking guy who had inherited a raffish sense of humor from his mother, he punctuated his witticisms by literally sticking his tongue in his cheek. The two Roberts (Peel and my brother), of the same age and sharing the same urges, were frequently together in the roadster headed for Juan-les-Pins, a nearby resort where the tempo was a bit quicker and the way of life a bit less self-conscious than at Eden Roc, where there was hardly a name that could not be dropped for effect. Peel lost his life in the ensuing war.

My photograph album includes a snapshot of Bill Tilden, the retired American tennis champion, sitting at a table with a couple of young men and a woman. His black, patent leather hair set off his handsome profile, with reflected back-lighting from the sea. In the water one was likely to bump into Elsie de Wolfe, the queen of Art Deco interior decorators, with the grand salons of the SS *Normandie* and the Waldorf-Astoria Hotel to her credit. Chatting gaily as she dog-paddled energetically, she was invariably outfitted in a volumi-nous black bathing costume and a pair of white gloves, to mask the hands that might give away the secret of her very advanced age.

Nearby in the bay of Cannes, Mme. Paternotre and her sister were entertaining on an enormous steam yacht that they had char-tered for the season from one of the Rothschilds. When they invited my brother and me to come along for a short cruise to the Greek Isles, my mother put her foot down firmly. We acceded, but only after a day on board during which we met the French premier, Paul Reynaud, and his notoriously influential mistress, Mme. la Porte. Both looked a bit seedy, having come from the cramped quarters of a small sailboat they were living on, moored nearby. Also among the Paternotre guests that day was an attractive young couple, the Prouvosts. He, the publisher of the journal *France Soir,* was known to advocate collaboration with the Germans.

Among our fellow guests at the Hôtel du Cap was Marlene Dietrich, who presided every morning at her Eden Roc cabana over an entourage that included her husband, her hairdresser, her close friend author Erich Maria Remarque, and her solidly Germanic daughter, wont to drive a tennis ball like a husky man. She was perhaps a suggestion of what her mother would have looked like without rigorous discipline. Dietrich, then at the pinnacle of her fame and beauty, emerged from her cabana one morning resplendent in a white bathing costume. "Everybady alvays vants to take my picture," she complained archly. "And here I am, all dressed up and no cameras." Taking the hint, I dashed back to my hotel room and returned breathless with my Eastman Kodak bellows camera. Dietrich went through a series of poses like a hard-working model. First the lotus position in the swimsuit, bathing cap wrapped in a turban, and a lei of mauve and pink coral. Then, donning a filmy white beachcoat, she stood up, with one leg slightly bent and toes pointed to the ground to expose the famous calf and foot. Head to toe, it was vintage Dietrich. My Kodak rose to the occasion, and I still have the evidence to prove it.

With a few cabanas between ours and theirs, an advance party of Kennedys appeared daily for the waterfront parade. Rose Kennedy had come down from the embassy in London accompanied by most of her brood. The ambassador himself arrived a week later. Memory, reinforced with photographs, attests to the presence of the two oldest boys, Joe and Jack, and sisters "Kick" (Kathleen) and Eunice. The youngest, Teddy, was a winsome six-year-old. Certainly the most junior member on the scene, he stuck close to his parents while the two oldest brothers spent mornings chasing a shapely brunette in and out of the swimming pool. My generation had met our Kennedy opposites a few summers earlier on Cape Cod, where we all frequented the Wiano Yacht Club. There we raced the sturdy little gaff-rigged Wiano-one designer sailboats and attended the club dances. The Kennedy kids were a high-spirited bunch, friendly with everyone, fiercely loyal to each other. At that time their oldest sister, Rosemary, who was markedly retarded, still went everywhere with the others, including the dances, where her brothers were remarkable in their sensitive protectiveness.

Young Joe was a solidly built, cocky heir apparent, in whom the family had invested its ambitions for the next generation. Jack, by contrast, was delicate, spare of frame, and inclined to introspection.

He seemed comfortable in his big brother's shadow. That summer people were whispering that Jack had only two years to live. It was rumored that he was suffering from some incurable, mortal ailment.*

In the summer of 1938 there was no doubt in my father's mind that Joseph P. Kennedy coveted his job as secretary of the treasury. Their relations in public were offhandedly civil, but in private, while Kennedy was contemptuous, Morgenthau harbored deep suspicions and hostility, which proved to be well founded. Later on it was not Morgenthau's job that Kennedy was after but FDR's.

After graduating from Princeton, I spent the first part of the summer of 1939, as I had done the year before, working at the Princeton Summer Camp. At Blairstown, New Jersey, near the Delaware Water Gap on the Pennsylvania border, teenage boys selected by New York City settlement houses were sent for two-week shifts to cope with the wilderness, under the supervision of more privileged Princeton students. It generally turned out to be a happy experience for all.

When camp was over, I joined the rest of my family on board the *Normandie* for yet one more summer holiday together in Europe. We were booked to return on the *Normandie*. Then, on September 1, the German Army invaded Poland, signaling the beginning of World War II. Three days later, a German submarine torpedoed and sank the British liner *Athenia* off the Hebrides en route from Liverpool to Montreal. Of the 1,400 passengers, 112 died, including twenty-eight Americans. The *Normandie,* deemed a particularly valuable prize, remained safely in port. We were in Norway at the time. My father, who was concerned about getting back to his post in Washington, summoned a U.S. Coast Guard cutter and shipped out for Newfoundland accompanied by my brother, the most seaworthy member of the family. From there they flew to Washington. The rest of us, after considerable pulling of rank, managed to scramble onto a small Norwegian liner for a stormy and seasick but otherwise undisturbed voyage to New York.

*My brother, Bob, organized Jack's presidential campaign in the Bronx with consummate success. Kennedy was appreciative and with appropriate gratitude appointed him U.S. attorney for the southern district in New York. But they never became intimates. On the morning of November 22, 1963, Bob Morgenthau was alone with Bobby Kennedy at his home in McLean, Virginia, when word reached him that Jack had been shot.

In September 1939, when I returned to the States from Europe, I went to Chicago to become a research fellow at the National Association of Housing Officials (NAHO), an institution dedicated to the advancement of public housing. It was a new and expanding field that provided an outlet for my earlier passion for architecture. (I had started out at Princeton as an architecture major and then shifted to history of art and architecture when it became apparent that I seemed cursed with a genetic ineptitude for this field of endeavor.)*

NAHO was one of a family of organizations under the umbrella of the Public Administration Clearing House, which in turn operated under the University of Chicago. Its goal was to coordinate various independent agencies, each determined to enhance professionalism in its particular area of service.

During the rest of my stay in Chicago in 1940 I answered many calls outside the line of duty. A lot of my colleagues at the Clearing House joined the United Office Workers Union. As an unpaid apprentice I became an "unemployed" member of the Welfare Workers Division, dues twenty-five cents per month, and was recruited to pass out literature in support of the striking workers at Michael Reese Hospital.

Come spring I had a number of job offers and my NAHO mentors advised me to accept one from Ernest J. Bohn, director of the Cleveland Metropolitan Housing Authority, as his research assistant. They pointed out that it would be a marvelous opportunity to work closely with the man who was arguably the most dynamic local public housing official in the country.

In those years when the United States was stepping up its defense industries, Cleveland was a wonderful, humanly warm place to live. I have often found that the quality of life in a city can be measured by the standing of its baseball team and its symphony orchestra. I have never been a baseball fan, but in those golden years of the Cleveland Indians' great right-handed pitcher, Bob Feller, it was difficult not to be swept up in the crowd heading for the Cleveland Stadium, which was close enough so that I could hear the cheering when the windows were open at the Housing Center on a

---

*As noted earlier, my father, who had been directed by his father to become an architect at Cornell, subsequently moved to agriculture. Earlier, my grandfather Morgenthau had switched from a very brief encounter with engineering to the law.

warm afternoon. Much closer to my heart was Severance Hall, the elegant, acoustically superb home of the Cleveland Symphony Orchestra. Under the Polish conductor Artur Rodzinski (who later revealed that he was a Jew), it easily maintained its position in the top ranks of great American orchestras.

As a natural extension of my earlier participation in the Deerfield and Princeton glee clubs, I joined a choir in Cleveland. Walter Blodgett, choirmaster and organist at Saint James Episcopal Church, recruited a chorus of outsiders who shared his musical enthusiasms. I especially remember singing the Fauré and Brahms requiems, which set off pleasurable echoes to this day whenever I hear them. With Walter Blodgett's encouragement I started taking private voice lessons at the Cleveland Institute of Music. As an early test of my skills I sang Schubert's "Ave Maria" at the big Catholic wedding of Ernie Bohn's secretary, with Walter Blodgett accompanying me at the church organ.

In a letter to my mother I mentioned difficulties our choir was having in mastering a Vaughn Williams composition. I also reported on my attendance "at the New Year Services at Rabbi Barnett Brickner's Temple." Anshe Chesod was one of the two big Reform congregations in Cleveland. "They put me right in the center of the front row [with] the rich Jews, and I was quite uncomfortable. They all talked in rather loud tones throughout most of the service." The next month Rabbi Brickner invited me to have dinner in his home with Max Lerner prior to the latter's lecture at the Temple. "He is one of the most brilliant and forceful speakers I have ever heard." I reported to my father that Lerner had commented favorably on his "proposal for an increased debt limit and increased taxes. . . . I particularly remember his pointing out how foolish and fallacious is the common practice of trying to compare the running of government and household finances."

In Washington as the 1940–41 social season approached, my mother set her sights on launching her eighteen-year-old daughter with a full array of debutante honors. When Mother spoke of her intention, Mrs. Roosevelt responded with characteristic generosity. Would Elinor like to have Joan come out at the White House? Mother was absolutely thrilled, and when she confided the news to me, so was I. Joan herself was not, but she was not party to the decision.

At her press conference on November 7, Mrs. Roosevelt said that it had "been decided not to hold a diplomatic reception because of war conditions in Europe [no mention of Asia] and the feeling that it might be embarrassing for diplomats here in Washington." At the same time she announced "a White House dancing party for Joan Morgenthau, on December 26. The society affair for the debutante daughter of Secretary and Mrs. Henry Morgenthau will be a glamorous party." It would also be the first time that a debutante other than a relative of the incumbent White House family had been so honored.*

Mother wrote me in Cleveland that she had formed a "strategy board" for Joan's party to prepare the guest list, making sure that everyone was invited who should be and that no one was inadvertently left off. She wanted me to come back for a weekend to lend a hand. Mother's chosen aides were eminently qualified to cover all bases. Mrs. Charles Glover, whose son and daughter were friends of ours, was the pre-eminent hostess for the young. The Glovers lived in a large, rambling house set on several acres of prime real estate on Massachusetts Avenue, in the heart of the District. They were an informal, congenial lot, but an open invitation to their regular Sunday afternoon volleyball games was a prized indicator of social acceptance. Another strategist, Mrs. James Houghteling, was the daughter of Sara Delano Roosevelt's brother, "Uncle Fred" Delano. Both Mr. Houghteling and Uncle Fred had been given Treasury jobs. Like the Glovers, the Houghtelings had a son and daughter who were our good friends. The other two strategists were seasoned pros: Anne Squire, Mother's social secretary, and Mrs. Edith Helm, widow of an admiral and White House social secretary. Mrs. Helm advised Mother that about "500 plus" was the right number of guests for an East Room dance but that "at the last moment literally hundreds must be added." Mother asked Joan to append some of her Madeira friends "even though she says they cannot come" (probably an indication of how Joan felt about the party herself).

There was concern among the party organizers about having

---

*Joan Morgenthau's White House debut was said to be "only the fifth presentation party in forty years" (Betty Hynes, *Washington Times-Herald,* December 27, 1940, society sec., p. 20). Two of those previous debuts included Teddy Roosevelt's daughter, who was Eleanor's cousin, "Princess" Alice, and Eleanor's niece and namesake. The latter had been presented at a much more low-key affair two years ahead of Joan.

enough boys. Mrs. Roosevelt had suggested a three-to-one ratio. When I arrived at campaign headquarters in Washington from Cleveland, I was given the assignment of organizing a floor committee whose members would collectively know all the guests. Above all they would be charged with making sure that there were no "wall-flowers": no young lady was to be left either sitting on the sidelines or stranded with an unlucky partner unable to pass her on. Like so many lieutenants, members of the floor committee would be ever ready to charge onto the battlefield and keep the situation fluid. Above all, they were to see that the honored debutante was in a constant whirl of changing partners throughout the evening, without respite.

The boys in New York who were invited to deb parties there were selected from a list of Social Register eligibles compiled by a Miss Cutting. With rare, if any, exceptions, there were no Jews on Miss Cutting's list, although my cousin Henry Fox was. "It seemed natural to me," Henry recalled. "I'm sure I would be the only Jew in the place at these parties . . . but [I] didn't even think about that particularly." When I interviewed Henry Fox in 1978 he was nearing the end of a long, distinguished career as a psychoanalyst. I was interested that he believed that as a young man he had "blotted out" his awareness of any manifest anti-Semitism that might have been directed toward him.

In New York the German Jews I grew up with replicated some aspects of Protestant debutante rituals. But they did it in an offhand way. The whole process was considered more of an option than a necessity.

We invited many out-of-town guests to Joan's White House party: some of my newfound friends from Cleveland, my brother Bob's Amherst friends, and those from other locations where we had acquaintances. The largest contingent was a group of long-time family friends from New York. They were all invited to a dinner given by Nathan and Helen Straus at the Shoreham Hotel. Colonel and Mrs. M. Robert Guggenheim gave a dinner in honor of his niece, Florence Straus (granddaughter of Oscar Straus), who came down from New York for the occasion. The largest dinner party, for fifty-four young people, was hosted by the Glovers in their home.

I was stationed at the Shoreham Hotel to shepherd the out-of-town guests to 1600 Pennsylvania Avenue after their repast. Joan, my parents, and my brother, Bob, attended a small dinner in honor of the debutante in the family dining room upstairs in the White House. One of the guests who remembered the occasion vividly — especially his friendly chat with FDR — was an old Deerfield friend, H. Stuart Hughes. His grandfather, the chief justice, was about to swear in the president for the third time.

The party, as reported in the next day's *Washington Times-Herald*, "gave the final burnish to one of the brightest holiday seasons that has ever dazzled the Capital's younger set." Everyone seemed to end up having a good time, even Joan. But perhaps no one enjoyed it more than Mrs. Roosevelt. Contrary to her image as a joyless do-gooder, she really loved parties. On the dance floor a good part of the evening, partnered by her extremely handsome son, Franklin Jr., and others, she proved herself a graceful, light-footed waltzer. In her next "My Day" column, she mentioned that Sidney's band (Washington's favorite), which supplied the music, was "particularly kind to me for they played many waltzes which I notice the young people were enjoying too."

The president devoted two and a half hours to the festivities, but Mrs. Roosevelt was "sorry that he could not have stayed away from work" longer. He had repaired to his upstairs study where he toiled until 3:15 A.M. on a fireside chat to be broadcast to the nation three days later.

All the young guests who had arrived at the White House that evening in an assortment of jalopies and limousines were on their best behavior. The party was "informal but not rowdy" as some guests sat on the floor and "sipped pink lemonade, ice water, and a mild sauterne punch that would not have harmed a milk barfly." The president's mother, Sara Roosevelt, "looked in on the blithe scene and held quite a court of her own." Supper at midnight was served from a buffet in the dining room. Guests ate on small tables placed in the Blue, Red, and Green Rooms.

At 3:00 A.M. Franklin Jr. told me firmly that the music was disturbing his father, so the band was ordered to play "Goodnight Ladies." But, as Mrs. Roosevelt noted, "no one paid any attention until finally they played 'The Star Spangled Banner' so that everyone had to stop dancing and join the singing. That ended what for me was a delightful evening."

· 25 ·

Pearl Harbor Remembered

ON SATURDAY, December 6, 1941, I flew from Cleveland to New York, joining my parents and my sister, Joan, to attend a symphony orchestra concert conducted by Arturo Toscanini. It was one of the special radio broadcasts that the Treasury had organized to promote the sale of Defense Savings Bonds.

On Sunday, shortly after 1:00 P.M., my parents' chauffeur, Charles Frazer, drove us all to Voisin's posh midtown restaurant. While we had lunch he sat in his parked car and listened to the radio. When we came out of the restaurant about two hours later, Charles broke the news that the Japanese had bombed Pearl Harbor. The extent of the destruction was still unknown. When we got back to the hotel where we were staying, there was a message for my father from the White House. A few moments later he was on the line with the president. "Sir, I have just heard the news," he announced grimly. "I have my Coast Guard plane standing by. I'll fly right back to Washington."★

"Be careful you don't get shot down, Henry," the president quipped cheerfully, responding to the lugubrious tone of his old friend.

I decided to spend a day or two of leave from my job in Cleveland and tag along with my parents to take in the excitement. That

★In 1941 the Coast Guard was under the command of the secretary of the treasury during peacetime, to protect U.S. shores against smugglers and to ensure the collection of revenues. Henry Morgenthau, Jr., had a twin-engine Lockheed Coast Guard plane outfitted for his official use. He found it handy for his weekend jaunts from the capital to his Dutchess County farm.

afternoon we had only a hazy picture of the extent of the disaster, but each fresh report deepened the gloom.

Around midnight I was in my father's Treasury office when he returned from the White House from an emergency cabinet meeting followed by a session with a few key congressional leaders. His "9:30 group" (close advisers who met him daily at that hour) was waiting for orders. In his head their boss had been preparing for the war for years. There could have been no Pearl Harbor in the Treasury.

Monday morning I was at the Office of Civil Defense (OCD) with my mother, who was working there as Eleanor Roosevelt's deputy. Mrs. Roosevelt was planning a trip with Mayor Fiorello La Guardia, head of the OCD, to the West Coast, which was thought to be a prime target for the next Japanese attack. She had asked my mother to manage her office while she was out of town.

Around eleven o'clock Mother and I left the OCD office at Dupont Circle, joined my father at the Treasury, and headed for the Capitol. Mrs. Roosevelt had given me permission to sit on the steps in the aisle of the White House gallery in the House where the cabinet and Supreme Court wives and a few presidential guests were to sit. At about 12:15 the first lady came in with her party and sat next to Mrs. Woodrow Wilson, who had come to witness history repeating itself. Harry Hopkins seated himself on a step next to me. Judge Sam Rosenman and the rest of the White House entourage sat or stood behind us. When the president entered the chamber, he was greeted with a tremendous burst of applause. Harry Hopkins let loose with a loud football game yell. The sound of cheering rolled above continuous waves of applause.

The president spoke of "a date which will live in infamy" with the clear, resonant ring that recalled the earlier days of his administration. Within a half hour the proceedings were over. The Supreme Court, the cabinet, and the diplomatic corps filed out. The senators left for their chamber to take action on the resolution to declare war.

At about 3:30 Monday afternoon, my father held a press conference. He was pleased to be able to tell the assembled reporters that the financial markets had remained steady without any support other than "the patriotism and horse sense of our businessmen." The night before, as a safeguard against panic, he had consulted with the secretary of agriculture, Claude Wickard, Attorney General Francis Biddle, and George Harrison, head of the Federal Reserve

Bank in New York. To be on instant call, Harrison had agreed to sleep on a couch in his office that night.

With my father sitting at his desk during the press conference, the reporters gazed out the window behind him, which was in line of sight with the Oval Office in the White House. One of the journalists remarked that the president must be about ready to sign the declaration of war just returned from Congress. I stepped to the window to witness the bursts of light from the photographers' flashbulbs exploding silently out of the Oval Office windows and dissolving in the grayness of the December twilight.

The night before, with a sense of having witnessed history in the making and having nothing to do, I had telephoned my good friend Clayton Fritchey, a *Cleveland Press* reporter who was a stringer for *Time* magazine. I divulged to him that the destruction at Pearl Harbor was much greater than what had been reported officially. This positioned *Time* for something of a scoop in the way it angled the bad news.

After Pearl Harbor, with the United States forced into active engagement in the war, there was a compelling surge in all aspects of defense activities. A regional headquarters for the Office of Emergency Management was set up in Cleveland to address the housing needs in the industrial heartland in Ohio, Michigan, West Virginia, and Kentucky. Philip M. Klutznick, the regional director in Washington, offered me a job as assistant director in the Division of Housing Coordination in Cleveland. I had met Phil while I was working for the National Association of Housing Officials when he was head of the Omaha, Nebraska, Housing Authority. At that time I had been appointed by the new Democratic mayor of Cleveland, Frank Lausche (later governor and senator), to serve on the Housing and Evacuation Committee of the local Civilian Defense Council. As the junior member of the committee, I became its recording secretary, writing up minutes and reports.

My new job was a big step up but not out of line considering the overall military and civilian manpower drain. For the first time in my life I had made a move without my father's intervention. Indeed he was rather unhappy, or at best ambivalent, about it. The job paid three thousand dollars a year, and there were murmurings in the press that the secretary's oldest son was at once wallowing in the public trough and escaping military duty. When questioned by a reporter, "unnamed Housing officials" responded that I "was on salary but declined to disclose the amount." The story went on to say that "the Treasury Secretary's second son, Robert, is now on active duty as an ensign in the United States Navy."

Following his junior year at Amherst Bob began the summer reading law with our great-uncle, Judge Irving Lehman. Then, before his vacation was over, he signed up with the navy V-7 officers'-training program in New York. In order to be accepted, he had to cheat on the hearing test by partially removing his finger plugging his good left ear while his deafened right ear was being evaluated. Immediately after graduating from Amherst in the spring of 1941, Bob completed his navy officers' training and was assigned to destroyer duty.

Sensitive to the criticism of my federal employment in Cleveland, my father arranged to have my salary returned to the Treasury, and he personally reimbursed me out of my mother's pocket. I did not attempt to obtain deferment from the draft because of my employment in defense work. On the contrary, I explored the possibilities of signing up with the navy and the marines but was told that I would be rejected because of poor eyesight.

Finally, I settled into my new job, knowing that I would eventually be called up by my draft board in Dutchess County, where I retained my voting residence. Four months later I answered the call and was shipped out of Beacon, New York, with 130 draftees headed for the induction center. A photograph in the Sunday *New York Herald Tribune* captioned "Another Morgenthau Son" shows my father beaming in my direction with warm pride, while I appear to be smiling off into space. By then I was looking forward to the army without regrets. It would be "the outdoor phase of my life," I declared in a letter home. If I had had any doubt about what I was getting into, I would still have found the pressure to join up irresistible. An article in the *New York Times* was headlined DAVID ROCKEFELLER TRAINS AS PRIVATE IN THE ARMY, with the subhead "Henry Morgenthau 3rd is also at Governor's Island."

During my three years of apprenticeship to life in Chicago and Cleveland, my parents had been inordinately supportive. My mother had visited frequently to check up on me and in between had written long, chatty letters. My father, while caught up in his own work, always made himself available to me at crucial moments. The day before my twenty-fourth birthday in 1941 I received a penciled note from him on official stationery embossed with the Treasury seal which was unusually revealing of his feelings toward me and himself.

> Dear Hen:
>
> I am sitting in the President's chair in his private [railroad] car trying to write you a letter. The two Elinors sit opposite me (I know I have misspelt one of them, but I gave Mother the breaks) and the President is asleep in his room.
>
> Many happy Birthdays to you. I expect to sing it to you some time tomorrow in person [on the telephone].
>
> You have given us much happiness and we are very proud of you. My only regret is we see so little of you. You don't [know] how you cheer both your Mother and me up when you are home.
>
> I am also pleased when I look back over the last year the way you handled the affair la Chicago.* I am sure you will not regret it as the years pass by.
>
> This week has been an extra difficult one. But I expect to give my all to help England get what it needs to *win*. US is not ready and most unfortunately will not be for two years. So the only way I know of keeping out of war is to help England keep fighting.
>
> Well it just shows how contious [*sic*] we are [thinking] of the war, that I can not write you a letter for your birthday without bringing in the War.
>
> Best love from,
Daddy

This letter froze for all time a rare moment when my father felt secure in his relationships with the Roosevelts and his own family, and confident of his mission in life. For that instant he was free from the doubts that so often clouded his outlook with angry suspicions. He could reach out to those he especially admired and loved with unfettered generosity. In this letter he appears to be savoring the moment, yet aware that no good fortune could long endure.

FDR, his boss and idol, had just been elected to an unprecedented third term, a happy and still healthy warrior. Sitting in the president's chair while he napped, Morgenthau had no thoughts of usurping the throne. But he had the satisfaction of knowing that

---

*While I was in Chicago I had become engaged to marry an intellectual red-haired beauty who was a graduate student at the University of Chicago. I was aware that my parents, especially my mother, were strongly disapproving, though they never discussed their true feelings with me. Shortly after I moved to Cleveland the engagement dissolved. For my part the cause was as much my own sense of unpreparedness for making a marital commitment as it was a response to parental pressure.

FDR trusted him to speak and act on his behalf while he found brief respite, or was otherwise preoccupied. Inches away, sitting directly opposite him, were the two women who, in partnership, had done more than any others to advance and protect my father on his perilous official journey. Eleanor Roosevelt had done it for a friend. Elinor Morgenthau had done it for her family. And as the sometimes vain, prickly recipient of my mother's grace, my father could momentarily extend his uncritical good will to us all. My handling of "the affair la Chicago," which to him seemed like an uncomfortably close escape from a misalliance, appeared to bring him only vicarious pleasure with no bitter aftertaste. What he had missed most on the road to success was the chance to have a little fun himself. A grim observer of the puritanical code that the Roosevelts, in their personal conduct, found so easy to abridge, he sternly adhered to the straight and narrow path. Many years later, after my mother's death, when my father plunged into a misalliance of his own, Mrs. Roosevelt observed wistfully, "Your father could never have kept a mistress. He had to marry his mistress."

Three months after my twenty-fourth birthday, my parents were preparing to celebrate their silver wedding anniversary. "I am not going to say a lot of nice things," I wrote them, "because you know how I really feel about both of you, but I couldn't begin to put it down in writing." Having said as much, I tried to do just that.

> You turned out to be pretty good parents, even if the products aren't exactly museum pieces. . . . The more I am away from home . . . the more I realize that there aren't many parents and children who form that very real something which is a family.
>
> Twenty-five years is a long time. It spans the distance between two periods of world chaos. I hope that the next twenty-five years will be as happy as the last, although I don't actually think that they will with things as they are today.

Within a year after the happy silver anniversary of their union, a sea change occurred — at first imperceptibly — which began to erode the strong, interdependent structure of our nuclear family. After the United States entered the war in December 1941, my brother and I were on active military duty, seldom able to return home.

My mother's activities were curbed drastically with the onset of menopause. Throughout her adult life her menstrual cycles had always brought on intense physical and emotional discomfort. A much-favored method for relieving this condition at this stage of life was a hysterectomy, which may have been misadvised in her case.

In the aftermath of her hysterectomy, Mother began to show symptoms of a separate unrelated disorder. It was an inherited tendency (seemingly from the Lehmans) to form blood clots, which when cut loose in the bloodstream could be life-threatening. Thereafter, as she began to withdraw from her habitual vigilance in monitoring her husband's performance, his office confidante, Henrietta Klotz, proceeded to step into her shoes. It was a subtle shift.

Players on the
Morgenthau Team

IN THE FALL OF 1941, when I was working at the Cleveland Housing Authority, I went to Detroit to join my parents, who were going there for a war bond rally. My father was to address the workers at the Ford Motor Company plant, which had been converted to make army tanks. But after lunch, just before his scheduled address, he was knocked out by a severe migraine. Without skipping a beat, my mother took over, jumping up on a tank turret and reading his prepared speech, lacing it with her own ad libs. She was eager for more action that would test her competence.

In September, New York mayor Fiorello La Guardia accepted a presidential appointment to organize the Office of Civilian Defense (OCD). He persuaded Mrs. Roosevelt to come on board as his deputy. Eleanor in turn invited my mother to be her assistant. It was the first and only time that either of these two women took a federal government job (albeit volunteer). The OCD was destined for disaster from the start. First of all, La Guardia tried to head the OCD on a part-time basis while retaining his job as mayor of New York City. Second, Mrs. Roosevelt became fair game for pot-shots taken by all the Roosevelt haters plus that especially vicious subgroup of Eleanor-haters. On top of this, Mrs. Roosevelt lacked the temperament for administration. She tended to surround herself with a group of friends, and appointed people to paid jobs on the basis of their needs rather than their abilities.

My mother began to see her situation as an unsettling replay of the events at the Women's Division of Democratic Headquarters in

1928. Once again she understood that in order to preserve her treasured friendship with Eleanor it would be prudent to bow out. Shortly after Mother quit her job, both La Guardia and Mrs. Roosevelt resigned as well. My mother came out of the OCD feeling emotionally drained and unsure of herself. At the same time, her private overseeing of my father's work and the careful advice she gave him declined.

It became evident in my father's newly awakened awareness of the plight of European Jewry and his determination to help. This was an area my mother preferred to see him avoid. Mrs. Klotz, on the other hand, was a militantly committed Jew. Then there was the way Henrietta used her position as "watchdog to the secretary of the treasury" to regulate access to her boss.★ The person who benefited most from this situation (through his deft manipulation of Henrietta) was Harry Dexter White. Having been in the Treasury since the end of 1934, White advanced to become the secretary's most influential adviser at the end of his tenure in office.

My mother had realized my father's attraction to his good-looking, intelligent, and ambitious young secretary. On one occasion when she came in to the Treasury to visit her husband, she first dropped in on Mrs. Klotz, handing her a crudely written anonymous note that had been sent to my mother. "Get rid of this woman," it read. "She has lunch with your husband every day. I don't trust her." My mother took back the letter and dropped it in the wastebasket. Klotz fished it out, gave it to her boss, and insisted that the author be unmasked, otherwise she would resign. The culprit turned out to be a Treasury guard posted at the "private" entrance used by my father and Klotz. The guard had become disgruntled when Klotz stopped responding to his incessant pleas on behalf of friends seeking job favors.

That was that. But there were other incidents. Shortly after he was seated in the cabinet, the May 1934 issue of *Fortune* devoted the lead story to a family portrait of the new secretary of the treasury. There were photos of each of us, plus photographs of my father in the front seat with FDR driving his open Buick touring car, and one of my mother and Eleanor Roosevelt as horseback-riding compan-

★This characterization of Henrietta Klotz appears in a letter my father wrote to her; it was a term he used frequently and she considered an honor. It appeared in her obituary, undoubtedly through her prearrangement.

ions. There were only two nonfamily pictures. One was of an ex–Texas cowboy who had become the secretary's administrative assistant. The other was "the Secretary's private secretary, who keeps large secrets gracefully," Henrietta Klotz. Afterward, when (through my mother) she was ordered not to submit to further interviews, Henrietta couldn't understand why.

The Henry-Elinor-Henrietta triangle that supported the secretary's job performance was stressed in many complicated ways. Henrietta could be a tough and dirty player; she was also naive. At seventy-seven, looking back, she recalled that my mother "might have resented her . . . today I would understand it . . . I was young. I didn't understand why. I never did anything." My mother was "wonderful," Henrietta told me, and I believed her sincerity. She did indeed admire Elinor Morgenthau for her college education and her social position. Henrietta Klotz named her daughter Elinor and tried to have her follow in my sister Joan's footsteps. This was difficult for many reasons, not the least being that Elinor was nearly blind. When a doctor recommended that she attend a special school, my mother offered to pay for it. "I wouldn't accept it, but she offered it, and I loved her," Henrietta told me.

The relationship between the secretary and his watchdog was that of master and servant, with the latter at times outwitting the former in the classic manner of a Figaro. With great self-discipline Klotz played on the vanities of her boss, as he in turn was the loyal courtier at FDR's beck and call. But the secretary of the treasury and his secretary were two extraordinarily sensitive creatures. Lacking the kind of emotional detachment that sometimes derives from a solid liberal arts education, they often trod painfully on each other's toes throughout the long, grueling hours of work in the office. As Morgenthau developed his own sense of White House priorities, Klotz developed hers. As a result, the Treasury employees sometimes courted her as a useful ally when they had difficulty selling an idea to the boss. Of course this procedure could backfire. In one instance, an assistant secretary, Earle Baillie, had tried to persuade Morgenthau to take a different position when he testified on the Hill, a position to which Morgenthau was firmly opposed. Baillie appealed to Klotz. She didn't really understand what he was talking about. But since she "adored that man" (Baillie) and "respected him," she told him, "He'll kill me . . . but I've been killed before." She was determined to have her boss "do the right thing, no matter what the punishment would be." So when she and my father were having lunch together in his office, she broached the subject.

He was infuriated. And without quite realizing what he was doing, he threw his fork directly at her face. It hit her forehead, which began to bleed profusely. "It was pure temper," she recalled. "I didn't need any stitches . . . I didn't mind the bleeding, but I hoped in view of the fact that I had a hole in my head . . . [that he would] do the right thing. And he did . . . I don't think if I had not been hit in the head he would have done it . . . When I got home he sent me roses. He always sent me roses when he punished me."

After years of on-the-job training, Henrietta had become a fearsome watchdog who could bark and bite, sometimes to protect her boss and on other occasions in her own self-interest. Gabrielle Forbush, Elinor Morgenthau's college chum who had been Henrietta's boss, now found their roles reversed. Gabrielle's Treasury job, answering the secretary's mail, put her under Klotz's authority. Gabrielle had many unpleasant recollections of being trampled roughshod by Henrietta. "I remember once that I did something she didn't approve of, and I said, 'I think the secretary will understand when I explain [it to him].' Henrietta snapped back, 'You won't get a chance. I'll be there.'"

There were many other occasions, however, when Klotz saved the day for her boss, like the time when he blew up at the feisty young *New York Post* financial reporter, Sylvia Porter. She was one of the few journalists with whom he had managed to forge a bond of mutual respect and trust. So Porter thought she had earned the right to address him by one of the more cheerful nicknames invented for him by FDR, which was popular in Washington circles but not with Morgenthau. With the exception of the Roosevelts and their inner circle and his own family, my father wanted everyone to call him "Mr. Morgenthau" or "Mr. Secretary."★ So that morning when she greeted him with a cheery "Hi, Henny Penny," Sylvia Porter was stunned by his angry response. Mrs. Klotz, who was in her boss's office at the time, said she "almost died" because Porter

★This was the practice adhered to by the Treasury staff. Randolph Paul, the distinguished New York tax attorney who came to the Treasury as chief counsel, developed his own way of dealing with this behavior. He addressed the secretary without any salutation at all.

was one of his few journalist friends. She slipped out to her office and called Porter. She apologized for Morgenthau, explaining that he was terribly upset about something quite unrelated. Klotz pleaded: "'Would you do me a favor and call him back because he's upset . . . that he talked to you like that' . . . She called him. I waited in my room, and then he rang for me and said, 'What do you think happened? I knew I was right. She called me back.'"

Arriving at the Treasury, Morgenthau got off on the wrong foot with the press. Sylvia Porter recalled him as "unprepared" and "unsure of himself." He was "afraid the press would ask him something he couldn't answer and the only way he could respond was to get angry." The press luminaries, like Walter Lippmann and Arthur Krock, contemptuously dismissed Morgenthau. Henry Luce's publications, with no love for the New Deal anyway, regularly spattered FDR and his henchmen with terse invective. In the 1934 *Fortune* feature article, Morgenthau was described as "the son of a Jewish philanthropist" who had "spent most of his life farming . . ." But *Fortune* conceded that "elsewhere you hear that Mr. Morgenthau is a humdinger executive, that he knows a financial brain when he meets one, that he is a terrific worker, and that he is certain to leave the Treasury a great deal better than he found it." Indeed, during the eleven succeeding years that Morgenthau remained at the Treasury's helm, he earned considerable respect from the press. But he was never comfortable with them.

Giving a public address was an even more difficult experience for my father than facing the press. His speeches were always vetted by a team of experts. When it came time for delivery, he would submit to his wife's coaching.

Secretary of the Treasury Morgenthau remained enthusiastic about Roosevelt's initial campaign promise to balance the budget, but he was dismayed when he saw his boss's resolve weakening in the face of what he found to be the unconvincing arguments of the disciples of John Maynard Keynes. In the 1930s Keynes became the most famous and influential economist in the Western world. His theories were widely respected by the New Dealers and intellectuals shuttling between Washington and their university perches. On Febru-

---

*John Maynard, Baron Keynes of Tilton (1883–1946), had been elevated to the peerage in 1942. His seminal *General Theory of Employment, Interest and Money* was published in 1936.

ary 1, 1938, Keynes wrote an unsolicited letter to President Roosevelt about the business recession in the United States, which had become serious the year before. As a cure Keynes had suggested countercyclical government spending, especially in such fields as housing, which affected a broad spectrum of Americans nationwide. Roosevelt turned the Keynes letter over to Morgenthau and asked him to draft an answer; this the president signed. In doing so Morgenthau ducked the central issue of spending, choosing instead to agree with Keynes on housing needs and other matters. For his part, Morgenthau remained firmly in favor of balancing the budget. Though he strongly favored relief measures and the New Deal social reforms, he believed that massive capital expenditures would lead to runaway inflation and ruin.

Faced with the implications for political as well as economic disaster stemming from the 1937–38 business downturn, Morgenthau found himself with few allies either in the administration or on Capitol Hill. In Washington one of the strongest proponents of the Keynes solution was Marriner Eccles, chairman of the Federal Reserve Board. A brilliant, self-assured Mormon banker from Utah, Eccles had originally come to town as special assistant to Morgenthau on housing. Morgenthau had advocated Eccles's appointment to the Federal Reserve Board and helped gain Senate confirmation against stiff opposition. Later, however, Eccles not only opposed Morgenthau's budget-balancing policy, but also disparaged him personally off the record.

The popular Keynesian philosophy had influenced some of Morgenthau's staff. However, Professor Jacob Viner, Morgenthau's senior economic adviser, maintained his position for a balanced budget. Viner, a Canadian Jew, was then an eminent conservative economist on the faculty of the University of Chicago. He had often represented and advised the U.S. government on international trade and monetary matters. But he disdained joining the bureaucracy and had designated a young, Harvard-trained economist, Harry Dexter White, to serve on the Morgenthau staff. When Viner asked White, in Morgenthau's presence, if he would be happy with a billion-dollar deficit, White tried to laugh it off, stating, "On advice of counsel I refuse to answer." Viner pinned him down, and White admitted that if the recession continued to worsen he would not favor trying to balance the budget.

Morgenthau realized that he was up against a stone wall with the president and began to hedge his position. Finally, on April 13, feeling terribly depressed, he offered to resign. It was not the first or last time he would do so. Perhaps he counted on the knowledge that his boss would never let him go. Or perhaps he had come to realize that there was one more cause ahead for him to champion even more important than balancing the budget. And Morgenthau knew that in their dark forebodings regarding the threat of Fascism to the democracies, he and Roosevelt were absolutely as one. When it came time to finance the arsenal of democracy, both men accepted the reality that it would have to be a massive deficit operation. In the face of widespread indifference and opposition to active U.S. support of the enemies of Fascism, Morgenthau was quick to shoulder a considerable share of responsibility. Then, as he came to fathom the complexities of a wartime economy and of the peace to follow, he began to depend increasingly on the advice of Harry White, placing great faith in his intelligence and judgment.

I can remember observing White on occasions when my father invited me to sit in on one of his daily 9:30 staff meetings in his large office. Harry would walk into the room with the quick, coordinated step of the good tennis and Ping-Pong player that he was. A man of medium stature and compact frame, he wore dark, conservative suits and ties. His high, bald forehead set off a trim, black mustache of the Charlie Chaplin, Adolf Hitler variety. When he spoke, his rapid-fire comments sounded disdainfully critical, though he always tried to show respect when addressing my father directly.

Harry Dexter White was born in Boston in 1892, a year after my father. His parents had emigrated from Lithuania or Russia. The family name at that time has been given variously as Weit or Wiett. In his youth Harry worked in his father's hotel crockery and hardware business, and taught Sunday school at the Home for Jewish Children in Dorchester. In 1917 he enlisted in the army six days after the United States declared war on Germany. White served overseas, and ended up as a first lieutenant in the infantry. After the armistice in November 1918, he remained in Europe for two years to run an AEF orphanage. On his return to the United States, he became head of Corner House, a Jewish settlement house in New York City.

Always an ambitious student, White was compelled to delay his education for financial reasons. Before enlisting in the army, he had completed one term at the Massachusetts Agricultural College in

Amherst (now the University of Massachusetts). From his job in New York he went on to Columbia and then to Stanford University in California, where he received bachelor's and master's degrees with highest honors. He then went to Harvard, where he studied for a doctorate in economics and supported himself as an instructor.

Under the reign of President Abbott Lawrence Lowell, Jewish students at Harvard were made to feel less than welcome, and Jewish junior faculty were shunted off to less prestigious institutions. White was intensely bitter when he could land nothing better than a job at Lawrence College in Wisconsin, where he taught for two years, ending in 1934. At that point he was rescued and brought to Washington by Jacob Viner at the beginning of Morgenthau's term at the Treasury.

On his arrival at the Treasury in 1934, Morgenthau was already committed to devaluing the dollar. Earlier, at Farm Credit, he had seen this as a tactic for raising commodity prices. But with a broader perspective from the Treasury, he saw the situation as much more complex and as having far-reaching implications. At the end of 1934, shortly after Roosevelt had handed the exchequer over to him, Morgenthau sent Jacob Viner to Europe to study the likely effects of devaluing the dollar. Afterward, Viner placed Harry White in the Treasury to implement his suggested policies. When White was himself sent to London in 1935, he succeeded in impressing British bankers and economists with the brilliance of his knowledge and logic. Even John Maynard Keynes, whom White found intimidating, was a willing listener.

During his first six years at the Treasury White augmented his staff with several highly qualified men who were subsequently charged with being involved in a Communist conspiracy. He also developed a network of contacts in various branches of government service, a number of whom were later suspected of providing a conduit to Russian intelligence.

White, by nature short-tempered and arrogant, was meticulously civil to anyone in a position to afford him access to the powerful. One, who later puzzled over the extent to which she might have been used, was Henrietta Klotz.

Mrs. Klotz first encountered Mr. and Mrs. White at a party shortly after White's arrival in Washington. Klotz attended alone, as at the time her husband was in New York. "I couldn't stand the people that were there and I sat in a corner alone," she recalled.

"There was [another] woman sitting alone too and we gravitated toward each other."

Henrietta Klotz and Anne White left the party together that night and became "very, very good friends." Anne and Harry subsequently became Henrietta's mentors. Henrietta had been compelled to drop out of school and go to work as a teenager. "I really got my education from these two people," she said. "I was hungry for an education and I learned a hell of a lot from them." They were both born Jews but "didn't know the first thing about being Jewish," Mrs. Klotz told me. (This in fact was a gross misconception of Harry, though he may have chosen to distance himself from his heritage at that time.)

Mrs. Klotz credited Anne White with teaching her about psychiatry. "She knew that I needed help in relation to my daughter, Ellie." By her own admission, Mrs. Klotz became a very frequent visitor to the Whites. "I was in Harry's house at least two or three times a week." At the same time she was also taken up by their friends the Nathan Gregory Silvermasters and the Ludwig Ullmans. Mrs. Klotz said that she assumed at the time a lot of Harry's friends were Communists. But, thrown into a situation that confused her, she "didn't know what a Communist was to begin with."

Eventually Klotz and daughter Ellie were invited to spend two weeks at the Silvermasters' vacation home near Atlantic City, New Jersey. Herman Klotz, who was then working in New York, drove them out and left them there. Henrietta recalled Silvermaster as "a great artist." Ullman, who lived nearby, "could do everything. He built homes and made a fortune." He was also "an excellent photographer." Henrietta went to his darkroom to watch him develop his film. Later, she would be questioned closely about this. He had taken "marvelous pictures of Ellie, who could never look into the sun," she recalled.

Even in retrospect, it was "still all very confusing." In the 1930s "a Communist was like a martyr . . . I didn't understand it." White continued to befriend Klotz. She insisted to me that "he never . . . never pumped me, never. My loyalty of course . . . was to your father."

In 1940 White invited a rising thirty-year-old Harvard-trained economist — the youngest full professor at the University of North Carolina in Chapel Hill — to come on board in Washington. Edward Bernstein had already published a book that gained him an

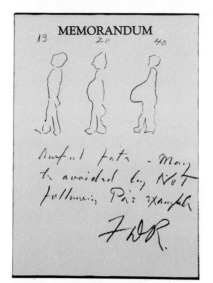

MEMORANDUM

13   20   40

Awful fate — May
to avoided by Not
following Pa's example.

FDR

FDR loved to tease his devoted, serious-minded friend "Henry the Morgue." In 1930, when he was forty and putting on weight, I accompanied him on a visit to the governor's office in Albany. Roosevelt dashed off a doodle depicting me at thirteen, twenty, and forty, with the warning: "Awful fate — May be avoided by NOT following Pa's example."

Henry and Elinor Morgenthau mastered a difficult balancing act, which kept them on good terms officially and personally with the two often rivalrous Roosevelts. It was said that the Morgenthaus were the only Jews the Roosevelts knew well socially. In this photograph taken at the University of Virginia in 1931, Elinor and Henry Jr. were in the back seat with FDR's bodyguard, Gus Gennerich. The chauffeur, Monty Snyder, had previously worked for the Morgenthaus.

August 29, 1938, Henry Jr., flanked by Eleanor and Elinor, whose loving counsel and skillfully plotted strategies kept his career on course.

At the onset of the New Deal in 1933, Henry Morgenthau, Jr., had aspired to be secretary of agriculture, but after Henry Wallace got the job Morgenthau became one of his most steadfast supporters.

In 1934 FDR asked a surprised Morgenthau to take over the Treasury as undersecretary and acting secretary. William Woodin (left), then secretary, was dying of cancer. Dean Acheson (right), then undersecretary, was dismissed for stubbornly opposing the president's gold-buying policy. Despite their differences, Acheson and Morgenthau had great respect for each other and continued to be mutually supportive.

In January 1944, at Morgenthau's urging, Roosevelt appointed him, along with Secretary of State Cordell Hull (left) and Secretary of War Henry Stimson (right), to a three-man War Refugee Board. Morgenthau was the board's principal activist champion.

Left to right: Secretary Morgenthau, standing next to Joe Kennedy, who coveted his job; Harry Hopkins, with whom he generally agreed on social issues; Daniel Bell, director of the budget; Harold Ickes; Charles West; and Rexford Tugwell.

Morgenthau, overcoming painful shyness, eventually put himself at ease with his peers. At the January 8, 1936, Jackson Day dinner, he is here with (left to right) Vice President Jack Garner, Postmaster General James Farley (standing), Attorney General Homer Cummings, and Secretary of Agriculture Henry Wallace.

Henrietta Klotz, Morgenthau's confidential secretary, watches anxiously while her boss responds uncomfortably to questions from the press.

Morgenthau, caught in a rare moment of levity, appearing before the Senate Finance Committee in a finger-wagging exchange with Republican Senator Arthur Vandenberg on June 12, 1940.

Secretary Morgenthau and Mexican Finance Minister Eduardo Suarez, signing a stabilization agreement in October 1941. Back row, left to right: treasury aides Daniel Bell, Harry Dexter White (Morgenthau's most influential and controversial adviser during the latter part of his treasury tenure), unidentified man, Edward H. Foley, Jr., and Bernard Bernstein.

Henry Morgenthau, Jr., and John Maynard Keynes at Bretton Woods, New Hampshire, in July 1944 when they were presiding over the international monetary conference that gave birth to the World Bank and the International Monetary Fund (IMF).

The First Lady with the Cabinet wives at the White House. Elinor Morgenthau is seated in the front row, far left. In the back row, second from the left, is Secretary of Labor Frances Perkins, the first woman appointed to the Cabinet. In addition to her official duties, she was expected to assume the obligations of a Cabinet wife.

THE WHITE HOUSE
WASHINGTON

How do you like
madam Perkins
new hat?

C H I C(K)

CLUCK! CLUCK!

Madam Secretary Perkins was frequently the butt of male chauvinist jokes exchanged on chits of paper passed between Morgenthau and Roosevelt during slow moments at Cabinet sessions.

Eleanor Roosevelt and Elinor Morgenthau on horseback in Rock Creek Park, Washington, D.C., 1934. The closest of friends, they maintained a conspiracy of goodwill to promote their husbands.

On summer vacation in 1937, the Morgenthau family toured the Hollywood studios. When FDR caught sight of this photograph shot on the MGM lot of *The Bride Wore Red,* starring Joan Crawford, he teased Henry mercilessly, saying that Ellie looked as though she had jumped into the breach just in the nick of time to save Henry's virtue.

During the summer of 1938 the Morgenthaus vacationed in Cap d'Antibes, the fashionable French Riviera resort where many notables gathered. The Kennedy clan came south from the U.S. embassy in London. Ambassador Joe Kennedy found a moment to confide in his youngest offspring, Teddy.

Léon Blum, France's first Jewish and first Socialist premier, came to lunch at Ambassador William Bullitt's elegant Chantilly retreat. Left to right: Ambassador Bullitt, Elinor Morgenthau, Léon Blum, and Henry Morgenthau.

At the French Treasury offices in the Louvre, top financial officials gathered to express their appreciation for the American treasury secretary's staunch support of the franc. From left: George Bonnet, foreign minister; Secretary Morgenthau; wearing a white pocket handkerchief, Paul Reynaud, minister of justice and later finance minister and premier; Pierre Mendès-France (directly behind Reynaud), undersecretary of the treasury at thirty-one and future premier; and Vincent Auriol (wearing glasses), former finance minister and future president, conferring with William Bullitt, U.S. ambassador to France.

After Pearl Harbor, the secretary of the treasury was successful in raising unprecedented sums to finance the war. War bond drives were as important for raising morale as for raising dollars. Morgenthau (seated at a desk at far right) frequently took part in live "We the People" patriotic radio broadcasts.

Courtesy of the FDR Library.

At a Second War Loan rally at Carnegie Hall, March 12, 1943, Morgenthau was flanked by AFL-CIO President Phillip Murray and New York's Republican Governor Tom Dewey, who was gearing up to run against Roosevelt in the next presidential race.
On the far right is the 1924 Democratic presidential candidate, John W. Davis.

Artists and entertainers turned out en masse to contribute their talents. A rising young Broadway and Hollywood star, Ronald Reagan, joined the secretary for this Fourth War Loan broadcast in 1944.

At the Chrysler tank plant in Detroit in January 1942, when Secretary Morgenthau was temporarily put out of action with a migraine attack, Elinor, despite a sprained ankle, jumped on top of a tank to deliver his lines.

Joan with her adored father, dressed for her White House debut in December 1940, which she submitted to reluctantly to please her mother.

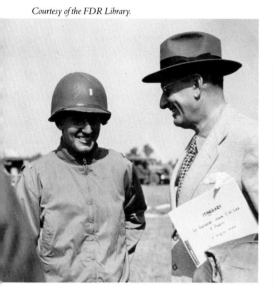

In August 1944 my father toured the Normandy front and arranged a rendezvous at General Omar Bradley's headquarters.

When Robert Morgenthau received his commission as a naval ensign in the summer of 1941, a proud "Grandpa" Morgenthau was the first to congratulate him.

BEADUTCH garment Corp. WORKERS WANT ROOSEVELT

WE WANT PENDELL for MAYOR

THE PARTY and THE MAN of the FUTURE VOTE LIBERAL for ROOSEVELT

WOMEN'S DEMOCRATIC ★ CLUB ★ for ROOSEVELT

The day before FDR's election to a fourth term, Morgenthau sat shivering and worried next to his gaunt chief, who insisted on making his traditional tour of the Hudson Valley in an open car during that final campaign.

Four Morgenthau veterans of many wars (left to right): Henry III, Henry Jr., Henry Sr., and Robert. The occasion was a B'nai B'rith dinner in New York honoring Henry Morgenthau, Jr., in 1946, when Henry Morgenthau, Sr., was ninety, a few months before he died.

In June 1945 a grim-faced Morgenthau stands by as his successor, Fred Vinson, is sworn in while President Truman was heading for Potsdam. After twelve years in Washington with FDR, Morgenthau could not tolerate a new boss.

Photo by Alexander Archer.

Out of government, the retired secretary of the treasury dedicated himself to the new State of Israel.

Gathered at the Waldorf-Astoria in New York to promote the Weizmann Institute (left to right), Meyer W. Weisgal, General George C. Marshall, Henry Morgenthau, Jr., and Dorothy (Dolly) Schiff.

Courtesy of the FDR Library.

Henry Montor became Morgenthau's mentor in Jewish affairs and chief of staff at the United Jewish Appeal and the Israel bond drives that Morgenthau chaired.

Courtesy of United Jewish Appeal.

When Morgenthau went to the White House in 1946 to gain a presidential blessing for the United Jewish Appeal, he and President Truman eyed each other warily as Herbert Lehman and Adele Rosenwald Levy looked on.

UPI/Bettmann Photos.

UPI/Bettmann Photos.

President Chaim Weizmann receiving Morgenthau at his home in Rehovet, Israel, October 21, 1948.

Prime Minister David Ben-Gurion decorates Morgenthau with a golden Israel Army emblem at Government House, Tel Aviv, October 28, 1948.

Courtesy of United Jewish Appeal.

Morgenthau at Lake Tiberias, Israel, in 1950, with (left to right) Finance Minister Eliezer Kaplan, Labor Minister Golda (Meyerson) Meir, and Henrietta Klotz.

Henry III and Ruth Schachter were wed on May 9, 1962, at Brandeis University, Waltham, Massachusetts, flanked by Henry's father and Eleanor Roosevelt.

A proud and loving father cradles his first-born, Sarah Elinor Morgenthau, June 1963, Cambridge, Massachusetts.

Henry III with sons, Kramer and Ben (Henry IV), at Jerusalem's Western Wall, 1973.

international reputation as what we would now call a monetarist, a fiscal conservative. At the Bretton Woods Conference in 1944 he served as White's principal assistant and sometimes his alter ego. As a fellow economist from Harvard, Bernstein always admired White, although they often disagreed on both theory and tactics. Bernstein remained true to White on several critical occasions. Like many of his peers Bernstein found White "temperamental" and "foul tempered" but possessed of a very good mind. "He really wasn't a top-notch technician, but if you could think of somebody having a mind for economic policy, he had it."

Bernstein speculated at length on White's Communist associations and came up with a perceptive analysis of the tangled course of events. It is his contention that, whatever Harry White's sympathies and connections with the Communists may have been, he changed his tack abruptly at the end of the summer in 1939. This was after Molotov and Ribbentrop, the foreign ministers of the Soviet Union and Germany, respectively, negotiated a nonaggression pact, sealed in Moscow. White's sense of shock was deepened by evidence that many American Communists and fellow travelers were willing to go along with this cynical alliance. Nothing that happened subsequently, including the German invasion of the Soviet Union two years later, seems to have induced White to reverse his course again. Above all, he feared Europe would be engulfed by German militarism. As a Jew, he felt powerful subterranean undercurrents. It was White's anti-German passion that made him particularly attractive to my father, blinding him to the more complex, sometimes contradictory facets of White's persona. Morgenthau himself had long harbored an admiration for the Soviets. Like many liberals in the post–World War I era, he had a rather romantic view of the Soviets as liberators of the Russian people from czarist tyranny. One didn't have to be a Communist or socialist to discount the completely undemocratic nature of the new dictatorship. Furthermore, many Russian Jews had supported the revolution and held top positions in the Lenin regime, although these Jews, along with Christians, had renounced their religion in favor of the new secular faith.

My father had taken the lead in negotiating the resumption of U.S.-U.S.S.R. diplomatic relations. The affable, urbane Maxim Litvinov and his British wife, Ivy Low, were very much at home with the Morgenthaus in Washington.

According to Edward Bernstein and others best qualified to comment, White was never a member of the Communist party. Whittaker Chambers, who would implicate White as conspirator and author of one of the famous "pumpkin" papers, concurred on this point, adding that his relationship with White was "never especially close. I had the impression that he did not like me nor did I especially like him."

Bernstein assumed "there's no doubt that Harry was close to the Russians" prior to the Molotov-Ribbentrop agreement. "It was just like Harry to think he could give advice to everybody." But he couldn't take orders. "He was a very undisciplined man." After the Russo-German agreement and his disillusionment with his Communist friends, who condoned it, he set about cleaning house. Specifically, he got rid of his two principal Treasury assistants, Harold Glasser and Frank Coe. Glasser was shipped out to become an adviser to the Equadoran government. "Coventry is putting it gently." Coe resigned; later he went to China. Both men took the Fifth Amendment when they were investigated by the House Un-American Activities Committee.

As their replacements, White brought in two clean "country boys," Frank Southard from Cornell and Edward Bernstein. But for reasons that are not at all clear both Glasser and Coe were back in the Treasury in 1943. Bernstein credits himself with bringing Glasser back for Bretton Woods, believing that he was indispensable. Ludwig Ullman and Gregory Silvermaster were also back on White's team. In the fall of 1943 Coe was a key representative of the Treasury during the Lend-Lease Phase II negotiations with the British.

Handwriting on the
Wall Misread

I N 1934, when asked if he thought German Jewry had a future, Max Liebermann, the eminent German portraitist, answered, "German Jewry is like a man who is mortally wounded and in addition has a cold. So he calls in a doctor to stop his snuffling." Adopting the dark, conservative suits of his Berlin industrialist father, highly assimilated and honored, Liebermann had been ousted by the Nazis the year before from the presidency of the Berlin Academy of Art. He died two years later. In 1943 his widow, on learning that she was to be deported by the Gestapo, committed suicide.

In the United States, Liebermann's black humor was quoted by, among others, the distinguished archivist of American Reform Jewry, Dr. Jacob R. Marcus. Having brushed against the truth for a disturbing moment, Marcus concluded that Liebermann's "ironic answer" and "bitter skepticism is hardly justified. . . . Barring wholesale expulsion or massacre, which seem rather remote even under the implacable hatred of the National Socialists . . . it does not seem that their [the Nazis'] weight can be sufficient to turn the scales against survival."

It is doubly ironic that, after thoroughly documenting the mounting virulence of Hitler's anti-Semitic program, Dr. Marcus should have been so blind to the facts that he had published. Yet this was typical of the conventional wisdom of that time among concerned American Jews and Christians. In Germany itself there were many who felt the same way. Men like the banker Max Warburg, dean of the Jewish community in Frankfurt, who had served as a director of the Reichsbank under its president, sometime Hitler confidant and cabinet minister Dr. Hjalmar H. G. Schacht, found it hard to believe that things were entirely beyond repair while his old friend Schacht held such a privileged position. Warburg was hardly naive. In the 1920s he had turned down an offer from the Weimar Republic to be minister of finance because he foresaw the collapse of the German economy and wanted to avoid having the Jews blamed for it.

The Jewish population in Germany had always been small compared with that in Eastern Europe and also in percentage (under 1 percent). By the 1930s, with a low birthrate, increasing emigration, and assimilation, the Jewish population had been in steep decline for some time, even though the assimilationists had been reclassified as Jews. From the post-Napoleonic Enlightenment, around the time Lazarus Morgenthau was born in Bavaria in 1815, the absorption of Jews into the mainstream had been greater in Germany than anywhere else in the world. To be sure, it had been erratic, marred by a number of unsettling reverses. Yet the net gains had been impressive. Thus one can understand the position of those who believed the dreaded Nazis represented just one more temporary setback.

Mein Kampf is often cited as Hitler's advance blueprint for his "final solution of the Jewish problem." Yet his policy too was not executed in a straight line. There were changes and significant choices made along the way.

Observing what was taking place in Germany, some American Jews were considerably disturbed by what seemed like parallel developments in the United States. However, there were some very important differences. Above all, there was no American equivalent to the national humiliation suffered by the Germans in the aftermath of the First World War. Furthermore, Americans had experienced nothing comparable to the German economic, social, and moral collapse. Our Great Depression was indeed severely destabilizing. It was eventually overcome, not by New Deal recovery measures but by meeting the production requirements of the Second World War. In the meantime, we experienced a significant rise in extremism, including the anti-Semitism of Father Coughlin, the radio priest, and others. Yet in the midst of all this we selected not an Adolf Hitler but a Franklin Roosevelt to get us back on track.

When it came to supporting FDR, the Jews, for all their internal divisiveness, closed ranks behind him. Without seriously questioning anything he did or failed to do, they remained loyal throughout the twelve years of his presidency. They reconciled their position — though it hardly seemed to require any justification — by joining hands with other liberals in a grand anti-Fascist coalition. Any special worry about Jews was included in general concern for victims of totalitarianism or refugees (but not specifically Jewish refugees).

Before hostilities exploded in Europe, my father too avoided any pleading for his fellow Jews. Yet by 1938, the ubiquitous secretary of the treasury was fully aware that war was imminent and that the United States would and should be actively engaged in it.

Morgenthau Welcomes Stimson on Board

I N 1939, after the war broke out in Europe, Morgenthau had
become the most ardent advocate of preparedness and aid to the
Allies in the Roosevelt cabinet. With isolationist Harry H. Woodring as Roosevelt's first secretary of war, Morgenthau sometimes
acted on behalf of the president to counteract both army and navy
foot-dragging. In military as in foreign affairs, Morgenthau intervened to carry out the president's wishes, especially when he shared
Roosevelt's convictions. Morgenthau, however, found no pleasure
in the exercise of power per se and welcomed Woodring's replacement in the summer of 1940.

When Henry L. Stimson joined the Roosevelt cabinet as secretary of war that summer, the seventy-three-year-old veteran Republican statesman was pleasantly surprised by the "gratifying cordial-
ity" proffered on his arrival by the young New Deal secretary of the
treasury. Later on he remembered the "friendly and tactful help in
learning the ropes" and "the kindness [Morgenthau] had shown him
when he most needed it."

Morgenthau welcomed the arrival not only of Stimson but also
of the able Wall Street lawyers brought in as assistant secretaries,
particularly John J. McCloy and Robert Patterson. McCloy, who
often dealt directly with my father, spoke respectfully of him as
"practically another War Department in seeing to it that the American war production got quickly into the battle." He recalled that a
lot of people were critical of Morgenthau because he lacked financial experience. "But he turned out to be a pretty damned good

secretary of the treasury. . . . He was an adroit manipulator in getting munitions into the line against the German effort. He was brilliant. He knew where every six-inch mortar was coming out of the line, and he saw to it that it was put to good use against the Germans."

Still, there were times when Stimson and McCloy worried that Morgenthau was pushing to arm the Allies at the expense of American preparedness. In this regard they were reflecting the president's position, that of the consummate politician, highly sensitive to strong and vocal isolationist opinion.

"Your father wanted to use every gun we were producing here and get it over there," McCloy told me, "and have it used by people . . . who weren't under the impediment of neutral inhibition, and get it used . . . in favor of the achievement of victory against the forces of Hitler."

Morgenthau supported Stimson's outspoken belief that U.S. involvement in the war was inevitable. His major concern was that in the interval the Allies might go under — as France in fact did and Britain nearly did — and it was expected that the Soviet Union would be rapidly overrun by Nazi invaders following their short-lived alliance. So it was that from the time Stimson joined the cabinet, when the United States was preparing for and then fighting the war, he and Morgenthau were in complete agreement on a policy of aggressive pursuit. It was only when they began anticipating the peace that the two men moved toward a fundamental policy split.

Although Morgenthau had never met Stimson before they became cabinet colleagues, he had long looked up to him with respect. Stimson had started off in public life as a Grover Cleveland Democrat. Disturbed by the corruption in New York City's Democrat-bossed politics and attracted to the strenuous reformer Teddy Roosevelt, he became a liberal Republican.

In 1910 he chaired a citizen's commission to investigate the tragedy of the Triangle Shirtwaist Company fire with Frances Perkins, then a young social worker, as the commission's secretary. In 1911, when President Taft appointed Stimson secretary of war, the senior Henry Morgenthau stepped into his shoes as chairman. Some two decades later, when serving as Governor Franklin Roosevelt's conservation commissioner, the younger Morgenthau vacationed at the Ausable Club, a favored Adirondack mountain haunt of Stimson, who by then had become President Hoover's secretary of state.★

The Ausable regulars were a group of congenial families with no inclination toward the extravagant ostentation practiced in the Newport and Palm Beach colonies. They thought of themselves as a true cross-section of the establishment — businessmen, professionals, intellectuals, and clergy. They had no conscious policy of exclusion; they were simply disinclined to reach out beyond their accustomed social boundaries. For many years Henry L. Stimson had cherished his retreats to the Ausable Club "particularly on account of the character of the people who are assembled there." In stressful times he could relax with members of the club who "maintain the same characteristics that their fathers and mothers had twenty or thirty years ago."

I can remember my parents talking about the arrival of Stimson, a regular at the club during one of the summers we were there. Awestruck, they kept their distance. But by 1940 they were friends in need in a very divided nation, and the bond of agreement held until 1944.

The infamous attack on Pearl Harbor radically altered the political balance in the United States. Overnight the country was united. With two sons destined for combat, my parents were apprehensive, but the resolution of the country's divisiveness liberated my father in a profoundly personal way that led to a new public commitment.

★On the whole, though not entirely consistently, the Morgenthaus avoided accepting token hospitality where other Jews would be unable to follow. During the 1928 Winter Olympics at Lake Placid we did not accept guest privileges at the Lake Placid Club. But in August 1930 my parents were extended a warm welcome from the Ausable Club.

· 29 ·

The War Refugee Board

I N THE LAST YEARS of the Roosevelt presidency, the younger
Henry Morgenthau's career in government rose to a resounding
crescendo in courage in an arena he appeared to have been
avoiding all his life. His lonely, embattled stand on behalf of the
condemned remnant of European Jewry, seemingly out of character
with his upbringing, started late in the tragic course of events. The
results were small in terms of counterbalancing the enormous load
of human destruction. Yet in the darkest moments of despair he
appeared as a bright beacon for the rescue of the surviving remnants
and the hope for regeneration.

In the early 1920s Henry Morgenthau, Jr., had hitched his wagon to FDR's rising star, with total loyalty and increasingly convincing demonstrations that he was an able administrator. He had been
groomed by his father to serve not as a Jew but as the 100 percent
American the elder Morgenthau could never be.

Thereafter Henry Jr. had gained a unique position within the
Roosevelt inner circle. He and Elinor were the only Jews the Roosevelts knew socially on a family basis. Because of Elinor Morgenthau's close friendship with Eleanor Roosevelt, Henry Jr. achieved
the impossible in managing to remain in good standing with both
of the two often-rival camps in the administrations.

For the first time in history a president of the United States had
appointed a large number of Jews to middle- and top-level jobs.
Roosevelt detractors were wont to call it the "Jew Deal." Along
with his Jewish peers, Morgenthau tended to avoid representing the
special interests of coreligionists, which was usual behavior. Bernard Baruch from his park bench, Felix Frankfurter on the Supreme

Court bench (and a Brandeis Zionist retainer), and Sam Rosenman at the president's elbow were all anxious to appear above parochial concerns that might tend to limit the range of their influence.

In later years Roosevelt was criticized for his insensitivity to the plight of the Jews and his failure to come to their rescue. But much of the blame must be placed on those Jews who worked so closely with him. Almost without exception, they avoided or downplayed the significance of Jewish questions. Through the 1930s my father, along with the president's other "court Jews," misinterpreted news of the Nazi scourge.

In 1938 Roosevelt called an informal White House conference to discuss the full range of refugee problems. When the President's Advisory Committee on Political Refugees (PAC) was appointed, Morgenthau and Baruch were its two Jewish members. Neither of them had any record of involvement in or knowledge of Jewish organization. There is no indication that they were active on behalf of the PAC. As an afterthought, Rabbi Stephen Wise was invited to serve on the committee. At the time, Wise was the most forceful leader in the United States in the cause of world Jewry. His long association with Roosevelt had cooled when he continued to support the presidential aspirations of Roosevelt's rival, Governor Alfred E. Smith in 1932, but subsequently they were reconciled.

However, in 1938, except for Wise, the strongest voices demanding that attention be paid came from Christian leaders. James G. McDonald, former League of Nations high commissioner for refugees from Germany (later the first U.S. ambassador to Israel), was the PAC chairman. But since McDonald had no access to the White House and no clout in the State Department, his good will went for naught.

When my father finally became converted to the cause, he found himself very much on his own. Throwing his misgivings to the winds after the nation's declaration of war on Germany, he proceeded to risk the use of his unique relationship with his boss.

In his book *The Abandonment of the Jews,* David Wyman claims that "except for Morgenthau, Jews who were close to the President did very little to encourage rescue action." Prominent delinquents listed by Wyman included Bernard Baruch, Herbert Lehman, and Felix Frankfurter. Roosevelt's special counsel, Samuel Rosenman, "consistently tried to insulate Roosevelt from [the rescue issue]. . . . When Morgenthau was getting ready to urge the President to form a rescue agency, Rosenman objected."

In this climate of Jewish evasiveness it is significant that the initial breakthrough to my father's conscience was achieved by three zealous Christian Treasury lawyers he trusted and respected. The senior member of the triumvirate was Randolph Paul, whom my father had brought to the Treasury to draft tax reform legislation. The two junior members were John Pehle, then thirty-five, director of the Foreign Funds Control Board (subsequently director of the War Refugee Board), and Josiah E. DuBois, the thirty-two-year-old assistant to the general counsel. Their smoldering moral indignation caught fire when Pehle became aware that the State Department was actively blocking the transfer of funds from private Jewish organizations intended for refugee rescue. Moreover, they discovered that the State Department was suppressing critical information from its own official sources.

John Pehle said in an interview with me that he and his colleagues had been attracted to the Treasury by the idealism prevalent in the secretary's inner circle. "It was an organization that went into all sorts of things that weren't the Treasury's business primarily. The secretary just encouraged this."

While the three Treasury lawyers were the activists in shaping and moving my father's rescue campaign, Henrietta Klotz was the catalyst.

John Pehle believed that "some of us in the Treasury were the ones that got your father interested. He valued above everything else his relationship with the president, and to get him to act in this area took a bit of doing. But I would say that once he saw what was really going on he was very supportive all the way through." I asked Pehle if he thought my father believed his being Jewish was an impediment. "Oh, yes," Pehle declared. "He didn't want to stand out as a Jew. He wanted to stand out as secretary of the treasury. It was doubly hard, I would think, for him, but he did it."

Henrietta recalled one of the incidents that had gotten her boss involved. "Stephen Wise . . . came into the Treasury and told your father what was going on in Germany." Since Rabbi Wise and Henry Sr. had had a falling-out over Zionism, Henry Jr. and Wise had managed to find few occasions to meet again. At this reunion in the Treasury, Klotz remembers her boss imploring, "'Please, Stephen, don't give me the gory details.' Of course [Wise] went into their making soap [out of the concentration camp victims], and your father was just getting paler and paler, and I thought he was going to keel over."

Morgenthau's involvement in refugee affairs picked up momentum in 1943 when he and his alert Treasury colleagues were shocked into awareness that the State Department not only was impeding the issuance of passports and flow of funds destined for the rescue of Jews, but was actively preventing the communication of vital information. In Switzerland, Gerhart Riegner, a German Jewish refugee, ran the headquarters of the World Jewish Congress. The WJC served as the coordinating agency for rescue activities, including the disbursement of private funds and the flow of information to the United States, where most of the funds were being collected. It was Riegner's practice to send cables to Rabbi Wise, the WJC representative in the United States, through Leland Harrison, the U.S. minister in Bern.★ There was a pair of cables that finally brought everything out in the open.

On January 21, 1943, Harrison, in Bern, sent cable number 482 to the State Department in Washington. It contained information from Gerhart Riegner to be relayed to Rabbi Wise detailing in a precise manner the massacres and the ghettoization of the Jewish people in Poland; the deportation of Romanian Jews to Transnistria (a bleak portion of the Ukraine under Romanian control); the starvation of Jews in Germany, Austria, and Czechoslovakia; and the apparent systematic extermination of many thousands of Jews throughout Europe. After receiving that cable, the State Department responded with cable number 354, which referred to "your 482 of January 21," and then went on to say that information such as this should not be sent to the State Department in the future because it violated the neutral countries' censorship regulation. A reply was given to Undersecretary of State Sumner Welles to initial, without any explanation as to its significance. Welles was most likely not aware of what he was doing, because shortly after that he himself sent a cable to Bern asking for further information from Harrison.

Within the State Department, attitudes ranged from outright hostility to benign neglect. Cordell Hull was sympathetic but ineffective in these matters as he was in most others. Roosevelt had made a conscious choice in the distinguished-looking, silver-haired senator from Tennessee. He wanted to be his own foreign minister

---

★In 1917 Leland Harrison, then a young foreign service officer in the State Department, had been assigned by Secretary Robert Lansing to facilitate the preparations for Ambassador Henry Morgenthau's "secret mission" to explore a separate peace with the Turks.

and often short-circuited Hull, going directly to the brilliant Undersecretary Sumner Welles. An old family friend, Welles had been a page at Eleanor and Franklin's wedding. His sympathy for the Jews was unusual in the State Department. Thus beleaguered and overworked, he too was largely ineffective, though not for lack of trying. Welles was forced to resign on August 16, 1943, much to Roosevelt's chagrin, after he was entrapped in a homosexual scandal that had surfaced largely through the self-serving intrigues of William C. Bullitt.

Twenty-three of the forty-two divisions in the State Department were directly under the supervision of Assistant Secretary Breckinridge Long. Descended from the aristocratic Breckinridges of Kentucky and the Longs of North Carolina, he had been a Roosevelt friend since the Wilson administration. In 1932, on the floor of the Chicago Democratic Convention, Long had garnered significant support in gaining the Democratic nomination for FDR.

Among other duties at State, Long was in charge of the passport division. Hostile to foreigners and particularly Jewish refugees, Long, in the name of national security, seemed to be doing everything he could to impede immigration of all kinds. (After he took office in 1940, the immigration level, already below the allowable quotas, had receded drastically.)

DuBois caught wind of what was going on and informed Secretary Morgenthau, who urged him to proceed further, and he did.

> I went ahead and did a little investigating on my own. I had good relations with Donald Hiss, the head of the Foreign Funds Control Division in the State Department, who incidentally was the brother of Alger Hiss. Donald Hiss gave me copies of the original cables, which was crucial because later on, when the Treasury asked for them, they were supplied with paraphrased cables which had deleted the critical cross-references. All of this caused delays of six to eight months, and cost the lives of many thousands of French and Romanian Jews, who very likely would have been saved. Morgenthau finally arranged a showdown with Cordell Hull at a meeting to which Hull was accompanied by Breckinridge Long.

In his diary, Morgenthau noted the meeting, which took place on December 20, 1943, with Secretary Hull and Long. The latter tried to pass the blame on to an assistant, Bernard Meltzer, one of the few Jews in the State Department. Long held that he "was one of the fellows who had been raising technical difficulties. I think you ought to know that; I know he had been creating a lot of trouble." Morgenthau knew this was contrary to fact, that indeed Meltzer and Herbert Feis (also Jewish) had been fighting a lonely battle against their colleagues.

"Breck, we might be a little frank," Morgenthau replied. "The impression is all around that you particularly are anti-Semitic." Long said he knew that to be the case and hoped Morgenthau would use his "good offices" to correct the impression "because I am not."

"After all, Breck," Morgenthau said, "the United States of America was created as a refuge for people who were persecuted the world over, starting with Plymouth. And as Secretary of the Treasury for 135 million people, I am carrying this out as Secretary of the Treasury and not as a Jew."

This meeting with Hull and Long finally convinced Morgenthau that he would have to lay his influence on the line in person to persuade President Roosevelt to remove refugee affairs from the State Department. At this time, when the ailing president was preparing to run for a fourth term, Morgenthau's tactic was to play up the politically explosive nature of the problem.

Back in April 1943 an Anglo-U.S. conference in Bermuda had appeared effectively to whitewash the plight of the Jews. But almost immediately thereafter, frustrated Jewish leaders outside of government began to take action. At first, unfortunately, much of their energy was sapped by infighting. However, despite the opposition of some of the established leaders, the gruesome reality of events led to the formation of the Joint Emergency Committee, inspired by the young charismatic Peter Bergson from Jewish Palestine.* By fall 1943, the committee's intense public relations campaign had attracted broad support, including that of Eleanor Roosevelt, though not that of her husband. FDR, taking his solid Jewish support for granted, was more concerned by strong anti-Semitic opposition. However, some of his closest political advisers, Morgenthau in particular, became alarmed when identical resolutions were introduced, November 9, 1943, in the Senate and the House. Urging the creation of a presidential commission to save the surviving Jewish people from extinction at the hands of the Nazis, the resolutions

*Hillel Kook adopted the name of Peter Bergson in the United States to separate his militant political activities from identification with his late uncle, Abraham Isaac Kook, former chief rabbi of Palestine.

seemed destined for passage. It was in this climate that Morgenthau, who wanted Roosevelt to grab the initiative, and the president, who wanted some leeway to soften the demands made on him, were both ready for an executive act.

Morgenthau told his staff, "[This] is a boiling pot on the Hill. You can't hold it; . . . you have either got to move very fast, or the Congress of the United States will do it for you. At the beginning of the new year he ordered his chief counsel, Randolph Paul, to give him a fully documented briefing.

Paul turned the assignment over to his fiery assistant DuBois. The result was the "Report to the Secretary on the Acquiescence of the Government to the Murder of the Jews." Morgenthau edited and composed a preface for the report himself, toning down some of the inflammatory language but retaining all the implications that a nasty political scandal was in the offing.* Feeling well armed, he marched across the street from his office to the White House, accompanied by Pehle and DuBois. He personally delivered the revised document, retitled "Personal Report to the President." Following this meeting the War Refugee Board was established on January 22, 1944, by executive order from the president under the shared oversight of the State, Treasury, and War Departments. With Hull and Stimson as his two reluctant associates, my father assumed the active leadership of the board. After a fruitless search for a "big name" head, John Pehle became the magnificently effective director.

In their partnership in rescue, Pehle found my father "a great person to work for" who made "everybody conscious of participating in the effort. He was a rather austere person. Nobody called him anything except Mr. Secretary . . . He kept his distance . . . but he worked very hard and people worked very hard for him." But he made it known that his personal access to FDR was sacrosanct. "I remember I once had a meeting with the president," Pehle said. "I hadn't cleared it with [Morgenthau] and he found out about it. Eleanor [Roosevelt] or somebody told him and the next day he called me in and gave me unshirted hell. . . . He said the most

---

*DuBois told me that as my father was preparing to deliver the Treasury report to the president, he told the secretary, "If it means anything and if you want to, you can tell the president if he doesn't take any action on this report, I'm going to resign and release the report to the press." Morgenthau never used this kind of high-pressure tactic in dealing with Roosevelt. Nevertheless DuBois believes that he impressed his boss with the depth of his feelings.

important thing to him in his life was his relationship with the president and nobody was going to get in between them. I was brought up real short. Not because he objected to what I was doing . . . but he wanted it to be cleared with him and be fully a part of it all. And I suppose he was right."

On the whole, the War Refugee Board under Pehle's direction moved aggressively, carrying out many daring rescue maneuvers. Though millions had already perished, many precious lives still remained to be saved.

Jo DuBois's readiness to venture beyond the limits of propriety, at the risk of his reputation, struck a warm, responsive chord in my father, who was prepared to jeopardize his own favored position with FDR for the cause. DuBois recalled an incident that occurred April 6, 1944.

A group of rabbis came in to see your father. They were headed by the now famous, or infamous, depending on how you want to look at it, Rabbi [Baruch] Korff. They told their story — and some of them literally cried during the meeting — that there were about 232 rabbis who were in France. They had Latin-American passports, but in order to get to the various countries in Latin America they had to pass through the United States. Our State Department had taken a position that these passports were invalid. Indeed, they undoubtedly were forged. They had been bought and paid for. And at this point our State Department would not recognize them. The situation was terribly urgent because if the rabbis did not get immediate passage through the United States, they were going to be sent back to their doom.

The atmosphere . . . became so emotional that your dad excused himself and left the room for about ten minutes. He was obviously terribly shaken by it. Then he came back, and he tried to get Secretary Hull but was told that he had left for the day. This was rather late on a Friday afternoon. Then he tried to get Undersecretary of State Sumner Welles;* he wasn't in. He did speak to someone lower down — I can't remember who it was — but apparently without success. The guy didn't know much of what it was all about. So the meeting broke up. I was very upset. So I decided to take matters into my own hands. It was the first time I ever attempted to — let's say — leak information. I called Drew Pearson. I told him who I was and told him very briefly what the story was. [Thereupon as agreed] he met with my wife and me Saturday for lunch.

*Welles had resigned in 1943 and was replaced by Edward R. Stettinius.

Sunday night, on the radio, he made it one of the key topics of his regular broadcast, giving the full story of the terrible plight of these rabbis. Monday morning early, Secretary Hull personally called your dad and said that the State Department had decided to recognize the rabbis' passports. As it turned out, they had acted too late because the rabbis had already been sent back to their fate. Then I received a summons to the secretary's office. Your dad had a wonderful way about him. He said, "Secretary Hull just called me. He said they're going to recognize these passports."

And I said, "Oh, I'm glad to hear that."

He said, "I guess that broadcast last night had something to do with it."

I said, "It probably did."

He said, "I wonder who leaked that story."

I said, "It must have been someone who cared a lot." I said no more. He didn't ask me whether I'd leaked it or anything else; but he had a pretty good idea, I think. It was a very moving incident, believe me.

There are some factual errors in DuBois's statements to me of which I was not aware until after his death on August 1, 1983. The incident he described concerned three rabbis who called on Secretary Morgenthau on April 6, 1944, to plead for the lives of 238 very pious Jews (not primarily rabbis) who had been sent from Poland to a specially privileged detention camp outside Vittel, France. These Jews were protected by "bogus" passports purchased from Latin-American officials. The Germans had chosen to recognize them as valid, with the intention of trading Jewish detainees for interned Germans.

Then suddenly, a group of Orthodox rabbis in the United States, Vaad Hahatzala (Rabbis' Rescue Committee), learned that these passports were going to be invalidated. This did not mean, as DuBois had stated, that the Vittel Jews would be unable to pass through the United States on their way to an ultimate destination, but that they would be immediately transported to a Nazi death camp. The rabbis realized the extreme need to get the U.S. State Department to bring pressure through the Swiss government to have the Germans reinstate these passports.

This was the basis of the very emotional meeting in the office between Secretary Morgenthau and the three rabbis. Rabbi Abraham Kalmanowitz (born in Belorussia in 1891 the same year as the secretary) used his broken English to serve as spokesman for the group. Rabbi Aaron Kotler, head of Vaad Hahatzala, spoke no English. The guide and wily expediter for the group was Rabbi Baruch Korff. At a very early age Rabbi Korff had gained the ear and confidence of many prominent American politicians, winning special access to Congressman John McCormack of Massachusetts (then House majority leader, later Speaker) and Senator James M. Mead of New York (the best man at Korff's wedding).

At the conclusion of the Friday afternoon meeting, April 6, when he found that Secretary Cordell Hull had left for the weekend, Morgenthau undoubtedly tried to reach Undersecretary Edward R. Stettinius.

The matter of DuBois's leak to Drew Pearson concerning the State Department's delaying tactics remains somewhat ambiguous. His widow, Dorothy DuBois, remembers clearly that, as her husband told me, the two of them lunched with Pearson the Saturday before the Sunday evening broadcast. Rabbi Korff on the other hand has reconstructed an account of how he was roundly chastised by an infuriated Secretary Hull for being responsible for "the lies on the radio . . . by that chronic liar." This account, based on his memory, is indirectly substantiated by an entry in the Morgenthau diaries which indicates that Morgenthau asked his press secretary, Herbert Gaston, to try to track down the leak. Gaston reported that it had probably come from "the Rabbis," or from Congressman McCormack or Senator Mead. However, since Pearson was sympathetic to the plight of the Jews and his broadcast was a primary Sunday evening event, it is entirely possible that both Korff and DuBois, each unbeknownst to the other, approached him independently.

Tragically, the effort Morgenthau personally spearheaded, to rescue the Jews in Vittel, came too late. They were deported to Auschwitz and exterminated.

Henrietta Klotz had a similar account of when and how my father committed himself to saving Jews. The tale is weighted with the same emotional freight, but the cast of characters is different.

It was a time when all foreign funds were frozen. Some rabbis came to your father and wanted to bring out some very, very important rabbis from Poland and wanted some money unfrozen for that purpose. Well, most rabbis are very small, but this Rabbi Kalmanowitz was six feet tall — the most handsome man you ever saw.

They didn't know that I was Jewish and I spoke the language, that I understood everything they were saying. Kalmanowitz had another rabbi as his interpreter. Kalmanowitz kept saying to his interpreter [in Yiddish], "Press him more. He looks like the kind you can get away with an awful lot of things with." Words to that effect. If you understood Yiddish, it would be much better.

Your father said, "Well, gentlemen, I will have to take it under advisement, and speak to my subordinates."

And Kalmanowitz said to his interpreter, "Once you hear the words *taking it under advisement,* forget it. He's going to do nothing." I understood everything, of course, but they didn't know it. And just at that point Kalmanowitz falls on the floor and goes into a faint. Your father was very sensitive. He was terribly upset. He had a lot of buttons to push behind his desk when he wanted this one or that one or the Secret Service. He pushed all the buttons at once, and the Secret Service came in with guns, and everything seemed to happen at once. Then I thought your father would faint too. A nurse and a doctor arrived, and your father said, "Henrietta, take the rabbi out through my private entrance, and get him into my car, and go back with him to the hotel."

Rabbi Kalmanowitz was talking to his interpreter in Yiddish. He was saying, "Well, did I cry well?" And the other rabbi said, "Sehr gut, sehr gut." I almost died when I heard this. Of course I wouldn't tell your father, because if I told it to him, he'd never let another rabbi in. I am Jewish, and their cause was justified. It wasn't that he was a crook or that he wanted any money for himself. I didn't say a word. I didn't look Jewish at that time. I was young and I was very, very blond, and they didn't know I was Jewish, so I didn't say a word. Eventually your father arranged to have the funds released. They got the rabbis out, and after the war was over, they gave your father a big dinner and medals and all kinds of things.*

As a macabre dividend produced by the tragedy of the Vittel Jews, in April 1944, the U.S. State Department was pushed in-

---

*The aftermath of this tale took place in New York late in 1945.
According to Henrietta Klotz, about 8:30 one morning [your father] was sitting in his office . . . They were planning all kinds of things, and I came in and looked at the calendar and noticed that Rabbi Kalmanowitz was down for an appointment. I said, "I wonder what he wants this time?" They were in fact planning a dinner, which was held December 17, 1945, to honor Morgenthau, William O'Dwyer, and John Pehle.
  Your father said to me, "Every time you hear that man's name, you curdle." So I thought to myself, It's about time now that I tell him what happened.
  So I said, "Mr. Morgenthau, I guess you've been bar mitzvahed." And then I told him the whole story, as it really happened.
  Your father looked at me sternly, and said, "Henrietta, you should have told me the truth."
  And I said, "Well, Mr. Morgenthau, I guess I'm entitled to one lie in my life and this was it."

to regaining German and international acceptance of the "bogus" passports. Thereafter, overriding the hostility in the Latin-American countries that had issued them, thousands of Jews in Nazi-occupied countries who had bought these passports were able to survive.

This came at a time when the British were strongly resisting Jewish immigration into Palestine. The response of many of the Allied and neutral nations was one of callousness and in some cases outright hostility. While the British people themselves were most generous in their reception and treatment of refugees, Britain's Commonwealth colleagues were not. Australia, Canada, and New Zealand remained unyielding in their restrictionism. Vast, under-populated Australia had previously announced at the Évian Conference on Refugees in 1938 that "as we have no real racial problem, we are not desirous of importing one."

At the instigation of the War Refugee Board, a secret message was sent by courier from the State Department to the U.S. embassies in Latin America. The message notified the ambassadors that the Germans had begun to check the authenticity of the passports of the interned Jews, and that their names would be submitted to Latin American countries for verification. If the passports were declared invalid, the Jews would be doomed, because they would then serve no useful purpose to the Nazis as hostages to be exchanged for Germans in South America. The news, of course, leaked out to the press.

The Peruvian newspaper *Verdades* exemplified the attitude in that country. In an article entitled "Latin America and European Refugees," it declared that hospitality should not be extended to "elements that might endanger the solid basis of the Ibero-American personality, our Catholic tradition, and the intangibility of our respective nationalities. Under no circumstances should we accept the imposition of offering asylum to foreigners of contrary religious beliefs, of excessive liberal customs, and of moral norms different from our own."

When he took the helm at the War Refugee Board early in 1944, John Pehle hoped to reverse the virtually universal recalcitrance toward rescuing the remnants of European Jewry by demonstrating active U.S. leadership. Pehle and Morgenthau believed that the key to any meaningful rescue operation was to provide places for the refugees to go. Countries such as Turkey and Spain stood ready to serve as exit conduits if they were assured that the human traffic would not back up on their soil.

While pressing for the long-promised refugee camps in North Africa, the WRB also sought a major commitment from the United States that would set an example for others to follow. In March the WRB prepared a message for President Roosevelt, declaring that the United States would offer temporary haven to all who could escape from Nazi-controlled lands. The offer was to be based on the free-port concept wherein shipments of goods were temporarily held in warehouses, duty free. In this way those seeking temporary haven could be held without the usual immigration restrictions. The refugees would be placed in camps, to be returned to their homelands after the war was over.

Pehle and Morgenthau understood that before the message was submitted to Roosevelt, it would have to be approved by the other two members of the board. Hull, as usual, played no active role. Stimson, however, was firmly against the president's exercising executive power without consulting Congress on what might be considered a violation of the immigration laws. Confirmed restrictionist that he was, Stimson foresaw this proposal as a move to open the doors for the entry of an unlimited flood of refugees, who in all likelihood would never leave the country. Along with the U.S. State Department and the British Foreign Office, he shared the fear that Hitler might use Roosevelt's declaration to dump countless refugees in a manner, he believed, which could damage the war effort.

Morgenthau, although philosophically at odds with Stimson, was persuaded by his argument that again raised the specter of a heated congressional dispute. With a presidential election looming in the months ahead, Morgenthau was unwilling to expose his boss to such a potentially dangerous political confrontation. As he told Pehle, his first duty was, as always, to look out for his boss's best interests. Indeed there was smoldering opposition to moves that suggested a major violation of the immigration quotas. But ironically, over 90 percent of the quotas for countries in Nazi-controlled Europe had been unfilled.

Meanwhile, time was slipping away. At a cabinet meeting on June 26, Morgenthau brought up the refugee situation in Italy. On July 1, Morgenthau and Pehle met with the president and obtained his agreement to admit one thousand refugees to be housed in an unused army camp.

In August, 982 refugees (89 percent of them Jewish) arrived at Fort Ontario in Oswego, New York, having been transported by an army troop ship returning otherwise empty from Italy. As things turned out, this "token payment to decency" was the sum total of the American safe haven response. Its supporters were pleased that something had been done, yet bitterly disappointed by the meagerness of the gesture. On the other hand there was loud, cantankerous opposition voiced by those who saw this as a dangerous opening wedge. The restrictionists were joined by Zionists who considered safe havens abroad as sidetracking their objective to have all Jews go to Palestine. Furthermore, the general infighting among Jewish groups in a struggle for power added to the general confusion.

On September 20, my mother accompanied Eleanor Roosevelt on a visit to the Oswego camp. Both women were disheartened by what they found there. Although the camp director and his staff attempted to treat the refugees humanely, they were compelled to deal with internment conditions. Along with many other disturbing indignities, refugees were allowed a maximum of six hours leave within the confines of the town and were required to return by midnight.

On the upper levels of power, Pehle continued to rely almost exclusively on Morgenthau, with Hull, Stimson, and Attorney General Francis Biddle all negative influences. Secretary of the Interior Harold Ickes, whose department operated the Fort Ontario camp, was fully sympathetic to the refugees. But Ickes, the irascible chronic complainer, had long since worn out his welcome at the White House.

After D-Day in June, both the military and civilian brass thought the war would be over in a very few months. When my father met me at General Omar Bradley's Normandy headquarters in August, it was at the very moment when he was anticipating a quick victory. Significantly, my father was somewhat skeptical of the prevalent optimism. Nevertheless, he was persuaded that it was time for the WRB to wind down its affairs. On this assumption he arranged to have Pehle head the Treasury's Procurement Division, which had the task of disposing of surplus military property, while at the same time he was continuing to direct the WRB on a part-time basis. Pehle was then succeeded by General William O'Dwyer, also on a part-time and unsalaried basis.

Throughout its existence the WRB received most of its funding from private charitable sources. The initial $1 million in government funding was later expanded by another $4 million. When the WRB finally went out of business, some of this money was returned unspent.

While serving as the WRB's principal champion, Morgenthau was continually frustrated by the crippling limitations imposed by indifference, outright prejudice, and the self-serving infighting on the part of those who should have been the board's friends. In the end some 200,000 lives had been saved — a not insignificant, yet heart-rendingly disappointing number. Not one to sit back and mourn, Morgenthau harnessed his anger to the task of building institutions to safeguard and ensure a lasting peace.

· 30 ·

Bretton Woods

O N DECEMBER 14, 1941, the Sunday following Pearl Harbor, Secretary Morgenthau asked Harry White for a memorandum on the establishment of an inter-Allied stabilization fund. Thereafter White was the principal architect at the Treasury of planning for financial stability in a postwar world. By May 1942 he had "completed his first elaborate proposal" for a United Nations Stabilization Fund, which ended up as the IMF (International Monetary Fund), and a Bank for Reconstruction and Development, the official title of what is now popularly known as the World Bank. In transmitting his proposals to the secretary, White suggested that they be implemented by calling a conference of the finance ministers of the United Nations. This eventuated two years later in a meeting at Bretton Woods in New Hampshire.

Harry White's concepts, though arrived at independently, often paralleled those of Keynes, the reigning economic genius who so greatly overshadowed him. White's ideas, according to Edward Bernstein, "weren't really overwhelmingly new . . . there are very few things that are 100 percent new." But they were "bold," and "up to that time nobody had talked of [them] being institutionalized." The first important step in that direction had been the Tripartite agreement in 1936 among the United States, Britain, and France, with the Dutch, Belgians, and Swiss tagging along. The primary objective then was to stabilize the ratio of the dollar, the French franc, and the British pound. That year President Roosevelt had confided to Morgenthau that he believed the chances of war breaking out in Europe were one in three.

In the face of Germany's aggressive economic warfare and heavy domestic demands for increased expenditures on arms, France was especially vulnerable. According to Bernstein, the Tripartite agreement was able to help "France through currency crises in 1936, '37, and '38, thus strengthening international security — temporarily." The arrangement was a relatively simple system in which "each treasury dealt with the other directly, not through the intervention of an institution." Bernstein noted that "there was of course an institution your father didn't like and Harry White hated. That was the Bank for International Settlements [the central bank of Europe's central banks, founded in Basel, Switzerland, in 1930] . . . I didn't care for it very much either." All of them considered it a tool of the private banking interests.

White's general premise, endorsed by Morgenthau, was that through two proposed international institutions, a bank and a monetary fund, countries with favorable balances should extend credit to deficit countries in a regulated manner. The United States, as the dominant creditor nation, would be locked into these institutions, which would be controlled by the collaborating national treasuries. To Morgenthau, who deeply mistrusted private bankers and their influence over national central banks, this strategy was enormously appealing.

Once these concepts and means of realizing them were laid out in Harry White's 1942 memoranda, the arduous task of consultation with all the interested parties abroad and at home began. Edward Bernstein recalled, "First we had a big period in the Treasury with many meetings in your father's office." As discussions became more technical, there were interdepartmental meetings of the State Department, the Treasury Department, and the Federal Reserve, with reinforcement from the Commerce Department and the War Production Board. "Ben[jamin] Cohen [from the famous Corcoran and Cohen team of New Deal kibitzers] used to come to the meetings. And any hanger-on from any department that thought it would have an interest would send somebody . . . we didn't try to keep the group small." At first Adolf Berle, assistant secretary of state, was his department's principal representative. Berle, who had been a child prodigy, appeared to Keynes as "a queer attractive unattractive figure in disequilibrium with himself, helpful and generally tending to take our side."

Later the State Department shifted the responsibility for its stake in these international monetary negotiations to Dean Acheson, who became an enthusiastic, effectively articulate member of the team.★

Acheson also developed a fondness and respect for Eddie Bernstein, who was assigned to brief him at Bretton Woods. The feeling was mutual. "He was a wonderful man to brief," Bernstein recalled. "You talked to him for ten minutes and he could spout back what you said to him in elegant English, nicely organized."

The Bretton Woods conference became reality as the issues of a revised postwar international economic order rose to the top of the Allied nations' agenda. After years of preparation, at home and abroad, and a final session of intense preparatory negotiation in Atlantic City, luck seemed to favor the internationalists. Following the Normandy Beach landings in June 1944 the smell of victory in Europe was in the air. At the same time the shadow of a protracted struggle in the Far East grew ever darker, as news filtered through of our crumbling, corrupt Chinese allies. The bridgehead across the English Channel made possible a reinvigorated British military initiative. But the successful conclusion in this greatest of global struggles also demanded the full and sustained engagement of the Soviets. While this reality was fully appreciated by the U.S. military, especially General Dwight D. Eisenhower, it was only reluctantly accepted by the State Department and the civilians in the War Department, already busy sowing the seeds of the Cold War.

Bretton Woods was conceived as a design to maintain the triangular U.S.-British-Soviet alliance as a strong economic frame for a sustained peace among the United Nations. The Allies were winning, but such good luck would only matter if they were prepared to seize the moment. Preparations had been made under determined Morgenthau-White leadership, with major, though reluctant cooperation from Lord Keynes. The Soviets, intransigent and hypersensitive, remained elusive to the very end of the negotiations.

At Bretton Woods a grand international assembly gathered to fashion — some said rubber-stamp — an Anglo-American plan for a system of fixed rates of currency exchange. The plan provided for two institutions: the International Monetary Fund, to regularize and stabilize the international exchange of currencies, and the World

★Although Acheson had been replaced by Henry Morgenthau, Jr., as undersecretary of the treasury, Acheson courteously bowed out and continued on respectful terms with his successor. Though they differed on some important policies, they were usually in fundamental agreement. In 1941 Acheson credited Morgenthau as "entirely responsible for the fact that . . . between Dunkirk and the first of the year the English kept on fighting."

Bank for Reconstruction and Development of impoverished war-torn nations. Together these two institutions were intended to function as a kind of multinational pacemaker for the economic heartbeat of the postwar world. The hope was to avoid the kind of chaos and crash that followed World War I.

In early July 1944, Lord Keynes, heading an eminent British delegation, arrived at the huge, sprawling, old-fashioned New Hampshire summer hotel that had been reopened to house representatives of forty-four members of the newly designated United Nations. "The monkey house," as Keynes called the site of the conference, was, he complained, "still semi-prepared following its wartime closure." The first night he was there, opting out of the preliminary ceremonies, "he chose instead to give a small dinner party to celebrate the 500th anniversary of the Concordat between King's College Cambridge and New College Oxford."

Impoverished by the war and with an eroding empire, Britain found itself in the humiliating position of begging at the doorstep of its rich, powerful former colonials. The dollar had taken the place of the pound sterling as the predominant world currency and the English had little to fall back on. But there was the still fresh memory of that finest hour when Britain had bled itself white — economically as well as militarily — to prevent the extinction of European democracy.

Keynes could be as disdainful of the British Establishment — often operating outside and even against it — as he was of the American. Yet his countrymen understood that he was pre-eminently qualified to bargain for the restoration of British financial and economic authority with American underwriting. And the American negotiators recognized Keynes's unique creative abilities.

History in the making often goes on unnoticed. The events in New Hampshire were never intended to attract popular attention, and they didn't. In the preceding month the successful D-Day landing on the Normandy beaches had seized the attention of Americans and Europeans. In the weeks that followed, that foothold extended inland at great human cost to American and British forces. Then, for a brief moment on July 20, the Bretton Woods delegates paused for word of the aborted attempt by German officers on Adolf Hitler's life. It is little wonder that the *New York Times,* the newspaper of record, when it took note of Bretton Woods at all, buried the stories in the back pages.

The master builder at Bretton Woods was Harry Dexter White, whose ideas were eventually combined with similar ideas long incubating in the fertile mind of Keynes. But the one who turned these ideas into lasting institutions was White's boss. Morgenthau, without intellectual pretensions or verbal grace, seemed to have an intuitive grasp of his objectives. In the end he demonstrated considerable skill in steering Keynes and White through the treacherous diplomatic, bureaucratic, and political shoals to safe harbor.

At this critical moment the secretary was especially skillful in keeping Congress in line, though not without stirring up some serious grumblings to be sure. First, there was dissatisfaction when leaks from London showed that Capitol Hill had not been fully informed as to how far the Treasury had progressed in formulating a U.S. position. Second, there were Republicans with Wall Street connections who were politicizing the debate in a manner calculated to favor a Republican in the 1944 presidential election, or at least to ensure a Republican majority in the House of Representatives.

Harry White, who had been handling the negotiations with the British and the Soviets, had been frustrated by their extended foot-dragging. He continually pressed his worries on the secretary, who had by then become uncharacteristically self-confident. In March and April 1944 an anxious White had warned Morgenthau of the urgency of completing the work of the proposed conference before the Republican convention in June. "Don't worry," Morgenthau assured him, "I haven't let you down yet. I have it very much in mind and I promise you that I will see the President." For some time White had been depressed by FDR's apparent lack of interest in postwar monetary concerns. Morgenthau tried to console him, explaining that the president "very seldom, Harry, shows any enthusiasm these days. It is very rare. So don't be disappointed."

Despite his reassurances to White, the secretary was also becoming impatient with the agonizing delays before the conference as he saw the crucial moment slipping away. He too had hoped to have everything in place before FDR announced that he would run for a fourth term. But that wasn't to be. Thomas Dewey, the Republican nominee, was by then advancing his own plan for an international monetary agreement. Meanwhile the Russians and British had still not officially come on board.

Morgenthau, as always, was stubborn. But he also displayed confidence, skill, and courage. He relied on Harry White's brilliance but not without protecting himself against the man's tactlessness. He also enjoyed the crucial support of Acheson, who was not averse to circumventing the obdurate Secretary Hull on matters that reached beyond the narrow limits of his own initiatives.

At Bretton Woods, Morgenthau assumed command with a greater display of authority than he had ever shown before. By that time Roosevelt's attention span on all matters had shortened, and what energy he had left was focused on the military and political campaigns. More and more he tended to shift his burdens onto the backs of a few tried and trusted old colleagues, of whom Morgenthau was one. Morgenthau had a vision of the long-range importance of the "penultimate" round of negotiations in New Hampshire, and he was quite willing to commit the full "prestige of his office and influence with the President." He understood that the initiative he had taken "was very important for [FDR]. He may have to sit at the peace conference. He should have a record of success for his first conference. If it is a failure it is a black mark against him."

Morgenthau was "not worried about getting a bad press personally." He was "used to it." Nor was he worried about "Hull running out on him." He would simply do "everything in the President's interest, because the President's interest are [sic] the country's interest." He could afford to let the boss "have what is good" while he settled for "what is bad." After all, he could always go back to Dutchess County "and raise apples." But this time the president seemed to be more grateful than Morgenthau had hoped for. "In excellent humor," he approved with considerable attention to detail everything Morgenthau had done. "Here's where you get a medal, Henry," he beamed.

While chairing the conference, Secretary Morgenthau led what might be called an all-star U.S. team. The vice chairman, Fred Vinson, then the deputy chief of the Office of Economic Stabilization, was destined to succeed Morgenthau as secretary of the treasury in two years, and shortly thereafter to become chief justice of the Supreme Court. Dean Acheson, who would become President Truman's secretary of state, had been designated to represent that department at Bretton Woods. Other American delegates included Edward E. Brown, the gruff president of the First National Bank of Chicago, respected by his peers yet, unlike most of them, open-minded about the Bretton Woods objectives; Leo T. Crowley, head of the Foreign Economic Administration; Federal Reserve Chairman Marriner Eccles; and one woman, Mabel Newcomer, professor of economics at Vassar College, a likely Elinor Morgenthau suggestion.

Eccles was determined not to fight with Morgenthau and to do what he could "to get some sense in the fiscal policy." With this intention, he had joined in the general enthusiastic support of the Treasury's proposal for the Bretton Woods agreements, calling them "the most important in the international field from a monetary standpoint."

Morgenthau hadn't hesitated to include in the U.S. delegation men who had been critical of him. He was equally determined to have strong bipartisan congressional representation for the agreements Congress would have to ratify. During his years in the Treasury he had developed an excellent behind-the-scenes working relationship with the leaders of both houses. This was something the press and the public discounted because of the secretary's painfully shy, seemingly ill-informed performances when called to testify on the Hill.

Consequently, the congressional delegation at Bretton Woods was embellished by Senator Alben W. Barkley; the majority leader (later vice president), Robert F. Wagner, chairman of the Senate Committee on Banking and Currency; and senior Democratic and Republican members of the House, Congressman Brent Spence and Congressman Jesse P. Wolcott, respectively. Robert Taft, the distinguished Republican senator from Ohio, had cosponsored major New Deal domestic legislation and would have appeared the obvious Republican counterbalance to Wagner at Bretton Woods. But Taft, a die-hard isolationist who had stated publicly that the proposed IMF would be "like pouring money down a sewer," was bypassed. When the Republicans succeeded in forcing through the appointment to the delegation of Senator Charles W. Tobey of New Hampshire, known as a rabid anti-British isolationist, the administration was dismayed. But Tobey fooled them all. Lord Keynes, like everyone else, was taken completely by surprise when three days after setting foot on his home turf the senator delivered a public address with the press in attendance, "calling down the blessings of God on the conference and saying we should be untrue to Christ if we did not put these plans through, since the countries to be succored had also been suffering from a crown of thorns." "What a strange country!" Keynes observed.

As the conference got under way, the job to be done fell mostly to its two commissions. Commission I, charged with formulating the IMF, was chaired by Harry Dexter White, with Edward Bernstein serving as the U.S. spokesman. Commission II, which charted the World Bank, was chaired by Lord Keynes, with Dean Acheson serving as the U.S. spokesman. Acheson was backed by Ansel F. Luxford (the U.S. delegation's chief legal counsel, later assistant secretary of the treasury), who was positioned to see that the Treasury's objectives didn't get lost in the shuffle.

Maynard Keynes, ever fearful of British interests being overwhelmed by the Americans, found himself pleasantly surprised by the positive drift of events and particularly by a newfound, warm relationship with Morgenthau.

"One remarkable bit of news," he wrote home to a friend, Lord Catto, on July 4. "For the first time in my life I am really getting on with Morgy. In all the years I have known him there has never been a moment which was not sticky. Now all that is changed . . . and we can chat together like cronies by the hour. Of course, I have not yet tried any difficult subjects. The atmosphere was altogether too good to risk spoiling it." Keynes also found Harry White, remarkably, "all smiles, kindness and geniality." The American position was clearly "that we are allies and the common foe is from without. In spite of the immense volume of criticism in the press and great doubts expressed by bankers and Congressmen, my judgment is (and I think Harry shares it) that the real position is extremely good. . . . There is no steam in the opposition." Keynes knew that the general public found the whole matter so "boring" that "no enthusiasm can be roused for discussing the details" and that anyone with "isolationist origins" would think twice before "sabotaging the first international scheme."

Keynes's relationship with White had been complex and mercurial, with jarring ups and downs over a period of several years. But in September 1943, with the long, protracted negotiations picking up momentum, Keynes had reported, "Most interesting and exciting discussions with Harry White and his associates in an atmosphere singularly free from unnecessary controversy . . . we all of us have high hopes that joint and common effort will emerge," adding, "I hope I am not being too optimistic." A couple of weeks later he was complaining bitterly that White was "overbearing, a bad colleague, always trying to bounce you, with harsh rasping voice, aesthetically oppressive in mind and manner; he has not the faintest conception of how to behave or observe the rules of civilised intercourse." Then, unaccountably, without dropping a beat, he continued, "At the same time, I have a very great respect and even liking for him . . . he is the best man here. A very able and devoted public servant, carrying an immense burden of responsibility and initiative, of high integrity and clear sighted international public purpose, genuinely intending to do the best for the world."

Keynes admired White's ability to "get things done" and found him a noble adversary "not open to flattery in any crude sense." Keynes, the wily seducer, discovered he could "arouse [White's] genuine interest in the merits of an issue and then tell him off very frankly and firmly without finesse, he has gone off the rails of relevant argument or appropriate behavior."

White's tendency toward grating behavior seemed to be exacerbated by an intense fear in Keynes's presence. Edward Bernstein recalled an occasion when "White was so afraid of Keynes that he had to take to his bed." Besides sharing an inclination for ripostes administered with acerbic language, both men suffered from serious heart conditions; Keynes succumbed two years after Bretton Woods and White two years after him. In those heated sessions "White was addressing Keynes as 'your majesty,'" which Bernstein felt was "not really a very nice way of addressing Lord Keynes, even though he was in the nature of royalty, at least as an economist."

Keynes was contemptuous of American economic jargon. According to Bernstein, "He called it 'Cherokee' and contrasted it to his own 'Christian English.'" Early in 1943 White had in lumbering turgid prose prepared a proposal for the fund and, for the first time, the bank. The document was mimeographed on 150 legal-size pages and circulated within the Treasury and among other interested parties. But before Harry White's proposal saw the light of day, Keynes came out with his own "White paper," covering the same ground in somewhat different form, and it was big news. "Keynes had the great advantage over White apart from reputation," Bernstein noted, "that he could write succinctly," putting everything in "30 or 40 pages where White had taken up 150 pages or so."★

In the Bretton Woods hotel suite he occupied just below Lord

★Keynes also used his verbal legerdemain to settle scores with both White and Bernstein.

and Lady Keynes, my father had the company of Elinor and Joan, who remembers being urged by her father to attend what he assured her would be a historic occasion. Joan, a student at Vassar, at first demurred because of an overdue history paper but finally submitted. Today her only recollection of the event is that when she got back to Vassar she managed to finish her paper and get an *A*.

The secretary's retinue of course also included Henrietta Klotz. She especially remembers being pursued by Fred Vinson, the vice chairman of the conference.

> He chased me all over the lot. No matter where I sat, he sat next to me. So I got Lud Ullman to follow me and sit with me . . . Lud Ullman was there and [Nathan Gregory] Silvermaster was there . . . Harry [White] worked with them. Just before we left, Vinson asked me to come up to his room and I wouldn't go. He came down and said he very much wanted to get to know me . . . He was very apologetic. He was a low, cheap nothing . . . a dirty, filthy dog . . . I couldn't imagine a man like that becoming chief justice. I lost my respect for a lot of things.

Dean Acheson was, by contrast, Klotz recalled, "the most perfect gentleman I have ever met in my life . . . we were very, very good friends."

According to Bernstein, one of the few hitches that developed during the negotiations on the IMF resulted from a misunderstanding between the United States and the U.S.S.R. "that Harry White created inadvertently." In a preliminary meeting at the Treasury in Washington with some two hundred members of the press, White had suggested a "hypothetical" $1 billion quota for the Russians and Chinese. To keep the whole fund within bounds, this figure had to be reduced to $800 million. The Russians insisted on being on a par with the British, who were being offered $1.5 billion, although this included their colonies and commonwealth. White tried to make a deal with the Soviets by reducing their gold requirements. Dean Acheson opposed this on a number of grounds, especially that the

---

Certain currency and investment proposals that Keynes held were "the exact opposite to reality" were, he believed, "largely the fruit of the brain not of Harry [White] but of his little attaché, Bernstein. And when we seduce Harry from the true faith, little Bernstein wins him back again in the course of the night. Bernstein is a regular little rabbi, a reader out of the Talmud, to Harry's grand political high rabbidom . . . the chap knows every rat run in the local ghetto, but it is difficult to persuade him to come out for a walk with us on the highways of the world."

Soviets would "feel that if they press hard enough they're more likely to get a larger quota." Before matters were resolved, with a compromise $1.2 billion quota, the Soviets saw fit to enter a formal protest against Harry White.

During the anxious days when the Russian holdout threatened to disrupt the entire conference, Morgenthau more than anyone else, including White and Bernstein, was steadfast in his belief that they would ultimately cooperate. Up to this point, everything in his personal dealings with Soviet authorities, dating back to his initial negotiations for the resumption of diplomatic recognition with Maxim Litvinov, had produced positive results. Bernstein, who was inclined to cast a suspicious eye on all parties involved in international negotiation, held that Morgenthau's trust was justifiable. "In dealings we had . . . the Russians always did what they said they were going to do. They didn't hide anything and there was nothing very subtle about what they did."

The Soviets weren't the only ones who continued to bicker over their quotas, but the other complaints seemed insignificant by comparison. Then on July 22 at 7:00 P.M., "one hour before the final plenary session, Stepanov [M. S. Stepanov, deputy people's commissar of foreign trade and chairman of the Russian delegation] called on Morgenthau" and announced that he had received word from Molotov that "he is happy to agree to your proposition . . . to increase our quota . . . to one billion two hundred million dollars."

"Well, you tell Mr. Molotov that I want to thank him from the bottom of my heart," Morgenthau replied. "This confirms the long-time respect and confidence that I have in the Union of Soviet Socialist Republics."

When the secretary announced the good news in his farewell speech to the delegates, the formal banquet was transformed into a frenetic celebration. "My last memory," Keynes recalled, "is of Dr. Harry White with vine leaves (or were they cock tails?) in his hair, leading into the dining room a Bacchic rout of satyrs and Silenuses from Latin America loudly chanting the strains of 'Onward Christian Soldiers.'"

For all his laid-back good humor at the finish line, Keynes had fought ferociously for victory at Bretton Woods. At home his colleagues considered it "one of the greatest triumphs of his life," Lionel Robbins recorded in his diary. It was held that "Keynes was without doubt quite the dominant figure . . . frail in body but will-power and mental brilliance and flexibility enough for 10."

Notwithstanding his toughness and loyalty to London, the empire and the commonwealth, Keynes in the end was magnanimous in conceding that

> we have before us a proposal the origins of which we owe primarily to the initiative and ability of the United States Treasury, conceived on sound and fruitful lines . . . a contribution of fundamental value and importance to those difficult, those almost overwhelming tasks which lie ahead of us, to rebuild the world when a final victory over the forces of evil opens the way to a new age of peace and progress after great afflictions.

As Keynes retired from the revels that final night, the whole company (no doubt led by the British and Americans) rose to their feet to sing "For He's a Jolly Good Fellow." "As an experiment in international cooperation the Conference has been an outstanding success," Keynes wrote his friend Hoppy (Sir Richard Hopkins). Then he could not help chortling, "The Americans are virtually pledging themselves to untied loans on a vast scale." And with a final condescending poke at his hosts, he signed off from "this land of flowing abundance, infinitely remote from trouble, where there is no sense of strain, nothing but grilled steaks as big as your plate and ice cream."

In his closing remarks on that night of momentarily united nations, Morgenthau was "perfectly certain . . . that none of us has found any incompatibility between devotion to our country and joint action . . . The only safeguard for our national interests lies in international cooperation."

Dean Acheson told Morgenthau, "The last minute concession of the Russians was almost unbelievable . . . a great diplomatic victory" and "a matter of great political significance." Later Morgenthau told Roosevelt that Acheson had complimented him on possessing "a sixth sense" in dealing with the Soviets. "At first he told me that I had handled the Russian situation entirely wrong, and then he was man enough to come around at the end and say I was completely right and Keynes said the same thing."

Keynes had been pleasantly surprised at Bretton Woods when personal relations with the Soviets were "very cordial." Yet he was forced to admit that while "they *want* to thaw and collaborate . . . they are put in a most awkward, and sometimes humiliating position by the lack of both suitable instructions and suitable discretion from Moscow." To the extent that such things are allowed, it was a great personal triumph for Stepanov that he had succeeded in the "somewhat appalling job of making clear to Moscow what it was all about."

Still riding high after the victory celebration Keynes understood that the U.S. Congress, with some strong links to the financial community, was not about to give its approval without a fight. Thus, Bernstein recalled, "Keynes, who had unbelievable confidence in his persuasive power, went to New York and had a meeting at the Federal Reserve Bank." In the course of his session he praised the drafted agreement, adding, "We can thank Bernstein for that." "Knowing that if White heard of this" he would feel Bernstein was somehow "deliberately elbowing him out," Bernstein fired off a letter to Keynes stating, "I can think of nothing of any consequence in the two projects that didn't come from White's own fertile mind. . . . I was only a Levite serving the priests in their holy work." Keynes wrote back, "My dear Levite, . . . I will only comment in reply that perhaps priests cannot get on without Levites any more than the Queen Bee without her workers." It was a proud moment for "little Eddie Bernstein," but "thereafter things got progressively worse" in his relations with White.

The afternoon following the celebration, the secretary and his wife received Eddie Bernstein for tea. Bernstein was "really exhausted," having "hardly slept in the twenty-one days I was there. When we were through at Bretton Woods, I went off with my wife to Cape May and I slept for two weeks."

In later years Bernstein reflected that Bretton Woods was "one of the most successful conferences I've ever been at" because "it was thoroughly well prepared." Indeed that thoroughness was the hallmark of the Morgenthau style.

While Bernstein was flat-out exhausted at the end of the conference, my father seemed to have gained an extra charge from the success. Yet, perhaps more than any of his colleagues, American and foreign, he knew he was only halfway home. Morgenthau was aware that his increasingly frail boss could do no more. He himself would have to score the winning touchdown on the Hill. Without congressional approval everything else would be meaningless.

In the summer of 1944 the ubiquitous secretary of the treasury was passionately determined that what appeared to be an inevitable Allied military victory must be locked into a long-term peace, assuring that Germany would never again regain the strength to terrorize the civilized world. He envisioned a world order that involved long-term cooperation among the wartime partners. The British and the Soviets were to be appropriately rewarded for having made the major sacrifice, with the United States remaining the number-one superpower, serving the best interests of all the united nations.

At that time this concept enjoyed a broad consensus among American officials, politicians, and experts, though not the bankers. Furthermore, it provided a blueprint for strategies that would endure for a generation and institutions that continue to operate today, though in a very different and still evolving context.

· 31 ·

The Morgenthau Plan
for Germany

M Y FATHER, like everyone else in Washington in 1944, was first and foremost absorbed in the final push for military victory. At the same time he had been deeply shocked on learning the full facts of the Jewish genocide. Thereafter he became obsessed with the problems of rescuing the survivors and trying to make sure that history would never again repeat itself. He remembered his father's warning after World War I that the Versailles Treaty was merely an intermission, and that Germany would rise again even more powerful and aggressive than before. With these thoughts uppermost in his mind, he became the unyielding advocate of, first, the landmark Bretton Woods agreements to sustain world economic stability, and second, the so-called Morgenthau Plan, intended to stop yet another phoenixlike rise of German militarism.

On July 6, 1944, while presiding over the Bretton Woods conference, Morgenthau temporarily relinquished his chair to Deputy Chairman Fred Vinson and went to the White House to confer with the president. He asked permission "to go to France to see how the [U.S. occupation] currency was getting along" and was pleased with Roosevelt's "instantaneous" positive reaction. He also received permission to invite Assistant Secretary of War John McCloy to accompany him. Morgenthau had been out in front leading his Washington peers on the home front; now he was eager to move within range of the sound, smell, and agony of battle.

But he also had personal reasons. Both my brother, Bob, and I were on active duty. I was serving in General Patton's Third Army in Normandy, where a reunion was arranged at General Omar Bradley's First Army Headquarters. Early that spring Bob's destroyer, the *Lansdale,* was sunk while on convoy duty in the Mediterranean. Losses were heavy, but Bob was rescued after twenty-four hours in the water. This incident concerning "the son of the Secretary of the Treasury" was reported in the press just as the Second Cavalry Group, in which I was serving, embarked for Europe. Believing that my ship had gone down, the families of my outfit were distraught.

At the end of 1943, in Teheran, Roosevelt, Churchill, and Stalin had sat down face to face for the first time. Although the pervasive concern was still the conduct of the war in Europe, the Big Three began to exchange ideas on plans for a defeated Germany. The gap between the Briton and the Russian was immediately apparent. The Soviets clearly wished to dismantle Germany and punish the Nazi perpetrators of aggression. The British, despite heavy losses, were intent on reviving the European economy, including the German, as a safeguard against a financial collapse similar to the one that occurred after World War I. Roosevelt found himself in the middle, but tending to gravitate toward Stalin rather than Churchill. And there the matter rested. Although the Allied chieftains agreed on a joint strategy for concluding the war both in Europe and in Asia, their differences concerning the fate of postwar Germany were, for the time being, papered over.

At Teheran the Big Three had also endorsed a European Advisory Commission (EAC), which began to meet in London early in 1944. The senior U.S. representative was the American ambassador to Britain, John G. Winant. Serving on the EAC in London, Winant was swayed by his knowledgeable advisers' deep-seated mistrust of the Russians, especially by the brilliant Soviet expert George F. Kennan. With no guidance from Washington, the EAC in London came up with a plan for postwar recovery that Roosevelt eventually vetoed, finding it too soft.

After General Eisenhower assumed command of SHAEF (Supreme Headquarters, Allied Expeditionary Forces), other plans began emanating from SHAEF's headquarters at Bushey Park outside of London. In general, they advocated a harsher policy toward the Germans than that communicated by Winant. They not only empowered Eisenhower to arrest Nazi leaders and embark on a program of total de-Nazification, but also provided for revitalization of German agriculture. As an aid to carrying out the SHAEF plan, the military government officers released a draft of the *Handbook for Military Government in Germany*. In consonance with military priorities, its primary objective was a German society and economy that operated as efficiently as possible, so as to relieve the occupation overlords of excessive demands.

Meanwhile in Washington, without any effective overall coordination of the various initiatives under way, the State Department proceeded to develop its own plan. Although State's document was designed to support a State Department policy of "a stern peace with reconciliation," it appeared to ignore completely the basic tenets endorsed by the Big Three at Teheran. Far from advocating a stern peace, it was in fact a blueprint for the reconstruction of the German economy in the European community. It recommended against partitioning the country and against dismantling German industry. Reparations were to be paid out of current production rather than with capital equipment. The German people were to be restored to a tolerable standard of living as soon as possible.

On August 6, just two weeks after the triumph at Bretton Woods, my father boarded a military transport plane at Presque Isle, Maine, to make the sixteen-hour flight to Prestwick, Scotland. While Eddie Bernstein and others who had participated in the round-the-clock sessions in New Hampshire were flattened by exhaustion, Morgenthau and Harry White were experiencing a high that stimulated their hunger for a new challenge. Ostensibly their mission was to investigate financial conditions in Europe and formulate plans for the currency to be used by the Allied occupying forces. On the plane Harry sat right next to his boss. Two other members of the Treasury entourage, Josiah DuBois and Fred Smith, were seated to the rear.

Trained as a lawyer, Jo DuBois had been the junior member of the group of Treasury staffers who had pushed Morgenthau into the creation of the War Refugee Board. He tended to display an unrestrained enthusiasm for the causes he believed in. Fiercely anti-German, he supported, and at times goaded my father into taking, extreme positions.

Fred Smith was a swarthy, heavy-jowled public relations man who resembled a cheerful (if that is possible) Richard Nixon. Smith, who had experience in advertising and promotion, had proved to be highly useful to Morgenthau in publicizing and selling war bonds. In later years he billed himself as "confidential adviser" to the secretary. One of Smith's talents was his ability to get along with Harry White, who alienated so many with his abrasiveness.

DuBois recalls that once when he was in White's office,

> he [White] showed me a document that he had received from the State Department. Generally speaking, it said that we were going to require . . . the Germans to supply us with enormous amounts . . . of products in the form of reparations. . . . Harry says, "If we take reparations from Germany in the form of goods, all that means is we're going to be rebuilding their factories and making them again a very strong industrial nation." He said, "What we ought to be doing is making Germany basically a deindustrialized nation, not rebuilding them and making them a strong industrial nation. Therefore reparations should [take the form of dismantled] factories that are manufacturing heavy goods."

White disagreed with the State Department proposal and knew that it "was not in line with the Secretary's views." But even White was unprepared for the shattering violence of Morgenthau's reaction. My father had inherited his father's hatred of the Germans and a fear that after each successive war they would reemerge even stronger unless their military-industrial base was dismantled. Unlike Keynes and Stimson, both of whom had been intimately involved in European affairs at the end of the First World War, Henry Morgenthau, Jr., attributed the rise of Hitler not to an excessively harsh peace but to insufficient Allied restraints on the Germans. Faced with the hostility of the State Department and the relative indifference of the War Department, he became a magnet both for the appeals for help and the criticisms for not doing more, a situation that set off an inextinguishable firestorm in his brain.

"I can tell you how the Morgenthau Plan got started," DuBois confided.

> On the way over in the plane, White and your dad sat together, and though I wasn't deliberately eavesdropping, it was obvious from the conversation that what they were talking about was the whole notion of how we should get reparations from Germany. And by the time we arrived in England, there was no question in my mind that your dad was at this point completely convinced that the approach that the State

Department had suggested was the wrong approach . . . So at that point he began pushing what later became known as the so-called Morgenthau Plan for Germany, and wherever he went, whoever he talked to, he would hammer this point home.

On August 7, the morning after he arrived in Britain, my father had an appointment with General Eisenhower at Portsmouth, the English Channel headquarters where Eisenhower had launched the D-Day invasion two months earlier. My father was accompanied by Harry White and Fred Smith; DuBois was not in the party. It was about 12:30 when they sat down for lunch in Ike's mess tent.

"We started right in with General Eisenhower to find out where he stood on this business of how he is going to treat Germany when he first gets there," Morgenthau told his staff when he got back to Washington. Eisenhower replied "that he was going to treat them rough."*

On their arrival in Scotland, White, and Morgenthau were briefed by Colonel Bernard Bernstein, a former Treasury lawyer, then on duty with the SHAEF Civil Affairs section. Colonel Bernstein tipped them off as to the directives being prepared for the occupation of Germany. He advised them that in tune with military logic the SHAEF staff believed it was the mission of their Civil Affairs section to bolster the German economy to keep our troops "from bogging down in a morass of economic wreckage." At lunch with Eisenhower, White pointed out that under the proposed plan "life would be re-established on as high a plane as feasible, as quickly as possible." Until this moment Eisenhower had been totally absorbed in masterminding solutions to the tactical and inter-Allied political problems of the invasion. This was perhaps the first time he had been confronted with posthostility challenges. "Eisenhower became grim," Smith recalled, stating, "'I am not interested in the German economy and personally would not like to bolster it if that will make it any easier for the Germans.'" He thought the Germans had punishment coming to them: "'The ringleaders and the SS troops should be given the death penalty without question.'" Beyond that

---

*The transcripts of Morgenthau's reports to the Treasury staff and to the president on August 19 are the closest thing to an on-the-spot report that exists. All of the other comments were written in the late 1940s and 1950s when the Morgenthau Plan had been repudiated in U.S. and European official circles, and Harry White was under suspicion as a Communist agent. In 1954 Fred Smith claimed to have written his account based on notes he made "directly after the meeting" in Eisenhower's tent.

he held that the entire German people were guilty of supporting the Nazi regime and that he personally "'would like to see things made good and hard for them for a while.'"

Morgenthau's harsh sentiments toward the Germans were consonant with Eisenhower's at the time of this trip. The day of the secretary's arrival Eisenhower had received a lurid account of atrocities being committed in the Nazi death camps. But perhaps more than anything he had painful memories of the D-Day decisions he had made, knowing that many American lives would be lost.

Now, two months later, with the ultimate triumph of "the great crusade" in Europe in sight, Eisenhower was not about to return his costly gains. Another important factor in his thinking was the Russians. No one understood better than he that keeping the Soviets fully engaged would be vital to winning the war. Despite the rising tide of fear in the United States and Britain that the Soviet Union would dominate postwar Europe, Eisenhower was more concerned about the danger of unraveling the Soviet military partnership before the battle was over. He remained steadfast in opposing any signs of favoring "the soft peace" so abhorrent to the Soviets. On August 7 he reiterated to Morgenthau and White that "the whole German population is a synthetic paranoid. All their lives the people have been taught to be paranoid in their actions and thoughts, and have to be snapped out of it. The only way to do that is to be good and hard on them. I certainly see no point in bolstering their economy or taking any other steps to help them."

Years later Eisenhower would be "plagued" with the accusation that he had inspired or even authored the Morgenthau Plan. When he searched his records for some evidence of exactly what he had said, he came up with nothing. He reconstructed the situation as best he could in a memorandum that he circulated as his authorized document, quoting it in his autobiography. His grandson, David Eisenhower, who researched the matter painstakingly, stated, "Eisenhower would never deny — in so many words —" that he had been "the inspiration behind the Morgenthau Plan." In the general's reconstructed memo there is no backing away from his stance that "the German people must not be allowed to escape a sense of guilt, of complicity in the tragedy that has engulfed the world."

Eisenhower did claim to have differed with Morgenthau's suggestion during their Portsmouth meeting "that the Ruhr mines be flooded. This seemed silly and criminal to me," he wrote. In fact, there is no indication that proposals for the Ruhr were discussed at that time.

Morgenthau took Eisenhower's words in the tent at Portsmouth as a clear signal that he could advocate a tough policy for Germany with the general's complete approval. Eisenhower had agreed that he could be quoted, adding, "I will tell the President myself, if necessary."

· 32 ·

Views from the Battlefronts

BY THE TIME my father arrived in Europe, I had been in England and France with the Second Cavalry for over three months.* Ours was one among a mixed bag of American units crowded on the *Mauretania,* a former British Cunard luxury liner that had been converted into a troop carrier. Some years earlier I had sailed on the same ship as a first-class passenger in a small cabin by myself. This time I shared similar quarters with three other lieutenants. But this too was luxury compared with the quarters of the enlisted men, who slept in hammocks in the ship's hold. Since the *Mauretania* was a fast ship, it was deemed safer to have her cross the Atlantic unescorted rather than proceeding in a much slower and therefore supposedly more vulnerable convoy. We disembarked in Liverpool on April 30, 1944, and proceeded to a bivouac area in Bewdley.

There we learned that the Second Cavalry was to be part of a new Third Army in formation, commanded by the legendary, controversial, "old blood and guts" himself, General George Patton. The entire staging area where all the troops were located had been cordoned off with barbed wire. No unauthorized personnel were allowed in or out. Our squadron had been moved to Torquay, a shabby, working-class resort on the English Channel, which had been closed for the duration. Here we transported equipment and medical personnel to old hotels converted into hospitals for the

---

*The Second Cavalry group was a light armored mechanized reconnaissance regiment consisting of the Second and Forty-second Squadrons. I was in B Troop of the Second Squadron.

anticipated casualties. We had the sense of a gigantic build-up of tension, as though we were poised on a mammoth spring coiled for release. Of course we knew nothing of what was going on at General Eisenhower's headquarters at Portsmouth. I learned later on that the possibility of prolonged stormy weather had delayed the supreme commander's final decision until 4:14 A.M. on June 5. On June 6 we had the predicted break in the foul weather. It was to be D-Day. Looking out over the channel from the verandah of one of the Torquay hotels, we could see the sky become darkened by continuous waves of bombers and fighter planes flying directly over our heads eastward to France with thunderous roaring that shook us to the bone.

Word soon filtered back that our troops — U.S., British, and Canadian — had made successful landings on the Normandy beaches. There had been heavy, bloody losses. Though in reality there was still little to support it, optimism ran high. As for the Second Cavalry, dispersed as service troops to aid the First Army's launching, our turn to get into the battle still lay ahead.

On June 9, three days after D-Day, as the Second Squadron was reassembling from scattered posts, I was ordered to report to our squadron commander, Lieutenant Colonel Walter Easton. At his quarters I found him with my troop commander, Captain Bill Potts. A special order had just arrived assigning me and a platoon from B Troop as a security guard for the supreme commander at SHAEF Headquarters. A number of things about this special order made both me and my superiors uneasy. I was then troop executive officer and had no platoon of my own. Then too, assigning a specific junior officer by name was rather odd, as was indeed the entire operation.

Some weeks later I received orders alerting our platoon that we were to go to France to guard the SHAEF forward CP (command post). Next morning we traveled to the London docks where we were promptly loaded onto a small landing craft and proceeded to cross the English Channel, which by then was quite secure.

For the duration of my detachment from the Second Cavalry, the SHAEF forward CP was situated at Reims, well behind the rapidly advancing front. There were three house trailers: one for General Eisenhower, the supreme commander; one for the deputy supreme commander, Air Marshal Sir Arthur Tedder; and one for Ike's chauffeur and secretary, Kay Summersby. None of them was present, and little security was needed beyond that already provided by a detachment of MPs. So to keep us occupied, our platoon sergeant and a squad of his men set off for Reims with a dump truck to bring back a load of finely crushed gravel. At the CP we were ordered to shovel it out carefully along a connecting path between the entrance doors of the Eisenhower and Summersby trailers, which were further embellished with awnings and heavy carpets from North Africa spread out on the turf. However, during the time I was stationed at Reims, the supreme commander and his driver never put in an appearance.

On August 9, two days after his long talk with Eisenhower, my father went from Britain to the once great French port of Cherbourg, which he found "to hell and gone," having been mined by the Germans and bombed and shelled by the Allies. I had received orders through SHAEF to join him at General Omar Bradley's headquarters on the Normandy front.

Bradley made "an excellent impression" on my father: "very quiet, complete self-control, complete balance. . . . He planned our trip." As it happened, on the very day of our visit that taciturn, modest man was as close to euphoria as he ever got. "In briefing Morgenthau that morning," Bradley recalled, "I pointed to where the German line hooked back below Mortain and showed him how we were hemming the enemy in with troops on our open flank. 'This is an opportunity that comes to a commander not more than once in a century,' I told him. 'We're about to destroy an entire hostile army.'" Bradley explained that there was a good chance to close the escape route between Argentan and Falaise (the so-called Falaise gap), trapping the German Seventh Army. "'He'll have nothing left with which to oppose us. We'll go all the way from here to the German border.'" Bradley thought the secretary reacted skeptically to his prediction. "I'm not sure Morgenthau believed me. The border was still 350 miles further east." Bradley didn't understand that his civilian guest was thrilled literally beyond words. "They let me go down within 5000 yards of the Germans . . . but they wouldn't let me go any further, because the thing is so fluid . . . we were due south of St. Lô . . . where the fighting is most severe and they had five German Divisions right opposite there. Three were SS Divisions . . ."

At the time of my father's visit Bradley believed the war in Europe might be over by the end of the following month. However, during the next few days his hopes were considerably reduced.

Faulty intelligence reports on the movement of German troops and the disappointing progress of General Montgomery to the north would postpone the final victory for nine months. In the meantime General Patton from the south was proceeding to move against orders to close the gap on his own. But while my father was his guest, Bradley had scrupulously refrained from criticizing his British and American colleagues. Thus the secretary came away with the impression that "General Patton has been perfectly magnificent."

On a tour of the battlefront in France, Morgenthau visited the evacuation hospitals, where he came in intimate contact with the maimed, the dying, and the dead. It was a searing experience for him, dampening the exhilarating mood of victory. "The loss of lives was something terrific — in American troops something like 16,000 dead and when I left there were 78,000 wounded." The possibility of American vulnerability was something my father had never before conceived of.

Patton's Third Army had been committed to combat in Normandy a week before I arrived at Bradley's headquarters. It was there that I learned of their spectacular advances on the Brittany peninsula. I felt like a deserter, even though I had nothing to do with my separation from the Second Cavalry and transfer to SHAEF. As a result, though, I was happy to see my father. I was quietly outraged by the humiliation of his well-meant manipulations, which I strongly suspected had led to my transfer to SHAEF. However, I never confronted him with my surmise, nor was I ever enlightened as to the facts of the matter. At the time of our rendezvous, he certainly greeted me with unabashed affection and pride. On August 11, from Claridge's back in London, he wrote my mother of

> a wonderful 31 hours in France with Henry. He is in fine shape and in a grand humor . . . [but] now that I look back on the trip I remember so many questions I wanted to ask him. We slept together in a little town on cots between blankets. No sheets, no pillows. I had the best night's rest that I can remember. From now on when I want to sleep I shall throw away the sheets.
>
> The war is going unbelievably well. We went thru St. Lo. In my whole life I have never seen such complete destruction.
>
> We lunched with General Bradley who made a *very* good impression and was very nice to us . . . They let me go and see everything I wanted to.

I felt awful when I left Henry and was glad I had my dark glasses. Let us pray and hope that this terrible war will be over soon.

After his tour of the battlefront my father spent several days on the British home front, which he discovered was as much a war zone as the Normandy countryside. He was especially moved by the determination of the plucky British people to stick it out. "Any idea of a negotiated peace or anything like that, is finished." But after five long, grim years, he found ordinary English men and women impatient in the face of the indiscriminate V-1 bombings of civilians. "These little buzz bombs go over — they make a noise very much like a single-engine fishing vessel — the damage is unbelievable; it is terrific." Pent-up frustration was vented in angry attacks on government leaders. Churchill had been publicly jeered. When Morgenthau asked to be taken through the air-raid shelters, there was difficulty in finding guides who would not fuel resentment. "Finally they decided on Mrs. Churchill and Lady Mountbatten."

The climax of Morgenthau's visit was two hours spent with the prime minister. "He took me through his map room — which was quite a thrill. He is a great fellow." Churchill told the secretary, "As soon as the war was over he would resign and be the most unpopular man in England . . . I got the impression he wanted the Germans treated in a stern manner — he and I got along very well. He put it right on the line . . . He started off bang, on how England was busted." During the course of their conversation Churchill kept returning to the point that England "was broke." Indeed, the whole purpose of his masterfully staged performance seemed aimed at impressing this single fact on Morgenthau and winning his sympathy for the upcoming negotiations over Lend-Lease, Phase II.

Churchill's strategy was successful. He won Morgenthau's personal support, and when the secretary returned to Washington he transmitted Churchill's message to Roosevelt. Morgenthau himself was surprised by the impact this news had on his boss. "The President kept coming back to England's being broke. He said, 'This is very interesting. I had no idea that England was broke. I will go over there and make a couple of talks and take over the British Empire.'"

Toward the end of his stay in London, Morgenthau came to understand that not all the British favored severe peace terms for the Germans. Confirmed Tories, including the secretary's opposite number, Sir John Anderson, chancellor of the exchequer, wanted to maintain the German economy at a level that would make the country a good market for British goods as well as provide a buffer against the Soviets. Coming away from a cordial luncheon with the foreign secretary, Anthony Eden, my father believed that he had Eden's support for his German policy. But in fact he had misinterpreted the suave diplomat's silence for assent.

On August 12, while staying at an elegant country house in Wiltshire which the British government had provided for his comfort, Morgenthau invited the U.S. ambassador, Gil Winant, and a group of his advisers to discuss plans for postwar Germany. E. F. Penrose, who was present, recalled that "as we lounged on the grass, Mr. Morgenthau in brief, simple terms expounded his views." Thereupon Harry White attempted, as Penrose conceived it, to clothe "a bad thesis with an appearance of intellectual respectability." All of those present, including Winant, were hostile to the Morgenthau-White plan to "smash" the German economy and dismember the state. Once again Morgenthau found himself confronted with State Department officials who were operating contrary to what he assumed to be the intentions of the president to which he personally was strongly committed. He moved quickly to delve deeper and put the pieces together. These matters were clearly well off Treasury turf, but if such a thought ever occurred to my father, it didn't give him a moment's hesitation. Then as always he thought of himself not only as the secretary of the treasury, but also as ambassador plenipotentiary with a license to hunt down and even act on what he believed to be the president's wishes. Always reporting back promptly, he counted on receiving the boss's gratitude and approval — though at the same time FDR might be encouraging others to sail forth on an entirely different tack, as Morgenthau, to his chagrin, sometimes discovered.

Just before he left England, Morgenthau had another talk with Eden at the Foreign Office. Eden seemed very much surprised to hear that Ambassador Winant was pursuing a course contrary to the agreement reached by the Big Three at Teheran, though Eden was not in disagreement with him. At that point Eden sent for the minutes of the meetings and read for my father's benefit the Big Three's specific instructions to the EAC to study the problems of partitioning Germany. Thus my father discovered that "Stalin . . . strongly favored dismemberment. Roosevelt backed him wholeheartedly, and Churchill reluctantly agreed."

The exchange of intelligence between Morgenthau and Eden on this occasion was mutually revealing. "Eden and I were both amazed to learn that EAC was cheerfully drawing its plans on the basis not of German dismemberment, but German unity. Winant had been at Teheran. But having received no instructions from the State Dept. to proceed along the Teheran lines, he felt that they might not know of the Big Three decision and that it was not his business to inform his superiors of such matters."

As soon as Morgenthau got back to Washington, he took pains to call on Secretary of State Hull at the State Department. Hull had conflicting feelings about Morgenthau. He admired "the excellent organization in the Treasury, ably headed by Harry White," but resented "the Secretary of the Treasury's persistent inclination to try to function as a second Secretary of State." Hull's personal feelings concerning a policy for postwar Germany were erratic. Most of the time he was influenced by the positions developed by his staff. In his view, "emotionally upset by Hitler's rise and his persecution of the Jews, [Morgenthau] often sought to induce the President to anticipate the State Department or act contrary to our better judgement." Morgenthau respected Hull personally but realized that he was often duped by his staff and continually locked out or ignored in matters of foreign policy by the president. When Morgenthau spoke of what he had learned about the Teheran meeting from Anthony Eden, Hull was shaken. "Henry, this is the first time I have heard this," he gasped. "I have never been permitted to see the minutes of the Teheran Conference." Morgenthau was flabbergasted, noting that "if Eden hadn't actually read from the minutes of the Teheran Conference and Hull hadn't told me face to face that he hadn't seen them, I wouldn't believe it."

Once again Hull had been placed in an untenable position. His fury at the secretary of the treasury was mitigated by Morgenthau's having voluntarily reported to him first, before seeing the president. Yet Hull found himself not only circumvented by his boss, but betrayed by subordinates who had short-circuited him by communicating directly to the president themselves. So although peevish with Morgenthau, he could hardly escape the truth.

From what Morgenthau had been able to piece together in London and from what Hull told him on his return, he was convinced that the policy for postwar Germany the Big Three had made in Teheran had gone adrift. In the absence of any clear directive from the State Department, Morgenthau decided that it was incumbent on him, personally, to lay all the facts as he saw them before the president, and urge him to recapture the initiative — a very tall order for any one man to carry out. Yet, driven by a passionate sense of being in the right, Morgenthau found little need to look over his shoulder to see whether his supporters were still behind him. With the recent victory at Bretton Woods, he could logically assume that with the same team and personal determination he could succeed again. In that earlier instance it had been an idea of Harry White's, backed up by competent Treasury staff work, that had attracted broad American and international support.

Although the so-called Morgenthau Plan seems to have been conceived in the mind of Harry Dexter White, Morgenthau's response to White's proposals went far beyond anything that White himself had hoped for. In no time Morgenthau was proceeding with a driving fury, confounding even his most ardent and loyal supporters.

Hull had no consistent policy in relation to Germany. His attitude shifted perhaps more in reaction to how he was treated personally than because he held to any basic tenets. When Morgenthau met with him on August 17 he found the secretary of state's views very much in tune with his own. Hull told Morgenthau, "You know the reason I got along so well with the Russians was because when I was in Moscow I told the Russians that I would hold a secret trial before which I would bring Hitler and his gang and Tojo and his gang and I would shoot them all." But when Morgenthau asked what he was going to do about Germany, Hull answered petulantly, "I don't have a chance to do anything. I am not told what is going on . . . I am told that that is a military affair . . . I am not even consulted."

Observing how miserable Hull was, Morgenthau tried to level with him. "You know, Cordell . . . I appreciate the fact that this isn't my responsibility, but I am doing this as an American citizen, and I am going to continue to do so, and I am going to stick my nose into it until I know it is all right . . If I find out anything I will come over and tell you about it."

Morgenthau departed convinced that "if Hull got a directive on the dismemberment of Germany he would go to town." In sum, as he told his Treasury staff, his "trip to Europe was many, many times worthwhile just for what I learned and what I told, and we will see what happens when I see the President."

Morgenthau reported to his boss on August 19. He immediately confronted Roosevelt with Hull's pique at not having been informed about the understandings reached at Teheran. "The President didn't like it, but didn't say anything," Morgenthau noted in a memo dictated right after his meeting. "He looked very embarrassed, and I repeated it so that he would be sure to get it."

Morgenthau went on to inform the president that Churchill, Winant, and the army all favored a policy that would lead to the rebuilding of Germany. "Nobody," he said, "has been studying how to treat Germany roughly along the lines you wanted."

"We have got to be tough with Germany and I mean the German people not just the Nazis," Roosevelt insisted. "We either have to castrate the German people or you have got to treat them in such a manner so they can't go on reproducing people who want to continue the way they have in the past."

Morgenthau left the White House with "no doubt whatsoever" that the president "personally wants to be tough with the Germans." All fired up, he proceeded to set up a special Treasury committee consisting of Harry White, John Pehle, and Ansel Luxford to define the budding Morgenthau Plan. The secretary himself monitored their work assiduously and though they followed his demanding instructions each was left with some misgivings. Harry White set out to gain for his thinking a broad basis of support. Later on some of the alleged proponents of the plan, including John Maynard Keynes and Bernard Baruch, contended that they had been misquoted or misinterpreted.

Morgenthau's uncompromising commitment to his German policy created a serious rift among his staff that failed to heal during the final year he remained in office. The most formidable opposition to the Morgenthau philosophy began to coalesce around an eminent colleague whom Morgenthau greatly respected.

Stimson versus Morgenthau

O
N AUGUST 23, 1944, Henry Stimson had a brief opportunity
to discuss German policy with the president during an appointment that was abruptly cut short by other pressing
business — but with a promise to continue the discussion two days
later. That same day Stimson and John McCloy lunched with Morgenthau. As usual, Morgenthau had been briefed by Harry White,
who gave him misleading assurances that he had the support of
Bernard Baruch (the ubiquitous adviser to Democratic presidents
and other high officials), James Conant (then president of Harvard
and Roosevelt's chief scientific adviser), and John Maynard Keynes.
White's report that "Keynes seems to be wholly in our corner" was
entirely contrary to the truth.

At lunch Morgenthau and Stimson seemed to be talking past
each other. Morgenthau himself later noted that Stimson complained that the proposed elimination of industry and pastoralization schemes would mean "that you might have to take a lot of
people out of Germany." Morgenthau answered, "Well, that is not
nearly as bad as sending them to gas chambers."

Morgenthau was left with the impression that "Stimson thought
this was a very important subject — but he hasn't given much
thought to it." In any case, the two men agreed to propose to the
president that he appoint a cabinet committee of Hull, Morgenthau,
and Stimson to prepare a policy memorandum on Germany so that
"he will have it before he meets Churchill again [at Quebec]."

Two days later, on August 25, both Morgenthau and Stimson
arranged appointments for themselves with the president. "Stimson
and McCloy knew of Morgenthau's appointment, and Morgenthau
knew of Stimson's. Neither was bothered because neither realized

how profound their differences were." As Morgenthau noted in his diary, "I called on the President this morning and I really was shocked for the first time because he is a very sick man and seems to have wasted away." But the secretary was nonetheless relentless in scoring his points. During his visit to England, Colonel Bernard (Bernie) Bernstein had handed him a draft of the SHAEF military *Handbook for Germany,* which, as a member of the G-5 (civil affairs) staff, Bernstein had been working on. Bernstein disagreed with the general tone of the *Handbook,* which stressed establishing efficient, orderly operation of civil affairs under German supervision, as a priority for the Allies' occupation forces, and he shared Morgenthau's concern that with the rapid advance of the Allied troops toward the German border, the draft document could soon be locked in as operating policy. In fact, the *Handbook* had not been finalized; it had not even been seen by General Eisenhower or anyone in the War Department. The highly irregular manner in which Bernie turned over this draft document was something which both men were sensitive to. Bernie learned later on that it cost him a much-coveted promotion to general and a Distinguished Service medal.

Morgenthau for his part felt quite justified in showing the draft of the *Handbook* to the president. "If we hadn't gone to Europe and dug this stuff up," he told his staff, "that *Handbook* would have gone into effect."

Although giving the *Handbook* to the president was a calculated and unorthodox maneuver, Morgenthau was entirely aboveboard in the way he performed it. "Look, Mr. President," he said, "this is based on a handbook which we picked up in England and which I understand has not yet been approved, but lacking a directive from the top this is what is going to be used . . . I told McCloy to tell Stimson that I was going to speak to you about it — I don't want to annoy him so I think maybe you'd better give me back [my] memorandum and the *Handbook*." "No," Roosevelt replied. "If you don't mind, I would like to keep it and read it tonight and then I will return it to you."

Later that day Stimson took lunch with Roosevelt, and during the cabinet meeting immediately thereafter the president announced his appointment of the three-man cabinet committee of Hull, Morgenthau, and Stimson, to be coordinated by the pre-eminent White House adviser, Harry Hopkins. That night the president carefully read through the *Handbook* and Morgenthau's memorandum.

The next day FDR wrote Stimson, "This so-called *Handbook* is pretty bad." It was an unusually blunt rebuke. "I should like to know how it came to be written and who approved it down the line. If it has not been sent out as approved, all copies should be withdrawn." In his own language Roosevelt reflected the outrage Morgenthau had conveyed to him: "It gives me the impression that Germany is to be restored just as much as the Netherlands or Belgium, and the people of Germany brought back as quickly as possible to their pre-war estate. . . . The fact that they are a defeated nation, collectively and individually must be so impressed upon them that they will hesitate to start any new war — the whole nation has been engaged in a lawless conspiracy against the decencies of modern civilization." Thereupon the president concluded, "Please let me see the revision of this and also let me have this original copy back."

On September 1 Harry Hopkins went to see Hull to inform him that the president had ordered him to give top priority to advancing the cabinet committee toward a consensus. On Saturday, September 2, Hopkins convened two meetings of the cabinet members and advisers in his White House office. At these sessions, with Harry White representing Morgenthau, and McCloy standing in for Stimson, as these two often did, the adversarial positions of the Treasury and the War Department became more sharply defined. The collective wisdom of the State Department supported the Stimson position, though Hull's stance was unclear. Hopkins, while representing the president, managed to convince both the Morgenthau and the Stimson proxies that he was on their side.

From the Ausable Club Stimson remained "in constant touch by direct line telephone, which the Army had put in, with McCloy." Morgenthau, from his farm in Fishkill, kept on the line with Harry White and John Pehle. Reviewing the memorandum they were preparing, he found it not tough enough. "I'd like to approach the thing from . . . just putting the whole Ruhr out of production . . . and the Saar. . . . I mean England, Belgium and Russia could take care of the customers that Germany used to have . . . with coal and steel." White was skeptical, but Morgenthau remained adamant. Edward Bernstein and John Pehle would beg off from this assignment along with other old Treasury hands.

Fortifying himself against mounting dissent from all quarters, Morgenthau prepared to play his trump card. On that Saturday, September 2, Franklin and Eleanor Roosevelt motored over from Hyde Park to Fishkill, to call on Henry and Elinor Morgenthau.

That evening Morgenthau dictated his impressions of the meeting at great length for his presidential diary. This candid, detailed, and immediate recall gives us a self-portrait of Morgenthau, passionately intense as he pushed to gain presidential support for his plan to crush Germany once and for all. Although he believed he succeeded in nailing down Roosevelt's full endorsement, a careful reading of the diary entry suggests that the president was merely avoiding a confrontation, while his good friend's rantings punctured the tranquility of a beautiful, crisp afternoon in the countryside both men loved so much. "The President listened very closely and seemed to be in complete sympathy with what I was saying," Morgenthau noted. "I don't think he had done any thinking along these lines." He had shown the president the draft memorandum that his staff had prepared, adding, "My own criticism of it was that it didn't go nearly far enough."

He was pleased that the president "was keenly interested in the memorandum and read it very slowly and very carefully." But he didn't appear to understand that Roosevelt was deflecting a discussion by making three rather trivial suggestions tinged with that humor he used as an avoidance maneuver. The Germans, he said, should be allowed "no aircraft of any kind, not even a glider." Second, "nobody should be allowed to wear a uniform." Third, there would be no marching: "That would do more to teach the Germans than anything else that they had been defeated." Morgenthau accepted these suggestions at face value, and they were dutifully appended to what became the final draft of the Morgenthau Plan.

Morgenthau also "felt it had been distinctly worthwhile to see Mrs. Roosevelt because I never knew just how she might feel toward treating the Germans so harshly." Since she was a close friend of his wife, Morgenthau had often found her eager to push his interests with the president. Nevertheless, in this instance he wanted to test the water because Eleanor "had been slightly pacifist before the war and I thought she might think we should go a little easy on the Germans, but she doesn't," he reported.

Back in Washington, on Labor Day morning Morgenthau summoned to his office in the Treasury White, Pehle, Edward Bernstein, and the others who had been working all weekend on the memorandum. Emboldened by blessings from on high, Morgenthau would brook no compromise, even when his staff members expressed their misgivings about the boss's stance, White again suggested that the Ruhr be internationalized. Morgenthau responded angrily: "Harry you can't sell it to me . . . You just can't sell it to me at all . . . you have . . . only so many years and you have an Anschluss and the Germans go in and take it. . . . Just strip it. I don't care what happens to the population. . . . I would take every mine, every mill and factory and wreck it . . . steel, coal everything. Just close it down . . . I am for destroying it first and we will worry about the population second."

Stimson had of course been especially at odds with Morgenthau's "very bitter — personal resentment against the entire German people without regard to individual guilt." It made him "very much afraid that it will result in our taking mass vengeance." Stimson believed this would not only be "ineffective" but that it would "inevitably produce a very dangerous reaction in Germany and probably a new war."

On the morning of September 4, Stimson flew back to Washington from the Adirondacks, where he had arisen before dawn for a full day of catching up on the fast-moving military situation in both the European and Asian theaters. He discussed a wide range of pressing problems with General George Marshall, including "my troubles in regard to the treatment of Germany. . . . It was very interesting to find that Army officers have a better respect for the law . . . than civilians . . . who are anxious to go ahead and chop everybody's head off without trial or hearing." Marshall supported Stimson in favor of using civilians rather than army officers on tribunals to try the Gestapo, though he thought that in the case of joint tribunals the Soviets would insist on military men as their representatives. Marshall favored setting up regional commissions for trials at the locations of the crimes. This would be an easy way of assuring speedy "justice" while escaping responsibility for the predictable results. "In such a case as the Lublin mass murder a large group of the Gestapo might be tried together."

At the end of a long, tiring day Stimson went home and "rested for an hour" before keeping a dinner engagement at Morgenthau's home, with McCloy and White serving as seconds for the two principal adversaries. (Stimson, who was seventy-seven, was just then ending convalescence from minor surgery.) During an evening intended as a dress rehearsal for the meeting of the president's cabinet committee the next day, Morgenthau "unveiled his newly completed plan for Germany." Stimson found Morgenthau "not unnaturally very bitter and as he is not thoroughly trained in history or even economics, it became very apparent that he would plunge out for a treatment of Germany which I feel would be unwise." Despite their emotionally charged differences, the two men, restrained by long-term mutual regard for each other's strength, continued to talk matters over "with temperateness and good will [which] was as much as could be hoped from the situation."

When he got home late that night Stimson learned that Hull, in whose office the cabinet committee was to meet the next morning, had advanced the time from ten to nine-thirty. Stimson stayed up until the early hours of the morning to inform himself as best he could. The briefing continued when McCloy picked him up after breakfast and rode with him to the State Department. Only the three cabinet officers and Harry Hopkins attended this session. Hull was his usual ambivalent self, resenting trespassers while at the same time remaining unwilling or unable to make a move. Stimson, fearful that Hull regarded this as a "reflection upon the prerogatives of the State Department," was even more worried about "drifting into a chaotic situation," leaving Eisenhower's troops poised to enter Germany with vital points of policy not yet decided."

Stimson had found that Morgenthau, equally concerned, for his own reasons, "had been rooting around the scene and greased the way for his own views by conference with the President and others." As the meeting progressed, Stimson to his "tremendous surprise found that Hull was as bitter as Morgenthau against the Germans. . . . He and Morgenthau were determined to wreck completely the immense Ruhr-Saar area of Germany and turn it into a second-rate agricultural land regardless of all that that area meant not only to Germany but to the welfare of the entire European Continent."

At this point Harry Hopkins seemed to be in accord with the Morgenthau-Hull line. Afterward on the phone Hopkins said to Morgenthau that Stimson had been "terrible . . . it hurts him to think of the non use of property. . . . I think it's fruitless to talk with him any more . . . and . . . I feel confident . . . about where the President is going to land."

Stimson was devastated. As "a minority of one I labored vigorously but entirely ineffectively against my colleagues. In all the four years that I have been here I have not had such a difficult and unpleasant meeting although of course there were no personalities.

We all knew each other too well for that. But we were irreconcilably divided." The thin skin of gentlemanly civility was stretched to the breaking point. On the phone with Hopkins, Morgenthau recalled, Stimson said "kindness and Christianity" were called for in the reconstruction of Germany, and referred to Morgenthau's "understandable bitterness" and his demand for a "Carthaginian peace." And McCloy, for all his proclaimed admiration of Morgenthau as "a man of culture [and] sensitivity," nevertheless pigeonholed him as "a deeply passionate member of the Jewish race. He felt his racial position was affronted by the activities of the Hitler regime." And though McCloy said he "would hesitate to use the word *vindictive*," he repeatedly applied it to the Morgenthau stance, perhaps not incorrectly. Morgenthau had indeed become the avenging angel for the remnant of world Jewry. He alone among his peers was committed to a final solution for what he believed to be the German threat to a lasting peace.

It pained my father to be called a Jewish champion or the champion of the Jews, yet it was something he could accept. Stimson was not anti-Semitic in his advocacy of a Christian solution and was doing a magnificent job in winning the war, for which he was receiving and acknowledging Morgenthau's active cooperation. But when it came to participating on the War Refugee Board, Stimson had been, as Morgenthau expected, passive and aloof. In Stimson's view, refugees could be best served by the winning of the war; any direct intervention would only prove an impediment. Moreover, he was concerned that Jews who were given temporary haven would end up staying in the United States after the war. A long-time restrictionist, he was opposed to anything that might loosen the immigration laws. In his grudging way, Cordell Hull, as the third member of the board, which had been born as a challenge to the State Department, had gone along with Morgenthau.

Outnumbered three to one (including Hopkins) at the September 5 cabinet meeting, Stimson recognized that he had lost yet another crucial round. Having failed to negotiate a unified position to present to the president, he went back to his office and "spent the rest of the day in hammering out a careful but vigorous statement of my views." They were views that had ripened over three decades of cabinet-level service. In the twilight of his career Stimson was determined "to leave a record for history that the entire government of this Administration had not run amuck at this vital period."

The Morgenthau Plan had stolen the lead in the battle to set the course of Germany's future. Although people in the State Department had done a great deal of work on the question, they lacked the necessary coordination and focus. Above all, Hull failed to provide leadership at the top, remaining unaware of much that his staff was doing. Initially he seemed against their moderate proposals, aligning himself closely with the tough Morgenthau position. Stimson, having served as secretary of state himself, had found it inappropriate to initiate foreign policy from the War Department. It was only when he learned that Roosevelt and an administration he found deplorably out of control had "run amuck" that he took matters directly in hand.★

The memo that Stimson prepared on the afternoon of September 5 for the next day's cabinet committee meeting was the first of several that would bring the full weight of his intellect, experience, and political savvy to bear on the president. At first Stimson had despaired of this man who seemed to have his mind made up and to be too weary to think the issues through afresh or listen to reasoned counsel for any length of time. But in the days and weeks ahead, Stimson discovered that he had many allies, and that the president's moorings were less firmly anchored than he had reckoned.

Stimson and Morgenthau had the common objective of making it impossible for Germany to start another world war, yet their perception of the German people was significantly different, especially their assessment of the conditions in Germany following World War I which led to the rise of Hitler. Morgenthau believed that Hitler's assumption of power resulted from the Allies' weakness and from an isolationist United States' failing to enforce the terms set down at Versailles. Stimson believed, on the contrary, that the fault lay with Germany's economic devastation in the 1920s.

As far as Morgenthau was concerned, the German people were to subsist as best they could (or if they could) in an agrarian economy. Whatever suffering this might incur seemed slight in comparison with the acts of sadistic brutality visited upon the Jews and other innocent Nazi victims. Shocked and sickened when he learned

---

★Stimson, who served six presidents, and in the cabinets of four, found President Franklin D. Roosevelt "the poorest administrator I have ever worked under in respect to the orderly procedure and routine performance. He is not a good chooser of men and he does not know how to use them in co-ordination" (diary entry, March 28, 1943).

of these atrocities late in the course of events, it permanently altered the course of his life.

From then on Morgenthau accepted the mission of waging a lonely, unpopular campaign against the indifference of his colleagues, the governments of friendly nations, and the anti-Semitism that prevailed in the State Department. My father, who was so often put down as a Roosevelt yes man, found the guts to risk all his influence and friendship with FDR for something he believed in. And for a while it seemed to be paying off.

In 1917 Henry Stimson, at fifty, who had been President Taft's secretary of war, volunteered as an artillery colonel with the U.S. forces in France. Though a Republican, he shared the Wilsonian hope that the United States would join the League of Nations. Later, as Hoover's secretary of state, he worked for disarmament. Visiting the Weimar Republic in 1931, he was sympathetic to Chancellor Heinrich Brüning's efforts to ward off opposing Nazi and Communist extremism. He found a sentimental affinity with Brüning personally when the two old veterans discovered that they had been "opposite each other in the same sector of the lines in 1918." There is nothing that makes men feel closer than the revelation that once upon a time they had been in a position to kill each other.

In 1931 there was a widespread sentiment among the Allies that Germany had been a good loser. At that time Stimson had advocated a revision of the Versailles Treaty, which he believed would have lightened the burden on the German economy, relieved the nation's bitterness, and allowed the Weimar democracy to survive. In retrospect, he came to view the rise of Hitler as a "tragedy of timidity" on the part of the Allies, including the Americans. In his analysis of the failure, Stimson was close to John Maynard Keynes, who, as a young adviser to the British Treasury delegation at Versailles, had resigned in disgust for much the same reason.

At the meeting of the cabinet committee with the president on September 6, Stimson masterfully attacked the Morgenthau Plan, zeroing in on the controversial proposal for destroying the Ruhr and the Saar. "I cannot treat as realistic the suggestion that such an area in the present economic condition of the world can be turned into a nonproductive ghost territory," he argued. "I can conceive of endeavoring to meet the misuse which Germany has recently made of this production by wise systems of control or trusteeship or even transfer of ownership to other nations." (Morgenthau had overruled

Harry White's suggestion of a United Nations trusteeship over the Ruhr.) Stimson "could not conceive of turning such a gift of nature into a dust heap. . . . Moreover speed of reconstruction is of great importance if we hope to avoid dangerous convulsion in Europe."

Morgenthau reported back to his staff after the September 6 session in the White House that it was a "very unsatisfactory meeting." During the course of the afternoon, while Hopkins stuck with Morgenthau, Hull had seemed to retreat from his previous position and to line up with Stimson. But the truly important thing was the president's shift. Not wanting to expose himself directly, he had fallen back on his old trick of telling a long, rambling story and then terminating the discussion abruptly, thus cutting off debate. Rather than oppose the destruction of the Ruhr directly, he appeared merely to favor postponing it. "You can do this economic thing in six months . . . a year; there is no particular hurry." Morgenthau insisted there was. He asked for a rehearing the next day and got it. FDR took the occasion of a one-on-one meeting to try to smooth Morgenthau's feathers. "Don't be discouraged about yesterday's meeting," the president told him. "The whole question seems to be about closing down the plants, and we have got to do the thing gradually." The secretary didn't pick up the implication that the proposed delay of the destruction of the Ruhr might be permanent, noting, "The amazing thing was that he should have greeted me the way he did because he must have realized the way I felt and this was most encouraging."

On September 8, Morgenthau called on Hull and "found him looking very tired and very badly." Hull was indeed both tired and sick. He told Morgenthau that the president had invited him along to the impending summit meeting with Churchill in Quebec but that he had declined, pleading exhaustion. But then "he went on another of his tirades complaining that the President didn't consult him."

When the cabinet committee met again with Roosevelt the next day, Morgenthau noted, "Hull just wouldn't get into the discussion and just what his game is I don't know." The president again asked Hull "whether he didn't want to come to Quebec, and he said he was too tired." (Hull had earlier told Morgenthau that he hoped the Quebec meeting would be confined to military matters, although he knew this was an empty wish.) Roosevelt told his cabinet committee, "I think there will be two things brought up in Quebec.

One is military and the other is monetary because Churchill keeps saying he is broke. . . . If they bring up the financial situation I will want Henry to come to Quebec."

Stimson was extremely perturbed by the dire prospects for "Octagon" (the code name given to the Quebec conference). Making his strongest statement yet against the Morgenthau proposal for the Ruhr, he contended that "it would breed war, not peace; it would arouse sympathy for Germany all over the world; it would destroy resources desperately needed for the reconstruction of Europe."

Morgenthau was hopeful that the president's hints would lead to a summons to the summit, but he was not counting on it. He had his staff prepare a "Black Book" for the president, containing three memoranda for handy reference. One was on German and British problems. Another was designed to prove that "the British could supply all the coal for coking purposes if we lose the coal mines in the Ruhr." And, finally, a succinct statement of his plan for postwar Germany.

The third memorandum, titled "Program to Prevent Germany from Starting World War III," was a concise statement of what would soon see the light of day as "The Morgenthau Plan," a spare, fourteen-point outline, just over three typewritten pages long. Prepared by Harry White to Morgenthau's specifications, it was more harshly explicit than White himself wanted. The provisions for the total destruction of the Ruhr were incorporated over his objections, as were certain suggestions that Roosevelt himself had insisted on. Edward Bernstein recalled White urging Morgenthau to be at least "a little vague" about his intentions for the Ruhr. But Morgenthau stuck to his intransigence. "I'm not going to budge an inch," he told his staff. "I don't know any other way than going to the heart of the thing which is the Ruhr . . . I can be overruled by the President, but nobody else is going to overrule me." At this point Morgenthau appeared to have the president completely sold on his plan.

Boiled down to its dispassionate essence, the memo, which the president took with him to Quebec, started with a call for "the complete demilitarization of Germany in the shortest possible time." The intention was not only to remove the weapons but also to dismantle or destroy all industrial equipment that could contribute to military strength, directly or indirectly.

Next came a proposed geographic dismemberment of the German state. "Poland should get that part of East Prussia which doesn't go to the USSR and the southern portion of Silesia." France was to get the Saar and the territory between the Rhine and Moselle rivers. The Ruhr and surrounding industrial areas would become an international zone. The remaining German territory would be partitioned between a northern, essentially Prussian, state and a southern state primarily including Bavaria, Württemberg, and Baden.

The separation of the greater Ruhr zone, to be governed by the United Nations, was the heart of the proposal. The intent was that the area "should not only be stripped of all its presently existing industries but so weakened and controlled that it could not in the foreseeable future become an industrial area." No more than six months after the cessation of hostilities all remaining plants and equipment were to be "completely dismantled and transported to Allied nations as restitution." All the mines were to be closed, with equipment removed. Thus, "restitution and reparation" were to be effected through "the transfer of existing German resources and territories" and *not* in the form of "future payments and deliveries." The unstated intent was to eliminate the incentive to foster German production as the means of reparations.

In addition to tapping existing resources and territories, Morgenthau proposed that restitution and reparation be made through the use of forced German labor outside the Reich. The entire German education system and media were to be completely closed down. Elementary schools would be reopened "as quickly as appropriate teachers and textbooks are available," but institutions of higher learning would remain shut for "a considerable period of time." All radio stations, newspapers, and periodicals would be shut down until desirable programs and controls could be formulated, and all the "policy-making officials of the Reich" would be dismissed. A decentralized government would be encouraged to look toward eventual federation of the states (*Länder*). For a period of "at least twenty years after surrender the United Nations would control foreign trade and the international flow of capital."

Curiously, there is little in this document about what later became the hallmark of the plan — the reduction of Germany from an industrial to an agrarian economy, what Churchill termed the "pastoralization" of Germany. The only reference to that idea was the call for the breakup of the large estates to redistribute the land among peasant farmers.

The punishment of "certain war crimes" is briefly noted without specifics. Following this section were Roosevelt's dicta preventing Germans from wearing uniforms of any sort, banning military parades or bands, and forbidding the operation of aircraft of any sort, even gliders.

The document concluded by staking out a U.S. claim to "full military and civilian representation" on international commissions established for "the execution of the whole German program." But "under this program U.S. troops could be withdrawn within a relatively short time," leaving the primary responsibility for the policing and civil administration of Germany to the "military forces of Germany's continental neighbors."

· 34 ·

Summons to the Summit

O N THE MORNING of September 11 Roosevelt and Churchill met in Quebec for a second summit in that city to consider questions concerning the North Atlantic alliance. Though in private many old acquaintances, including Churchill and his physician, Lord Moran, would express grave concern about Roosevelt's dramatic weight loss, his wide, confident grin exuded the heartiness that the public had grown to expect. Mrs. Roosevelt had come along on the trip because she knew that Mrs. Churchill's presence made it desirable for her to be there as well. Having nothing to do beyond the demands of protocol, however, she felt trapped.

Churchill too was in poor health. Just before departure he had been running a temperature of 103 degrees and was obliged to consider canceling the rendezvous, but with the American presidential election less than two months away he realized that a postponement was out of the question.

"Elinor dearest," Eleanor Roosevelt wrote my mother on stationery embossed with the Citadel crest, "the ladies' duties here are all social and it would be boring except for the meals with a few people when the PM and F are entertaining. I like Mrs. Churchill and Princess Alice,* but I don't grow intimate quickly."

In order to obscure the true nature of *Octagon,* spokesmen told the press that the discussions were exclusively concerned with military matters, particularly the war in the Pacific and Asia, and so the highest-ranking uniformed personages were put on display. Roose-

---

*Princess Alice, granddaughter of Queen Victoria, was the wife of the Earl of Athlone, Canadian governor general.

velt and Churchill posed for pictures on the terrace of the Citadel with ten generals, field marshals, and admirals. The Americans included General George C. Marshall, chairman of the Joint Chiefs of Staff; Admiral Ernest J. King and General Henry H. ("Hap") Arnold, the top-ranking naval and air force officers, respectively; and Admiral William D. Leahy, the president's military chief of staff. Later on, when first Morgenthau and then British Foreign Minister Anthony Eden arrived in Quebec, their presence was given low-key newspaper coverage, without photographs. The president's press secretary, Steve Early, issued a vague communiqué that Morgenthau was coming to Quebec "to study economic problems affecting the United States and economic conditions throughout the world."

Grace Tully, FDR's personal secretary, remembers receiving "a call at the Citadel from the Secretary of the Treasury in Washington asking me to inquire of the President whether he could come to see him. The answer being yes Morgenthau arrived the next day."

Morgenthau was thrilled. It was the first time in his career that he had been asked to participate in a meeting of heads of state. On September 12, the day after Roosevelt arrived in Canada, the president made the summons official with a cable: PLEASE BE IN QUEBEC BY THURSDAY, SEPTEMBER 14TH NOON ROOSEVELT. As things turned out, Morgenthau would be the only cabinet-level adviser present. It was dizzying and not altogether enviable exposure. Hull, despite having turned down several Roosevelt overtures, was peeved by the Morgenthau alternative. Stimson hoped Roosevelt would reject Morgenthau's "very dangerous advice."

Harry Hopkins, who had chaired the cabinet committee on Germany through its contentious sessions, would have been the logical person for the president to take with him to Quebec. He had been become the adviser Roosevelt relied on most heavily, after the death of Louis Howe, often sending him on missions to serve as his alter ego. Hopkins took up residence in the White House in 1940 and remained for three and a half years. Robert Sherwood, Hopkins's biographer, noted that at this time his relationship with the president had cooled. But Sherwood also recognized other factors that help explain why Hopkins was left behind. He and Winston Churchill, opposites in background and personality, had been strongly attracted to each other. Over the years when Hopkins served as presidential emissary, he and Churchill formed a bond of mutual affection and esteem which led Roosevelt to mistrust Hopkins's impartiality in any matter involving the charismatic British prime minister. Furthermore, Roosevelt, as candidate for a fourth term, wanted to keep Hopkins, the prime target for attack on New Deal ultraliberalism, out of the limelight until after the November election. Finally, there was something that may have been most disturbing of all to Roosevelt. Though he never spoke of his own increasingly poor health, it seemed to depress him to have ailing people around him. Harry was not only a very ill man, but his brown, tobacco-stained lips, teeth, and fingers, his pallor, and his rumpled, cadaverous appearance were an uncomfortable reminder of the physical limits of fellow mortals under stress. The time had come, with victory close at hand, when the men who had worked the hardest behind the lines were showing the physical and emotional strains of battle. Those close to Roosevelt and Churchill took note of their two leaders' condition with increasing apprehension. There were ever more frequent comments in Morgenthau's presidential diaries on his boss's poor health and fatigue, though Morgenthau usually seemed too absorbed in his own mission of the moment to appreciate the full gravity of the signs before his eyes.

On October 13 Morgenthau flew to Quebec, accompanied only by Harry White. From September 13 to 15 White wrote a series of memoranda "for the Secretary's files" in which he described much that took place and quoted from the conversations. In most instances White himself was present. To cover occasions when he was not, Morgenthau took pains to recall what had occurred for him to record.

Shortly after Morgenthau's arrival Mrs. Roosevelt invited him for tea. Grace Tully greeted him and said "the boss" wanted to see him. As he was ushered into the president's suite, FDR commanded his Scottish terrier, Fala, to "say hello to your Uncle Henry." Morgenthau was heartened by Roosevelt's warmth.

"I have asked you to come up so that you could talk to 'the Prof,'" Roosevelt announced, referring to Lord Cherwell, a professor of physics at Oxford University who had become Churchill's "one man brain trust" and influential confidant. Churchill "had been very glum," the president told Morgenthau, until asked if he would "like to have the steel business of Europe for 20 or 30 years." Thereupon he perked up and seemed "much excited over the possibility." The president went on to explain that in the evening at dinner they were scheduled to discuss shipping but added, "You might as well come too." Morgenthau asked how freely he could talk with Cherwell.

"You can talk about anything you want."

"Anything?"

"I wouldn't discuss with him the question of the zones to be occupied by our armies," Roosevelt replied. "That's a military question. Nor would I discuss the question of partitioning as that's a political question. But you can talk about the fact that we are thinking of internationalizing the Ruhr and the Saar, including the Kiel Canal. If Holland has a lot of land inundated by Germany we can give her a piece of Western Germany as compensation."

The president kept referring to "the book" Morgenthau had prepared for him. After going over the section on Germany item by item he remarked, "I have sent for Eden. Churchill, Eden, yourself and I will sit down to discuss the matter." Roosevelt had sent for Eden largely because Morgenthau had reported after his meeting with the foreign minister in London in August that Eden was an advocate of the same "tough" policy for Germany that he wanted (a complete misreading of Eden's true position.) "Don't worry about Churchill," the president continued. "He is going to be tough [on Germany] too."

At 8:00 that evening Morgenthau (without Harry White) sat down at a round table for a stag dinner in the Citadel with the president and the prime minister. Others who attended were Lord Cherwell; Admiral William Leahy; the president's physician, Admiral Ross McIntire; the prime minister's physician, Lord Moran; and two men who had been invited as authorities on shipping: Lord Leathers, the British minister of war transport; and Admiral Emory S. Land, the chief of the U.S. Maritime Commission.

Shipping, supposedly the evening's topic of discussion, was hardly mentioned. When the president turned to the prime minister to explain that he had invited Secretary Morgenthau to come to Quebec to talk about Germany, and that he was scheduled to begin with Lord Cherwell the next day, Churchill asked, "Why don't we talk about Germany now?" Thereupon the president told Morgenthau to explain what he had in mind. When Morgenthau began to lay out the plan for the destruction of the Ruhr, it was apparent that Churchill was in a foul mood and very much opposed to Morgenthau's proposals, growling that they were "unnatural, un-Christian and unnecessary." Churchill lit into all the Morgenthau arguments, including the advantages to Britain of taking over German markets.

The president said very little. Morgenthau interpreted this silence "as part of his way of managing Churchill. He let the Prime Minister wear himself out attacking me; he used me, so to speak, to draw the venom." Knowing what he was in for didn't make the tirade any easier to take. "It is quite an experience to be on the receiving end of one of Churchill's blasts . . . his language biting, his flow incessant, his manner merciless. I have never had such a verbal lashing in my life."

Churchill looked on the Treasury plan, Morgenthau said, as he would "on chaining himself to a dead German." The prime minister pointed out that "there were bonds between the working classes of all countries." The English people "will not stand for a policy which prevents Germans from living decently. I agree with Burke," he submitted. "You cannot indict a whole nation . . . At any rate what is to be done should be done quickly. Kill the criminals, but don't carry on the business for years."

The conversation around the dinner table continued for three hours. When it strayed to India and other topics, Roosevelt steered it back to Germany with deft good humor. He reminded Churchill that at Teheran Stalin had said, "Are you going to let Germany produce metal furniture? The manufacture of metal furniture can be quickly turned into the manufacture of armament." At one point Churchill demanded, "Is this what you asked me to come all the way over here to discuss?" During the course of debate Morgenthau received little support from any of the other dinner guests, with one conspicuous exception. Among the Americans, only Admiral Land spoke out on his side, and then only perfunctorily. Admiral Leahy was unsympathetic, as was the British minister of war transport, Lord Leathers. But Lord Cherwell stood up against the prime minister with cool arrogance.

Late in the evening Roosevelt wound things down, saying, "Let the Prof go into our plans with Morgenthau in the morning." Cherwell said that he wanted to talk about Lend-Lease, Phase II. Morgenthau answered that the president had summoned him to talk about Lend-Lease "after they had had the conversation about Germany." Later some would claim that Morgenthau had blackmailed Britain into supporting the Morgenthau Plan with a $6 billion Phase II program.

Wednesday, September 13, had been a long day for the secretary.

He had risen early on his farm in Dutchess County to fly to Quebec, where he was greeted cordially first by Eleanor and then by Franklin Roosevelt as an old friend. He had looked forward to a reunion with Churchill, whom he greatly admired. But when he retired late that evening he recalled that he had "never seen him more irascible and vitriolic than he was that night . . . I went unhappily to bed and spent a sleepless night."

The next morning at ten Morgenthau sat down with Lord Cherwell. Like Churchill, Cherwell had an American mother. He was born in Baden-Baden, where she had gone to take the cure. His father came from Alsace. Tall, skinny, balding, with a mustache, Cherwell was a stereotypic upper-class university man. When Morgenthau learned that he would be dealing with Cherwell, he asked (via his Treasury office in Washington) his wife's cousin, Arthur Goodhart, professor of jurisprudence at Oxford, what he thought of Cherwell. Word came back that "Arthur likes him personally but says he is not popular at Oxford because he is more interested in politics than scientific work . . . is strong conservative and has individual influence but not popular generally."

That Thursday morning the secretary had Harry White at his side. Cherwell was accompanied by two British civil servants. As the meeting commenced, Cherwell suggested that by transferring German markets to the British, England could be saved from bankruptcy. However, before pinning down an agreement on Germany, he wanted to set the terms for Lend-Lease, Phase II,* which, all agreed, should be deferred to a joint Anglo-American committee. After the morning session Cherwell and Morgenthau went off to meet with the prime minister and the president. At this session Morgenthau discovered that Cherwell had already effected a "sharp right-about turn" in the prime minister's thinking. The previous evening's hostility toward the Morgenthau Plan had been replaced by an equally vehement commitment to accepting it. When someone said the plan wouldn't work, Churchill snapped back, "Why shouldn't it work? I have no patience with people who are always raising difficulties."

*Lend-Lease, Phase II, was planned in anticipation of victory in Europe, to continue U.S. financial aid to Great Britain during the period between then and the end of the war with Japan. The British hoped the U.S. would be generous in easing their war-induced economic distress. Morgenthau, who was among the most sympathetic to the British plight, was faced with strong pressure in the U.S. for retrenchment.

Lord Moran, dismayed by his patient's complete change of heart, later blamed it on Lord Cherwell, "a very clever man," who had "learnt a good deal about Winston's mental process." He had a way of simplifying complex questions, reducing them to graphs and explaining them with "that quiet confident air that he was right." To Churchill, who was deeply concerned about Britain's finances, it suddenly seemed obvious that "if Germany were left without industries Britain must step into her shoes."

Churchill also feared that during the period between the defeat of Germany and a possibly prolonged demise of the Japanese, U.S. assistance to the British would be perilously scaled back. He accepted the proposal for a joint U.K.-U.S. committee. He suggested his old friend Harry Hopkins rather than Morgenthau as chairman, but later took no exception to Roosevelt's choice of Morgenthau. A memorandum setting up the committee was before them. Churchill was "nervous and eager" to have it initialed. FDR delayed by "interrupting with stories." Impatient to get on with it, Churchill burst out angrily, "What do you want me to do? Get on my hind legs and beg like Fala?"

After the Thursday meeting Cherwell drafted a memo for Churchill summarizing the conversations. But it didn't satisfy Morgenthau. "It's two steps backwards," he declared. Surprised and delighted by the prime minister's overnight conversion, the secretary thought "they ought to begin where Churchill left off and go forward." He had already spoken of "diverting [*sic*] Germany to an agricultural state as she was in the last quarter of the 19th century."

When they all met again on Friday, Churchill asked for the minutes of the previous day's session. Morgenthau, who thought they presented "much too weak a case," said there weren't any minutes. When Churchill "seemed quite put out" by this, Roosevelt quipped that the reason they had no minutes was that "Henry had interspersed . . . too many dirty jokes." Churchill then restated his case very "forcefully" and "clearly," to Morgenthau's way of thinking, and asked Morgenthau and Cherwell "to withdraw and try to put their ideas down in writing." Morgenthau recalled, "It only took us a few minutes, and we came back up to the room where they were meeting and just calmly walked in." When Churchill read their very short redrafted memorandum he snapped, "No, this isn't what I want," and started to dictate.

"I don't know what the rules of the game are," Morgenthau

queried, "but is there any reason why we can't have a stenographer present, then you could dictate directly to her?"

"By all means," Churchill replied.

Cherwell then went to find Churchill's secretary. Morgenthau noted that Churchill "dictates extremely well because he is accustomed to doing it when he writes his books . . . He used the memorandum which I had dictated as a sort of text."

The final memo stood just as Churchill dictated it that Friday afternoon. Roosevelt's principal contribution was to insist on the words *in Germany* in reference to safeguards against reconversion of industries from peace to war production. Morgenthau thought this was "terribly important" because Roosevelt wanted to make it clear that "he didn't have just the Ruhr and the Saar in mind but . . . entire Germany."

The Churchill memorandum set off one of the hottest international controversies at the end of the war. Four short paragraphs outlined the concept of a pastoral Germany: "The program for eliminating the war-making industries in the Ruhr and the Saar is looking forward to converting Germany into a country primarily agricultural and *pastoral* in character."

Anthony Eden, who arrived at the last moment, just in time to witness the prime minister's dictation, "seemed quite shocked at what he heard." "You can't do this," he protested. "After all you and I publicly have said quite the opposite."

Churchill's main point was that Britain would pick up Germany's export trade.

"How," Eden asked, "do you know what or where it is?"

"Well," Churchill answered testily, "we will get it wherever it is. Now I hope, Anthony, you're not going to do anything about this with the War Cabinet. After all the future of my people is at stake, and when I have to choose between my people and the German people, I am going to choose my people."

During the squabble Roosevelt remained silent. Morgenthau involved himself "in a small way," later noting that he "kept throwing things in." Ironically, Eden's presence served Morgenthau's purpose, for, as Eden fought against Churchill's newfound position, he triggered the prime minister's resolute stubbornness.

That very day, Friday, September 15, Roosevelt accepted the Churchill memo on Germany, signing it "OK. FDR." Churchill added his "W.S.C. 15 9."

Morgenthau was overjoyed. "Of course," he confided to his diary, "the fact that Churchill has dictated this himself strengthens the whole matter tremendously. Naturally, I am terrifically happy over it as we got just what we started out to get."

The next evening Roosevelt sent for Morgenthau again. Several times Morgenthau "tried to get up to go because I thought the President wanted to rest, but he evidently just wanted to sit and talk. We haven't had a talk like this since almost going back to the time when he was governor. He was completely relaxed and the conversation was entirely on the week's work." In the course of this long, rambling entry in his diary my father noted several times that Roosevelt seemed "not at all tired," as though trying to reassure himself against his anxieties as he looked closely at his old friend's increasing frailness.

After Quebec the Churchills accompanied the Roosevelts to Poughkeepsie, as their guests at Hyde Park. Morgenthau rode with them and went to his farm. On Sunday afternoon the prime minister and the president came to call on the Morgenthaus in Fishkill. They had tea on the open west portico facing the afternoon sun. Later, while Roosevelt watched from his chair, the others strolled under the huge oak tree back of the house. Then they were all given a tour of the orchards, the trees laden with apples, ripe for picking.

Returning to Washington from Dutchess County, Morgenthau was elated by his Quebec triumph. Reporting to his staff, he said that things at Quebec had been "unbelievably good. . . . It was the high spot of my entire career in government."

Hull and Stimson were as appalled by the turn of events as Eden had been. For Hull, it was as usual largely a matter of personal pique. For Stimson, it was a matter of principle rather than personality. Morgenthau had informed him immediately — "modestly and without rubbing it in," Stimson noted in his diary. "But it was the narration of a pretty heavy defeat for everything we had fought for." He was contemptuous of the two men Churchill and Roosevelt had so ill-advisedly selected as their aides at a most critical moment. As Stimson worried during the weekend, a "heavy cloud seemed to have settled over my head." It was terrible "to think that the total power of the United States and the United Kingdom . . . is in the hands of two men, both of whom are similar in their impulsiveness and their lack of systematic study." In his estimation, Cherwell was "an old fool . . . who had loudly proclaimed that we could never cross the Channel and . . . the robots [V-1 and V-12 "buzz bomb" rockets] could never do any damage. He is a pseudo scientist . . . for whose attainments nobody has much respect." Morgenthau fared hardly better. Stimson felt that he was witnessing the realization of the "'Carthaginian' attitude of the Treasury. It is semitism gone wild for vengeance and, if it is ultimately carried out (I cannot believe that it will be), it as sure as fate will lay the seeds for another war in the next generation."

With a good deal of assistance from McCloy, Stimson prepared yet another memo for the president. Though he despaired of its having any influence, he "wanted our record to be complete." They pitched their argument "on a higher level than anything that had before been written." The paper was designed as an appeal to Franklin Roosevelt, "the farsighted and greatly humanitarian President of the United States." It cited the language of the Atlantic Charter that "victors and vanquished alike are entitled to freedom from economic want." It concluded that "the sum total of the drastic political and economic steps proposed by the Treasury is an open confession of the bankruptcy of hope for a reasonable economic and political settlement of the causes of war."

Harry Hopkins carried this memo to the president at Hyde Park. Stimson received word that Roosevelt had read it and wanted to talk to him about it. "I hope this is a good symptom, but I dare not be too sure" he noted in his diary. Roosevelt had indeed been moved by the message and its moderate language. At the same time, though, something else was happening that had a great deal more to do with the president's reconsideration of his stance on postwar Germany.

Roosevelt was compelled to focus on his fourth-term presidential race against Governor Thomas E. Dewey of New York. Unlike the third-term campaign, when the Republican candidate, Wendell Willkie, had been taken seriously, this time Roosevelt's victory was considered inevitable, based on a consensus that it was important for him to stay in control until the end of the war. Nevertheless, the press, which on the whole had little love for Roosevelt and even less for Morgenthau, was looking for an issue, as was Governor Dewey.

As news of the rift within the cabinet over the Morgenthau Plan began to leak out, the press played it up. Stories tended to focus on the opposing points of view championed by Morgenthau and Stimson. The *Washington Post* published a Drew Pearson column favorable to Morgenthau and mentioning Roosevelt's harsh criticism of the *Handbook*. This story seemed to have leaked from a Treasury source, though Morgenthau tried to track it down without success.

Whatever the source and intention of the story, it served to set off a preponderantly negative reaction, linking — indeed blaming — Roosevelt along with Morgenthau for deviating from what was held to be the wiser and more appropriate position of the War and State Departments. By this time Hull had wholly realigned himself with Stimson. Arthur Krock, the influential *New York Times* columnist, a Roosevelt-hater friendly to Hull, published his version of the story on September 22. The following day the details of the Morgenthau Plan appeared in a damning *Wall Street Journal* article.

Immediately after the president felt the chilling draft of press criticism, the Roosevelt retreat from *Octagon* got under way. On September 29 he dissolved the three-member cabinet committee. That same day he told Hull privately, "No one wants complete eradication of German industrial productive capacity in the Ruhr and Saar."

Prompted by this news, Morgenthau marched across the street to the White House. The president's daughter, Anna Boettiger, was standing guard. "'I think he ought to get Hull, Stimson and me together . . . and tell us to stop talking,'" Morgenthau told Anna. The uproar in the press "'is bad politically and it is bad by inference on the Jewish angle. . . . I will stay here outside the President's door in case he should want to see me.'"

Anna went in to see her father and came out a couple of minutes later. "'All I know is that the President definitely doesn't want to see you,'" she told him. "Then she put her hand on my arm and sort of gently but forcibly started to move me toward the elevator."

The news coverage eventually took on disturbing implications — specifically that the Morgenthau Plan represented Jewish vengeance — and the notion that at Quebec Morgenthau had bought Winston Churchill's approval with a guarantee of a $6 billion loan for Lend-Lease, Phase II. Although these stories and speeches had absolutely no effect on the outcome of the election, they definitely made Roosevelt, who hated this kind of politicized controversy, distance himself from the Morgenthau program. Having already dissolved the cabinet committee on German policy, he dealt directly and separately with the opposing cabinet members.

At the same time, Churchill, under severe pressure from his own cabinet, repudiated his approval of the document that he himself had dictated at Quebec.

All the nasty public allegations were privately excruciatingly painful to my father. What hurt deep down to the father of two sons on active duty were the stories that the Morgenthau Plan was motivating the Germans to stay in the war. Governor Dewey struck the lowest blow of all when, in his wind-up speech the night before the election, he held that publishing the Morgenthau Plan had done as much good as ten fresh German divisions.

Father and Son at War

A FTER MY VISIT with my father at General Bradley's head-
quarter in Normandy in August 1944, I returned to duty
with my platoon at General Eisenhower's so-called forward
CP in Reims. There was virtually nothing for any of us to do there.
The next two months constituted the most unhappy time I spent in
the army. Then in October, I was able to determine the exact
whereabouts of the Second Cavalry and was granted permission
from SHAEF to visit. I reported to our Second Squadron CO
Lieutenant Colonel Walter Easton. He told me that there was a
Second Squadron first lieutenant who had succumbed to the strain
of battle and was absolutely of no use to the unit. Easton would be
happy to exchange him for me if I could arrange it with SHAEF.
This I managed to do. Not long after my return, the lieutenant who
replaced me and the entire platoon were sent back to our unit on the
grounds that they were no longer required at SHAEF. This strongly
reinforced my suspicion that the whole maneuver had been engineered by my father for my protection.

From the fall of 1944 until mid-December, when the Second
Cavalry became involved in the Battle of the Bulge, we advanced
rapidly against only minor resistance, though we did have many
small engagements with the enemy.

On the evening of December 22, Colonel Reed reported to the
Twelfth Corps advance CP at Luxembourg where he received orders for the Second Cavalry Group to move out at 0700 the next
morning. At the time we were still patrolling and guarding bridges
at Sarreguemines, as the Third Army was making rapid advances
into the Saar. Some rumors of the disaster to the north had filtered

through to us, but as we were completely absorbed in the frantic business of gathering our men and equipment for the move, there was no time to ponder over where or why we were going.

In the predawn black of December 23, it was so cold that we had to use blowtorches to loosen up the tracks on the tanks and half-tracks. Chow lines for an early hot breakfast formed behind the mess trucks, which were packed up ready to go. When we moved out at seven it was still dark. Standing in the open turret of my armored car, with a knitted wool scarf wrapped around my face, I rolled out on the road heading back west toward Metz, along with the rest of our outfit. The hurried move had us almost sweating, but as we stood in our cold, iron vehicles, the damp chill penetrated to the bone. At Metz troops were converging from all directions, heading north toward Luxembourg: Sherman tanks, troop-carrier vans, and rolling artillery. MPs were frantically waving us on, somehow avoiding a mammoth traffic jam. In any town where we slowed up, women rushed out with hot coffee, which a lucky few would manage to grab.

During combat one seldom sees or hears very much beyond one's own small unit. Now, as the clanking, roaring mass of troop-carrying vehicles barreled through Metz (bearing battle scars from two World Wars), it was a war scene resembling those in the movies. As we moved steadily along the road toward Thionville, the halts were so brief and uncertain there was hardly time to get out to urinate. Then, as we pulled up a long hill, the heavy clouds broke. Almost immediately we heard a droning crescendo as the sky filled with our bombers. You could see the bombs dropping and hear the thud of their explosion. Too close for comfort, it seemed as if they were going to bomb us. But then it was over, with nothing left but the vapor trails in the sunny sky. Although we didn't know it, this sudden liberation of our great air force lent critical major support to our advance on the ground.

By nightfall we had arrived at our designated bivouac on the vulnerable side of Luxembourg. Here the expanded Second Cavalry Group, heavily reinforced by tank destroyers, engineers, and field artillery, became Task Force Reed. Our mission was to protect the right flank of the Third Army, which was advancing to free the First Army units trapped in Bastogne. As we came to know it, it was the Battle of the Bulge. The whole operation had proceeded through the snow with unbelievable speed, exactly according to plan. A week later General von Rundstedt's offensive dragged to a halt, never to regain momentum. General Omar Bradley held that "Patton's brilliant shift of the Third Army from its bridgehead in the Saar to the snow covered Ardennes front became one of the most astonishing feats of generalship of our campaign in the West."

By December 24 the frantic northward dash was over. The Second Cavalry settled into relatively comfortable billets in barns and houses in the evacuated villages that nestled in the Moselle valley. The mountainous area to the north is known as little Switzerland, but all of Luxembourg has the same diminutive, picturesque charm. As the sudden break in the leaden skies held, the frozen snow sparkled in the brilliant sunlight, and everyone's mood lifted. "Hey, lieutenant," my South Carolinian jeep driver drawled. "This kind of shit would look good on a Christmas card."

The day after Christmas, von Rundstedt's main advance to the north ground to a standstill. The tide had turned. From the Second Cavalry outposts concealed in villages on the edge of the Moselle River, one could look "smack into German held territory and . . . see 'Heinies' crawling around against the white snow background." We frequently sent out patrols to gather information and if possible capture prisoners. The patrols set out at night in inflated rubber boats made to carry four men. Fashioned like wide, squared-off canoes, they were propelled by two men paddling furiously at bow and stern against the strong current. On one bright moonlit night an OSS team (Office of Strategic Services) showed up at our squadron CP, prepared to reconnoiter across the Moselle deep into enemy territory. They were outfitted as German soldiers. I escorted them down to the B Troop CP on the riverbank where they planned to go across. I had recently been there on a number of occasions, observing how our patrols launched their rubber boats and took off. A fearless young trooper named Burke always seemed to be literally dancing on the gleaming white, frozen snow while waiting to move out on patrol. He had gained a reputation for bravery that he was compelled to live up to. I had quizzed him on how he handled these operations. He made it appear at once exciting and simple. Ferrying the OSS men across the Moselle and coming right back seemed easy enough; as a youngster I had become adept at maneuvering canoes and Adirondack mountain guide boats. I was also a strong swimmer.

I asked the B Troop commander, Captain Bob Langley, for

permission to take off with Burke. This was a routine assignment for B troopers. Langley had frequently led patrols himself, but volunteers were gratefully accepted. Burke and I shoved off with our OSS passengers. Channeled in the partially frozen river, the current was stronger than I had anticipated. We started to slip rapidly downstream sideways until Burke and I synchronized our forward and back paddling strokes. Soon we began to make head-way while still slipping a bit. In a matter of minutes we dragged the boat up on the far bank. Our passengers got out and immediately disappeared into the night. That was my first foothold on German soil, but not for long. We headed back across the river immediately, having the good luck not to attract enemy attention. I don't recall any verbal exchange with the OSS men during the entire operation. I never saw them again. Bob Langley later told me that they managed to get back. I have no idea how.

Knowing that my father could and would yank me out to safety again if I gave him the faintest signal of assent was probably at the root of my compulsion to expose myself to danger. Driven by a belief that my privileged position generated resentment among my peers, I was constantly bent on proving myself, whereas my protected status, in fact, mattered little to them. GIs had a realistic sense of their powerlessness and were fatalistic about the kind of breaks they got. "I knew people who had staff jobs all the time we were overseas," Bob Langley recalled. "Our S-4 [supply officer] stayed back in Paris 'couchezing' with a French lady he was living it up with. Some people got to stay in a nice warm house. Some people got combat. It was all part of the game."

With political power, as with money or arms, it is difficult to possess it without using it. The secretary of the treasury, who perhaps had been more effective than any other American except his boss in spurring the Allies toward victory, was at times tempted to use his influence for the welfare of two sons in the service. His natural fatherly instincts and pride, moreover, were intensified by the anxieties of my seriously ailing mother, whose health was ravaged by a series of embolisms in 1944–45. To err on the side of protecting one's children is human. But to fail to exercise prudent restraint is asking for trouble.

It was quite natural for my father to turn to his top-echelon peers when he wanted to get something done, even in a private matter. He was following in the old family tradition, of going straight to the top when seeking a favor. Nevertheless he understood that at times he could achieve his goals more expeditiously by dealing with people he knew on a lower level. Thus he would also employ the good offices of Colonel Bernard Bernstein or the president's confidential secretary, Grace Tully. Still, there were moments of embarrassing overkill.

"Mother worries because she hasn't heard from Henry," my father wrote my brother and me. "Yesterday I told Mr. Stimson that Mother was worrying and asked him whether he couldn't find out about you, Henry, and he promised he would. I asked Mr. Forrestal (secretary of the navy) to do the same thing about Bob, and within three days he got me a message from Bob that you, Bob, were well and happy which, of course cheered us all up." A week later my father wrote that "through the courtesy of the Secretary of War" he had received word that I was well "and that was the best medicine that Mother had gotten in a long time because she had been worried, as was I, because we hadn't heard from you . . . I'm curious to know if you are conscious of the fact that the Secretary of War was checking up on your whereabouts, Henry. He was terribly nice about it, and seemed pleased that he was able to locate you promptly."

I responded, "With your high level briefing you probably know a hell of a lot more about what I'm doing than I do." Though I wasn't directly aware of these probes I was worried that he was again planning to have me transferred to some safe desk job behind the lines.

My father's principal on-the-spot agent in the European theater of operations was Colonel Bernard Bernstein, the devoted Treasury hand, who had been commissioned in the army as a financial adviser to General Eisenhower, serving first in North Africa and then at SHAEF. Bernie was a brilliant lawyer and an intensely loyal friend of my father.

"I think you may see Bernie in the not-too-distant future," my father wrote me. "I also gave your address to Judge Sam Rosenman, who is going over on a mission to France and Belgium for the President, and expects to go to the front, but I cautioned Judge Rosenman, particularly, not to send for you or in any way do anything that might embarrass you."

Bernie did visit me on a number of occasions, sometimes acting as courier for an exchange of letters and gifts. On one such visit while I was on detached service with SHAEF at Reims, an associate of Bernie's, Commander Joel Fisher★ (another able Treasury lawyer in uniform), facilitated the shipment of two cases of magnums of Pommeroy Greno 1929 champagne from me: one for my parents, the other for President and Mrs. Roosevelt. In a birthday letter to my mother, February 6, 1945, I reported that "I received — much to my surprise, and with great pride — a letter from FDR thanking me for the champagne and telling me of New Year's eve spent with you and Daddy."

I wrote to my parents on February 24 that Bernie had come to see me in the city of Luxembourg. He brought me some Grand Marnier brandy, red caviar, and captain's bars [I had just received my promotion]. After rambling on at some length, I zeroed in on my true concerns. Bernie had "spent some time trying to interest me in G-5 [military government] work; transferring into something in that line. I hope he doesn't take it upon himself to do something about it. After all I went to enough trouble getting out of SHAEF without getting back in right away.

"First of all, I am satisfied to stay where I am.

"Secondly, after personally witnessing the tremendous waste of manpower and expenditures that exist at SHAEF, I would hate to have to identify myself with such an organization."

"Henry," my father replied on March 9, "I got your letter after the visit from Bernie, in which you said you hoped he wouldn't do anything about trying to get you transferred from your outfit to the Military Government Branch of the Army, in view of your experience, when along came a letter from Bernie saying how he'd had a nice visit with you, and how you had told him you wanted to be left alone for the next several months. Then he said that riding home in the car, he decided that he was going to have you transferred anyway."

Quietly, but firmly, I seemed to have succeeded in scoring my point this time. "I was very much disturbed," my father continued. "I talked it over with Mother, and decided that we just had to do something to stop Bernie from carrying out this plan of his. So I got hold of our man Taylor [William H. Taylor, the Treasury's representative on the Combined Civil Affairs Committee in Lon-

---

★All of the men who visited me in the ETO at my father's request — Colonel Bernstein, Sam Rosenman, Joel Fisher, and Isadore Lubin — happened to be Jewish.

don] and told him to tell Bernie not to do anything. Then I also asked Mr. McCloy to get word to Bernie, which he did by phone, and asked him not to do anything. So I think we've stopped Bernie in his tracks."

In this case my father slammed the entire official machinery into reverse. He didn't hesitate to use the full force of his influence to block an action he'd probably endorsed. While he felt that "Bernie's motive was good," he took the position that Bernie had "no business asking for your transfer when you made it so plain that you wanted to be left with your own outfit. . . . Mother and I feel so strongly about how fine your attitude has been, and we don't want anybody to step in and spoil it, and we want you to know that whatever your wishes are as to your present and future plans, we will back you up 100%. We are both very proud of you, and we don't want anybody interfering with your present Army life. Certainly we haven't tried to interfere, and we don't want anybody else to."

Bernie Bernstein remained a good family friend over the years. I spoke to him shortly before his death in 1990 about this incident. He recalled that he laid out his strategy for my transfer while dining with my parents in Washington. They listened without comment, which he interpreted as giving their consent.

Death and Transfiguration

THE SENTIMENT against the Morgenthau Plan when Roosevelt was elected president for the fourth time turned out to be a definitive turning of the tide. Yet for Morgenthau this major shift in the balance of opinion seemed like just another temporary aberration. His personal clout within the administration had never been stronger. However far he had strayed off Treasury turf, he had earned general respect by having fulfilled his primary responsibility, financing the war, with stunning success. As he prepared to mount a seventh war bond drive, he could look back on a record of raising unprecedented sums. He had enjoyed the cooperation of patriotic citizens, industry, labor, and even, grudgingly, Wall Street. No one was more delighted with Morgenthau's success than FDR, who had gambled on his "favorite farmer," untutored in the ways of high finance, uneasy in the limelight, and won, while "Henry the Morgue" remained gloomily unsure of himself and uncertain as to where he stood with Roosevelt. By 1945 the ailing president became ever more dependent on those surviving old stalwarts. If he was evasive as he wearied of Morgenthau's obsession with Germany's destruction, his door was still open for his old friend.

When a sick and disgruntled Hull finally bowed out of the State Department, Morgenthau was an influential supporter of his replacement, Edward Stettinius. He thought Stettinius rather weak but probably as much secretary of state as Roosevelt could stomach while intending as always to manage foreign affairs himself. "What he wanted was merely a good clerk." Stettinius disapproved of the Morgenthau Plan, but the two men handled their differences with the utmost civility. However, Morgenthau's main reason for backing

Stettinius was his opposition to two of the other chief contenders, Jimmy Byrnes and Henry Wallace. Morgenthau strenuously opposed Byrnes, stating that if he were appointed "it would only be a matter of a couple of months before I would want to get out."

At the time, Henry Wallace, who had been dropped as vice president, was looking for a job. Morgenthau thought him unsuitable for the foreign portfolio but vigorously supported him when he was appointed secretary of commerce. Wallace almost didn't make it through the Senate confirmation proceedings; his opposition held that he was a fuzzy-minded liberal. But Wallace was the essence of New Deal idealism to Morgenthau, who believed that Wallace's defeat would enfeeble the fourth Roosevelt administration.

After the Battle of the Bulge in December 1944, the Allied victory in Europe seemed to be inevitable, although the war in Asia dragged on endlessly. As the armies of Generalissimo Chiang Kai-shek crumbled under his corrupt administration, the Japanese strengthened their stand on mainland China. Contrary to his involvement in Western affairs, however, Morgenthau knew little about the turmoil in the East. During Mme. Chiang's visits to the United States, he had been put off by several petty incidents that he interpreted as tokens of her selfish arrogance, reflecting the spirit of her husband's regime. But the suave charm of T. V. Soong (Mme. Chiang's brother), serving as ambassador to the United States and later as president of China, had turned his thoughts back around. Against the insistent warning of Harry White and White's assistant, Frank Coe, that American gold shipments would disappear down the Chinese rat hole, Morgenthau continued to advocate generous financial and commodity aid to China. White was aware of — and was sympathetic to — the Chinese Communists' growing strength. Whatever the ideological basis of his assessments, they also happened to be correct.

At Quebec, Roosevelt had named Morgenthau to lead the American team working out negotiations for Lend-Lease, Phase II with the British. Lord Keynes, heading the British delegation, was apprehensive that his own disparagement of the Morgenthau Plan would embitter his old friend "Morgy." He turned out to be wrong, for Morgenthau was convinced that bolstering Britain was indeed an important facet of his plan to counteract the revival of a strong Germany. Ultimately, although Keynes didn't get as much American commitment of aid as he wanted, he got far more than he would have, had it not been for Morgenthau's effective leadership — and Keynes knew it.

Another strenuous battle that Secretary Morgenthau led at the onset of the fourth term was the fight for congressional approval of the Bretton Woods agreements. American bankers who had never accepted the idea of moving financial control from the hands of private interest to government institutions, sustained their powerful lobby, with Senator Robert Taft, intellectual and ideological leader of conservative Republicans, as kingpin of the opposition. When Harry White was called to testify at a Senate committee hearing, Taft pressed his questions. White, with his notorious arrogance, responded, "There is no use my trying to explain it to you, Senator, you wouldn't understand anyway." White's aides were appalled. Ultimately, Morgenthau himself managed to repair the damage, by-passing Taft to tap the reservoir of congressional good will he had established during the Bretton Woods sessions. But most of the leading bankers and the Federal Reserve directors remained intransigent. Ironically, they were unable to appreciate that the World Bank and especially the IMF could become the major bulwarks of international capitalism.

When Roosevelt went to meet Stalin and Churchill in Yalta at the end of January 1945, taking his new secretary of state, Stettinius, and Jimmy Byrnes with him, Morgenthau was the ranking cabinet member in Washington. At the last cabinet meeting before his departure Roosevelt announced that if anything happened (short of his death) in his absence he wanted Morgenthau to call the cabinet together. Referring to the time of President Wilson's illness in 1920, when Secretary of State Robert Lansing called a cabinet meeting without orders from his chief, who subsequently dismissed him, Roosevelt wanted to make his wishes clear. My father wrote to my brother and me that he hoped "the occasion will not arise because it does place considerable responsibility on my shoulders, but, frankly, it rather thrills me."

At about the same time, Morgenthau (with Roosevelt's approval) designated Harry White as an assistant secretary and submitted his name for Senate confirmation. Morgenthau was pleased to advance "people like Harry White who made good rather than political appointments." He had overridden the opposition of the Democratic party's national chairman, Bob Hannegan, who "tried to hold up White's appointment so that he could appoint a 'fat cat' who had made a large contribution." Hannegan had been Harry Truman's primary supporter for the vice presidency.

When Roosevelt returned from Yalta, Morgenthau noticed that he seemed "very tired" and had "lost a great deal of weight," although when he and Elinor shared a train ride from Washington to Hyde Park with Franklin and Eleanor, he found the president "very talkative, very friendly, and very informative."

On February 21, my parents were ecstatic about the arrival of their first grandchild, Bob and his wife Martha's daughter, Joan.

Bob had met Martha Pattridge while he was at Amherst and she was at Smith. During their junior year, Bob purchased a sporty little Buick hatchback with the thousand dollars Grandpa Morgenthau had given him for not smoking before he was twenty-one (supplemented with other twenty-first-birthday funds). That year the Buick was well exercised on the road between Amherst and Northampton. Martha was a tall, good-looking honey-blonde who shared his enjoyment of tennis and encouraged him in his ambitions. Martha had been reared in Minneapolis. Her parents were Protestants with family roots in Vermont. Everyone in our family loved Martha and soon took it for granted that she would join us.

In the midst of the war, Bob obtained a week's leave from the navy to marry Martha on December 30, 1943. The civil ceremony was performed by Uncle Irving Lehman, in his judicial capacity, in the New York townhouse he shared with his wife, Sissie (daughter of Nathan Straus). Uncle Irving officiated at all the mixed marriages in the family, though, as an observant Jew and president of Temple Emanu-El, he encouraged Jews to marry within their faith. But my parents accepted Martha on her own merits with enthusiasm.

I had managed to wangle a seventy-two-hour pass from my colonel in South Carolina, where I was then serving with the Second Cavalry. Bob had invited me to be his best man. Almost two decades later he returned the favor when I married Ruth Schachter at Brandeis University.

In spring 1944, a few months after he was married, Bob had yet another brush with death. He was then the executive officer of the destroyer *Landsdale,* which was on convoy duty in the Mediterranean, off the coast of North Africa. The convoy was attacked by German bombers, and the *Landsdale* was sunk. Bob was one of the fortunate men to be rescued.

With the advent of victory in Europe, Bob was assigned to

another destroyer on duty in the Pacific. "I enjoyed your letter, Bob," my father wrote in one of his letters addressed jointly to both his sons. "I read part of it to President Truman . . . about hoping that the Russians would come in so we could get their air bases . . . He was very much interested, as was I." Shortly thereafter Bob's destroyer was put in for repairs, and a miraculously unexploded Japanese bomb was found lodged in its hull. At the end of the war, Bob returned to the States, was separated from the navy, and was introduced to his daughter, Joan (Jenny), born while he was at sea.

During the first week of April 1945, while my parents were vacationing in Daytona Beach, Florida, my mother suffered what was diagnosed as a heart attack. It came seemingly without warning, though it was probably caused by one of those blood clots with which she was known to be afflicted. In this instance the clot had moved to the heart, causing considerable damage. My father wrote to my brother and me to assure us that Mother was expected to make an excellent recovery, but one could read his worry between the lines. In fact, Mother had been placed in an oxygen tent, for she was gravely ill.

On April 11, Mother was well enough for him to head back to Washington. In transit he arranged to stop off at Warm Springs, Georgia, to take dinner with the vacationing president. "I was terribly shocked when I saw him," he dictated in a long memo early the next morning. (Morgenthau arrived in Washington at 3:45 A.M., April 12, by plane. The memo, dated April 11, may have been recorded on the Ediphone machine in his house during the wee hours of the twelfth.) "His hands shook so that he started to knock the (cocktail) glasses over . . . I have never seen him have so much difficulty transferring himself from his wheelchair to his regular chair, and I was in agony watching him." He seemed, nevertheless, in a jovial mood.

In addition to my father there were four other guests at the dinner on April 11. On the host's right was his friend Lucy Mercer Rutherfurd. Also present were his cousin Laura (Polly) Delano, Margaret (Daisy) Suckley, an old Hyde Park friend, and Mme. Shoumatoff, an artist commissioned by Mrs. Rutherfurd to do a portrait of Franklin for her.

After dinner Morgenthau told Roosevelt what he intended to do about postwar Germany. Noting that Roosevelt "didn't answer me directly," he bulldozed ahead. "Look, Mr. President, I am going to fight hard, and this is what I'm fighting — a weak economy for Germany means that she will be weak politically, and she won't be able to make another war . . . I have been strong for winning the war, and I want to help win the peace." The president said, "Henry, I am with you 100 percent." Then, as though on cue, their dinner companions re-entered the room to break up the conversation. Morgenthau said goodbye to his old boss. It was the last time he saw him alive.

At 3:00 P.M., April 12, Polly Delano phoned Eleanor Roosevelt at the White House to tell her that Franklin had fainted and had been carried into his bedroom. His physician, Admiral McIntire, gave Mrs. Roosevelt the impression that he was not alarmed and urged her to continue with her scheduled appointments. She drove to the Sulgrave Club for the annual thrift shop benefit, where she received a telephone call from Steve Early, the president's press secretary, summoning her back to the White House at once. At quarter to six she phoned Morgenthau at his office and asked him to come over immediately, "the purpose being to tell me [that the president had died] so that I could get word to Mother before the announcement came over the radio. I thought it was one of the most considerate and kind acts I've known anyone to do."

To the press Morgenthau stated, "I have lost my best friend." That evening Truman presided at his first cabinet meeting. At nine the following Saturday morning, Morgenthau had his first private meeting with his new boss. "He didn't keep me waiting a minute," Morgenthau noted in his diary. He wasted no time in telling Truman that Roosevelt had encouraged him "to do a lot of things that aren't strictly Treasury business." He wanted to talk to Truman about Germany and "explain the Morgenthau Plan." On the whole he felt good about that initial session. "I want you to stay with me," Truman had told him. Morgenthau replied, "I will stay just as long as I think I can serve you," to which the new president responded, "When the time comes that you can't you will hear from me first, direct." Morgenthau concluded that "the man has a lot of nervous energy and seems to be inclined to make very quick decisions. He was most courteous with me and made a good impression, but, after all he is a politician, and what is going on in his head only time will tell."

Saturday night, the Roosevelt family, along with relatives and close friends of Franklin and Eleanor, boarded the special train bound for Hyde Park. The passengers included President Truman and two men who would bridge the gap between the Roosevelt and Truman administrations, Bob Hannegan and Jimmy Byrnes.

Bearing the shock of FDR's death following on the heels of Elinor's heart attack, my father was lonely and grief-stricken. With my brother and me overseas and my mother in a Florida hospital, the only person close enough to lend him comfort was my sister, Joan, still in Poughkeepsie at Vassar College. But in his pain and disorientation he had momentarily blocked her out. "Sunday morning as we pulled into the station I suddenly remembered that I had forgotten about Joan." He tried to call her on the phone, only to discover that he "had her number wrong." He dispatched a Secret Service man who "caught her just as she was leaving for the laboratory. She . . . got there in time to see one of the most beautiful ceremonies I suppose I will ever see in my life. It was a brilliant, clear, spring day, and the flowers around the grave stood out like so many jewels . . . When they finally blew taps it got to me. Joan cried like a baby. She was terribly 'emoshed' about the whole thing. I was awfully glad I had her with me."

On that final evening he spent with FDR my father's public career in government ended, except for the short, unhappy coda, played out with Harry Truman, whom he found it difficult to address as "Mr. President." Their alienation from each other was predetermined in both their attitudes. My father, after twelve years in Washington and a total of twenty-five years at Roosevelt's side, was unwilling to adjust his ways to a new boss. His relationship with Roosevelt had never been easy, and on many painful occasions he had allowed himself to serve as whipping boy. Yet he also had license to prowl freely on other people's turf and to exercise an extraordinary degree of initiative. In authority among the president's men he was exceeded only by Harry Hopkins.

Truman moved into the White House with his own cronies, mostly men who had served with him in the Congress. He was remarkably expeditious in seizing the reins. On the train back to Washington after the funeral at Hyde Park, Morgenthau confronted Bob Hannegan to tell him that if, as was rumored, James Byrnes was to be appointed secretary of state, he would not be able to get along with him. In fact, the day after Roosevelt died Truman had told Byrnes he intended to appoint him to the top cabinet position.

The Morgenthau-Byrnes feud dated back to 1942 when they had

fallen out over control of tax policy in Roosevelt's presence, much to his irritation. Trying to smooth things over, Morgenthau had suggested they could reach an agreement. But Byrnes retorted, "I wouldn't agree with you on anything." In 1944, when Byrnes's name came up for consideration as Cordell Hull's replacement, Morgenthau opposed him in no uncertain terms.

The letters my father wrote to my brother and me during the beginning of the Truman administration gave the impression that all was well between him and his new boss. Entries in his diary, however, indicate a swift deterioration of the relationship. First, Truman saw no reason for Morgenthau to concern himself with affairs outside the Treasury, particularly in determining the fate of postwar Germany. Under Truman the Morgenthau Plan's vehement antagonists quickly closed ranks, reconstituting the opposition originally led by Henry Stimson. Truman viewed Stimson as an elder statesman and confidently relied on him. Stimson and Truman joked privately that Morgenthau and Bernard Baruch were alike in their obsessive meddling in German affairs; in fact, Baruch had worked vigorously to undermine the Morgenthau Plan. This mistaken linking had some ugly anti-Semitic overtones; earlier, Stimson had referred to Morgenthau's "Jewish vengeance." Further, with the rising tide of anti-Soviet feeling grew a tendency to think in terms of a Jewish-Communist bond (though Stimson had nothing to do with this).

These undercurrents surfaced as Truman prepared to leave for the Potsdam Big Three Summit in July 1945. At that time, without a vice president, and before the constitutional amendment altering the order of succession, the secretary of the treasury was two heartbeats away from the presidency: if Truman and Secretary of State Byrnes, who were traveling together to Potsdam, died, Morgenthau would become president. This thought disturbed many, including President Truman. The possibility of having a Jewish president seems to have been one of the concerns.

By this time Morgenthau was aware that Truman intended to install Fred Vinson as secretary of the treasury and have Vinson accompany him to the Potsdam meeting with Churchill and Stalin. Vinson and Byrnes, Southerners with similar backgrounds, were often seen as a pair. Both had served in Congress, a top-priority recommendation for Truman appointees. Both men subsequently served on the Federal Court and then stepped down to accept New

Deal appointments. Byrnes had recommended Vinson to take his place as economic stabilization administrator in 1943 when he became head of the Office of War Mobilization (later also Reconversion). It was hardly a surprise when they turned up in the number one and two seats in the Truman cabinet, though ideologically the two men had fundamental differences. Byrnes, from South Carolina, was a confirmed segregationist and states' rights proponent. Vinson, from Kentucky, was a great advocate of a strong federal government. Morgenthau heartily disliked Byrnes but had found the homespun amiability of his successor less difficult to accept.

Yet Henrietta Klotz remembered how desolate her boss felt when Vinson was sworn in. He had no family with him. Standing alone in a corner he looked crushed. Henrietta went over to comfort him. "And your father felt much better," she told me. When he realized that he was about to be dumped, Morgenthau insisted on resigning immediately. At the last minute, as the presidential party was setting sail for Potsdam, Vinson was literally yanked off the boat and sworn in. Truman had not told Morgenthau about his intentions himself as he had promised. He had designated Sam Rosenman, a holdover from the Roosevelt White House and a Jew, as his messenger. Rosenman had implied that if Morgenthau resigned gracefully a deal could be struck making him the U.S. representative on the World Bank and the International Monetary Fund. This was Rosenman's idea, as it turned out, not Truman's.

By the end of 1945 our family was reunited, though somewhat bruised and battered. My mother was increasingly ill. However, my brother and I returned unscathed. Bob resumed his education at Yale Law School. I returned to my work in public housing, this time in New York City, where I could be close to my mother. My sister, Joan, started medical school at the Columbia University College of Physicians and Surgeons.

My father's Treasury policies had made him few friends in the financial world, and he had refused to use his clout in Washington to line up opportunities in the private sector. Finding himself at loose ends and somewhat drained financially, he accepted the chairmanship of the Modern Industrial Bank, which catered primarily to small New York City business interests and labor unions. He was still trying to gain acceptance for his ideas on Germany and to secure his niche in history. The result was a book, *Germany Is Our Problem,* a series of articles in the *New York Post,* and another series in *Collier's* magazine, ghostwritten by Arthur Schlesinger, Jr. He also gave weekly broadcasts on radio station WMCA, owned and operated by his old friend Nathan Straus. In the summer of 1945, after Morgenthau's resignation, the Morgenthau Plan enjoyed a short afterlife implanted in the regulations for administering the military German occupation, JCS (Joint Chiefs of Staff) 1067. This was in part the handiwork of Morgenthau's former assistant, Colonel Bernard Bernstein, and other Treasury hands planted in Eisenhower's staff. However, without Morgenthau and his privileged Roosevelt connection, the elements of JCS 1067 for enforcement of a tough peace were ultimately ignored.

For my father, who was essentially an activist, the sum of his new endeavors did not satisfy him, and no one knew it better than Henrietta Klotz. She herself had been frustrated in her work in the post-Morgenthau Treasury. Technically protected by her Civil Service status, she was, nevertheless, "a Morgenthau person." With strong professional and personal motivation, Klotz hit on a seemingly ideal solution to her old boss's problems as well as, incidentally, her own. She had links to the organized Jewish community, and was well aware of its need for new, vigorous, far-reaching leadership.

When the doors of Washington closed behind Morgenthau, a combination of historic and personal events served eventually to redirect the course of his life as he sought a new commitment for his energies and idealism. During the war in Europe, American Jews had discovered to their delight a new confluence of their patriotism and their Jewishness. Gentiles and Jews alike had been aroused by the horror of Nazi genocide and had fought side by side in the armed services for its destruction. But at the outbreak of peace Morgenthau's plan to prevent any possibility of yet another resurgence of German militarism was not shared by those who were more troubled by the threat of Communism and, further, the burden of supporting an indigent German people.

During the last days of the war in Europe, American troops were confronted with the reality of the German death camps: the pitiable survivors and the heaps of human remains, a token of the millions who had perished. There were also reports of thousands of starving, homeless wanderers uprooted by the war and without any prospects for refuge. Morgenthau asked his new boss if he could bring up the urgent matter of these displaced persons at a cabinet meeting. Truman, who considered that this was none of the secretary of the treasury's business, ignored his requests. Ironically, shortly after he had gotten rid of Morgenthau, the president accepted a suggestion, which, unbeknownst to him, Morgenthau had planted in the State Department, to have a U.S. representative investigate conditions in the displaced persons camps.

At this point Morgenthau was being given information and plans for relief by Meyer Weisgall, a feisty Zionist who was Chaim Weizmann's representative in the United States. Weisgall got word to Weizmann that Morgenthau had been "very kind and cooperative in a certain important matter he was asked to do." Through Morgenthau's intervention, the State Department designated Earl G. Harrison as their man to investigate the DP camps. Harrison's scathing report on the concentration camp conditions where Jewish DPs were being held was submitted to Truman at the end of August 1945, and it made a lasting impression on the president.

From Washington
to Jerusalem

WHEN THE ALLIED FORCES began their occupation of Germany they could account for some 35,000 Jews. By the end of 1947 the number had risen to about a quarter of a million. Helped by the Haganah (the Jewish underground military organization), refugees filtered in from the east. During the war, the Soviets had transported some 400,000 Jews from Central Europe to the Asian regions of the Soviet Union beyond the Urals. The Soviets demanded their labor and subjected them to extreme hardships but, whatever their motives were, they also saved many lives.

The remnant of European Jewry stranded in Europe were shepherded by the Haganah, with some cooperation from the U.S. military, to sixty-four collection points, almost all in the U.S. sector in Germany. Fearful of resettling in Europe, where so many of their fellow Jews had perished, most of them looked forward to emigrating to Palestine. They had few other choices. The British, meanwhile, had turned 180 degrees since the Balfour Declaration thirty years earlier, which favored a Jewish homeland.

The Jewish DPs were quite different from others, who were on the whole hopeful of returning to their European homelands. The occupying forces' attitudes toward displaced persons, particularly Jews, varied under different commanders. General Eisenhower and his chief of staff, General William Bedell Smith, were consistently sensitive and helpful, but General George Patton, the emotional commander of the Third Army, was not. When he saw the concentration camps he was so shocked that he burst into tears. Later, however, he became more interested in corralling and repatriating strayed Lipizzaner horses to their original home, the Spanish Riding School in Vienna, than in the plight of the DPs.

In the end, aid to the Jews came largely through unofficial channels. A twenty-seven-year-old Third Army chaplain, Rabbi Herbert Friedman, discovered the Haganah and attached himself to it. He became a principal conduit for Joint Distribution Committee funds, providing a lifeline for Jews in the German camps. At a critical time the JDC was able to add a thousand calories a day to the two-thousand-calorie daily rations being provided by the U.S. Army. The JDC was one of the three constituent agencies of the United Jewish Appeal (UJA), the other two being the United Palestine Appeal (UPA, later the United Israel Appeal) and the National Coordinating Committee for Aid to Refugees (NCCR, later the National Refugee Service and today NYANA). Of these the UPA represented the Zionist interests. Its chief professional was Henry Montor, who had risen through the ranks of Zionist organizations, handling public relations for the United Palestine Appeal and becoming its professional leader before taking on the top-paid job at UJA. Montor had a vision of a unified, dynamic American Jewish community that would rise to the challenge of supporting the independent Jewish state about to be born. In 1946 the Morgenthau-Montor team headed the UJA, with Morgenthau as general chairman and Montor as executive vice president. Then its often rivalrous constituent agencies joined together to become an integrated whole. Morgenthau was not yet a committed Zionist, though he bore none of his father's hostility toward the movement and its goal of an independent Jewish state. His motives were primarily humanitarian. But all differences of motivation were overwhelmed by the rescue imperative.

It soon became clear that the financial burden for resettlement of the surviving European Jews would have to be shouldered by the 5 million Jews in the United States. During the war American Jews reached a new level of acceptance and a secure sense of their Americanism. Many served in the armed forces, and others amassed fortunes that were rapidly expanding at the war's end.

But the strident factionalism that had long distracted Jewish organizations persisted. A power struggle between generations arose: David Ben-Gurion versus Chaim Weizmann, Rabbi Abba Hillel Silver versus Rabbi Stephen Wise. Peter Bergson (Hillel Kook) took a militant stand against all comers. The German Jewish "establishment" still tended to fear the dual-allegiance implications of Jewish nationalism, a concern shared by some of the more recent immigrants from Eastern Europe. A generation earlier Louis Brandeis had championed the Zionist cause, and by dint of his personal prestige he gained a degree of support and respectability for Zionism in the United States, only to go down in defeat before Weizmann.

. Faced with the necessity of raising money quickly, Jewish organizations seemed ready to put their differences aside and to rally behind a leader who could, like Brandeis, stand above the fray. He would have to be someone with no attachment to organized Jewry (though sympathetic to the overall cause) and who stood tall in the nation at large. Since the Brandeis heyday no one seemed to have both the stature and the inclination to fill such a role as did Franklin Roosevelt's secretary of the treasury.

Shortly before he died in 1946 at the age of ninety, the senior Henry Morgenthau gave his son a final piece of advice: "Don't have anything to do with the Jews. They'll stab you in the back." But Henry Morgenthau, Jr., by then very much his own man, proceeded to accept the general chairmanship of the United Jewish Appeal. After the humiliating denouement of his career in government, he was aching to find a cause that would put him back in public service, that would absorb his energy and passion. He needed the respect and love that the Jewish community was ready to offer him, and they in turn needed his stamp of ecumenical respectability. It was a perfect match. This time Morgenthau was accepting a challenge with a reservoir of experience and confidence.

Beyond financing the most rudimentary maintenance, no public funds were available for the care and relocation of the DPs, an undertaking that exceeded the scope of anything previously envisaged. The dream of raising $100 million from private sources in one year seemed impossible. In 1945 fund-raising had reached the all-time high of $35 million. But having juggled billions at the Treasury, Morgenthau found these sums less mind-boggling than did his peers. In 1946 the UJA went over the top with $102 million.

Morgenthau's almost pristine innocence concerning Jewish tradition was regarded by the UJA as yet one more asset. At the end of March 1945 he had written my brother and me that while he and Mother were on vacation at Daytona Beach, Florida, they had attended a Seder organized by the community for the servicemen and -women stationed in the area.

"I had never been to a Seder service before. . . . I am sure that you boys have when you were younger."

My father went on to explain that the Seder "is the celebration of the freedom of the Jews from bondage in Egypt . . . It was awfully nice. The young rabbi . . . took a lot of trouble to explain it. . . . I enjoyed the whole thing. They asked me to speak, but I felt that I didn't know enough about the service to get up and make a semi-religious speech."

As a way of showing their respect and affection for this man who had risen so far and had volunteered to help his fellow Jews fight their battles, Jewish leaders joked good-humoredly about Morgenthau's innocence of Jewish ways. Mrs. Mathilda Brailove, whom my father and Montor picked as chairman of the UJA Women's Division, remembered that when she sat with him at fund-raising dinners he would ask, "What am I eating?" To which she would reply, "If I told you, you wouldn't eat it."

Mrs. Klotz thought "he became a little Jewish after a while." He learned how to play the game, intermittently scolding and reaching out to his audiences until they began outdoing one another with their donations. Klotz remembers an occasion when he had been warned that a particular group would be icily resistant. "He wasn't the greatest speaker," Klotz said, and he knew that he hadn't moved the audience with his words from the podium. So he stepped down and did the rounds of the potential big givers on the floor. He put his arm around each man, looked him straight in the eye, and expressed confidence that he would come through. It worked. "They raised a fortune," Klotz recalled.

In February 1947 the UJA staged an impressive campaign kick-off in Washington, with Chairman Morgenthau joined by President Truman and General Eisenhower. That spring in New York the National Christian Committee, organized by Eleanor Roosevelt and Nelson Rockefeller, designated Thomas J. Watson, founding president of IBM, as its chairman and pledged itself to raise large sums of money in 225 cities. In March, when commercial airliners were grounded by foul weather, Morgenthau chartered planes and visited seven cities in seven days, stirring up great enthusiasm. In April one of his pilots lost his license for making a prohibited landing during a snow and ice storm.

In between these strenuous rounds of barnstorming across the country, Morgenthau ran his New York headquarters with the same efficiency that he had been noted for in the Treasury. Each morning when he was not on the road he started off with a 9:00 meeting of UJA department heads. The rest of the day was spent on the phone and meeting in person with communal leaders on their fund-raising problems and pushing them to forward cash.

Despite the frenetic campaigning, by the summer of 1947 fund-raising results had fallen disappointingly short of expectations. An emergency conference was called in Philadelphia in July, and the top leadership flew in from all over the country. The principal attraction, four-star general Joseph T. McNarney, General Eisenhower's successor in command of the European occupation forces, didn't show. As a most unlikely pinch hitter Henry Montor had flown in the young chaplain who had been the unofficial Haganah agent in Europe for the past two years, Rabbi Herbert Friedman. As the meeting got under way a short, Napoleonic man, Max Firestein, stood up on the floor and began to attack Morgenthau for having flown him in across the country for nothing. Firestein was the son-in-law of Max Factor, founder of Max Factor Cosmetics, and president of the Los Angeles Jewish Community Council. With hostile arrogance, he demanded to be told something new to report to his community. Not "just the same old crap."

Everyone in the room was looking in embarrassment at Morgenthau. Rabbi Friedman recalls Morgenthau's gaze falling on him, catching him "with those calm eyes of his I got to know so well." With a simple nod he signaled Friedman to stand up and answer Firestein. "I felt the deftness of an old experienced hand. He knew exactly what was required to turn that attack into an opportunity for history." With righteous fury the Third Army chaplain shot back, "What kind of people are you in Los Angeles? We haven't had enough blood? We haven't had enough gassing? You want to start a fire so that we can smell charred bodies? If that's what the people in Los Angeles need then the hell with you. There is nothing new, Mr. Firestein. These people are sitting in the mud and the filth and the hopelessness of the DP camps. And they're waiting for something new, too."

There was a moment of stunned silence. Then Firestein stood up and began to applaud. Instantly everyone in the room joined in. Firestein began again. "My trip is now worthwhile. I'm going back to sock it to my people and we're going to do the right thing. And I'm going to personally get a million dollars from my own family."

Sometimes while Morgenthau was traveling with Friedman he would speak about his father. "He was proud to be doing in his generation what his father had done in his generation." However, Friedman came to understand the generational chasm between father and son. The senior Morgenthau's goal had been 100 percent Americanism and that Americanism was not to be diluted by any potentially conflicting loyalty. To his way of thinking, affinity to Jewish separatism and Jewish dreams of a national homeland were considered to be threats to one's pure Americanism. "Your father's attitude was much healthier," Friedman told me. "He had lived through the agony of the Holocaust period. He saw that most of the world didn't give a damn. He became more and more deeply involved himself. 'If nobody else will do anything, at least I have to do my best.' Day by day he became more convinced that Palestine was the only solution. This put him in touch with the people he was soliciting. He was not just a passive chairman. He was an active chairman."

As he rose to become the pre-eminent lay Jewish fund raiser in the United States, Morgenthau coupled his effectiveness to the talents of the maverick professional, Henry Montor. Montor had seen in Morgenthau the unique qualities of both an avid leader and an adept pupil. Morgenthau for his part recognized in Montor the skills, the driving energy, and the ruthlessness needed to get the job done. An acknowledged genius flawed by impatience and abrasiveness, Montor was to play a role similar to that played by Harry Dexter White in the Treasury. Morgenthau grew to depend on Montor and to give him his unquestioning loyalty.

Israel Goldstein, the wise and broadly respected veteran of many Jewish wars, believed that "Montor must have conditioned a good deal of [Morgenthau's] thinking because he came in more or less as a stranger to Jewish life and Jewish communal activity, and Montor had to teach him a lot of things, a lot of facts of life about the Jewish community and how it functions." Yet Goldstein believed Morgenthau was no mere tool in the hands of an ambitious professional. "He was a man of convictions, and once he came to his conclusions he stuck by them. He was very, very helpful to the United Jewish Appeal, not only because of the prestige he brought to it, but also because of the understanding he brought to it."* The 1947 UJA campaign showed an increase over the previous year, reaching a total of $124 million. During the end of 1947 and the beginning of 1948 excitement in the American Jewish community was fueled by the on-again, off-again imminence of a full-fledged Jewish state. Eleanor Roosevelt, who was part of the U.S. delegation to the U.N. at Lake Success, was the most ardent and visible supporter of the Jewish cause. Harry Truman, who was personally committed to the creation of a Jewish state, was as usual undercut by his own State Department. The result was mixed signals that were particularly embarrassing to the president at the beginning of an election year.

On May 15, 1948, when the British Mandate in Palestine was officially over, the Jews, led by David Ben-Gurion, gave birth by declaration to the state of Israel. The United States was the first nation to recognize Israel, followed by many others, including the Soviet Union.

But Israel's Arab neighbors hadn't waited for the inevitable. Toward the end of 1947 they began skirmishes, and Jewish forces immediately counterattacked. Since they were outnumbered and underequipped, their prospects for holding out were grim. The United States had placed an embargo on arms shipments, but also tended to look the other way when the "Sonneborn Institute" and other clandestine groups stepped up illegal shipments.† Then, miraculously, the tide began to turn, when Jewish soldiers carved out a corridor bordering the "Burma Road" linking Jerusalem with the coastal area.

The American Jewish community had reached a historic, unprecedented consensus in support of embattled Israel. Overnight, pictures of Jewish warrior-heroes were having an electric effect. Pride in the new Jewish self-image was enormous. American Jews identified with brave exploits of these soldiers, and some actually joined their ranks. Others stayed at home to cheer them on and to outdo one another in financial support. In 1948 the UJA drive peaked with an all-time high of $148 million.

---

*Israel Goldstein was an American-born Conservative rabbi and an ardent Zionist. In addition to serving his prominent New York congregation for forty-three years, he was the lay head of some of the most important Jewish and interfaith organizations, including the UJA, where Montor was the professional executive.
†The "Sonneborn Institute" was financed by Rudolph Sonneborn, a wealthy member of the German Jewish establishment.

In October, with the war still on, Morgenthau made his first trip to Israel. It was carefully orchestrated by Henry Montor, in cooperation with the top officials of the new state, to maximize positive feedback to constituencies in the United States and Israel. Meyer Steinglass, Montor's star publicity man, accompanied by a photographer, documented Morgenthau's every move. Not least important was the impact this visit had on the always emotionally driven UJA chairman himself. Immediately on arriving at the airport the Morgenthau delegation was escorted up the Burma Road, its shoulders littered with recently burned-out enemy armored vehicles, to the Holy City. On October 24, Morgenthau eagerly scrambled through a tunnel to emerge where he could view the Arab-occupied Old City of Jerusalem. While he was inside the Notre Dame Church, two mortar shells exploded outside, followed by an exchange of small-arms fire. That evening Morgenthau told the guests, "After traveling over the 'Burma' I am convinced more than ever there can be no State of Israel without a Jewish Jerusalem. [It] without Jerusalem would be like the Jewish people without its history." All of this had been stated in the context of opposition to inclusion of Jerusalem in the Jewish state by the U.S. government, the Arabs, and dignitaries of the Christian churches.

The next evening Morgenthau visited David Ben-Gurion at his house in Tel Aviv. It was Simchas Torah.★ Outside, throngs were dancing in the street and singing religious and patriotic songs. Ben-Gurion and his guest, coming out to join them, were handed sacred scrolls, and they entered into the dancing. Those who stood near Morgenthau observed there were tears in his eyes.

During the course of the visit Ben-Gurion recalled how his guest's father, Ambassador Morgenthau, had saved his life along with that of his companion, Yitzhak Ben-Zvi (who later became the second president of Israel). At the outbreak of World War I these two young Zionists were in Jerusalem. There Djemal Pasha, commander of the Ottoman Fourth Army Corps, was distinguishing himself by his persecution of the non-Muslim population. Ben-Gurion and Ben-Zvi were jailed and charged with treason, which was punishable by death. In March 1915, Ambassador Morgenthau intervened on behalf of several persecuted Jews and arranged to

---

★Simchas Torah means in Hebrew "Joy of Torah" (the law), and is a holiday falling at the end of the High Holy Days.

have them exiled to Alexandria, Egypt, transported by the U.S. Navy. In Alexandria, Ben-Gurion and Ben-Zvi were again jailed, this time by the British. Again, with Ambassador Morgenthau's help they were released and proceeded to New York.

On October 27, 1948, the Israeli government prepared to confer a high honor on Morgenthau by giving his name to a new settlement, Tal Shachar (the English translation being "valley of the dew" as the English translation of the German Morgenthau is "morning dew"). At Tal Shachar a few hastily constructed frame buildings had sprouted on the still contested Judean hill region. The settlement was planned as a *moshav* (an agricultural collective). The first inhabitants were new immigrants from Turkey and Greece. For the noon dedication ceremonies a delegation of dignitaries headed by President Chaim Weizmann arrived with a large military escort.

Speaking under a canvas canopy that provided the only shade on the barren hill site, Morgenthau acknowledged the occasion as "one of the greatest moments of my life." To the assembled military he declared, "You are showing the world that the Jew is a fighting man, and in that way you have raised the standard of the Jew in the eyes of the Christian world. Unfortunately, the young Republic of Israel has very few friends in the outside world. You will therefore have to depend on your own strong right arm." Reported in the American press the next day, this was the kind of exultant militancy that inspired the American Jewish community. The Israelis themselves seemed more philosophically resigned to their fate. "We are people of peace," Dr. Weizmann insisted at the ceremony. "But now we must live with one hand on the plough and one on the sword. I trust that very soon we will be able to put both hands on the plough."

On this sentimental occasion and during the course of many subsequent meetings, Weizmann and Morgenthau did not choose to recall the former's encounter with Ambassador Morgenthau at Gibraltar in 1917. However, when Weizmann published his memoirs a year later he devoted a chapter to snide recollections of the Gibraltar incident with the senior Morgenthau, but in a separate entry praised the junior Morgenthau as a valued friend of Israel who took his responsibilities as head of UJA "very seriously, like everything else to which he devotes his attention."

The 1948 UJA campaign broke all previous fund-raising records, yet Henry Montor, who had set the precedent-shattering agenda of the previous three years, was not satisfied. The announced goal for 1948 had in fact been $250 million. Montor was impatient with the labyrinth of organizations impeding the flow of funds from American donors to the ultimate recipient, the new state of Israel.

As early as July 8, 1948, Morgenthau, probably at Montor's urging, wrote to Ben-Gurion suggesting that the Israeli government authorize a U.S. agency, the American Friends of the State of Israel, to be the sole clearinghouse for all American funds. Almost no one else thought this a good time to rock the boat. Henry Montor calculated that the only way to pull the plan off would be to gain complete support from his boss. Morgenthau, with no stomach for internecine warfare and no institutional loyalties, was equally impatient to get on with the job. So he and Montor together resigned from the UJA on December 31, 1948, to operate independently through the Palestine Economic Corporation. Eliezer Kaplan, Israel's first finance minister, was horrified. According to his calculations the Morgenthau defection would cost the campaign an intolerable $20 million. Two months later Morgenthau and Montor were persuaded to come back on board.

In 1949, with Arab-Israeli hostilities at a temporary standstill, fund-raising declined substantially. The next year the total fell further to the $102 million level of 1946. To perk things up Morgenthau called on his war bond drive experience in the Treasury, which had both financed the war and sold it to the American people. Similarly, he decided, the government of Israel bonds sold in the United States provided a way for American Jews to invest directly in Israel and indirectly in their Jewishness. The sale of Israel bonds would also fulfill Montor's dream of a direct channel from the United States to Israel.

In the meantime, my mother was sinking in a painful illness. At the New York Hospital she suffered a stroke and lapsed into a coma, and on September 21 she died at the age of fifty-eight. My father was distraught to the point of becoming ill himself and was hospitalized in a room down the corridor from hers when she passed away. Her death marked the end of a four-year period during which the three people whose counsel and affection my father most relied on had left him. Franklin Roosevelt's death in 1945 had been a sudden shock. At the same time his father and wife withdrew into themselves as their energies waned. During the span of my father's career when he had been influenced by their judgment, both had steered him away from entanglements in Jewish affairs. After they passed from the scene the course of his life changed as he became the devoted servant of the Jewish community. Was it partly an act of self-definition, a rebellion against his upbringing, a craving for love, a respect that he couldn't find anywhere else at that time? Perhaps the answer is yes to each.

Starting at the end of 1949, Morgenthau's involvement in Jewish activities reached its peak. At the beginning of 1950 he made his second trip to Israel, this time including Henrietta Klotz in the party. His every move was photographed. Henrietta, poised and elegantly turned out, appears constantly at his side. One picture particularly captures the significance of the Morgenthau visit. Captioned "An important business conference," it shows Israeli Finance Minister Eliezer Kaplan, Mr. Morgenthau, Minister of Labor Golda Meyerson (Meir), and Mrs. Klotz. It was at this session that the scenario for the Israel bond drive was hammered out by the ex-secretary of the treasury and his opposite member, Israel's first finance minister. Golda Meyerson was the most effective UJA speaker in 1948.

Following the Morgenthau visit, a formal conference was held in the prime minister's office. Henry Montor acted as Morgenthau's surrogate. Herbert Friedman, also present, recalls that Montor was irascible in demanding that Israel Bonds should replace the UJA, with its apparently diminishing fund drives. In a few years, he predicted, UJA would be back to the $25 million level. Friedman and a majority of those attending the meeting argued that the tax-exempt UJA gifts and the fully taxable bonds would reinforce rather than compete with each other. The compromise agreed on provided for the UJA to continue, but Morgenthau and Montor would leave to head the Israel Bond drive. A four-point program to provide guidance for the external funding of Israel's financial needs was drawn up.★

As Morgenthau prepared to chair the bond sales campaign, he asked President Truman if the White House would object to his becoming what was essentially the agent of a foreign government. He was informed that as a private citizen he was free to act as he chose.

★The plan included (1) issuance of state of Israel bonds, (2) a UJA of enlarged scope, (3) private foreign investment in Israeli enterprises, and (4) government grants, primarily from the United States. In the long term, point number 4 provided by far the largest share of the funding.

Early in 1951 the bond drive got off to a flying start when Morgenthau and Montor persuaded Ben-Gurion to come to the United States to make a whirlwind tour of major American cities exclusively for bonds. The UJA was ignored completely. From then on there was mounting fury among its leaders.

Montor was itching to cut loose and set up an independent organization to sell bonds, but Morgenthau urged him to explore other channels. First came the normal underwriting procedures of the Wall Street financial houses. However, the uncertainty of the continued existence of the embattled fledgling state made its bonds unattractively risky. Second was the idea of coattailing on the UJA or the Jewish Welfare Board, but both rejected this idea. Legal questions had arisen about a charitable organization sponsoring a commercial operation. Senator William Fulbright had questioned the tax-exempt status of the UJA itself in 1948 because a foreign government was the ultimate recipient of charitable donations, but Morgenthau succeeded in regaining clearance. Above all there was the fundamental concern that an independent bond organization would threaten Israel's capacity to respond directly to the network of Jewish institutions in communities nationwide.

In direct opposition to this position, Montor held that the Jewish communal interests were getting a free ride on the wave of euphoria for embattled Israel. With uncompromising arrogance he proceeded to stage spectacular bond-drive rallies across the country. In 1951, after being criticized for having campaigned exclusively for bonds, Ben-Gurion managed to smooth things over temporarily by declaring that both the UJA and bonds were essential to Israel. However, the following year, Golda Meyerson came back for bond rallies that conflicted directly with the UJA spring campaign.

Morgenthau, while continuing to be loyal to Montor, remained above these internal squabbles. But he was increasingly unhappy with a situation that seemed so unnecessary and so destructive. And he had found other attractions.

On November 21, 1951, my father married a French woman living in New York, Marcelle Puthon Hirsch. She was divorced from a French Jew who had made a small fortune selling gold braid to the French Army. Marcelle was nominally a Catholic, and when she and my father became engaged, he arranged for her to convert to Judaism. Some ten years younger than he, she had short blonde hair, expertly bleached and coiffed, and was very nearsighted, her eyes blurred behind heavy glasses.

The wedding ceremony was performed by Rabbi Julius Mark of Temple Emanu-El in Marcelle's New York apartment. About ten guests were present, including my brother, sister, and myself. They divided their honeymoon appropriately between Paris and Jerusalem. Marcelle was not interested in Israel or in any of the activities that had absorbed my father's energies. Most of his close associates ascribe his diminished interest in Israel Bonds to her influence. Yet, considering his tendency to dominate and hers to recede, perhaps she was more the instrument than the instigator. During the next two years he did in fact continue to provide effective, if less driven, leadership to the bond campaign, though he probably exerted less control over Montor's behavior.

As a result the strained relations between those promoting bonds and the UJA worsened. The final showdown came when the leaders of the Detroit Jewish community demanded some rational division of time. Montor responded with a vitriolic memorandum titled "The Nonsense of Timing." He had thrown a hand grenade that blew up in his face. Federations all across the country banded together to pepper the Israel government with complaints that couldn't have come at a worse time. David Ben-Gurion was preparing to resign as prime minister, and Kaplan, the finance minister, had died. The entire government was shaky. Moshe Sharett, who took Ben-Gurion's place, and Levi Eshkol, who took Kaplan's, were both more cautious than their predecessors, fearful of alienating the American Jewish community.

In the spring of 1953 Morgenthau, fed up with the bickering, announced his intention to resign. At the beginning of December, Eshkol was dispatched to New York with orders to get matters settled. Eshkol understood that he could no longer sit still and accept Montor's bulldozing actions. Israel couldn't sell its bonds without American help and good will, and if someone had to play the sacrificial lamb it should be Montor, not Morgenthau.

On December 9, 1953, Eshkol, Morgenthau, and Montor had a breakfast meeting. Morgenthau dictated a four-page memo detailing the conversation which turned out to be the last entry in the *Morgenthau Diaries*. Eshkol had learned that Ben-Gurion had made good on his promise to resign, and that he was upset Morgenthau was resigning simultaneously. Morgenthau seems to have been in a sour mood, determined to pull out yet wanting to be wooed back. Eshkol, however, distracted by the cabinet crises, was less effusive than Morgenthau had hoped he would be.

"I got the feeling that Eshkol is not too sure what his own position is. He was not at all warm or friendly with me at any time during our visit," he recalled. "I got there promptly, Montor was a little late . . . Breakfast had not been ordered and didn't come for an hour." At this meeting there were some overtones of his last encounters with the Truman administration as Morgenthau virtually invited rejection. "I told you last spring that I was going to resign," he recalled saying to Eshkol. "I am not like Montor who resigns regularly and expects to be called back . . . I am finished." But his ambivalence showed through as he continued, "Israel's position today in the diplomatic world is worse than it was last spring. She is in trouble and I want to be helpful. I helped when you were at war with the Arabs." When Morgenthau asked Eshkol if there were anything he wanted him to do, Eshkol was open to suggestions. Then, noting that Morgenthau was "of German extraction," Eshkol asked him to intervene with the U.S. government in getting $20 million in German reparations owed to Israel. Morgenthau tried to explain that Germany was without doubt the place where he was least likely to be effective.

At the end of the meeting, "Eshkol followed me out mumbling something about how nice it was of me to come to see him and he would always remember, if he had a difficult problem, that there was always a Morgenthau around. . . . Coming down[town] in the taxi alone, it was very obvious to me that they have written me off as a total loss and do not expect anything from me and do not want anything from me in the future. So the thing for me to do is to bow out gracefully and not look for anything or expect anything further from the Government of Israel."

Caught up in his own disappointments, Morgenthau had sadly misread the genuine affection and respect he had earned from both the American Jewish community and the Israelis. With no mentor to steer him back on course, he made his resignation effective early in 1954. Within a year Montor was dismissed, and he entered private business. Together this team had led the way in selling $190 million worth of state of Israel bonds, though they had not attained their $500 million goal. Yet with Israel Bonds and UJA combined, Morgenthau and Montor had broken all records of amounts raised. And for a fleeting moment, with Morgenthau at the helm, something almost unknown in Jewish affairs happened. There was a consensus.

Harry Dexter White
Revisited

IN 1948, while busily engaged with the UJA, Morgenthau was shocked by headlines alleging that his esteemed and trusted Treasury aide, Harry Dexter White, had been a master Soviet spy. He was incredulous. The news had sprung from the House Un-American Activities Committee (HUAC) that Morgenthau had little respect for. Its two chief witnesses were the avowed ex-Communists Whittaker Chambers and Elizabeth Bentley, who were spinning bizarre tales of Soviet agents lodged in the upper reaches of the federal government.

Fred Vinson had kept White on as assistant secretary. In international monetary affairs Vinson found White as uniquely valuable as Morgenthau had. The following January, after Congress approved the Bretton Woods agreements leading to the creation of the World Bank and the International Monetary Fund, Vinson recommended that Truman appoint White the U.S. director of the IMF. Prior to the Senate confirmation hearings, the FBI delivered a letter to President Truman's aide, General Harry H. Vaughan, stating that a number of government employees, including White, were involved in Soviet espionage. The FBI made no specific charges against White, and the White House paid no attention to the letter.

One of the ideas that had sparked FBI concern was that White, as the reputed father of the Morgenthau Plan, had been put up to it by the Kremlin for the purpose of softening up Germany for Communism and eventual Soviet occupation. The FBI warned the White House again in a second letter, this time sending copies to other key officials, including Secretary of State James Byrnes. Byrnes tried to get Truman to withdraw White's appointment, which had just been confirmed. The president believed this would not be correct and did nothing. After serving at the IMF for a year White offered his resignation, and Truman accepted it "with sincere regret and considerable reluctance." More than fourteen months after the second FBI warning, John W. Snyder, then secretary of the treasury, wrote a warm collegial letter to White stating, "You have every reason to be proud of your career in government service."

In 1948, when HUAC was ripping into colleagues and friends of White's, several of whom had been members of the Communist party and took the Fifth Amendment, White testified on their behalf. His contemptuous, disrespectful responses to questions brought the committee's fury down on his head. His pleas for respite because of a chronic heart condition were denied with sarcastic remarks about his Ping-Pong and tennis prowess. On August 16, during a weekend recess while resting at his summer home in New Hampshire, White suffered a heart attack and died at the age of fifty-six. Two days later Morgenthau wrote Mrs. White, "I am sure you know how I feel about my association with Harry in the Treasury, but I want to try to put it in words in the hope that it will be of some comfort to you." It wasn't. Mrs. White was very bitter that Morgenthau had not spoken out in her husband's defense. He did not attend the funeral in Boston. "To sum it up," Morgenthau concluded his long, rambling condolence letter, "Harry was a top flight public servant who served his country well. If I get around to writing the real story of my life, Harry will occupy an important place in the book. He served his country well." Mrs. Klotz recalled being questioned closely by the FBI about her attendance at the White funeral, and was mystified until she later learned of the rumor that White had committed suicide, some said with an overdose of sleeping pills, others by shooting himself in the temple. The FBI was curious to know whether she had viewed the body. The coffin had been closed at the time of her arrival.

Morgenthau was not privy to any of the information about White which the FBI had transmitted to the Truman White House. All that he knew was already public knowledge. With the 1948 presidential election in the offing, little attention was paid to White's prior association with Morgenthau. But as the unresolved mystery persisted amid the general anti-Communist hysteria, Morgenthau was bothered by the gnawing suspicion that he might have been duped by White. After repeated inquiries to two attorneys general, Tom Clark and J. Howard McGrath, and others produced nothing substantial he requested an appointment with J. Edgar Hoover in January 1952. Hoover did not make himself available. Instead Morgenthau met with one of his top assistants, who afterward reported to Hoover that "Mr. Morgenthau stated he . . . has been very much concerned, and naturally is very much upset to learn that there appears to be no question but that White was working for the Russians, but that now that he has the information he feels much better. He stated he had no suspicion . . . during the time that White was working for him."

In 1953, with the Republicans controlling both the presidency and Congress, the White affair erupted again with a vicious new twist. President Eisenhower's attorney general, Herbert Brownell, made a speech accusing retired president Truman of having retained White in the Treasury and then promoting him to the IMF in the face of repeated FBI warnings. HUAC subpoenaed Truman, whose refusal to comply on constitutional grounds was ultimately upheld. Morgenthau, out of the line of fire, was only indirectly touched by the free-floating accusations, partly because the fabled Morgenthau diaries were believed to be an unmined treasure trove of information that could confirm the darkest suspicions about White.

In the spring of 1955, after the Democrats had regained control of the Senate and censured Senator Joseph McCarthy, the Senate Internal Security Subcommittee, chaired by a Mississippi Dixiecrat, James O. Eastland, had assumed much of the McCarthy committee's witch-hunting role. Morgenthau was invited to appear before the subcommittee in closed session. He was flattered when the chairman, Senator Eastland, and the ranking minority member, Indiana Republican senator William E. Jenner, came to New York to confer with him on the plan of approach.

At this time my brother, Robert, an attorney with the New York law firm of Patterson Belknap & Webb, was informally representing our father. Bob recalls that he continued to stand his ground firmly in response to the alternating flattery and pressure emanating from the Eastland committee. Meanwhile the committee's chief staffer, Jay Sourwine, was informing the FBI of everything that took place. Reporting on the meeting in New York, he said Morgenthau's "attitude was excellent. He is mad at White and those who played him for a sucker . . . He will be a friendly witness." This information is incorporated in an FBI memo with a marginal comment initialed by Hoover: "I would never be too certain of Morgenthau's sincerity." At the hearing Morgenthau again stated that while he served in the Treasury he never had reason to suspect White's "integrity or loyalty to the United States." His word was accepted without challenge. At the conclusion of the hearing on June 4, Morgenthau thanked the committee for their "consideration," adding, "Anything I have got that can help my government is yours . . . you ask for it and you will get my whole-hearted cooperation." Senator Eastland went on the record with his praise of Morgenthau, to which the latter responded, "I would not want anything better on my tombstone."

What the committee really wanted was not Morgenthau's testimony but his diaries. Without them the committee would be unable to document Sourwine's contention that "White was in touch with the Russians as was Morgenthau." The plan was to unearth evidence that "they would never get if Morgenthau knew what was in the offing."

Morgenthau had given the original set of his diaries to the Roosevelt Library at Hyde Park, a branch of the National Archives, which at that time was a division of the General Services Administration (GSA). Morgenthau had kept two microfilm copies. When Bob learned of the existence of these copies, he quickly arranged to have them turned over to the National Archives so that our father would be removed from any dispute over the availability of the diaries to the subcommittee. Thus it would be a matter to be worked out between the executive branch and the Congress.

When Hoover was informed of this maneuver, he scrawled another marginal note: "Reversal by Morgenthau doesn't surprise me. It serves the Committee right which went all out in nauseating commendation of Morgenthau." However, since Senator Eastland's nephew held a key job at the GSA, the committee members managed to cut through administrative red tape and got their hands on the diaries within a couple of weeks. Eventually they published substantial excerpts, which proved nothing except that White had indeed been a trusted and influential Treasury aide. In due course, the investigation petered out with no significant results.

Morgenthau, troubled that White might have abused his absolute trust, wondered whether he and the United States had been betrayed. Though my father was never able to resolve the question of White's Communist affiliations in his own mind, he seems to have had no doubt as to the major importance of White's contribution as a U.S. governmental official. This is made clear in the many references to his work in *From the Morgenthau Diaries,* written by John Morton Blum with my father's collaboration and approval. Blum gives a straightforward record of the close working relationship between the two men. The account was quite clear as to the extent Morgenthau valued (though not uncritically) White's contributions. Morgenthau's letter to Anne White at the time of her husband's death appears to represent his sober assessment of an eleven-year association.

> Harry had a keen and original mind. I threw many problems at him but sooner or later he always came up with the answers. Starting with Sept. 3, 1939, when England went to war with Germany, Harry was ceaselessly doing his part to see that the United States would have a preparedness program . . . After we got into the war, Harry was most helpful in seeing that everything was done to wage war successfully against the enemy.

From Generation
to Generation

B Y 1954 Morgenthau was worn down from the strain of relentless campaigning to raise money for Israel. He was ready to retire to his first love, his Dutchess County farm. Each time, as the shadow of death crossed his path, it seemed to inch a little closer. He adopted a popular song as a kind of personal anthem: "Enjoy yourself, it's later than you think." Like everyone else he wanted to wind down his life in an orderly and pleasurable fashion. But as is usually the case, life, especially its ending, is seldom tidy.

My father soon discovered that after years of stressful engagement in the public arena an unfocused life of leisure was intolerable. Furthermore, it had long been on his mind to set the record straight concerning his public career. A dignified monument in the form of a biography would be appropriate but was not something to be trusted to others. He would not attempt to write it himself, but did, however, want to shape and control the end product.

Meticulous preservation of ephemera was an old family custom. The first Henry Morgenthau had saved every scrap of evidence concerning his life, public and private. He wrote (with collaborators) four autobiographies. The senior Henry's father, Lazarus, also preserved a collection of documents, including the short memoir he wrote as a young man, the so-called *Diary,* privately printed by my father. Although the senior Henry was deeply resentful of the way Lazarus had misused his family, particularly his wife, he nevertheless preserved the records.

My father carried the family archival propensities to the utmost extremes during his years at the Treasury. The task of organizing the material was carried out under the vigilant eye of Henrietta Klotz, who in turn made it the full-time occupation of a devoted and experienced librarian.*

By the time Secretary Morgenthau left Washington in 1945, the Morgenthau diaries had swollen to some nine hundred volumes of transcripts: telephone conversations, stenotype verbatim reports, letters, and supporting documents. There was also the twelve-volume "Presidential Diary," consisting of memos my father dictated after each of his meetings (or telephone conversations) with FDR. No one in the Roosevelt administration, or for that matter before or since, kept such an extensive and well-ordered record of day-to-day official proceedings.

When my father left the Treasury, he deposited the Morgenthau diaries and most of the rest of his papers at the Roosevelt Library in Hyde Park, New York. The job of sifting through this mountain of undigested material was a gargantuan task demanding the skills and tireless energy of an exceptionally talented historian. There were several false starts. In 1954 John Morton Blum turned out to be the right person at the right time.

Morgenthau and Blum were introduced to each other in 1954 by their mutual friend, Arthur Schlesinger, Jr. At thirty-three, Blum was a rising young historian at MIT. In 1957 he became a tenured professor at Yale. He was also a cheerfully nonobservant Jew. Though each man was impressed by the other's credentials, the beginning of their collaboration was, to say the least, rocky. My father approached the task like the administrator he was, treating Blum like some junior staffer. For his part, Blum wanted to portray his subject with all the frailties as well as the strengths that combined to make him an interesting human being.

Early on my father arranged to have Blum interview his two surviving sisters, Helen Fox and Ruth Knight. But when he began to write about his subject's close and highly dependent relationship with his father, Blum found himself in the midst of a minefield. Throughout his career my father had been accused of being his father's puppet. Henry Jr. had in fact moved considerably beyond his father's most ambitious expectations on his own. Theirs was a

---

*The librarian, Isabelle Diamond, was nominated for the Treasury assignment by Elinor Morgenthau's old friend Gabrielle Elliot Forbush.

complex relationship. While the old man's support seemed to be an essential prop, it had also undermined Henry Jr.'s self-confidence. In sum, my father, who was not much given to reflection, chose to exclude this personal material from his commissioned biography. His father was not to be portrayed even as a source of inspiration; he even preferred to credit his motivation for going into public service to Lillian Wald of the Henry Street Settlement rather than to his old man.

On the whole, Blum abided by my father's wishes not to interview people likely to reminisce about touchy subjects. But he had his way of getting the information he needed. One person declared off-limits was Henrietta Klotz. Blum never set up a formal interview with Klotz. There was, however, an occasion when, at my father's request, Blum spent four hours with her rummaging through old files and pictures in a New York warehouse. Blum found Klotz very careful "because she knew your father didn't want her talking to me . . . but she answered any question I could think of."

The other person notably absent from the Blum biography is my mother. Along with Henry Jr.'s father, she was most effective in advancing his career. "Your father would never talk about her," Blum told me. There seemed to be two principal reasons. First, he was probably tired of hearing that she had secured his influence with FDR through her friendship with Eleanor Roosevelt. Second, Marcelle (his second wife) was almost always present when he met with Blum. Though she never opened her mouth except to greet "Mr. Bloom," she was known to be keenly jealous of her predecessor.

Eventually, Blum learned about Elinor Morgenthau from Eleanor Roosevelt. Like Blum, Mrs. Roosevelt was often a guest for Sunday supper at the farm. She always ordered her chauffeur to pick her up at 10:00 P.M. "Your father went to bed at nine," Blum recalled, and so he and Mrs. Roosevelt "would have an hour together alone when she talked freely about your mother, and that's how I got some sense of her."

John Blum completed the third and final volume of *From the Morgenthau Diaries* just before my father died in 1967. True to his agreement, my father had "let the chips fall where they may." I think he understood that buried in the mountain of raw material that constituted his diaries was the self-image that he himself had never been able to project. He intended Blum to sculpt a true and enduring likeness from the solid rock placed in his skilled hands.

On July 1946, during a brainstorming session in preparation for a series of articles on Morgenthau to be published by *Collier's,* the recently retired cabinet member told some magazine staffers in a rare flash of candor that he wanted to try to explain the real nature of his relationship with Roosevelt.

> I worked and slaved for this fellow the way I never would in a lifetime for anybody else . . . You could fight with Roosevelt and argue with him up to a certain point . . . He never did let down the bars beyond a certain point. And, if we are going to be completely truthful, he never let anybody around him have complete assurance that he would have the job tomorrow. That gave you a sense of uneasiness, of insecurity, of his playing one person off against another, which I am not going to talk about [in the articles] but was there . . . The thing that Roosevelt prided himself the most about was, "I have to have a happy ship." But he never had a happy ship . . . Just the opposite of the way I ran my own outfit, where people would know that I would see them through hell and high water . . . I don't know why I said all this. But I want to get over the terrific difficulty of giving the picture.

My father struggled with the unfamiliar exercise of retrieving the past, which was made more difficult by his nagging self-doubts. "This fellow [Roosevelt] was my friend; I was with him through sickness and health. Sure I thought as he did; sure he tested me with the various jobs that he gave me before he put me in the Treasury; sure I was independent and ran the job very independently." Yet the president, true to form, had played on Morgenthau's insecurity, always keeping him off-balance. What my father didn't fully realize was that in the process of playing the game according to his boss's rules he had in fact gained tremendous strength. Though Roosevelt would never give Morgenthau all the assurance and love he craved, there was between these two men a bond of trust and fondness that held firm until the very last night of Roosevelt's life.

Blum's writings, like the diaries, describe my father's life to the end of his career in public office. The diaries (except for a few scattered entries) did not cover his subsequent service on behalf of the Jewish people and were therefore not included in the Blum volumes.

John Blum happened to be Jewish. Once, after he and my father had become comfortable with each other, Morgenthau broached the subject, rather obliquely. "One of my children tells me that your wife's Christian. Is that true?" Blum said, yes, it was true. Morgenthau said cheerfully, "My God, you're as bad as my son Bob."

My father was very proud of his son Bob, who represented the third generation of Morgenthaus attracted by the aroma of politics. Our father, like his father before him, had encouraged his family to observe the official and private doings of the nation's top office holders, including the president and himself. So it was that when we could be in Washington during the Roosevelt presidency, we saw the New Year in at the White House. After the Quebec Conference in 1944, where the Morgenthau Plan had been briefly accepted, Roosevelt, with Mr. and Mrs. Winston Churchill as house guests, drove from Hyde Park to the Morgenthau farm. Bob, who was on leave from the navy, mixed mint juleps for the distinguished company. He was rather surprised that the prime minister, who was not noted for abstinence, drank only one julep. Perhaps he had little fondness for bourbon.

When Bob graduated from law school, Robert Patterson, former secretary of the army, hired him as his assistant at his law firm. One afternoon, as the two men were heading for La Guardia Airport to depart on a business trip, Patterson discovered that he had left some important documents behind. He sent Bob back to the office to retrieve them and take a later flight. Patterson's life ended that afternoon when his plane crashed. For many years thereafter Bob limited his travels to surface transportation.

In New York, as a young lawyer and family man, Bob managed to find time to become actively involved in politics. In 1949 he worked in the senatorial campaign of the state's most popular Democratic veteran, our "Uncle Herbert" Lehman. That year Lehman beat John Foster Dulles. Then, during the 1960 John F. Kennedy presidential campaign, Bob — who was living at the time in the posh Riverdale section of the Bronx — led a Bronx Citizens for Kennedy drive. It was a smashing success. After the election, Bob was given his choice of several jobs. He decided on one that enabled him to remain in New York, distancing himself from the Washington scene, to run his own shop with relative independence.

John Blum told me a story that my father had recounted with great relish. On a crisp, bright morning in the fall of 1961, Henry Morgenthau, Jr., and old Joe Kennedy were crossing Park Avenue from opposite directions when the traffic light changed and they were momentarily stranded together on the center island. There had never been any love lost between them, and they hadn't spoken to each other for years. Morgenthau, as he told Blum, was in no mood for reconciliation. But Kennedy broke the ice with a cheerful "Hello, Henry. I've been hearing great things about that boy of yours." Morgenthau, with what he himself referred to as "the ultimate chutzpah," responded, "Joe, I hear great things about that boy of yours too."

In 1961 President Kennedy appointed Robert Morgenthau the U.S. attorney for the prestigious New York Southern District. From then on, with some notable interruptions, Bob rose to become recognized as the pre-eminent prosecuting attorney, with a nationwide reputation for aggressive perseverance and incorruptibility. He particularly enjoyed nailing big shots involved in white collar crime. He was able to convict the Democratic boss Carmine DeSapio. He was less successful, however, in his long pursuit of Roy Cohn, who had been Senator Joseph McCarthy's counsel and Robert Kennedy's archenemy. Cohn always insisted that Morgenthau had taken up the Kennedy vendetta.

As the New York gubernatorial election approached in 1962, Bobby Kennedy, the attorney general and Bob Morgenthau's boss, encouraged Bob to run for governor in New York, promising to take him back if he were unsuccessful. Indeed, the chance to run against the Republican incumbent, Nelson Rockefeller, then at the height of his popularity, was hardly an attractive opportunity. Then when the Cuban missile crisis put a freeze on all campaigning, the odds became absolutely overwhelming. After losing the election, Bob Morgenthau resumed his job as U.S. attorney and remained in office throughout the Johnson administration.

When he had been back in private law practice for four years, the elected office of district attorney for New York County became available. Frank Hogan, the incumbent until his death, had become a legendary figure. Bob seemed determined to maintain — indeed, to enlarge — the legend. As of 1991, he was serving his fourth consecutive four-year term, having run each time (after an initial primary contest in 1974) with no serious opposition. The Manhattan D.A.'s office engages in the rough-and-tumble business of pursuing murderers, sex offenders, and other heinous criminals. The staff of that office includes many able young assistants who are compensated primarily by the prestige and experience gained in serving under an illustrious and grateful boss. As urban crime becomes ever more vicious and incumbent officials become more vulnerable, Bob has continued in office. Of course he is not without detractors. Some of his best friends find him at times inordinately stubborn. His enemies believe him to be vindictive. I can little understand what gives him the courage to continue on this essentially thankless assignment. Though it hardly goes to the heart of the matter, there are hints that his perseverance is linked to a hereditary trait. "You know I always liked to be a policeman," my father wrote to Bob and me about his "activities in investigating black market and tax evaders . . . I'm really aroused about these men who, during the middle of a war, aren't satisfied to make reasonable profits but are going to . . . cheat their own government, and also cheat the public through [the] excessive prices that they charge."

After two long bouts with breast cancer, Martha Morgenthau died, leaving her husband with their five children. Five years later Bob married a spunky Pulitzer Prize–winning journalist, Lucinda Franks. His second wedding, like his first, was performed by a judge in a civil ceremony. But despite his marriages to two Christian women, Bob has always thought of himself as Jewish. And indeed the Jewish community has reciprocated by welcoming his service. Today he sits as a trustee on a number of boards, including that of Temple Emanu-El on Fifth Avenue. He is also cochairman of the New York Holocaust Commission. He has been a staunch supporter of the state of Israel, which he visits frequently. Though he personally adheres to a rather hard-line position, his close Israeli friends range from Mayor Teddy Kollek to Ariel Sharon.

Blum completed his final volume of *From the Morgenthau Diaries* just before my father's death. During this period their relationship became ever more trusting as they worked out a modus operandi for dealing with some significant differences of opinion. When the Morgenthau Plan came up for discussion, Blum said he thought Morgenthau had been wrong. Blum also thought Morgenthau had been wrong in his insistence on balancing the budget. So they made a deal that Blum would refrain from personal criticism but would be free to quote anyone else who thought Morgenthau had been wrong.

When Blum wanted to criticize Morgenthau's budget policy, he would quote the Federal Reserve chief, Marriner Eccles, who vigorously opposed most of Morgenthau's actions on financial matters. When it came to criticizing the Morgenthau Plan, he would quote

Henry Stimson. This was fine with my father. Of course, there were exceptions to this rule. Just before Truman dismissed him, Morgenthau had indicated that he planned to be in Europe at the time of the Potsdam conference to protect the implementation of the Morgenthau Plan. When word reached Secretary Stimson, he went to Truman in a white heat and said that if Morgenthau were going, he (Stimson) wouldn't go. As Blum told Morgenthau, Truman replied, "Don't worry, neither Morgenthau nor Baruch nor any of the Jew boys will be going to Potsdam." Morgenthau asked Blum to delete this Stimson quote, adding, "I'm sure if Mr. Stimson wrote it in his diary, President Truman said it. But I don't like the phrase 'Jew boy' in the mouth of any President of the United States. And since it's not in *my* diary couldn't we keep it out of *our* book?" Blum complied.

As Morgenthau insisted on cleansing his book of what he considered the anti-Semitic mouthings of a president, he was also sensitive about possible misinterpretation of some of his own casual remarks. He occasionally indulged in expressing that brand of ironic self-hatred that Jews prefer to share with each other only. In the first draft of the opening chapter, Blum had included an account of an incident that took place in 1916. Shortly after Ambassador Morgenthau returned from Turkey, he and his son were on the train from New York to Washington and were seated in a parlor car with Jacob Schiff. The ambassador explained to Schiff that his son had taken temporary leave from his farm to serve as his unpaid private secretary. "What do you do on the farm?" Schiff wanted to know. The young man explained that he was planting apple orchards and had a herd of dairy cattle. He added somewhat diffidently that he sometimes raised hogs. "Are they profitable?" Schiff inquired. Assured that they were indeed, he responded, "That's good. Then they are kosher." When Morgenthau demanded that the story be deleted because it was anti-Semitic, Blum was nonplused. "But you told me that story yourself," he argued. "I know," Morgenthau chortled. "But sometimes I'm anti-Semitic myself."

I cannot recall ever having a serious discussion with my father about Jewish matters; in fact we found talking intimately about anything difficult. It was not that there weren't warm feelings between us — to the contrary they were sometimes too hot to handle face to face. Often it seemed a little easier to talk on the telephone.

So it was that at the beginning of April 1962, just as he and

Marcelle returned from one of their frequent sojourns in France, I rang him up to announce that I was going to get married. At first he was incredulous. My younger brother and sister were already married and had produced grandchildren. I had established myself as a confirmed bachelor. I had met Ruth Schachter, who was fourteen years my junior, a year earlier when, as producer of *Eleanor Roosevelt: Prospects of Mankind* for public television, I had been sent to Ruth for expert advice for a program on the Congo crisis. Ruth was teaching in the Boston University African Studies Program. She was also weaning herself from cigarettes by chewing cloves. Facing me across a desk Ruth opened a small silver box and offered me a clove. I was intrigued by the cloves, by her lively, Nefertiti-like good looks, and a voice that sang softly in an accent I couldn't quite identify. As I discovered later it consisted of a top layer of Oxford English acquired with a D.Phil. degree, and a base of Viennese beginnings, with some Cuban Spanish and Upper West Side New Yorkese in the middle. Shortly after our first meeting, I took off on a trip around the world to recruit candidates for a State Department–sponsored seminar on communications I was to administer at Brandeis University. Afterward, a wise old friend compared me to someone he knew who took his honeymoon before his wedding.

When I introduced Ruth to my father, he preened as he told her she should have known him when he really was somebody. He didn't know what to make of this unexpected event, which he viewed with characteristic suspicion. Here was a young woman walking into our family with the self-assurance of someone who had firmly established her professional credentials and who had paid dearly for the privilege of being Jewish. Of Grandpa Morgenthau's twelve grandchildren, all of whom had already married at least once, about half had wedded Christians. The other half had Jewish spouses who favored the thoroughly assimilated life that our family had cultivated. (Barbara Tuchman's husband, Lester, was a notable exception. Contentious in his Jewishness and in his general attitude toward life, he had become increasingly committed to the traditions of his ancestors, with due adjustment to suburban Connecticut living.) Most of us were inclined to be apologetic about our Jewishness, or somberly rational, always on guard against setbacks in preserving our hard-won social advancements.

Ruth's parents had both been born in the province of Galicia (then in Austria-Hungary, now in Poland) in Bolechov, a small town near the city of Lemberg (Lvov). After the First World War, they married and went to live in Vienna, where Ruth and her sister, Alice, were born. One night shortly after Kristallnacht, November 9–10, 1938, when they were all gathered in their comfortable apartment overlooking the Danube canal, there was a knock on the door. They didn't answer. They heard men's voices. Someone said, "No, not this one," and they moved on. Ruth's mother fainted.

Before the end of the year the family managed to get out of Austria and headed for the United States, with several detours, including almost two years spent in Cuba. Both of Ruth's parents had been raised in Orthodox homes. Her father had become more rigidly observant in reaction to the ordeal he had suffered. Ruth's mother, on the other hand, became increasingly relaxed and optimistic, despite the fact that most of her relatives had disappeared in Poland during the Holocaust. Later she learned that both of her parents had been shot by German soldiers in a cemetery on the outskirts of Bolechov.

The Schachters were the living embodiment of the remnant of European Jewry that my father had agonized over and fought for. On the whole, both families were delighted, though both anticipated the union with some apprehension. Later, when Ruth's mother and I became very good friends, she confessed, "When Ruth told me she wanted to marry a Morgenthau, I told her, 'Watch out.' What is behind the name and the money? I hope there is a worthwhile human being.'"

Prior to the great event, Ruth's family treated me as though I were a Presbyterian. Moses (Mo) Feuerstein, the lay head of the Orthodox Jewish community, who had welcomed Ruth when she first came to Boston, handled the necessary negotiations with authority. He selected an Orthodox rabbi, William Weinberg, from Malden, Massachusetts (home base of the Feuerstein knitting mills). The rabbi in turn dispatched Mo to New York to check on my Jewish credentials with Rabbi Julius Mark at Temple Emanu-El who assured him that all my progenitors had been Jewish for at least three generations. Rabbi Weinberg was assisted in the wedding ceremony by a cantor imported from the synagogue the Schachters regularly attended in Washington Heights in New York and also by a close friend of mine, Fred Vogel, a Conservative rabbi who was the Brandeis chaplain.

Ruth and I were married on May 9, 1962, Israel Independence Day (according to the Jewish calendar of that year). The date had been selected to accommodate Orthodox restrictions as well as Eleanor Roosevelt's tight schedule.

The night before the ceremonies my brother, Bob, who was my best man (as I had been his), arranged a dinner for the two families in a private dining room at Boston's venerable Locke-Ober restaurant. In deference to her father, Ruth asked Bob to conform with the laws of kashrut, not an easy thing to do in a nonkosher restaurant. Of course we would have to eschew the lobster Savannah for which the establishment was famous. We settled on a main course of poached salmon, but this was hardly a satisfactory solution for Ruth's strict constructionist papa. After all, who knew what the cooking pots and serving plates had been exposed to? He finally agreed to a can of salmon that he would open himself and eat directly from the tin.

The next day, in Brandeis University's Berlin Chapel, Abram Sachar, the university's founding president, was delighted to have "Henry's father, the former Secretary of the Treasury, on the platform sitting near the Ark trying to cope with a skullcap, and with Mrs. Roosevelt smiling benignly at him and the couple from her seat in a front pew."

It was a beautiful, short, and simple ceremony that I thoroughly enjoyed, having memorized my part in Hebrew with difficulty. We drank wine from a silver cup that had been supplied by my great-uncle Irving Lehman for my parents' wedding in 1916. At the end, according to tradition, I crushed a glass with my foot. Mo Feuerstein came forward and gathered up all the pieces, placing them in a leather pouch as a keepsake. Afterward, my father descended into the small basement carved out below the chapel. Many years later Mo told me, "I followed him. He stood at the bottom of the stairs with his back to me, took out a handkerchief and began to dab his eyes. I went up to him. 'Is there anything wrong, Mr. Secretary?' I asked. 'You know he is my oldest son,' he answered. There were tears in his eyes. He was a very private person. With all his responsibilities, he was very emotional about private things."

A year later, our daughter Sarah was born. As new parents we were consumed at once with delight and concern. To the consternation of friends and, particularly, older relatives, whenever we accepted their hospitality we would arrive carrying Sarah with us in a wicker laundry basket.

Thirteen months after Sarah arrived, our son Ben was born. A chubby, self-assured baby, he soon wanted to do everything for himself, insisting in a deep, gravelly voice, "Ben do it." On his birth certificate he carries the name Henry (IV).

When our youngest child was born in December 1966, my father was too ill to see him. We named him Kramer, in honor of Chaim Kramer, the revered grandfather of Ruth's mother (our Kramer's great-great-grandfather). Though we were seasoned parents by the time Kramer came into the world, he nevertheless tried our composure when he became something of a skateboard prodigy, endowing the name of the hangout he frequented, Zero Gravity, with alarming verity.

These three latter-day Morgenthaus, well-differentiated individuals all, have one thing in common: more than a smattering of the Jewish education of which the author and his parents had been deprived.

My sister, Joan, my brother, Bob, and I had planned a festive ingathering of family and friends to celebrate our father's seventy-fifth birthday, May 11, 1966, but it never took place. Severe arterial sclerosis was rapidly slowing the flow of blood to his extremities. In a desperate remedial effort, the doctor amputated one of his legs above the knee. His mind fogged; still, there were painful lucid moments. On one such occasion while I was sitting at his bedside, he asked me in that old demanding way of his, "Was I a good father?" I told him that he was and felt sad that he needed that kind of reassurance. I wanted to hug him and ask him if I had been a good son, but I didn't.

Henry Morgenthau, Jr., died February 6, 1967, at Vassar Hospital in Poughkeepsie. On the day of the funeral all the workers of the major Jewish organizations in New York City were given the morning off to attend the funeral at Temple Emanu-El on Fifth Avenue.

Acknowledgments

Sources

Notes

Index

Acknowledgments

This book represents the wisdom, skills, and good will of many people who supported me in my effort to shape a vast body of documents and opinions into a readable story of a Jewish family transplanted from Germany to the United States, where it has thrived with uncommon vigor.

A number of people who encouraged me along the way are, sadly, no longer here to see the completed work. I am especially thankful to two of them.

Barbara Tuchman, with whom I share the Morgenthau ancestry, was particularly forthcoming with vivid memories of our grandfather. But she went far beyond that to encourage me, and to read through the early drafts of my manuscript, commenting and correcting in minute detail.

Gabrielle Elliot Forbush, my mother's close companion from their Vassar years until the end, reflected on what might have been the happiest moments of their lives and some of the frustrations that closed in on them in later years. As a writer and editor she too combed through "*the* book," as she called it, with a keen professional eye.

At the Roosevelt Library in Hyde Park, the director, Dr. William Emerson, was probably my most enthusiastic booster. Without his resourceful insights and the generous assistance of his wonderful staff, this book would have been well nigh impossible. My thanks and gratitude go especially to Elizabeth Denier, Susan Elter, Paul McLaughlin, Frances M. Seeber, and Raymond Teichman.

John Morton Blum, the distinguished Yale historian, as a young man had combed through the Morgenthau diaries and had reduced a mountain of material to three manageable volumes. These are the primary resource on the official career of "Henry the Morgue." With sagacity and humor, John divulged a great many humanizing anecdotes which, at the request of my father, he had refrained from including in his own books.

Rabbi Ben-Zion Gold of Harvard Hillel, a scholar and a generous friend, was my principal mentor in matters of Jewish thought and history.

He also translated Hebrew publications published at the time of Ambassador Morgenthau's visit to Palestine in 1914.

The staff of the Manuscript Division of the Library of Congress guided me through the Henry Morgenthau, Sr., papers, which my grandfather had given to them. I am particularly grateful to Dr. James Hutson, the director of the manuscript division at the time; to Garry Kohn, reference librarian; and to Allen Teichrow, who reorganized the Morgenthau papers preparatory to having them microfilmed.

At the New York headquarters of the Leo Baeck Institute, which is devoted to the study of German Jewry, Dr. Fred Grübel, formerly its director, steered me to appropriate resources in Germany and gave me access to the institute's incomparable archives. Dr. Sibyl Milton, Jonathan Sperber, and Frank Mecklenberg provided many important references.

At the Hochschule für Judische Studien in Heidelberg, members of the staff guided me to locations in Germany where Morgenthau ancestors had resided. Benno Szklanowski, a graduate student at the Hochschule, fluent in German, Hebrew, and English, took me on an extended tour of locations mentioned in Lazarus Morgenthau's diary.

In Mannheim, the last place where my forebears lived before emigrating to the United States, Dr. Karl Otto Watzinger, the leading authority on Mannheim Jewry, became a valuable mentor and friend. In the Mannheim Stadtarchiv, Dr. Friedrich Teutsch unearthed significant family records and other documents.

After I returned to the United States with a considerable collection of German materials, my friend Ernest Nathan in Rhode Island spent long hours translating them for me. My good neighbor in Cambridge, Gisela Warburg Wyzanski, translated additional documents and family letters.

Two experts on modern Armenian history, who understood the key role played by Ambassador Morgenthau in this tragic saga, were very helpful in throwing light on a vast body of conflicting opinions. Marjorie Housepian pulled together an annotated dossier of background material and got me back on course on difficult terrain with some strong critical jolts. Susan Blair treated me liberally to her rich assembly of research and writings, published and unpublished. Her husband, Richard Gould, then an archivist at the National Archives, ferreted out Morgenthau material and discovered a trove of documents shedding light on the ambassador's post-Armenian missions.

Eugene Black, a noted historian at Brandeis University, recruited some exceptionally able graduate students to assist me. John Hill helped me broaden the base of my research on Ambassador Morgenthau's 1917 secret mission and 1919 Polish mission. Sandra Gereau meticulously organized the source notes and the index.

In tracking down the Sykes and Himmelreich (changed to Heavenrich) antecedents of my Morgenthau grandmother, I had a lot of help from Bill Morris, the leading authority on the Jews of Manchester, England. Others in England who were most helpful include June Jacobs, Rosalyn Libshin, Arnold Lister, and Barry and Sonia Supple. Samuel Heavenrich provided key documentation of both the Himmelreich and Sykes families. And Joan Auerbach Dumont, a Sykes descendant, produced the only known photograph of our great-grandfather Samuel Sykes.

Some delightful anecdotal material about my mother's family came from several of her relatives, including Arthur and William Goodhart, Phyllis Goodhart Gordan, Frances (Peter) Lehman Loeb, and her late sister Helen Lehman Buttenwieser, for the Lehmans. The late Amy Spingarn and her daughter, Honor Tranum, spoke for the Fatmans.

A large batch of letters to Elinor Morgenthau from her devoted friend Eleanor Roosevelt, written in her barely decipherable hand, were transcribed for me by her former secretary, Maureen Corr, as a labor of love.

Others who aided me in producing the largest part of this book, that devoted to my father, include Mathilde Brailove, Frank W. Brecher, Rabbi Herbert Friedman, John Kenneth Galbraith, General Edward S. Greenbaum, Peter Grose, Bernard (Jack) Heineman, Jr., Henrietta and Herman Klotz, Phillip M. Klutznick, Lori Lefkowitz, Dan Ocko, Mark Sexton, Meyer Steinglass, and Frances Morgenthau Treguboff, as well as my brother and sister, Joan Morgenthau Hirschhorn and Robert M. Morgenthau.

The chain of events leading to this publication began when I wrote a playful, highly personal sketch of my family for *Moment* magazine. It caught the keen editorial eye of a lifelong friend, Jean Sulzberger, who brought it to the attention of the venerated literary agent Julian Bach. Julian, who became an enthusiastic advocate, assured me that publishers would take notice.

I was indeed blessed that John Herman, a sensitive and courageous editor, saw both the possibilities and problems of nursing the embryonic beginnings of my work to full maturity. A number of people, mostly under John's guidance, were helpful in bringing this about.

John Stuart Cox undertook the task of reducing an overgrown manuscript to a manageable size.

Daphne Abeel helped me abbreviate the opening chapters to an appropriate length.

At Ticknor & Fields, Caroline Sutton continued the process of refining. Margo Shearman went beyond copy editing to raise many challenging questions that brought clarity to both the substance and the style of my prose.

I am grateful for the all-important word processing of two friends and neighbors. Rosemary Brown accepted the lion's share of the job until the onset of her terminal illness. Barbara Swanson undertook to complete the job with great good humor and skill.

Finally I want to acknowledge with my love the support and affection of my immediate family, who gave me the courage to go on. My three children, Sarah, Ben, and Kramer, were rightfully concerned about the way I documented their past. My mother-in-law, Mizia Schachter, who makes her home with us, was as interested in what I was up to as were her grandchildren, and she read every revision of the manuscript with a critical eye.

Now that all is said and done, the one person indispensable to my carrying this book to its completion was my wife, Ruth. Having written many books and articles herself, she empathized with my frequent mood swings. She read every word with critical leniency while urging me onward. This was the ultimate mitzvah.

Sources

I collected material for this book for more years than I am willing to admit. Writing is hard work, but research is a pleasurable addiction. However, I finally faced the painful reality that enough has to be enough. What follows is an account of how and where I gathered substance for my writing, to guide those who may wish to pursue these matters further.

For each of the three parts of the book there proved to be successively larger amounts of source material. Yet even for Lazarus, enough written and visual documentation existed to bring him back to life.

Though he was not a public figure like the two Henrys, Lazarus nonetheless desired to leave his mark in the communities where he resided; the diary he wrote at twenty-seven is a remarkable testament to that wish. The writing could not have been an easy task for a young tailor, with only two years of formal schooling, who was struggling to earn a living. This little book, the first Morgenthau autobiography (published with the Louise Heidelberg "Sketch"), set me on the course that led to this family memoir.

I soon discovered rich veins of source material in two great libraries. My grandfather, Henry Morgenthau, Sr., donated the bulk of his papers to the Manuscript Division of the Library of Congress. I should note that he greatly disliked the appendage "Sr.," insisting that he was *the* Henry Morgenthau. (My father was "Jr." and I, the grandson, have become "III.") In my use of "Sr." I have accepted the librarians' labels, to avoid confusion.

The Library of Congress collection includes personal and official papers supported by family correspondence, documents, publications, and memorabilia. The Morgenthau propensity for autobiography went hand in hand with a strong archival instinct. Henry Morgenthau, Sr., saved everything he could lay his hands on, and he must have influenced other members of the family to turn their papers over to him; many predate his birth.

The second and larger collection of source material is at the Franklin D. Roosevelt Library, a division of the National Archives, in Hyde Park,

New York. My father gave this wonderful library most of his official and personal papers, and the family donated additional materials after his death in 1967. The FDR Library mother lode includes the Morgenthau Diaries and the Presidential Diaries. The former consists of about nine hundred volumes of official and supporting documents assembled while my father was secretary of the treasury. The latter consists largely of dictated memoranda documenting my father's relationship with his boss. The diaries include transcripts of his recorded telephone conversations and meetings. At that time it was not common to record conversations, and regulations controlling the practice were vague. Although my father deemed it inappropriate to tape his telephone conversations with the president, a few were recorded, probably inadvertently.

The Hyde Park collection also includes family correspondence and other documents of my grandfather's. At his death, my father, as executor, presented them to the FDR Library along with his own papers.

The State Department documents in the National Archives contain a great deal of material concerning my grandfather's official missions.

The Lazarus Morgenthau material at the Library of Congress led me to the New York offices of the Leo Baeck Institute, which is dedicated to the history of German Jewry. With the help of their knowledgeable staff, I was able to place the Morgenthau material in historical context. Dr. Sibyl Milton, then the chief archivist, guided me through a maze of documents and a series of historical maps of all the Jewish communities in Germany with their dates and sizes. The maps show many of the hamlets mentioned in Lazarus Morgenthau's diary that no longer exist. For example, Hürben, where Lazarus Morgenthau settled and was married, has merged with the neighboring town of Krumbach.

My briefings at the Leo Baeck Institute assisted me when I went to Germany in the summer of 1982 to gain a sense of the region where my ancestors lived. I started in Heidelberg at the Hochschule für Judische Studien, a center for Jewish studies and research established after World War II. With their staff I planned my trip through the territory described by Lazarus Morgenthau. In his diary he had indicated distances in days and hours of walking or cart riding. Most of the communities he wrote about were within a well-defined area of southern Germany, primarily in Bavaria. The cities and towns were in the river valleys of the Main, the Rhine, the Neckar, the Danube, and their tributaries.

In Mannheim, the Morgenthaus' final German home, I was warmly received by Dr. Karl Otto Watzinger, the leading authority on the history of Jewish Mannheim. He has written several articles and a book, *Geschichte der Juden in Mannheim 1650–1945* (*History of the Jews of Mannheim 1650–1945,* Stuttgart: Verlag W. Kohlhammer, 1984). In the Mannheim Stadtarchiv, with the assistance of the archivist, Friedrich Teutsch, I found the complete records of the Morgenthau family residences. Continuing this research in my behalf, Teutsch unearthed some real gems, such as an article in the *Mannheimer Anzeiger,* May 25, 1860, describing the visit to the Morgenthaus of the reigning archduke and duchess.

Henry Sr.'s journals and memoranda at the Library of Congress date back to his teenage years. They are at once blueprints of his good intentions and an uncensored balance sheet of the results. He also left a vast correspondence: letters received along with drafts, copies, or, in some instances, retrieved originals of his own letters. There is a large body of family letters exchanged among siblings and with Henry Sr.'s mother (in German) and later with his wife, children, and grandchildren.

At various times of his life Henry Sr. corresponded with mentors and peers. Probably the most important of these letters are those exchanged with Rabbi Stephen S. Wise. While Morgenthau was serving as ambassador to the Ottoman Empire, the two men sometimes wrote several times a week. Of special interest is the contemporary view of then Turkish Palestine, Egypt, and Syria.

Henry Sr. produced three autobiographies: *Ambassador Morgenthau's Story, All in a Life-Time,* and *I Was Sent to Athens.* (The privately printed *My Trip Around the World* was written for family and close friends only.) The stiffly formal portraits painted by his ghost writers bear scant resemblance to the feisty grandfather I loved. However, the account of the massacre of the Armenians in *Ambassador Morgenthau's Story* has become gospel to the survivors, and its author is remembered as their apostle.

Much, of course, overlaps in the writings pertaining to Henry Morgenthau Senior and Junior. Henry Jr. immeasurably advanced the family propensity for record keeping and preservation. While Lazarus and Henry Sr. were their own archivists, my father institutionalized the procedure. During his tenure at the Treasury he employed the fulltime services of a dedicated librarian, Isabelle Diamond, who under the watchful eye of his confidential secretary, Henrietta Klotz, assembled the volumes of papers known as the Morgenthau Diaries.

Writing letters was a daunting experience for my father, but when pressed he managed to express himself with an appealing if awkward directness. My mother, Elinor, was much more prolific and wrote lots of wonderfully revealing letters. In addition to her family correspondence there is a large body of letters she received from Eleanor Roosevelt. Though for the most part my mother's letters to her have vanished, the Roosevelt letters tell a great deal about the ups and downs of this friendship that was so important to our family.

My father could wax eloquent when he dictated. In 1945, when my brother and I were serving overseas, he began a remarkable series of letters to us that continued through the end of his tenure at the Treasury. The letters detail his impressions of historic events, including his evening with FDR the night before the president's death.

In dealing with the Morgenthau years in government, John Morton Blum's masterful three-volume *From the Morgenthau Diaries* remains the ultimate resource. Blum took on the prodigious job of sifting, selecting, and evaluating the entire body of material in the diaries, which he enriched by checking with his subject and related sources. Where I have referred directly to the Morgenthau Diaries, I have used Blum's system, in which the volume number of the diary precedes the colon, and page numbers or dates follow it. In an interview I had with Blum recently, he was very candid about what he had left out of his books and why. His anecdotes were at once entertaining and informative.

The interview with Blum was one of many I have listed below as a major resource for this book. In talking with relatives, family friends, and official associates I have garnered recollections that in some instances extend back to the closing years of the nineteenth century.

Among the many interviews concerning my family, Barbara Tuchman's was the most comprehensive. Representing my mother's side of the family, a cousin, Phyllis Goodhart Gordan, and Gabrielle Elliot Forbush, Vassar 1912, were especially helpful.

Harold Hochschild, my father's closest boyhood friend, and Henrietta Klotz both had much to say that was meaningful, if subjective.

I interviewed a number of men who had served as Secretary Morgenthau's key aides. Edward Bernstein's perception of the Bretton Woods agreements and the roles played by John Maynard Keynes and Harry Dexter White were especially helpful. John Pehle, Josiah DuBois, and Colonel Bernard Bernstein helped me understand the War Refugee Board and the Morgenthau Plan.

In the latter portion of the book, where I describe Henry Morgenthau Jr.'s activities as secretary of the treasury, I have gone to considerable lengths to examine the influence of his controversial adviser, economist Harry Dexter White. Many people shed light on the Morgenthau-White relationship, but I learned the most from Edward Bernstein. As White's principal assistant in formulating the Bretton Woods agreements, Bernstein best understood White's professional brilliance and personal limitations, as well as his relationship to Morgenthau.

The FBI dossiers, including the comments of J. Edgar Hoover, which are now available, reveal no incriminating evidence of White's disloyalty. Indeed, in all of the voluminous congressional and government records of investigations, nothing would convince an objective observer that White was anything but a loyal public servant. What does emerge is that Morgenthau, who had fully trusted White, was greatly shaken by the allegations made after he himself was out of government. Morgenthau's efforts thereafter to get to the bottom of the White affair were stymied, and his personal doubts remained unresolved. Since then the Freedom of Information Act has made it possible, though by no means easy, to examine the relevant documents. My daughter, Sarah, started the process of gaining access to the Morgenthau-White files, and Dan Ocko carried through in the arduous search. My brother, Robert, who counseled our father during his postwar dealings with the FBI and the Eastland Committee's Senate investigation, was able to recall some significant details of these proceedings.

After my father left the Treasury, he no longer kept voluminous records of his activities. I have interviewed many of his associates at the United Jewish Appeal and the Israel Bond drives that he headed. They include Mathilde Brailove, Rabbi Herbert Friedman, Rabbi Baruch Korff, and Meyer Steinglass. I also used written and photographic materials from the extensive UJA archives.

Throughout the writing of this book I have relied heavily on primary sources and my personal recollections, and I have attempted to place my remarks in historical perspective. Jacob Katz's *Out of the Ghetto* provided an understanding of Lazarus Morgenthau's Germany. For the Roosevelt-Morgenthau connection and the Roosevelt era, I benefited particularly from the writings of Frank Freidel, Joseph P. Lash, and Arthur M. Schlesinger, Jr. Two works that reflect Secretary Morgenthau's attempts to enlist the U.S. government in countering the Nazi destruction of the Jews are *The Politics of Rescue* by Henry Feingold and the *The Abandonment of the Jews* by David S. Wyman. Supplementary conversations with Wyman opened the way to other valuable resources. I gained some understanding of the controversy over the Morgenthau Plan from *On Active Service in Peace and War* by Henry L. Stimson and McGeorge Bundy as well as from Stimson's diaries (Henry L. Stimson Papers, Manuscripts and Archives, Yale University Library). In writing the final portion of the book, devoted to Morgenthau's involvement in Jewish affairs, I found the analysis in Peter Grose's *Israel in the Mind of America* consistently dependable and brilliant.

The notes, sources, and bibliography that follow will provide those who are interested with more comprehensive information.

INTERVIEWS

Bagiotti, Josephine
Bernstein, Bernard
Bernstein, Edward
Blair, Susan
Bloomfield, Dorothy
Blum, John Morton
Brailove, Mathilde
Doyle, Marian

DuBois, Josiah
Eliachar, Menache
Forbush, Gabrielle Elliot
Fox, Henry M.
Friedman, Herbert
Frisch, David
Goodhart, Arthur L.
Gordan, Phyllis

Halle, Peter
Hochschild, Harold
Joseph, Louise
Kahn, Virginia Lewisohn
Klotz, Henrietta
Korff, Baruch
Langley, Robert
Lowe, Charles U.
Morgenthau, Joan E.
Morgenthau, Robert M.
Pehle, John

Porter, Sylvia
Rosenman, Dorothy
Sagalyn, Arnold
Spingarn, Amy
Steinglass, Meyer
Straus, Flora Stieglitz
Straus, Helen Sachs
Sulzberger, Iphigene Ochs
Sulzberger, Louise Blumenthal
Tranum, Honor
Tuchman, Barbara

NEWSPAPERS

American Hebrew
American Israelite
New York Nachrichten
New York Post

New York Times
Washington Daily News
Washington Herald
Washington Post

BOOKS AND ARTICLES

Adler, Cyrus. *Jacob Schiff: His Life and Letters.* 2 vols. New York: Doubleday, 1928.

Agar, Herbert. *The Saving Remnant: An Account of Jewish Survival.* New York: Viking Press, 1978.

Arlen, Michael J. *Passage to Ararat.* New York: Farrar Straus Giroux, 1975.

Baker, Leonard. *Brandeis and Frankfurter: A Dual Biography.* New York: New York University Press, 1984.

Bauer, Jehuda. *My Brother's Keeper: A History of the American Jewish Joint Distribution Committee, 1929–1939.* Philadelphia: Jewish Publication Society of America, 1974.

Bierstadt, Edward Hale. *The Great Betrayal. A Survey of the Near East Problem.* New York: Robert M. McBride and Co., 1924.

Birmingham, Stephen. *"Our Crowd": The Great Jewish Families of New York.* New York: Harper & Row, 1967.

Blair, Susan. "Excuses of Humanity: The Official German Response to the 1915 Armenian Genocide." *American Review* 37 (1984):14–30.

———. "America's Greatest Act: Near East Relief in Retrospect." In *Remembrance and Hope.* New York: Prelacy of the Armenian Church, 1985.

———. *Windows in Heaven: The Story of Near East Relief.* Unpublished manuscript.

Blum, John Morton. *From the Morgenthau Diaries.* Vol. 1: *Years of Crisis, 1928–1938.* Boston: Houghton Mifflin, 1959.

———. *From the Morgenthau Diaries.* Vol. 2: *Years of Urgency, 1938–1941.* Boston: Houghton Mifflin, 1965.

———. *From the Morgenthau Diaries.* Vol. 3: *Years of War, 1941–1945.* Boston: Houghton Mifflin, 1967.

Bryce, Viscount. *The Treatment of the Armenians in the Ottoman Empire, 1915–1916.* Beirut: G. Donoguian and Sons, 1979.

Burton, J. Hendrick. "Henry Morgenthau, Diplomat." *World's Work* 32 (1916), 97–110.

Clarke, Elspeth McClure, and Court Carroll Walters. *The Joy of Service, Memoirs of Elizabeth Dodge Huntington Clarke.* New York: National Board of the Young Women's Christian Association, 1979.

Daniels, Josephus. *The Life of Woodrow Wilson.* New York: Will E. Johnston, 1924.

Des Pres, Terence. "On Governing Narratives: The Turkish-Armenian Case." *Yale Review* (1986):517–31.

Donovan, Robert J. *Tumultuous Years: The Presidency of Harry S. Truman, 1949–1953.* New York: W. W. Norton, 1967.

———. *Conflict and Crisis. The Presidency of Harry S. Truman, 1945–1948.* New York. W. W. Norton, 1977.

DuBois, Josiah. *The Devil's Chemists.* Boston: Beacon Press, 1952.

Eisenhower, David. *Eisenhower at War: 1943–1945.* New York: Random House, 1986.

Evans, Laurence. *United States Policy and the Partition of Turkey 1914–1924.* Baltimore: Johns Hopkins University Press, 1965.

Feingold, Henry L. *The Politics of Rescue: The Roosevelt Administration and the Holocaust, 1938–1945.* New York: Holocaust Library, 1970.

Freidel, Frank. *Franklin D. Roosevelt: A Rendezvous with Destiny.* Boston: Little, Brown, 1990.

Friedman, Isaiah. *The Question of Palestine, 1914–1918: British-Jewish-Arab Relations.* London: Routledge and Kegan Paul, 1973.

Furman, Bess. *Washington By-Line: The Personal Story of a Newspaperwoman.* New York: Alfred A. Knopf, 1949.

Gidney, James B. *A Mandate for Armenia.* Kent, Ohio: Kent State University Press, 1967.

Glazer, Nathan, and Daniel P. Moynihan. *Ethnicity: Theory and Practice.* Cambridge, Mass.: Harvard University Press, 1975.

Goldstein, Alice. "Some Demographic Characteristics of Village Jews in Germany: Nonnenweier, 1800–1931." In Paul Ritterband, ed., *Modern Jewish Fertility.* Leiden: E. J. Brill, 1981.

———. "Urbanization in Baden, Germany: Focus on the Jews, 1825–1925." *Social Science History* (1984):43–66.

————. "Aspects of Change in a Nineteenth-Century German Village." *Journal of Family History* (1984):145–57.

Goodhart, Arthur L. *Poland and the Minority Races.* New York: Brentano, 1920.

Greenbaum, Edward S. *A Lawyer's Job.* New York: Harcourt Brace Jovanovich, 1967.

Grose, Peter. *Israel in the Mind of America.* New York: Schocken, 1984.

Halpern, Ben. *The American Jew: The Zionist Analysis.* New York: Theodor Herzl Foundation, 1956.

Han, Paul Y. *Directives for the Occupation of Germany: The Washington Controversy.*

Handlin, Oscar. *A. L. Smith and His America.* Boston: Little, Brown, 1958.

Hartunian, Abraham H. *Neither to Laugh Nor to Weep: A Memoir of the Armenian Genocide.* Trans. Vartan Hartunian. Boston: Beacon Press, 1968.

Hellman, Geoffrey T. "Profiles: Any Bonds Today? Henry Morgenthau, Jr." *The New Yorker,* Jan. 22 and Jan. 29, 1944.

Housepian, Marjorie. "The Unremembered Genocide." *Commentary* (1966):55–62.

————. *Smyrna, 1922: The Destruction of a City.* London: Faber and Faber, 1982.

————. "What Genocide? What Holocaust? News from Turkey 1915–1923: A Case Study." In *Toward the Understanding and Prevention of Genocide,* 1982, pp. 100–12.

Hughes, H. Stuart. *Gentleman Rebel: The Memoirs of H. Stuart Hughes.* New York: Ticknor & Fields, 1990.

Hull, Cordell. *The Memoirs of Cordell Hull.* New York: Macmillan, 1948.

"The Israeli Connection: Who Israel Arms and Why." *Armenian Review* 30 (1977–78):16–17.

Jacob, Gustav. *Mannheim: so wie es war.* Düsseldorf: Droste Verlag, 1971.

Kaplan, Marion. "Family Structure and the Position of Jewish Women." In Werner Mosse, Arnold Pauckert, and Reinhard Ruerup, eds. *Revolution and Evolution: 1848 in German Jewish History.* Tubingen: J. C. B. Mohr, 1981.

Katz, Jacob. *Exclusiveness and Tolerance: Jewish-Gentile Relations in Medieval and Modern Times.* New York: Schocken, 1962.

————. *Out of the Ghetto: The Social Background of Jewish Emancipation. 1770–1870.* Cambridge, Mass.: Harvard University Press, 1973.

Keller, Volker. "Die ehmatige Hauptsynagoge in Mannheim." *Mannheimer Hefte* (1982):2–14.

Kloian, Richard D. *The Armenian Genocide: First Twentieth-Century Holocaust.* Berkeley: Anto Offset, 1980.

Korff, Baruch. *Flight from Fear.* New York: Elmar Publishers, 1955.

Kranzler, David. *Thy Brother's Blood: The Orthodox Jewish Response during the Holocaust.* New York: Mesorah Publications, 1987.

Lambert, A. L., and G. B. Layton, eds. *The Ghosts of Patton's Third Army.* Second Cavalry Association. Munich: n.d.

Lash, Joseph P. *Eleanor and Franklin: The Story of a Relationship.* New York: W. W. Norton, 1971.

————. *Eleanor: The Years Alone.* New York: W. W. Norton, 1972.

————. *Love, Eleanor: Eleanor Roosevelt to Her Friends.* New York: Doubleday, 1982.

————. *A World of Love: Eleanor Roosevelt and Her Friends, 1943–1962.* New York: Doubleday, 1984.

Lebow, Richard Ned. "The Morgenthau Peace Mission of 1917." *Jewish Social Studies* 32 (1970):267–85.

Lehman, Herbert H. *Tributes and Other Documents.* Stanford: Overbrook Press, 1946.

Lehman Brothers 1850–1950: A Centennial. New York: privately printed, 1950.

Leighton, Isabel, and Gabrielle Forbush. *My Boy Franklin.* As Told by Mrs. James Roosevelt. New York: Ray Long and Richard Smith, 1933.

Lemkin, Raphael. *Axis Rule in Occupied Europe: Laws of Occupation, Analysis of Government Proposals for Redress.* 1944.

Link, Arthur S. *Wilson: The Road to the White House.* Princeton: Princeton University Press, 1946.

Loewenstein, Steven. "Voluntary and Involuntary Limitation of Fertility in Nineteenth-Century Bavarian Jewry." In Paul Ritterband, ed., *Modern Jewish Fertility.* Leiden: E. J. Brill, 1981, pp. 94–111.

Magnus, Philip. *Kitchener: Portrait of an Imperialist.* New York: E. P. Dutton, 1915.

Marcus, Jacob. *The Rise and Destiny of the German Jew.* Cincinnati: Department of Synagogue and School Extension, 1934.

Margolis, Max, and Alexander Marx. *A History of the Jewish People.* New York: Meridian, 1958.

Moggridge, Donald, ed. *The Collected Writings of John Maynard Keynes.* Vol. 25: *Activities 1940–1944. Shaping the Postwar World: The Clearing Union.* Cambridge: Cambridge University Press, 1980.

Moran, Lord. *Churchill Taken from the Diaries of Lord Moran: The Struggle for Survival, 1940–1965.* Boston: Houghton Mifflin, 1966.

Morgan, Ted. *FDR: A Biography.* New York: Simon and Schuster, 1985.

Morgenthau, Henry, Jr. *Germany Is Our Problem: A Plan for Germany.* New York: Harper Brothers, 1945.

————. "The Morgenthau Diaries. Part 1: The Fight to Balance the Budget." *Collier's,* Sept. 27, 1947, pp. 11–13, 80–82.

———. "The Morgenthau Diaries. Part 2: The Struggle for a Program." *Collier's,* Sept. 27, 1947, pp. 10–12, 45–47.

———. "The Morgenthau Diaries. Part 3: How FDR Fought the Axis." *Collier's,* Oct. 11, 1947, pp. 20–21, 72–75, 77, 79.

———. "The Morgenthau Diaries. Part 4: The Story Behind Lend-Lease." *Collier's,* Oct. 18, 1947, pp. 16–17, 71–72, 74–75.

———. "The Morgenthau Diaries. Part 5: The Paradox of Poverty and Plenty." *Collier's,* Oct. 25, 1947, pp. 24–25, 83, 85–86.

———. "The Morgenthau Diaries. Part 6: The Refugee Run-Around." *Collier's,* Nov. 1, 1947, pp. 22–23, 62, 65.

Morgenthau, Henry, Sr. *Ambassador Morgenthau's Story.* New York: Doubleday, Page, 1918.

———. "The Jews in Poland." *World's Work* (1922):617–30.

———. *All in a Life-Time.* New York: Doubleday, Page, 1926.

———. *I Was Sent to Athens.* New York: Doubleday, Page, 1929.

———. *My Trip Around the World.* Privately published.

Morgenthau, Lazarus. *Lebens Geschichte von Lazarus Morgenthau aus Hürben bei Krumbach.* Trans. Louise Heidelberg. Speyer, 1842.

Morse, Arthur D. *While Six Million Died: A Chronicle of American Apathy.* New York: Random House, 1967.

Mowrer, Edgar Ansel. *Germany Puts the Clock Back.* New York: Reynal, 1960.

"Mr. Roosevelt's Men." *Fortune,* February 1934.

Murphy, Bruce Allen. *The Brandeis-Frankfurter Connection: The Secret Political Activities of Two Supreme Court Justices.* New York: Oxford University Press, 1982.

Nevins, Allan. *Herbert L. Lehman and His Era.* New York: Scribners, 1963.

"One of Two of a Kind." *Fortune,* May 1934.

Phillips, Harlan. *Felix Frankfurter: Reminisces.* New York: Reynal, 1960.

Piper Schmitt, Judy. *The Prince Remembers: One Hundred Years of the Daily Princetonian, 1876–1976.* Princeton: Daily Princetonian Publishing Co., 1977.

Raphael, Marc Lee. *Understanding American Jewish Philanthropy.* New York: KTAV, 1979.

———. *A History of the United Jewish Appeal 1939–1982.* Chico, Calif.: Scholars Press, 1982.

Richter, Julius. *A History of Protestant Missions in the Near East.*

Roosevelt, Eleanor, *This Is My Story.* New York: Harper and Brothers, 1937.

———. *This I Remember.* New York: Harper Brothers, 1949.

———. *On My Own: The Years Since the White House.* New York: Harper Brothers, 1958.

Roosevelt, James. *My Parents: A Differing View.* Chicago: Playboy Press, 1976.

Rose, Peter I., ed. *The Ghetto and Beyond: Essays on Jewish Life in America.* New York: Random House, 1969.

Rosenman, Samuel I. *Working with Roosevelt.* New York: Harper Brothers, 1952.

Rossbach, Mabel Limburg. "Summering: Memoirs of Mabel Limburg Rossbach." *Adirondack Life* 2 (1971):8–13.

Sachar, Abram. *A Host At Last.* Boston: Little, Brown, 1976.

Schlesinger, Arthur M., Jr. *The Age of Roosevelt.* Vol. 1: *The Crisis of the Old Order.* Boston: Houghton Mifflin, 1957.

———. *The Age of Roosevelt.* Vol. 2: *The Coming of the New Deal.* Boston: Houghton Mifflin, 1959.

———. *The Age of Roosevelt.* Vol. 3: *The Politics of Upheaval.* Boston: Houghton Mifflin, 1960.

"Secretary Morgenthau." *Fortune* 9 (1934):60–64.

Shaw, Carolyn Hagner. *The Social List of Washington, D.C.* 1946.

Sherwood, Robert E. *Roosevelt and Hopkins: An Intimate History.* New York: Harper Brothers, 1948.

Shirer, William L. *The Rise and Fall of the Third Reich: A History of Nazi Germany.* New York: Simon and Schuster, 1960.

Silberman, Charles. *A Certain People: American Jews and Their Lives Today.* New York: Summit, 1985.

Sklare, Marshall. *America's Jews.* New York: Random House, 1971.

———. *The Jew in American Society.* New York: Behrman House, 1974.

Stimson, Henry L., and McGeorge Bundy. *On Active Service in Peace and War.* New York: Harper Brothers, 1947.

Straus, Flora Stieglitz. *Bits and Pieces.* Privately printed.

Straus, Oscar S. *Under Four Administrations.* Boston: Houghton Mifflin, 1922.

Synnott, Marcia Graham. *The Half-Opened Door: Discrimination and Admission at Harvard, Yale, and Princeton, 1900–1970.* Westport, Conn.: Greenwood Press, 1979.

Tuchman, Barbara. *The Guns of August.* New York: Macmillan, 1962.

———. "Ambassador Morgenthau's Story." *Commentary* 63 (May 1977):58–62.

Tully, Grace. *FDR My Boss.* New York: Scribners, 1949.

Voss, Carl Hermann, ed. *Stephen Wise: Servant of a People.* Philadelphia: Jewish Publication Society of America, 1969.

Warburg, Edward M. M. *As I Recall.* Privately printed, 1978.

Warburg, Frieda Schiff. *Reminiscences of a Long Life.* New York: privately printed, 1956.

Watzinger, Karl Otto. *Geschichte der Juden in Mannheim, 1650–1945.* Stuttgart: Kohlhammer, 1984.

Weinstein, Allen. *Perjury: The Hiss-Chambers Case.* New York: Alfred A. Knopf, 1978.

Weizmann, Chaim. *Trial and Error: The Autobiography of Chaim Weizmann.* 1949; reprint: Westport, Conn.: Greenwood Press, 1972.

Williams, Bill. *The Making of Manchester Jewry, 1740–1875.* Manchester: Manchester University Press, 1976.

———. *Manchester Jewry: A Pictorial History, 1788–1988.* Manchester, Eng.: Archive Publications, 1988.

Wise, Stephen. *Challenging Years.* New York: G. P. Putnam and Sons, 1949.

Wyman, David S. *The Abandonment of the Jews.* New York: Pantheon Books, 1984.

Yahuda, A. S. *Dr. Weismann's Errors on Trial.* Privately printed, 1952.

Yale, William. "Ambassador Henry Morgenthau's Special Mission of 1917." *World Politics.* 11 (948):308–20.

Notes

ABBREVIATIONS

ALT   Henry Morgenthau, *All in a Life-Time* (New York: Doubleday, Page, and Co., 1921)

AMS   Henry Morgenthau, *Ambassador Morgenthau's Story* (New York: Doubleday, Page, and Co., 1918)

Blum   John Morton Blum, *From the Morgenthau Diaries,* Vol. 1: *Years of Crisis, 1928–1938*; Vol. 2: *Years of Urgency, 1938–1941*; Vol. 3: *Years of War, 1941–1945* (Boston: Houghton Mifflin, 1959, 1965, 1967)

DLM   Lazarus Morgenthau's diary (*Lebens Geschichte von Lazarus Morgenthau* [Speyer: privately printed, 1842]), translated by Louise Heidelberg

FDRL   Franklin Delano Roosevelt Library, Hyde Park, New York

FRUS   *Foreign Relations of the United States,* reports of the U.S. State Department

LC   Henry Morgenthau, Sr., Papers, Manuscript Division, Library of Congress

MD   Henry Morgenthau, Jr., diaries, FDRL

MPD   Henry Morgenthau, Jr., Presidential Diaries, FDRL

page

CHAPTER 1. *Trying to Survive in Early Nineteenth-Century Bavaria*

3   All quotes in chapter 1, unless otherwise noted, are from the Lazarus Morgenthau diary, *Lebens Geschichte von Lazarus Morgenthau aus Hürben bei Krumbach,* translated by Louise Heidelberg (Speyer: privately printed, 1842). This edition includes a biographical "Sketch" prepared by Louise Heidelberg. The Morgenthau family will be forever grateful to our cousin for having preserved, translated, and annotated this extended memoir. The Diary of Lazarus Morgenthau (abbreviated hereafter as DLM) and the Max Morgenthau memo are both available in the Henry Morgenthau, Sr., Papers, Manu-

script Division, Library of Congress, Washington, D.C. These papers are abbreviated hereafter as LC.

CHAPTER 2. *An Ambitious Tailor Cuts a Few Corners*

20   "paid very close": DLM, pp. 94–96.
21   "I took my whole": Ibid., pp. 98–99.
22   "this speculation": Ibid., pp. 100–101.

CHAPTER 3. *Mannheim: Success and Failure in the Cigar Business*

27   M1-10: Mannheim Stadtarchiv. Dr. Fred Grübel at the Leo Baeck Institute in New York told me that Dr. Karl-Otto Watzinger was the foremost authority on Jewish life in Mannheim. Dr. Watzinger has written several articles and a book, *History of the Jews of Mannheim 1650–1945 (Geschichte der Juden in Mannheim 1650–1945* [Stuttgart: Verlag W. Kohlhammer, 1985]). After leaving Krumbach I hastened to Mannheim with high hopes for my prearranged rendezvous at the hotel, where I found Dr. Watzinger waiting and ready. This courtly, silver-haired Christian gentleman had been imprisoned in Dachau by the Nazis. After the war, the U.S. military government made him the administrative bürgermeister of Mannheim. Dr. Watzinger had already collected basic information on the Morgenthau family. On the evening of my arrival he drove me around the city, and we saw the location of the two successive Morgenthau residences. The buildings had been destroyed when the central city was leveled by U.S. bombers toward the end of the war. In addition to his personal briefings and his writings, Dr. Watzinger led me to the Mannheim Stadtarchiv and introduced me to one of the archivists, Dr. Friedrich Teutsch, who was able to dig out the complete residency records. Dr. Watzinger also sent me to the Riis Museum, which houses an extensive collection of paintings, photographs, and artifacts spanning the entire history of Mannheim. The neighboring Theater Museum has a collection of playbills and other memorabilia of performances, some of which Lazarus attended.
     "Swarms of fugitives": Karl-Otto Watzinger, "Die Jüdische Gemeinde in Mannheim in der Grossherzoglichen Zeit, 1803–1918 [The Jewish Community of Mannheim in the Time of the Archduchy]," in *Sonderdruck aus der Zeitschrift,* Mannheimer Hefte, 1981/2, p. 22. English translation of text by Ernest Nathan.
     "acts of blind": Ibid.
29   "The problem with": Memorandum by Maximilian Morgenthau, December 19, 1929. This memo was probably written at the request

of Louise Heidelberg. In her "Sketch," she credits Max as her main source of information about the family subsequent to what Lazarus covered in his diary.

"rejected about": Ibid.

30   At the beginning: Mannheim Stadtarchiv.

A woodcut print: See Gustaf Jacob, *Mannheim — so wie es war* (Düsseldorf: Droste Verlag, 1971), p. 41.

33   The words had been: Hermann Levi, a Jew, conducted the first performance of Wagner's *Parsifal,* at the composer's behest. Wagner, an overt anti-Semite, "never had any objection to accepting money from Jews, nor to calling on their assistance in the production of his operas." Ernst Newman, *Wagner, As Man and Artist* (Garden City, N.Y.: Garden City Publishing Co., 1937), p. 129.

The synagogue ledger: DLM, p. 115.

At about that same time: Ibid.

To the Society: Ibid.

34   Carl arranged: Ibid.

"The zenith": Max Morgenthau memo.

"In November": Ibid.

35   "Unfortunately": Henry Morgenthau, Sr., *All in a Life-Time* (New York: Doubleday, Page and Company 1921), p. 4, hereafter abbreviated as *ALT.*

"He took out patents": Max Morgenthau memo, p. 20.

"and though": Ibid.

37   The festive atmosphere: Henry Morgenthau, Sr., date unknown, LC.

"My dear son:" Max Morgenthau memo, and *ALT*, pp. 4–5.

CHAPTER 4. *The Morgenthaus Transplanted in New York*

38   "At our arrival": *ALT,* p. 13.

39   He invented: DLM, p. 117.

"In the course of settling": *ALT.*

"He knew the power": Ibid.

40   The rabbi, Dr. David Einhorn: Ibid.; and *Encyclopedia of the Jewish Religion*, p. 125.

41   As his enterprise: "The Golden Book," *Jewish Times,* September 1871.

42   Dr. Einhorn eulogized: *Jewish Times,* March 21, 1871.

"requesting of him": Henry Morgenthau, Sr., to Samuel Schlessinger, September 24, 1872, LC.

"This day ought to be": Henry Morgenthau, Sr., diary, September 23, 1872, LC.

"orphan girls": Ibid.

43   "about seventy-five": *Jewish Times,* March 21, 1871.
      would "likely cut": Henry Morgenthau, Sr., "Centennial Reminiscences," LC.
48   "contact with other": *M. N. Figaro,* undated article (c. 1888), LC.

CHAPTER 5. *Ambition and Idealism*

54   "We were given": *ALT,* p. 3.
55   "These letters gave": Ibid.
      "On the stormiest": *Hermann* manifest listing, Lazarus Morgenthau, LC.
56   "to restore my mother": *ALT,* p. 14.
      "I was full": Ibid., p. 15.
57   He began at: Ibid., p. 7.
58   "Though 'stumped'": Ibid., p. 13.
      "how so rich": From a memorandum dated Nov. 17, 1872, and signed by Henry Morgenthau, Sr., LC.
59   "formed the habit": *ALT,* p. 15.
      "He was the physician": Ibid. Henry Morgenthau, Sr., diary, April 26, 1872, mentions the book *No Cross, No Crown* as a gift from Dr. Samuel S. Whitall.
60   "lacked the requisite": *ALT,* p. 18.
      "til September 16th": Henry Morgenthau, Sr., "Autobiography," 1871–72, LC.
61   "Stenographers": *ALT,* p. 12.
      "when his individual": From a long and generally laudatory — though strikingly candid — obituary of Lazarus Morgenthau published in the *American Israelite* with the dateline New York, September 1, 1897.
62   "I shall relate": Henry Morgenthau, Sr., to Sam Schlessinger, September 29, 1872, LC.
      "[Grant] is a mere": Ibid.
      "If any of our": Henry Morgenthau, Sr., diary, January 1, 1872.
63   "This will help": Ibid.
      "I eat for my": Ibid.
64   "We have all": Henry Morgenthau, Sr., to Sam Schlessinger, September 24, 1872, LC.
      The proceedings: The *Sun,* New York, December 3, 1872; and *Neue Yorker Tages-Wachrichten,* December 3, 1872, LC.
      "[I] shall never": *ALT,* p. 18.
      "No man": Ibid., p. 20.
      "the president": Ibid., p. 21.
65   When Henry reached: Ibid., pp. 21–22.
      "had not lived": Ibid., p. 22.

CHAPTER 6. *An Eye-opening Return to Germany*

67   "where I listened": Henry Morgenthau, Sr., diary, August 1874. The spellings found in the original source have been retained here. "C.S. weighed": Ibid., p. 49.

CHAPTER 7. *Studying Law at Columbia*

70   "the country [is]": Henry Morgenthau, Sr., "Centennial Reminiscences," 1876.
71   "even if I": Ibid.

CHAPTER 8. *On the Bumpy Road to Love*

73   "He was about": *ALT,* p. 31.
74   "plots of three": Ibid.
75   "two inches smaller": Henry Morgenthau, Sr., to Ida Ehrich, October 21, 1882, Franklin Delano Roosevelt Library, Hyde Park, New York, hereafter abbreviated as FDRL.
      "I neither expect": Ibid.
76   "Probably this": Julius Morgenthau to Henry Morgenthau, Sr., December 15, 1882, LC.
      "Ever since": Josephine Sykes to Henry Morgenthau, Sr., December, 1882, FDRL.
77   "I insist on": Henry Morgenthau, Sr., to Josephine Sykes, December 8, 1882, FDRL.
      "a tiny bit": Dorothy Bloomfield, interview with the author, 1984.
78   Three important clues: Most of the leads that I was able to track down were provided by Bill Williams, an engaging Welshman who has written a definitive history of the Jews of Manchester (*The Making of Manchester Jewry, 1740–1875* [Manchester: Manchester University Press, 1976]), as well as a pictorial history (*Manchester Jewry: A Pictorial History, 1788–1988* [Urmston, Manchester: Archive Publications, 1988]). He is also the prime mover behind the Manchester Jewish Museum, established in the former Spanish-Portuguese synagogue.
      It was one of: Ibid., p. 179.
      "voluntary ghetto": Williams, *The Making of Manchester Jewry,* pp. 176–77.
      It was one of: Ibid., pp. 179.
      Manchester Guardian article: This was discovered by Bill Williams after his two books on Manchester Jewry were published.
      Scholar Bill Williams: *The Making of Manchester Jewry,* pp. 176, 362.
80   "help-mate to dear": Samuel Heavenrich memo, 1929, LC.

81   "Sykes thought": Ibid.
      "The Sykeses were": Bloomfield interview.
      "Henry asserted": Josephine Sykes to Henry Morgenthau, Sr., December 1882, LC.

82   "With Papa": Henry Morgenthau, Sr., to his mother, April 16,1883, FDRL.
      "The 5 months": Henry Morgenthau, Sr., to Julius Morgenthau, undated.

83   "At lunch": Henry Morgenthau, Sr., to Julius Morgenthau, May 22, 1883, FDRL.
      "how happy": Henry Morgenthau, Sr., to Julius Morgenthau, May 11, 1883, FDRL.

84   "Let me state": Henry Morgenthau, Sr., to Julius Morgenthau, May 22, 1883, FDRL.

85   "I remind myself": Josephine to Henry Morgenthau, Sr., July 3, 1891, FDRL.

86   "My dear little": Henry Morgenthau, Sr., to Josephine, July 6, 1884, FDRL.

87   "With much love": Josephine to Henry Morgenthau, Sr., July 22, 1884, FDRL.
      "I'll calm your": Henry Morgenthau, Sr., to Josephine, July 24, 1884, FDRL.
      "Yesterday was": Josephine to Henry Morgenthau, Sr., August 6, 1891, FDRL.

CHAPTER 9. *The Law, Real Estate, and Politics: Comfortable Bedfellows*

88   "a number of": *ALT,* p. 48.

89   "very, very anxious": Josie to Henry Morgenthau, Sr., August 4, 1891, FDRL.
      "I have firmly": Henry Morgenthau, Sr., to Josie, July 16, 1891, FDRL.
      "know any one": Henry Morgenthau, Sr., to C. A. McCall, March 1, 1892, FDRL.

90   "most of the [Jewish]": *ALT,* pp. 34–38.
      "that night": Ibid., p. 37.
      "Why not induce": Ibid., p. 57.

91   "suddenly catapulted": Ibid., p. 63.
      "and through this alliance": Ibid., pp. 58–59.

92   "thus returned": Ibid., p. 89.
      "devote the rest": Ibid., p. 129.

93   "unreserved moral": Ibid., p. 132.

"great honor": Henry Morgenthau, Sr., diary, February 26, 1872, LC.

95   "I have a very high": Oscar Straus, *Under Four Administrations* (Boston: Houghton Mifflin, 1922), p. 210.

"The life of men": *New York Times,* May 12, 1911. See also Irving Howe, *World of Our Fathers* (New York: Harcourt Brace Jovanovich, 1976), p. 305.

CHAPTER 10. *The Discomforting Jewish Slot*

99   "duty to pay back": *ALT,* p. 128.

"which appealed to you": Felix Adler to Henry Morgenthau, Sr., May 1, 1903, LC.

100   "the Governor": *ALT,* p. 151.

"the ill-humored rivalries": Henry Morgenthau, Sr., to William Gibbs McAdoo, August 15, 1912, LC.

101    $25,000 left in the kitty: Arthur S. Link, *Wilson: The Road to the White House* (Princeton: Princeton University Press, 1947), pp. 481, 484–86.

"Have you heard": Stephen Wise to Henry Morgenthau, Sr., 1913, LC.

102   "Bull Mooser": Judge Ben Lindsey to Woodrow Wilson, February 5, 1913, LC.

"Morgenthau's attitude": Charles Strauss to Sen. James A. O'Gorman, March 8, 1913, LC.

"he had been requested": *ALT,* p. 159.

"We talked of": Diary of Col. Edward M. House, May 2, 1913, pp. 384–85, LC.

"The two posts": *ALT,* p. 160.

103   "was aggressive": Ibid., pp. 160–61.

"In compliance": Henry Morgenthau, Sr., to Woodrow Wilson (draft), June 12, 1913, LC.

104   "the post tendered": Josephus Daniels to Henry Morgenthau, Sr., June 10, 1913, LC.

"Your letter": Henry Morgenthau, Sr., to Josephus Daniels, June 12, 1913, LC.

105   "You may rely": Samuel Untermyer to Henry Morgenthau, Sr., July 6, 1913, LC.

"I am through": Henry Morgenthau, Sr., to William Gibbs McAdoo, July 10, 1913, LC.

He cautioned: Henry Morgenthau, Sr., to Colonel House, July, 10, 1913, LC.

"It is all important": Ibid.

106 "Your sentiments": Henry Morgenthau, Sr., to Colonel House, July 28, 1913, LC.
"a grievous mistake": *ALT*, p. 167.
"that not only I": Ibid.

107 "of warm friendliness": Stephen S. Wise, *Challenging Years* (New York: Putnam, 1949), pp. 40–48.
"I was tempted": Stephen Wise to Henry Morgenthau, Sr., August 7, 1913, LC.
"Sincerely glad": Cable from Woodrow Wilson to Henry Morgenthau, Sr., undated, LC.
"Now that you": Samuel Untermyer to Henry Morgenthau, Sr., August 15, 1913.

108 "I should be very glad": William McAdoo to Henry Morgenthau, Sr., August 14, 1913, LC.
"that it was most": Ibid.

CHAPTER 11. *The American Ambassador*

109 "Uncle Henry": Wise, *Challenging Years*, pp. 40–41.
110 "10:30 A.M.": Henry Morgenthau, Sr., diary, Nov. 1, 1913, LC.
112 "certain persons": Stephen Wise to Henry Morgenthau, Sr., August 7, 1913.
113 "I[srael] Zangwill": Henry Morgenthau, Sr., diary.
115 "not pessimistic": Ibid.
116 "Was met at": Ibid., November 27, 1913.
The "instinctive ambition": *ALT*, p. 78.
117 "every American interest": Henry Morgenthau, Sr., *Ambassador Morgenthau's Story* (New York: Doubleday, Page and Company, 1918), p. 187, hereafter abbreviated as *AMS*.
"Prussia and modern Germany": Ibid., p. 183.
118 Sir Louis Mallet: Ibid.
"as nearly as I": Ibid.
Marquis Pallavincini: Ibid., p. 10.
119 "You can't imagine": *ALT*, p. 188.
"Never in my life": Ibid., p. 190.
"next to the place of honor": Ibid.
"Wangenheim asked me": Ibid.
121 "if it were possible": Julius Richter, *A History of Protestant Missions in the Near East*, p. 72.
122 "There were constantly": *ALT*, pp. 211–12.
125 "extreme desire": Henry Morgenthau, Sr., to family, January 22, 1914, LC.
"It is really pathetic": Ibid.
"Talaat Bey": *AMS*, p. 90.

126 "much surprised": Ibid.
"a very strong": Ibid.
"Let us not criticize": Ibid., p. 13.
"has at times": Ibid., p. 14.
127 "I am not here": Ibid.
"particularly [in their] stubborn": Henry Morgenthau, Sr., to Josephine Morgenthau, December 29, 1913, LC; Henry Morgenthau, Sr., diary, December 12, 1913, FDRL.

CHAPTER 12. *The Jewish Ambassador*

129 "You will of course": Louis Marshall to Henry Morgenthau, Sr., November 11, 1913, LC.
"requiring Jews": Ibid.
"Of course": Ibid.
"a list of recent": Henry Morgenthau, Sr., to Louis Marshall, December 7, 1913, LC.
"the Holy Land": *ALT,* p. 212.
131 "Schmavonian is": Ruth Morgenthau to Henry Morgenthau, Jr., 1914, FDRL.
"of what abject slavery": Henry Morgenthau, Sr., to family, May 13, 1914, FDRL.
"received a deputation": Ibid.
"The Jews absolutely": Ruth Morgenthau to Henry Morgenthau, Jr., 1914, LC.
132 "a very nice frank": Ibid.
Lord Kitchener: Philip Magnus, *Kitchener, Portrait of an Imperialist* (New York: Dutton, 1915).
"a forceful courageous": Henry Morgenthau, Sr., to family, May 13, 1914, FDRL.
"talked of the Colonies": *ALT,* p. 226.
133 "many attractive": Magnus, *Kitchener.*
"so as to secure": Henry Morgenthau, Sr., to family, May 13, 1914, FDRL.
"It was a very curious": Ibid.
"He talked about Egyptianism": Ibid.
"pupils were seated": Ibid.

CHAPTER 13. *The Holy Land*

135 "in a very rough sea": Henry Morgenthau, Sr., to family, May 13, 1914, FDRL.
"Everyone who can afford it": Henry Morgenthau, Sr., letter, April 11, 1914, LC.

"drove to Tellavi": Ibid.

"a clean nice little town": Ibid.

136 "They have raised oranges": Ibid.

"The latter are very peculiar": Ibid.

"that there are no leaders": Ibid.

138 "As an American": Louis Lipsky to Henry Morgenthau, Sr., January, 7, 1914, LC.

"Isn't it a thousand pities": Stephen Wise to Henry Morgenthau, Sr., January 21, 1914, LC.

"bitter and divisive": Stephen Wise to Henry Morgenthau, Sr., February 16, 1914, LC.

139 "it might be unwise": Ibid.

"There are evidently": Henry Morgenthau, Sr., to Stephen Wise, February 14, 1914, LC.

"The name of": Menache Eliachar, interview with the author, July 8, 1980.

140 "an energetic": Henry Morgenthau, Sr., to children, May 3, 1914, LC.

"His title": Ibid.

141 "about whom": Ibid.

"They informed me": Ibid.

"At the end": *ALT,* p. 217.

"we all thought": Henry Morgenthau, Sr., to children, May 3, 1914, LC.

142 "a large contingent": *Ha-Heruth,* April 19, 1914, p. 5.

"Fortunately": Henry Morgenthau, Sr., to children, May 3, 1914, LC.

"But I shall not": *ALT,* p. 217.

143 "The same looks": Ibid.

"They explained": Ibid., p. 218.

"I did so": Ibid., pp. 218–19.

144 "tremendous importance": Henry Morgenthau, Sr., to children, May 3, 1914, LC.

"the greatest enthusiasm": Ibid.

"We had a": Ibid.

"each carrying": Henry Morgenthau, Sr., diary, April 11, 1914, LC.

145 "They looked": *ALT,* p. 233.

"traced his lineage": Ibid.

"the most delightful": Henry Morgenthau, Sr., to Stephen Wise, April 21, 1914, FDRL.

"I am impressed": Henry Morgenthau, Sr., to Stephen Wise, March 6, 1914, LC.

"Has it ever": Ibid.

146 "retain their religion": Ibid.
147 "Such a jontefdick": Henry Morgenthau, Sr., to family, May 12, 1914, FDRL.
"he told us": Henry Morgenthau, Sr., diary, April 19, 1914.
148 "all were suddenly": *Ha-Heruth,* April 29, 1914, p. 2.
"It is again": Letter from Sen. Hamilton Lewis to Henry Morgenthau, Sr., dated April 27, 1914, LC. The Hamilton Lewis letter marked "Copy" suggests that it might be a typewritten transcript of a handwritten note with a U.S. Senate letterhead.
149 "truly happy": Stephen Wise to Henry Morgenthau, Sr., May 25, 1914, LC.
"to survey": Wise, *Challenging Years,* p. 183.
150 "failure to keep": Stephen Wise to Henry Morgenthau, Sr., May 18, 1914, LC.
"Personally": Stephen Wise to Henry Morgenthau, Sr., February 23, 1914, LC.
"It is too bad": Henry Morgenthau, Sr., to Stephen Wise, June 17, 1914, LC.
"by no means enthusiastic": Henry Morgenthau, Sr., to Stephen Wise, April 11, 1914, LC.
"I am sure": Henry Morgenthau, Sr., to Stephen Wise, July 6, 1914, LC.

CHAPTER 14. *Witness to the Armenian Massacre*

152 "became a big": Barbara Tuchman, interview with the author, June 28, 1979.
"the daughter": Barbara Tuchman, *The Guns of August* (New York: Macmillan, 1962), p. 138.
"do a book": Tuchman interview.
153 "I hope": Stephen Wise to Henry Morgenthau, Sr., n.d., LC.
154 Ambassador Morgenthau: *AMS,* p. 92.
"not so much": Ibid., p. 8.
"the Kaiser's personal representative": Henry Morgenthau, Sr., to family, January 22, 1914, LC.
"I think Liman": Ibid.
155 "that he was using": *AMS,* p. 34.
"As you ride": Ibid., p. 4.
One could obtain: Ibid., p. 66.
"amounted to wholesale": Ibid., p. 64.
"his success in raising": Ibid., p. 66.
156 "the *Goeben*": Ibid., p. 79.
"Down went the mines": Ibid., p. 79.

157 "as targets": J. Hendrick Burton, "Henry Morgenthau, Diplomat," *World's Work* 32 (1916): 109.
"an ingenious German scheme": Ibid.
"finally consented": Ibid.

158 "Palestine Jews": Henry Morgenthau, Sr., to Jacob Schiff, August 28, 1914, LC. See also Cyrus Adler, *Jacob Schiff, His Life and Letters,* vol. 2 (New York: Doubleday, 1928), pp. 227–28.
"accepting your suggestion": Adler, *Jacob Schiff,* p. 278.
"We had a meeting": Ibid.

159 "There was a large": Arthur L. Ruppin to Henry Morgenthau, Sr., October 1, 1914, LC.
Barbara Tuchman: Barbara Tuchman, "The Assimilationist Dilemma: Ambassador Morgenthau's Story," *Commentary* (May 1977).
"the same tour": Arthur Ruppin to Henry Morgenthau, Sr., October 1, 1914.
"and requested them": *Ha-Heruth,* April 29, 1914, p. 20.
"On Sunday": Ibid.

160 "visit to Palestine": Stephen Wise to Henry Morgenthau, Sr., December 14, 1914, LC.
"All the members": *AMS,* p. 171.
"His private life": Ibid., p. 173.
"alarming news": Arthur Ruppin to Henry Morgenthau, Sr., October 19, 1914, LC.

161 "He despised": *AMS,* p. 174.
"The government here": Henry Morgenthau, Sr., to Louis Marshall, February 23, 1915, LC.
In January 1915: Confidential memo, Commander Renton C. Decker to secretary of the navy, *Report of Conditions in Palestine with Reference to Zionism,* February 10, 1915. pp. 2–3, LC. Commander Decker was captain of the USS *Tennessee,* which was stationed at Alexandria, Egypt.

162 "wholly destitute": Arthur Ruppin to Henry Morgenthau, Sr., January 6, 1915, FDRL.
"cannot afford": Arthur Ruppin to Henry Morgenthau, Sr., July 13, 1915, FDRL.

163 "The existence of Zionism": Commander Decker to secretary of the navy, *Report of Conditions,* LC.
"We had a splendid meeting": Stephen Wise to Henry Morgenthau, Sr., June 29, 1915, LC.
"It is rather dangerous": Henry Morgenthau, Sr., to Stephen Wise, August 2, 1915, LC.

164n Although the term: Raphael Lemkin: *Axis Rule in Occupied Europe:*

Laws of Occupation, Analysis of Government Proposals for Redress (1944).

165   As Ambassador Morgenthau: Henry Morgenthau, Sr., diary, August 3, 1914, LC.

Overruling the top: Susan Blair, *Windows in Heaven: The Story of Near East Relief,* unpublished manuscript about Armenian massacre, chap. 5, pp. 6–7.

They had been selected: Ibid., chap. 5, p. 8.

166   "among Turks": Henry Morgenthau, Sr., April 24, 1915, LC.

167   Babies were born: Blair, chap. 7, pp. 6–7.

168   Franz Werfel: See the *New York Times,* September 23, 1915, for a news story on which the 1930 Werfel novel was based. This tale of the mountaintop holdout of a little band of Armenians rescued by a French warship has assumed the proportions of a great epic saga. In writing his novel, Werfel, an Austrian Jew, was mindful of the Masada parallel, though the novel has a bittersweet rather than a tragic end. *Musa Dagh* is "Mount of Muses" in Armenian. See also Peter Stephan Junck, *Franz Werfel,* translated by Anselm Hollo (New York: Grove Weidenfeld, 1990), pp. 129, 138.

"nailing horseshoes": *AMS,* p. 307.

169   "We don't want the Americans": Ibid., p. 309.

"They must never": Ibid., p. 350.

"We have got to finish": Ibid., pp. 338–39.

"I have accomplished": Ibid., p. 342.

Since they lacked: Ibid., p. 339.

"It is difficult": Ibid., p. 12.

170   "however much": Ibid., pp. 13–14.

"I told him": Ibid., p. 17.

171   "could think of no": Ibid., p. 379.

"My failure to stop": Ibid., p. 385.

172   "You seem to represent": Henry Morgenthau, Sr., to family, January 19, 1916, FDRL.

CHAPTER 15. *The Homecoming*

174   "You have thrown": Telegram from Nathan Straus to Henry Morgenthau, Sr., April 26, 1915. This telegram was delivered to Morgenthau at the reception for him in the Great Hall of City University of New York.

175   "Lowering himself": *New York Tribune,* February 23, 1916.

176   "While I realize": Robert Lansing to Henry Morgenthau, Sr., February 21, 1916.

The full membership: *New York Times,* February 23, 1916.

177 "I could trace": Morgenthau clipping scrapbook, no source, n.d., LC.
"Mr. Dodge's son": Ibid.
"When I went": Ibid.
"As [Morgenthau] stated": Ibid.

178 "with sharp emphasis": *New York World,* February 23, 1916.
"If this reception": Morgenthau clipping scrapbook, no source, n.d., LC.
"How are the Jews": Ibid.

CHAPTER 16. *The Secret Mission*

179 Morgenthau, who knew: Robert Lansing, secretary of state, desk diary, June 10, 1917, p. 14, LC.
"That is not fantastic": Ibid.

180 With the Germans de-fanged: Woodrow Wilson Papers, vol. 42, p. 317, LC.
"give up Palestine": Ibid., p. 316.
Whether Morgenthau had: *Letters of Louis D. Brandeis,* vol. 4: 1916–1921, p. 288.

181 "one chance in fifty": Lansing memo, June 10, 1917, p. 104, LC.

182 "where he could": Ibid.
Meanwhile Balfour: Ibid., p. 105.
"to attempt to alleviate": Ibid.

183 "being any more foolish": Harlan Phillips, *Felix Frankfurter Reminisces* (New York: Reynal, 1960), p. 151.

184 "closely connected": Richard Ned Lebow, "The Morgenthau Peace Mission of 1917," *Jewish Social Studies* 32 (1970): 279.
"Mr. Morgenthau": Ibid.

186 As an alternative: William Yale, "Ambassador Henry Morgenthau's Special Mission of 1917," *World Politics* 1 (1949): 312; and Isaiah Friedman, *The Question of Palestine, 1914–1918: British-Jewish-Arab Relations* (London: Routledge and Kegan Paul, 1973), p. 216.
The other factor: Yale, "Ambassador Henry Morgenthau," p. 313.

187 "Jewish energy": Peter Grose, *Israel in the Mind of America* (New York: Schocken, 1984).
"leave nothing undone": *Foreign Relations of the United States, 1917,* supplement 2, vol. 1 (Washington: Department of State, 1932), p. 109. Hereafter referred to as *FRUS.*
"British and French": Ibid., p. 108.

188 Frankfurter soon: Phillips, *Frankfurter Reminiscences,* p. 149.
In addition: Chaim Weizmann, *Trial and Error* (1928), p. 199.
Years later: A. S. Yahuda, *Dr. Weizmann's Errors on Trial* (privately printed, 1952), pp. 14–16.

Because Weyl: Weizmann, *Trial and Error*, p. 198.

He had arrived: *FRUS, 1917*, supp. 2, vol. 1, pp. 604–5.

Morgenthau offered: Weizmann Papers, A, 7, pp. 461–62.

189   Frankfurter recalled: Phillips, *Frankfurter Reminisces*, pp. 149–50.

He recognized: Weizmann Papers, p. 463.

They both argued: Wilson Papers, vol. 43, p. 159, n. 1.

190   "in view of the fact": Weizmann Papers, A, 7, p. 464.

Frankfurter urged: Phillips, *Frankfurter Reminisces*, p. 151.

191   Wilson had: Wilson Papers, vol. 43, p. 172.

Morgenthau was instructed: Ibid., p. 160; and *FRUS, 1917*, supp. 2, vol. 1, p. 129.

Colonel House: Wilson Papers, pp. 183–84.

He suggested: Ibid., p. 210; and *FRUS, 1917*, supp. 2, vol. 1, pp. 130–31.

Despite his: Robert Lansing, desk diary, August 13, 1917, LC.

192   "In July 1917": *ALT*, p. 255.

CHAPTER 17. *The Polish Mission*

195   After the November: *ALT*, p. 348.

He left: Ibid., p. 345.

"the establishment": Ibid., p. 350.

"have to have a Jew": Phillips, *Frankfurter Reminisces*, pp. 147–48.

196   "foreign manufacture": Grose, *Israel*, p. 94.

"a scarcely veiled": Ibid., p. 94.

197   "we are enjoying": *ALT*, p. 355.

"had done more mischief": Grose, *Israel*, p. 94.

"While I thoroughly": Jacob Schiff to Henry Morgenthau, Sr., July 3, 1919, LC.

"I realize": Henry Morgenthau, Sr., to Jacob Schiff, July 4, 1919, LC.

But when the president: *ALT*, pp. 353–54.

198   He kept: Arthur L. Goodhart, *Poland and the Minority Races* (New York: Brentano, 1920).

"massacres, and other": Secretary Robert Lansing to Henry Morgenthau, Sr., June 30, 1919.

200   "takes the part": Goodhart, *Poland*, pp. 22–37.

"The Polish public": Ibid., p. 22.

"At first they were": Ibid., p. 23.

"suggested that a Polish": Ibid., p. 108.

201   "the Armenian affair": Richard Diran, ed., *The Armenian Genocide*, 2nd ed. (Richmond, Calif.: Armenian Commemorative Committee, 1981), p. 84.

"Everyone took": Ibid., p. 76.

They "were our": *ALT,* p. 363.

202 Morgenthau believed: Ibid., p. 364.

"ransacked the entire": Ibid., p. 366.

203 Without General Jadwin: Ibid., p. 414.

"This was the first time": Ibid., p. 376.

204 in "his official capacity": Ibid., p. 374.

his official report: American Commission to Negotiate Peace, "Mission to Poland," Paris, October 3, 1919. See *ALT,* Appendix p. 407.

"One of the deep": *ALT,* p. 384.

lay with "undisciplined": Ibid., p. 415.

205 "political rather than anti-Semitic": Ibid.

"American public opinion": *New York Times,* date unknown.

A "Dear Henry": Frank Polk to Henry Morgenthau, Sr., February 21, 1920, LC.

"there is that defiance": Henry Morgenthau, Sr., to Frank Polk, March 1, 1920, LC.

206 "in that land of turmoil": Robert Lansing to Henry Morgenthau, Sr., March 25, 1920, LC.

"a thousand congratulations": Stephen Wise to Henry Morgenthau, Sr., May 24, 1920, LC.

"I do not agree": "The American Hebrew and Jewish Messenger," *National Jewish Weekly* 109 (1921): 365, LC.

CHAPTER 18. *Great Expectations*

214 To sister Helen: Henry Morgenthau Fox, interview with the author.

"ought to send her": Henry Morgenthau, Jr., to Henry Morgenthau, Sr., 1906. Reply, Henry Morgenthau, Sr., to Henry Morgenthau, Jr., (postmark on envelope January 24, 1906), FDR Library.

216 "lacked the requisite": *ALT,* p. 18.

219 "The only trouble": Louise Sulzberger, interview with the author, June 17, 1978.

"the most beautiful": Harold Hochschild, interview with the author.

CHAPTER 19. *Henry and Ellie*

221 "a blue stocking": Fox interview.

"Nobody knew Ellie": Gabrielle Elliot Forbush, interview with the author.

222 But, "to us": Ibid.

223 "I have often": Henry Morgenthau, Sr., to Henry Morgenthau, Jr., May 17, 1914, FDRL.

224 "have some wonderful": Henry Morgenthau, Jr., to Elinor Fatman, December 20, 1915.

226 "It was a great": Forbush interview.

230 "suggestion of sending": André Tardieu to Herbert C. Hoover, February 1918; and Joseph Gaer, "All for Tomorrow" (unpublished manuscript), p. 308. This is a ghostwritten autobiography of Henry Morgenthau, Jr., through 1920, FDRL.

231 "I am the only": Henry Morgenthau, Jr., to Elinor Morgenthau, April 3, 1918, LC.

232 She was also taking: Gaer, "All for Tomorrow."
"our tractor plan": Ibid., pp. 312–13.
The following week: Ibid., p. 314.
"Women do not receive": Ibid., p. 315.

CHAPTER 20. *Morgenthaus, Fatmans, and Lehmans*

237 "I had to": Louise Sulzberger interview.

CHAPTER 21. *Henry and Franklin, and Elinor and Eleanor*

246 "He is an awfully nice": John Morton Blum, *From the Morgenthau Diaries,* vol. 1: *Years of Crisis, 1928–1938* (Boston: Houghton Mifflin, 1959), p. 12 (hereafter Blum, 1); Franklin Delano Roosevelt to Louis Howe, August 12, 1918.

248 "money, jewels and sables": Joseph Lash, *Eleanor and Franklin: The Story of a Relationship* (New York: Norton, 1971), p. 214.

249 Both Morgenthaus gleefully: Ibid., p. 279.
"Al nominated with great": Ibid.

250 "We are looking": FDR to Elinor Morgenthau, July 16, 1925, FDRL.
"There is nothing": Henry Morgenthau, Jr., to Henry Morgenthau, Sr., n.d. (c. 1921 or 1922), LC.

251 "lovely ash-blonde hair": Forbush interview.
"He looked at me": Henrietta Stein Klotz, interview with the author.

252 Once Henrietta started working: Forbush interview.

253 had "become awfully": Elinor Morgenthau to Henry Morgenthau, Jr., n.d. (c. 1923–1924), LC.

254 "I do wish": Ibid.

256 "Elinor and Henry": Lash, *Eleanor and Franklin,* p. 319.
"There was no doubt": Blum, 1, p. 14.
"Franklin will definitely": Ibid., p. 15.

259 "To say that your letter": Eleanor Roosevelt to Elinor Morgenthau, November 13, 1928, FDRL.
"I have always felt": Ibid.

263 "I feel tremendous": Elinor Morgenthau to FDR, December 14, 1930, Blum, 1, p. 553.

264 "I hope it will be": Elinor Morgenthau to Henry Morgenthau, Jr., May 8, 1932, Blum, 1.

265 "My trip is going fine": Ibid., p. 24.

CHAPTER 22. *Passing the Baton*

266 "I will never forget": Tuchman interview.

267 "Please at least": Eleanor Roosevelt to FDR, n.d., FDRL.

268 "No one close": Lorena A. Hickok, Associated Press, March 4, 1933.

269 "All that I say": Edgar Ansel Mowrer, *Germany Puts the Clock Back* (New York: Morrow, 1933), p. 241.

270 "the aim of": Ibid., p. 239.

271 "a warm friendly man": Blum, 1, p. 57.

272 This was Henry Jr.'s: Author's interviews with Louise Sulzberger, Iphigene Sulzberger, Harold Hochschild, and Henrietta Klotz.
But when, after: Blum, 1, p. 73.

273 "the President wanted": Ibid., p. 74.

CHAPTER 23. *Princeton, a Painful Awakening*

281 "Here was something": Tuchman interview.

283 "Europe seemed full": Walter Lord, "25 Years to Remember," '*39 in '64, 25th Yearbook; Princeton University Class of 1939* (privately printed, 1964), p. ix.

284 Bob and I: Igor Cassini, "Petit Point," *Washington Times,* January 2, 3, 1939.

285 "until some men": Unidentified newspaper article. January 1, 1939.
"my niece Eleanor": Eleanor Roosevelt, "My Day," *Washington Daily News,* January 3, 1939.

CHAPTER 24. *World War II Shall Not Take Place*

293 "at the New Year Services": Henry Morgenthau III to Elinor Morgenthau, October 8, 1940, author's papers.

294 At her press conference: Eleanor Roosevelt's press conference, November 7, 1940.
that "at the last": John Morton Blum, *From the Morgenthau Diaries,*

vol. 3: *Years of War, 1941–1945* (Boston: Hougton Mifflin, 1967) (hereafter, Blum, 3); Elinor Morgenthau to Henry Morgenthau, n.d.

295　"It seemed natural": Fox interview.
296　One of the guests: H. Stuart Hughes, *Gentleman Rebel* (New York: Ticknor & Fields, 1990), p. 126.
　　"gave the final": Betty Hynes, *Washington-Times Herald,* December 27, 1940, p. 20.
　　In her next: Eleanor Roosevelt, "My Day," *Washington Daily News,* December 28, 1940.
　　The party was: *Time,* January 6, 1940.
　　Sara Roosevelt: *Washington-Times Herald,* December 27, 1940.
　　"no one paid any": Eleanor Roosevelt, "My Day," *Washington Daily News,* December 28, 1940.

CHAPTER 25. *Pearl Harbor Remembered*

297　On Saturday, December 6: Recollections of the events of December 6–8, 1941, are based on the author's undated memorandum and a letter to Robert Morgenthau (brother), who was on duty in Puerto Rico at the time with the U.S. Navy. These items are included in the Morgenthau Papers, FDRL.
300　The story went on: Unidentified newspaper clipping.
　　"Henry Morgenthau 3rd": Ibid.

CHAPTER 26. *Players on the Morgenthau Team*

305　"Get rid of this woman": Klotz interview.
306　"might have resented her": Ibid.
　　"I wouldn't accept it": Ibid.
307　"I didn't need any stitches": Ibid.
　　"I remember once": Forbush interview.
　　"Hi, Henny Penny": Klotz interview.
308　"afraid the press": Sylvia Porter, interview with the author.
　　"the son of a Jewish": *Fortune,* May 1934, p. 6.
311　From his job in New York: *Encyclopedia Judaica* (Jerusalem: Keter Publishing House, 1972), vol. 16, p. 481.
　　"I couldn't stand": Klotz interview.
313　"He really wasn't": Edward Bernstein, interview with the author, January 27, 1979.
314　"never especially close": Whittaker Chambers, FBI summary report no. 3220, pp. 106–10, in Allen Weinstein, *Perjury: The Hiss-Chambers Case* (New York: Knopf, 1978), pp. 238, 616.

"there's no doubt": Bernstein interview.
"He was a very": Ibid.
"Coventry is putting": Bernstein interview.

CHAPTER 27. *Handwriting on the Wall Misread*

315   "German Jewry is": Jacob R. Marcus, *The Rise and Destiny of the German Jew* (Cincinnati: Union of American Hebrew Congregations, 1934), p. 300.
"bitter skepticism": Ibid.

CHAPTER 28. *Morgenthau Welcomes Stimson on Board*

318   "friendly and tactful": Henry L. Stimson and McGeorge Bundy, *On Active Service in Peace and War* (New York: Harper, 1947), p. 332.
"practically another War": John McCloy, interview with the author. John McCloy developed to a fine art the ability to be well liked by his peers and superiors. Behind my father's back he often joined his sharpest critics.
320   "particularly on account": Henry L. Stimson diaries, August 26–September 3, 1944, Yale University Manuscript and Archives Library.

CHAPTER 29. *The War Refugee Board*

322   But since McDonald: Henry Feingold, *The Politics of Rescue* (New York: Holocaust Library, 1970), pp. 25–26.
"consistently tried": David S. Wyman, *The Abandonment of the Jews: America and the Holocaust, 1941–1945* (New York: Pantheon, 1985), pp. 315–16.
323   John Pehle said: interview with the author, January 29, 1979; and Josiah DuBois, interview with the author, February 26, 1981.
"Stephen Wise": Klotz interview.
325   "I went ahead": DuBois interview.
326   "After all": Henry Morgenthau, Jr., diaries (hereafter MD) 688, II, pp. 156–67, 164–65, FDRL.
327   "[This] is a boiling pot": Wyman, *Abandonment of the Jews,* p. 203.
"everybody conscious": Pehle interview.
328   "A group of rabbis": DuBois interview.
330   "the lies on": Baruch Korff, *Flight from Fear* (New York: Elmar Publishers, 1955), p. 46.
the Morgenthau diaries: MD, 719:158–59.

Tragically, the effort: Sources for the discussion here: David Kranzler, *Thy Brother's Blood* (New York: Mesorah Publications, 1987); Korff, *Flight from Fear*; and the author's conversations with Rabbi Korff.

334   "token payment": I. F. Stone in *PM,* May 11, 1944; also Wyman, *Abandonment of the Jews,* pp. 266, 400.

CHAPTER 30. *Bretton Woods*

336   On December 14, 1941: MD, 473:16.
By May 1942: MD, 526:111–12.
White's ideas: Bernstein interview.

337   "a queer attractive": Donald Moggridge, ed., *The Collected Writings of John Maynard Keynes* (hereafter Keynes), vol. 25: *Activities 1940–1944. Shaping the Postwar World: The Clearing Union* (Cambridge: Cambridge University Press, 1980), Keynes to Wilfrid Eady, October 3, 1943, p. 354.

339   "The monkey house": Keynes, 25, p. 71.
"he chose instead": Ibid.

340   "Don't worry": Blum, 3, p. 246.
"very seldom, Harry": Ibid., p. 238.

341   "prestige of his office": Ibid., p. 252.
"not worried about": Ibid., p. 250–51, and notes, pp. 495–96.

342   "to get some sense": confidential interoffice memo from a major news magazine.
"the most important": MD, 528:321–22, reply in MD, 529:7.
But Taft: MD, 744:84.
"calling down the blessings": Keynes, 25, letter to Lord Catto, July 4, 1944, p. 82.

343   "For the first time": Ibid.
"that we are allies": Ibid.
"sabotaging the first": Keynes to L. Rasmunsky, September 18, 1943, Ibid., p. 390.

344   "At the same time": Ibid., p. 356.
"arouse [White's] genuine": Ibid., p. 356, Keynes to Sir Wilfrid Eady, October 3, 1943.
"White was so": Bernstein interview.
"White was addressing": Bernstein interview.
"He called it": Blum, 3, p. 244.

345   "He chased me all over": Klotz interview.
"that Harry White": Bernstein interview.

346   "feel that if": Ibid.
"In dealings we had": Ibid.

"Well, you tell": MD, 757:13a (July 22, with Morgenthau's thanks to Molotov), MD, 757:1–2, 15–16, 100–14, 115; "Morgenthau's closing comments," August 25, 1944, Henry Morgenthau, Jr., Presidential Diaries (hereafter MPD), FDRL.

"My last memory": Keynes, 25, p. 232.

"one of the greatest triumphs": Ibid., p. 112.

"Keynes was without": Ibid., p. 113.

347   "we have before": Ibid., p. 71.

"For He's a": Ibid., p. 232.

"As an experiment": Ibid., pp. 108–9, 112.

"perfectly certain": Blum, 3, p. 276–77.

"At first he told": MD, 756:282; 757:1–2, 15–16, 104–14, 115; MPD, August 25, 1944.

"they *want* to": Keynes, 25, p. 109.

348   "somewhat appalling job": Ibid., p. 112.

"deliberately elbowing him": Bernstein interview.

"I can think of": Keynes, 25, p. 193, Edward Bernstein to Keynes, May 15, 1945.

"My dear Levite": Keynes, 25, p. 193, Keynes to Edward Bernstein, May 29, 1945.

"thereafter things": Bernstein interview.

"really exhausted": Ibid.

"one of the most": Ibid.

CHAPTER 31. *The Morgenthau Plan for Germany*

350   "to go to France": MPD, July 6, 1944.

352   Two other members: Of the three men who crossed the Atlantic with Secretary Morgenthau on August 6, 1944, Harry Dexter White, Josiah DuBois, and Fred Smith, there are no longer any survivors. But on February 26, 1981, I recorded a long interview with DuBois on his recollections of his association with my father, while serving in the Treasury as an assistant to the general counsel and then as assistant to the secretary. During that period he had a number of important special assignments, including that of general counsel of the War Refugee Board. During the 1947–48 War Crimes Trials at Nuremberg, he was the chief prosecutor of the I. G. Farben case. DuBois carefully reviewed the transcript of my interview, writing in his corrections and addenda. The following DuBois quotes are from this interview, pp. 13–15.

353   White disagreed: MD, 767:176.

354   My father was: Fred Smith, "Rise and Fall of the Morgenthau Plan," *United Nations World,* November 23, 1954; and notes for Fred Smith interview by Robert Collins, November 14, 1953.

"We started right in": Blum, 3, p. 335.

"Eisenhower became grim": Smith, "Rise and Fall."

355 "the whole German": Ibid.

"Eisenhower would never": David Eisenhower, *Eisenhower: At War, 1943–1945* (New York: Random House, 1986), p. 403.

"the German people": Dwight Eisenhower, *Crusade in Europe* (Garden City, New York: Doubleday, 1948), p. 387.

"that the Ruhr mines": Ibid.

356 "I will tell": Smith, "Rise and Fall."

CHAPTER 32. *Views from the Battlefronts*

357 We disembarked: *The Ghosts of Patton's Third Army: A History of the Second U.S. Cavalry* (History Section, Second Cavalry Association, privately printed), p. 53.

358 A special order: Ibid., p. 61.

359 "very quiet, complete": Blum, 3, pp. 336, 500.

"In briefing Morgenthau": Omar Bradley, *A Soldier's Story*, pp. 375–76.

"They let me": Blum, 3, p. 336.

360 In the meantime: On the evening of August 12 he telephoned Bradley from his forward CP. "We've got elements in Argentan," he reported. "Let me go on to Falaise and we'll drive the British back into the sea for another Dunkirk." "Nothing doing," an irritated Bradley ordered him firmly. Bradley was convinced that the Third Army did not have the strength to seal the gap alone (see his book *A Soldier's Story*, p. 376). Furthermore, Monty would have been outraged at this humiliation.

"The loss of lives": MD, 763:103–5, 111–12.

361 "Any idea": Ibid.

"Finally they decided": MPD, August 19, 1944.

"He took me through": MD, 763:103–5, 111–12.

362 "as we lounged": E. F. Penrose, *Economic Planning for the Peace* (Princeton: Princeton University Press, 1953).

"Stalin . . . strongly favored": Henry Morgenthau, Jr., *New York Post,* November 25, 1947.

363 "the Secretary of the Treasury's": Cordell Hull, *The Memoirs of Cordell Hull* (New York: Macmillan, 1948), p. 207.

"emotionally upset": Ibid.

364 "You know the": MD, 763:202–5.

"I don't have a chance": MPD, August 19, 1944.

"trip to Europe": Ibid.

365 "The President": Ibid.

"Nobody has been studying": Ibid.

they followed his: Bernstein and Pehle interviews.

Morgenthau's uncompromising: Bernstein and DuBois interviews.

CHAPTER 33. *Stimson versus Morgenthau*

366   "Keynes seems to be": Blum, 3, p. 343.

"Well, that is not": MD, 765:14–16, 39–43.

"Stimson thought": Ibid.

"he will have it": Blum, 3, p. 345.

"Stimson and McCloy": Paul Y. Hammond, "Directives for the Occupation of Germany: The Washington Controversy," in H. Stein, ed., *American Civil-Military Decisions* (University, Ala.: University of Alabama Press, 1963), p. 354.

367   "I called on": MPD, August 25, 1944.

"If we hadn't": Blum, 3, p. 350.

"if you don't mind": Ibid., p. 345.

"This so-called *Handbook*": Ibid., p. 349.

368   "in constant touch": Stimson Diary, August 26–September 3, 1944.

369   "The President listened": Blum, 3, pp. 352–54.

370   "my troubles in": Stimson Diary, September 4, 1944.

"In such a case": Ibid.

"unveiled his newly": Blum, 3, p. 359.

371   "not unnaturally very bitter": Stimson Diary, September 4, 1944.

"with temperateness": Ibid.

"reflection upon the": Ibid., September 5, 1944.

"drifting into a chaotic": Ibid.

"had been rooting around": Ibid.

"terrible . . . it hurts": MD, 769:1–19.

"a minority": Ibid.

372   "a deeply passionate": McCloy interview.

A long-time restrictionist: Feingold, *Politics of Rescue,* p. 262; Wyman, *Abandonment of the Jews,* p. 362.

"spent the rest": Stimson Diary, September 5, 1944.

"to leave a record": Ibid.

375   "could not conceive": Stimson memo, September 5, 1944: Stimson and Bundy, *On Active Service,* pp. 571–73.

"very unsatisfactory": Blum, 3, p. 362.

"You can do this": Ibid.

"Don't be discouraged": Blum, 3, p. 365; MD, 769:118–45.

"Hull just wouldn't": Blum, 3, pp. 568, 501; MPD, September 9, 1944.

"whether he didn't": Ibid.

"I think there will": Ibid.

376   "it would breed war": Stimson and Bundy, *On Active Service*, pp.
      574–75; Stimson Diary, September 9, 1944.
      "I don't know any": Blum, 3; pp. 355, 501.
378   "military forces of Germany's": Henry Morgenthau, Jr., "Program
      to Prevent Germany from Starting a World War III," in *Germany Is
      Our Problem* (New York: Harper, 1945).

CHAPTER 34. *Summons to the Summit*

380   "to study economic problems": *Quebec Journal Telegraph,* Septem-
      ber 14, 1944.
      "a call at the Citadel": Grace Tully, *FDR My Boss* (New York:
      Scribner's, 1949).
      "Please be in Quebec": Blum, 3, p. 368; MD, 771:140.
      Stimson hoped: Blum, 3, p. 369.
381   To cover occasions: MPD, September 13, 1944.
383   "as part of his way": Henry Morgenthau, Jr., *New York Post,* No-
      vember 27, 1948 (ghostwritten by Arthur Schlesinger, Jr.).
      "It is quite": Ibid.
      "You cannot indict": Lord Moran, *Churchill, Taken from the Diaries
      of Lord Moran* (Boston: Houghton Mifflin, 1966), p. 190.
      "Are you going": MPD, September 13, 1944.
384   "Arthur likes him": MPD, September 14, 1944.
      "Why shouldn't it": Moran, *Churchill,* p. 101.
385   "that quiet confident": Ibid.
      "What do you want": Harry Dexter White memo for Henry Mor-
      genthau, Jr., MPD, September 15, 1944.
      "much too weak": MPD, September 15, 1944; and MD, 772:1–3,
      153–63, 208–12.
      "seemed quite shocked": Ibid.
387   "Of course,": Ibid.
      "tried to get up": Ibid.
      "unbelievably good": Ibid.
      "modestly and without": Stimson and Bundy, *On Active Service,* p.
      577; Stimson Diary, September 16–17, 1944.
388   "the farsighted": Stimson and Bundy, *On Active Service,* p. 578.
389   "Then she put": MD, 777:1–18, 21–22, 29–30, 90.

CHAPTER 35. *Father and Son at War*

393   "Patton's brilliant shift": Bradley, *A Soldier's Story,* p. 472.
      "smack into German": Henry Morgenthau III to parents, January
      11, 1945.

394 "I knew people": Robert Langley, conversation with the author.

395 "Mother worries": Henry Morgenthau, Jr., to sons, April 21, 1945.

CHAPTER 36. *Death and Transfiguration*

398 "What he wanted": MPD, November 27, 1944.

399 "it would only be": Ibid.

400 "the occasion will not": Henry Morgenthau, Jr., to sons, January 21, 1945.
"tried to hold up": Ibid.

401 "very talkative": Henry Morgenthau, Jr., to sons, March 9, 1945.

403 "the purpose being": Henry Morgenthau, Jr., to sons, April 12, 1945.
"I have lost": MPD, April 12, 1945.
"the man has a lot": Ibid., April 14, 1945.

404 "caught her just as": Ibid., April 16, 1945; and Henry Morgenthau, Jr., to sons, April 21, 1945.

405 "I wouldn't agree": Blum, 3, p. 70.

406 "And your father": Klotz interview.
The result was: See Henry Morgenthau, Jr., *Germany Is Our Problem* (New York: Harper, 1945); Henry Morgenthau, Jr., "Morgenthau's Inside Story," a series of articles in the *New York Post,* November 24, 25, 26, 28, 29, 1947; and Henry Morgenthau, Jr., "From the Morgenthau Diaries," a series of articles in *Collier's* magazine, September 27, October 4, 11, 18, 25, and November 1, 1947.

407 In the summer of 1945: Joint Chiefs of Staff, p. 1067; See Blum, 3, pp. 383–90.

408 "very kind and": Wyman, *Abandonment of the Jews,* p. 197.

CHAPTER 37. *From Washington to Jerusalem*

412 "is the celebration": Henry Morgenthau, Jr., to sons, March 25, 1945.
"he became a little Jewish": Klotz interview.

413 The rest of the day: Marc Lee Raphael, *A History of the United Jewish Appeal, 1939–1982.* (Providence, R.I.: Brown University, Judaic Studies 140034), pp. 29–30.
"My trip is now": Rabbi Herbert A. Friedman, interview with the author, 1989.

414 Israel Goldstein: Rabbi Goldstein retired to his home in Jerusalem, where I called on him in 1973. However, the quotes here are in his own words as they appeared in Abraham J. Karp's *To Give Life: The UJA and the Shaping of the American Jewish Community,* pp. 100–101.

416   "After traveling over the 'Burma'": *New York Times*, October 25, 1948.

417   "But now we must live": *New York Herald Tribune*, October 28, 1948.

      "very seriously": Weizmann, *Trial and Error*, p. 457.

422   "Eshkol followed me": All these quotes are from MD entry, pp. 1814–17, December 9, 1953.

CHAPTER 38. *Harry Dexter White Revisited*

425   "Mr. Morgenthau stated": FBI office memorandum, to the director from D. M. Ladd, January 24, 1952.

426   "I would never": FBI memo, L. B. Nichols to Mr. Tolson, June 1, 1955.

      "I would not want": Undated FBI memo, L. B. Nichols to Tolson.

      "they would never get": FBI memo, June 4, 1955.

      "Reversal by Morgenthau": undated FBI memo, L. B. Nichols to Tolson.

427   "Harry had a": Henry Morgenthau, Jr., to Anne White, August 18, 1948; see also *New York Times*, November 12, 1953.

CHAPTER 39. *From Generation to Generation*

430   "because she knew": John Morton Blum, interview with the author.

      "Your father went to": Ibid.

431   "I worked and slaved": These quotes from Henry Morgenthau, Jr., are excerpted from transcripts of one of the many brainstorming sessions he participated in with members of the *Collier's* magazine staff and Mrs. Henrietta Klotz in preparation for a series of articles by Henry Morgenthau, Jr., "The Morgenthau Diaries," published in fall 1947. The session quoted occurred July 26, 1946, FDRL.

434   "You know I": Henry Morgenthau, Jr., to sons, May 25, 1945.

437   "When Ruth told me": Mizia Schachter, interview with the author.

438   "Henry's father, the former": Abram Sachar, *A Host at Last* (Boston: Little, Brown, 1976), p. 138.

Index

Mann, Thomas, 282

Mannheim, Germany, 5, 26, 27–37, 38 40, 48, 53, 55, 66

Marcus, Jacob R., 315

Mark, Julius, 421, 437

Marshall, George, 370, 380

Marshall, Louis, 128, 129, 146, 158, 161, 176, 186, 197

Marx, Bernice, 219, 220, 222

Massachusetts Agricultural College, 311

Massachusetts Institute of Technology (MIT), 429

McAdoo, William Gibbs, 99, 100, 101, 103, 105, 108, 148, 248

McCall, C. A., 89

McCarthy, Joseph, 425, 433

McCloy, John, 318–19, 350, 366–68, 370–72, 388, 397

McCombs, William, 100

McCormick, John, 330

McDonald, James G., 322

McGrath, J. Howard, 425

McIntire, Alfred, 73

McIntire, Ross, 382, 403

McNarney, Joseph T., 413

Mead, James M., 330

Measell, Joe, 284, 285

Meir, Golda (Meyerson), 419, 420

Meltzer, Bernard, 325, 326

Menuhin, Yehudi, 238

Miller, Heinrich von, 34

Molotov, Vyacheslav, 346

Molotov-Ribbentrop pact, 313, 314

Moltke, Helmuth von, 66

Montefiore, Claude Joseph Goldsmid, 113, 114, 138

Montefiore, Sir Moses, 113, 201

Montor, Henry, 412–22

Moran, Lord, 379, 382–90

Morgan, Anne, 96

Morgan, J. P., 96

Morgan family, 94

Morgenthau, Alma. *See* Wertheim, Alma Morgenthau (Mrs. Maurice)

Morgenthau, Babette Guggenheim (Mrs. Lazarus), 4, 9, 24, 26, 30, 33, 40, 43, 44, 46, 47, 53, 55, 75, 82, 110

Morgenthau, Bernhard, 9, 12, 14,15, 16

Morgenthau, Bertha, 26, 40, 45, 46, 47, 83

Morgenthau, Brunhilda (Breule) Lebrecht, 7, 9,10, 11,12, 19

Morgenthau, Elinor Fatman (Mrs. Henry, Jr.), 114, 216, 220–33, 304–14, 321, 368, 379, 395, 401–2, 411–12, 418, 429n, 430, 432; and Eleanor Roosevelt 243–65, 288, 293–96, 298–303

Morgenthau, Gerson, 9, 14, 19

Morgenthau, Gustav, 43, 44, 46, 54

Morgenthau, Heinrich (Heyum), 19,29

Morgenthau, Helen, 119, 126, 212

Morgenthau, Henry, Sr., 4, 5; in Germany, 31, 53–55; in New York, 35–49; youth, 53–65; return to Germany, 66–68; at Columbia Law School, 69–71; law practice and businesses, 72–75, 88–97; and Josephine, 75–87; and public life, 92–97; and ambivalence about Turkish embassy, 93, 102, 103, 108, 109–27; with Woodrow Wilson, 98–102; as ambassador, 127–51; and visit to Holy Land, 129–51; and Armenian massacre, 152–72; and homecoming, 173–78; and secret mission 179–94; as opponent of Zionism, 193–94, 206–8; and Polish mission, 195–209; and

Schiller, Friedrich von, 33
Schlesinger, Arthur M., Jr., 407, 429
Schlessinger, Sam, 62
Schmavonian, Arshag K., 116, 129–31, 140, 172, 188, 191
Schnaitoucher, Carl, 29, 34, 36
Schneiderman, Rose, 95
Schoffield, Carl Schurz, 218
Schurz, Carl, 61
Schwabacher, Solomon, 17
Schwartz, Gordon, 60
Seligman, Isaac, 176
Seligman family, 38, 40
Shaffer, Chauncy, 69, 73
Sharett, (Shertok) Moshe, 421
Sharon, Ariel, 434
Sherwood, Robert, 380
Shoumatoff, Mme., 402
Silver, Abba Hillel, 410
Silvermaster, Nathan Gregory, 312, 314, 345
Simon, Carl, 44, 67, 68
Simon, Edward, 40, 45, 65–67
Simon, Pauline Morgenthau, 40–45, 65–67, 83
Simon, Robert E., 92
Smith, Alfred E., 96, 208, 248–49, 256, 258, 322, 352–54
Smith, William Bedell, 409
Smith College, 401
Snyder, John W., 424
Society for Ethical Culture, 63, 99, 110
Society for Freedom of Religion, 33
Sonneborn, Rudolph, 415n
Sonneborn Institute, 415
Soong, T. V., 399
Sourwine, Jay, 425, 426
Southard, Frank, 314
Soviet Union, 275, 287, 319, 345, 346, 423

Spence, Brent, 342
Speyer, James, 176
Speyer, Bavaria, 24, 26
Spring-Rice, Sir Cecil, 184
Stalin, Josef, 269, 351, 363, 400, 405
Standard Oil Company, 91, 158, 187
Stanford University, 310
Stanley, Arthur P., 142n
Stein, Henrietta. See Klotz, Henrietta Stein (Mrs. Herman)
Steinglass, Meyer, 416
Stepanov, M. S., 346, 348
Steppacher, Abraham, 18
Stern, Leopold, 33
Stern Bros., 90
Stettinius, Edward, 330, 398, 399, 400
Steuer, Max, 96
Stieglitz, Alfred, xvi
Stieglitz, Julius Oscar, xvi
Stillman, James, 91
Stimson, Henry, 96, 318–20, 335, 353, 366–78, 382–90, 395, 405, 435
Straus, Flora Stieglitz (Mrs. Hugh Grant), xvi, 275
Straus, Florence, 295
Straus, Helen Sachs (Mrs. Nathan), 295
Straus, Hugh Grant, xvi
Straus, Isador, 72, 94
Straus, Jerome (Jerry), xv-xvi, 275, 276
Straus, Jesse, 249, 267
Straus, Nathan, 72, 94, 138, 174, 238, 295, 401, 407
Straus, Oscar, xv, 72, 94–95, 98–99, 101, 103, 267, 272, 295
Straus family, xvi, 38, 94, 238
Strauss, Charles, 102
Strauss, Lewis, 230

Suckley, Margaret (Daisy), 402
Sulzberger, Arthur, 219
Sulzberger, David, 219
Sulzberger, Iphigene Ochs (Mrs. Arthur), 219
Sulzberger, Louise Blumenthal (Mrs. David), 219
Sulzberger family, 38
Summersby, Kay, 358
Supreme Headquarters Allied Expeditionary Force (SHAEF), 351–54, 358–60, 391, 395–96
Swarthmore College, xvi, 281
Sykes, Caroline, 78, 214
Sykes, Charles, 77
Sykes, Emma 87
Sykes, Helen Himmelreich, 76, 77–84
Sykes, Henry, 78
Sykes, Josephine. *See* Morgenthau, Josephine Sykes (Mrs. Henry, Sr.)
Sykes, Morris, 79
Sykes, Samuel, 78–81
Sykes, Sophie, 87
Sykes, Susan, 78
Sykes, Willie, 47, 81
Sykes, Mrs. Willie, 47, 77
Sykes family, 75, 88
Szklanowski, Benno, 5
Szold, Henrietta, 146

Taft, Robert, 319, 342, 374, 400
Taft, William Howard, 98, 99, 106
Talaat Bey, 119, 124–26, 144, 153–55, 164–69, 171, 179, 182, 188
Tardieu, André, 230
Taylor, J. A., 218
Taylor, William H., 395
Tedder, Sir Arthur, 358
Teheran Conference, 351, 352, 363, 365
Tel Aviv, 135

Temple Beth El, 58
Temple Beth Israel, 93
Temple Emanu-El, 92, 401, 421, 434, 437, 439
Temple of Humanity, 42
Tilden, Samuel J., 70
Tilden, William (Bill), 289
Tilton, Theodore, 70
Time magazine, 299
Tobey, Charles, 342
Tojo, Hideki, 364
Toscanini, Arturo, 297
Triangle Shirtwaist Company fire, 95–97
Truman, Harry S., 401–8, 415, 419, 422, 423, 435
Tuchman, Barbara Wertheim, xvi-xvii, 152, 159, 266, 281, 436
Tuchman, Lester, 436
Tully, Grace, 380, 395

Überbruck-Rodenstein, Anna (Countess Forini), 30
Überbruck-Rodenstein, Baron Heinrich von, 30, 36
Ullman, Ludwig, 312, 314, 345
Ulm, Bavaria, 14, 26
Underwood Typewriter Company, 115, 216
United Jewish Appeal (UJA), 410–22
United Palestine Appeal (UPA; later United Israel Appeal), 410
University of Chicago, 292, 309
University of Pittsburgh, 130
Untermyer, Samuel, 100, 104–5, 107, 128, 208

Vaad Hahatzala (Rabbis' Rescue Committee), 329, 330
Vanderbilt, Mrs. Frederick W., 247
Vanderbilt family, 94
Vanderlip, Frank, 177